Countering Terrorism and Insurgency in the 21st Century

COUNTERING TERRORISM AND INSURGENCY IN THE 21ST CENTURY

INTERNATIONAL PERSPECTIVES

VOLUME 3: LESSONS FROM THE FIGHT AGAINST TERRORISM

Edited by James J. F. Forest

PRAEGER SECURITY INTERNATIONAL

Westport, Connecticut • London

Library of Congress Cataloging-in-Publication Data

Countering terrorism and insurgency in the 21st century : international perspectives /
edited by James J. F. Forest.
    p. cm.
    Includes bibliographical references and index.
    ISBN 978–0–275–99034–3 (set : alk. paper)—ISBN 978–0–275–99035–0 (vol 1 : alk.
    paper)—ISBN 978–0–275–99036–7 (vol 2 : alk. paper)—ISBN 978–0–275–99037–4 (vol 3 :
    alk. paper)
    1. Terrorism—Prevention—Cross-cultural studies.   2. Terrorism—Government
    policy—Cross-cultural studies.   3. Counterinsurgency—Cross-cultural studies.
    I. Forest, James J. F.
  HV6431.C69183   2007
  363.325′17–dc22   2007007938

British Library Cataloguing in Publication Data is available.

Library of Congress Catalog Card Number: 2007007938
ISBN-10: 0–275–99034–6 (set)   ISBN-13: 978–0–275–99034–3 (set)
          0–275–99035–4 (vol. 1)   978–0–275–99035–0 (vol. 1)
          0–275–99036–2 (vol. 2)   978–0–275–99036–7 (vol. 2)
          0–275–99037–0 (vol. 3)   978–0–275–99037–4 (vol. 3)

First published in 2007

Praeger Security International, 88 Post Road West, Westport, CT 06881
An imprint of Greenwood Publishing Group, Inc.
www.praeger.com

Printed in the United States of America

The paper used in this book complies with the
Permanent Paper Standard issued by the National
Information Standards Organization (Z39.48–1984).

10 9 8 7 6 5 4 3 2 1

CONTENTS

EDITOR'S NOTE

Governments have been countering the threat of terrorism and insurgency since the establishment of the Westphalia system of nation-states. However, the rapid evolution of science and technology over the past 100 years—from the invention of dynamite to commercial air travel and the Internet—has enabled new forms of terrorist and insurgent activity. It is thus likely that further technological advances over the next 100 years will yield similar results, as today's terrorist and insurgent groups have proven to be adaptable, learning organizations. This three-volume set, *Countering Terrorism and Insurgency in the 21st Century*, seeks to encourage the development of learning organizations among national security professionals by examining what we currently know about the strategic application of hard and soft power in countering the sources and facilitators of terrorism. As a collection, the thematic essays and focused case studies represent an ambitious effort to capture existing knowledge in the field of counterterrorism and counterinsurgency, and draw lessons (from successes as well as failures) that will inform new, adaptable strategies to counter the new threats that—judging from historical trends—will no doubt emerge over the next century.

At the outset, it is necessary to address why this publication covers both terrorism and insurgency, as there is confusion about these terms among many in the academic, media, and policymaking communities. In some countries that have faced the threat of violence for many years—including Colombia, Ireland, Spain, Sri Lanka, and Turkey—societies have grappled with additional terms like "paramilitaries" and "freedom fighters," but the general view reflected throughout the chapters of this publication is that all groups or individuals (including insurgents) who engage in the act of terrorism can be considered terrorists. In essence, the act of terrorism defines its perpetrator as a terrorist, regardless of the ideological motivation behind such acts.

According to the U.S. Department of Defense, terrorism is defined as "the calculated use of violence or threat of violence to inculcate fear; intended to coerce or to intimidate governments or societies in the pursuit of goals that are generally political, religious or ideological," while insurgency is defined as "an organized resistance movement that uses subversion, sabotage, and armed conflict to achieve its aims.... [and which] seek to overthrow the existing social order and reallocate power within the country." In teaching my classes on these topics to future U.S. Army officers at West Point, the distinction I make is that insurgents can and do use terrorism (among other forms of violence), but insurgents are but one type of violent nonstate actors who may choose to use terrorism. In other words, not all insurgents use terrorism, and not all terrorists are part of an insurgency. Further, while the use of violence by insurgents to target governments is driven by a particular ideology, terrorists use violence against a range of targets (including governments) to advance their ideology.

While such distinctions may seem academic to most readers, they are actually quite important when formulating strategic, tactical, and policy responses to the threat posed by terrorism and insurgencies. As described in Volume 1 of this publication, strategies and tactics for countering insurgency are an important aspect of our knowledge base on countering terrorism, and vice versa. In both cases, experts have emphasized that the use of force to counter an organization whose objectives resonate with a larger disaffected population yields limited (if any) success. Instead, it is argued, the ideology, political, and socioeconomic aspects of an organization— through which it derives its financial support, recruits, and sympathizers from amongst the local population—must be addressed. In other words, the use of hard power in countering terrorism (including insurgencies that employ terrorist tactics) must be complemented by elements of soft power.

The link between counterinsurgency and counterterrorism is also informed by recent analyses which suggest that the al Qaeda movement can be described as a global insurgency, seeking to replace the existing Westphalia-based system of nation-states with a global caliphate in which Islamic law reigns supreme. Recent terror attacks in Bali, Madrid, London, and Cairo, as well as disrupted terror plots in Denmark, the Netherlands, and the United Kingdom, are all seen as examples of how individuals and groups around the world have been inspired by al Qaeda's ideology to commit violence as part of a strategy to change the policy and behavior of these nation-states. In other words, it is argued, al Qaeda uses terrorism tactically and operationally to advance its global insurgent strategy. When described in these terms, the U.S.-led global effort against al Qaeda can be considered to be fighting both terrorism and insurgency. Thus, *Countering Terrorism and Insurgency in the 21st Century* addresses the many challenges that stem from both types of threats to our security.

Another source of confusion in the study of terrorism and insurgency involves disagreement over the proper spelling of certain groups (or, rather, the spelling of the transliteration from the original language into English). For example, a brief survey of the literature reveals that a certain

Lebanese militant group can be spelled Hizballah, Hezbollah, Hizbullah, Hezballah, and Hizbollah. For these volumes, we have standardized the spelling of certain common names across all the chapters, such as al Qaeda (because this is how several agencies of the U.S. government are now spelling it), Hizbollah (because this is how the group spells it on their English language Web site), and Osama bin Laden (rather than Usama). Finally, it is important to note that while many chapters discuss aspects of the "global war on terrorism (GWOT)," we recognize that this term has fallen out of favor among many in the academic and policy communities. However, there currently is a worldwide effort to reduce the capabilities of globally networked terror movements like al Qaeda, and in the absence of an equally useful short-hand reference for this effort, GWOT serves an important role.

At this point in the development of the global counterterrorism effort, it is particularly important to pause for reflection on a number of critical questions. What do we know about effectively countering terrorism and insurgencies? What are the characteristics of successful or unsuccessful counterterrorism and counterinsurgency campaigns? What do we need to learn in order to do these things more effectively? *Countering Terrorism and Insurgency in the 21st Century* addresses these and related questions, and in doing so contributes to national security policy as well as to our understanding of the common threat and how it can be defeated. Chapters of this publication address many different aspects of the unconventional warfare puzzle, examining the most important diplomatic, information, military/law enforcement, and economic/financial dimensions to regional and global cooperation in countering terrorism and insurgency, and providing specific examples of these dimensions in practice.

Authors in the first volume address issues of important strategic and tactical concern, organized around the primary instruments of power through which nations pursue their counterterrorism and counterinsurgency efforts. These instruments can generally be described as either hard power (the use of force by military and law enforcement) or soft power (including diplomacy, information, and intelligence). The second volume provides a variety of insights on how to assess and combat the sources and facilitators of political violence, including state sponsors of terror, authoritarian regimes, criminal network activity, border insecurity, and the global struggle for influence among societies. As highlighted by several authors in this volume, the community of responsibly governed democracies faces uniquely complex challenges in combating terrorism and insurgencies while maintaining civil freedoms. And contributors to the third volume offer in-depth analyses of historical events and lessons learned in counterterrorism and counterinsurgency. Each volume contains a preface and introductory chapter, describing the contributed essays and providing an intellectual background for the discussions that follow.

This project is the final installment of an ambitious trilogy published by Praeger Security International. The first of these—the three-volume *The Making of a Terrorist: Recruitment, Training and Root Causes* (published in 2005)—intends to help readers understand the nature of the threat by exploring what transforms an ordinary individual into a terrorist. This was followed by the three-volume *Homeland Security: Protecting America's Targets* (published in 2006), which explored the ongoing efforts in the United States to secure our borders and ports of entry, and to protect our public spaces and critical infrastructure from future terror attacks. The volumes of *Countering Terrorism and Insurgency in the 21st Century* complement these earlier publications by focusing our attention on the broad, worldwide effort to actively confront those who threaten or use political violence against our communities. Together, these nine volumes are meant to provide a central, authoritative resource for students, teachers, policymakers, journalists, and the general public, as well as stimulate new ideas for research and analysis.

ACKNOWLEDGMENTS

The views expressed herein are those of the author and do not purport to reflect the position of the United States Military Academy, the Department of the Army, the Department of Defense, or the U.S. Government.

PREFACE

The chapters of the final volume of *Countering Terrorism and Insurgency in the 21st Century* provide dozens of case studies from which students and scholars can draw useful lessons and insights to further the study of critical challenges in the global security environment. Readers will undoubtedly note that some of history's prominent terrorist groups are not addressed in these chapters, such as Algeria's Armed Islamic Group and Salafist Group for Preaching and Combat, Indonesia's Jemaah Islamiyah, the Basque separatist group *Euskadi Ta Askatasuna* in Spain, and the Irish Republican Army (and its ideological cousins) in Northern Ireland. A number of books and articles have been published on these and other groups, and many are summarized in the new *Annotated Bibliography of Research on Terrorism and Counterterrorism* published by the Combating Terrorism Center at West Point (available online at: http://ctc.usma.edu). However, in order to manage the overall size of this volume, it has proven impossible to be all-inclusive. Instead, the topics selected for the volume are meant to offer a significant amount of geographic diversity: all the major regions of the world are covered in these chapters, and each country represented in this volume has had significant experience countering terrorism and insurgency.

As with the other two volumes in this book, an introductory chapter is provided in order to frame the discussions that follow. In addition to a brief review of concepts and the existing literature, this chapter also provides a discussion on the value of comparative analyses in general and specifically within the context of studying terrorism and insurgency. Next, Professor Stephen Sloan, who has studied and written about terrorism for several decades, provides his thoughts on necessary changes in counterterrorism education. He addresses the historical context of terrorism studies and why such studies had such a slow and sometimes tortuous path in finding their place as a discrete specialization within both the social and hard sciences. Based on that assessment, the chapter then examines the state of the counterterrorism art as it stands today and suggests critical questions and areas of investigation that must be addressed in order to meet both the short and longer-term evolution of the strategies and tactics of terrorism. The discussion then focuses more specifically on the elements necessary to evolve the new educational programs that are required to assist the counterterrorism specialist in the academic, public, and corporate sectors to not only achieve the necessary corpus of knowledge, but also disseminate it to those who are on the frontline in combating terrorism. Together, these two introductory chapters frame the case studies offered in this volume and highlight their contributions to the study of countering terrorism and insurgency in the twenty-first century.

The volume is then organized around two types of case studies: examinations of discrete events and discussions of a state's multiyear struggle with terrorism and insurgency. In both sections, authors were asked to provide a brief overview of a particular terrorist event or group (including motivations, aims, organizational strength, leadership, and prominent attacks), and then address how the state responded, what successes or failures resulted, and what lessons (good or bad) we can draw from the case study that can improve our understanding (and practice) of counterterrorism in general. In their analyses of these events, authors were also asked to address topics such as intelligence gathering, surveillance, communication, hostage situations, guerilla warfare, policymaking, legal and ethical considerations, and long-term implications.

PART I: CASE STUDIES OF TERRORIST ATTACKS AND COUNTERTERRORISM OPERATIONS

The section begins with a case study by Rick Wrona, a U.S. Army officer and a faculty member at the U.S. Military Academy at West Point, in which he analyzes the hijacking of TWA Flight 847 in June 1985. He writes that this event highlighted an atypical aspect of terrorism—instead of sowing fear among their target audience, the terrorists generally succeeded in convincing spectators to sympathize with the hijackers' cause. After providing a brief historical overview of the Lebanese civil war, the rise of Hizbollah, and the Afwaj al-Muqawamah al-Lubnaniyyah (AMAL, or "Lebanese Resistance Brigades"), as well as Palestinian Liberation Organization (PLO), and the actions taken by Israel (particularly, the prisoner exchanges that preceded the attack on Flight 847), Wrona describes the events that transpired in June 1985 and the role played by different governments, including Algeria, Israel, Iran, and Syria. Two noticeable differences separated the TWA 847 crisis from earlier hijackings, and particularly from the contemporary hijackings by Arab factions in the Middle East. First, TWA 847 received more media attention and direct media involvement than any previous hijacking. Second, the hostages' role in the media coverage of the hijacking was something not previously seen in similar events. Finally, Wrona highlights a number of lessons that can be drawn from this event that inform counterterrorism strategy, particularly in viewing terrorist acts as combat, not as crime.

Another hijacking is the focus of the next chapter by Sean Anderson of Idaho State University and Peter Spagnolo of the Government Training Institute in Boise, Idaho. In October 1985, Palestinian fighters took control of the *Achille Lauro*, a cruise ship owned by the Italian government. Although there had been numerous aircraft hijackings during the early 1980s, the taking of a civilian passenger ship was unprecedented. Consequently, the security measures on the ship were lax: only a passport was required to buy a ticket, there were no checks of luggage, and very little observation of persons embarking other than to ensure that they were paid passengers. After describing the events that took place during this hijacking, the authors provide a brief overview of the pursuit of the culprits and the political fallout in Italy, Israel, Egypt, and the United States, and note that at the time these actual events were unfolding, disagreements over how to interpret and assess the crisis caused significant rifts and conflicts among allies both in the North Atlantic Treaty Organization (NATO) as well as in the Arab world. They conclude that it is impossible to rule out that events similar to the *Achille Lauro* hijacking will not be repeated in the twenty-first century.

Next, Daniel Baracskay of Valdosta State University provides an analysis of the February 1993 attack on the World Trade Center (WTC) in New York. He notes that this event warrants analysis for several reasons. First, it signaled a turning point in American history; where beforehand, terrorist attacks were waged primarily on foreign soil, the events of February 26, 1993 revealed that Americans no longer enjoyed immunity from this form of violence. Second, the WTC bombing indicated that foreign terrorist organizations can successfully penetrate American borders with a significant attack that embodies a political and religious plot for restitution against American presence overseas, particularly in the Middle East. Third, the attack signified the expanding nature of ad hoc terror groups that come together exclusively for violent purposes and exist as organizations that are linked together by the like-minded ideologies of their extremist members. Finally, the event in 1993 was a precursor to the September 11 attack on the two World Trade Center towers 8 years later, indicating that al Qaeda may seek to revisit targets until it succeeds in destroying them. Overall, the implications and lessons from this incident suggest that time and cooperation, both domestically and internationally, will create a more unified front to combat terrorist behavior.

Attacks on a country's major urban centers are not uncommon, as Jim Robbins—a professor at the National Defense University—observes in the next chapter. His analysis of the Chechen attack on (and takeover of) the autonomous region's capitol city, Grozny, in August 1996 reveals the challenges that urban guerilla warfare pose to a nation's government and military leaders. In one of the few cases of an insurgency prevailing in an urban takeover, Chechen rebel forces took the city in a matter of days and were able to hold it for several years. However, he notes, the reason for the Chechens' success had less to do with their battlefield prowess than the unwillingness of the Russian government to pay the costs necessary to take the city back. Thus, Robbins concludes that the 1996 Battle of Grozny is a cautionary tale for countries involved in counterinsurgency operations under conditions of diffident leadership and weak public support at home.

This analysis is followed by a case study on the bombing of the U.S. embassies in Kenya and Tanzania in August 1998, authored by Sundara Vadlamudi of the Monterey Institute of International Studies. This event was the first major al Qaeda attack against U.S. targets that resulted in a large number of casualties. The meticulous planning, sophistication of the attack (involving near simultaneous bombings), and the number of casualties served as a significant wake-up call to the U.S. intelligence and law enforcement community. The attack brought into sharper focus the danger posed by transnational jihadists, and forced the U.S. government to readjust its counterterrorism policies. The chapter is divided into six sections. The first provides an overview of the bombing plot and lists the key individuals involved in the plot. The second section describes the immediate U.S. response to the bombing and the third section provides an overview of U.S. counterterrorism efforts against Osama bin Laden from the early 1990s until the attack in August 1998. The fourth section describes the cruise missile attacks on al Qaeda targets in Afghanistan and Sudan, launched by the United States as a response to the embassy bombings. The fifth section examines U.S. counterterrorism policies and efforts after the cruise missile attacks. And finally, the conclusion highlights some of the lessons learned from the U.S. response to the embassy bombings.

The next chapter, co-authored by Gary Ackerman of the University of Maryland and Sundara Vadlamudi, describes the history, exploits, pursuit, and capture of Ramzi Yousef, the mastermind of the 1993 attack on the World Trade Center in New York, among several other Islamist extremist terror plots. During his relatively brief career as an international terrorist, crisscrossing the globe from 1993 to 1995, Yousef succeeded in attacking one of the world's most prominent structures, plotting the assassination of several heads of state, winning over dozens of Muslim radicals, and planning what would have been one of the deadliest and most complex terrorist attacks of all time, all the while being pursued by several nations' law enforcement and intelligence agencies. Yousef has been variously described as a "mastermind" and—at least while he was active—as "the most dangerous man in the world," monikers that he egotistically appreciated; yet much about this chameleon-like villain remains a mystery. This chapter describes what is known about

Yousef's origins and his development as a terrorist, and traces his global exploits of mayhem. At the same time, the authors examine the nature and efficacy of the ultimately successful counterterrorist effort directed toward capturing a man who quickly rose to the rank of the world's most wanted terrorist. Lastly, the chapter draws lessons from the campaign against Yousef, lessons which can be applied to both current and future counterterrorism operations.

Next, Ruth Margolies Beitler of the U.S. Military Academy provides a case study of the attack on the USS *Cole*, a U.S. Navy destroyer refueling in Aden's harbor off the coast of Yemen on October 12, 2000. With 17 sailors dead and more than 38 wounded, the attack shocked the United States and its allies, and brought into sharp relief the relations between Yemen and the United States. Her chapter explores the events leading to the bombing of the USS *Cole*, the challenges of executing an investigation on foreign soil, and the ramifications of the *Cole* attack for U.S. counterterrorist policy. Regarding the latter, the investigation into the bombing of the USS *Cole* indicated clear shortcomings on a variety of levels. First, agencies within the United States must work together to increase the effectiveness of the investigations. Second, the United States must recognize the indigenous capability of a host nation, such as Yemen, and capitalize on those areas where the host nation retains a clear advantage over American investigators. Third, the U.S. government must grasp the flexible and ever-changing tactics utilized by al Qaeda. Overall, by assessing how the *Cole* investigation was handled, this chapter provides lessons for future investigations and counterterrorism cooperation.

Next, U.S. terrorism expert Robert Wesley describes the hunt for Khalid Sheik Mohammad, the tactical mastermind behind the 9/11 attacks, who was captured on March 3, 2003, in the Pakistani city of Rawalpindi. This chapter highlights the complex process that led to his detainment and the lessons underlined by this process. His capture serves to emphasize how the United States will be operating in the future to ensure continued progress in disrupting both the traditional leadership and those who replace them. Mohammad's case study allows for reflection on several counterterrorism issues likely to have an impact on the future of this global conflict. For example, governments must recognize the importance of developing strong international partnering relationships; harnessing the core competencies of joint operations, involving U.S. and host-country organizations; creating and exploiting actionable intelligence; identifying and provoking security mistakes by al Qaeda operatives; and targeting "partner organizations" of al Qaeda.

The next case study by Adam Dolnik of the University of Wollongong, Australia, describes the siege of School No. 1 in the North Ossetian town of Beslan, Russia. On September 1, 2004, a group of terrorists took more than 1,200 hostages on the first day of school in what became the deadliest hostage crisis—and the fourth deadliest terrorist attack—in history. After a 52-hour standoff, the detonation of explosive devices inside the school triggered a chaotic rescue operation in which 31 terrorists and 331 innocent victims were killed, 176 of them children. This chapter analyzes the myths and facts of the attack, with a clear purpose of identifying the lessons learned. The central focus is devoted to the Russian response, namely, the crisis negotiation approach and management of the tactical assault. In addition, the chapter examines events that occurred before Beslan that in retrospect could have provided an intelligence picture concrete enough to prevent the attack, as well as the media management and investigation aspects of the incident. The Beslan school hostage crisis was an unprecedented terrorist attack, both in its scale and targeting. It is clear that understanding the lessons of Beslan is one of the key prerequisites of designing counterinsurgency and counterterrorism strategies for the twenty-first century.

This is followed by a chapter from Rogelio Alonso of King Juan Carlos University in which he examines the terrorist attacks of March 11, 2004, in Madrid. Although Spain had been constantly targeted by various types of terrorism since the late 1960s, violence from the ethno-nationalist Basque terrorist group *Euskadi Ta Askatasuna* (ETA, or Basque Fatherland and Freedom) being by far the most intense, never before had a terrorist attack in the country been so indiscriminate and lethal. On that day, ten bombs planted in four different trains filled with thousands of commuters on their way to Madrid were detonated between 7:37 and 7:40 A.M., killing 191 people. As it would soon emerge, the killings on March 11 were carried out by a group of Islamist terrorists, some of whom were closely linked to individuals who were also part of the al Qaeda network. The chapter examines the events that led to this terrorist attack, analyzes how and why such an atrocity was perpetrated, as well as its implications for counterterrorism in the country, and concludes with an analysis of the main counterterrorism measures implemented as a response to this tragedy.

Next, Tom Maley of Cranfeld University examines the terrorist attacks of July 7, 2005, in London, England. After describing in detail the events that took place and the subsequent police investigation, Maley examines the motivations of the bombers, concluding that Muslim disadvantage, under-achievement, and under-representation at the hands of Western influence and policies seem to have been key motivational themes; thus, they sought martyrdom operations in their quest to right these wrongs. He then describes the government's response to the attacks within the context of the UK's long-term counterterrorism strategy. Operationally, this strategy is based upon four pillars: prevention, pursuit, protection, and preparedness, known colloquially as the "Four Ps." The first two pillars were designed to reduce the threat, whereas the remaining two pillars focused upon the UK's vulnerabilities with respect to international terrorism. Overall, Maley's analysis provides several important insights into the most likely type of self-organized and motivated terrorist attack we may see in other large Western cities, as well as how to cope with and counter the threat from local al Qaeda-inspired terrorist cells.

The final chapter of this section by Daniel Baracskay examines the April 1995 bombing of the Murrah Federal Building in Oklahoma City. He notes that this was a significant event for three principle reasons. First, the bombing established that American cities are vulnerable not only to the threats of external terrorist groups, but also to the impulses of internal extremists that are willing to use violence to advance their objectives. Second, the Oklahoma City bombing was the second large-scale assault on a public building in a 2-year period. The use of terrorism as an instrument of destruction is becoming more pervasive in the United States, if not expected. Finally, trends have shown that terror groups purposefully identify large and densely populated urban centers for targets in the United States and intentionally use violence in these cities to gain media coverage. This chapter analyzes the Oklahoma City bombing incident in detail and examines several implications and lessons that have surfaced in the decade following the event.

PART II: CASE STUDIES OF THE LONG-TERM FIGHT AGAINST TERRORISM AND INSURGENCY

The second section of the volume explores the struggle between nation-states and terrorist groups operating within their borders. The first chapter of this section, by Tom Marks of the National Defense University, examines the response of the Sri Lankan government to the persistent threat posed by the Liberation Tigers of Tamil Eelam (LTTE). He notes that the LTTE is labeled "terrorist" by any number of governments, but in reality, it is an insurgency in intent and methodology. It has, however, gone from using terror as a tool for mass mobilization to using it as a strategy for insurgency. The success of the LTTE reveals the ability of a radical, institutionally totalitarian movement to recruit, socialize, and deploy manpower so rigidly indoctrinated that combatants prefer death by cyanide or self-destruction to capture. Having gained control of certain areas early on, LTTE was able to recruit manpower at young ages and then guide them in ways that produced entire units comprising young boys and girls who had never known alternative modes of existence. Meanwhile, this case study reveals several mistakes of strategic approach and operational implementation on the part of the government. These began with a persistent failure to assess the insurgency in terms appropriate to framing a correct response, attacking the symptoms to the near-exclusion of the causes of the violence, and misinterpreting that violence once it appeared. To focus upon the tactical acts of terror, then, was precisely the wrong approach.

Certainly repression was a necessary element of state response, but the se-curity forces should only have been an instrument for the accomplishment of a political solution.

Next, Joanne Wright, the Pro-Vice-Chancellor at Sussex University, pro-vides a case study of West Germany's Red Army Faction (RAF, a.k.a. the Baader Meinhof Gang). Examining the RAF, its motivating ideology, and particularly the West German government's counterterrorism policies can provide valuable lessons and insights into twenty-first-century terrorism. It can illustrate, for example, how a relatively small and seemingly irra-tional group can create a physical and psychological impact way out of proportion to size and threat. Perhaps even more usefully, it can illustrate that whatever sympathy terrorist groups do manage to generate among national and international audiences is largely derived from government responses to terrorism. Her chapter suggests that the RAF was able to gen-erate some degree of success and attach some degree of credibility to its analysis of a repressive state in three areas: security force behavior, pris-oners and prison conditions, and legislative changes. Overall, the West German experience highlights the need to review the impact of policies on the motivations and support of terror groups within a society.

This is followed by a chapter from David Scott Palmer of Boston Uni-versity in which he examines the case of Sendero Luminoso (Shining Path) in Peru. Beginning in May 1980, the government of Peru faced the first attacks from a Maoist insurgency originating in the Andean high-lands known as Shining Path, attacks that expanded dramatically over the decade. By 1990, more than 20,000 Peruvians had been killed, $10 billion of infrastructure had been damaged or destroyed, and some 9 million inter-nal refugees and emigrants had fled their homes. This chapter offers an ab-breviated account of the rise and fall of Shining Path. It discusses the con-ditions contributing to the initial formation and growth of the insurgency, the largely counterproductive responses by the Peruvian government and its security forces, and the key elements of the major strategic and tac-tical overhaul that turned the tables on the insurgents. The conclusion draws together the lessons to be learned as to how a guerrilla movement could come close to succeeding, as well as how a besieged government could overcome the threat—lessons of possible use to other governments in the formulation of their own counterinsurgency and counterterrorism policies.

A similar analysis of counterinsurgency in Latin America is provided in a chapter on the Revolutionary Armed Forces of Colombia (FARC), co-authored by Nicolás Urrutia Iriarte and Román Ortiz of Los Andes University (Bogotá). Traditionally, FARC has been considered the oldest guerilla movement in Latin America, with a history of nearly 40 years. It has also proven to be one of the more adaptable movements, as an analysis of their military tactics and financial dealings reveal. The group had its origins in an essentially rural country with scarce social mobility and deficient political participation mechanisms. However, the long-term evolution of their attack capabilities, the multiplication of its financial resources—particularly resulting from an increase in the demand for cocaine in the new markets of Eastern Europe and the expansion of heroin production in Colombia, which provided FARC with new options to increase the volume of income from drug trafficking—and the renewed capacity to project its political message has turned FARC into a formidable threat. Their research highlights how clandestine networks for exchanging technology and military information between terrorist groups and criminal organizations have offered FARC critical channels through which they could expand their fighting capability, creating enormous challenges for the government's counterterrorism and counterintelligence efforts.

Another insurgency with a considerable history is examined in the following chapter by Thomas Sherlock of the U.S. Military Academy, which explains the origins of the Chechen crisis, assesses the costs to Russian pluralism of the Kremlin's efforts to pacify Chechnya, and suggests what the West might do to help resolve one of Russia's most important political problems. Throughout numerous brutal encounters with Russia, Chechen civilian casualties have been high and there is deep animosity throughout the region, rooted in decades of government repression. Sherlock notes that promoting democratization in Russia and working to resolve the crisis in Chechnya are important goals for the West, but it should not oscillate between condemnation and approval of Russian behavior in Chechnya, even in the face of dramatic intervening events, such as the terror attacks of 9/11, which led Washington to adopt generally supportive language regarding Kremlin policies in Chechnya. Putin and Russia's political elites fear that instability in Chechnya will spread throughout the Caucasus. Meanwhile, the recent, unexpected, and tumultuous "revolutions" on Russia's borders are viewed as threats by Russia's ruling elites, who since Putin's accession to power have been drawn in large part from the security services, and who worry that Russian influence is yet again receding in post-Soviet space. Such perceptions of vulnerability strengthen the desire to treat the problem of Chechnya as a completely "internal" matter. Sherlock concludes that while holding Russia publicly and privately accountable for atrocities committed in Chechnya by Russian and pro-Russian Chechen forces, the West should repeatedly reassure the Kremlin of its support for Russia's territorial integrity, while promoting even-handed proposals that may effectively compel Russia to negotiate with moderate elements to reach a final solution to the Chechen insurgency.

Next, Erica Chenoweth of Harvard University examines one of the most durable and evasive terrorist groups of the 1970s and 1980s in Italy—the Red Brigades. Her investigation into the history of this group illuminates the successes and failures of the Italian government in confronting the Red

Brigades, providing several observations that should inform current U.S. policy in fighting insurgency and terrorism. For example, Italian counterterrorism efforts initially failed because of shadowy complicity between elements of the state and right-wing terrorism; refusal of the government to acknowledge the destructive potential of the Red Brigades; knee-jerk reactions resulting in undemocratic policies that raised some ethical considerations; and a failure to appreciate the escalatory effects of intergroup rivalries among terrorist groups. However, according to Chenoweth, the eventual successes of Italian counterterrorism included a unification of intelligence units and a coordination of their activities; creation of special commando forces with training in hostage crises; and finally, the introduction of policies that exploited internal divisions within the Red Brigades and led to the defection of many members.

Rick Wrona follows with a case study on the Lebanese terror organization Hizbollah. After describing the origins of Hizbollah, he examines the group's ideology and its sponsorship by Iran and Syria. Today, he notes, the organization acts as a political, economic, social, and military leader in Lebanese society. Responding to such an organization is a daunting challenge for the United States and its allies in the region, most notably Israel. As a case study, Hizbollah demonstrates the lack of American consistency when dealing with organizations that resort to terrorism. America's focus on Hizbollah has been sporadic and, in many instances, poorly timed. Further, American support of the Lebanese regime in the early 1980s had the unintended consequence of turning the Shi'a population against the United States, because support of the regime equated to support of the Maronite factions controlling the government. Likewise, American support of Israel, particularly after the 1973 Yom Kippur/Ramadan War, came to be viewed by Hizbollah as both an indirect attack on the Lebanese people and direct support for Israeli regional expansion. Hizbollah's history demonstrates that integration into the political process has simply given the organization more tools by which to achieve its goals, raising questions about the role of democratization in countering terrorism. Finally, the example of Hizbollah demonstrates the power of organizations that combine national, religious, and class appeal successfully. While some terrorist organizations (most notably several European groups of the 1970s) have been unable to expand beyond a small core of radicalized supporters, Hizbollah is the textbook case of an organization that has built a constituency that guarantees the group's longevity and importance for the foreseeable future.

The next chapter by Lydia Khalil of the New York Police Department examines the Partia Karkaren Kurdistan (PKK, or the Kurdistan Workers Party). Founded by a small group of communist Kurdish students of the University of Ankara and led by Abdullah Ocalan, the PKK was originally a Marxist-Leninist-Maoist group attempting to establish socialism in the Kurdish populated areas of the Middle East. In the late 1980s, the PKK came to focus more on promoting Kurdish nationalism and the establishment of a Kurdish nation-state. Turkey's fight against the PKK is a good example of how a military defeat of a terrorist insurgency does not automatically translate into permanent peace. Although the group is currently not operating with the full military and political force it had before Ocalan's arrest, the lack of a political settlement on Turkey's Kurdish question allowed the PKK to continue hit and run operations against Turkish forces and civilian targets. Clashes between PKK rebels and Turkish security forces have increased since the PKK called off their unilateral ceasefire in the summer of 2004. After a study of Turkey's different counterterrorism policies toward the PKK, this analysis highlights lessons learned from Turkey's successes and failures in dealing with the PKK.

This is followed by a chapter from Joshua L. Gleis of Tufts University on counterterrorism measures adopted by Israel in its fight against terrorist organizations. His description of Israeli tactics is particularly interesting. For example, narrow alleys require infantry to move house to house, blowing holes through walls in order to limit the danger to them from snipers and explosives planted in the entrances. His chapter also addresses issues of doctrine, education, preemption, targeted assassinations, and technology, including civilian antiaircraft missile systems, counterterrorism measures implemented on buses, and long-range explosives detectors. He notes that the U.S. armed forces, and particularly the Marine Corps, have joint training exercises with Israeli forces and are learning from Israel's urban warfare tactics. However, in the intelligence field there is still an extreme lack of trust toward the Israeli intelligence and security agencies. Overall, he concludes, there is much that can be learned from Israel's long experience in combating insurgency and terrorism.

Next, Brian Fishman of the Combating Terrorism Center at West Point provides a case study of Syria's struggle against the Muslim Brotherhood during the 1970s. This chapter examines the efforts of Syrian President Hafez al-Asad to defeat several armed groups operating in the streets, many of whom were associated with the Syrian Muslim Brotherhood (Brotherhood). Although the focus is on Asad's campaign against the militant Islamic opposition, it is impossible (and would be entirely improper) to separate Syria's counterinsurgency policies from Asad's efforts to build a social and political system that would enable him to dominate the Syrian state. Asad's strategy for defeating the Brotherhood contained four elements employed by all governments fighting counterinsurgencies: (1) strengthen and legitimize the government, in this case Asad himself; (2) target the insurgent's support networks domestically and internationally; (3) de-legitimize the insurgents; and (4) use violence to eliminate the insurgents and deter sympathizers. In order to understand Asad's approach to counterinsurgency, one must understand the social bases of both the Ba'th party in Syria and the Brotherhood. The chapter begins by reviewing the rise of Asad's Alawite-dominated Ba'athist regime in Syria and the Sunni Brotherhood-associated movement that violently challenged his authority. This leads naturally into a discussion of the struggle for legitimacy between Asad and the Brotherhood. Overall, this case study is an excellent example of how counterinsurgency in an autocratic state represents the struggle of an individual or party to fend off challenges to its power and legitimacy.

Militant Islamism is also the focus of the next chapter, by Sherifa Zuhur of the U.S. Army War College, in which she provides a detailed history of Egypt's long (and recently resurgent) conflict with several Islamist groups, some of which have proved more violent than others. For much of this history, Egypt's leaders have sought to contain Islam as a political force and suppressed an array of Islamist groups. While officials disagree that their stringent counterterrorist actions could encourage further jihad, she argues, torture and imprisonment of Islamists in the 1960s produced several results in the 1970s: uncompromising radicalism and aims to immediately overthrow the state; or accommodation and commitment to a gradual Islamization of the state, this being the path of the Muslim Brotherhood. Torture and imprisonment in the late 1970s and 1980s led to further organizational development in prisons themselves, including the forming of new radical groups and the spread of "global jihad" or the quest for sanctuary somewhere outside of Egypt. She notes that in recent years, Egypt has accepted moderate Islamism in other dimensions (intellectual and social), but recent acts of religious violence (including attacks in Cairo, Sharm al-Shaykh, and Dahab) have renewed the state's efforts to counteract the rise of moderate Islamism in its political form.

In the next chapter, Vera Eccarius-Kelly of Siena College provides another case study in which a nation-state's counterterrorism policies and tactics may have contributed to the strength of a violent insurgency. Her analysis of Peru's response to the *Movimiento Revolutionario Túpac Amaru* (Revolutionary Movement of Tupac Amaru, or MRTA) reveals a repressive and corrupt national security state. This chapter examines the government's management of the media, its collusion with corrupt military and police, and its embrace of tactics of intimidation, abduction, torture, and a series of other horrific human rights offenses. She describes several of the major confrontations between the Peruvian government and the MRTA, and offers a detailed analysis of the counterterrorism policies employed during the 1996–1997 hostage crisis at the Japanese Ambassador's residence in the capital city Lima. Several significant insights can be gained from investigating the measures utilized to defeat the MRTA during both the García and Fujimori presidencies between 1985 and 2000. Overall, an evaluation of the Peruvian government's handling of the MRTA is an important case study of counterinsurgency and counterterrorism measures in a society with fledging democratic institutions.

A similar case of a fledging democracy battling a terrorism-inclined insurgency can be found in the Philippines, as Robin Bowman of the U.S. Air Force Academy describes. Her chapter addresses the "whys"—goals, motivations, and leadership—and "hows" (including organization and tactics) behind the violent Muslim separatist movements in the Philippines, and their well-documented connections with foreign jihadists, as well as Manila's responses to its home-grown insurgencies and international terrorism. The country is considered highly vulnerable to foreign terrorist penetration and prolific domestic attacks due to its abundant Christian and Western targets, its fluid borders, weak political institutions and responses, and general lack of governmental reach into the Muslim regions. Bowman begins the chapter with a look at the formation of Moro identity, and how and why this community turned to violence and militancy in order to assert their goals of a distinct and independent Muslim homeland. She then profiles each of the violent separatist movements (particularly the Moro Islamic Liberation Front and the Abu Sayyaf Group) before describing the government's response. Overall, this chapter offers an interesting case study of political violence.

The struggle for a distinct and independent Muslim homeland is also a centerpiece of the next chapter by Johua Sinai of The Analysis Corporation in which he describes the Islamic Movement of Uzbekistan (IMU) and its struggle with the secular regime of President Karimov. Uzbekistan is the former Soviet Union's largest Muslim nation, with a population of 25.1 million people. The government believes that its counterinsurgency and counterterrorism strategies will enable it to avoid the fate of its smaller southern neighbor Tajikistan, which has been engulfed in a civil war since independence. So far, these strategies have not succeeded in rooting out Uzbekistan's extremist Islamic insurgency because its military campaign has been ineffective and solutions still need to be provided to tackle the country's internal problems, particularly the lack of full political participation in the form of free, fair, and competitive elections. Sinai notes that an effective response to the radical Islamic insurgency in Uzbekistan must be found and implemented, because this insurgency is part of a wider series of insurgencies facing the Central Asian states that pose a major threat to regional stability, democratization, and economic well-being. However, until Uzbekistan adopts a more democratic course, he argues, there will be few internal or external allies to help it defeat the IMU's insurgency.

The next chapter addresses another critical insurgency/separatist movement in this region: Kashmir. Authored by retired Indian Army officer Behram A. Sahukar, the chapter examines the origins of the Kashmir issue and the role of Pakistan in sponsoring or supporting Islamic militant groups engaged in terrorist attacks. He explains how the Soviet invasion of Afghanistan in 1979 made Pakistan a frontline state in the United States-funded jihad against the Soviet Union, and the infusion of CIA-funded arms, equipment, and other forms of support into Pakistan legitimized the use of Islam to fight an Islamic holy war. The end of the Afghan jihad in 1989 left Pakistan flooded with surplus arms and equipment, as well as a cadre of fighters with experience in a prolonged low intensity conflict. Mujahideen who had completed their successful mission against the Soviets were diverted to Kashmir to continue their fight for Islam in Kashmir against "infidel" Hindu India. Since 1989, separatist violence in Kashmir has been backed by a radical Islamist ideology that aims to annex Kashmir to Pakistan and extend Islamic rule over India. Pakistan considers the issue of Kashmir as the "unfinished agenda of partition," and remains in occupation of one third of the Indian state. It has tried to take the rest of the state by force several times in the past and failed. However, both sides have now realized that continued hostility and acrimony is counterproductive to the peace and stability of the region. This realization led to the beginnings of a comprehensive dialogue and peace process in April 2003, and a series of confidence building measures. Unfortunately, the jihadi factor and the anti-India military in Pakistan has been a hindrance to any lasting peaceful solution to Kashmir. Sahukar concludes that unless Pakistan abandons its fixation with Kashmir and returns to a democracy, the military and the Inter Services Intelligence agency will continue to fuel a proxy war against India.

Nearby this troubled region, another insurgency has grown in strength and prominence since 1996, led by the Communist Party of Nepal (Maoist), or CPN(M), in which more than 13,000 Nepalis have lost their lives, many to insurgent torture and murder. The chapter by Tom Marks of the National Defense University describes the socio-political roots of the insurgency and the influence on the CPN(M) by other communist movements, notably *Sendero Luminoso* in Peru and Maoists in India. In Nepal, the Maoists seized territory over a period of years, enlisting a growing number of recruits until by 2003 the government estimated the movement's strength to be roughly 5,500 combatants, 8,000 militia, 4,500 cadre, 33,000 hardcore followers, and 200,000 sympathizers. Marks then describes the government's response to this "people's war" as anything but adequate. Patrols sent to the scenes of incidents were ambushed, while numerous small police stations were overrun, attacked in the dead of night in assaults initiated with homemade explosives, then overwhelmed by human wave assaults. The police then abandoned outlying stations and consolidated their forces in a defensible mass, and by early 2003, half of all police stations nationwide had been abandoned. Once the police presence was eliminated, the insurgents became the state. Marks also criticizes the Nepalese government for the lack of a political component to its counterinsurgency strategy. He concludes that counterterrorism should be an important element, but only one element of many in a comprehensive approach, a blend of the violent and the nonviolent that addresses the roots of conflict and creates good governance.

The next chapter examines a unique form of terrorism with roots in Japan, but affiliations in other Asian countries as well. As James Smith of the U.S. Air Force Academy's Institute for National Security Studies writes, the case of Aum Shinrikyo—a Japanese "new religion" and cult that also embraced and practiced chemical and biological terrorism—and of the restrained and delayed Japanese government response provides significant lessons for those seeking to better understand and respond to terrorism, domestic religion-based terrorism, and weapons of mass destruction (WMD) terrorism. The chapter also illustrates the utility to terrorism of "sanctuary under national law," and of the acquisition of chemical and biological materials and production equipment under the sanctuary of legitimate business operations. Smith explores important issues of—and consequences from—governmental restraint and the persistent challenge of balancing civil liberties and national security. Finally, the case of Aum Shinrikyo also illustrates the utility of a culturally based analytical framework in examining terrorist groups and political violence, terrorist decisions and actions regarding WMD acquisition and use, and government response options and constraints.

The final chapter of this volume brings us back to the United States, where Eric Shibuya of the U.S. Marine Corps Command and Staff College examines the struggle with violent right-wing extremist groups. After describing several different types of groups, he identifies three trends as most significant when considering the threat these groups pose to the United States. The first is that the use of a WMD in a terrorist attack is clearly not beyond the scope of possibility for violent right-wing actors, in terms of motivation or in (growing) capability. The second trend is the increasing value of the Internet in putting the leaderless resistance form of operation into practice. The Internet has been a boon to the movement by allowing for the creation of virtual communities of interest that are more anonymous and physically disconnected, making investigation and surveillance much more difficult. The third and perhaps most significant trend is the growing statements of common cause between the violent right-wing movement and other terrorist movements. It may be an exaggeration to consider groups like al Qaeda and the Aryan Nations to be part of a single "movement," but it is certainly true that both groups find common cause in their hatred for the U.S. government. While strategic alliances may be less likely, tactical relationships may increase as both groups find areas of mutual benefit to work together. Overall, this chapter demonstrates that the threat from violent right-wing groups must be included in our national strategies for countering insurgency and terrorism in the twenty-first century.

CONCLUSION

As a collection, these chapters demonstrate the truly global challenge of combating terrorism and insurgency. Further, there is unfortunately a wealth of additional case studies worth exploring beyond what is covered in this volume. Clearly, there is much that any country can learn from the experience of others in how to meet these challenges in new and increasingly successful ways. Thus, this collection will hopefully stimulate the reader to pursue further research on their own, in order to expand our collective understanding of countering terrorism and insurgency in the twenty-first century.

ACKNOWLEDGMENTS

The views expressed herein are those of the author and do not purport to reflect the position of the United States Military Academy, the Department of the Army, or the Department of Defense.

ACKNOWLEDGMENTS

This project is the final installment of an ambitious trilogy, which began with *The Making of a Terrorist: Recruitment, Training and Root Causes* (published by Praeger in 2005) and continued with *Homeland Security: Protecting America's Targets* (in 2006). Together, these volumes are meant to provide a central resource for understanding the global threat of terrorism, how America is working to defend against it, and how the international community is actively seeking to disrupt, deter, and defeat those who seek to conduct terror attacks. I would like to thank Hilary Claggett at Praeger Security International for her vision and encouragement throughout this effort. Each of these multivolume projects required significant coordination, and Hilary and her staff have been enormously professional and helpful collaborators during the past 3 years. Also, the Advisory Board members for this project—Bruce Hoffman, Rohan Gunaratna, and James Robbins—have been extremely helpful in identifying authors and topics to be addressed, in addition to serving as outstanding guest lecturers to the cadets in my terrorism studies courses at West Point.

New contributions to the study of counterterrorism and counterinsurgency have never been more urgently needed. Each of the chapters in these three volumes is the product of thoughtful research and analysis, and I offer my sincere thanks to the authors for their hard work and commitment to excellence. The insights and suggestions they have provided in these pages will undoubtedly inform discussions and debate in a variety of policymaking and academic settings for the foreseeable future.

For their continued support and encouragement, I extend my gratitude to the faculty and staff of the Combating Terrorism Center (CTC) at West Point. General (R) Wayne Downing, Lieutenant Colonel Joe Felter, Dr. Jarret Brachman, and Brigadier General (R) Russell Howard have been especially important sources of mentorship and guidance. Colonel Kip McCormick, Major Rick Wrona, Mr. Brian Fishman, Mr. Clint Watts, Mr. Jim Phillips, and Ms. Lianne Kennedy Boudali have also contributed significantly to my understanding of terrorism and counterterrorism. I would also like to thank the leadership of the Department of Social Sciences—Colonel Mike Meese and Colonel Cindy Jebb—along with the Dean of the Academic Board, Brigadier General Patrick Finnegan, and the former Dean, Brigadier General (R) Daniel Kaufman, all of whom have been supportive of my publishing efforts over the last several years. I am also sincerely grateful to Mr. Tom Harrington, Deputy Assistant Director of the FBI's Counterterrorism Division, for his role in sustaining and expanding the CTC's educational mission. And of course, the CTC would not exist without the generous commitment, support, and vision of Mr. Vincent Viola, USMA Class of 1977.

My faculty colleagues throughout West Point continue to be a source of inspiration as both academic mentors and members of the U.S. armed forces. I joined West Point as a civilian faculty member and assistant dean in early Fall 2001, and the attacks of September 11 had a tremendous impact on my personal and professional life. The United States Military Academy is a very unique place to work as an academic, particularly given the current global security challenges. Upon graduation, the students I teach are commissioned as officers in the U.S. Army, and very soon find themselves on the front lines of the global counterterrorism effort. Some have been injured, some have been killed. Many of the officers who serve on the faculty and staff at West Point have also been deployed to Afghanistan, Iraq and elsewhere; some of them have fallen as well. I have never before encountered such a willingness to sacrifice, and I am continually awed by so many men and women (and their families) who are committed to a life of service to our nation. I offer them my deepest gratitude and best wishes for a long and successful military career.

Finally, my wife and daughter—Alicia and Chloe Lynn—have been sources of great motivation and support, and I thank them sincerely for their patience and tolerance during my scholarly adventures.

James J. F. Forest
January 15, 2007

Chapter 1

AN INTRODUCTION TO THE COMPARATIVE STUDY OF COUNTERTERRORISM

James J. F. Forest

The primary goal of this volume is to distill lessons and insights from past conflicts involving terrorism or insurgency that will help inform new approaches to fighting current and future counterterrorism and counterinsurgency campaigns. Volumes 1 and 2 of *Countering Terrorism and Insurgency in the 21st Century* address important themes in a mostly international and comparative perspective. The chapters of this third volume provide a more detailed analysis of the experiences of many countries and regions, adding greater qualitative depth to the comparative perspectives offered in the other two volumes.

A comparative perspective helps us identify phenomena that, while framed by different political and social arrangements, lead to a better understanding of a complex world and our place within it. In the study of counterterrorism and counterinsurgency, we are so often bound by the constraints of national thinking that a comparative perspective becomes especially valuable, because the security challenges facing the global community of responsible nations have many common characteristics. As a collection, these chapters complement each other in highlighting important themes and issues that transcend the many differences in history, culture, and experience that occur among nations. Lessons learned in counterterrorism policies and practices in different countries can offer valuable insights to those officials responsible for setting policy.[1] Further, while it is important to review cases where governments have had success, it is also vital to examine instances where things did not go so well for the government, or the terrorists actually succeeded in carrying out their deadly mission.

A SAMPLING OF SUCCESSFUL COUNTERTERRORISM OPERATIONS

On January 7, 2005, a group of suspected Islamic militants were arrested in Manila, the capital of the Philippines. The group was discovered in the process of assembling bombs for what was intended to be an attack on the Christian festival of the Black Nazarene, an annual event that attracts tens of thousands of devotees. When police examined the improvised explosive devices and bomb components, including timing gadgets and cables, they realized that the death toll of the explosions, had they occurred, would have been considerable.[2] On November 9, 2005, state and federal police forces in Australia raided dozens of properties in Melbourne and Sydney, arresting 17 men and seizing large quantities of alleged precursor chemicals, laboratory equipment, instruction manuals on the production of the explosive triacetone triperoxide (TATP), and maps and photographs of potential targets. Police and political leaders declared that the operation had foiled an imminent attack of enormous magnitude.[3]

In June 2006, London police conducted a series of arrests after uncovering a plot to explode up to 12 aircraft in mid-flight between Britain and America. Authorities said that the would-be terrorists planned to carry the explosive material and detonating devices onto aircraft disguised as drinks (or other liquids that appeared innocuous on their own but could be potentially deadly when mixed) and seemingly harmless electronic devices. Subsequently, it was revealed that authorities had been monitoring the meetings, movements, travel, spending, and the aspirations of a large group of people since December 2005, and it was this surveillance effort that led to the disruption of the plot and arrest of the cell's members.[4] Clearly, as described at length in Volume 1 of this book, intelligence plays a critical role in countering terrorism. For example, in September 2006, a sting operation conducted by authorities in Odense, Denmark, resulted in the arrest of nine men charged with suspicion of plotting to carry out a bomb attack on Danish soil. Police uncovered chemicals used to make bombs, along with computers, telephones, and CD-ROMs suggesting that a radical Islamist-inspired terror attack was imminent.[5]

Similar counterterrorism investigations conducted in the United States have resulted in arrests and convictions that, in the end, help make our nation safer. For example, on September 13, 2002, the FBI arrested five U.S. citizens near Buffalo, New York (Sahim Alwan, Faysal Galab, Yahya Goba, Shafal Mosed, and Yasein Taher), charging them with "providing, attempting to provide, and conspiring to provide material support and resources to a designated foreign terrorist organization." In addition,

Mukhtar Albakri, also a U.S. citizen, was arrested in Bahrain on the same charges. All six individuals were indicted on these charges on October 21, 2002. The arrests and indictments were based on information indicating that these individuals traveled to an al Qaeda training camp in Afghanistan in 2001, where they received military training and were visited by Osama bin Laden. All six pled guilty to terrorist related charges and received prison sentences ranging between 7 and 10 years.[6]

In Portland, Oregon, six individuals (Ahmed Bilal, his brother Mohammad Bilal, Habes Al-Saoub, Patrice Ford, Jeffrey Battle, and October Lewis) were indicted on October 3, 2002, and subsequently arrested on federal charges, including conspiracy to levy war against the United States, conspiracy to provide material support and resources to a terrorist organization, conspiracy to contribute services to al Qaeda and the Taliban, and possessing firearms in furtherance of crimes of violence. With the exception of Al-Saoub, these subjects have pled guilty to terrorism related and money laundering charges and have received federal sentences ranging from 3 to 18 years. The only subject who has not been brought to justice, Al-Saoub, is believed to have been killed in Pakistan, by Pakistani military authorities.[7]

In Los Angeles, an investigation led by the FBI's Joint Terrorism Task Force discovered that Irving Rubin and Earl Krugel—active members of the Jewish Defense League (JDL), a known violent extremist Jewish Organization—were planning to attack the Islamic Muslim Public Affairs Council (IMPAC) office in Los Angeles, or possibly the California office of United States Congressman Darrell Issa. Statements made by Krugel indicated that the motivation for the attack was to serve as a "wake up call" to the Muslim Community. Rubin and Krugel were arrested for conspiring to build and place an improvised explosive device at the IMPAC office.[8]

These cases, as well as those developed by Philip Heymann and his colleagues for use at Harvard University's John F. Kennedy School of Government, offer important learning opportunities in courses on terrorism and counterterrorism.[9] But in addition to examining successful examples of counterterrorism, it is also important to explore situations in which authorities made mistakes that could have—or did—prove lethal for those people whom they intended to protect.

EXAMINING QUESTIONABLE "SUCCESSES" IN COUNTERTERRORISM

Sometimes intelligence fails, and luck is all that prevents a terrorist attack. For example, in August 2006, German authorities disclosed a botched plot to bomb two trains. In this case, two men left suitcases stuffed with crude propane-gas bombs on trains heading for the western cities of Hamm and Koblenz, but the explosives failed to detonate because of a "technical defect," according to the German federal prosecutor. If they had detonated as intended, the police said, they would have killed a "high number" of passengers.[10]

A more dramatic example of questionable success in countering terrorism is drawn from the recent siege of a theater in Moscow. At 9 P.M. on October 23, 2002, 41 Chechen separatists calling themselves the Islamic Suicide Squad took more than 800 Moscow theatergoers hostage.[11] This precipitated a 57-hour crisis that captured the world's attention. The Chechens were armed with small arms and machine guns. They also carried a large amount of explosives, much of which was strapped to their bodies to ward off attempts by Russian authorities to take the theater by force. They sought negotiations with Russian authorities in a quest to meet their demands for an end to the war in Chechnya, withdrawal of Russian forces, and Chechen independence. On October 26, they set a deadline of 12 hours for the Russian government to comply with their demands before they would "start shooting the captives." A second deadline (7 days) demanded "to bring an end to the war . . . or they would blow up themselves, the hostages and the theater."[12] But the Russian government was never willing to cooperate or negotiate, as evidenced by the lack of official government negotiators at any point in the process. In the early morning hours of October 27, the hostage crisis ended when Russian Federal Security Service (FSB) special forces (Spetsnaz) pumped an aerosol version of a potent, fast-acting opiate named fentanyl into the theater and then stormed it by force.[13] The gas prevented the Chechens from mounting any resistance to the assault. The fentanyl, however, had a stronger effect than expected. By the end of the incident, 129 hostages and 41 hostage-takers had died—all but two of the hostages' deaths were due to the effects of gas inhalation.

As Adam Dolnik recounts in his chapter of this volume, the Russians faced a similar hostage-taking challenge a year later at a school in Beslan, with similarly disastrous results. Naturally, the authorities in Russia have little interest in "hanging out their dirty laundry" for the rest of us to see, but in cases like these the counterterrorism community would gain tremendously from a critical, introspective analysis from the strategists, tacticians, and policymakers involved about what mistakes might have been prevented, and what other countries might do to avoid similar mistakes when faced with their own terrorist hostage crisis.

LEARNING FROM INSTANCES IN WHICH THE TERRORISTS SUCCEEDED

Unfortunately, there are far too many instances where the terrorists succeed with their deadly mission, and evidence collected during post-attack investigations offer important insights for the counterterrorism community. Thus, it can be argued that authorities need to provide as much detail as possible to members of the academic community (without, of course, jeopardizing their case for possibly prosecuting the perpetrators) who are responsible for teaching the next generation of national security professionals. A recent example from Indonesia is particularly instructive.[14]

In October 2005, three men walked into separate restaurants in Bali and blew themselves up, killing 15 Indonesians, 4 Australians, and a Japanese tourist. In the course of their investigation, Indonesian police discovered the step-by-step plan of the attack, a 34-page document startling in its scope and detail. Even the smallest aspects of the attack were carefully choreographed. For example, the author identifies the intended targets as "foreign tourists from America and its allies," but recognizes that the bombers would have trouble determining the native country of many tourists. "So," he notes, "we will consider all white people the enemy." A few weeks before the attacks, the three men who would carry out the operation were sent to Bali to do a "survey" of possible targets for themselves. Beforehand, they were told to learn what they could about Bali (a popular tourist island) on the Internet, and to get tourist brochures and a map. As part of their surveillance, the men were told to "pay attention to clothes worn by local tourists" and note what kind of day packs or shoulder bags they carried and whether they carried more than one. The document, titled "The Bali Project," was found on the computer of Azhari Husin, a Malaysian-born engineer educated in Australia and Britain who became a master bomb maker and was one of the most dangerous terrorists in Southeast Asia until he was killed in a shootout with the police in November 2005. His co-planner was Mohammad Noordin Top, who has narrowly escaped capture several times and remains on the run.

Documents like these serve an important purpose beyond their primary investigative purposes—they shed light on the strategic mindset and capabilities of modern terrorist groups who have embraced the tactic of suicide bombing. For example, the author describes how the group decided that discos and nightclubs offered potential targets because most of the patrons were foreigners, and there was "no security to speak of, easy to enter." But those sites were ultimately rejected, because backpacks would be suspicious at the time of night when the clubs got crowded, after 9 P.M. That led the men to consider restaurants in Kuta, one of the most popular tourist districts, as well as the seafood restaurants on the beach at Jimbaran. "Of all the places," the document says, "this may be the easiest, God willing." The team explained how the tables at Jimbaran were arranged in the sand, about a yard apart with three to seven diners at each. "Almost 80 percent of the patrons are white," they said. Others were Chinese or Japanese, they noted, using a derogatory term. The best time to attack would be around 7:30 P.M., when the restaurants were the most crowded and a backpack would not be suspicious. There was also a further reason for choosing the restaurants at Jimbaran: many of the patrons were businessmen. "The death of foreign businessmen will have a greater impact than that of young people," the document says.

The backpack bombs were to be assembled by Mr. Azhari, and the team determined that the backpacks should not be mountaineering backpacks, but student day packs, in order to avoid suspicion. For that reason, Mr. Azhari constructed relatively light bombs, weighing roughly 22–26 pounds. He devised two elaborate detonating systems that the report explains in detail, including schematic diagrams of the wiring system and drawings of a man with the wired backpack. The first system was "direct" and connected to the explosives in the backpack. The other was on "delay," for explosives in a fanny pack worn by the bombers, with a delay time of 30 seconds; the bomber would flip the switches for that one as he approached the restaurant. That way, if he were stopped by a guard and could not set off the main bomb, the fanny pack would still explode.

Within the last 10 years, the number and lethality of terrorist attacks like this has increased worldwide. In the Palestinian Territories, a young woman by the name of Wafa Idris—a paramedic who lived in Ramallah—entered a shopping district in Jerusalem on January 27, 2002, and detonated a 22-pound bomb filled with nails and metal objects, killing an 81-year-old man and injuring more than 100 bystanders. Idris, a member of the Al Aqsa Martyr's Brigade, was the first known *istish-hadiyat* (female martyr) of the Islamic fundamentalist movement in the Middle East—but others soon followed, including Dareen Abu Aisheh, who wounded two Israeli policeman when she detonated her bomb at a roadblock near Maccabim on February 27, 2002; Aayat al-Akhras, who strolled into a supermarket in the neighborhood of Kiryat Yovel in Jerusalem and killed two Israeli civilians and wounded 22 more on March 29, 2002; and Hanadi Jaradat, a 29-year-old lawyer who calmly entered a highly popular restaurant on October 4, 2003, and killed 21 Israeli and Arab men, women, and children.[15]

Of course, while extreme militant Muslims have been a primary source of terrorism in the past decade (and are the main source of suicide bombings worldwide), they are by no means alone, as terror attacks from Sri Lanka to Ireland to Colombia demonstrate. For example, on August 15, 1998, a car bomb packed with 500 lbs. of explosives detonated in the popular shopping district of Omagh, a small town in county Tyrone, Northern Ireland (about 70 miles west of Belfast).[16] The entire front wall of SD Kells clothes shop was blasted into the building, and the roof collapsed onto the top floor. At the Pine Emporium, a furniture shop, the blast was such that furniture could later be seen sticking out the windows at the back of the building. A water main under the road was exposed by the blast, and this began pouring gallons of water over the wreckage, washing bodies down the hill. All in all, 28 people were killed by the blast, and hundreds more were injured.

We can learn much from studying what transpired to make these and other terrorist attacks successful in order to prevent new ones. This is the primary goal of the chapters in this volume. Counterterrorism professionals in the military, law enforcement, intelligence, diplomacy, and policymaking communities must all have a comprehensive understanding of the issues addressed in the first two volumes of this book, and must draw lessons from the application of hard and soft power (both successful and unsuccessful) reflected in the cases provided in this volume. As the world's superpower and leader of the global war on terrorism, the United States has a particular responsibility to learn from the successes and avoid the failures of other nations in countering terrorism and insurgency.

CONCLUSION

Studying the history of terrorism—using case studies to examine a diverse array of groups including anarchists, ethnic separatists, and religious extremists—helps us recognize that the global threat is not new, but rather, presents itself in new forms, partly due to the evolution of transportation and communications technologies. It is also important to explore the organizational strategies of terrorist groups and the individual motivations of their members, as well as specific dynamics such as recruitment, training, ideology, and communication. As demonstrated by the chapters of Volume 2, we must examine various facilitators of terrorism—such as transnational financial and criminal networks—as well as the local circumstances that support terrorism, including the political, economic and social conditions that existed before political violence erupted.

Throughout history, as Yonah Alexander observes, governments challenged by terrorism have responded in different ways. Politically, one response was to seek political means of conciliation to resolve underlying issues in an effort to undermine popular support for terrorist acts. Another response was widespread repression, not only of terrorists but of innocent civilians as well. Other responses included military attacks and police raids on supposed terrorist sites, freezing the financial assets of individuals believed to be connected to the terrorists, arranging for training in counterterrorism practices, and rallying international support, to name but a few.[17]

In formulating counterterrorism strategy and tactics for the twenty-first century, it is obviously necessary to reflect on historical examples of what has worked and what has not. Unfortunately, there are many such examples to choose from, as the diverse case studies in this volume demonstrate. The chapters of this volume provide a significant amount of geographic diversity: all the major regions of the world are covered in these chapters, and each country represented in this volume has had significant experience countering terrorism and insurgency.

New security environments and new roles and expectations require new forms of education for the counterterrorism profession. In addition to appreciating the enemy's strategies, motivations, goals, and tactics, we must develop an understanding for how complex, networked, decentralized, loosely organized groups operate. From this understanding, we can identify the political, cultural, organizational, and financial seams within those networked organizations, so that ways can be found to exploit these seams in order to degrade their operational capabilities. And equally important, we must understand the nonkinetic dimensions of today's conflicts. An insurgency is conducted in numerous locations simultaneously, including the information battlespace. Counterterrorism professionals must think in terms of influence and combined actions, as well as the impact that military and law enforcement operations will have on local perceptions. They must have a full appreciation of many forms of technology and understand what skill sets are needed for conducting strategic communications and cyber-warfare.

To some degree, the lessons contained in the chapters of this volume mirror a set of observations produced by a Rand study of counterinsurgency published in April 1962, which highlighted the need to:

- Identify and redress the political, economic, military, and other issues fueling an insurgency;
- Gain control over and protect the population, which the counterinsurgent must see as the prime center of gravity in any counterinsurgency conflict;
- Establish an immediate permanent security presence in all built-up areas cleared of enemy forces;
- Accumulate extensive, fine-grained human and other intelligence on insurgent plans, modes of operations, personnel, and support networks;
- Avoid actions that might antagonize the population; and
- Convince the population that they represent the "winning side" and intend to prevail until complete victory is secured.[18]

The salience of these observations for the current global security environment—45 years later—is striking, and hopefully not reflective of our inability to learn important lessons from our own history. Overall, a predominant theme in the literature on counterterrorism and counterinsurgency, both old and new, highlights the need to have more situational awareness and strategic understanding than the enemy. The case studies provided in this volume, combined with the chapters of the previous two volumes of *Countering Terrorism and Insurgency in the 21st Century*, thus provide a comprehensive understanding at the strategic and would pursue what was viewed to be an unconventional path. The fact that terrorism was not recognized to be of strategic importance or a threat to U.S. national security—coupled with the inherent inertia and generally conservative aspects of curriculum development at all universities, as well as the bureaucratic inertia within the civilian and military bureaucracies—in large part accounted for the slow pace of the evolution of terrorism as a systematic, identified field of study. These impediments continue to slow the evolution that continues today. The fact is that conventional members of the academy, as well as the military establishment (with their focus on the Soviet threat during and at the end of the Cold War and their continuing emphasis on conventional warfare), failed to grasp a new reality—namely that while terrorism may have come from an ancient tradition, it was as Brian Jenkins succinctly and very insightfully noted "A New Mode of Conflict."[6] That is, the modernization of terrorism could be seen as a result of two profound changes, notably the introduction of commercial jet aircraft as the primary means of international travel and the maturation of television as the rapidly growing dominant medium for global communication.

As a result of these interrelated developments terrorists could literally strike at global targets in a matter of hours, and in the conduct of their operations they could ignore the arbitrary boundaries of nation-states as they seized aircraft flying at over 500 miles an hour. In effect, the terrorists were engaging in what could now be called low intensity aerospace warfare; a form of warfare that would be refined with murderous efficiency with the events of 9/11. Moreover, they could use the television and its profound visual impact to have an instantaneous and international form of "armed propaganda" or "propaganda by the deed" that would greatly exceed the wishes and capabilities of the most dedicated terrorists that preceded them. The first generation of new terrorists was transforming their operational art by engaging in what some refer to as "non-territorial terrorism—a form of terror not confined to a clearly delineated area."[7]

This first generation would be replaced by a second one, who further amplified their capabilities of spreading fear and intimidation to a global audience through the use of the Internet. Unfortunately, while the terrorists very effectively utilized technology to greatly enhance their capabilities, the lack of flexibility and imagination that characterized the academic response to the threat was mirrored in what could be called the doctrinal response of a counterterrorism community that was only beginning to understand and organize to meet a new challenge. Both the civilian bureaucracies responsible for national security and especially the military still thought and relied on a spatial approach to countering a nonterritorial, nonspatial threat and adversary. In effect, they were unwilling to "think out of the box," a term that that has been used so much that is has too often become an empty slogan. Those involved in doctrinal, policy, and operational developments in combating terrorism stayed "in the box" because they either could not or would not let go of the restraints created by organizational, legalistic, or operational boundaries in meeting the nonterritorial nature of the threat.

Organizationally, the terrorists increasingly relied on the use of compartmentalized cells that provided them with security as well as considerable operational flexibility, and cost them the ability to coordinate their attacks—a cost that would diminish in the anonymity of cyberspace with the coming of the Internet.[8] Moreover, counterterrorism organizations and forces relied on traditional top-down hierarchies where there was not a lateral sharing of information and there were often cumbersome divisions between line and staff functions. Instead of the flat organizations that could develop cadres of counterterrorism professionals to mirror the terrorists and have the necessary flexibility, conventional organizational doctrine acted as a serious barrier to the creation of new types of organizations to meet an increasingly decentralized adversary who did not suffer from the impediments caused by administrative "stove piping." Admittedly, there were (and still remain) valid issues about having the necessary oversight and accountability, but that concern was employed at times as one of the ways of justifying and protecting existing bureaucratic turfs. The situation was excerbated by the fact that the turf battles often led to bureaucratic and legalistic boundaries. While the terrorists were transnational and transorganizational, existing governmental organizations even lacked the capacity and willingness to achieve a unity of command that is essential in combating those who are not limited in their operations by physical, legal, or bureaucratic boundaries. As in the case of academia, the governmental response to terrorism—where it existed—during this period was fragmented, as each civilian and military entity defined its mission based on achieving its own bureaucratic place under the sun.

The concept, for example, of "the lead agency" had more to do with affecting a bureaucratic compromise than achieving a unity of purpose and operational capability in combating terrorism.[9] The military's organizational emphasis on having a physically delineated bureaucratic field of operations even when confronted with the nonspatial nature of nonterritorial commands could also be readily seen in the geographically defined commands and the unfortunate continuing interservice rivalries, despite the calls for "jointness." The problem was also manifested within the intelligence community that, while it did recognize terrorism as a global issue like narcotics and organized crime, still emphasized a traditional Cold War geographic approach in meeting such threats. In addition, the agencies unfortunately did not share even the limited information they had with other community members prior to the very costly lessons that perhaps have been learned in the post-9/11 period.

In the 1970s and into the 1980s, bureaucratic warfare often took precedence over the war on terrorism, as the forces of inertia led to a situation where the United States at the federal level (and even much more so at the state and local level), failed to adjust to the truly international challenges created by nonterritorial terrorism. Moreover, especially in the area of operational doctrine, the traditional focus on placing terrorism as a subset of tactics under the general term insurgency also reinforced the spatial orientation. For example, "the hearts and minds approach" applied to a territorially based insurgency might be appropriate; but how could it be implemented when the nonterritorial terrorists operated beyond the boundaries of a particular geographical conflict arena? Whose government could be strengthened under Internal Defense and Development (IDAD) Programs and what psychological techniques could be used to win over populations when the conflict was in the fullest sense global in nature? Moreover, the "battle for hearts and minds" has now been changed with the rise of religious extremism to become "the battle for hearts and souls," creating yet another new development to challenge existing doctrine.

FINALLY RECOGNIZING THE THREAT: THE 1990S AND BEYOND: REACTION AND THE LACK OF INTEGRATION

In assessing developments within the terrorism studies academic, policy, and operational areas since the 1970s and 1980s, one sees a pattern of responses to the threats and acts of terrorism ranging from reluctant awareness, very cautious incremental responses, a failure to recognize the growing strategic threat, and above all a failure—which has aptly been called "a failure of imagination"—to recognize the profoundly changing nature of terrorism.[10]

While there were a number of events that finally led to the recognition of the changing nature of the threat and the concomitant requirement for innovative programs, three incidents tend to stand out. The first was the initial bombing of the World Trade Center on February 26, 1993. That event should have been a wake-up call that other attacks would follow—a warning that was confirmed by a perpetrator who, when caught, stated that his accomplices would seek the complete destruction that they failed to achieve that day. But, while there was public shock and concern that (in a sense) terrorism had come home to the United States, there nevertheless was the view that any other major attack would somehow not take place in the interior of what was called "the heartland" of the country. Terrorism may have spread to the urban centers on the coasts, but the sense of insularity remained. Somehow, people believed, terrorism would remain an urban, coastal affair.

This insularity would change with the bombing of the Federal Building in Oklahoma City on April 19, 1995. The myth of insular safety was destroyed as the shock waves of fear generated outwardly from the very center of the country. If a major bombing happened in Oklahoma City, what other Midwestern city would be safe? Ironically, while there was a forced recognition that there were no safe havens against terrorism in the United States, the recognition led to an overreaction, as officials and the public assumed the bombing was the result of Middle Eastern terrorists. It would take time for them to recognize that terrorism is not limited to various boundaries or nationalities. The perpetrators forced the public to accept the reality that American terrorists were quite capable of killing their fellow Americans. However, the bombing of the Murrah Building was not (despite claims made to the contrary) the end of American "innocence in the heartland," but the end of American insularity.

Those two bombings and other incidents did initiate a plethora of legislative action and training programs to prepare the national government and state and local communities for effectively responding to terrorist incidents. The primary focus of these was the training of first responders. As a result, such entities as the Memorial Institute for the Prevention of Terrorism (MIPT) in Oklahoma City—supported by federal funding—developed a variety of programs to enable fire and police departments, medical personnel, and others involved in disasters to respond, contain, and lessen the impact of terrorism and natural disasters. Clearly this was an important first step. But there would also be a need to develop programs where the research would, through the effort to achieve a degree of integration within academia and with the government, take the initiative in preventing and deterring incidents. There was, and still is, the need to develop the specializations required to understand, forecast, and ideally go on the academic, operational, and policy offensive in regards to short-, mid-, and long-term threats. This focus on reactive measures and the training of field personnel and emergency managers, however laudable, took precedent over the broader types of research and analysis required in both the academic and intelligence community to effectively engage in strategic assessments of future dangers and how to prevent them. The events of 9/11 would unfortunately affirm the danger of such a gap in research.[11]

It was, of course, the tragedies of 9/11 that finally mobilized the United States as the major superpower to take the initiative both within its homeland and overseas to address terrorism as a major threat to national and international security; a threat that had been recognized by a number of countries who were forced how to learn to live with terrorism. The response to the attacks on the Pentagon, the World Trade Center, and the United Airlines Flight 93 were a manifestation after a major incident to "do something now," instead of also developing an integrated strategy and approach between governmental departments, the military, and academia to acquire the capability to systematically encourage the development and refinement in the chaotically growing field of terrorism, where instant expertise was often the rule and real knowledge the exception. There was, and more than ever now is, a vital requirement to educate and train highly qualified terrorism professionals.

Not only at the national level, but also increasingly at the state and local levels, governmental authorities have been heavily involved in establishing funding and research for programs on terrorism. The funding for the Department of Homeland Security Centers of Excellence illustrates the current focus on developing a research agenda and operationalizing preventing and responding to terrorism. As of now there are six major Centers that are initially funded for three years, each headed by a university in partnership with other institutes of higher education and outside organizations. These include The John Hopkins University, with the creation of its Center for the Study of High Consequence Event Preparedness and Response; the University of Southern California's Homeland Security Center for Risk and Economic Analysis of Terrorism Events (CREATE); Texas A&M University's Homeland Security National Center for Foreign Animal and Zoonotic Disease Defense; the University of Minnesota's Center for Homeland Security for Food Protection and Defense; the University of Maryland and its Homeland Security Center of Excellence for Behavioral and Social Research on Terrorism and Counterterrorism; and Michigan State University's Center for Advancing Microbial Research Assessment (CAMRA). While it is difficult to make generalized observations about the aims and activities of these Centers and other governmental programs and how they may impact on the present and future educations of counterterrorism professionals, a number of observations are nevertheless in order.[12]

In the first place, while the Centers' activities relate to government-sponsored research and not the development of undergraduate and graduate programs leading to a degree, it is interesting to see that the major research problems involve addressing the challenges created by terrorism that reflect concerns primarily based on current threat assessments. In a sense, these are the threats *de jour,* and while each of them are certainly important, one does not see a broader, longer-term integrated research strategy that takes into account those strategic threats that, as the Duke of Marlborough said, "May be over the horizon." Certainly, topics ranging from defense against agro-terrorism to understanding suicide bombers are important, but they are (in a sense) an expression of "conventional wisdom." What should also have been—and must in the future be—considered is promoting the understanding of future longer-term threats that may not presently be recognized. Just as the slow growth of Islamic Fundamentalism was not perceived to be important until after the fall of the Shah and the seizing of the hostages in Iran, will academics, policymakers, and operators be blindsided by other emerging threats? The understandable government sponsored "do something approach" certainly has validity in meeting present threats, but does it continue a reactive short-term response to what is a long-term protracted conflict?

Secondly, while there certainly is a broad scope of research topics that will be carried out by each Center, that broad scope creates difficulties in developing a wide variety of programs to, in the fullest sense, educate a new generation of counterterrorism professionals. That is, there does not appear to be a central core of areas, a canon on terrorism studies that can provide a more integrated approach to fully developing the discrete field of terrorism studies and subspecializations that emerge from the canon within what could be viewed as an emerging new academic discipline.

The lack of integration is further seen with the emphasis on separate Centers of Excellence. This is not to suggest that such an approach may not be needed to focus on particular problem areas, but as in the case of bureaucracies, we may be emulating the development of intellectual-academic "stove piping," something that unfortunately has already taken place in government organizations. "Stove piping" acts as a barrier to lateral integration of effort. Moreover, such an approach may also emulate the type of turf battles that have too often characterized organizational responses to terrorism.

Thirdly, the lack of integration may also be seen in the absence of a Center whose task is to act as an overarching coordinator of research agendas and efforts. Perhaps even more troubling is the fact that at a time when there is a need to educate terrorism professionals in the state of the art, there is, in a sense, no basic uniform requirement—something that would be similar to the core courses in a college or university. Perhaps there should or will be new centers established both in and out of government to address the issues raised here—centers for the development and advancement of terrorism studies. Moreover, the specializations—with the two exceptions of the John Hopkins' program and the University of Maryland's—tend to favor technological innovation in regards to preventing or countering terrorism. Unquestionably the technological threats are there, but does this approach rely too much on scientific and technological fixes to address the at once complex and yet human intensive terrorists threats?

There may be a lesson to be learned from the experience of the intelligence community in combating terrorism. That is, it is widely understood that the United States has relied too heavily on technical intelligence (TECHINT) and not enough on human intelligence (HUMINT) in combating terrorism. Recent changes, including the newly established Director of National Intelligence, are committed to addressing this problem. In the organization of academic research on terrorism, are we running a similar risk of becoming technologically muscle-bound against an emotional and often value- or religious-driven, highly committed asymmetric adversary?

THE ACADEMIC ARENA: SEEKING TO FIND A PLACE FOR TERRORISM RESEARCH AND TEACHING—THE QUEST FOR IDENTIFYING DISCIPLINES

If the governmental response to addressing the challenges engaging in research on terrorism is characterized by the lack of a central direction—or an intellectual core—the problem is also manifested in academia, where there is still no agreement on where terrorism "fits" and therefore what type of organization of knowledge should be used in establishing the boundaries and direction of terrorism studies.

As noted earlier, prior to the 1970s there was a body of literature on the history of terrorism, but only as part of a broader examination of the French Revolution and the development of terrorism as an aspect of regime repression before and during the Russian Revolution. There was also a focus on the role mass terrorism played as an integral part of the rise of modern totalitarian governments. But one of the first treatments of terrorism as a potential field in itself took place within political science, especially in reference to those who were addressing a new area of investigation in reference to comparative politics and international relations. This focus could be expected, since the pioneering studies of modern terrorism primarily addressed the political purposes of terrorism in the conduct of international affairs, and especially the challenges democratic states face in reconciling the need for security with the traditions of due process and individual rights. In the 1980s, the emphasis on the political aspects of terrorism would slowly grow within the discipline of political science in the United States, as there was recognition of how such threats and acts could influence the conduct of foreign affairs and broader issues of national security.

By the same token, there were relatively early studies in the discipline of psychology that explored the motivation behind terrorism. In addition, as a result of the hostage-takings of the 1970s that culminated in the Iranian hostage crisis, there was a growing emphasis on hostage behavior. This emphasis on hostage behavior, both academically and operationally, was carried over to the field of law enforcement, where there was growing literature—and concomitantly, training courses—dealing with hostage negotiation and what (at the time) was referred to as "siege management." This emphasis was not solely the result of acts of terrorism; rather, it was necessitated by the increasingly rapid response of police forces arriving on scene before the perpetrators could escape. As a result, there were more hostage-barricade situations, ranging from domestic disputes to bank robberies to terrorist's incidents, which required skilled negotiators. At the same time, operationally, there was also an increased concern for learning how to train, equip, and deploy special weapons and tactical teams to be activated and take action as required; especially if negotiations failed. The development of the literature in the tactical arena was also seen with the emergence of highly trained national counterterrorism forces, including the U.S. Delta Force, the British SAS, and other specialized units. But, it would take time before those involved in the discipline of law enforcement and the administration of justice, particularly in the United States, would begin to systematically address the whole spectrum of challenges created for police and other security forces at all levels—from national, to state and local.

The reason for this slow evolution was that—with the exception of various extremist groups in the 1960s (for example the Weathermen)—the long-enduring attacks by Puerto Rican separatist groups and the existence of various right-wing extremists, domestic terrorism were not viewed to be a major threat to the maintence of law and order. Moreover, law enforcement studies did not address the then-psychologically "distant" threat of international terrorism, which was still viewed to be "what happened to other people in other countries." Certainly, there were other disciplines that had emerging specialists who drew on their expertise in regards to violence as a means of beginning to understand the comparative and interdisciplinary aspects of both domestic and international terrorism, but such approaches were largely individual and not part of a large coordinated research agenda.

Within the hard sciences, there were indeed pioneering studies on (for example) early concerns over what was in the 1970s and early 1980s often called "super terrorism," before the term "weapons of mass destruction" became popular, but such studies languished in the face of the continuing resort to more conventional bombings by terrorists.[13] Nevertheless, there were particular advances in the fields of engineering, where there was a recognition of the need to "harden targets," especially those with symbolic meaning as well as those considered a part of the "critical infrastructure," whose destruction could greatly disrupt the social, economic, and political order of a community or a country. However, such studies were not part of the academic program in engineering schools.

Finally, while there certainly were a wide variety of courses at medical schools and health science centers related to threats to public health, there were virtually no courses that specifically focused on terrorism as a potentially major threat. Such events as the Aum Shinrikyo attack, where sarin gas was used, would help change the traditional orientation that did not take into account the impact on health (and indeed literally life or death) within a community. Therefore, in looking back to the early days, while historians and political scientists may have dominated terrorism studies, their efforts were often not recognized as a legitimate field within the discipline; at the most they were on the intellectual edges.

WHERE DOES TERRORISM FIT WITHIN ACADEMIA: SHOULD THERE BE A SEARCH FOR A HOME?

It is ironic that whereas at one time terrorism studies were an academic orphan, today so many disciplines want the subject to be a member of their family. One wishes this desire was primarily the result of a genuine intellectual interest in the topic; and perhaps to a degree it is. But the realities of the long-coming recognition, especially in the United States, is based on the combination of funding and empire building as universities—like government organizations and the corporate sector—try to find their place in what tragically has now become a new market. Moreover, whereas in the past a specialization in terrorism was viewed to be an esoteric skill, now reputations, tenure grants, and promotions can be acquired from research and publication on a myriad of terrorism-related topics.

In discussing where terrorism "fits" in academia, it would be useful to assess the areas based on requirements in general undergraduate education, possible majors, or courses of study, and then focus on graduate education. There obviously is no clear fix, but there are alternatives that should be considered when creating curriculum and programs to educate the next generation of counterterrorism professionals. At the outset, more than ever the requirement for a solid liberal arts education is important to the potential counterterrorism professional. First and foremost, the ability to engage in critical thinking, as well as having an excellent ability to express oneself in written and oral form, is absolutely vital. The requirement for critical thinking is especially important given the need for the ability to identify and separate significant information from the growing mass of unimportant data, information, and misinformation that surrounds the current avalanche of material on terrorism. The ability to engage in critical thinking is also important in order to develop the imagination and accompanying creativity to discern future trends and outthink (and outcreate) those who, in their own nefarious way, have developed their own arts of destruction and carnage. The benefits and requirements of a good liberal arts education provide a fundamental contribution to the education of the would-be counterterrorism professional. Moreover, a broad-based understanding of the social and behavioral sciences coupled with the requirement for international studies would provide the foundation that could be readily applied to terrorism studies on both the undergraduate and graduate level, as well as applied in the field.

It might also be advisable to have a required undergraduate liberal arts course on terrorism that would assist the students in developing an appreciation of the changing security environment they will be working in, irrespective of their profession, with particular emphasis on a solid overview of what is, and where, terrorism would fit in their potential careers.

This course, much like other survey courses, could serve not only as an introduction to terrorism per se, but be a gateway for students who have or might become interested in terrorism studies as a rapidly expanding area of educational, professional and policy concern. Such a course could also be offered in schools of engineering, business, and other professionally oriented colleges as a means of providing a basis through which students might consider applying their newly found knowledge to an important field of specialization. Candidly, it is troublesome to see, for example, that schools of business that are training the executives of the future, or those now involved in continuing education do not require at least one basic course on security and terrorism. It is, and will increasingly be, a vital skill-set in the conduct of doing business both domestically and overseas.

As far as specific undergraduate programs on terrorism studies, there are various alternatives to be considered, developed, and implemented for the would-be professional in counterterrorism. At the outset, political science will continue to be a major focal point for the study of terrorism, not only because a number of pioneers came from the field but also as a result of the fact that ultimately there has been an agreement over the years that one of the major elements of terrorism is its political nature. Moreover, the study of terrorism as a political phenomenon may fit well into the subfields of comparative politics and international relations; the former because it provides the foundation for developing comparative analytical analysis and the latter because of the increasing significance of terrorists as major international actors. In addition, political science programs that offer courses on national security with a particular emphasis on the application of military power and the basics of intelligence could readily be adjusted to meet the unique educational challenges in these areas caused by the requirements necessary to combat terrorism.

A second, readily identifiable discipline involves programs associated with criminal justice and the administration of justice. Particularly in regards to domestic terrorism—which is still first and foremost viewed to be a criminal act—it is indeed essential that those who will be involved in law enforcement are knowledgeable about the nature of terrorism and the means to combat it through the legal system. The emphasis on this approach has of course accelerated as a result of the Murrah bombing, the attacks on the World Trade Center and the Pentagon, and the emerging recognition that other incidents and possibly campaigns of terrorism—including those from abroad—will increase in the years to come. One may also suggest that, given the increasingly international dimensions of terrorism, any new or extant program on terrorism would have to have a comparative/international scope to assist in educating those who are working with foreign countries or stationed overseas.

This requirement can be readily seen, for example, with the greatly expanded effort of the Federal Bureau of Investigation's operations throughout the world in its new role of combating terrorism. Certainly the behavioral sciences, most notably psychology, have a key role to play and a specialization on the motivation and behavior of terrorists is necessary. While there are impressive strides being made in the systematic long-term study of individual and group behavior among terrorists and their supporters, such studies need to be intensified by addressing the psychological impact on individuals and the sociological and economic impact on the community at large. In addition, other disciplines within the social and behavioral sciences can also make major contributions ranging from understanding the historical roots and perceptions of terrorists to anthropological examinations of how terrorism and terrorists evolve and are conditioned through the complex processes of acculturation. Still other disciplines, such as economics and finance, also have their contributions to make, ranging from the cost of the impact of terrorism on the economy and the existing financial order. One may, of course, suggest that other departments could independently create ad hoc interdisciplinary entities, collaborating across their departments to advance research and educate a new generation of terrorist professionals. However, it is important to have an integrated core of areas of investigation along with those yet to exist, a canon of knowledge that can lead the way to achieving a unified field, as contrasted to the often-fragmented approach to addressing terrorism.

Achieving a meaningful degree of intellectual unity of action that can compete with what unfortunately has characterized terrorists operations will not be easy, especially since, as noted, the field of terrorism studies is certainly not (and should not be) the monopoly of any particular discipline. The comments of one particularly thoughtful authority in the field have relevance to the requirements for interdisciplinary studies on the undergraduate and graduate level:

> The field of terrorism does not neatly fit into one discipline. Terrorism is truly a multidisciplinary subject, and I believe future terrorism specialists need to know this from the very beginning. I was very grateful in my BA and MA programs and policy analysis Ph.D. program that allowed me to take courses relevant to the field of terrorism and political violence in the fields of political science, history, sociology, forensic science, political psychology, public health, peace studies, emergency management, religion and area studies.... I also benefited from course work in communications, which I found highly relevant since terrorism is communication.[14]

The author's points are quite well taken and one can emphasize, starting on the undergraduate level, that the importance of participating in the interdisciplinary area-studies approach is especially valuable, since there remains a paucity of terrorists "specialists" who are trained in the language and culture of a society based on extensive study and, especially in the graduate arena, field work. The authors' concern of overspecialization in one department also has validity in that:

> What worries me is that a new generation of "terrorism specialists" will be birthed out solely of political science departments and have a concentration of Middle Eastern studies. This will create a bias in understanding. Much like the vast generation of Sovietologists who never saw the Soviet collapse and would not offer assistance in the post-Cold War world full of ethnic and asymmetric warfare/terrorism.[15]

The observer's point is also especially well taken since, as noted earlier; the focus on funding programs tends to be on current, not future threats. We need an off-the-shelf capability to constantly monitor the global threat environment based on overarching area programs and an ability to have experts immediately available before and when a new threat location becomes significant. The current reliance of an academic "surge approach" may be useful as an aspect of short-term crisis management in the academic and operational arena, but it does not provide the scope or consistency of effort needed to monitor, prevent, and respond to future threats from areas where terrorists plan and launch regional or international operations.

The importance of the interdisciplinary approach is readily apparent, but as in previous programs there will continue to be problems associated with coordination and communication between and among different disciplines. Moreover, in regards to such real concerns to the academic such as tenure, promotion, and funding, the importance of having an academic department or home cannot be dismissed. But a creative approach to integration can and should take place. As in the case of bureaucracy, academic administrators cannot afford to engage in turf battles when addressing terrorism.

At the graduate level, there certainly can and should be more narrowly based specializations in regards to combating terrorism both on the MA and Ph.D. levels as well as postdoctoral studies. Flexibility is key. For example, one may envision a 3-year intensive terrorism studies program that would include a 1-year general overview of the field followed by 2 years of specializing in the social, behavioral, or hard sciences ranging from history to public health. Perhaps one could consider developing a professional terminal degree entitled the MA or MS in Terrorism Studies (M.A.T.S., M.S.T.S.) similar in length and recognition to a Masters in Public Administration (M.P.A.) or a Masters in Fine Arts (M.F.A.).

Programs for the Ph.D. could be offered as a continuation of the specialized M.A.T.S./M.S.T.S., with a very heavy emphasis placed on original and applied research. In addition, one may suggest that—especially at the graduate level—an internship or residency should be required in the public or private sector to begin a vital process of creating the necessary interconnectivity to the academic, bureaucratic, operational, and policy sectors. All of these programs can also benefit by the use of distance education and continuing education. The traditional campus setting would remain important, but there are so many other alternatives available to deliver the necessary knowledge.

It is beyond the scope of this chapter, but the issue of accreditation must also be addressed. Unfortunately, there has been a massive growth of terrorism programs without the establishment of appropriate standards and requirements. In part, this is because of the rapid emergence of the field and the lack of a body of prior knowledge and sufficient authorities to evaluate a growing field. The accreditation can ultimately take place at the university-wide association level, the respective schools and disciplines, and other agencies. Moreover, one could also model accreditation of a degree based on such certification programs as the American Society for Industrial Security's CPP Program (Certified Professional Program), which includes core courses on security and terrorism. The developing standards is absolutely essential, especially now in a period of often chaotic change, when anyone can "put up a shingle" that they are a terrorism specialist.

In addition to these civilian programs, there is (and will be) a growing need to educate a new generation of uniformed terrorism specialists in the respective military academies, as well as the staff and war colleges. While the need for present courses of studies will most certainly be required, as in all things it will be necessary to finally move beyond the verities of traditional military thinking as well as the strategies and doctrine associated with the Cold War. Innovation is required to address and understand the transformation of warfare, in which the changing nature of terrorism is but one manifestation. Positive advances are taking place in this arena. The privately funded Combating Terrorism Center (CTC) at the United States Military Academy is clearly an advance, along with the announcement that the academy's first minor's program will be on terrorism studies.[16] In addition, the Department of Defense's Counterterrorism Fellowship Program, with selected universities and overseas partners, has provided a venue in which future leaders can learn the arts and sciences, tactics and strategies of terrorism early in their careers, instead of essentially learning how to combat terrorism on the battlefield with occasional short courses in professional military studies.[17] This approach to training and education should also be utilized by the intelligence community, whose members are often on the forefront of combating terrorism. As noted earlier, there are no quick fixes in educating the next generation of counterterrorism professionals, but one thing is clear: civilian and military educators, institutions, and programs do not have the luxury of engaging in a slow, incremental process of curriculum-building to meet a very real threat. Yet, by the same token, those educators face the daunting task of bringing rigor and standards to a field of study that may be drawn from many traditional disciplines but is as new as the next incident.

THE NEED FOR A BODY OF KNOWLEDGE: THE QUEST FOR A CANON ON TERRORISM

In the final analysis, it is important to recognize that despite attempts at academic organization and funding, it will be very difficult to achieve the recognition of terrorism as a field of study until there is an extensive body of knowledge ranging from general theory to classic works. The development of a canon on terrorism will take time, since it is still such a recent specialization, much less a formally recognized and academically sanctioned field of study. As one authority astutely notes:

> The blunt truth is that we have failed as a community to create or identify a 'canon' of counterterrorism theory which would represent a foundation for new research and policy recommendations. While . . . the strategist can resort when in trouble to the almost eternal verities of Sun Tsu or Clausewitz, there are no essential writings which illuminate all potential challenges in the field of counterterrorism.[18]

It is not that studies do not exist. Indeed, they have vastly proliferated since the 1970s where one could have a core library of the major academic works on terrorism numbering no more than 200–300 books. The problem now, of course, is there has been a massive proliferation of books, articles, monographs, and other publications as well as databases on the Internet. There certainly are excellent sources, but quite candidly the would-be specialist is confronted with material of very uneven quality. In a real sense, the problem today, as in other areas, is that there is too much information and data, and therefore the scholar and the professional face the very demanding task of information handling and, more traditionally, engaging in a critical evaluation of source material. It would be beyond the scope of this chapter to provide a bibliography of terrorism source material. Such bibliographies are numerous and readily available.[19] Rather one can suggest areas where those who would develop a canon to guide professionals should address. In part this gap is the result of the fact that terrorism still lacks an academic home. But more specifically, there are other gaps that are a manifestation of the failure of institutions of higher education to recognize the need for an emerging specialization in one or field or in an interdisciplinary arena.

Firstly, there is an absence of overarching theories that can provide integrative conceptualizations to achieve a level of unity and direction in the field. This does not mean to suggest that there needs to be plethora of grand or general theory, but the field must acquire what could be called its own "intellectual center of gravity." Secondly, one can readily draw on theories, especially in comparative politics, to develop the necessary foundation for the analysis of terrorists groups and movements from international politics to place such an analysis in a broader context. These, coupled with the existing and growing sophistication of political methodology, will greatly enhance the ability to refine the new field. Thirdly, there already exists a body of knowledge that can be readily built upon to further develop the canon—most notably the extensive theories and associate studies related to counterinsurgency; this especially since now terrorism is often viewed to be an aspect of global counterinsurgency. There is recognition of both continuity and change in regards to understanding the mutation of both insurgencies and terrorism. Fourthly, in developing the canon there will be a particular need for theoretical "yardsticks" that can be refined to measure and evaluate the operational effectiveness of counterterrorism operations, strategies and policy. Finally, a canon on terrorism faces the ultimate task of addressing where terrorism fits within the most fundamental areas of inquiry: the role of violence in political life, the transformation of warfare, and the concomitant transformation of terrorism. None of these are going to be easy tasks in an international arena where the classic state system is now undergoing fundamental assaults of change created by nonstate actors, the impact of the global web, and the acceleration of technological change.[20]

Faced with these challenges, a new generation of counterterrorism specialists may have a very daunting challenge, but it can also place them at the forefront of researching and, consequently, understanding the fundamental change that characterizes and challenges our human existence.

CONCLUSION

There is, unfortunately, every reason to believe that a new generation of terrorists—even as they may pursue highly different causes—will increasingly forge their own form of academic alliances through their use of the Internet. They may not belong to particular institutions of higher education or be drawn from a particular discipline; but whether they have shared outlooks or engage in marriages of convenience, in too many instances, they are professionals without the need for core courses, master's theses or dissertations. They are engaged in developing their own areas of specialization and interdisciplinary capabilities, and the completion of their studies may end in the death of their victims as well as their own.[21] Like it or not, they have forged both a virtual and real community of the committed—committed to a protracted conflict that can and will increasingly test the resolve of their global targets. Confronted with these realities, it is absolutely essential that the United States and other governments, organizations, and regions educate, in the fullest sense, a new generation of counterterrorism professionals, a generation that has the knowledge and commitment to not only help lead and guide those who are in the forefront of combating terrorism, but also help to educate both traditional, modernizing, and developed societies who are confronted by adversaries who are rapidly developing their own body of murderous knowledge. We can not afford the luxury of long curriculum committee meetings, drawn out bureaucratic competition, or the lack of operational unity in the face of "the men and women of violence" who, in too many instances, are rapidly completing their undergraduate and graduate education where the degree requirements lead to fear, injury, and death of so many whose only "crime" in many cases was that they were adjudged "guilty by location," guilty of being at the wrong place at the wrong time. The semester for the counterterrorism professionals must begin, since today's terrorists are now completing their advanced studies.

NOTES

1. Sean K. Anderson and Stephen Sloan, *Historical Dictionary of Terrorism*, 2nd ed. (Lanham and London: Scarecrow Press, 2002).

2. Crane Brinton, *The Anatomy of Revolution* (Upper Saddle River, NJ: Prentice-Hall, 1965).

3. Hannah Arendt, *The Origins of Totalitarianism* (New York: Harcourt, 1966).

4. It is beyond the scope of this chapter to provide a list of many of the excellent books on insurgency—both classics and new. Unlike books on terrorism where few have weathered the passing of time to validate them given the recent origins of the emerging field, one can readily argue over who are the best strategists, theorists, and writers on insurgency. One of the author's favorites that in many ways is just as relevant today as when it was written is: Bernard Fall, *The Two Viet-Nams: A Political and Military Analysis*, 2nd ed., revised (New York: Praeger, 1967). The authors' analysis of insurgent organizations in a territorially based conflict remains valid today and certainly can be applied to what is now called Global Insurgency. For an excellent discussion of how traditional theories and concepts of insurgency apply to modern insurgency see: David Killcullen, "Countering Global Insurgency," *Journal of Strategic Studies* (August 24, 2005): 597–617. For fine a collections of articles that address the changing face of insurgency see: Robert J. Bunker (ed.), *Networks, Terrorism and Global Insurgency* (Oxford: Routledge, 2005). The contributors include representatives of a new generation of scholars who are, and will continue to, make their names in the field.

5. Brian Jenkins' studies at the Rand Corporation and Paul Wilkinson's contribution to the field were and still are very significant. They established the foundation and encouraged other pioneers who were finding their ways in a yet to be recognized field.

6. Brian Jenkins, *International Terrorism: A New Mode of Conflict* (Los Angeles, CA: Crescent Publications, 1974).

7. Stephen Sloan, *The Anatomy of Nonterritorial Terrorism: An Analytical Essay* (Gaithersburg, MD: International Association of Chiefs of Police, 1979).

8. J. K. Zawodny, "Infrastructures of Terrorist Organizations," *Conflict Quarterly* 1 (Spring 1981), 61–70. The author drew from his experience in the Polish underground to provide one of the earliest and best accounts of, not only the way clandestine organizations operate, but also how the organizational structure influences the behavior of both leaders and followers in a combat cell.

9. William Regis Farral, *The U.S. Government Response to Terrorism: In Search of an Effective Strategy* (Boulder, CO: Westview Press, 1982). If one reads this book they will be struck by how many of the problems that confronted Washington in 1982 remain today. Moreover Washington is still "In Search of an Effective Strategy."

10. The impact of the "failure of imagination" lack of vision, bureaucratic turf battles that helped to lead to the events of 9/11 will be subject to continuous historical investigation in the years to come. The following report provides a very readable work that seeks to address what took place before and during the attacks. Certainly there are areas in the respective accounts that are subject to debate and new questions are continually raised, but the report should be required reading for potential, present and future counterterrorism professionals. Steve Strasser (ed.) with an Introduction by Craig R. Whitney, *The 9/11 Investigations: Staff Report of the 9/11 Commission* (New York: Public Affairs Reports, 2004).

11. The author served on the steering committee that was charged with establishing the goals, organization, program, and funding The Memorial Institute for the Prevention of Terrorism. Given the understandable concern and pride in how the first responders and the community reacted to the bombing along with the extraordinary assistance on the state, local and national level there was a desire to apply what was called "The Oklahoma Standard" to assist others who would face acts of terrorism.

12. U.S. Department of Homeland Security. No update listed, http://www.dhs.gov/dhspublic/interapp/editorial/editorial_0498.xml (accessed May 22, 2006).

13. Robert K. Mullen, "Mass Destruction and Terrorism," *Journal of International Affairs* 32 (1978): 63–89. Dr. Mullen wrote this very prescient study. The threat was readably recognized by those who had the imagination and talent to recognize the threat. It is ironic that after all these years weapons of mass destruction are part of the conventional wisdom on terrorism.

14. E-mail to author from Brian Houghton, Director of Research, The Memorial Institute for the Prevention of Terrorism.

15. Brian Houghton.

16. See the Combating Terrorism Center's excellent Web page for an overview of its activities and research, http://ctc.usma.edu/research.asp.

17. The Counterterrorism Fellowship Program comes from a long tradition in the United States Air Force to develop and teach courses for military personnel and their civilian equivalents in the counterterrorism field. In the early seventies, for example, the USAF pioneered the outstanding Dynamics of International Terrorism Course that is still given today at Hurlburt Airfield which is now home to the Special Operations University. An extensive discussion of the Counterterrorism Fellowship Program and the future course of terrorism studies was conducted from September 28 to October 1, 2004, in Orlando, Florida (despite the threat of a natural WMD) weather of mass destruction—a hurricane.

18. E-mail to author from Sebestyen Gorka (May 23, 2006).

19. There are now and will increasingly be a variety of references, encyclopedia and other works that will seek to provide definitive scope and detail on the current nature of terrorism research. There are two early studies however that not only provide "the state of the art" of the time but should be used as models for future detailed surveys in the field. They are: Alex P. Schmid with a bibliography by the author and A.J. Jongman, *Political Terrorism: A Research Guide to Concepts, Theories, Data Bases and Literature* (Amsterdam: Royal Netherlands Academy of Arts and Sciences Social Science Research Center (SWIDOC) and New York: Transaction Books, 1981). A second edition of this book authored by Alex P. Schmid, Albert J. Jogman et al. was published in 1988. More recently, see the two post-9/11 terrorism research bibliographies published by the Combating Terrorism Center at West Point, http://ctc.usma.edu.

20. For an outstanding study of the profound impact of the Internet on contemporary and future terrorism see: John Arquilla and David Ronfelt, *Networks and Netwar: The Future of Terrorism, Crime and Militancy* (Santa Monica, CA: Rand Corporation, 2001).

21. For more on this topic, please see *Teaching Terror: Strategic and Tactical Learning in the Terrorist World*, ed. James Forest (Lanham, MD: Rowman & Littlefield, 2006).

PART I

CASE STUDIES OF TERRORIST ATTACKS AND COUNTERTERRORISM OPERATIONS

Chapter 3

"BEGINNING OF A WAR": THE UNITED STATES AND THE HIJACKING OF TWA FLIGHT 847[1]

Richard M. Wrona, Jr.

June 14, 1985, began the most prolonged and media-intensive aircraft hijacking in the history of terrorism. Over a 16-day period, the American population was inundated with unprecedented access to the drama and coverage of unfolding events.[2] This public drama, when combined with precarious regional relationships and continuing hostage situations, led to a demonstration of American impotence in the face of a direct attack. The TWA 847 hijacking highlighted an atypical aspect of terrorism—instead of sowing fear among their target audience, the terrorists generally succeeded in convincing spectators to sympathize with the hijackers' cause.

BACKGROUND TO THE HIJACKING

Lebanon's Civil War

By 1985, Lebanon's civil war had been raging for close to 10 years. After the division of the Lebanese population along ethno-religious and familial lines, the country faced ongoing violence between sectarian militias. At the macro level, these militias could be identified by their religious allegiance—Maronite Christian, Sunni Muslim, Shi'a Muslim, and Druze. However, even within these sectarian groupings there were competitions for power. Most notably, the Shi'a Muslims were divided between organizations taking a more secular stand (like Afwaj al-Muqawamah al-Lubnaniyyah, or AMAL) and those taking a more religious position (Hizbollah,[3] Islamic AMAL, or "Lebanese Resistance

Brigades" and other smaller groups).[4] Additionally, the Shi'a organizations had competing state sponsors. While Syria backed AMAL (in support of Syrian efforts to subsume Lebanon into a "Greater Syria"), the Iranian Islamic regime supported Hizbollah and the other radical religious groups.

International intervention added fury and uncertainty to the boiling Lebanese cauldron. In 1976, an Arab League multinational peacekeeping force, overwhelmingly dominated by the Syrian military, entered Lebanon in an attempt to quell the civil war's sectarian violence. The Syrians used the excuse of the open-ended mandate to occupy Lebanon. Then, in June 1982, Israel invaded southern Lebanon, in order to combat escalating cross-border attacks by the Palestinian Liberation Organization (PLO). Two months later, Lebanon incurred a third introduction of foreign forces when American, French, and Italian forces (later joined by the British) of the Multinational Force (MNF) landed to evacuate Israeli-encircled Syrian and Palestinian forces. September 1982 found the peacekeepers assuming the role of peacemakers, when the MNF attempted to divide the warring Lebanese factions.

By 1985, war still raged in Lebanon. Israel had withdrawn to a security zone in the south. The Syrians roamed freely in the east. Beirut was a free-fire zone, with competing militias (Lebanese and Palestinian) raging against each other for control of sections of the city. The multinational forces had withdrawn in 1984 after suffering spectacular terrorist attacks against diplomatic and military targets. Their departure, however, did not occur before the development of a lingering antipathy resulting from their role in the conflict—particularly, a hate harbored by the Shi'a religious factions.

The Prisoners

In addition to the direct combat with their militia rivals, kidnappings of Western citizens became a weapon in the Lebanese militias' arsenals. Beginning in 1982 with the kidnapping of David Dodge, the president of the American University of Beirut, numerous individuals with a variety of national and occupational backgrounds were kidnapped. By 1985, militias held seven American hostages, but the United States had little information as to where the hostages were or what groups detained them.

The Lebanese also faced a hostage dilemma. After its 1982 invasion, Israel soon faced an unstable situation in southern Lebanon, as the domestic population revolted against Israel's continuing occupation. Israel's answer to the increasing guerrilla activity was to implement an "Iron Fist" policy, which included the raiding of Lebanese villages in the south, and, more importantly, the detention of large numbers of Lebanese Shi'a thought to be involved in the guerrilla actions. These detentions assumed a new dimension when, in April 1983, the Israelis moved 1,200 of the detainees to Israel.[5] Lebanese leaders protested the movement as a violation of the Geneva Convention—a position that the United States supported.[6] However, Lebanese opinion commonly held that the United States had not done enough to pressure the Israelis to abide by the convention and release the Shi'a.

The Lebanese Shi'a also faced other hostage/prisoner predicaments. The radical Lebanese Shi'a had ties to other radical Shi'a groups in the Middle East, which led to joint operations against some of the region's secular/autocratic Arab regimes. Lebanese Shi'a were involved in two particular cases of interest. On December 12, 1983, terrorists of radical Lebanese and Iraqi Shi'a factions attacked multiple targets in Kuwait. Soon after, Kuwait captured and tried 17 individuals, and delivered sentences ranging from 5 years' imprisonment to death.[7] Radical Shi'a groups made the release of these individuals, the "Dawa 17," their central demand during the hijackings and kidnappings of 1984–1985.[8] In addition to the Dawa 17, radical Lebanese Shi'a were concerned about two Lebanese Shiites incarcerated in Spain for the attempted assassinations of Saudi Arabians in 1984.[9]

TWA Flight 847's hijacking must be considered not only in the context of these prisoners, but also in the environment of prisoner exchanges that preceded the attack. While nearly every country had a public policy of refusing to negotiate with terrorists, two states that stood center-stage in the Flight 847 drama had established dangerous precedents. Israel, in the 18 months preceding the TWA flight, made prisoner exchanges an established norm when dealing with the Lebanese and Palestinian factions (see Figure 3.1.)

Likewise, Greece was perceived to be sympathetic to radical Arab regimes and movements. On two different occasions, it released individuals known or implicated in terrorist operations.[10]

Date	Hostages Released by Israel	Israeli Hostages Returned
November 1983	4,500 (Lebanese and Palestinian)	6 (Israeli)
June 1984	291 (Syrian), 21 (civilians—nationality not designated), 70 (Syrian bodies)	6 (Israeli), 5 (Israeli bodies)
May 1985	1150 (Palestinian and others)	3 Israelis
Total	5962 (alive)/70 (dead)	15 (alive)/5 (dead)

Figure 3.1 A Summary of Israeli Hostage Exchanges (November 1983–May 1985) *Source:* "The Beirut Hostages: Background to the Crisis" (Washington, DC: Foreign Affairs and National Defense Division, Congressional Research Service, The Library of Congress, June 21, 1985).

The Hijackings—A Target-Rich Environment

Aircraft hijackings became a regular part of the Middle East's décor during the 1970s and 1980s. A method refined by the PLO during the 1970s, by the 1980s many Arab nonstate actors accepted aircraft hijackings as an effective way to broadcast their appeals internationally. While attainment of their demands was only moderately successful, hijackers adopted the international air carrier as a podium for proclaiming their organizations' manifestos. After the operations, hijackers usually evaded prolonged imprisonment, either by escaping or as the result of ultimatums delivered to their captors.

Two important hijackings in the Middle East immediately preceded the TWA 847 incident. On June 11, a Shi'a Muslim hijacked a Royal Jordanian Airlines 727 departing Beirut Airport in an attempt to hasten the exit of Palestinian guerrillas from Beirut. Then, on June 12, a Sunni Palestinian responded to the June 11 operation by hijacking a Middle East Airlines 707.[11]

THE HIJACKING[12]

TWA 847, a passenger aircraft carrying 145 passengers and 8 crewmembers, was bound for Rome when two young male Arabs hijacked the plane at 10:10 A.M. (local time) on June 14, 1985.[13] Armed with pistols and hand grenades that they had smuggled through the X-ray machines at Athens airport, the hijackers violently subdued the crew and passengers. First-class passengers were forced to vacate the first-class section and join the rest of the passengers in coach. The hijackers then ensured that all male passengers were seated next to windows, in order to prevent attempts by the men to retake the plane.[14] The pilot, Captain John Testrake, acceded to the hijackers' demand of diverting the flight to Beirut International Airport. Throughout the flight, passengers were forced to remain incommunicado with their heads on their knees.

Landing at Beirut International Airport proved to be no easy feat. Because of its value as a transit node and a symbolic point of the city, Lebanon's sectarian groups continually fought to gain control of the airport. When TWA 847 approached Beirut, the airport's control tower initially denied the pilot permission to land. Moreover, he found the runway barricaded by the Druze militias that were fighting the Shi'a AMAL.[15] Testrake landed after AMAL defeated the Druze and removed the barricades.

The short stay at Beirut on June 14 began the cycle of violence that led to the death of the U.S. Navy's Robert Stethem. After releasing 17 women and 2 children, the hijackers beat Stethem because of the airport's hesitation in refueling the aircraft.[16] At Beirut, the hijackers read a prepared letter to the control tower and released their first of a series of demands—Israel had to release the 766 Arab prisoners held in Atlit prison.[17] TWA 847 then departed Beirut enroute to Algeria. Upon landing at Algiers, the terrorists increased their list of demands. In addition to Israel's release of the 766 Shi'a Muslims held at Atlit, the hijackers also demanded Spain's release of 2 Lebanese Shiites held for the attempted assassinations of two Saudi nationals, Kuwait's release of the Dawa 17, and an end to Arab oil and arms transactions with the United States.[18]

Algeria was a contentious place for the plane to land. Algerian President Chadli Bendjedid initially planned to refuse landing permission to the aircraft, but reconsidered after American appeals. American officials believed that Algeria was a far better alternative to other possible airports that the hijackers might request. In addition, Algeria had proved an effective negotiator in the past, particularly in 1979 when the Algerian government acted as the primary intermediary in the negotiations with Iran concerning American captives in Tehran.[19] Relying on Algeria proved to be beneficial. Algerian forces secured TWA 847 without incident. More importantly, the Algerians successfully gained the release of 21 additional passengers. During this initial stay in Algiers, the hijackers severely beat an American, Kurt Carlson, when the airport delayed the plane's refueling.[20] After approximately 5 hours, the hijackers demanded a departure.

TWA 847 landed a second time at Beirut in the early morning of June 15. Either because the Beirut control tower was delinquent in lighting the runway markings or because the hijackers' demand of a meeting with AMAL representatives was not satisfied promptly, the hijackers shot Petty Officer Robert Stethem and dumped his body from the plane.[21] Soon after, AMAL representatives approached the plane, and 10–12 gunmen reinforced the original hijackers. One of the reinforcements was believed to be Imad Mugniyeh, an individual implicated in the 1983 Marine barracks bombing and the kidnapping of Americans in Beirut.[22] During this second stop in Beirut, the hijackers made the strategic decision to separate the hostages. AMAL and Hizbollah captors segregated approximately 12 hostages with American government identification or "Jewish-sounding" surnames and spirited them away to different locations in the city. After only a few hours on the ground, TWA 847 was once again airborne for a second trip to Algiers.

TWA 847's second visit to Algeria was a mixed blessing. After communicating demands for the release of additional prisoners in Cyprus and Greece,[23] the hijackers (now the 2 original hijackers plus the 10–12 reinforcements from Beirut) entered into negotiations with the Algerian government and the International Red Cross. As a result of the negotiations, the Algerians secured the release of approximately 65 passengers, which included the flight's remaining women and children. The release, however, required a quid pro quo. In exchange for the release of Greek citizens (at least two fo whom were in Beirut), Greece agreed to release Ali Atwa, a third hijacker who had been unable to board the flight in Athens.[24] After he failed to secure a seat on the flight and raised a commotion, Greek authorities detained Atwa. When the hijacking was announced, Atwa readily admitted to his planned participation, and was subsequently arrested by the Greek government. After Atwa rejoined his companions in Algiers, TWA 847 began the final leg of its air travel at 8:00 A.M. on June 16, the third day of the ordeal.

Once again, upon approaching Beirut International Airport, Captain Testrake found the runway blocked. After he communicated the necessity of landing, even at the expense of a crash landing, airport personnel moved the obstacles, and TWA 847 landed for its final time at Beirut.[25] The hijackers demanded to speak to AMAL personnel, who were soon at the airport. After meeting with the representatives of AMAL, the hijackers reemphasized their demands for the release of Shi'a prisoners in Spain and Israel. This meeting also had the effect of positioning Nabih Berri, the leader of AMAL, as the middleman in the TWA crisis. Approached by both the hijackers and the United States,[26] Berri became the public negotiator and spokesman for the hijackers' demands. He publicly assumed responsibility for the hostages' safety.

June 16 showed the weakness of Lebanon's recognized government and the powerlessness of the United States government to respond to the hijacking. After the United States conducted a demonstration of force with attack aircraft in the skies over Beirut, AMAL and its allies reinforced the airport with scores of fighters, and the Lebanese Army withdrew its 180 soldiers.[27] Hostile militias completely controlled the airport and its surrounding area, negating the slim hopes for a rescue attempt. Also on June 16, the hijackers, in coordination with Berri, removed the passengers (but not the three-person flight crew) from the aircraft, divided them into groups, and transferred them to different locations in Beirut. While the AMAL militia gained control over the majority of the passengers, Hizbollah retained control of at least four hostages. Finally, June 16 brought Nabih Berri's first press conference, the beginning of his parley with Western negotiators, and the start of his dance with the international media. Berri had been educated in France and maintained a residence in the United States. National Security Adviser Robert McFarlane, who met Berri in 1983, believed that the AMAL leader "had in his hands the ability to end the hijacking."[28]

During the press conference, Berri masterfully presented a number of points. First, by assuming responsibility for the hostages, he placed himself at the center of the situation for the remainder of the crisis. Berri became the *de facto* spokesman for an operation and an organization (Hizbollah) over which he had little control. Second, in his reiteration of the terrorists' demands, he presented himself as the fair moderator between parties.[29] Knowing the reticence of the Kuwaiti regime, he convinced the hijackers to concentrate on the prisoners detained in Israel and Spain. In doing so, Berri fed perceptions that he could influence and moderate the hijackers' demands. Third, Berri tied the hostages' plight to the plight of the Lebanese prisoners in Israel's Atlit prison—a parallel that gained increasing public legitimacy throughout the crisis.[30] He consistently compared the remaining TWA hostages, now predominantly American men, with the Lebanese Shi'a held in Israel,

> I do not know why the policy of the U.S. differentiates between a kidnapper of a country and its people [Israel], and a hijacker of an airplane. Why should someone who defends his country be termed a terrorist, while the terrorism against our people is disregarded?[31]

After June 16, the hijacking of TWA 847 degenerated into a stand-off between competing entities with Berri acting as a churlish third party. By June 17, AMAL and Hizbollah controlled the Beirut airport, 36 hostages were held in various locations around Lebanon, 3 crew members remained on the aircraft, and the United States had few options. A military operation seemed to be impossible, as the United States had little information concerning the passengers' locations and few friends in Lebanon to aid in a rescue attempt.[32] Diplomatically, the United States also faced an impasse. Not only did it not have confirmation of the group affiliation of the hijackers (although most analysts assumed that they belonged to an organization tied to Hizbollah), but the United States did not control the foci of the hijackers' demands. On June 16, Spain had publicly announced that it would not release the two Shi'a prisoners held in its prison. On the same day, Israel had started to demonstrate its intransigence concerning the Atlit prisoners. As a result, circumstances forced the United States into a position of relying on mediators, particularly Berri, to protect the hostages and attempt to gain their freedom.

From June 17 through June 22, none of the major variables in the hijacking changed significantly. AMAL and Hizbollah moved the prisoners between locations in an effort to prevent rescue attempts. Berri shifted between stances of utmost concern for the hostages and a willingness to "wash his hands" of the hijacking.[33] The United Nations, the International Red Cross, and various European states offered to act as negotiators between the hijackers, the United States, and Israel. The Reagan Administration, facing the specter of the 1979–1980 Iranian hostage crisis, came under increasing domestic pressure to solve the situation in Lebanon.

As a result of this cumulative inertia, the United States increased its diplomatic traffic to Israel, Iran, and Syria. American messages centered on the question of the Shi'a prisoners in Atlit and the possibility of their release. Because of its public policy of "no negotiations" with terrorists, however, the United States refused to formally or publicly ask the Israelis for the prisoners' release. In communications to Iran and Syria, the United States sought assistance from those believed to be the state sponsors of

AMAL and Hizbollah. Advocates within the administration felt that the correct mix of incentives and deterrents toward these two states might gain the hostages' freedom. Unfortunately, the United States made little headway, and concern mounted that the TWA passengers faced a fate similar to the seven American hostages already in Beirut, some of whom had been held for longer than a year.

Days continued to slip by with little hope of a resolution. Even after the Israelis' release of 31 prisoners from Atlit on June 23, the hijackers refused to make a comparable release of TWA passengers. Berri approached France and Switzerland to enlist their embassies as way-stations for the hostages until the release of the remaining Shi'a prisoners, but France and other European states only agreed to shelter "released" persons. Berri unilaterally expanded the list of demands to include the withdrawal of American warships from Lebanese waters and an American guarantee against retaliation upon the conclusion of the crisis.[34] Israel and the United States publicly refused any attempts to tie TWA 847 and Atlit together as part of a hostage exchange bargain, but both states tacitly agreed to the step should the TWA hostages be released.

Soon, however, pressures outside Lebanon began to move the event toward a conclusion. Hafez al-Assad's influence and Syria's strength in Lebanon came to bear on AMAL, in an effort to (according to a CIA report) "extract Shia AMAL leader Nabih Barri . . . from a no-win situation" and to prevent Shi'a Islamists from gaining too strong a hold in Lebanon.[35] Syria's increasing pressure on Berri forced him to seek new ways to bring the situation to a hasty conclusion. Also, Israel's position shifted to one that viewed the release of the Atlit prisoners as a process interrupted by the TWA hijacking—a process that could be reinstated once the passengers were released.[36]

The hostages were released on June 30, 1985, but not without a number of missteps that delayed the process. Three days prior to the release, the United States hindered the negotiations, when it publicly demanded that the seven non-TWA American hostages held in Beirut be included in the release. Berri and Hizbollah, separately, refused to entertain such a notion. However, after Berri became satisfied that the demands concerning the Shi'a prisoners and American retaliation would be met, and after Syria agreed to accept responsibility for the hostages, the TWA passengers were consolidated in Beirut and shuttled to Damascus.[37] From Damascus, a U.S. Air Force transport plane carried them to American military facilities in Germany and to freedom. After 16 days of brinkmanship, the conclusion seemed anticlimatic, at least to everyone except the hostages.

TWA 847 IN CONTEXT

Two noticeable differences separated the TWA 847 crisis from earlier hijackings, and particularly from the contemporary hijackings by Arab factions in the Middle East. First, TWA 847 received more media attention and direct media involvement than any previous hijacking. Second, the hostages' role in the media coverage of the hijacking was something not previously seen in similar events. Beginning with Berri's press conference on July 16, through the final press conference by the hostages in Damascus on June 30, the international media gained unprecedented access to the event and its actors. In addition to interviews with released hostages,[38] the media publicized an interview and a press conference with hostages still held captive. The first event, on June 19, immortalized TWA 847 in media history, when journalists approached the aircraft on the Beirut tarmac to interview the captive crew. Then, on June 20, AMAL brought four hostages to the Beirut airport for a press conference. In addition to covering the hostages, the press gave unprecedented coverage to the captors. Nabih Berri became an overnight media sensation with almost-daily press conferences, interviews, and statements. AMAL gained international recognition as a result of its part in the stand-off, particularly after Berri negotiated the release of the hostages. Even the original hijackers, albeit with hooded masks, gained international recognition in a press conference conducted on June 30.

This nonstop coverage colored the Reagan administration's approach to the situation, causing it to seek the quickest resolution possible in an effort to maintain popular support of the president. While such media inundation may have proved inconsequential to the Middle East's autocracies or to Lebanon's failed state, it was all-important to an American population increasingly influenced by television coverage. As David C. Wills highlights in his excellent account of the hijacking, President Reagan's chief of staff, Donald Regan, raised the important point during the June 24 meeting of the National Security Planning Group,

> How long is the process [going to take]? We don't have the luxury of waiting. Public opinion will desert the President [and we'll face the] Carter Syndrome.[39]

WHY TWA 847?

Why did Ali Atwa, Mohammed Ali Hammadi, and Hasan Izz-Al-Din choose TWA 847? While we can never be sure of the true intentions of the hijackers or the organization that they represented, tactical and strategic considerations made the flight an ideal target.

The flight offered a number of advantages. Athens, the flight's departure airport, was known to have lax security—a deficiency that led to many successful and recent hijackings. In 1973, the PLO's Black September attacked passengers inside the airport, and, in 1976, members of the Popular Front for the Liberation of Palestine and Germany's Baader-Meinhof Gang hijacked an Air France flight.[40] In June 1983, a Romanian aircraft scheduled to fly the Athens-to-Rome route was hijacked to Libya. Then, in March 1985, an "Arab" fired a rocket-propelled grenade at a Royal Jordanian airliner after he breached the airport's perimeter fence.[41] In addition to this demonstrated lack of preventive measures, Greek reactive measures were weak. The Greek police were inefficient and poorly trained,[42] and according to Middle East analyst Spiros Kaminaris, Papandreou's government showed "[a] sympathy for radical Arab regimes and causes [that] was encouraged and, to some extent, exploited by Papandreou's ambition to promote Greek leadership of Third World states..."[43] Finally, the Greek government demonstrated on at least two occasions that it was willing to free hijackers and suspected terrorists, particularly in response to other hijackings of Greek citizens, aircraft, or ships.[44]

Strategically, the TWA 847's majority-American passenger list offered the hijackers the bargaining chips necessary to gain the freedom of their compatriots. While contemporary scholars viewed the hijacking merely as one-upmanship between the Lebanese Shi'a factions,[45] this analysis seems only accurate concerning the intervention of Nabih Berri and AMAL. Other evidence indicates that Hizbollah was primarily concerned with the Shi'a prisoners' release. First, Hizbollah and its affiliates (most notably, Islamic Jihad) made the release of Lebanese Shi'a prisoners their core demand after the Dawa 17's detention in 1983. Prior to the TWA hijacking, Islamic Jihad hijacked a Kuwaiti Airways aircraft and made demands similar to those presented by Hammadi and Izz-Al-Din.[46] Likewise, in May 1985, Islamic Jihad contacted Western news agencies with pictures of the seven American hostages held in Beirut in an effort to achieve the Dawa 17's release. On the heels of these events, TWA 847 seemed to be a more robust effort to gain the same objectives. As the United States was a patron of Israel, a patron of Kuwait, an ally of Spain, and a world superpower, the logic of forcing American pressure on these states through a hijacking of Americans appeared eminently sensible. Also, Hizbollah's decisions during the crisis indicated that Lebanese power politics was hardly the group's foremost consideration. For example, the original hijackers' demands of June 15 and 16 of only AMAL mediators, followed by a reinforcement contingent of AMAL and Hizbollah gunmen, showed little hesitancy by Hizbollah to share the spotlight with its sectarian rival.

THE LESSONS OF 847

Military Difficulties

From the second day of the incident until its conclusion, the lack of a military solution to the TWA hijacking frustrated the United States. In hindsight, an attempted rescue mission would have undoubtedly caused hostage fatalities and significant diplomatic problems for the United

States. Any rescue attempt first faced the problems of time and space. While much was made in the contemporary media about the deployment of Delta Force to the region,[47] the unit's deployment faced significant problems. One problem stemmed from the unit's position in the United States. Although it had the ability to react immediately to any deployment order, Delta still found itself 8–10 hours away from the Middle East. Bureaucratic inertia compounded this problem by delaying the deployment of the force until the second day of the crisis.[48] Related to this variable of proximity was the temporal window within which the United States could feasibly react. Even at the time of the hijacking, high-ranking American officials recognized that a rescue mission became impossible once the aircraft landed in Beirut for the second time (the early morning of June 15).[49] The Shi'a factions' ability to reinforce the airport and disperse the hostages to a variety of unknown locations made a successful rescue extremely unlikely.

Another problem facing military action and, particularly, a rescue attempt was the lack of agreement to such an operation by key regional actors. Even had the United States been ready to mount a rescue operation in the early hours of the crisis, Beirut was not a feasible location. The government, while friendly to the United States, did not have effective control over the airport or its surrounding area, as was demonstrated by the Lebanese Army's withdrawal from the airport on June 16. Likewise, the Algiers airport could not be the rescue location due to the Algerian government's adamant objection to any such operation.[50] While attempts had been made to force TWA 847 to land at a more hospitable location (Cyprus being the first choice as it was the staging location for Delta), the hijackers invariably controlled the aircraft's destinations.

Other problems concerning a rescue included the lack of coordination between entities that wanted to make such an attempt, and the lack of expertise of some of those actors. In addition to the United States, reports indicated that the Lebanese, the Jordanians, the Israelis, and a shadowy private entity expressed interest in staging a rescue operation.[51] Who would control such a rescue, particularly should two countries attempt simultaneous operations, became highly problematic.

Even after the hostages' release on June 30, the United States faced problems concerning the use of military force to retaliate for the hostage-taking. First, the United States faced the important question of who to retaliate against. AMAL and Hizbollah were obvious choices, but there were difficulties in distinguishing one group from another, particularly given Hizbollah's amorphous nature and the predilection of the terrorists to espouse membership in many different groups. Also, there was the question of what to retaliate against. In 1985, groups like AMAL and Hizbollah had little infrastructure for the United States to strike. Air attacks could have been conducted against Hizbollah's training camps in the Bekaa Valley, but doing so might have caused casualties among the camp's Iranian cadre or the seven Americans still held hostage in Lebanon. More importantly, conducting attacks after the United States government's June 30 reiteration of its foreign policy calling for the "preservation of Lebanon, its government, [and] its stability and security," would have caused multiple difficulties.[52] Berri and the Syrians took the statement as a guarantee against retaliation, and military action after the statement could have caused other states and movements to question American reliability in future negotiations.

Friends, Neutrals, and Adversaries

Given the difficulties of a military response, diplomacy became the instrument of necessity during the TWA 847 hijacking. In this arena, the United States experienced unexpected benefits and difficulties. Algerian intervention was one of the great advantages of the crisis. Former Secretary of State Henry Kissinger reportedly once said, "[I]f you want to find out what the Arab 'radicals' are thinking, go to Algiers."[53] In June 1985, the government of President Benjedid proved instrumental, particularly in gaining the freedom of so many hostages. While the Algerians were resistant to the idea of allowing American forces to attempt a rescue attempt at the Algiers airport, the Algerian performance mirrored the central role that they had played in the release of the Tehran hostages nearly 5 years earlier. Algeria was no democracy, but it certainly proved to be a valuable American friend during the crisis.

On the other hand, Israel proved to be more of an obstacle than an ally during the event. The hijackers' central demand focused not on a redress of American actions, but on the Israeli detention of Lebanese Shi'a. The Israelis had established a precedent of exchanging hostages. However, in the case of TWA 847, the Israelis demonstrated an intransigence that hindered American diplomatic efforts. At one point, according to David Wills' analysis of these events, Israeli Defense Minister Rabin told the media that "the Americans will have to crawl on all fours before we even discuss . . . releasing the detainees."[54] Israeli obstinacy, particularly during the first week of the hijacking, acted as a distraction to Reagan Administration officials who had expected and assumed far better support from the country thought to be the United States' best regional ally.

Lessons Learned Again, and Again . . . and Again

During and after the TWA 847 crisis, the United States undertook a number of actions in response to the incident. On June 16, the administration established the Vice President's Task Force on Combatting

Terrorism.[55] Directed to provide recommendations to President Reagan concerning responses to future terrorist threats, the task force presented its report in December 1985. On June 18, in his first public statement concerning the hijacking, President Reagan issued a travel advisory against travel to Athens International Airport and issued a directive for expansion of the Department of Transportation's sky marshal program.[56] Finally, the Department of Transportation implemented a ban on American airline traffic to Beirut International Airport and restricted the Lebanese national carrier, Middle East Airlines, from landing at American airports.

In retrospect, several recommendations stemming from the Task Force's review of TWA 847's hijacking failed to be implemented, and would haunt the United States in the aftermath of the September 11 attacks. For example, their final report observed that:

– Pre-flight screening of passengers and carry-on baggage is a cornerstone of our domestic security program . . . [t]he recent terrorist acts against international aviation and maritime interests indicate a need for continual monitoring and updated security procedures.

– Currently, while several federal departments and agencies process intelligence within their own facilities, there is no consolidated center that collects and analyzes all-source information from those agencies participating in antiterrorist activities.

– An increase in human intelligence gathering is essential to penetrate terrorist groups and their support systems.[57]

In short, the recommendations put forth by the 1985 task force are remarkably similar to the recommendations provided 16 years later in response to other, far more deadly aircraft hijackings.

Another failure displayed before, during, and after the TWA hijacking was the United States' inability to recognize terrorism as a form of warfare, rather than a criminal act. Statements made by President Reagan, Secretary of State George Schultz, and other administration officials showed a desire to arrest, prosecute, and "bring to justice" the perpetrators and supporters of the hijacking.[58] Likewise, the Task Force's report to the president reflected a similar mindset. Unfortunately, this approach has not always produced a lasting justice for the atrocities committed by terrorists. For example, after his arrest in Germany in 1987 on other charges, Mohammed Ali Hammadi was tried for the hijacking of TWA 847 and the murder of Robert Stethem, and subsequently sentenced to life imprisonment. However, his "life" sentence only lasted until December 2005, when German authorities released Hammadi. He is now thought to reside somewhere in Lebanon.

CONCLUSION

This study of TWA 847's hijacking offers specific lessons concerning antiterrorist and counterterrorist strategies. Military action, while seemingly the default response of the United States, is not the best (or a feasible) response in many circumstances. In this case, the terrorists offered little opportunity for a rescue attempt to be executed. Beirut offered too many impediments, the Algerian government would not allow any such operation in Algiers, and the hostage-takers would not allow the plane to land elsewhere. Another lesson centered on the diplomatic efforts employed during the incident. While diplomatic solutions became difficult, particularly because of strained or nonexistent relations between some parties (as in the case of American-Iranian exchanges), diplomacy was productive when the United States enlisted the aid of a third party (Algeria) that had credibility with the hijackers. Yet another lesson stemming from the incident concerned the importance of the media in the modern battle against terrorism. When countering terrorist actions, states must gain and maintain the initiative when dealing with the media. During the TWA crisis, Nabih Berri's preeminence in the media spotlight gained popular legitimacy for an incident that was an act of war, and showed the dangers of allowing terrorists to shape the media environment. Finally, TWA 847 demonstrated that states must be able to adjust their tactics and strategies in an effort to recognize terrorism for what it is—war. Whether terrorist organizations act to further their own interests or on behalf of state sponsors, their actions are a means of combat, not of crime. As such, continuing efforts to treat terrorists as criminals (even after September 11) accord the terrorists a freedom of action that hinders antiterrorist and counterterrorist efforts.

ACKNOWLEDGMENTS

The views expressed herein are those of the author and do not purport to reflect the position of the United States Military Academy, the Department of the Army, or the Department of Defense.

NOTES

1. The phrase "beginning of a war" in relation to the TWA hijacking was attributed to Secretary of Defense Caspar Weinberger in David C. Wills, *The First War on Terrorism, Counter-Terrorism Policy during the Reagan Administration* (Lanham, MO: Roman and Littlefield, 2003) 137.

2. Barry Rubin, "The United States and the Middle East, 1984–1985," in Itamar Rabinovich and Haim Shaked, *Contemporary Survey, Vol. 9, 1984–1985* (Boulder, CO: Westview, 1987), http://meria.idc.ac.il/us-policy/data1984.html (accessed May 2006).

3. The "correct" English spelling of the group's Arabic name is Hizb'Allah or Hizbu'llah, however it is more usually spelled "Hizbollah," "Hizbullah," or "Hezbollah." In order to standardize across all three volumes, the editor has chosen "Hizbollah" because that is the spelling employed in the URL designating the group's official homepage.

4. AMAL is an acronym of *Afwaj al-Muqawamah al-Lubnaniyyah*, or "Lebanese Resistance Brigades." *Amal* is also the Arabic word for "hope."

5. Robert B. Bowie, "Hostages: American and Shiite," *Christian Science Monitor* (June 28, 1985): 16.

6. Bowie: p. 16.

7. "ITAC Intelligence Note (IIN 88-58): The Dawa 17 and Islamic Jihad Terrorism: Attempts to Win the Release of Dawa Party Prisoners in Kuwait," (declassified cable) Intelligence and Threat Analysis Center, US Army Intelligence Agency, June 22, 1988, http://nsarchive.chadwyck.com (document number TE00958) (accessed June 2006).

8. "Dawa" (Arabic for "call") was a movement started in Najaf, Iraq, under the tutelage of senior Shi'a clerics Ayatollah Ruhollah Khomeini and Ayatollah Baqir al-Sadr. Its belief structure centered on the need for the establishment of Islamic regimes in the Middle East, even if such establishments required radical action. Dawa became the font from which many of the radical Shi'a regional movements (to include the Iranian Islamic regime and Lebanon's Hizbollah) developed. See "ITAC Intelligence Note . . . " (pp. 4, 7) for a description of the numerous hijacking and kidnapping operations that involved demands for the release of the Dawa 17.

9. Charles Waterman, "Islamic Jihad—hostage-takers with an Iranian connection," *Christian Science Monitor* (June 17, 1985): 11; Wills: p. 96.

10. Spiros Ch. Kaminaris, "Greece and the Middle East," *Middle East Review of International Affairs* 3, no. 2 (June 1999): 37–38.

11. "TWA Hijacking: A Chronology of Events" (Washington, DC: Foreign Affairs and National Defense Division, Congressional Research Service, The Library of Congress, July 15, 1985) 12.

12. For an excellent day-by-day account of the hijacking that focuses particularly on the American decision-making process, see David C. Wills, *The First War on Terrorism, Counter-Terrorism Policy during the Reagan Administration*.

13. "The Beirut Hostages: Background to the Crisis" (Washington, DC: Foreign Affairs and National Defense Division, Congressional Research Service, The Library of Congress, June 21, 1985) 9.

14. Kurt Carlson, *One American Must Die, A Hostage's Personal Account of the Hijacking of Flight 847* (New York: Congdon and Weed, 1986) 27–28.

15. Carlson: p. 32.

16. "He's Pulled a Grenade Pin," *The New York Times*, June 15, 1985: 1; Carlson: pp. 33–34.

17. "TWA Hijacking: A Chronology . . . ": p. 11; Wills: p. 92.

18. "TWA Hijacking: A Chronology . . . ": p. 11.

19. Wills: p. 92.

20. Carlson: pp. 46–50.

21. Different accounts exist concerning the cause and time of Stethem's murder. See Wills: p. 93 and Carlson: pp. 61–62.

22. Wills: p. 93.

23. Wills: p. 96.

24. Paul Anastasi, "Athens Discloses a Hijacker Deal," *The New York Times*, June 16, 1985: 12.

25. Wills: pp. 97–98.

26. Wills: pp. 99–101.

27. "TWA Hijacking: A Chronology . . . ": p. 10.

28. Larry Rother, "Passengers Taken From Hijacked Jet, Lebanese Reports," *The New York Times*, June 18, 1985: 1.

29. Berri reiterated the hijacker's demands concerning prisoners in Israel, Spain, and Kuwait, and then went on to say that, "I persuaded the hijackers not to include this demand [the prisoners in Kuwait] in the case of the American aircraft." See "Nabih Berri's June 16 Press Statement," declassified cable from Ambassador Reginald Bartholomew to the Department of State, June 18, 1985, http://nsarchive.chadwyck.com (document number TE00765) (accessed June 2006).

30. For example, 58 percent of Americans favored negotiating with the terrorists. See Wills: p. 109.

31. "Nabih Berri's June 16 Press Statement."

32. At one point, CIA Director William Casey even briefed President Reagan that some of the hostages may have been moved to Tehran. See Wills: p. 101.

33. "TWA Hijacking: A Chronology . . . ": p. 8.

34. "TWA Hijacking: A Chronology . . . ": p. 5; Wills: p. 126.

35. "Syria-Lebanon: Next Steps after the Hijacking," Center Intelligence Agency Analysis (declassified), July 9, 1985, http://nsarchive.chadwyck.com (document number TE00773) (accessed June 2006).

36. Wills: p. 128.

37. "TWA Hijacking: A Chronology . . . ": p. 1.

38. Joseph Berger, "Hijackers Release over 60 from Jet in Algiers Airport," *The New York Times*, June 16, 1985: 1.

39. Wills: p. 122, brackets in original.

40. The airport attack resulted in 3 killed and 55 wounded. The Air France flight was hijacked to Entebbe, Uganda, from which Israeli commandoes rescued the hostages. Kaminaris: pp. 36–37.

41. Patrick Quinn, "Lax security at Athens airport weakens anti-hijack efforts," *Christian Science Monitor*, June 17, 1985: 9.

42. Quinn: p. 9.

43. Kaminaris: p. 37.

44. Kaminaris: p. 37; Quinn: p. 9.

45. Bruce Hoffman, "Shi'a Terrorism, the Conflict in Lebanon, and the Hijacking of TWA Flight 847," *Rand Policy Paper* July 1985: 3, http://www.rand.org/pubs/papers/P7116 (accessed June 2006); Rubin: p. 1.

46. "ITAC Intelligence Note . . . ": p. 4.

47. Delta Force, better referred to as Special Forces Operations Detachment-Delta (SFOD-D), is the U.S. Army's premier counterterrorist force. See Bernard Gwertzman, "U.S. Said to Send Commando Squad," *The New York Times*, June 16, 1985: 1.

48. Wills: p. 94.

49. Peter Grier, "US finds it hard to use military might against terrorists," *Christian Science Monitor*, June 19, 1985: 1; Wills: p. 102.

50. "The Beirut Hostages . . . ": p. 11; Wills: p. 94.

51. Berger: p. 1 (Lebanese); Wills: p. 99 (Jordanians); "TWA Hijacking: A Chronology . . . ": p. 11 (Israelis); Carlson: pp. 147–148 (private).

52. "TWA Hijacking: A Chronology . . . ": p. 1.

53. John K. Cooley, "Hijacking emphasizes US need for friends in the third world," *Christian Science Monitor*, June 18, 1985: 11.

54. As quoted in Wills: p. 98.

55. Donald P. Gregg and Douglas E. Menarchik, "Vice President's Meeting with Admiral Holloway" (declassified briefing memorandum), July 16, 1985, http://nsarchive.chadwyck.com (document number TE00779) (accessed June 2006).

56. Ronald W. Reagan, "Presidential Remarks: News Conference Opening Statement Tuesday, June 18, 1985," June 18, 1985, http://nsarchive.chadwyck.com (document number TE00764) (accessed June 2006).

57. *Public Report of the Vice President's Task Force on Combating Terrorism*, February 1986: 24–26, http://www.population_security.org/bush_and_terror.pdf (accessed July 2006).

58. Ronald W. Reagan, "Presidential Statement on Release of the Hostages" (internal White House memo), June 30, 1985, http://nsarchive.chadwyck.com (document number TE00772) (accessed June 2006); "TWA Hijacking: A Chronology . . . ": p. 2.

CHAPTER 4

THE *ACHILLE LAURO* HIJACKING

Sean K. Anderson and Peter N. Spagnolo

In October 1985, tension between the State of Israel and the Palestinians was nothing new. Four major wars had been fought, the Israelis had invaded and occupied southern Lebanon in 1981, and countless attacks, counterattacks, preemptive strikes, and raids had been carried out by both sides over the larger questions of Israeli existence and Palestinian rights. One of the results of the 1981 invasion was the displacement of the Palestinian Liberation Organization (PLO) from Lebanon and the relocation of its headquarters to Tunis in 1982.

On September 25, 1985, three Israeli citizens were killed on their yacht as it was anchored off the coast of Larnaca, Cyprus. Credit for this attack was claimed by Force 17, an elite unit of the PLO whose main function was the personal protection of the PLO leadership but, who also conducted terrorist strikes as well as attacks on rival Palestinian factions.

On October 1, 1985, Israel launched a long-range air strike against the PLO headquarters in Tunis, killing over 73 people and wounding about 100 others. Israel announced this attack on Tunis in a press conference held by Israeli Minister of Defense Yitzhak Rabin, Chief of Staff Moshe Levy, and Air Force Chief Amos Lapidol. During the press conference, the three Israeli leaders announced a new policy whereby terrorist targets would be attacked wherever they were located and that no terrorist would be safe. According to Israel's official account of these events:

> Mounting wave of terror against Israelis and Jews, in Israel, in the areas and abroad, culminating with the murder of three Israelis in Larnaca's harbour, led the government of Israel to seek new ways to combat terror. Since it was evident that the attacks were masterminded by the PLO and the various

organizations under its umbrella, Israel decided to attack the PLO headquarters in Tunis. In a daring, long distance aerial raid, Israeli planes bombed a PLO base in Tunis, some 4800 kilometers round-trip from Israel. 60 terrorists were killed, including some senior members of "Force 17." Arafat was not in Tunis at the time, but his headquarters was hit.[1]

Some claim that the three Israelis killed in Cyprus were Mossad agents, while the official Israeli position is that they were civilians. While many considered the aerial attack on Tunis as specifically a retribution for the Larnaca incident, the Israeli government insisted it was simply a part of their wider ongoing war on terrorism.

EVENTS LEADING UP TO THE HIJACKING

When the *Achille Lauro* attack occurred, at first many believed that it had been conducted in retaliation for Israel's attack on Tunis. However, the hijacking operation had been planned in advance for over 10 months, involving two previous journeys on the *Achille Lauro* by Masar Kadia,[2] who posed as a Greek shipping magnate under the name "Petros Floros," and was accompanied on at least one of these trips by the man who would lead the hijacking, Magied al Molqi. These scouting trips were intended— among other things—to assess security measures, meal times, the normal activities of passengers and crew, the relative competence and aggressiveness of specific crew members, the likely response of the ship's captain and crew, and the layout of the ship.

On September 28, 1985, accomplices smuggled four Soviet-made Kalashnikov automatic rifles, eight hand grenades, and nine detonators aboard the Tunis-to-Genoa ferry, the *Habib*, which were then carried aboard the *Achille Lauro* by the four hijackers in their uninspected baggage on October 3, 1985.[3] Masar Kadia, the previous scout who was also the handler of the four hijackers, booked a cabin separate from the others, and did not associate with them apart from one private meeting with their tactical commander, Magied al Molqi, after which he debarked in Alexandria. Later, it was learned that only Kadia and al Molqi knew of the full hijacking plan. Prior to arriving in Alexandria, after consulting with Kadia, al Molqi gave orders to the other three to unpack their weapons and prepare to seize the vessel.[4] Although the other three attackers had been kept in the dark until that moment, the original plan had apparently been to hijack the ship on the high seas.[5] Technically, such an operation would violate the PLO's declared policy since 1974, which ruled out terrorist attacks "outside the territory of Occupied Palestine."[6]

While adhering to the 1974 policy had made the PLO and its factions more respectable as "freedom fighters" in the view of the international community (apart from the United States and Israel, who still regarded them as terrorists), it also reduced the strategic effectiveness of their military struggle. The group that would seize the *Achille Lauro* had conducted seven major actions in the period 1978–1983, all of which involved attempts to take hostages, and all but one involved attempts to infiltrate Israel. Only three of the six infiltration attempts succeeded, while in only one case did the terrorists succeed in seizing hostages, but in no case did they win the release of any Arab prisoners. In April 1979, four Palestinian fighters landed on a beach near Nahariyah, Israel, on a mission to seize hostages. Three Israeli civilians were killed by the terrorists, two of whom were killed and the other two captured. The political and military payoffs of such actions were minimal: Israel was able to defend its territory and citizens effectively while the rest of the world, whose citizens were no longer in the cross-fire of the Arab-Israeli conflict, could regard it now with relative indifference.[7]

The *Achille Lauro*, a vessel owned by the Italian government, was a 23,629-ton cruise ship that was 643-feet long, capable of serving 900 passengers, having two swimming pools, a movie theater, and a discotheque. The Italians had leased the ship to the Chandris-Italy Company, which offered low-cost cruises throughout the Mediterranean. Some 748 passengers had boarded the ship at Genoa on October 3 for a 12-day Mediterranean cruise, with calls at Naples, Syracuse, Alexandria, Port Said, Ashdod (Israel), Limassol (Cyprus), and Rhodes (Greece). Cruise manager Max Fico later reported that a party of several young men kept to themselves and displayed none of the friendly behavior usual on cruises. Some passengers tried to strike up conversations with the men during a meal, but they seemed reluctant to interact with their fellow passengers and merely said they were from Argentina. When a female passenger who was fluent in Spanish tried to speak with them, none seemed to understand anything she said to them. The terrorists boarded with passports issued from Norway, Argentina, and Portugal.[8]

According to a document seized later, the four had planned to attack the Port of Ashdod upon arrival, but when a crew member saw them cleaning their weapons, they were forced to change their plans. Excerpts of this document read as follows:

> The Ashdod Port Operation: When the Zionist enemy carried out an air strike against the Palestinian HQ in Hamam al-Shatt in Tunis in October 1985, the Front reacted to this aggression by attempting a sea landing in Ashdod port … This operation was unsuccessful, forcing the Front's fighters to change the original plan … Once they were uncovered on the ship taking them. They

took over the ship known as "Achille Lauro"...The organization found itself fighting on several fronts, [including] directly against the American enemy. This, especially after American aircraft hijacked a civilian Egyptian aircraft that carried the comrade Abu al-Abbas, General Secretary of the Front and Member of the PLO Executive Committee, and other comrades, and forced them to land in the Sicily airport in Italy.[9]

Although there had been numerous aircraft hijackings during the early 1980s, the taking of a civilian passenger ship was unprecedented. Consequently, the security measures on the ship were lax: only a passport was required to buy a ticket, there were no checks of luggage, and very little observation of persons embarking other than to ensure they were paid passengers. Therefore the *Achille Lauro*'s distress call would receive immediate international attention. Fortunately, before the actual hijacking occurred, most of the passengers had debarked at Alexandria for a tour of the Pyramids, planning to travel overland to Port Said (the next port of call) to continue their voyage. This was on Day 5 of the planned 12-day cruise, and the next stop after Port Said was to be Ashdod, Israel, the terrorists' supposed target. The people remaining on board included the 350 members of the crew (Italian and Portuguese citizens) and 97 passengers of various nationalities.[10]

Another reason this hijacking would captivate the worldwide attention that the terrorists were seeking was the nature of their immediate victims—namely, tourists from about 20 nations, including, Belgium, Brazil, Britain, France, Holland, Italy, Spain, Switzerland, the United States, and West Germany. No Israelis were on the passenger list, however. A group of elderly Jewish Americans would eventually be singled out for "special treatment" by the hijackers, and thus receive the anxious attention from the on-looking global audience. This group included Leon and Marilyn Klinghoffer, along with eight of their closest friends—three retired couples and two older women who shared the Klinghoffer's summer homes in the same group of condominiums in Long Branch, New Jersey. The Klinghoffers were celebrating their 38th wedding anniversary, but their voyage also had some urgency behind it: Marilyn, age 58, had been diagnosed as having an incurable colon cancer and had less than a year to live. Leon Klinghoffer, a 69 year-old retired small appliance manufacturer, had suffered two strokes and was partly paralyzed and confined to a wheelchair. He had limited ability to use his hands, which were tremulous, while his speech was often slurred. Fellow hostages recalled afterwards that the hijackers seemed irritated and uneasy with his slurred speech and erratic motions.

Neither spouse expected to long survive the demise of the other, but both had decided to make the most of this twilight honeymoon voyage in the company of their closest friends. However, the hijackers would also radio threats to kill all of the over 400 people aboard if their demands were not met or if escape were attempted, so anxiety was shared among the several nations, families, and friends who had other passengers and crew members aboard the cruise ship.

EVENTS DURING THE HIJACKING

The passengers first realized something was amiss when the hijackers burst into the dining room toward the end of the noon meal of October 7, firing over their heads and shouting barely intelligible commands. Some passengers fled into the kitchen, pursued by one of the hijackers who beat two of the kitchen staff to the floor and then forced everyone back to the dining room. Two crew members were reportedly shot, but received only minor wounds, while another Italian sailor was slightly wounded by shrapnel from a bullet.[11] As the hijackers consolidated their control over the vessel, they took command of the ship's bridge and radio room.

After securing the passengers in the dining room, the hijackers ordered the crew to summon Captain Gerardo de Rosa, who later testified that "As soon as I got there, I faced the machine guns. First they fired some shots at the deck, shouting in Arabic. Then they told me to head for Tartus."[12] The ship then turned for the Syrian port, which was about 300 miles to the northeast. The hijackers then allowed the crew to return to running the ship, telling the captain that any attempts by him or the crew to thwart them would result in harm to the passengers held hostage.

After the initial shooting spree, the terrorists herded all passengers—except for Anna Hoerantner, a 53-year old Austrian—into the dining room, and instructed Captain de Rosa to order the crew to carry on with their normal duties but avoid all contact with the hostages. Hoerantner had been knocked down a stairwell when the hijackers had rushed into the dining room. In the confusion, she escaped and hid in a bathroom in an unoccupied cabin for the duration of the hijacking and was found hiding there 15 hours after the hijacking had ended. The terrorists told the crew that there were 20 hijackers on board; this was probably a ruse to discourage any attempts to retake the ship.

The treatment of the hostages was erratic, going from considerate one minute to brutal the next: when one passenger asked for a cup of water, the hijackers handed one to her, but when an exhausted Marilyn Klinghoffer attempted to lay down on the floor, one of them struck her with the butt of his weapon, ordering her to get up. The terrorists also tried some form of political statement by occasionally proclaiming "Reagan no good! Arafat good!"[13] and then later forced the passengers into a common area, the Arazzi Lounge. After the terrorists directed the ship into the Mediterranean and turned off the ship's transponders, the ship blended into the busy sea lanes, and in spite of extensive tracking efforts by the United States, Egypt, Italy, Great Britain, and Israel, it disappeared for much of the next 36 hours.

To further exacerbate the confused situation, it was unclear exactly who the hijackers were and with what (if any) group they were affiliated. Early on, the terrorists claimed to be part of the Palestinian Liberation Front (PLF), and this seemed to be confirmed by the fact that the only prisoner named in the release demand was a member of the PLF. However, the PLF was no longer a single entity but had splintered into no fewer than three factions.

The original PLF had been founded in 1961 by Ahmed Jabril, who coordinated the group's efforts with Fatah in 1965. In 1967, a group from the PLF, which included Jabril, founded the Popular Front for the Liberation of Palestine (PFLP) under Dr. George Habash. Soon after the founding of the PFLP, Jabril became disillusioned with the group's emphasis on ideology, and broke away to form yet another splinter group—namely, the Popular Front for the Liberation of Palestine-General Command (PFLP-GC)—while still sharing the parent group's goal of the eradication of Israel in favor of a Palestinian state. In 1977, yet another split took place when the current PLF broke away from PFLP-GC over Jabril's support of Syria's policy in Lebanon. In late 1983, the PLF split when founder Abu Abbas decided the group was growing too subservient to Syria. He and his followers left for Tunis in order to align themselves closer with Arafat's al Fatah. The PLF faction remaining in Damascus was headed by Talat Yaqub, but was itself split when Abdal Fatah Ghanim tried unsuccessfully to seize power over the PLF in January 1984. The Yaqub faction remained in Damascus, while Ghanim and his followers established their rival PLF office in Libya. While the PLF had been recognized by Yassir Arafat in April 1977 as a member of the PLO, this recognition continued to be extended only to the faction led by Abu Abbas,[14] who was eventually made a member of the PLO Executive Committee.[15] With all of these factions and shifting loyalties and alliances, the authorities did not initially know which PLF faction they were dealing with in the hijacking of the *Achille Lauro*.

On the following day, the hijackers sought to separate Jewish and American passengers from the others. When the hijackers asked if there were any Jews present, two elderly Austrians identified themselves, whom the hijackers immediately beat and manhandled. Having seen this, the small group of Jewish Americans held their tongues. The hijackers separated the 2 Jewish Austrians—as well as the 12 Americans and 5 British women belonging to a dance troupe—from the rest of the hostages, and forced them to climb up to an upper open deck, where they were forced to sit or lie under the burning sunlight and where they were surrounded by tins of gasoline or diesel fuel. The hijackers told these hostages that they would be shot, blown apart by grenades, and burned alive if anyone attempted to rescue them. When there was difficulty in moving Leon Klinghoffer's wheelchair up the stairs to the upper deck, the hijackers separated him from the rest, over the protests of Marilyn Klinghoffer, who was forced to leave him at the point of a gun. The hijackers took Mr. Klinghoffer's watch and cigarettes from him at that time. This was the last time that Marilyn Klinghoffer would see her husband alive. The hijackers took the passports of these 19 selected passengers and shuffled them, telling them that they would be killed one by one in the order of the shuffled deck of passports.

Meanwhile, the hijackers ordered Captain de Rosa to sail toward Syria and radioed their demands in the name of the PLF for the release of 50 Palestinian prisoners in Israel, naming only Samir al-Qantari, a PLF member arrested for the murders of an Israeli man and his five year-old daughter during a 1979 raid on the Israeli town of Nahariya on the Mediterranean coast. Once they had come into radio contact with the Syrian port authorities in Tartus, they repeated demands to talk to International Red Cross officials, and to the Ambassadors of Italy, West Germany, and Britain, whom they wanted to pressure the Israelis to comply. While they claimed to have seven Israeli captives aboard, this claim was denied by Israel.

The Voice of Lebanon, a Christian radio station in Beirut, intercepted radio communications between the hijackers and the Syrian authorities, providing the first indication that a hostage had been killed. At 2:42 P.M. [local time], the voice of a hijacker demanded: "[Where are the] negotiators? We will start killing at 1500 hours." At 3:23 P.M., the hijacker's voice then said: "What are the developments, Tartus? We will kill the second. We are losing patience." However this report was followed by another radio message from the captain in English stating that everyone aboard was "in very good health. Please, please, please don't try anything!"[16]

However, according to the later testimony of Captain de Rosa, around 3:05 P.M. he heard gunshots and when the hijackers appeared in the bridge with blood spattered over their pants and shoes, they told him that they had killed Leon Klinghoffer. The ship's bartender later testified that he witnessed the oldest hijacker shoot Klinghoffer in the forehead and in his chest. The ship's barber and one of the waiters were forced to pick up Mr. Klinghoffer in his wheelchair and to throw them both over the side of the ship. According to one of the women held hostage in the Arazzi room, the youngest hijacker had started to weep. When she asked him what was wrong, he replied that the other hijackers had killed the man in the wheelchair.

Refused landing rights in Syria, the hijackers ordered the captain to return to Port Said. Meanwhile, Yassir Arafat—who declared that he "totally dissociated himself" from this operation—sent PLO Executive Council members Abu Abbas and Hani al-Hassan to Cairo in order to help mediate the crisis. With the ship anchored 16 miles off Port Said, at

7:15 A.M. [local times] on October 9, 1985, Egyptian authorities contacted the ship and began negotiations. A boat containing some Egyptian officials, along with Abu Abbas and another unidentified man aboard, reached the *Achille Lauro*. The Egyptian and Italian authorities had agreed to grant the hijackers' demands of safe passage out of Egypt with no prosecution in exchange for their freeing all the hostages and their surrendering the ship, but only on the condition that no one had been harmed. Captain de Rosa was interviewed by Egyptian officials between 1:30 P.M. and 4:30 P.M., during which time he stated that "I am the captain. I am speaking from my office. And my officers and everyone is in good health." Based on this false assurance, the Egyptians agreed to the hijackers' demands, who in turn agreed to surrender at 4:20 P.M. They finally left the ship at 5:00 P.M., after they packed their guns and remaining weapons to take with them off the ship. The hijackers then disappeared from public view. In spite of the shipping company's and captain's wish to sail the *Achille Lauro* to its next intended destination of Ashdod, Egyptian officials insisted on it remaining in Port Said for their own investigation. The *Achille Lauro* was then steered into Port Said, arriving there at 4:00 A.M. the morning of October 10, 1985.

AFTER THE HIJACKING: FLIGHT AND PURSUIT

Immediately after the hijackers had left the ship, Marilyn Klinghoffer ran to the infirmary where the hijackers had told her they had left Leon Klinghoffer. Not finding him there, she was told by the infirmary staff to go see the captain. When she reached the bridge, the captain informed her that her husband had been murdered by the hijackers. In fact, the cruise came to an end at Port Said, with the 15 Americans returning to the United States by a military plane on October 12, after a brief stopover in Sicily to allow witnesses to identify the hijacking suspects who by then were in custody there. The other passengers were booked return passage by either the cruise line or their respective governments.

The repeated denials by the hijackers, by Abu Abbas, and by Yassir Arafat that anyone had been killed and that Leon Klinghoffer had merely died of a heart attack before they threw his body overboard were refuted on October 15 by the discovery of Klinghoffer's body on the Syrian coast. Subsequent forensic tests confirmed not only his identity but also his violent death by gunshots to his forehead and chest. Syria's actions in recovering and delivering the body (which eventually was returned to his widow on October 20, 1985, and buried later in New Jersey) may have been intended to undermine the international credibility of Yassir Arafat, with whom Syria had serious differences over his peace policies toward Israel.[17]

Throughout the hijacking, the United States had urged all governments to deny landing rights to the hijackers, as well as any safe passage or asylum to them and, if possible, either to extradite them to the United States or at least to arrest them pending other legal actions. After the hijackers had left the *Achille Lauro* and U.S. officials demanded that local officials arrest them, President Mubarak claimed that they had already left Egypt for an undisclosed destination. In fact, U.S. intelligence knew that they were being moved around the region by Egyptian authorities until they could be flown out on an EgyptAir 737 bound for Tunis. President Reagan was briefed about this at around 5:00 P.M. (all following times are GMT) on October 10, and he ordered the U.S. Defense Department and CIA to attempt an interception of the airplane. At 7:15 P.M., four F-14 fighter planes left the *U.S.S. Saratoga* stationed off the coast of Albania. Earlier, two E-2C electronic surveillance planes (smaller versions of the AWACS aircraft) had already left the *Saratoga* in order to track the EgyptAir flight. When the EgyptAir flight carrying the four hijackers, along with Abu Abbas and his bodyguard, took off from Cairo at 9:15 P.M., U.S. intelligence quickly informed President Reagan, who was aboard Air Force One en route from Chicago to Washington, DC, at that time. At 9:37 P.M. Reagan gave final approval to intercept the plane. At 10:30 P.M. the F-14s intercepted the EgyptAir flight that had been refused permission to land at either Tunis or Athens, and ordered it to land in Sicily. At 11:45 P.M. the plane had landed at the NATO Air Base at Sigonella, just outside Catania.[18]

Respecting diplomatic protocol, President Reagan telephoned Italy's Prime Minister Bettino Craxi just minutes before the plane was due to land at Sigonella to inform him of the operation. Craxi immediately ordered the Italian police and military at Sigonella to intervene on behalf of the Palestinians. The Italian prime minister had worked during his 26-month-long tenure in office to secure good relations with the PLO and the Arab states, but would claim later that he had intervened because the unauthorized landing of the EgyptAir flight at Sigonella violated the United States-Italian accord on the use of the NATO base.

Once the EgyptAir 737 landed at Sigonella and had come to a stop, several dozen U.S. Army Delta Force soldiers exited a nearby C-141 transport plane and surrounded the civilian plane. While their orders had been to take the four hijackers, along with Abu Abbas and his bodyguard off the civilian plane, rush them into the C-141 and to take off immediately for the United States, members of the Italian carabinieri arrived and surrounded the American soldiers. A tense situation took hold on the ground, with the Italian police being joined by Italian soldiers already on the base, facing off U.S. troops for three hours. As U.S. troops parked trucks in front of, and behind, the Egyptian plane to prevent it from moving, the Italians countered by doing the same to the C-141 to prevent it from being able to move. While the Italian and American troops each held their own ground for the next three hours, Reagan Administration officials tried in vain to persuade the Craxi government to relent and allow them to take into custody the four hijackers along with Abu Abbas and his bodyguard, Ozzuddin Badrakkan, who also was suspected of direct involvement in the hijacking conspiracy. At about 3:00 A.M. GMT President Reagan ordered the U.S. troops to "stand down" and allow the Italians to take custody of the six men.[19] The four hijackers were arrested and held in Sicily for several days, while Abu Abbas and his bodyguard again boarded the EgyptAir plane that flew them to Rome. The Craxi government refused several U.S. requests to arrest them, even stating that Abu Abbas, as a PLO official, enjoyed diplomatic immunity, and claiming a lack of evidence linking him to the hijacking. While the United States consistently demanded that Italy arrest the two men or at least prevent their departure, both were permitted to leave for Yugoslavia on October 12, in spite of U.S. claims of having evidence "based on sensitive intelligence" that Abu Abbas had actually directed the hijacking.[20] The Yugoslavians also refused to extradite or to try Abu Abbas, who later was reported to have left for South Yemen and who eventually found refuge in Iraq.

THE POLITICAL AND LEGAL FALLOUT OF THE *ACHILLE LAURO* AFFAIR

Prime Minister Craxi's decisions that stymied U.S. attempts to seize the hijackers and Abu Abbas led to strained relations between Italy and the United States. They also triggered the resignation of Craxi's government on October 18, 1985, after the Defense Minister Giovanni Spandolini withdrew his Republican Party from the governing five-party coalition government two days earlier in protest against Craxi's actions. Craxi then led an interim government and eventually won parliamentary approval on November 8, 1985, to form a new government. However, ironically, the Craxi government—which had tried so much to appease the PLO and Arab governments in its handling of the *Achille Lauro* affair—faced another Palestinian terrorist attack upon Italian soil on December 27, 1985, when gunmen of the Abu Nidal faction murdered 18 travelers and wounded 60 others in coordinated attacks in both Rome and Vienna.

While Washington was angry at President Mubarak for his deception and refusal to hand over the hijackers, the U.S. action in intercepting the EgyptAir flight itself triggered anti-United States resentment and demonstrations in Egypt and other Arab nations. The governments of Egypt and Jordan were also irritated and embarrassed by the duplicity of Yassir Arafat for his apparent involvement in the *Achille Lauro* hijacking at the same time that his PLO was involving their governments in purported joint peace initiatives with Israel. The Tunisian government, still in shock from the Israeli air raids earlier that month, now found itself embarrassed over the *Achille Lauro* operation that had been set in motion from its own territory, and also found itself accused by Egypt and other Arab states of caving in to U.S. pressures for having denied landing rights to the EgyptAir flight carrying the hijackers. Following the *Achille Lauro* fiasco, for which Abu Abbas and his followers were responsible, the Tunisian government ordered Abu Abbas and the PLF to leave; they then moved to Baghdad, Iraq.

On October 11, 1985, Marilyn Klinghoffer, with three other former hostages, identified the four hijackers in a police lineup in Sicily. On October 16, Israel's military intelligence chief, Maj. Gen. Ehud Barak, revealed the transcripts of intercepted radio communications between Abu Abbas and the hijackers, which indicated that he was not merely a mediatory as he and Yassir Arafat maintained, but rather was the mastermind of the operation and was giving orders to the four hijackers of the *Achille Lauro*.[21] Israeli authorities also claimed to have intelligence indicating that Arafat himself played a knowing and controlling role in these events.[22] By October 17, following much cross-examination of the four suspects along with ample testimony by Captain de Rosa and crew members, the Italian investigators in Sicily concluded that the hijackers' claim that they had originally intended to attack Ashdod—a position that seemed to crumble under interrogation—was a ruse, and that a stand-alone hijacking had been the original plan. According to this original plan, the ship would be sailed near the Syrian port of Tartus where PLF comrades ashore would take the American hostages off the ship and hold them in safe-houses until the 50 Palestinian prisoners were released.[23]

It should be noted that most American and Israeli experts continue to endorse the explanation that the PLF hijacking was a spontaneous improvised response to their having been discovered by an errant cabin steward. However, the Italian investigators concurred that the testimonies of both the accused hijackers and eye-witnesses did not confirm the account of their having been supposedly surprised and exposed, while there were serious discrepancies in the testimony claiming that the port of Ashdod was the intended target.

Ironically, the first suspect to break down and collaborate with Italian investigators was Magied al Molqi, the hijackers' leader, who had also killed Leon Klinghoffer: he confessed that the hijackers had been acting on the written orders of Abu Abbas.[24] As other hijackers broke down and began talking, naming accomplices and contacts, the judicial authorities began issuing more arrest warrants. Whereas Prime Minister Craxi had insisted that the United States lacked any proof of Abu Abbas' involvement, by October 23, 1985, the magistrates in Sicily had issued an arrest warrant for Abu Abbas. Genoa's magistrates lost little time asserting their right to try the case under Italian maritime law, since Genoa was the home port of the *Achille Lauro*, and they shortly assumed full jurisdiction over the case.

On November 11, 1985, Luigi Carli, one of the Genoa prosecutors assigned to the case, announced that 16 arrest warrants had been issued. The four captured hijackers, including the leader Magied Youssef al Molqi (23 years old), Ahmad Marrouf al-Assadi (23 years old), Ibrahim Fatayer Abdelatif (20 years old), and Bassam al-Ashkar (17 years old) were charged with hijacking, kidnapping, murder, and various charges involving the illegal possession of firearms and explosives. Also charged and already in custody were Mohammad Khalaf and Mohammad Issa Abbas, the latter a close relative of Abu Abbas, for their roles in bringing the arms and explosives from Tunis to the hijackers in Genoa. Those charged but still at large included Abu Abbas and his bodyguard, Ozzuddin Badrakkan, both of whom had left Italy on October 12; Ibrahim Hassir, a PLO official; Abu Kitah and Mohammad al-Khadra, who had procured the arms later sent to Genoa; Ziad al-Omar, who was believed to have directed the operation both in Tunis and Genoa; and Masar Kadia (49 years old), who had scouted out the *Achille Lauro* and who later handled and accompanied the four on the cruise ship as far as Alexandria, where he disembarked.

Those in custody were convicted on November 18, 1985, on the arms and explosives charges and sentenced to jail terms ranging from four to nine years. The most severe sentence of nine years was imposed on Muhammad Issa Abbas, who had delivered Abu Abbas' instructions to the four hijackers. Although he had been arrested in late September on charges of possessing falsified passports, while remaining in custody he had revealed nothing of the planned operation to the authorities. By securing the conviction of the hijackers on these lesser charges, prosecutors could hold them in prison while they could more thoroughly prepare to try them on the more serious charges of murder and piracy.[25] Later, on November 27, 1985, the Klinghoffer family filed two lawsuits, one in the State Supreme Court in Manhattan suing the PLO for $1.5 billion, and another in Federal District Court in Manhattan suing Chandris-Italy Inc, the Port of Genoa, and Club ABC Tours Inc., for compensatory and punitive damages.[26]

In 1986, Abu Abbas was tried in absentia in Italy and convicted on charges of conspiracy in connection with the *Achille Lauro* hijacking and murder of Leon Klinghoffer; however, he would never be extradited to Italy from his safe haven in Iraq. Similarly, Italy sought to extradite Masar Kadia from Greece in 1991. On May 30, 1990, members of the Abu Abbas faction of the PLF, with Libyan support, made a seaborne attack on Tel Aviv beaches that was quashed by the Israeli Defense Forces. Four of the PLF terrorists were killed and 12 captured. This raid occurred in the eighteenth month of talks between the United States and the PLO. While Yassir Arafat disavowed any PLO connection with the raid, he also did not publicly condemn the raid nor expel Abu Abbas from the PLO Executive Committee. This in turn prompted the United States to suspend its dialogue with the PLO. Later, in 1991, Abu Abbas resigned his membership in the PLO Executive Committee, but retained his seat on the Palestine National Council.

In 1995, an immunity accord was completed between Israel and the PLO constituting a general amnesty and granting immunity from prosecution for all PLO members for violent acts committed before September 1993. Subsequently Abu Abbas could travel freely from Iraq back and forth to the territories under control of the Palestinian Authority to take part in PLO business. On April 22, 1996, Abu Abbas—who was still wanted by the United States for his role in the *Achille Lauro* hijacking—attended the Palestine National Council meeting held in Gaza. During his presence at this meeting, Abu Abbas repeatedly stated to reporters that the *Achille Lauro* affair "was a mistake and it led to other mistakes." He claimed that his men did not know Leon Klinghoffer was Jewish or American, but that they had killed him "because he started to incite the passengers against them." By early August 1997, the PLO had agreed to settle the civil lawsuit brought against it by the Klinghoffer family. Rejecting the PLO claim that as a sovereign state it could not be sued, Federal District Judge Louis L. Stanton ordered Yassir Arafat to give a deposition.[27] Instead, the PLO moved to settle the dispute out of court and to pay the surviving Klinghoffer daughters an undisclosed sum.[28]

Following the U.S. invasion and occupation of Iraq, Abu Abbas was captured by U.S. troops on April 14, 2003. He was held as a prisoner in Iraq under U.S. custody until March 8, 2004, when he died apparently of natural causes.

CONCLUSION: PRE-PLANNED HIJACKING OR IMPROMPTU IMPROVISATION?

In retrospect it may appear to some that the entire operation had the foreknowledge and blessing of Yassir Arafat, and was just another example of a repeated pattern of covert attacks ordered by him and carried out by proxies, whose roles could then be covered up by plausible denials, followed by an offer from Arafat and the PLO to use their good offices as mediators to solve the crisis. Whereas many Western leaders and policy experts seemed to accept at face value Arafat's denial of PLO involvement in the hijacking, and to welcome his role as a mediator, by contrast both Egypt's President Hosni Mubarak and Jordan's King Hussein regarded Arafat as being directly responsible for the hijacking and guilty of duplicity and even of personal treachery in the matter. Egypt's role in trying to resolve the *Achille Lauro* crisis cost Mubarak political goodwill with the United States. Likewise it cost King Hussein his credibility with Britain for Jordan's recent efforts to mediate with Britain vouching for the PLO as a party earnestly seeking a peace settlement. For a while, King Hussein contemplated dissociating himself completely from the PLO and negotiating directly with Israel over the issue of the occupied territories in the West Bank[29]

The question remains: Was the takeover of the *Achille Lauro* merely a tactical blunder occasioned by the haphazard intrusion of a cabin steward upon the PLF gunmen while they were cleaning their weapons? Or was it instead a premeditated hijacking aimed at forcing the PLO's agenda back into the forefront of the world's consciousness by threatening to kill hundreds of citizens of nations other than Israel—in short, a quintessentially normal terrorist operation? While the consensus of U.S. and Israeli experts and commentators favors the view that an attack on Israeli soil was the original motive, there are problems with this hypothesis. First, previous attempts by the PLF to attack Israel using inflatable landing craft, hang-gliders, and the like, had not proven very effective. Although smuggling the arms and explosives aboard the *Achille Lauro* seemed relatively easy, the next stage of smuggling them into Israel through Ashdod customs and Israeli port security would not be so easy. If the plan had been to attack the port of Ashdod from the decks of the *Achille Lauro*, in effect using the civilian cruise liner and its passengers as human shields, then there was still a terrorist threat directed indiscriminately at all the nationalities on board and not directed simply at Israel in particular. In effect, this would have been no less heinous than simply seizing the cruise ship on the high seas and using its crew and passengers as hostages. The other problem was that noted by the Italian investigators: the testimonies of the suspects on the supposed Ashdod plan were inconsistent and contradictory. At one point, suspects said a crew member had spotted them cleaning their guns, but at another point, the suspects also claimed that they had been recognized by Egyptian port authorities and had decided to seize the ship then. Some of the suspects—in particular Bassam al Ashkar—stated that they had never been surprised by any crew member, that the Ashdod attack account was in fact a fabrication, and that he had been instructed by al Molqi that they were going to seize the ship.

While preparations for the *Achille Lauro* venture had been in the works for over 10 months prior to the hijacking, the inspiration for the final form of this operation more likely may have come from a recent and very dramatic hostage situation that proved itself very successful from the viewpoint of the terrorists who perpetrated it—namely, the hijacking of TWA flight 847 on June 14, 1985.[30] Shiite gunmen in this hijacking seized 145 passengers and 8 crew members. One American serviceman among the hostages was killed and 39 American men were held hostage in Lebanon until the leader of Lebanon's Shiite AMAL militia, Nabih Berri, negotiated their release in exchange for 119 Lebanese and Palestinian prisoners held in Israel's Atlit Prison. Berri, whose own gunmen played a principal role in the hijacking and hostage-taking incident, was portrayed in Western media as a negotiator and mediator. Thus, the *Achille Lauro* attackers may have felt that the seizure of a large number of Western hostages on a cruise liner could similarly lead to a negotiated settlement in which the PLO might wind up being hailed as a mediator and peacemaker, "saving" the hostages and conceivably gaining freedom for PLO prisoners in Israel.

There was also a Palestinian precedent for attempting such an operation—namely the "Black September" attack on the Israeli athletes at the 1972 Munich Summer Olympics, which also had been a hostage-barricade siege in which the hostage-takers demanded the release of 234 prisoners in Israel, including the surviving Japanese Red Army member who took part in the Lod Airport massacre of May 1972.[31] While the PLO denied responsibility for those attacks, it later became well-established that Black September was a PLO creation led by PLO Executive Committee member Salah Khalaf, also known as "Abu Iyad," who later even wrote about his role in the operation in his memoirs.[32]

Therefore, the problem for Arafat and the PLO was not any lack of willingness to engage in covert terrorist actions, under the cover of plausible denial, from which to reap political benefits. Nor was there any lack of motivation, since the outcome of the TWA 847 hijacking demonstrated that such an action could be successful and benefit the PLO. The problem, rather, was one of execution: to seize and hold a multideck cruise ship, full of myriad passageways, hidden service conduits and crawl spaces, with over 700 passengers and close to 350 crew members, would be a formidable task for a mere four hijackers. The success of Anna Hoerantner in evading capture illustrates this problem. This would explain why the hijackers would wait to seize the vessel until after the ship had unloaded over 600 passengers for their temporary sightseeing tour of the Pyramids. However, unlike the TWA 847 hijacking, or even the 1979 occupation of the U.S. Embassy in Tehran, the actual venue of the hijacking on the high seas remained isolated from any possibility of minute-by-minute instantaneous global press coverage. Therefore, the hijacking unfolded without creating the sort of constant coverage feeding high public emotion and outrage that had helped pressure the U.S. and Israeli government decision-makers into making concessions in the TWA 847 case, concessions that undermined their ability to maintain a steadfast and consistent position in the face of terrorist manipulation. Interestingly, there have been no noteworthy attempts by any other terrorist groups to try to replicate the *Achille Lauro* incident by hijacking another cruise liner.

Unfortunately, the only persons who could have verified whether the hijacking was intended as a PLO-sponsored stand-alone action—namely

Yassir Arafat and Abu Abbas—died without ever confirming this in spoken word or writing. The idea that Ashdod was the original intended target of the hijackers may be attractive to Western observers outside of Israel for a psychological reason: the need to believe that the Palestinian-Israeli conflict can in fact be mediated and solved through some combination of goodwill, rationality, self-interest, and skillful diplomacy. The images of Arafat's character and of PLO politics that are most consistent with the "stand-alone" hypothesis are those of a deceptive and intransigent party that in fact would be incapable of making a lasting peace. And that hypothesis clashes with the perennial optimism and faith in human progress and rationality that must underlie any hope for peace in the Middle East. Even with the 2006 Hamas political victory in the Palestinian Authority, United States and other Western diplomats—as well as well-meaning people elsewhere—continue to speak of the possibility of Hamas somehow accepting the existence of the State of Israel despite the Hamas Charter calling for the extermination of Israel, the repeated calls of Hamas leaders for destroying Israel, and the over 60 suicide-bombings sponsored by Hamas over the five-year period preceding their election. Even with so much evidence to the contrary, the United States and other Western observers wish to believe, hoping against hope, that there is still some possibility for reconciliation, compromise, and peace. Likewise, at the time of the *Achille Lauro* crisis, both the world public and Western leaders wanted to believe that Yassir Arafat and the PLO were earnestly seeking to mediate that crisis, and not simply exploiting it for political gain.

It is more perplexing to understand why Israeli analysts, who have had a much more pessimistic assessment of Arafat and the PLO leadership, endorsed the view that the hijackers originally intended to attack Ashdod and not simply hijack the ship. If the objective of an attack on Ashdod were ruled out, then the *Achille Lauro* incident would become almost completely detached from Israeli concerns, apart from the murder and mistreatment of Jewish individuals at the hands of the hijackers. After all, none of the passengers were Israeli citizens, the cruise ship was not an Israeli vessel, and the incident did not take place in Israeli territorial waters. Israel felt no need to make any concessions to the hijackers. However, for Israel, stressing the Ashdod connection helps to make it clear to nations such as Italy, France, and others, that as long as Israel remains the target of Palestinian terrorism, the nationals, ships, and territories of these other nations will not be protected from the scourge of that same terrorism no matter what separate political accommodations they make between their own nations and the PLO, and no matter how much they attempt to distance themselves from being associated with Israel.

The reader is left with two conflicting interpretations of the real purposes and motives behind the *Achille Lauro* hijacking. Nor is this a merely "theoretical" concern: at the time these actual events were unfolding, these same disagreements over how to interpret and assess the crisis also caused great rifts and conflicts between allies both in the NATO alliance as well as in the Arab world. Neither can anyone rule out that events similar to the *Achille Lauro* hijacking will not be repeated in the twenty-first century.

NOTES

1. Israeli Ministry of Foreign Affairs Web site: http://www.mfa.gov.il/MFA/Foreign%20Relations/Israels%20Foreign%20since%201947/1984-1988/92%20Press%20Conference%20Following%20Israel%20air%20Force%20Att (retrieved April 7, 2006).

2. Masar Kadia also went by names of "Petros Floros" and "Abdel Rahim Khaled." In the earliest Italian legal documents he is referred to as "Abdel Rahim Khaled" but in later extradition documents as "Masar Kadia." The name "Masar Kadia" is used throughout this chapter to avoid confusion.

3. John Tagliabue, "Italians Identify 16 in Hijacking of Ship," *New York Times*, November 20, 1985: A3.

4. This was learned from the youngest hijacker, Bassam al-Ashkar (only 17 years old at the time), who later denied a separate report that the weapons had been discovered by a cabin steward and they had seized the ship on the spur of the moment.

5. Tagliabue, "Italians Identify 16 in Hijacking of Ship," A3.

6. Sean K. Anderson and Stephen Sloan, "Palestine Liberation Organization," in *Terrorism: Assassins to Zealots* (Lanham, MD: Scarecrow Press, 2003) 308.

7. Sean K. Anderson and Stephen Sloan, "Palestine Liberation Front," in *Terrorism: Assassins to Zealots* (Lanham, MD: Scarecrow Press, 2003) 304–305.

8. Robert D. McFadden, "15 Passengers, on Return to U.S., Tell of Terror on the Cruise Liner," *New York Times*, October 13, 1985: A1, A24.

9. Israeli Ministry of Foreign Affairs Web site http://www.mfa.gov.il/MFA/MFAArchive/2000_2002/9/The%20Palestinian%20Liberation%20Front-%20Headed%20by%20Abu%20al (retrieved April 7, 2006).

10. Vlad Jenkins, *The Achille Lauro Hijacking*, John F. Kennedy School of Government Case Program, 1988. This case was written by Vlad Jenkins at the John F. Kennedy School of Government for Professor Philip Heymann and the Project for the Study and Analysis of Terrorism, Harvard Law School. Funding was provided by the Central Intelligence Agency and the John D. and Catherine T. MacArthur Foundation. (0894)

11. Joseph Berger, "Even With a Name, It's Hard to Know Who the Hijackers Are," *New York Times*, October 9, 1985: A9.

12. Michael K. Bohn, *The Achille Lauro Hijacking; Lessons in the Politics and Prejudice of Terrorism* (Washington, DC: Brassey's Inc., 2004).

13. Anderson and Sloan, "Palestine Liberation Organization," 308.

14. NOTE: "Abu Abbas" or "Abu al-Abbas" was the *nom de guerre* of Muhammad Abbas. Throughout this chapter for sake of brevity he will be referred to always as "Abu Abbas" however in the official U.S. and Italian documents mentioned in this chapter he is generally referred to as "Muhammad Abbas" rather than "Abu Abbas."

15. Anderson and Sloan, "Palestine Liberation Front," 304.

16. John Tagliabue, "Hijackers of Ship Vow Again to Kill 400 Held Hostage," *New York Times*, October 9, 1985: A1, A9. On page A9 is an insert of the radio dialogue reported by Reuters on October 8, 1985.

17. Bernard Gwertzman, "U.S. Believes Body Found By Syrians Is Slain Hostage's," *New York Times*, October 16, 1985: A1, A13.

18. Francis X Clines, "U.S. Heads Off the Hijackers: How the Operation Unfolded," *New York Times*, October 12, 1985: A1, A9.

19. Bill Keller, "Aides Say Reagan Put End to Troop Standoff," *New York Times*, October 19, 1985: A4.

20. Philip Shenon, "U.S. Reported to Have Evidence Linking P.L.O. Aide to Hijacking," *New York Times*, October 14, 1985: A1, A11.

21. Thomas L. Friedman, "Israelis Say Tape Ties Top P.L.O. Aide to Ship Hijackers," *New York Times*, October 17, 1985: A1, A12.

22. Joseph Berger with E. J. Dionne, Jr., "Italy Said to Free 2 P.L.O. Aides; U.S. Issues a Warrant for One; Hostages Tell of a 'Death List:' Account of Ordeal," *New York Times*, October 13, 1985: A1, A22, col. 6, paragraphs 2 and 3.

23. John Tagliabue, "Italians Doubt View That Hijacking Was Improvised," *New York Times*, October 18, 1985: A10.

24. John Tagliabue, "Hijacker Is Reported to Implicate Abbas," *New York Times*, October 24, 1985: A3.

25. John Tagliabue, "Italy Convicts Palestinians in Arms Case," *New York Times*, November 19, 1985: A3.

26. Anonymous, "The Klinghoffers Sue P.L.O. for $1.5 Billion," *New York Times*, November 28, 1985: B7.

27. Anonymous, "Judge Rules P.L.O. Liable in Raid on the Achille Lauro," *New York Times*, June 9, 1990. Stanton's ruling: "Although [the PLO] claims the attributes of a state, it controls no defined territory or populace and is not recognized by the United States . . . [therefore there is no justification in] treating it as a foreign sovereign or state in this litigation. Rather, as its name indicates, the P.L.O. is an organization."

28. Anderson and Sloan, "Palestine Liberation Front,": 305–306.

29. John Kifner, "Warning by Arafat: Peace Will Not Exist Without the P.L.O.," *New York Times*, October 30, 1985: A1, A6; also, Ihsan A, Hijazi, "Arafat's Palestinian Foes Split on How to Challenge His Leadership," *New York Times*, October 30, 1985: A6: also John Kifner, "Hussein Reported to Weigh Leaving P.L.O. Out of Plan," *New York Times*, October 27, 1985: A1, A14.

30. Please see the chapter by Rick Wrona in this volume.

31. Sean K. Anderson and Stephen Sloan, "Munich Massacre," in *Terrorism: Assassins to Zealots* (Lanham, MD: Scarecrow Press, 2003) 270–271.

32. Joseph Berger, "Even With a Name, It's Hard to Know Who the Hijackers Are," *New York Times*, October 9, 1985: A9.

Chapter 5

THE FEBRUARY 1993 ATTACK ON THE WORLD TRADE CENTER

Daniel Baracskay

Recent decades have proven that large urban centers are particularly prone to terrorist attacks. They have reputations of national and international standing, are centers of trade in a capitalist society, and have dense populations of people who live and work within their borders. Over time, New York City has matured into a globally recognized bastion of commerce, entertainment, and industry. Composed of several soaring buildings, the World Trade Center has been a familiar landmark in the city for decades. The north and south towers, each with 110 stories of office space, were the tallest and most populated of the cluster. Scores of businesses are located in close proximity to these two towers, making it a congested but profitable location. New York City's population in 1990 was approximately 7.3 million people, making it the most populated American city.[1]

The World Trade Center (WTC) bombing in 1993 warrants analysis for several reasons.[2] First, it signaled that the threat of a terrorist attack is not solely confined to foreign soil. Second, the WTC bombing indicated that foreign terrorist organizations can successfully penetrate American borders with a significant attack that embodies a political and religious plot for restitution against American presence overseas, particularly in the Middle East. Third, the attack signified the expanding nature of ad hoc terror groups that come together exclusively for violent purposes and exist as organizations that are linked together by the like-minded ideologies of their extremist members. Finally, the event in 1993 was a precursor to the September 11 attack on the two World Trade Center towers in New York City 8 years later, indicating that further efforts are essential to prevent the ongoing prospect of similar incidents. This chapter will examine the WTC bombing of 1993 and present several lessons and implications of the event.

EXAMINING THE WORLD TRADE CENTER ATTACK OF 1993

On February 26, 1993, a terrorist group drove a truck containing more than 1,000 pounds of explosives into the underground parking garage of the 110-story north tower of the WTC in New York City. The truck exploded at 12:17 P.M., killing six Americans and injuring hundreds more. The explosion reduced daily activities to a standstill, and created a cloud that blanketed the area with smoke and debris. The physical structure of the building was significantly damaged but did not collapse. The immediate psychological ramifications of the incident were profound. It was believed that more than 50 thousand people were in the twin towers of the WTC at the time. Evacuees from the building walked down flights of stairs in complete darkness. Smoke inhalation was rampant among the survivors.[3] The bombing was testimony that American borders were penetrable, making us vulnerable to attack by outside terrorist groups. Besides the attack on Pearl Harbor in 1941, and a small number of isolated incidents, the United States had not witnessed an aggressive display of violence of such magnitude on American soil. In fact, with the absence of a continual wave of bombings like those that had historically affected London, Paris, Rome, and numerous other cities each year, the United States lived under a "myth of invulnerability." As Jeffrey Simon observes, "since international terrorists could find an abundance of U.S. targets overseas to strike with relative ease and avoid capture, it appeared as though they would be unwilling to risk traveling to the United States to carry out their violence ... Yet it was only a matter of time before America joined the rest of the world in encountering terrorist assaults on its soil."[4]

Victims at the scene directly experienced what millions of other American citizens viewed through the lens of journalistic reporting—a political act of aggression by a radical Islamic terrorist organization that was seeking retribution for what it perceived to be American oppression and interference in the affairs of Muslims in the Middle East. While the WTC bombing occurred inside the spatial borders of American territory, it was considered an act of international terrorism by a group that was not state-sponsored but still operated abroad. State-sponsored terrorism involves the actions of "rogue states" (e.g., Iran, Libya, and Iraq) that threaten adjacent or regional actors that pose a threat to that country's policies by using government-sponsored terrorist behaviors.[5] This pattern of behavior does not preclude an attack against democratic states, however. Terror groups have a different inclination. With the exception of Hizbollah and a few others, terrorist groups typically do not associate themselves directly with rogue states, but present a more pervasive display of power that transverses the international arena. CIA veteran Paul Pillar refers to these entities as "ad hoc terrorists," which are basically "small cabals of extremists who do not belong to any larger, established, previously known group. Although the individuals involved may gravitate toward particular political or spiritual leaders, they do not become a group until they become one for the purpose of conducting a particular terrorist operation. After the operation, they may dissolve and disperse."[6] These groups elude capture and are discernibly more challenging to trace, since they often roam across the penetrable borders of rogue states or other nations that are considered safe havens for terrorist activities.

The terrorists of the WTC attack in 1993 subscribed to a religious fundamentalism that is quite alien to many Americans. The conventional practice of separating church from state to prevent the fusion of religion and politics in democratic regimes is manifestly absent in the proscribed doctrines of several major world religions. With over 1.2 billion adherents, Islam is the world's second largest religion after Christianity and promotes unique views on the nature of politics and religion. Students of religion and philosophy have long observed that "from its very beginnings, Islam has viewed religion and politics (church and state) as necessarily and rightfully inseparable. To Muslims, the notion of religion as separable from the totality of the human context is unimaginable, even detestable."[7] For some adherents, these religious convictions are a key motivating factor behind various forms of political violence, including terrorism. Indeed, many kinds of religious extremists, including radical Islamic fundamentalists, employ the use of terrorist activities to bridge their beliefs with reality.[8]

An extremist interpretation of Islam served as the mutually reinforcing principle that guided the WTC conspiracy. Ramzi Yousef was acknowledged as the operational mastermind of the Trade Center bombing, although the FBI has ultimately determined that the activities were part of a broader plot by al Qaeda leader Osama bin Laden.[9] Removed from Palestine and raised in Kuwait, Yousef developed a militant posture and advanced his skills at a training camp in Afghanistan. For several decades, Afghanistan has been a haven for militant rebels, including those who fought the occupation of Soviet troops from 1978 to 1988. Presidents Carter and Reagan covertly provided aid from the United States to Afghan rebels during that decade to destabilize the left-leaning and Marxist Afghani government. Simultaneously, bin Laden pledged his own money, weapons, and resources to the Afghan cause. During the late 1980s, bin Laden helped form al Qaeda and funneled his extensive family fortune into supporting a global "jihad," or holy war against the West. When the Soviets left Afghanistan in 1988, as terrorism analyst Peter

Bergen observes, al Qaeda viewed it as a "victory against the communists in Afghanistan . . . a superpower had been defeated. It was an important lesson for the Afghan Arabs and for bin Laden himself, who applied it to his next holy war—a war against the United States."[10] Al Qaeda used its relationship with the amenable Taliban regime in Afghanistan to build a coalition of supporters for its cause. Bin Laden has specifically blamed his use of terror tactics on American support for Israel and its presence in Islamic holy lands like Saudi Arabia.[11]

After his experience with al Qaeda operatives in Afghanistan, Yousef traveled to the United States in 1992 using a falsified passport. Also traveling with Yousef was his colleague, Ahmed Ajaj. Ajaj was detained by American authorities for having a phony passport and documents in his luggage on how to construct a bomb. The name Abu Barra was printed on the documents. It was the alias used by another colleague, Mohhamed Jamal Khalifa.[12] Ajaj was arrested for the incriminating evidence and Yousef informed the authorities that he had lost his passport and wanted to claim political asylum. Ajaj remained in custody, serving as a decoy to draw attention away from Yousef, who was issued a temporary passport by the Pakistani Consulate in New York, allowing him to travel freely.

Late in 1992, Yousef initiated communication with Umar Abd al-Rahman, an Egyptian cleric known as the "Blind Sheikh" who preached to his followers at the al-Farouq mosque in Brooklyn.[13] Abd al-Rahman was an unlikely culprit for the World Trade Center plot. He was 55 years of age, blind, diabetic, and moderately immobile. Those who ultimately pledged support for Abd Al-Rahman's views did not originally migrate to the United States as an independent sectarian group. Rather, they forged a link from their analogous extremist views and contacts at New York mosques.[14] Abd al-Rahman was the self-professed leader of a holy war that he waged against the United States for being an enemy of Islam. Yousef, along with other Abd al-Rahman followers and coconspirators Mohammed Salameh, Mahmud Abouhalima, and El Sayyid Nosair, constructed the explosive device that was detonated on February 26. The result of the bombing fell short of Abd al-Rahman's optimism that the force of the explosion would collapse the north tower onto the southern one, destroying both in the process.[15]

Following the incident, Yousef fled to Pakistan. Based upon information conveyed by an informant,[16] several of the conspirators were captured by authorities in the months after the attack. They were brought to trial in September 1993 and subsequently convicted in March 1994. Yousef was later arrested in Islamabad in 1995.[17] His arrest came after an informant divulged Yousef's location in exchange for a $2 million reward that had been offered for information leading to his capture. During his deportation back to America, Yousef elaborated more of his plan to the FBI agents

Table 5.1 Defendants and Outcomes of the *U.S.A. v. Eyad Ismoil et al.* Trial

Defendant	Number of Counts Convicted	Prison Sentence and Fines Assessed
Ramzi Ahmed Yousef	18	8 life sentences, plus 240 years; Fined $4.5 million dollars
Mahmud Abdouhalima	9	240 years; fined $250,000
Mohammad Salameh	10	117 years; fined $250,000
Nidal Ayyad	9	117 years, fined $250,000
Bilal Alkaisi*	1	20 months and 2 years supervised release
Ahmad Mohammad Ajaj	9	115 years; fined $250,000
Abdul Hakim Murad	7	Life in prison, plus 60 years; fined $250,000
Eyad Ismoil	10	240 years; fined $250,000

*Turned states evidence to receive a lesser sentence
Source: Table derived from data from The National Memorial Institute for the Prevention of Terrorism, *Terrorism Knowledge Base* (Washington, DC), September 2006.

who accompanied him. As the plane holding Yousef and the agents passed by the WTC, Yousef allegedly stated that he would have succeeded in toppling one tower onto the other if he had been able to secure more money and explosives.[18]

Mohammed Salameh was one of the first to be arrested. Salameh had rented the truck used in the explosion, later reporting that it was stolen. He was captured at the truck company rental office when he attempted to get back his $400 deposit. The FBI also arrested Nidal Ayyad, an engineer who acquired the chemicals for the bomb, and Mahmoud Abouhalima who mixed the chemicals.[19] In the case *U.S.A. v. Eyad Ismoil et al* (93-CR-180-KTD), a total of ten radical Islamic extremists were convicted for the incident and sentenced to prison. The table above lists the defendants, number of convictions, and sentences for those involved in the WTC bombing case.

The WTC attack of 1993 was not Yousef's only plot. He was also allegedly involved in another bombing conspiracy. Yousef and his associates plotted to slip several bombs composed of liquid explosives onto 11 U.S. commercial aircraft.[20] The liquid explosives were designed to pass easily through airport metal detectors. The modes of transportation and expected destructive capacities for executing the plot were similar to what actually transpired on 9/11. However, Yousef's plan was foiled and he was forced to flee his apartment after a chemical reaction started a fire. The computer he left behind was salvageable and tipped the FBI and other criminal investigators off to his plans. It contained information that was used to help capture Yousef later that year.[21]

The Islamic cleric Abd al-Rahman was also arrested and convicted of five counts, including seditious conspiracy, solicitation and conspiracy to murder Egyptian President Hosni Mubarak, solicitation to attack a military installation, and bombing conspiracy. He was sentenced to life in prison, plus 65 years without the possibility of parole in the case, *U.S.A. v. Omar Ahmad Ali Abdel-Rahmen et al. (93-CR-181-KTD)*. Also on trial in the case were nine coconspirators, who were sentenced to various prison terms ranging from 25 to 35 years.[22] This case addressed the information supplied by an informant to the FBI detailing plots to bomb additional landmarks in New York City—namely the United Nations building, the FBI building in New York, and the Holland and Lincoln Tunnels.

Despite the favorable outcomes that these two trials had in bringing the assailants to justice, "an unfortunate consequence of this superb investigative and prosecutorial effort was that it created an impression that the law enforcement system was well-equipped to cope with terrorism."[23] This was not the case—the trial executed justice but did not bring bin Laden or his network to the attention of either the public or policymakers.[24] Overall, 1993 was a slightly more active year for terrorist activities globally.[25] In addition to these plots by Abd al-Rahman and his associates, the FBI also foiled an Iraqi-motivated plot to assassinate former Republican President George Bush while he visited Kuwait in April of that year. These attempts were more obscured in coverage by the media, indicating that efforts by FBI and CIA agents to successfully thwart an attack emit much less public attention than when an attack does occur.[26]

THE RESPONSE TO THE ATTACK

The World Trade Center had been attacked by foreign perpetrators and government inquiries were launched into two primary issues. The first issue probed whether the incident had state sponsorship. In such circumstances, the U.S. Department of State investigates whether the act was committed by a state or rogue terrorist group. If evidence suggests the latter, then the next step examines where the terrorists were residing prior to the incident, and whether the state that housed them covertly supported or had knowledge of their activities. Much of this analysis was predicated on foreign intelligence information gathered and supplied by the CIA. President Bill Clinton immediately charged the National Security Council (NSC) with coordinating the initial response, and the New York office of the FBI assumed control of the local investigation.[27] The NSC and its interagency Counterterrorism Security Group (CSG) both used their authority to respond to the attack with domestic and foreign counterterrorism measures.[28] In 1986, Congress had granted the FBI authority to investigate terrorist acts against Americans overseas, and in 1989 this authority was expanded to allow the FBI the authority to arrest perpetrators abroad without the consent of the host country. House and Senate intelligence committees likewise conducted their own series of investigations. The U.S. Department of Justice's investigation sought to identify and apprehend those responsible for the incident. It attempted to isolate where the breaches in public security occurred and develop a strategy for preventing similar attacks in the future. These investigations uncovered an integrated network of terrorists who spanned the globe. The reaction times for initiating these investigations were rapid, but the process itself was long and tedious, and spanned state borders—as the capture and deportation of Yousef from Pakistan demonstrated.

The governor of the state of New York at the time of the attack, Mario Cuomo, worked closely with David N. Dinkins, the mayor of the City of New York throughout the response and recovery. As mayor, Dinkins had the primary role of reassuring the city's residential and professional inhabitants of the government's resolve, and of coordinating the efforts of local law enforcement officers with federal agents, primarily from the FBI. Dinkins was perceived throughout his short mayoral tenure (1989–1993) as being weak and unresponsive to some of the city's more plaguing problems, despite his handling of the WTC attack in 1993. The 3-day Crown Heights Riot in August of 1991 and the perceptions citizens had of the growing crime problem were contributing factors to Dinkin's defeat in the fall 1993 election, when Rudy Giuliani assumed the city's leadership for two terms, and—like his predecessor—was also forced to respond to an attack on the WTC. The destruction of the two towers 8 years later on 9/11 indicated the persistence of bin Laden and those affiliated with (or inspired by) his al Qaeda network, which produced the level of destruction envisioned for the first WTC incident.

IMPLICATIONS AND LESSONS OF THE WTC ATTACK IN 1993

Perceptions and Culture in World Politics

Counterterrorism measures in the United States inherently take into account the unconventional ideologies and cultures embraced by terrorist groups. This has been a growing challenge over time. Political scientist John Rourke has explored the importance that perceptions have in international politics, and argues that perceptions create a "lens" through which reality is perceived. These lenses often create distortions in the images of both ourselves and other states in the world arena. How strongly the perceptual distortion is depends upon the strength of the beholder's beliefs. Misperceptions cause a misjudgment of others' actions and plausibly increase the likelihood of a conflict.[29] Given the low levels of knowledge that most Americans have of domestic and international politics,[30] citizens consequently have a difficult time identifying either a motive for the World Trade Center attack or an understanding of the assailants. American political culture was built upon fundamentals of democracy, which include values like freedom and independence. This has allowed the nation's borders to be porous and vulnerable to attack. Like-minded Americans find the acts of a terrorist organization morally reprehensible and inconceivable. Yet, the values embraced by terrorist groups encourage a merging of politics and religion. The two cultures find each other incomprehensible, if not disagreeable at times. This implies an innate difficulty that cannot be easily resolved.

Terrorism has become a favored tactic of several extremist religious sects, as well as groups from both the left and right of the ideological spectrum. Yet, religious doctrine itself is not to be blamed for acts of terror, but rather it is the interpretation of such doctrine. As terrorism scholar Cindy Combs has observed, "Islam is not, in any sense, a violent religion. Nor are Christianity, Judaism, or any of the other religions in whose name violence has been carried out. However, the mixture of religion and politics has quite often resulted in violence, frequently against innocent victims, which makes it . . . terrorism."[31] Combs likens the actions of extremist, self-sacrificing Islamic fundamentalists engaged in a jihad to the Brotherhood of Assassins from the Middle Ages. Though from different eras in world history, both groups promised their followers that they would be rewarded for their actions with paradise. However, Combs also observes that governments have been ineffective in preventing the proliferation of these fundamentalist groups or their use of terror to achieve their objectives. The problem has remained inherently insoluble over the years, partly because the difference in cultures and approaches has made the actions of terrorist groups difficult to predict and respond to with counterterrorism policies. Overall, the understated nature of these cross-cultural disparities, along with the inability for both sides to negotiate and bargain over perceived grievances, makes peace improbable.

Counterterrorism Measures That Target Terrorist's Growing Financial Resources

One poignant lesson of strategic importance involves tracing the financial resources of terrorist networks.[32] These resources have expanded over time and pose a significant threat in preventing acts of terrorism. Correspondingly, this trend has also commanded the attention of counterterrorism policymakers. The terrorists who conducted the WTC bombing in 1993 drew financial support from a well-funded network of like-minded Islamic fundamentalists. Rohan Gunaratna's research finds that this expansive network—particularly with the support of bin Laden—provided the necessary funding for Yousef's terrorist activities and numerous other

Islamic fundamentalists. Yousef also received financial backing from his uncle, Khalid Sheikh Mohmmad, who lived in Qatar at the time.[33] Al-Rahman's base of support came from Egyptian groups including the Muslim Brotherhood, as well as from Algerian, Afghani, and Pakistani elements in al Qaeda.[34]

The acknowledged father of al Qaeda is Abdul Azzam, a mentor of bin Laden. Together, they founded the Maktab al Khidmat lil Mujahidin al-Arab (MAK, or Afghan Service Bureau) to increase membership, raise money, and spread their jihad globally. The MAK has expanded al Qaeda influence exponentially over time and has allowed numerous terrorist groups to extract both money and capital to support their cause. From an operational and counterterrorist policy standpoint, the United States has found that preventing the spread of al Qaeda and other terrorist organizations requires considerable thought and effort to track the financial resources of such networks. These funds have allowed al Qaeda and other groups to successfully recruit a seemingly endless number of members, and to secure weapons and supplies for its activities. For instance, U.S. intelligence tracked a money trail used to fund an assassination attempt of Egyptian President Hosni Mubarak to the National Commercial Bank (NCB) of Saudi Arabia. Millions of dollars had been transferred to al Qaeda operatives via banks in New York and London, without the banks' knowledge. U.S intelligence has additionally traced over $100 million that went to support al Qaeda's efforts to recruit loyal Islamic groups, including the Taliban.[35]

The unregulated nature of banking systems in the Middle East allows members to easily transfer funds without much governmental scrutiny. This poses a significant threat to democratic nations and has burdened U.S. counterterrorism measures with having to respond to an ever-expanding terrorist network. The Al Taqwa and Al Barakaat banking networks have both been identified by the U.S. Justice Department as financial havens for terrorists, but hundreds more like these exist. The Dubai Islamic Bank, which is controlled by the United Arab Emirates (UAE), funneled millions of dollars in laundered money from Saudi businessmen to al Qaeda operatives.[36] The 1993 WTC attack demonstrates that the multinational character of al Qaeda has often made it difficult for the CIA to trace its funding sources. These sources are extensive and span several decades. For instance, the Bank of Credit and Commerce International channeled funds to support the Afghan rebels during the Soviet Occupation. This fueled the Afghani cause and jihad that spread to the United States. But as Gunaratna notes, "intelligence and security services worldwide, including the CIA and MI6, have never before encountered a global terrorist financial network as sophisticated as Al Qaida's ... [it] has built the most complex, robust and resilient money-generating and money-moving network yet seen."[37]

Globally interconnected relationships enable large terrorist groups like al Qaeda to generate funding from many sources. Much of al Qaeda's financial base is used for technical and logistical operations, and comes from Islamic philanthropists and foundations, notably the UAE, Kuwait, Saudi Arabia, and Qatar.[38] Many Islamic charities and NGOs pose as fronts for raising money. Other money has filtered into terrorist activities from the sale of drugs through organized crime connections.[39] The al Qaeda financial network has been analogized to a holding company, with associated Islamic terrorist groups functioning as its subsidiaries. According to numerous sources, the financial system of al Qaeda is overseen by a committee of Muslim bankers and accountants, and has supported an estimated 3,000 core Afghani and overseas members, along with 120,000 ancillary members who spread terrorism across the globe, and has an annual budget of under $50 million. Bin Laden's own family inheritance was in the range of $25–30 million, which he has used to substantially buttress the network.[40]

Prior to 9/11, efforts by the CIA to weaken the financial networks of terrorist groups were only nominally supported by other countries, particularly Canada and those in Western Europe. The attention devoted to funding sources has taken a new strategic importance in modern times as governments across the globe more readily link the growing monetary bases of terrorist groups to specific activities. The counterterrorism strategies of many of these countries have been revamped accordingly. Approximately 2,500 companies and individuals have been identified by the U.S. Office of Foreign Assets Control as entities that must have their assets blocked.[41]

The Sprawling Nature of Interconnected Terror Networks

Counterterrorism policies have required significant adaptation in the post-Cold War era. After World War II, conflict between the United States and former Soviet Union dominated American foreign policy throughout the Cold War. The official collapse of the Soviet regime in 1991 ended what was considered a contentious bipolar era.[42] This era seems to pale in light of a perceptibly different global system. The number of rogue and nuclear-capable states has grown, as have the terrorist organizations that use such failed or rogue states for shelter. This makes the post-Cold War era much more perilous for democracies.[43] These various groups are bonded together by a shared extremist ideology, and many of them seek to infiltrate American society with terror cells.

The declaration of war against terrorist activities was enunciated by President George W. Bush on the evening of September 11. The declaration represented the cumulative effects of prior terrorist acts like the first WTC bombing in 1993, and the culmination of an incremental shift toward a more guarded state of existence for the United States. In strategic terms, the creation of the cabinet-level Office of Homeland Security—and corresponding realignment of FBI, CIA, and Department of Defense communications and functions—demonstrates that the internal threat to our nation is not expected to recede in the foreseeable future. However, terrorist groups present a different operational challenge than was perceived during the Cold War or other points in American history. They represent a "borderless" war by groups of interconnected radical ideologues with different beliefs of political and religious idealism. Bergen argues that the end of the Cold War produced an environment conducive for the expansion of terrorist groups. His research on bin Laden and al Qaeda led him to conclude that "it was precisely the end of the Cold War, which brought more open borders, that allowed his organization to flourish . . . made possible by the changing rules of the New World Order."[44] Yet, despite the nature of this interconnected terrorist network, the end of the Cold War brought funding cuts in the U.S. budget for national security expenditures from 1990 to 1996, and led to flat budgets from 1996 to 2000.[45] This challenged the vibrancy of counterterrorism measures before 9/11.

Meanwhile, al Qaeda training camps in Afghanistan attracted an expansive coalition of followers. The WTC bombing in 1993 illustrates how terrorist groups are interconnected in nature. Yousef, the operational leader of the bombing, had trained at an al Qaeda camp in Afghanistan where he met an array of Islamic extremists. As Pillar notes, these acquaintances have allowed for "cooperation among groups—such as in procuring false documents, facilitating travel, and performing other support functions—even if they do not conduct joint terrorist operations."[46]

In order to successfully combat the sprawling and integrated nature of terrorist organizations, democratically based states must be willing to band together their own counterterrorist organizations more effectively to share information and effectively track down the vestiges of terror networks. This is not to say that such cooperation does not exist at present. The international police organization, INTERPOL, exists for just this reason—to gather information on terrorist and criminal activities, and disseminate it to countries for use in their counterterrorism measures. But such coordination and communication are increasingly complex endeavors that require significant levels of dexterity when spanning national boundaries.

One obstacle to counterterrorism measures has been the difficulty many states have had in distinguishing terrorists from viable nongovernmental organizations (NGOs) that are legitimately performing social service work. For instance, NGOs such as the Pakistani Maktab al-Khidamat exist for a valid reason, but are unwittingly used as pawns by terrorist groups that take advantage of them. Terrorists have been known to join the organization and use it as a vehicle to transport both money and materials across their organization. The NGOs provide jobs and make activities appear legitimate when members consequently travel to other regions.[47]

Another related lesson that has been learned has been the tendency toward cross-pollination of terror networks.[48] Members communicate, recruit across organizational boundaries, transfer tactical knowledge and ideas, and share financial resources. The effect of capturing and punishing one group's members only creates a small ripple in a larger sea of the network. This has required a broader application of counterterrorism policies. Similar to the building of vast interest group coalitions and advocacy networks in the United States,[49] terrorist groups recognize the advantages of linking human and material resources together in a nonhierarchical network. The ultimate effect generates a stronger force and mechanism for inducing chaos. For example, a partnership between the Japanese Red Army and a group of anti-Israeli Palestinian Arabs led to the May 1972 terrorist attack at Lod International Airport in Tel Aviv.

Additional illustrations pointedly suggest the proliferation of terror network coalitions. Renowned terrorism expert Bruce Hoffman calls this the "internationalization of terrorism," which he traces back to the hijacking of an Israeli El Al commercial flight from Rome to Tel Aviv. The incident took place in 1968 and was instigated by the Palestinian terror group Popular Front for the Liberation of Palestine (PFLP). What differentiated the hijacking of that flight from the 11 prior incidents was that it expressed a political statement, and successfully used the media as an outlet to propagate the group's actions and goals.[50] Following this, the Red Army Faction (RAF) of West Germany and the Action Direct (AD) of France formed a cooperative coalition in the 1980s to destabilize the North Atlantic Treaty Organization (NATO) through a series of attacks that spanned across Europe.[51] A meeting in Frankfurt, Germany, in 1986 provided a forum for several hundred terrorists from around the world to share agendas and ideas to spread a revolution across the globe.[52] This cross-pollinating tendency appears to be intensifying as time progresses and via the expansion of the Internet, thus future counterterrorism policies must evolve to respond to this trend.

Terrorists Are Well Trained and More Sophisticated

Counterterrorism measures in the United States and worldwide must address the changing nature of technology and its inherent use by terrorist organizations. The *9/11 Commission Report* found that the old Cold War intelligence community has been ill-equipped to handle the challenges of the new era. Congress failed to reorient itself to effectively respond to new threats. Advances in technology have forced counterterrorism measures to evolve incrementally, with an emphasis on new digital technologies and satellite systems rather than relying upon human intelligence or physical troops.[53] This new age of technology has necessitated a time-consuming but essential shift in the operational and strategic cultures of governmental bureaucracies.

With the progression of time, terrorists have also employed the use of technology to advance their cause. Modern terrorists are well trained. For instance, Yousef was educated in Wales and became an engineer with excellent communication skills and fluency in the English language. Yousef's training in terrorist activities began early. He attempted to assassinate Benazir Bhutto, Pakistan's first woman prime minister, elected in 1988.[54] His training continued in the Afghani al Qaeda camps operated under the auspices of bin Laden. Yousef's communication skills and militant training later facilitated successful contact with Abd al-Rahman and other likeminded Islamists in New York City. The execution of the 1993 bombing was not an isolated aim. Yousef's terrorist plots for the United States included smuggling liquid explosives onto several passenger jets, a plan to assassinate Pope John Paul II, and a scheme to crash a plane into the CIA headquarters in Virginia.[55] In effect, according to Bergen's analysis, "the 1993 World Trade Center bombing looks increasingly like a dress rehearsal for al-Qaida's devastating attack on the Twin Towers eight years later. Several of the 1993 plotters had ties to the Alkhifa Center . . . [Yousef] appears not to have frequented the Alkhifa Center, but he had close ties to al-Qaida members."[56]

Further, technological advances in the 1990s, particularly the Internet, have made communication easier for terrorist groups. Terror groups have used the Internet and DVD technology to recruit members to their cause. Many even used Internet chatrooms to open communications with their compatriots. Intelligence research has revealed that "the men who lead these movements are generally well-educated and utilize the latest in technology in their various jihads."[57] With data and information being exchanged at faster rates, terrorists have become more sophisticated in their plots. A charismatic leader like bin Laden need not set foot on American soil to successfully motivate a following to execute an attack.

Terror Cells Integrate Themselves Deep in Society

Terrorists have a propensity for patience. They devoutly spend years devising and preparing to execute the perfect plot. Despite the fact that the 1993 WTC attack did not produce the outcome envisioned by the perpetrators (the collapse of both the north and south towers), the event still called for increased vigilance. Al Qaeda plotters of the September 11 attack began arriving in the United States as early as 1994. They were as resolute as ever, just cognizant that more planning was necessary to execute the plot.[58]

BACKGROUND

The Chechen relationship with Russia is one of enduring enmity, dating back to Russia's annexation of the north Caucasus in the nineteenth century. The cycle of uprising, reprisal, suppression, and bitterness was well established before the Chechen uprising in the 1990s. The most noteworthy event during this period was Soviet leader Joseph Stalin's deportation of the entire Chechen nation to internal exile during World War II. It was the most comprehensive attempt in history to eradicate the Chechen people. The Chechens were permitted to return to their homeland in the 1950s during the Khrushchev period. Among the returnees was future Soviet Air Force General Dzhokhar Dudaev, who had been born in exile. Dudaev was the first and only Soviet General of Chechen ethnicity, and would play a central role in the attempt to secure the Chechens an independent state.

The Chechens, like other nationalities in the Soviet Union, sought to make use of the opportunity afforded by the gradual collapse of Soviet authority at the end of the Cold War. Lithuania was the first Union Republic to declare (or reaffirm) its independence, on March 11, 1990. The Lithuanians were gradually followed by other former Soviet states.[1] On November 23, 1990, Dudaev presided over a Chechen National Congress that called for free elections and the formation of a Chechen parliament. Two days after the August 1991 coup attempt in Moscow, a small Chechen parliament convened and selected Dudaev as the putative country's interim leader. The following month, Dudaev stormed the local parliament and killed the Soviet Communist Party chief for Grozny, Vitali Kutsenko. His men also seized the KGB (*Komitet Gosudarstvennoy Bezopasnosti*, or Committee for State Security) headquarters as well as radio and television stations in the capital. Dudaev easily won a referendum held October 27, 1991, which Moscow denounced, and immediately declared the independent Republic of Ichkeria. Russian President Boris Yeltsin flew troops to Grozny in November and Chechen forces immobilized them at the airport. Lacking political support for war, Yeltsin withdrew the troops, and the Chechens won their first bid for independence.

The Chechen Republic of Ichkeria existed as a de facto political entity for three years, unrecognized by Russia or the international community. The situation was barely tolerable to Moscow. The Russian Federation had many such minority enclaves within its borders, and there was concern that other nationalities might try to copy the Chechen experiment. There was also some fear of Chechnya serving as a base for the spread of Muslim fundamentalism, though this tendency was less prevalent in the early years of the Chechen conflict, which was largely a nationalist movement before 1995. Chechnya was also strategically located close to the Caspian oil fields and along some planned pipeline routes. Within

Chechnya, government controls were weak and black markets and other forms of transnational criminal activity began to proliferate, spreading to Moscow and other major Russian cities. Dudaev's rule was not without problems; he faced factional infighting (sometimes violent) and generally decreasing popularity after the flush of enthusiasm for independence waned.

The Yeltsin administration attempted various overt and covert means to suppress and subvert the Dudaev government, finally opting for direct military action in December 1994. Moscow was very optimistic; Defense Minister Pavel Grachev said Grozny could be taken with a single airborne regiment in 2 hours, and Russian Security Council Secretary Oleg Lobov predicted "a small victorious war." However, Operation WAVE—the campaign against Chechnya—was ill-planned and poorly executed, and became a case study in how not to conduct military operations against a separatist uprising, particularly in urban settings. Poorly trained and ill-supplied Russian troops made slow going against determined Chechen forces, and were frustrated by civilian protestors, poor weather, and the unwillingness of some of their commanders to press the offensive. By contrast, the Chechens were highly motivated, fought on their home ground, and enjoyed strong public support.

In January 1995, Russian forces attacked the Chechen capital of Grozny and suffered a humiliating setback as the Chechen guerillas used the advantages of defense in complex urban terrain to good effect.[2] The most notable example was the experience of the 131st Independent Motorised Infantry Brigade (the Maikop Brigade), which lost 20 of 26 tanks, 102 of 120 APCs, and suffered over 1,000 combat fatalities, including commanding officer Colonel Ivan Savin. Despite these initial setbacks, the Russians were eventually able to secure Grozny by exploiting Russia's advantage in firepower and inflicting tremendous damage on the city and its half-million inhabitants. On February 26, 1995, Russia declared the city secure, and by this time was already pushing its campaign into the region's southern highlands. Other Chechen urban centers—such as Argun, Shali, and Urus Martan—fell shortly afterwards, and Chechen guerilla bands sought sanctuary in the high mountains to the south, or over the border in the Republic of Georgia.

Throughout the next year, Russia engaged in a difficult and controversial counterinsurgency with the Chechens. The Chechen guerillas fought back creatively—for example, when rebel leader Shamil Basayev seized control of a hospital in Budyonnovsk in June, 1995, taking 1,000 hostages. Salman Raduyev undertook similar attacks in Gudermes and Kizlyar. But the Russian response was the traditional one: reprisals against Chechen villages thought to be sheltering guerillas, and war of no quarter on the frontier.

MARCH 1996: TESTING CAPABILITIES

After the reduction of major hostilities in early 1995, Grozny had been handed over to the special troops of the Interior Ministry (MVD), which was standard Russian procedure for Phase IV operations dating back to World War II.[3] The city was occupied by between six and twelve thousand troops of various types—special armed units of the MVD, MVD contractors (*kontrakniki*), local pro-Russian Chechen militia (OMON), police, and other security forces. All varied in levels of training, equipment, motivation, and loyalty to the regime. Russia installed Doku Zavgayev, a pro-Russian Chechen, as the leader of the region, and began an aid program to bolster the loyalist regime; however, such programs were plagued by corruption, and much of the money was embezzled or diverted, doing little to ameliorate conditions inside Chechnya.

On March 6, 1996, 1,500 to 2,000 Chechen guerillas attacked Grozny from five directions. Most were from bands that had filtered back to the city from the mountains. Some were members of Zavgayev's own militia, and many others wore the militia uniform, arriving on the morning trains without raising the suspicions of Russian security forces. The attack came one day after Defense Minister Pavel Grachev paid the city a visit to discuss peace talks. "I wanted to save him the trouble of finding me," Dudaev later joked.[4] It was also the day before the Russian Security Council was to meet to talk about Chechnya. General Vyacheslav Tikhomirov, commander of Russian troops in Chechnya, said the rebels wanted to "show off their strength on the eve of the meeting."[5]

Dudaev soon appeared on rebel television with field commander Shamil Basayev and stated, "The city of Grozny will be taken. There will be no mercy for Chechen traitors."[6] (The Chechens used mobile TV transmitters that could overpower state-run TV signals, and Dudaev would regularly appear on regular television channels, interrupting scheduled programming with his special announcements.) The guerillas burned two police stations, attacked the power station and main administrative building, and attempted to seize the Interior Ministry. The railway station and main bridges were occupied to impede possible Russian movements. Fifteen Russian checkpoints were destroyed, and at the height of the raid, the insurgent forces had free movement in 80 percent of the city. As well, on March 8, Chechen rebels hijacked a Turkish Cypriot airliner and flew it to Munich as a means of publicizing their cause.[7]

The assault lasted for 2 days. Russian forces initially paused to see what the OMON (interior ministry special forces) and local police would do, but they offered no effective resistance.[8] As the Russians began their counterattack on the third day, the insurgents withdrew quietly from the city, ending the attack. Some snipers and saboteurs remained behind to harass the Russians, and security forces were still trying to root out some of these as late as March 26.[9] Nevertheless, the main attack was over.

There were characteristically conflicting claims of damage. Russian television reported 70 government soldiers had been killed and 200 wounded. The Russian government claimed 170 rebels were killed and more than 100 were wounded, with about 100 civilians dead.[10] Dudaev claimed to have killed 91 Russian troops while losing just 8 of his own men. But regardless of the scale of damage, the Chechens had made their political point. "Chechen leader Dzhokhar Dudaev, Aslan Maskhadov and many other Chechen commanders studied in Soviet military academies, where they learned in detail about the Soviet-backed Cold War guerrilla campaigns in Algeria and Vietnam," one analyst wrote. "Many a pundit who remembers the Vietnam War will immediately notice the striking similarities between the latest Chechen attack on Grozny and the 1968 Vietcong Tet offensive."[11]

The attack also served as a dress rehearsal for future operations, according to Dudaev.[12] He called it "a little harassing operation ... a training exercise for 'a new dimension of war' that will include bolder attacks inside Russia proper."[13] Dudaev believed that the raid demonstrated that "it is no big problem for us to capture any city" including "military-industrial and political-administrative centers" in Russia and other former Soviet republics.[14] "We are prepared to fight indefinitely to add to our history of 437 years fighting against the Russian Empire," Dudaev stated. "Only independence and withdrawal of the federal troops can bring peace."[15]

Meeting while the fighting raged, the Russian Security Council adopted a plan for "peace through stabilization" in Chechnya, and sought to end fighting by March 28. Initially, this entailed increasing attacks on rebel concentrations in towns and villages, using the same encirclement techniques that had been used since the nineteenth century.[16] But a ceasefire agreement was signed on March 31. Politics were very much in play. President Yeltsin was running for reelection in a hard-fought campaign, and was not doing well in the polls. The war was a major issue, one on which he was vulnerable. The March ceasefire was portrayed as a political victory after the embarrassing attack, and Yeltsin promised an expeditious Russian troop withdrawal. On April 21, 1996, at a joint press conference with U.S. President Bill Clinton following the Moscow summit, Yeltsin declared that "there are no military operations in Chechnya."

Of course this was not true, and 3 days later the Russians scored a noteworthy success when they assassinated Dudaev by targeting a transmission from his satellite phone with an air-to-ground missile. Dudaev was in the village of Gekhi-Chu, talking to Russian negotiator Konstantin Borovoy at the time of the strike.[17] Dudaev had argued for some time that killing him was the main objective of the Russian plan. "We have made preparations so that in case of my death, the Russians' ordeal would increase tenfold," he once said.[18] Dudaev was quickly succeeded by Zalemkhan Yanderbayev, to whom Yeltsin immediately reached out with peace feelers. The two men met in the Kremlin on May 27. Three weeks later, in the first round of elections, Yeltsin gained 35 percent of the vote, followed by Communist challenger Gennady Zyuganov with 32 percent. Yeltsin was reelected in the second round on July 3, 1996 with 53 percent of the vote, and most credited the peace offensive with helping secure his reelection. Yeltsin was set to be inaugurated on August 9.

AUGUST 1996: THE ATTACK

In early August, there were no signs of an imminent attack in Grozny. The political climate likewise seemed pacific; Chechen leaders agreed to negotiate with Organization for Security and Cooperation in Europe (OSCE) representatives on various aspects of the current peace plan. For its part, Moscow announced that by September 1 all Federal soldiers would be withdrawn from Chechnya except for a few garrison troops. The moment seemed promising for some type of long-term settlement.

However, at a July 25 meeting Chechen commanders initiated Operation ZERO OPTION, the planned takeover of Grozny, with smaller scale attacks on Argun and Gudermes. The operation sought to change the correlation of forces in the struggle with the Russians by taking the fight unexpectedly to the symbolic center of Russian power in Chechnya. At base, the attack sought to serve as a reminder; Aslan Maskhadov, Yanderbayev's chief of staff, stated, "the actions in Grozny have a single aim—showing that the war in Chechnya is not over yet."[19] The attack was something of a gamble, as are all insurgent attacks of this nature, since they forego some insurgent strengths, such as mobility, and place the insurgency at risk of being surrounded, pinned down, and destroyed. But the Chechens may have been emboldened by their relative success in March, and perhaps felt that should events turn against them they could again withdraw to regroup and fight another day. As well, they may have felt that the risks were worth taking. A fierce, highly visible, and symbolic attack against an unmotivated enemy in an unpopular war led by a weak leader could turn the tide, or so they reasoned.

The attack was set for dawn on Tuesday, August 6, 1996. Shamil Basayev was given overall command of the ground forces, which were organized in the usual semiautonomous groupings based on family and tribal affiliations. Rebels began infiltrating the city and hiding in prepared apartments to await the attack. About 4,000 Chechen fighters faced approximately 6–7,000 Russian troops, primarily MVD with militia and police. (There were 30–40,000 Russian troops in theater.) Though they outnumbered the

Chechens, the Russians were hampered by lack of unity of command between the various types of Russian units, and no systematic information sharing or systems for coordinated action. As with the March raid, many members of the ostensibly pro-Russian Chechen government were actually in league with the rebels. One estimate had 75 percent of the Chechen police and security units being rebel sympathizers. Major Sultan Tuleyev of the Chechen Interior Ministry helped direct some of the rebel attacks, particularly those aimed at pro-Russian Chechen targets.[20]

The August attack plan did not differ significantly from the March plan. Rebel units first seized the communications apparatus and strategic choke points in the city such as bridges and rail stations. They then attacked government buildings, Russian defensive positions, and the Severny airport. They worked in small teams of 20 or less, as they had in 1995, armed with rocket launchers, small arms, and the occasional mortar. Snipers worked from predetermined positions with wide fields of fire. Supplies had been prepositioned in the city, dispersed at key points to support the attacking forces.

The Chechens achieved surprise at every level. Strategically, it was an embarrassing incident, made more so because it was successful. The attack generated a great deal of press coverage, and emphasized the growing sense of drift under Yeltsin. Tactically, surprise was complete, though it need not have been. Journalist Maria Eismont, who was in Chechnya covering the war for *Sevodnya*, stated that "only a blind man or the deaf and dumb did not know about the impending attack a week before it came. Talk about the coming offensive could be heard in offices and in markets, at home and in the barracks."[21] Chechen rebels had circulated leaflets a week before the attack asking civilians to evacuate, but these had been ignored by the Russians. A wounded Russian private told of the chaos in the early moments of the fight: "They attacked us at night. Nobody expected it. We just had no idea. They trapped us all at our posts or between buildings in groups of three or four. They would shoot from buildings and pick us off when we had no way to fight back. They had better weapons than we did and they were organized."[22]

The Chechens also won the intelligence war. Chechen rebels had effective human intelligence (HUMINT) in the city from their established networks, and creatively used off-the-shelf and stolen equipment to intercept Russian signals. They combated Russian attempts to collect signals intelligence by using a system of couriers. The smaller, flatter Chechen command hierarchy allowed intelligence to be exploited more quickly and for greater effect. Likewise, their decentralized organization allowed for better counterintelligence—it was difficult to penetrate the closely knit tribal organizations. The rebels also benefited from a long-term intelligence collection effort they had undertaken inside the city, amassing detailed information on the Russian defensive positions. They were aided by their preexisting knowledge of the city and the sympathies of many of the non-Russian inhabitants.

The Russian defensive plan for Grozny recognized that they lacked sufficient troop strength to guard the entire city. Instead, the Russians had established checkpoints along the major roads coming into Grozny, and strong points at various locations within the city. These bunkers were intended to form knots of resistance to any rebel attacks and were designed to be strong enough to withstand attacks until reinforcements arrived. Essentially, the main effort would come through counterattacks. However, this gave the insurgents several advantages. According to guerilla band leader Vakha Ramzanov, "at most checkpoints the soldiers ignore us; they don't want a fight. Or sometimes we pay a bribe."[23] The strong points were not always mutually supporting and could be isolated and sometimes destroyed. In addition, because they were by their nature defensive positions, the Chechens were able quickly to consolidate the areas the Russians had chosen not to defend. By the end of 4 days of fighting, the Chechens had control of most of the city. A Russian military spokesman stated that Federal units were "totally surrounded in Grozny, and they are not even trying to attack the rebels, only trying to defend themselves."[24]

By seizing most of the city and establishing their own defenses, the Chechens exposed another serious contradiction in the Russian defensive plan. Chechen leaders acknowledged that the Russians would probably be able to take back the city with a concerted effort, but they doubted that the Russians would be willing to absorb the estimated 15,000 casualties in the process. The Chechens planned for the Russian counterattack by establishing harassment positions at high points around the city, and mining the main highways. Some armored reinforcements were allowed to enter the city following the same playbook as 1995, in order to be surrounded and destroyed. The Russians had not learned the lessons of the first battle of Grozny, and the Chechens were again able to cut off and kill or capture a number of Russian units. Basayev told rebel gunners to attempt to disable rather than destroy Russian vehicles when possible, in order to use them later.[25] After a few days, the Chechens were able to field four tanks and six APCs captured from Russian forces.

Russian doctrine stressed the use of firepower, either artillery, stand-off air assets such as helicopters, or bombardment by fixed wing aircraft. However, in most cases the Russians lacked accurate, timely targeting information and these attacks were rarely effective (though helicopter-fired rockets could be useful against known sniper positions). Thus, though the Russians could mass firepower, the quick-moving Chechens were not often at the receiving end. This increased the level of damage to the city and the number of civilian casualties. Furthermore, the armed formations of the MVD generally lacked the fire support capabilities enjoyed by MOD units and were unable effectively to respond to Chechen attacks.

Human factors were another asymmetric element of the battle. The Russians were in poor morale, inadequately trained and supplied, generally unmotivated, and combat ineffective. A Russian official described the troops as "hungry, lice-infested and in rags," commanded by "indifferent, tired-out people."[26] By contrast, the Chechens were well trained, well supplied, and highly motivated. "We are much more interested in continuing the war than Russia is," Dudaev had declared after the March raid. "What is left for us? Our economy has been destroyed. Our people have no homes, no bread, no jobs, nothing. We have 500,000 men aged 15 to 50 who know only one thing: how to fight."[27] Akhmed Zakayev, a Chechen ground commander, said, "It's easier for us. After a year and a half of fighting, each of us is a strategist, a commander, a general. Each person knows what he's fighting for—which I can't say for the Russians."[28] A journalist covering the attack observed that "it is not difficult to demonstrate one's fighting ability with people going quite calmly to meet their deaths. Russian soldiers have nothing to die for—neither in Grozny nor in any other settlement in Ichkeria."[29]

Initially, official statements from Russian military sources during the attack were mostly upbeat, stressing the imminent collapse of the rebel force. Journalists inside the city could be counted on to give a reality check to these claims, when they could reach the outside. But after the first few days of fighting, Russia admitted to losing 8 helicopters, 15 armored vehicles, 50 dead, and 200 wounded. In the first week, Russia admitted to 221 dead and 766 wounded troops, having only previously admitted to 1,000 casualties since December 1994.[30]

MOSCOW REACTS

Boris Yeltsin was reinaugurated president of the Russian Federation on August 9 in Moscow, 3 days into the Chechen attack. Planned inauguration pageants had been cancelled the day after the attack began; the organizers cited financial concerns. During the inauguration ceremony, Yeltsin appeared wooden and slurred his words. He spoke for 45 seconds only, simply reciting the oath of office and then departing for a long vacation. Yeltsin lacked the fortitude to be a decisive wartime leader; one of his first official acts in response to the crisis in Grozny was to ask Prime Minister Victor Chernomyrdin to convene a commission to fix blame for the fiasco.[31]

A statement released the day after Yeltsin's inauguration vowed, "All acts of terrorism will be crushed with determination." Nevertheless, Yeltsin's office was largely silent on the developing crisis. On the second day of the battle, Doku Zavgayev, the pro-Russian Chechen leader installed by Moscow, said, "the situation in Grozny is perfectly under our full control now."[32] However, sporadic reports from reporters trapped in

Grozny told a different story. Six days into the fighting, Prime Minister Chernomyrdin threatened to declare a state of emergency "if that is what we need to do." But whether declared or not, a state of emergency had been imposed on the Russian leadership.

Yeltsin decided to hand the crisis to his national security advisor Aleksandr Lebed. Lebed was a charismatic former lieutenant general in the Soviet and Russian armies, an Afghan veteran, known for his outspoken views and sarcastic wit. He had run against Yeltsin as a peace candidate, opposing the war in Chechnya, and come in third with 15 percent of the vote. Two days later, Yeltsin named him his national security advisor, seeking to coopt the peace platform, and sacked Lebed's old rival, Defense Minister Pavel Grachev, who was made the scapegoat for the war. Grachev was replaced by Lebed's supporter General Igor N. Rodionov.

Lebed believed that the conflict in Chechnya could not be won by military means alone. "Regardless of the blood spilled in Grozny due to the Chechen opposition," he said, in the opening days of the battle, "the security council does not intend to resolve the sharpened crisis purely by means of force, even though this is how the leaders of the illegal military formations are acting."[33] Lebed was sent to Chechnya to lead negotiations, replacing hard line national security council member Oleg Lobov. Chechen spokesman Movladi Udugov saw the move as positive, and pledged that if Lebed dealt fairly with them they would help Russia preserve its interests in the Caucasus and "get out of this war while saving face."[34] For his part, Lebed felt certain that he had been sent to Chechnya by people playing "apparatchik games" who wished to see him "break his neck" in the process, but he did not shy away from the assignment.

Lebed met with Aslan Maskhadov in the village of Stariye Agagi on August 11. "We discussed the question of the possible [political] status of Chechnya and arrived at the conclusion that in order to implement any good intentions, it is first necessary to stop killing people," said Lebed. He said the two sides could reach agreement on 90 percent of the outstanding issues.[35] The solution began to take the form of an agreement along the lines of the treaty Russia had with the then-Republic of Tatarstan. Lebed also denounced nominal Chechen leader Zavgayev as a megalomaniac who had difficulties with reality. The next day, Mashkhadov negotiated an agreement with Russian ground commander Lieutenant General Konstantin Pulikovsky to separate the warring parties in Grozny. The ceasefire went into effect at noon on August 13, though it was soon being violated by both sides. One problem the Russians faced was that provisions had not been made in the agreement for the safe conduct or resupply of troops inside the city. The Chechens were more than willing to let the Russians starve in their bunkers, and some violations of the ceasefire occurred when attempts were made to bring rations to the isolated troops.

Lebed was adamant that the conflict had to end. "A country with a collapsing economy and armed forces cannot allow itself the luxury of waging a war, a democratic country cannot decide questions of nationality with rockets and shells," Lebed said on August 15. "This war should be ended and it will be." He called the war "a colossal loss for Russian prestige."[36] Lebed praised the fighting ability of the Chechens and said that the situation would be resolved not by fighting but by "humane considerations and common sense." Maskhadov, a former Soviet Colonel, said that Lebed's "guarantee is the word of honor of a Russian officer." But not all the Chechen leaders were impressed with Lebed. Shamil Basayev said, "I am glad that Lebed thinks highly of our skills...But I don't believe in the words of any Russian. I believe it was Winston Churchill who said an agreement with Russia isn't worth the paper it was written on. So agreements mean little to me."[37]

As exchanges of gunfire became more common over the next few days and tensions began to mount, General Pulikovsky—the acting ground forces commander during the absence of the equally hawkish General Vyacheslav Tikhomirov—issued an ultimatum to the citizens of Grozny, giving them 48 hours to vacate the city before he used extreme measures. "Grozny will be cleared of the rebels," he said, "The only way out of the current situation in Grozny is the use of force." This sparked an exodus of tens of thousands of people to refugee camps.

The breakdown in policy caused many to look to Moscow for guidance, but none was forthcoming. President Yeltsin was unavailable, looking for a new dacha; Parliament was on vacation; Prime Minister Chernomyrdin had no comment.[38] Lebed was left standing, having to make difficult decisions on his own, which suggested that he had been right—that he was being set up by his adversaries. However, he was true to his belief that the war had to end. Lebed went to Grozny around August 21 and again met with Maskhadov. A new and final ceasefire went into effect at noon August 23.

Lebed expected a hero's welcome in Moscow, but Yeltsin at first snubbed Lebed on his return to the capital. Yeltsin later congratulated him over the phone for achieving this "first step" toward peace.[39] By late October, Lebed would be forced out of office by his opponents. The day the peace agreement with the Chechens was announced, the newspaper *Moskovsky Komsomolets* ran a front-page headline, "They Won."

ANALYSIS

The Chechen victory in August 1996 was not primarily a military victory, but rather a political victory catalyzed by military means. The attack on Grozny forced Russia to face political contradictions that made continued fighting untenable. The defeat came from the top; Yeltsin was a weak leader of a war-weary country. The Chechens correctly diagnosed that one more dramatic, large-scale attack would set the conditions for a peace on their terms. The Russians could well have taken the city back by applying the ruthless force they had in the past, but in the summer of 1996, Russian society could not make the sacrifices necessary to win it in the same old way. A negotiated settlement and withdrawal was seen as the better option by the political leaders and most of the voters.

The Chechen rebels established facts on the ground at precisely the right time to achieve their political ends. Russian Army forces began pulling out of Chechnya that same week, and completed their withdrawal by the end of the month, as scheduled. A peace agreement was signed at Khasavyurt, Dagestan, which postponed consideration of Chechnya's political status until 2001, a de facto recognition of Chechen independence. It gave tacit recognition to the rebel Chechen government and ended Moscow's support for the opposition government. The two sides agreed to mount joint security patrols in the city, and television audiences saw Chechen guerillas and MVD troops trading cigarettes and making a show of cooperation. The Chechens began imposing sharia-based law, and taking vengeance on former collaborators with the Russian puppet government.

Chechen rebel leader Zelimkhan Yanderbayaev arrived in Grozny on September 6, the fifth anniversary of the original Chechen declaration of independence, and began organizing his government. Grozny was a shambles, the presidential palace was in ruin. There was little running water, natural gas, or electricity. But among the populace there was a feeling of expectation that perhaps this time peace would prevail. Most would agree with rebel troop commander Akhmed Zakayev, "We aren't taking over the city, we're liberating it."

During the conflict with Chechnya from 1994–1996, about 6,000 Russian soldiers, 2–3,000 Chechen fighters, and 80,000 civilians were killed. Another 240,000 persons were wounded, though estimates of total casualties ranged much higher. Chechnya's infrastructure was almost completely destroyed, its urban areas reduced to rubble, and its people impoverished spiritually as well as materially. But the Chechen rebels had again secured their independence.

In an interview in September 1996, Russian Interior Minister Anatoly Kulikov stated, "Personally, I have one concern: how to prevent the current tactical gain from becoming a future strategic loss."[40] The tactical gain he was referring to was the end of open warfare. The strategic loss he feared was the gradual establishment of sovereighty by Chechnya[41] Over time and through acquiescence—by Russia, by neighboring states, and eventually the international community—a fully independent country would be created. "The danger," he continued, "using the example of Afghanistan, is the Chechenization of the war. That is, a war for power, among Chechen groups, all hostile to Russia, against each other just like what happened in Afghanistan after the withdrawal of Soviet troops. It is possible that the irreconcilable Chechen opposition will be consolidated around some leader. Then indefinite prolongation of the war is not out of the question at all."

This was a sound prediction, and over the next 4 years, the Chechens squandered their opportunity to establish an internationally recognized state through infighting, criminal activity, and extending their Muslim uprising to neighboring states. In so doing, they lost sight of the fact that they had won their independence by exploiting a very particular set of political circumstances. They began to overreach, failing to understand the changing dynamics within Russia. By 1999, political conditions in the Federation had changed, and Yeltsin's successor Vladimir Putin demonstrated that he was unwilling to let Chechen provocations stand. Putin was not interested in letting the separatists have their own homeland, and would make the sacrifices necessary to resubjugate Chechnya. Russian forces returned to Grozny in February 2000 and leveled the city.[42]

ACKNOWLEDGMENTS

The views expressed in this chapter are those of the author and do not reflect the official policy or position of the National Defense University, the National War College, the Department of Defense, or the U.S. government.

NOTES

1. The Soviet Union officially recognized the secession of the Baltic States on September 6, 1991. Note that the Union Republics that comprised the Soviet Union had been guaranteed the right to secede by the Soviet constitution. Chechnya, as an independent *oblast* within the Russian Soviet Federated Socialist Republic, had no such right.

2. C. F. Stephen, J. Blank, and Earl H. Tilford, Jr., *Russia's Invasion of Chechnya: A Preliminary Assessment*, Strategic Studies Institute (SSI) monograph, January 13, 1995, available at http://www.strategicstudiesinstitute.army.mil/pubs/people.cfm?authorID=21; Mr. Lester W. Grau, "Changing Russian Urban Tactics: The Aftermath of the Battle for Grozny," Foreign Military Studies Office, Leavenworth, KS, July 1995, available at http://leav-www.army.mil/fmso/documents/grozny.htm; Timothy L. Thomas, "The Battle of Grozny: Deadly Classroom for Urban Combat," *Parameters* (Summer 1999): 87–102; Anatol Lieven, "Russia's Military Nadir: The Meaning of the Chechen Debacle," *The National Interest* (Summer 1996), 24–33.

3. Note that the term of art "Phase IV Operations" is appropriate, since the handover to the MVD was slated as Phase IV of the original Russian campaign plan.

4. Richard Boudreaux, "Chechen Leader Vows to Step Up Attacks on Russia," *Los Angeles Times*, March 18, 1996: A1.

5. *Moscow Times*, March 7, 1996: 1.

6. Ibid.

7. On November 9, 1991, Shamil Basayev had hijacked a Russian aircraft, diverting it to Ankara, also to gain publicity. No one was harmed.

8. Dmitry Balburov, "Russia Disgraced by Attack on Grozny," *Moscow News*, March 14, 1996. "The policemen sitting there in the office confided that they had more problems with federal troops than with Chechen fighters, and stressed the need for Russian troops to pull out of Chechnya as soon as possible. 'We'll take care of Dudaev's men on our own—it's our own problem,' they said. I came to believe them as I saw policemen and unarmed separatist fighters standing side by side on the porch chatting amiably."

9. Boris Kipkeyev, " 'Special Operation' Against Rebels in Grozny Begins," ITAR-TASS World Service in Russian 1331 GMT, March 26, 1996.

10. "Russia Takes Grozny," *Toronto Sun*, March 11, 1996: 3.

11. Pavel Felgenhauer, "Chechnya's Tet Offensive," *The Moscow Times*, March 14, 1996.

12. Carlotta Gall, " 'The Plan Is to Kill Me,' Dudaev Says," *The Moscow Times*, March 19, 1996.

13. Bourdreaux, "Chechen Leader Vows to Step Up Attacks on Russia," *Los Angeles Times*, March 18, 1996: A1.

14. Ibid.

15. Sergei Strokan, "Bad News from the Front Weakens Yeltsin," IPS-Inter Press Service, March 21, 1996.

16. "Federal forces in Chechnya are currently employing the tactic of gradually squeezing Dudaev's gunmen from the population centers where their headquarters and bases are situated. This tactic is well known from the history of fighting rebellious mountain detachments in the nineteenth century. It involves successively surrounding villages, offering a 'safe corridor' through the encirclement to women and children and to men prepared to surrender and lay down their arms. Anyone not accepting this ultimatum is considered an enemy. They are treated according to the laws of wartime." "Everything Calm in Bamut, Russian Military State in Response to Duma Deputies' Initiative Aimed at 'Averting a Military Operation' in Yet Another Chechen Village" *IZVESTIYA*, March 13, 1996.

17. Sharip Asayev, "Dudaev Said Killed in Rocket Attack on Chechen Village," ITAR-TASS World Service in Russian 1537 GMT, April 23, 1996. According to a transcript of the conversation released afterwards, his last words were "Russia must regret what it is doing..." Yuliya Kalinina, "Dudaev's Last Words: 'Russia Must Regret...' After That the Conversation Broke Off," *MOSKOVSKIY KOMSOMOLETS*, April 26, 1996.

18. Bourdreaux, "Chechen Leader ..." Note that the tribally based decentralized nature of Chechen organization made this type of attack less useful than it might have been, as events showed.

19. "Chechen Rebels Storm Russian Units in Grozny," *New York Times*, August 7, 1996: A6.

20. Alexander Tolmachev, "They Betrayed Us in Grozny," *Moscow News*, August 15, 1996. The Chechen experience should inform efforts in Iraq to build indigenous defense forces.

21. Michael Specter, "Chechnya Rebels Entrap and Shell Moscow's Troops," *New York Times*, August 10, 1996: 1.

22. Michael Specter, "Russians Failing to Wrest Grozny from Insurgents," *New York Times*, August 12, 1996: A1.

23. Kirill Belyaninov, "To Live and Die in Grozny," *US News and World Report*, September 2, 1996: 44.

24. Specter, "Chechnya Rebels ..."

25. Ilya Maksakov, "Inability To Resolve Chechen Problem Leads To New Casualties," *NEZAVISIMAYA GAZETA*, August 7, 1996: 1

26. "In Chechnya, Anything is Possible," *The Economist*, August 17, 1996: 40.

27. Bourdreaux, "Chechen Leader ..."

28. Lee Hockstader, "Chechen Guerrillas' Deadly Swagger; Despite Theatrics, Highly Disciplined Rebels Overwhelm Russian Troops," *The Washington Post*, August 18, 1996: A01.

29. Sergey Agaponov, "Itogi': Wage Real War in Chechnya or Withdraw Troops," Moscow NTV in Russian 1800 GMT, March 10, 1996.

30. Carlotta Gall, "Cease-Fire May Halt Grozny Battle," *The Moscow Times*, August 14, 1996.

31. Chernoyrdin had been the target of a small Chechen bomb in Moscow, coinciding with the opening of the battle in Grozny.

32. Michael Specter, "Rebels Overrun Russian Troops in Chechen City," *New York Times*, August 8, 1996: A1.

33. James Meek, "Russians are Hit Hard as Rebels Take Grozny," *The Guardian*, August 8, 1996: 10.

34. Specter, "Russians Failing ..."

35. "Opposing Chechnya Commanders Talk Truce," United Press International, August 12, 1996.

36. Ron Laurenzo, "Lebed Attacks Russian Interior Minister," United Press International, August 16, 1996.

37. Michael Specter, "Chechen Rebel Leader Savors Triumph in a Shattered City," *New York Times*, August 16, 1996: A3.

38. Jo Durden-Smith, "On Holiday from Blame," *The Moscow Times*, August 27, 1996.

39. A good analysis of the political problems Lebed faced came to be found in Jonas Bernstein, "Kremlin Duplicity Makes Minefield for Lebed," *The Moscow Times*, August 23, 1996.

40. "Chechnya: Black Hole of Russia," *Moscow News*, September 12, 1996.

41. See James S. Robbins, "Sovereignty-Building: The Case of Chechnya," *The Fletcher Forum of World Affairs* (Summer/Fall 1997): 17–36.

42. C. F Timothy L. Thomas, "Grozny 2000: Urban Combat Lessons Learned," *Military Review* (July–August 2000): 50–58.

CHAPTER 7

THE U.S. EMBASSY BOMBINGS IN KENYA AND TANZANIA

Sundara Vadlamudi

The bombing of the U.S. embassies in Kenya and Tanzania was the first major al Qaeda attack against U.S. targets that resulted in a large number of casualties. The meticulous planning, sophistication of the attack (involving near simultaneous bombings), and the number of casualties served as an extreme wake-up call to the U.S. intelligence and law-enforcement community. The attack brought into sharper focus the danger posed by transnational jihadists and forced the U.S. government to readjust its counterterrorism policies. This study examines the plot to bomb the U.S. embassies, the responses by the U.S. government, and the lessons learned from those responses. The study is divided into six sections. The first section details the bombing plot and lists the key individuals involved in the plot. The second section lists the immediate U.S. response to the bombing and the third section provides an overview of U.S. counterterrorism efforts against Osama bin Laden from the early 1990s until the embassy bombings in August 1998. The fourth section describes the cruise missile attacks on al Qaeda targets in Afghanistan and Sudan, launched by the United States as a response to the embassy bombings. The fifth section examines U.S. counterterrorism policies and efforts after the cruise missile attacks. And finally, the conclusion highlights some of the lessons learned from the U.S. response to the embassy bombings.

THE BOMBING PLOT

On August 7, 1998, two bomb-laden trucks were driven almost simultaneously into the U.S. embassies in Nairobi, Kenya, and Dar es Salaam, Tanzania, at approximately 10:35 A.M. and 10:39 A.M., respectively.

The attacks killed 213 people in Nairobi, including 12 Americans and 11 people in Dar es Salaam.[1] More than 5,000 people were injured in the attacks. The bombings, carried out by al Qaeda and Tanzim al-Jihad (Jihad Organization, also known as Egyptian Islamic Jihad) operatives, represented the first attack that was "planned, directed, and executed by al Qaida, under the direct supervision of bin Laden and his chief aides."[2] The attacks on the U.S. embassies in Kenya and Tanzania, code-named by al Qaeda as "Operation Holy Ka'ba" and "Operation al-Aqsa,"[3] respectively, were timed to occur between 10:30 and 11:00 A.M. when observant Muslims would be in the Mosque for their prayers.[4] The attacks took place 8 years to the day after U.S. troops landed in Saudi Arabia as part of an international effort in response to Saddam Hussein's invasion of Kuwait in 1990. In December 1998, bin Laden denied his involvement in the bombing, but added "I don't regret what happened there." Bin Laden said that "our job is to instigate [people against the Jews and the Americans], and by the grace of God, we did that, and certain people responded to this instigation."[5]

Al Qaeda established its presence in East Africa during the early 1990s in response to the presence of U.S. troops in Somalia, who went there to implement a U.N. program to supply food to Somali citizens. Al Qaeda viewed the U.S. troops' deployment as a step toward increasing U.S. hegemony in the region as well as targeting al Qaeda's infrastructure in neighboring Sudan.[6] At times, bin Laden and others have suggested that al Qaeda established its presence in Somalia even before the arrival of U.S. troops in order to unify the Somali militias and oppose the U.S. presence in the country.[7] It is difficult to ascertain the precise timeline of al Qaeda's entry into Somalia, but it is apparent that bin Laden has always been opposed to the U.S. presence in the Horn of Africa. After all, he explicitly stated that America must be stopped and called for cutting "the head of the snake and stop them [Americans]."[8] In 1992, Abu Ubayda al-Banshiri, al Qaeda's military commander at that time, established cells in East Africa, specifically in Nairobi, Kenya,[9] that acted as a transit point for al Qaeda operatives entering Somalia. Several al Qaeda members who went to Somalia and were involved in running the Nairobi cell participated in the embassy bombings. These operatives include Muhammad Atef (who became al Qaeda's military commander after the death of Abu Ubayda al-Banshiri), Abdullah Muhammad Abdullah (also known as Ali Salih or simply Salih), Muhammad Siddiq Odeh, and Fazul Abdullah Muhammad (also known as Harun Fazil).[10]

By late 1993, al Qaeda, then based in Sudan, initiated reconnaissance efforts to identify targets in Kenya. Ali A. Muhammad[11] cased the U.S. Embassy in Nairobi, the USAID building, the French embassy, the French Cultural Center, and other British and Israeli targets. In 1994, Ali

Muhammad went to Djibouti to conduct surveillance on several facilities, including the American and French embassies and French military installations. For some unknown reason, additional trips to Senegal to gather intelligence on French targets[12] were cancelled. It is believed that bin Laden examined the surveillance photographs of the U.S. embassy in Nairobi and pointed to the exact spot where an explosive-laden truck should enter the building.[13] The exact reason why al Qaeda did not immediately carry out attacks on U.S. targets is not known. One possible reason is that some al Qaeda members feared that such attacks would invite retaliation from the Kenyan government, which would affect the flow of al Qaeda operatives into Somalia.[14] Another possible explanation is that a combination of factors, such as al Qaeda's relocation to Afghanistan, the resulting loss of financial resources in Sudan, the death of al-Banshiri in a ferry accident in May 1996, and the time taken to rebuild the organization in Afghanistan, contributed to the delay in carrying out the attack. In any event, the U.S. withdrew its troops in March 1994, and al Qaeda's cell in Nairobi remained active as a logistics base but did not plan any attacks.[15]

In May 1996, bin Laden was forced to leave Sudan and seek refuge in Afghanistan. Shortly thereafter, in August 1996, bin Laden declared war on the United States. Later, in February 1997, Wadi al-Hajj was summoned to Afghanistan, at which point bin Laden asked al-Hajj to "militarize" the cell in Nairobi.[16] Later, in August 1997, U.S. officials investigating bin Laden's role in financing terrorist attacks on the United States, raided al-Hajj's house and confiscated his computer and several documents. Al-Hajj was then ordered to appear before a Federal jury in New York. After al-Hajj left Nairobi, Fazul Abdullah Muhammad took over the management of the Nairobi cell. Then, in February 1998, bin Laden issued the fatwa ordering Muslims worldwide to kill Americans and their allies wherever possible. The timeline of the plot and the subsequent attacks indicate that the final decision on the selection of targets and the date of attacks was probably taken around the same time that the fatwa was issued. Beginning in March, the preparations for the bombings moved forward at great speed. The attack planners rented safe houses for building the bombs, prepared false documents, and acquired delivery vehicles and explosives.[17] By the first week of August, most of the attack planners had left Kenya and Tanzania, and the remaining members included only the actual perpetrators of the attack and a couple of al Qaeda operatives who were responsible for clearing up any traces of the group's involvement in it.[18]

Al Qaeda had several reasons for attacking the U.S. embassy in Kenya. According to Muhammad al 'Awhali, Abdullah Muhammad Abdullah provided the following reasons for choosing the U.S. embassy in Nairobi,[19]

a. a large American presence at the embassy;

b. the U.S. Ambassador was a female, whose killing might generate large publicity for the attack;

c. U.S. embassy personnel were also managing some duties in Sudan;[20]

d. a number of Christian missionaries were at the embassy in Nairobi; and

e. it was an easy target.

Abdullah explained that if multiple attacks were launched against U.S. targets outside the United States, it might make it easier to launch attacks inside the United States.[21]

Al Qaeda's basic operational strategy in carrying out terrorist attacks was outlined by Abu Jandal, bin Laden's bodyguard, following his capture and interrogation. According to Abu Jandal, al Qaeda pursues a method or principle that calls for "centralization of decision and decentralization of execution." In action, this principle means that the decision to attack is made centrally but the method of attack and execution is decided by the field commanders. For example, in the *USS Cole* operation, the target was set by al Qaeda operatives on the ground. Then it was referred to a higher military central committee in al Qaeda called the Military Affairs Committee that approved the operation and provided the support and the funds for the operations.[22] Muhammad al 'Owhali said that the training at the al Qaeda camps for operating a cell divided cell into four sections: the intelligence section, the administration section, the planning and preparation section, and the execution section.[23] L'Houssaine Kherchtou, an al Qaeda operative who turned an informant and testified in the embassy bombings trial, stated that there were four parts in an operation, namely, surveillance, targeting, facilitators, and the executors.[24] Table 7.1 provides a brief list of the committees and members involved in planning and executing the 1998 attack on the U.S. embassies.

Before examining the U.S. response to the embassy bombings, it is useful to look at whether or not the United States possessed any intelligence information that could have helped to prevent the attacks. The Accountability Review Board's report on the embassy bombings, prepared by Admiral William J. Crowe, stated that there was no "credible intelligence that provided immediate or tactical warning of the August 7 bombings." The report, however, acknowledged that there were rumors of threats to diplomatic missions, including the embassies in Nairobi and Dar es Salaam, but added that the information was "discounted because of doubts about the sources." The Board's analysis termed other threat reporting as "imprecise, changing and non-specific as to dates."[25] The first clue about a possible attack came, ironically, as a result of the U.S. investigation into bin Laden's role as a terrorist financier. Officials from the CIA and the Department of State were pursuing associates of bin

Table 7.1 Key Members of the 1998 Embassy Bombings Plot

Military Committee: Osama bin Laden, Muhammad Atef (killed in
  Afghanistan), Abu Ubayda al-Banshiri (killed in ferry accident)
Surveillance: Ali A. Muhammad, Anas al-Liby (Anas Al-Sabai, Nazih
  Al-Raghie, Nazih Abdul Hamed Al-Raghie)
Mastermind: Abdullah Ahmed Abdullah (Abu Mohamed Al-Masri, Saleh, Ali
  Saleh, Abu Mariam)
Bomb Builder: Muhsin Musa Matwalli Atwah (Abdul Rahman, Abdul Rahman
  Al-Muhajir, Abdel Rahman, Mohammed K.A. Al-Namer)
Nairobi Attack Facilitators: Wadi al-Hajj, Fazul Abdullah Muhammad (Haroon
  Fazul, Fadil Abdallah Muhamad, Abdallah Mohammed Fazul), Muhammad
  Siddiq Odeh, Fahid Mohammed Ally Msalam (Fahid Mohammed Ali
  Musalaam, Fahid Muhamad Ali Salem)
Nairobi Attack Executors: Muhammad Rashid Daoud al 'Awhali, Jihad
  Muhammad Ali (Azzam)
Dar es Salaam Attack Facilitators: Fahid Mohammed Ally Msalam (Fahid
  Mohammed Ali Musalaam, Fahid Muhamad Ali Salem), Ahmed Khalfan
  Ghailani, Khalfan Khamis Muhammad, Sheikh Ahmed Salim Swedan
  (Sheikh Ahmad Salem Suweidan)
Dar es Salaam Attack Executor: Hamden Khalif Allah Awad

Sources: "Most Wanted Terrorists," Federal Bureau of Investigation. Accessible at http://
www.fbi.gov/wanted/terrorists/fugitives.htm. (Accessed on July 16, 2006); and FBI Executive Summary of FBI's investigation into the embassy bombings. The document
can be found at http://www.pbs.org/wgbh/pages/frontline/shows/binladen/bombings/
summary.html (Accessed on July 4, 2006).

Laden, and their investigations led to Wadi al-Hajj, who was managing
an NGO called Help Africa People in Nairobi. Kenyan police officials and
U.S. investigators raided al-Hajj's house and confiscated his computer
as well as several documents.[26] The presence of an al Qaeda associate in
Nairobi should have alerted investigating officials about the possibility
that other al Qaeda operatives were in the country. Additionally, investigators found a letter by al-Hajj's deputy Fazul Abdul Muhammad, who
expressed alarm about the deteriorating security situation of the Nairobi
cell members. Muhammad warned that "there are many [r]easons that
lead me to believe that the cell members in East Africa are in great
danger" and added that "we are convinced one hundred percent that
the Kenyan intelligence are aware about us and that indeed our security
situation is extremely bad." Muhammad goes on to state that he was
extremely concerned about a report in the *Daily Telegraph*, which stated
that "a leading associate [of bin Laden] ... [known as] Abu Fadhl, the
terrorist alias for Sidi Tayyib" was being held by Saudi authorities, and
that the information provided by the captive was being passed to U.S. and
British intelligence officials.[27] Muhammad wished to confirm whether the
al Qaeda operative mentioned in the news article was in fact Abu al-Fadhl

al-Makki, since precautionary measures would have to be taken if such an important operative was in the custody of security officials.[28] Muhammad asked his superiors, in lieu of the dangerous security situation, "are we ready for that big clandestine battle?"[29] The discovery of the letter should have alerted U.S. officials about the presence of a larger al Qaeda cell in Nairobi. Later, in November 1997, an Egyptian named Mustafa Mahmud Sa'id Ahmad informed U.S. intelligence officials at the Nairobi embassy about a plot to target the U.S. embassy. Mr. Ahmad revealed that the plot involved the use of several vehicles and stun grenades and the detonation of a truck bomb inside the underground parking garage. The CIA, acting on Mr. Ahmad's revelations, sent two reports to the Department of State. In response, the level of security was raised for several weeks but was lowered after no attack materialized. The CIA also cautioned that the effort might be an attempt by al Qaeda to observe the defensive measures adopted by the embassy. Mr. Ahmad was later arrested in Tanzania for his role in bombing the U.S. embassy in that country.[30]

Based on the general threat information, the Department of State and the CIA issued general threat advisories on two occasions. On June 12, 1998, the Department of State issued a statement indicating that it was stepping up the security at embassies and government sites in the Middle East and South Asia following "serious" reports of a terrorist attack.[31] The announcement, which did not contain information on Africa, followed bin Laden's interview with the ABC television network in May 1998, in which he repeated his intentions to attack U.S. targets, including civilians. Curiously, a large map of East Africa was prominently displayed on the wall behind bin Laden during this interview. On July 29, the Counter Terrorism Center (CTC) at the CIA issued a general alert about a CBRN attack by bin Laden. Nairobi and Dar es-Salaam were classified as medium threat posts, but the embassy security officers were as worried about muggings and carjacking as they were about terrorism.[32] The U.S. Ambassador to Kenya, Prudence Bushnell, twice requested that the embassy to be relocated to a different place, since its current location posed great risks. Ambassador Bushnell's requests, however, were rejected by the Department of State.[33]

INITIAL RESPONSES

Immediately after the embassy bombings, Richard Clarke, the National Coordinator for Counterterrorism, convened the Counterterrorism and Security Group to respond to the bombing. Plans were made to evacuate the injured to Europe, deploy the Navy's Fleet Anti-Terrorism Support Team (FAST)—a specialized team trained to provide force protection at sensitive locations—to provide security for the damaged embassies, and send the Department of State's Foreign Emergency Support Team (FEST) to provide highly trained staff to assist the U.S. ambassadors in both the countries.[34] The FBI launched a massive investigation, collecting evidence from the bomb sites, interviewing suspects, and arresting people. The Kenyan and Tanzanian investigations, supervised by the New York field office, were codenamed "KENBOM" and "TANBOM" respectively.[35] In the first few days, some 400 FBI agents went to Africa from several field offices in the United States. The Washington, DC, office sent bomb experts and lab technicians; computer specialists were called from Pocatello, Idaho; and counterterrorism experts arrived from the New York office. The FBI conducted more than 1,500 interviews and collected about 8 tons of material that was shipped back to the United States for evidence analysis.[36] During the investigation in Kenya, the FBI paired agents with the local Criminal Investigative Division (CID) in order to elicit better cooperation during the investigation.[37]

On the day of the bombings, the first break into the investigation occurred in Karachi, Pakistan, when Pakistani immigration officials detained Muhammad Siddiq Odeh based on the suspicious nature of his passport. The Pakistani officials did not reveal details of the arrest for another 3 days.[38] Later, Odeh was taken into U.S. custody. Within a week, Kenyan police arrested Muhammad Rashid Da'ud al-Awhali, the alleged passenger in the truck that was used in the bombing. The original attack plan, if carried out successfully, would have resulted in the death of al-Awhali. However, he escaped the attack with some injuries.[39] The arrests of Odeh and al-Awhali provided the investigators with crucial details about the plot and the identities of the al Qaeda and Egyptian Islamic Jihad operatives involved in the attack. Within a week, the CIA was able to attribute the attacks to bin Laden, and on August 14, George Tenet, the Director of Central Intelligence (DCI), delivered his formal judgment that bin Laden and his senior Egyptian aides were responsible for the attacks.[40]

Shortly after the bombings, U.S. intelligence agencies became aware of a plot to bomb the U.S. embassy in Tirana, Albania. The CIA, in collaboration with Albanian officials, disrupted an al Qaeda forgery cell as well as the plot to attack the embassy.[41] Similarly, in the months after the embassy bombings, the CIA and the FBI, working with foreign intelligence agencies, managed to disrupt al Qaeda cells in several countries. In Uganda, the CIA and the FBI foiled a plot to attack the U.S. embassy in Kampala.[42] The disruption efforts were aided by the National Security Agency's (NSA) efforts in reviewing the communications made from al Qaeda safe-houses in Nairobi.[43] U.S. intelligence agencies also received assistance from some Muslim countries. The arrested members were involved in logistics, fundraising, and communications. U.S. intelligence agencies realized the difficulties involved in apprehending the bombing teams, which are usually mobile, and hence came to the conclusion that these bombing teams might find it difficult to operate if the infrastructure and the support networks were disrupted. The number of apprehended members revealed the extent and depth of the organization.[44] The United States made an important breakthrough when German officials arrested Mamduh Mahmud Salim, also known as Abu Hajir, a senior aide to bin Laden.[45]

After the bombings, the Counterterrorism Security Group examined the security levels of U.S. diplomatic missions around the world and identified 40 missions that needed urgent evaluation. Seven Embassy Security Assessment Teams (ESAT) comprising officials from several agencies, including the Department of State, the Pentagon, and the CIA, traveled to these posts to make their assessments. The U.S. Congress, in the meantime, acted on a $1.8 billion request from the White House for improving the security of U.S. diplomatic posts, and appropriated $1.5 billion for improving the security of U.S. diplomatic missions worldwide. The money was used to buy "radios, surveillance cameras, and armored cars" and to increase the number of diplomatic security personnel and improve the physical security of the buildings.[46]

U.S. RESPONSE TO AL QAEDA: PRE-EMBASSY BOMBING

Prior to examining the set of U.S. responses to the embassy bombings, it is useful to look at U.S. counterterrorism efforts against bin Laden prior to 1998, since it will help us both to evaluate the extent to which the U.S. government was focused on bin Laden and the al Qaeda network, and to better understand the response measures taken after the embassy bombings, since some policies involved building upon (or improvising) existing counterterrorism measures.

Following the first bombing of the World Trade Center in February 1993, and the subsequent discovery of a plot to target important landmarks in New York City, U.S. intelligence officials became aware of the threat posed by Osama bin Laden, although his role was identified primarily as a terrorism financier.[47] Over the years, however, U.S. intelligence officials noticed increased reporting on bin Laden, and his stay in Sudan became a contentious issue between Sudan and the United States.[48] After the United States withdrew its diplomatic staff from Sudan, citing threats and hostile surveillance of that staff, Sudanese officials attempted to mend ties with the United States. In those meetings, the sojourn of bin Laden and his supporters in Sudan figured prominently in the discussions.[49] After the assassination attempt on Mubarak in June 1995, the Counterterrorism Security Group also considered taking direct action against bin Laden, who was suspected of being involved in the attack. The retaliation plans included targeting "Veterans' Housing for Afghan War Fighters," a bank believed to contain bin Laden's money, as well as a few other options.[50]

Eventually, Saudi Arabia, Egypt, and the United States forced Sudan to evict bin Laden, who then sought refuge in Afghanistan.

In January 1996, David Cohen, chief of the CIA's Directorate of Operations, created a "virtual station"—like a CIA field station, but located in CIA's headquarters in Langley, Virginia—that was supposed to focus on terrorism financing. The focus was then shifted to Osama bin Laden based on the recommendation of Michael Scheuer, the first chief of the station, which was named "Alec station"[51] and had an initial staff of 10–15 officials.[52] The intelligence gathered by this station enabled the United States to respond immediately and aggressively after the embassy bombings.

During the summer of 1997, the CIA-funded Afghan tribal unit that was used to capture Mir Amal Kasi[53] was transferred to the bin Laden unit to help capture bin Laden. The unit was renamed as FD/TRODPINT (a CIA codename). The proposed strategy was to capture bin Laden and simultaneously work toward obtaining an indictment that would enable the United States to prosecute him or, in the absence of an indictment, send him to another country such as Egypt or Saudi Arabia to stand trial.[54] By early 1998, the Principals Committee[55] gave its "blessing" to the plan. Meanwhile, the FBI's New York field office, working with the U.S. Attorney for the Southern District of New York, was preparing to indict bin Laden on charges of conspiring to attack U.S. defense installations.[56] The court issued a sealed indictment in June 1998, which was revealed in November 1998, and the earlier indictment was superseded by another indictment issued after the embassy bombing.[57] During the spring of 1998, a CIA plan to capture and remove bin Laden from Afghanistan was cancelled due to a lack of precise intelligence and an increased risk of failure.[58]

After the CIA plan to capture bin Laden was cancelled, Richard Clarke asked the Pentagon to prepare a military option to target bin Laden. The chairman of the Joint Chiefs of Staff, General Hugh Shelton, asked CENTCOM Commander Anthony Zinni to develop a plan. The Pentagon plan was presented in the first week of July. The Pentagon's plan involved cruise missile strikes against eight terrorist camps as well bin Laden's compound in Tarnak Farms near Kandahar, Afghanistan.[59] Between 1996 and 1998, the Department of State's South Asian bureau focused attention on bin Laden, especially after his relocation to Afghanistan, but the bureau's agenda was dominated by the nuclear arms race between India and Pakistan, ending the civil war in Afghanistan, and improving human rights conditions under the Taliban's rule in Afghanistan.[60]

While looking for options to evict bin Laden from Afghanistan, the CIA approached Saudi Arabia and requested that the Saudi rulers utilize their influence on the Taliban to force bin Laden out of Afghanistan. Saudi Prince Turki bin Faysal, then head of Saudi Arabia's General

Intelligence Directorate (GID), met with Mullah Omar in June 1998; subsequently, Omar agreed to hand over bin Laden and promised to work with the Saudis in implementing the hand over.[61] Of course, that never happened.

As things stood on August 7, 1998, certain elements within the U.S. government became increasingly concerned about bin Laden's pronouncements and activities. However, the government's options were limited due to the lack of a legal indictment against bin Laden (at least until June 1998), the absence of U.S. influence over the Taliban regime, and poor intelligence on bin Laden's movements.

OPERATION INFINITE REACH

On August 8, a day after the bombing, the CIA received intelligence that senior leaders of Islamist groups linked to bin Laden planned to meet on August 20 at the Zawhar Killi camp near Khowst in eastern Afghanistan in order to discuss the embassy bombings and plan additional attacks. George Tenet informed the Principals Committee at the White House about the planned meeting. The Principals Committee decided to target the meeting using cruise missiles. Air strikes seemed to be a likely option due to their past use in both the 1986 bombing of Libya, in response to a terrorist attack in Berlin, and the 1993 retaliatory strikes against the Iraqi intelligence headquarters after the discovery of an Iraqi plot to assassinate President Bush, Sr., during his visit to Kuwait. The Principals hoped that the missiles would hit bin Laden, but the National Security Council (NSC) recommended that the attacks be launched regardless of the meeting.[62] The Zawhar Killi camp, besides being the location of the upcoming meeting, also had historical linkages to bin Laden that made it an attractive target. Bin Laden fought his most famous battle at that location and later issued his February 1998 fatwa against "Jews and Crusaders" from there, while announcing the creation of the World Islamic Front. The camp also served as a training ground with a base headquarters and five satellite training areas.[63] An interagency group of officials prepared a list of 20 targets in Afghanistan, Sudan, and an unnamed third country.[64] The decision to attack al Qaeda's infrastructure outside Afghanistan was based on the desire of President Clinton and his foreign policy aides to launch a global response to al Qaeda's attack on U.S. targets in two different countries.[65] At a high-level meeting on August 19, it was decided to launch the attacks on the Zawhar Killi complex in Afghanistan and two Sudanese targets, the al-Shifa pharmaceutical plant and a tannery. The al-Shifa plant was included on the grounds that bin Laden was using that facility to produce nerve agents that could be used in a future attack on the United States.[66] The chairman of the Joint Chiefs of Staff (JCS), Hugh Shelton, intervened to remove the tannery from the list of targets.

On August 20, as part of Operation Infinite Reach, 75 Tomahawk missiles—each costing more than $750,000—hit the training camp complex in Afghanistan. At the same time, 13 Tomahawk missiles hit the al-Shifa facility in Khartoum, Sudan.[67] The missile attack killed between 20–30 people[68] in Afghanistan and 1 person in Sudan. But bin Laden remained unscathed, since he was not present when the cruise missiles struck the camps.[69] The cruise missiles targeted the training camp complex, which included the Zawhar Killi al-Badr base camp, support complex, and four primary training camps.[70] President Clinton issued a statement explaining that he ordered the cruise missile attack for the following four reasons: a) the groups' involvement in the embassy bombings, b) the groups' involvement in the past attacks on Americans, c) to prevent additional attacks planned by the groups, and d) because the groups were seeking to acquire chemical weapons and other dangerous weapons.[71] Since international law prohibited acts of revenge, the Clinton administration portrayed the cruise missile attacks as self-defense measures aimed at disrupting the planning and execution of future attacks.[72] Clinton administration officials cautioned that the missile attacks would not prevent further attacks, but would have certainly disrupted attacks being planned for the not-too-distant future. Secretary of State Madeleine Albright, reiterating President Clinton's remarks, stated that "while our actions are not perfect insurance, inaction would be an invitation to further horror."[73]

POST-OPERATION INFINITE REACH ACTIONS

The U.S. response to the embassy bombings did not end with the cruise missiles attacks on Sudan and Afghanistan. The United States saw the bombings as a wake-up call that brought into clearer focus the danger posed by religious terrorists in general and by Osama bin Ladin in particular. After the cruise missile attacks, officials involved in designing and implementing counterterrorism policies discussed several options to capture bin Laden, disable elements of his network (that are spread across several countries), and cripple his financial infrastructure. The discussion below considers some elements of the U.S. strategy aimed at addressing the threat posed by the al Qaeda network, and deals primarily with the efforts undertaken by the CIA, the Department of Defense, and diplomatic efforts, chiefly led by the Department of State, since a major portion of the Clinton administration's counterterrorism efforts relied on these agencies. Other agencies, such as the FBI and the Department of Treasury, played crucial roles as well, and where appropriate they will also be discussed. However, because of space limitations, this section will not examine the responses to several threat reports that arrived immediately after the embassy bombings and throughout 1999.[74]

Operation Infinite Resolve

After the cruise missile attacks, some officials wished to carry out a sustained campaign of missile strikes against targets in Afghanistan. JCS Chairman General Shelton issued a planning order for additional missile strikes, and President Clinton expressed his desire to carry out such attacks sooner rather than later. The Pentagon named the planned strikes Operation Infinite Resolve. But some officials advised against further attacks. Undersecretary of Defense for Policy Walter Slocombe advised Secretary Cohen that the list of targets did not seem promising and suggested defining an "articulate rationale for military action." Some officials also feared that the missile strikes might cause large civilian casualties and stressed the need to collect better intelligence on bin Laden. Department of State officials cautioned that, after the bombing campaign in Kosovo and Operation Desert Fox in Iraq, the United States might be perceived as a mad bomber if it carried out additional cruise missile strikes in Afghanistan. President Clinton also feared that the additional missile attacks might increase the list of volunteers wishing to join al Qaeda's training camps.[75]

During the fall of 1998, Richard Clarke developed a plan called "Political-Military Plan Delenda"[76] to deal with the al Qaeda network. It was a multifaceted plan that involved bringing together several agencies of the U.S. government to attack the al Qaeda network. However, this plan was never formally adopted by the Principals Committee at the White House. In the plan's military component, Clarke suggested a sustained campaign against bin Laden's bases in Afghanistan or elsewhere whenever the situation provided a set of targets. Clarke advised against solely relying on targeting terrorist leaders, thereby implying that a sustained campaign might persuade the Taliban's leaders to hand over bin Laden. Defense Secretary William Cohen and JCS Chairman Shelton did not support Clarke's idea of "rolling attacks," since the primitive terrorist training camps offered poor targets for the expensive cruise missiles. President Clinton and Sandy Berger were also concerned about the "blowback" effects that might result from such a sustained campaign.[77]

The CIA's Role

The CIA, working with the FD/TRODPINT unit, developed plans to kidnap bin Laden as well as assist the Pentagon in launching cruise missile strikes on bin Laden whenever sufficient intelligence was available to carry out such an action. Sandy Berger ordered the Pentagon to deploy U.S. Navy ships and two cruise-missile-carrying submarines to the Arabian Sea. The submarine crew rehearsed the launching of the missiles and reduced the time gap between a presidential order and the missile impact in Afghanistan to about 4 hours.[78] On three occasions between August 1998 and December 1999, the U.S. government seriously considered launching cruise missiles to kill bin Laden.[79] The first chance occurred in December 1998 when intelligence information suggested that bin Laden might stay in the Haji Habash house that was part of the residence of the Governor of Kandahar. The strike was called off due to fears of causing large civilian casualties as well as concerns regarding the reliability of the intelligence source.[80] Again, in February 1999, the tribal unit in Afghanistan provided information that bin Laden was at a desert hunting camp that belonged to visitors from a Gulf state believed to be UAE, a U.S. counterterrorism ally in the region. Once again, the option of using cruise missiles was discussed, but it was dropped after NSC officials considered the intelligence to be unreliable. Certain officials have hinted that the strike was called off to avoid injuring or killing members from the UAE royal family or senior officials from the UAE who were believed to be in that camp.[81] The last attempt—and possibly the one with the best opportunity to kill bin Laden—was made in May 1999, when intelligence indicated that bin Laden will be staying in or near Kandahar for a period of 5 days. CIA field officers thought that this was the best piece of intelligence on bin Laden's location. The strike was once again called off at the last minute, citing unreliable intelligence as a pretext.[82] On all three occasions, the field officers at the CIA, officers in the bin Laden unit, and working-level military officials were unhappy with the decisions not to follow through with the missile strikes.

In addition to collecting intelligence to facilitate cruise missile strikes on bin Laden, the CIA was also working with the FD/TRODPINT unit to kidnap bin Laden and bring him to trial. The effort was put on hold during the spring of 1998 but was reactivated after the embassy bombings. Following those attacks, President Clinton signed a Memorandum of Notification (MON) authorizing the CIA to let the FD/TRODPINT unit use force to capture bin Laden and his associates and also to attack bin Laden in other ways. However, this MON only allowed the tribal unit to use force in self-defense.[83] As the tribal unit expressed its desire to conduct a raid to kidnap bin Laden rather than wait and lay an ambush, the initial MON was modified to include the use of firepower. The final draft of the MON included language that seemed to indicate that it was permissible to kill bin Laden only if it was not feasible to capture him during a raid.[84] In February 1999, the CIA received White House sanction to employ troops from the Northern Alliance to hunt and capture bin Laden. However, the MON authorizing the action only allowed the use of force as a measure of self-defense during the capture operation.[85] Divisions arose between White House officials and CIA field officers and officials working at the bin Laden's unit over the ambiguity regarding the use of lethal force in attempts to capture bin Laden. CIA's field officers felt that the White House was engaging in legal doubletalk concerning the use of lethal force, while unnecessarily criticizing the CIA for failing to capture bin Laden. The White House, on the other hand, felt that the CIA field officers were risk averse and purposefully misinterpreting the MONs to justify their inaction against bin Laden.[86]

In the fall of 1999, the CIA developed a new strategy called "The Plan." Its elements included disrupting bin Laden's operations, channeling and capturing bin Laden, conducting psychological operations to help capture bin Laden, targeting bin Laden's associates, and increasing the technical capability to conduct surveillance and gather more information.[87] The plan included a program for hiring and training better officers with counterterrorism skills, recruiting more assets, and trying to penetrate al Qaeda's ranks.[88] Meanwhile, in July 1999, Clinton authorized the CIA to develop plans, in collaboration with foreign governments, to capture bin Laden. This authorization allowed the CIA to make plans to work with the governments of Uzbekistan and Pakistan.[89] Uzbekistan provided basing rights for small aircraft, trained a commando unit to hunt bin Laden, allowed the NSC and the CIA to install monitoring equipment to intercept Taliban and al Qaeda communications, and later allowed Predator reconnaissance planes to be based on Uzbek soil.[90]

The Pentagon's Role

After the embassy bombings, while discussing retaliation options against the al Qaeda network in Afghanistan, the Clinton administration did not consider a full-scale military invasion of Afghanistan as an option, since it was not considered feasible at that time. Key members of the Clinton administration, such as Sandy Berger and Madeleine Albright, as well as Clinton himself, did not believe that the United States could obtain domestic approval and external support for such an invasion. An option to employ Special Forces was considered and then rejected, since the operational plans presented by General Shelton involved extensive logistical planning and a long deployment time.[91] Similarly, after the effort to attack bin Laden in December 1998 using cruise missiles was dropped due to fear of extensive collateral damage, the Pentagon proposed to use the AC-130 gunship instead of cruise missiles in order to reduce the extent of collateral damage. This proposal, however, was not implemented because its implementation would have involved extensive preparations and basing rights in neighboring countries, which the United States did not possess at that time.[92]

Unfortunately, during this period, the Pentagon missed an opportunity to reorient its counterterrorism strategies. In the fall of 1998, lower level officials in the Office of the Assistant Secretary for Special Operations and Low-Intensity Conflict suggested a broad change in the national strategy and the Pentagon's approach to counterterrorism, hinting at large-scale operations across a whole spectrum of U.S. military capabilities. The authors suggested an eight-part strategy that was more "pro-active and aggressive." The authors warned that when faced with horrific attacks in the future, the Pentagon might not have a choice or a plan to respond to the attack. For unknown reasons, the concept paper did not advance much higher in the decision-making hierarchy.[93]

Diplomacy

Diplomacy was also a major element of U.S. counterterrorism policy, as the United States tried to build alliances in its fight against the al Qaeda network and persuade countries that were providing safe haven to al Qaeda operatives to desist from continuing such support. During bin Laden's stay in Sudan the United States—in collaboration with Egypt and Saudi Arabia—forced the Sudanese government to evict bin Laden. After bin Laden fled to Afghanistan, the United States was faced with a difficult situation, since Afghanistan was roiled by a civil war between the Taliban movement and the several factions that constituted the Northern Alliance. The United States did not have any diplomatic presence in Afghanistan. After the Taliban movement captured Kabul and assumed power, the issue became even more complicated, since the United States did not recognize the Taliban government. Only three countries, Pakistan, Saudi Arabia, and the United Arab Emirates, recognized the newly formed Taliban government. Therefore, the United States at times relied on Pakistan and Saudi Arabia to negotiate with the Taliban government, especially its reclusive leader Mullah Omar, regarding the handover of bin Laden to the United States or to any other Arab country. As described earlier, Prince Turki bin Faysal visited Mullah Omar in June 1998 to discuss the possibility of handing over bin Laden to Saudi Arabia, and Omar initially seemed favorably disposed toward the idea. However, when the Prince visited Mullah Omar again in September 1998, after the cruise missile attacks, Omar reneged on his pledge and instead railed against the Saudi Kingdom. Immediately after this event, Saudi Arabia withdrew its diplomatic personnel from Afghanistan. Similarly, the United States requested that Pakistan engage the Taliban leadership in diplomatic efforts to evict bin Laden as well as cooperate with the CIA in its efforts to capture bin Laden. Pakistan stalled, however, and at times refused to provide such assistance. Sections within the Pakistani government, especially the Inter Services Intelligence Directorate (ISI), were helping the Taliban government and did not wish to cooperate with the United States in apprehending bin Laden, who in turn was helping the Taliban government with money and supplying troops for fighting the Northern Alliance. Even within the U.S. government, there was a significant debate on defining a policy to deal with the situation in Afghanistan. Some officials felt that the United States should help negotiate an end to the civil war and aid in the formation of a unity government. Other officials felt that the United States should label the Taliban movement as a terrorist group and funnel assistance to the Northern Alliance to help defeat the Taliban government. In addition, the Department of State's South Asia bureau was chiefly concerned with preventing hostilities between nuclear-armed India and Pakistan, so the issue of bin Laden ranked lower in its list of priorities.[94] Finally, in July 1999, Clinton declared the Taliban regime to be a state sponsor of terrorism and in October 1999, the United Nations imposed economic and travel sanctions on Afghanistan. Unfortunately, these actions did not change Mullah Omar's behavior toward bin Laden. Later in 2000, the United Nations passed *Resolution 1333,* imposing an embargo on arms shipment to Afghanistan. Pakistan, however, continued to ship arms to Afghanistan.[95]

Terrorist Financing

On August 20, on the same day that the United States launched cruise missile attacks on targets inside Sudan and Afghanistan, President Clinton—using powers under the International Emergency Economic Powers Act—signed *Executive Order 13099,* which prohibited transactions with terrorists "who threaten the Middle East peace process," and included the names of Osama bin Muhammad bin Awad bin Ladin (a.k.a. Osama bin Laden), Islamic Army (a.k.a. Al Qaeda, Islamic Salvation Foundation, The Islamic Army for the Liberation of the Holy Places, The World Islamic Front for Jihad Against Jews and Crusaders, and The Group for the Preservation of the Holy Sites), Abu Hafs al-Masri, and Rifa'i Ahmad Taha Musa.[96] Senior Clinton administration officials described the objectives of the executive order as "identifying the network, asserting jurisdiction, denying material support, technological, financial, provision of services and fundraising, and then working with allies to take similar steps, [through which] we will seek to identify a financial trail."[97] The Clinton administration also hoped that this measure would force other countries to adopt similar anti-terrorism financing regulations.[98]

Until President Clinton signed *Executive Order 13099,* there was no systematic effort within the U.S. government to examine bin Laden's financing apparatus. This was a strange situation, since bin Laden was initially identified in U.S. investigations as a terrorist financier. Conventional wisdom within the CIA stated that terrorists carry out attacks cheaply, and hence that bin Laden did not need large amounts of money to operate his network. Also, the prevailing wisdom held that bin Laden inherited a vast fortune that was being used to finance his organization. Investigations by Clarke's team and the Department of Treasury's Office of Foreign Assets Control (OFAC) revealed that bin Laden needed vast sums of money to operate his worldwide network, and that al Qaeda generated and moved large sums of funds through a vast financial network. The investigation revealed that bin Laden raised significant amounts of funds through generous donations from wealthy patrons in the Gulf States, circulated the money through regional banking centers, and then used Islamic NGOs operating as front organizations to deliver the funds to al Qaeda operatives.[99] Discussions with Saudi officials and bin Laden's family members revealed that his financial inheritance was not being used to finance the al Qaeda network.[100] The U.S. government received limited assistance from Saudi Arabia in regulating its banking system and sharing the information requested. The U.S. government considered using covert operations against key financial nodes that were involved in money laundering operations. U.S. officials, however, feared that such actions (if discovered) might damage confidence in the international financial system, leading to massive losses. Therefore, U.S. officials adopted a policy of "naming and shaming" organizations involved in money laundering operations.[101]

CONCLUSION: LESSONS LEARNED

> You can't fight this enemy simply in defense. You also have to be prepared to go on the offense.
> —Sandy Berger, National Security Advisor to President Clinton[102]

President Clinton, in his address to the nation on August 20, 1998 following the launch of cruise missiles, stated that there are certain occasions when "law enforcement and diplomatic tools are simply not enough" and that the United States "must take extraordinary steps to protect the safety of our citizens." Implying that the struggle against terrorism did not end with the cruise missile strikes, President Clinton indicated that the fight will be a "a long, ongoing struggle between freedom and fanaticism, between the rule of law and terrorism" and warned that the United States "is and will remain a target of terrorists precisely because we are leaders; because we act to advance peace, democracy and basic human values; because we're the most open society on earth."[103]

The cruise missile attacks and the counterterrorism policies outlined by Clinton administration officials revealed a shift in the U.S. counterterrorism strategy. According to Congressional Research Service analyst Raphael Perl, the cruise missile attacks represented the first time that the United States assigned such "primary and public prominence to the preemptive, as opposed to the retaliatory, nature and motive of a military strike against a terrorist organization or network." Perl's evaluation of the

Clinton administration's response to the embassy bombings is very informative and worth repeating in its entirety. Perl argued that the new counterterrorism policy was:[104]

1. more global, less defensive, and more proactive;
2. more national security oriented and less traditional law enforcement oriented;
3. more likely to use military force and other proactive measures;
4. less likely to be constrained by national boundaries when sanctuary is offered to terrorists or their infrastructure in instances where vital national security interests are at stake; and
5. generally, more unilateral when other measures fail, particularly if other nations do not make an effort to subscribe to like minded policies up front.

U.S. counterterrorism policies since the September 11, 2001 al Qaeda attacks on New York and Washington, DC, have built upon the Clinton administration's aggressive response to the embassy bombings. After 9/11, which served as a far more traumatic wake-up call, all the relevant agencies of the U.S. government that are involved in formulating and implementing counterterrorism policies have made significant progress in increasing their capabilities to address the threat from the transnational jihadists and self-starter cells inspired by al Qaeda's ideology. Despite such improvements, significant gaps remain in our understanding of the nature of the evolving threat and the means to address it. The limited scope of this chapter precludes a detailed examination of either the improvements made in U.S. counterterrorism capabilities since 9/11 or the shortcomings that still need to be addressed. However, some of the lessons learned from the U.S. responses to the embassy bombings can be identified:

– Terrorism financing: The imposition of economic sanctions on al Qaeda and its top leaders led to a better understanding of al Qaeda's financial network. The investigations into al Qaeda's financial network enabled the U.S. government to map the major nodes in the financial network that were used for collecting and routing money.
– Liaisons with local governments: The FBI made every effort to work closely with Kenyan and Tanzanian officials and actively involve them in the investigative process. This outreach effort helped the investigators gain the cooperation of local investigative agencies.
– Sharing intelligence with foreign governments: The CIA provided intelligence and worked closely with the governments of Albania and Uganda to disrupt plots to attack U.S. embassies in those countries. Similarly, the CIA worked with several foreign intelligence agencies to disrupt several al Qaeda cells.
– Importance of good actionable intelligence: The success of an aggressive strategy of targeting terrorists and their infrastructure is dependent on the ability to

collect accurate intelligence on the targets and striking the targets with limited collateral damage.

Hopefully, further lessons can be learned that will enable U.S. government agencies to interdict or forestall future terrorist attacks.

NOTES

1. In Kenya, the number of casualties would have been significantly higher if it were not for the guards who refused to allow the truck inside the compound. In Tanzania, due to good fortune, a water tanker stood between the bomb-carrying truck and the embassy building and absorbed a lot of the bomb's impact.

2. *The 9/11 Commission Report: Final Report of the National Commission on Terrorist Attacks Upon the United States* (New York: W.W. Norton & Company, 2004) 67–70.

3. Prosecution's closing argument presented by Kenneth Karas, *United States of America v. Usama Bin Laden et al.,* [henceforth USA v Usama bin Laden et al.] United States District Court, Southern District of New York, s(7) 98 cr. 1023, May 1, 2001, p. 5376. In February 1998, while issuing the *fatwa* against the Americans and announcing the formation of the World Islamic Front Against Jews and Crusaders, bin Laden stated: "[I]t is an individual duty for every Muslim who can do it to kill Americans and their allies—civilian and military—in any country where it is possible to do so, in order to liberate the Al-Aqsa Mosque and the Holy Mosque [the Al-Haram Mosque in Mecca, home of the Kaba] from their grip ... " See Randall B. Hamud, ed., *Osama Bin Laden: America's Enemy in His Own Words* (San Diego, CA: Nadeem, 2005) 60.

4. Peter Bergen, *Holy War Inc.: Inside the Secret World of Osama bin Laden* (New York: The Free Press, 2001) 108.

5. "Bin Laden hints he instigated embassy attacks," *The Ottawa Citizen*, January 3, 1999.

6. According to Abu Jandal, whose real name is Nasir Ahmad Abdallah al-Bahri, who served as bin Laden's bodyguard, "The impact of international developments on Somalia and the entry of the U.S. forces into it were [Osama bin Laden's] justification for the entry of al Qaida into [the country]. Al Qaida viewed the entry of the Americans into Somalia not as a move that is meant to save the Somalis from [famine], but to control Somalia and then spread U.S. hegemony over the region. This will achieve several goals. First, it will strike the growing Islamic movement in Sudan. Second, it will setup a rear U.S. base in the Gulf, since Somalia was the closest point to the Arabian Gulf." See Abu Jandal's interview, Khalid al-Hammadi, "Part 2—Al Qa'ida from Within, as narrated by Abu Jandal (Nasir al-Bahri), bin Laden's bodyguard," *Al Quds al-Arabi*, March 19, 2005: 19.

7. Abdel bari Atwan, who interviewed bin Laden in 1997, said "Bin Laden told me that he was expecting the [Americans] to come to Somalia and he sent people a month before their arrival to be prepared. And when they came actually he attacked them. But unfortunately, according to him, they ran away. And he wanted them to stay in order to fight them. He told me that the American

soldiers were cowards in comparison with the Soviet soldiers." Also Abu Jandal, bin Laden's bodyguard said "the Al-Qa'ida Organization mujahidin were already there when the United States entered because they had a program and camps and a vision to unify the country. They aspired to make of Somalia a stronghold for them close to the Arabian peninsula because the brothers in the Al Qa'ida had an aim to liberate the Arabian peninsula later on." For Atwan's comments see Peter Bergen, *The Osama Bin Laden I Know: An Oral History of al Qaeda's Leader* (New York: Free Press, 2005), pp. 137–138.

8. Testimony of Jamal al-Fadl during the trial of *USA v Osama bin Laden.* Quoted in Bergen, *The Osama Bin Laden I Know*: 137.

9. *9/11 Commission Report*: 65.

10. *USA v Osama bin Laden*, Summation of Prosecutor: pp. 5253–5261; For names of the operatives see the declassified FBI Executive Summary of FBI's investigation into the embassy bombings, http://www.pbs.org/wgbh/pages/frontline/shows/binladen/bombings/summary.html (accessed July 4, 2006).

11. Ali Muhammad was a former major in the Egyptian Army and later became a supply sergeant in the U.S. Army's Special Forces base in Fort Bragg, North Carolina. In 2000, Muhammad pled guilty to five counts of conspiracy to kill nationals of the United States and officers or employees of the U.S. government on account of their official duties, to murder and kidnap, and to destroy U.S. property.

12. Bin Laden wanted to attack French targets as a result of France's role in Algeria.

13. Daniel Benjamin and Steven Simon, *The Age of Sacred Terror* (New York: Random House, 2002), pp. 129–130.

14. Khalid al-Hammadi, "Part 9 - Al Qa'ida from Within, as narrated by Abu Jandal (Nasir al-Bahri), bin Laden's bodyguard," *Al Quds al-Arabi*, March 28, 2005: 21.

15. Benjamin and Simon, *The Age of Sacred Terror*: 130. In fact bin Laden expected the U.S. troops to stay and planned for a long fight in Somalia. See Bergen, *The Osama Bin Laden I Know*: 137–138.

16. *USA v Osama Bin Laden*, Summation by Prosecutor Karas: 5225.

17. *9/11 Commission Report*: 69.

18. Ibid.; Zahid Hussain, "Suspect Reportedly Says Hired Hands Left Behind to Carry Out Bombings," *Associated Press*, August 20, 1998.

19. Bergen, *The Osama Bin Laden I Know*: 222–223. Interestingly bin Laden is also believed to have provided some rationale for attacking the embassies in Kenya and Tanzania. According to Abu Jandal, bin Laden's bodyguard, bin Laden told Abu Jandal and others that the two American embassies were big detention centers for Muslims. They were also described as the "plotting minds" of the events in Rwanda where more than "80,000 Muslims were killed." The fight between the Hutus and the Tutsis was characterized as a fight between Muslims and Christians. The American embassy was portrayed to be behind that struggle. See Khalid al-Hammadi, "Part 3—Al Qa'ida from Within, as narrated by Abu Jandal (Nasir al-Bahri), bin Laden's bodyguard," *Al Quds al-Arabi*, March 25, 2005: 19.

20. In February 1996, after evaluating the threat to U.S. diplomatic personnel in Sudan, the U.S. embassy staff was withdrawn and 2,100 Americans living in

Sudan were urged to leave. Then Ambassador Timothy Carney moved to Nairobi and monitored Sudan. See Benjamin and Simon: *Age of Sacred Terror* pp. 244–245. In 1993, Sudan was designated a State Sponsor of Terrorism.

21. Bergen, *The Osama Bin Laden I Know*: 223.

22. Ibid.: 253.

23. Ibid.: 220–221.

24. Prosecution's closing argument presented by Kenneth Karas, *United States of America v. Usama Bin Laden et al.*, May 1, 2001, p. 5248.

25. Report of the Accountability Review Boards: Bombings of the US Embassies in Nairobi, Kenya and Dar es Salaam, Tanzania on August 7, 1998, U.S. Department of State, http://www.state.gov/www/regions/africa/board_introduction.html (accessed June 30, 2006).

26. Oriana Zill, "A Portrait of Wadih El Hage, Accused Terrorist," PBS Frontline, http://www.pbs.org/wgbh/pages/frontline/shows/binladen/upclose/elhage.html(accessed on July 4, 2006).

27. Hugh Davies, "Saudis detain member of anti-American terror group," *The Daily Telegraph*, August 2, 1997. The news article stated that Sidi Tayyib was providing information about the financial methods of bin Laden. The article also mentioned that another al Qa'ida operative named Jallud is also in the custody of the Saudis. Sidi Tayyib is also known as Madani al-Tayyib. Even though the article correctly stated that Tayyib was in U.S. custody, it incorrectly assumed that Saudi Arabia was passing on the information provided by Tayyib. In fact, Saudi Arabia blocked U.S. attempts to interview Tayyib. After the embassy bombings, U.S. officials made several requests to interview Tayyib during their investigations of al Qaeda's financial network. See *9/11 Commission Report*: 122.

28. "The Letter From El Hage's Computer," PBS Frontline, http://www.pbs.org/wgbh/pages/frontline/shows/binladen/upclose/computer.html (accessed July 4, 2006).

29. Ibid.

30. Raymond Bonner and James Risen, "Nairobi Embassy Received Warning of Coming Attack," *The New York Times*, October 23, 1998, Section A: 1.

31. "US increases security following 'serious' threats of terrorist attack," *Agence France Presse*, June 13, 1998.

32. Steve Coll, *Ghost Wars: The Secret History of the CIA, Afghanistan, and Bin Laden, From the Soviet Invasion to September 10, 2001* (New York: Penguin Books, 2004) 404.

33. Bergen, *Holy War Inc.*: 109.

34. Richard Clarke, *Against All Enemies: Inside America's War on Terror* (New York: Free Press, 2004), pp. 181–183.

35. "The War on Terrorism: Remembering the losses of KENBOM/TANBOM," Federal Bureau of Investigation, http://www.fbi.gov/page2/aug03/kenbom080603.htm (accessed July 5, 2006).

36. Angie Cannon, "Searching Hell," *The Advertiser*, October 10, 1998; David E. Kaplan, "On Terrorism's Trail," *U.S. News & World Report*, November 23, 1998: 30.

37. Kaplan, "On Terrorism's Trail."

38. Ibid. At least one report suggested that U.S. intelligence officials, after intercepting conversations between bin Laden's associates, alerted Pakistani

officials to watch for suspicious individuals, thus resulting in the capture of Odeh. See Gregory L. Vistica and Daniel Klaidman, "Tracking Terror," *Newsweek*, October 19, 1998: 46.

39. Karl Vick, "Assault on a U.S. Embassy: A Plot Both Wide and Deep," *The Washington Post*: A1.

40. Coll, *Ghost Wars*: 406–407.

41. *9/11 Commission Report*: 127. The U.S. Embassy in Albania was closed on August 14. See Philip Shenon, "Security Experts Assessing U.S. Embassies," *The New York Times*, September 8, 1998: 6.

42. In September 1998, Ugandan officials, acting on information provided by the CIA and assisted by the FBI, arrested 18 members, including 7 Somalis, who were planning an attack on the U.S. embassy. See Neely Tucker, "U.S. Deals Serious Blow to Bin Laden's Network," *Times-Picayune*, September 20, 1998. Another news report suggested that 20 people were arrested during the raids. See "CIA reportedly thwarted plot against embassy in Uganda," Deutsche Presse-Agentur, September 25, 1998.

43. John Miller, Michael Stone, and Chris Mitchell, *The Cell: Inside the 9/11 Plot, and Why the FBI and CIA Failed to Stop It* (New York: Hyperion, 2002), p. 213.

44. Benjamin and Simon, *Age of Sacred Terror*: 267–268. The countries in which the cells were disrupted include Italy, Britain, and Azerbaijan. *9/11 Commission Report*: 127. See also James Risen, "U.S. Directs International Drive on Bin Laden Networks," *The New York Times*, September 25, 1998: 3.

45. Benjamin Weiser, "U.S. Says Bin Laden Aide Tried to Get Nuclear Material," *The New York Times*, September 26, 1998.

46. Benjamin and Simon, *Age of Sacred Terror*: 266; Eric Schmitt, "Administration to Ask $1.8 Billion for Embassy Security," *The New York Times*, September 22, 1998; Shenon, "Security Experts Assessing U.S. Embassies."

47. Eleanor Hill, "Joint Inquiry Staff Statement—Part I," Joint Inquiry Staff, September 18, 2002: 13.

48. Barton Gellman, "U.S. Was Foiled Multiple Times in Efforts To Capture Bin Laden or Have Him Killed; Sudan's Offer to Arrest Militant Fell Through After Saudis Said No," *The Washington Post*, October 3, 2001: A1.

49. "1996 CIA Memo to Sudanese Official," *The Washington Post*, October 3, 2001.

50. Clarke, *Against All Enemies*: 141.

51. It was named Alec station after Michael Scheuer's son. Mark Mazzetti, "C.I.A. Closes Unit Focused on Capture of bin Laden," *The New York Times*, July 4, 2006.

52. Hill, "Joint Inquiry Staff Statement—Part I": 13.

53. Mir Amal Kasi was a Pakistani who, in 1993, shot five and killed two CIA employees outside the CIA headquarters at Langley, Virginia. Kansi was eventually captured in June 1997 and convicted in a U.S. court and was awarded the death sentence. Kansi was killed by lethal injection in November 2002.

54. Coll, *Ghost Wars*: 375–376.

55. The Principals Committee of the National Security Council (NSC) is a cabinet level policy formulation and implementation group of the U.S. government.

56. Al Qa'ida was involved in bombing two hotels in Eden in December 1992 where U.S. troops were staying on their route to Somalia. Two people, but no Americans, were killed in the attack. U.S. troops left before the bomb went off. Al Qa'ida was also involved in the attack on U.S. military personnel in October 1993 when 18 U.S. troops were killed in a firefight in Mogadishu, commonly known as the "Black Hawk Down" incident.

57. *9/11 Commission Report*: 110.

58. Ibid.: 111–114.

59. Ibid.: 116. It is certain that the Zinni's plan to use cruise missiles was influenced by previous U.S. responses to terror attacks or plots. In 1986, responding to the bombing of a disco in Berlin, the United States launched air strikes against Libya. Similarly, in 1993, after uncovering a failed Iraqi plot to assassinate President Bush, Sr., Clinton ordered cruise missiles attacks on the Iraqi intelligence headquarters.

60. Ibid.: 110; Coll, *Ghost Wars*: 382.

61. Ibid.: 115; Alan Cullison and Andrew Higgins, "Strained Alliance: Al Qaeda's Sour Days in Afghanistan—Fighters Mocked the Place; Taliban, in Turn, Nearly Booted Out bin Laden—A Fateful U.S. Missile Strike," *Wall Street Journal*, August 2, 2002: A1.

62. *9/11 Commission Report*: 116; Coll, *Ghost Wars*: 409. The level of accuracy of the information regarding bin Laden's presence at the facility varied. The source of the intelligence on the meeting is not known. Peter Bergen a journalist, has suggested that the information was provided by a Pakistani source. Bergen, *Holy War Inc.*: 121.

63. Coll, *Ghost Wars*: 409–410.

64. James Risen, "To Bomb Sudan Plant, or Not; A Year Later, Debates Rankle," *The New York Times*, October 27, 1999.

65. Ibid.

66. The decision to attack the Al-Shifa pharmaceutical plant was closely contested within the U.S. administration. The Clinton administration was severely criticized across the world for targeting that facility. An evaluation of the information available in the public domain indicates that the intelligence on chemical weapons production at the Al-Shifa plant was not entirely accurate. For more information on the debates within the Clinton administration and the controversy surrounding the decision, see Michael Barletta, "Chemical Weapons in the Sudan: Allegations and Evidence," *The Nonproliferation Review* 6, no. 1 (Fall 1998):115–136; James Risen, "To Bomb Sudan Plant, or Not; A Year Later, Debates Rankle," *New York Times*, Oct. 27, 1999: A1; Tim Weiner and James Risen, "Decision to Strike Factory in Sudan Based on Surmise Inferred From Evidence," *The New York Times*, September 21, 1998: 1.

67. Coll, *Ghost Wars*: 411.

68. *9/11 Commission Report*: 119; Barletta, "Chemical Weapons in the Sudan: Allegations and Evidence": 116.

69. Several reasons have been offered to explain bin Laden's absence at the camps. One explanation offered was that bin Laden expected the missile attacks and went into hiding. Another explanation offered was that Pakistani officials noticed the presence of U.S. Naval vessels and probably alerted bin Laden

through the Taliban. Another explanation was that the evacuation of U.S. diplomatic staff from Pakistan alerted bin Laden to the cruise missile attacks. Another explanation, offered by bin Laden's bodyguard, attributed bin Laden's escape to pure luck.

70. "U.S. DOD DoD news briefing," *M2 Presswire*, August 21, 1998. The training camps are used for training terrorist tactics, indoctrination, weapons, and the use of improvised explosive devices. See Ibid.

71. Statement by President Clinton, August 20, 1998, http://www.state.gov/www/regions/africa/strike_clinton980820.html (accessed on July 5, 2006).

72. "Press Briefing by Madeleine Albright and Sandy Berger," *M2 Presswire*, August 21, 1998; Coll, *Ghost Wars*: 409. National Security Advisor Sandy Berger, while replying to a question whether the attacks represented assassination, denied that the missile attacks were an act of assassination and stated that the camps were a "military target" and "it is appropriate ... for protecting the self-defense of the United States ... for us to disrupt and destroy those kinds of military terrorist targets."

73. "Press Briefing by Madeleine Albright and Sandy Berger," *M2 Presswire*, August 21, 1998; See also "White House: Press Briefing by National Security Advisor Sandy Berger and Mile McCurry," *M2 Presswire*, August 24, 1998. Berger stated that "We can't guarantee that something like this will prevent further attacks on the United States. But I am absolutely certain that had we not done this we would have been the victim of other terrorist attacks in the not too distant future."

74. For a discussion of the threats faced during 1998 and 1999, see *9/11 Commission Report*: 128–130, 141.

75. Coll, *Ghost Wars*: 413; Benjamin and Simon, *Age of Sacred Terror*: 283–284; *9/11 Commission Report*: 120–121, 134.

76. Delenda in Latin meant "[something] must be destroyed." See *9/11 Commission Report*: 120.

77. Clarke, *Against All Enemies*: 196–198; *9/11 Commission Report*: p. 120.

78. Coll, *Ghost Wars*: 421.

79. Benjamin and Simon, *Age of Sacred Terror*: 280–281.

80. *9/11 Commission Report*: 130–131; Coll, *Ghost Wars*: p. 422.

81. *9/11 Commission Report*: 137–138. For a detailed description of the events see Coll, *Ghost Wars*: 445–450.

82. *9/11 Commission Report*: 140–141.

83. Ibid.: 126, 131.

84. Ibid.: 131–132.

85. Ibid.: 139.

86. For a good description of the debates on both sides, see Coll, *Ghost Wars*: 424–430.

87. "Testimony of J. Cofer Black—Director of CIA Counterterrorist Center (1999–2002)" National Commission on Terrorist Attacks Upon the United States, April 13, 2004: 2.

88. *9/11 Commission Report*: 142; "Written Statement for the Record of the Director of Central Intelligence" National Commission on Terrorist Attacks upon the United States, March 24, 2004: 14–15. The decision to sue the Predator reconnaissance aircraft grew out of a policy decision to gather more real-time intelligence on

bin Laden's movements. See Coll, *Ghost Wars*: 526–530; Clarke, *Against All Enemies*: 220–222.

89. *9/11 Commission Report*: 142.

90. Coll, *Ghost Wars*: 459–460, 531–532.

91. Ibid, 407–408; Benjamin and Simon, *Age of Sacred Terror*: 294–295. Peter Schoomaker, Commander of the Special Operations Command, however, stated that it was possible to deploy Special Forces to attack bin Laden. During 1998, the Special Operations Command was not a "supported" command, rather it was a "supporting command" that meant it only acted to support other force commands and could not develop plans on its own. In this case, the elaborate plan for deploying Special Forces was prepared by CENTCOM Commander Anthony Zinni. *9/11 Commission Report*: 136.

92. Ibid.: 135.

93. Ibid.: 121.

94. Coll, *Ghost Wars*: 441–443; *9/11 Commission Report*: 121–124; Ahmed Rashid, *Taliban: Militant Islam, Oil, & Fundamentalism in Central Asia* (New Haven, CT: Yale University Press, 2000), pp. 183–196.

95. *9/11 Commission Report*: 125–126.

96. Clarke, *Against All Enemies*: 190; "The White House: Executive Order," *M2 Presswire*, August 25, 1998. Abu Hafs al-Masri is commonly known as Muhammad Atif, al Qaeda's military commander. Rifa'i Ahmad Musa Taha is the leader of the Egyptian Islamic Group who signed the statement announcing the creation of the World Islamic Front for Jihad against Jews and Crusaders.

97. "The White House: Background briefing by Senior Administration Officials," *M2 Presswire*, August 24, 1998.

98. Ibid.

99. Clarke, *Against All Enemies*": 190–193; Benjamin and Simon, *Age of Sacred Terror*: pp. 268–270.

100. *9/11 Commission Report*: 122.

101. Benjamin and Simon, *Age of Sacred Terror*: 270.

102. Raphael Perl, "Terrorism: U.S. Response to Bombings in Kenya and Tanzania: A New Policy Direction?" CRS Report for Congress, September 1, 1998: 2.

103. "Address to the Nation by the President: The Oval Office," *M2 Presswire*, August 20, 1998, http://www.state.gov/www/regions/africa/strike_clinton980820a.html (accessed July 5, 2006).

104. Perl, "Terrorism: U.S. Response to Bombings in Kenya and Tanzania": 2–3.

CHAPTER 8

THE CASE OF RAMZI YOUSEF

Gary A. Ackerman and Sundara Vadlamudi

Despite being replete with all sorts of colorful and dastardly characters, the annals of terrorism contain few more brazen and ambitious rogues than Ramzi Ahmad Yousef (also sometimes spelled Yusuf). During his relatively brief career as an international terrorist, crisscrossing the globe from 1993 to 1995, Yousef succeeded in attacking one of the world's most prominent structures, plotting the assassination of several heads of state, winning over dozens of Muslim radicals, and planning what would have been one of the deadliest and most complex terrorist attacks of all time, all the while being pursued by several nations' law enforcement and intelligence agencies. Yousef has been variously described as a "mastermind"[1] and—at least while he was active—as "the most dangerous man in the world,"[2] monikers that he himself no doubt appreciated; yet much about this chameleon-like and egoistical villain remains a mystery. This chapter will describe what is known about Yousef's origins and his development as a terrorist as well as trace his global exploits of mayhem. At the same time it will examine the nature and efficacy of the ultimately successful counterterrorist effort directed toward capturing a man who quickly rose to the rank of the world's most wanted terrorist. Lastly, the chapter will attempt to draw lessons from the campaign against Yousef, lessons that can be applied to both current and future counterterrorism operations.

ORIGINS

During his operational period, Yousef utilized a slew of aliases (more than 40 in all) and was known to periodically alter his external appearance—for instance, by changing the length and color of his hair. This penchant for disguising his identity to confuse his adversaries was sufficiently successful that to this day there exist those who doubt his true origins,[3] although most commentators believe that he was born Abdul Basit Mahmud Abdul Karim[4] on April 27, 1968, in a working-class suburb of Kuwait City.[5] His father was a Pakistani from Baluchistan who worked as an engineer for Kuwaiti Airlines and his mother was a Kuwaiti of Palestinian lineage. Although Yousef's father apparently became radicalized by Wahhabi doctrine while Yousef was still a teenager (and allegedly later joined the anti-Shi'i terrorist group Sipah-e-Sahaba in Pakistan[6]), Yousef is believed to have had a relatively standard Islamic education. Yousef showed great promise as a student, especially in mathematics and the sciences, and was conversant in Arabic, Urdu, and English. Contemporaries recalled him even then as being charismatic and seeking to lead, and several of his childhood friends later on ended up joining him in his terrorist pursuits.[7]

At the age of 18, Yousef traveled to Britain, and shortly thereafter, in August 1987, he began studying at the West Glamorgan Institute of Higher Education in Swansea, Wales. After receiving his diploma in 1989, Yousef returned to Kuwait, where he was likely swept up in the Iraqi invasion of Kuwait in August 1990. By this stage his militant attitudes were almost certainly already crystallized, and by mid-1991, he was associating and training with fellow militants in Pakistan, to which his family had moved in 1986. It was at this time that Yousef and one of his brothers married the sisters of a Pakistani militant, and Yousef bought a house in Quetta. Shortly afterwards, in late 1991, Yousef reportedly accompanied the future founder of the Abu Sayyaf terrorist group, Abdurajik Abubakar Janjalani, whom he had befriended, to the Philippines to help him train militants.[8] By the middle of 1992, Yousef was back in Pakistan, serving as an instructor at the *University of Dawa and Jihad*, a terrorist training camp, ready to embark on his campaign of violence. Physically, Yousef was a rather unimposing individual, being described as "tall with a long and skinny neck and face, ... a large, bulbous nose and flared ears."[9] Intellectually and psychologically, however, he certainly had the tools to become one of America's more lethal adversaries.

CHRONOLOGY OF ATTACKS

The first major terrorist attack that Yousef was involved in was the 1993 bombing of the World Trade Center (WTC) in New York City.[10] In the early 1990s, a group of followers of an imprisoned extremist named al-Sayyid Nusayr began formulating plans to carry out acts of *jihad* against the United States.[11] Mahmud Abu Halima, a burly, red-bearded Egyptian who had fought in Afghanistan against the Soviets realized that the group needed an explosives expert, and sent for Yousef, whom he had presumably met a few years earlier in one of the training camps in Pakistan or Afghanistan. Yousef, using a false passport, entered the United States on

September 1, 1992, and within a short space of time took de facto control over the group's planning and activities.[12]

Soon Yousef, using the alias Rashid, had developed a plan to conduct a large-scale bombing and settled on the WTC as the target. The core group of conspirators now consisted of Yousef, Abu Halima, a simpleton named Muhammad Salama, Salama's close friend Nidal Ayyad (who was a chemical engineer and helped acquire difficult-to-obtain chemicals through the company for which he worked), and an Iraqi named Abdul Rahman Yasin. Beginning in November, Yousef and Salama had begun ordering chemicals from chemical suppliers, storing them in a public storage facility and building the bomb in a rented apartment in Jersey City. Yousef directed the production of a 1,500 pound urea-nitrate bomb, the most difficult part of which was the production of the notoriously unstable nitroglycerine that was needed as a primary explosive. Salama, a somewhat incompetent driver, involved himself and Yousef in a car accident in late January 1993, resulting in Yousef's hospitalization and nearly derailing the entire plot. After returning from the hospital, Yousef continued work on the bomb, the force of which he enhanced with various chemicals and bottled hydrogen, and the conspirators began surveilling their target.

Then, on February 26, 1993, having loaded the bomb into a rented Ford Econoline van, the conspirators drove the van into the parking garage of One World Trade Center, lit four fuses, and left. At 12:17 P.M. the bomb exploded, creating a huge crater in the parking garage and collapsing several floors. However, the blast did not succeed in bringing down either of the twin towers, as Yousef had intended.[13] Yousef later claimed that he would have made a more powerful bomb if he had not run out of money.[14] Ultimately, 6 people lost their lives and over 1,000 were injured in the blast.[15] A few hours later, Yousef departed the United States for Pakistan.

After the WTC attack, Yousef's star was on the rise amongst extremists and in July 1993 he was approached in Karachi, Pakistan, and offered $68,000 to assassinate then prime ministerial candidate Benazir Bhutto.[16] After spending a week scouting and preparing, Yousef was ready to place the bomb but was wounded when the explosive detonated unexpectedly. Despite requiring several weeks of recuperation, Yousef doggedly persisted, and plotted to kill Bhutto with a sniper rifle. Unfortunately, when the rifle was not delivered on time, Yousef was forced to abandon the plot.

Undaunted, Yousef traveled to Bangkok in early 1994 to begin assembling a new terrorist cell to attack U.S. or Israeli targets there. Yousef assembled a 1-ton bomb, but the plot was aborted when the driver of the truck with the bomb had an accident on the way to the Israeli Embassy, and Yousef was forced to flee back to Pakistan. In May 1994, he began to display rising animosity toward Shi'i Muslims and, when recruited by the Mujaheddin-e-Khalq (MEK) organization, he agreed to lead an attack in Iran. On June 20, 1994, Yousef's efforts resulted in the detonation of a small bomb comprising high-explosive in a shrine in Mashhad, Iran, which killed 26 people and injured at least 200.[17] Yousef did not rest on his laurels; during the summer of 1994, he was involved in a series of incipient plots, prolific networking activities, and training other extremists in bomb-making in the Philippines.

It is alleged that Osama bin Laden requested that Yousef assassinate President Bill Clinton during his upcoming November 1994 visit to the Philippines.[18] While Yousef was enthusiastic, for once he demurred and decided that the security surrounding Clinton would be too great to conduct a successful attack. Thereafter, he refocused his attention toward assassinating Pope John Paul II, who was scheduled to visit the Philippines on January 15, 1995. One tactic he considered was to use a suicide bomber dressed as a Filipino priest, who would detonate an explosive when the Pope approached the "priest" to kiss him,[19] while an alternative plan consisted of the detonation of a remote-controlled device on the Pope's scheduled route.[20]

The envisaged attack on the Pope would also serve to divert attention from Yousef's single most ambitious plan, potentially even more destructive than the WTC attack, which carried the rather lyrically-sounding codename of "Bojinka."[21] From mid-1994, Yousef—together with his uncle, Khalid Shaykh Muhammad[22]—developed a plot to use 5 operatives to place timed explosives on 12 different flights that would explode on subsequent legs (mostly en route to the United States) after the attackers had disembarked during stopovers.[23] This was to be accomplished using a novel bomb devised by Yousef that could pass through airport security. While in Pakistan, Yousef recruited Abdul Hakim Murad, Wali Khan Amin Shah, and others and trained them to build his bombs. Yousef also did extensive background work on airport security and even obtained Boeing 747 blueprints to determine where to place his bombs so as to maximize their damage.

Yousef traveled to Manila in September 1994 to implement "Oplan Bojinka," and was later joined first by Murad and then by Amin Shah. Yousef wanted to test his explosive creation before the final attack, so he set off a similar device in a generator room in a shopping center in Cebu City in November, and on December 1 arranged for another device to be placed under a seat in a Manila movie theater, the detonation of which injured several patrons. On December 11, 1994, as a final test, Yousef succeeded in smuggling his device on Philippines Airlines Flight 434 from Manila to Japan, planted it under a seat, and left the plane at a stopover. During the next leg of the trip, the device exploded, killing one passenger and causing an emergency landing. At the same time, in mid-December 1994, he even came up with the idea of having his friend Murad fly a plane laden with chemical weapons or explosives and either crashing it into CIA headquarters, or spraying chemicals over the area.[24]

The Bojinka plot was nearing completion when, on January 5, 1995, roughly 2 weeks before it was to be activated,[25] a fire started while Yousef was mixing chemicals in an apartment in Manila. Yousef was forced to flee and both Yousef's friend Murad and a laptop detailing the plan were captured. The plot was aborted and Yousef returned to Pakistan, where, after considering several further terrorist plots (mainly aimed at the Philippines, with the ostensible aim of securing Murad's release), Yousef was captured before he could engage in any further violence.

TRAINING AND ORGANIZATIONAL LINKS

Yousef did not take his terrorist career lightly; he applied his intellect and energy toward developing the skills he would later use so adroitly in his attacks. While completing his diploma in computer-aided electrical engineering, Yousef took a course in microelectronics, which probably facilitated his later bomb-making. Although he did not actually fight in the Afghan conflict, it is believed that as early as 1988, Yousef spent time there and in Pakistan learning how to make explosives.[26] He also claimed to have studied numerous chemical encyclopedias in order to become a more proficient bomb-maker.[27] This allowed Yousef to create some genuine innovations in bomb-making, including the ingenious device consisting of nitroglycerine in a contact lens case, a Casio databank wristwatch as a timer, and an ignition circuit made from a light bulb filament and a standard 9-volt battery. It was this bomb that he intended to use in the Bojinka attacks and tested successfully in the Philippines in 1994.

However, it was Yousef's networking skills that arguably contributed the most to his success as a terrorist. Neil Herman, one of the investigators tasked with tracking down Yousef proclaimed, "The real eye-opener for me, the thing that brought it all together, was the ease with which Yousef was traveling around the world.... That's when I realized he had to have a sizeable organization behind him."[28] While there are still questions about the extent to which Yousef acted on his own initiative or was following the guidance of others, there is no doubt that Yousef maintained strong links with several Islamist leaders in the Middle East, South Asia, and the Philippines,[29] most prominent among these being Osama bin Laden.

Yousef's links to bin Laden are circumstantial but varied. First, the camps in Pakistan and Afghanistan in which Yousef trained and taught were linked to bin Laden and al Qaeda. Second, several of Yousef's friends and contacts, including Wali Khan Amin-Shah and Ibrahim Munir[30] had strong ties to bin Laden. Third, Yousef was the nephew of Khalid Shaykh Muhammad, with whom he maintained close contact and who would later become bin Laden's chief operational strategist and the architect of the 9/11 attacks. Fourth, during the preparations for the 1993 WTC bombing there was a trail of money leading to bin Laden,[31] and Yousef was in constant contact with several overseas parties during the course of the plot, including his uncle and perhaps even bin Laden himself. Fifth, according to police interviews with a senior member of Abu Sayyaf, Yousef introduced himself as an emissary of bin Laden in 1991.[32]

Despite some assertions to the contrary, there is no concrete evidence of Iraqi involvement in most of Yousef's activities. However, there are two, albeit tenuous, indications of possible linkages between Yousef and the Iraqis. First, it is reported that Yousef maintained close links to the MEK, on behalf of whom he may have participated in the bombing in Mashhad.[33] The MEK was supported by the Iraqi regime of Saddam Hussein at the time. Second, Abdul Rahman Yasin, one of Yousef's accomplices in the WTC bombing, was an Iraqi who fled to Baghdad after the bombing and was allowed to remain there in safety; however, this may have been more of a function of Iraq's post-1991 relations with the United States than a result of any direct links between the regime of Saddam Hussein and Yousef.

PERSONALITY TRAITS AND MOTIVATIONS

Yes I am a terrorist and I'm proud of it.
                                —Ramzi Yousef during sentencing at his 1997 trial[34]

A preliminary step in countering the terrorists of today and tomorrow is to understand the terrorists of yesterday and why they chose to act as they did. In short, we need to answer the questions "what kind of man is Ramzi Yousef?" and "what can we learn from his behavior that will help us catch the next Yousef?" To begin with, Yousef himself was something of an enigma in that, unlike many of his associates and coconspirators, he was not a religious zealot and did not practice Islam devoutly. For instance, he engaged in frequent womanizing while married, frequented bars and strip clubs, and did not always (or perhaps ever) fast during the month of Ramadan. Nevertheless, he harbored an intense hatred for the United States, Israel,[35] and Shi'ite Muslims. For example, he was quite ready to kill thousands of American civilians in the WTC bombing in order to punish America for supporting Israel,[36] and justified this by appealing to notions of collective punishment and the visiting upon his enemies of the same suffering he believed had been inflicted upon those he identified with, namely the Palestinians and Pakistani Sunnis. He therefore reasoned that only by sustaining a level of casualties on the scale of that inflicted by the United States on Hiroshima and Nagasaki, would the American public realize it was at war.[37]

It is unclear exactly when this intense hatred developed, but it is known that Yousef flirted with the Muslim Brotherhood while in Britain, but rejected their orientation as too moderate. Perhaps like many other impressionable and dissatisfied young Arabs, he felt simultaneously hopeless about the plight of the Palestinians and emboldened by the success of the mujahideen against the Soviets in Afghanistan. Despite the familial connections through his mother, Yousef's ostensibly strong identification with the Palestinian people might be viewed as somewhat curious, considering that he has never visited Palestinian areas, and most of his knowledge about their situation is second-hand. This leads one to entertain the notion that a search for the source of much of Yousef's hostility might prove more productive by examining the make-up of his personality.

While clearly intelligent and inventive, Yousef is hardly the humble type. Indeed, he displays all the signs of being a narcissist. A self-proclaimed genius, he has consistently displayed a great arrogance and sense of self-belief—for example, electing to defend himself during his first trial (wherein he was charged with capital offenses) despite lacking any legal training. His ambition has led him to contemplate attacks of enormous scale and impact, even though his resources were sometimes limited and he was being hunted by counterterrorism forces. At the same time, his supreme confidence has enabled him to maintain a calm demeanor in stressful or adverse situations. Examples of such behavior include his unhurried departure from the United States in the wake of the WTC bombing and his rapid resumption of terrorist activities after the interruption of the Bojinka plot when his computer was seized. He proved to be single-minded—such as when he continued with the plot to bomb the World Trade Center even though he had been hospitalized in a car accident in January 1993—and at times even a little foolhardy, for instance, when he continued his terrorist plots in the United States despite being aware that the Federal Bureau of Investigation was monitoring members of his cabal in New York and New Jersey in 1992–1993. At other times, however, he displayed evidence of pragmatic thinking, replying to a question about why he had sought to attack the United States rather than Israel by stating that Israeli targets were too well defended.

Another aspect of Yousef's character that greatly facilitated his terrorist activities was his ability to quickly surround himself with willing accomplices. A master manipulator, who could in turn be domineering and charming, Yousef displayed the capacity for at once attracting others to his cause and steering them toward doing his bidding.[38] Yet his apparent lack of concern for the well-being of his colleagues, as expressed by his willingness to risk or sacrifice their freedom and safety before his own,[39] ultimately proved to be his undoing, leading to his betrayal by one of his erstwhile protégés.

U.S. EFFORTS TO CAPTURE RAMZI YOUSEF

Immediately after the bombing of the World Trade Center, the FBI was able to arrest key members involved in the attack, including Muhammad Salama, Nidal Ayyad, and Ibrahim El-Gabrowny. The breakthrough in the investigation came as a result of a combination of good luck and good investigative efforts. The first break came when explosive forensics experts at the bombing site found the Vehicle Identification Number (VIN) of the truck used in the bombing. Using the VIN, the FBI was able to trace the make of the vehicle and subsequently its registration information. Further investigation revealed that the truck, a Ford Econoline, was rented by Salama, who had reported the truck stolen prior to the day of the bombing. Luckily, investigators found that Salama had visited the rental agency to recover the $400 deposit money. The rental agency, acting per the FBI's request, asked Salama to come back the next day to collect his money. After luring Salama into the trap, FBI agents arrested him as he came out of the rental agency after collecting $200 of his $400 deposit money.[40] Other members of the plot, including Yousef, Muhammad Abu Halima, Abdul Rahman Yasin, and Iyad Ismoil fled the country. Soon Abu Halima was arrested in Egypt, and in July 1995, Ismoil was arrested in Jordan. The local police in Egypt and Jordan cooperated with U.S. officials and easily identified and arrested the two suspects.[41] Yousef, on the other hand, would prove far more difficult to track and apprehend.

Following the capture and interrogation of several suspects involved in the attack, the FBI was able to determine the identity of Yousef, and by mid-March of 1993 was able to single him out as a major player in the plot.[42] The U.S. government—specifically, the Joint Terrorism Task Force (JTTF) led by the FBI—launched an international manhunt to capture Ramzi Yousef. Six agents were specifically assigned "to build up the evidence against Yousef, find him, capture him, arrange an extradition, get him back to the U.S. and secure a conviction in the U.S. court."[43] The six-member team was assisted by several investigators from the Department of State, New York City Police Department, Immigration and Naturalization Service (INS), and the Port Authority.[44] The JTTF got one of its early breaks in the hunt for Yousef when it was able to get a copy of his passport and his picture. Investigators searching through Salama's house discovered legal documents related to Ahmad Ajaj and were able to determine that Yousef arrived on the same plane with Ajaj. Since Yousef used an Iraqi passport belonging to Ramzi Ahmad Yousef, investigators were able to recover a copy of his passport submitted on arrival.[45] Based on Yousef's passport, the FBI discovered that Yousef had visited the United Kingdom several times between 1986 and 1989. The FBI therefore requested that Scotland Yard and the South Wales Police Special Branch help provide a history of Yousef's stay in that country. The FBI also contacted officials in several countries, and requested their assistance in tracing the addresses of the telephone numbers called by Yousef during his stay in the United States.[46] As the investigation began to reveal Yousef's international linkages, the FBI notified Interpol that issued an international "Red Notice," alerting all countries about Yousef. Also, on April 2, 1993, the FBI added Yousef as an eleventh member to its list of "Ten Most Wanted" fugitives.[47] In addition, the U.S. Department of State offered $2 million for any information leading to Yousef's capture, as part of its Rewards for Justice program. The reward announcement was printed on the covers of matchboxes, and they were distributed across parts of South and Central Asia.[48]

The JTTF received and followed a multitude of leads, most of which led to dead-ends. JTTF representatives visited the Baluchistan province in Pakistan several times, but were unable to achieve significant progress in the investigation there. On the Pakistani side, Rehman Malik, the Director-General of the Federal Investigation Agency (FIA), assumed supervision of the investigation. Malik, based on his investigation of Pakistani Islamists, identified Yousef's location in Quetta, Baluchistan, and sent a team of Pakistani agents and two agents from the U.S. Department of State's Diplomatic Security Service (DSS) to raid the house. Yousef, however, evaded capture and fled to Peshawar in the Northwest Frontier Province (NWFP) of Pakistan.[49] Following other leads, FIA agents, in another attempt to capture Yousef, raided the Peshawar house of Zahid al Sheikh, another of Yousef's uncles and a senior official in Mercy International, a Saudi charity for the Afghan mujahideen and Arab-Afghans. But Yousef and his uncle fled before the FIA officials raided the house.[50] While the JTTF was exploring overt options to capture Yousef and legally extradite him to the United States (or bring him back to the United States using the Rendition program),[51] the CIA also explored the possibility of covertly kidnapping Yousef and bringing him back to the United States.[52] Both efforts, however, were hampered by the lack of precise and actionable intelligence regarding Yousef's location.

So, despite such sweeping measures deployed against him, Yousef proved a difficult quarry, primarily due to the extensive nature of his network of contacts. Unlike Abu Halima or Ismoil, whose arrests were accomplished relatively easily, Yousef had numerous contacts around the world who helped him evade capture by providing him with shelter and other resources. Yousef knew veteran Arab-Afghans[53] in several countries, wealthy bankers from the Gulf countries, several sectarian militants within Pakistan, Afghan mujahideen leaders, and several recruits in Southeast Asia.[54] In fact, Yousef seemed unfazed by the efforts to capture him, and (as described earlier) even planned and carried out several attacks while on the run. As part of the investigation of the WTC bombing, the FBI found several numbers called by Yousef during his stay in the

United States, and created a database of telephone numbers that was used as late as 1998 to help track terrorists worldwide.[55] Factors that impeded the FBI's efforts to capture Yousef included a lack of human intelligence agents within the rapidly proliferating Islamist cells worldwide, a lack of strategic focus on the threat of religiously inspired terrorism, and a period of uneasy United States–Pakistan relationship as a result of Pakistan's nuclear weapons program, as well as Pakistan's displeasure with the sudden U.S. withdrawal of support to Afghanistan following the departure of Soviet troops.

Ultimately, Yousef's arrest came as the result of a lucky break, but one that was precipitated by Yousef's own arrogance and domineering demeanor. Yousef had recruited Ishtiaque Parker, a South African Muslim, to assist him in his operations. In one such attempt, Yousef involved Parker in a plot to kidnap the Philippine Ambassador to Thailand to secure Abdul Hakim Murad's release. In another plot, Yousef asked Parker to deliver suitcases packed with explosives on airplanes departing from Bangkok, Thailand, so that they would explode over U.S. cities. Parker failed to execute this mission due to heightened security measures that were implemented after the discovery of the Bojinka plot. After these plots failed, Yousef called Parker back to Pakistan and involved him in another attempt to kidnap the Philippine Ambassador to Pakistan, following which he planned to exchange the Ambassador for Murad. Yousef also ordered Parker to assist him in another plot to bomb a Shiite shrine in Islamabad, Pakistan.[56] Parker panicked, and on February 3, 1995, informed the U.S. Embassy in Pakistan that he wished to provide U.S. authorities with information on Yousef. Parker's decision to turn in Yousef was also partly based on his revulsion at Yousef's attempts to kill innocent people in his plots.[57]

Initially, DSS Agents Jeff Riner and Bill Miller interrogated Parker and became convinced that he was telling the truth. The agents informed Regional Security Officer Art Maurel, who then informed the Department of State about the new informant. The Department of State in turn passed the information to John Lipka, the Special Agent responsible for coordinating overseas liaisons in Yousef's case at FBI's Counterterrorism Section. John Lipka informed Neil Herman about the informant and a decision was made to utilize Parker to locate Yousef. On February 6, 1995, Parker informed his handlers that Yousef was in Islamabad and was planning to leave soon for Peshawar. An impromptu snatch team was hastily formed at the U.S. Embassy, and Art Maurel sought assistance from Pakistan's security agencies to capture Yousef. On February 7, officials from the U.S. Embassy and seven heavily armed Pakistani security officials, tipped off by Parker, apprehended Yousef at the Su-Case guesthouse in Islamabad's F7/2 sector. Yousef was identified by Agent Riner and was taken to the airport, where a JTTF team from the United States was waiting to take him back to the United States. Parker received $2 million for the information that led to the capture of Ramzi Yousef.[58]

SUCCESS AND FAILURE

Clearly, the capture of Ramzi Yousef was a significant victory for the JTTF. The long and intense manhunt provided a wealth of information on Yousef and several other terror operatives who were linked to him. At the beginning of the investigation, after realizing the extent of Yousef's connections, the JTTF forged overseas alliances to assist in the international manhunt. Similarly, FBI's Legal Attaché (Legat) in Bangkok, Thailand, proved to be quite useful for gaining the assistance of Asian security services in tracking Yousef. Another counterterrorism tool that played a role in successfully capturing Yousef was the Rewards for Justice Program. Even though Parker was not solely motivated by the reward, the $2 million prize certainly influenced his decision to turn Yousef in.

The manhunt, however, revealed at least two glaring absences in U.S. counterterrorism efforts. First, and foremost, the United States did not possess agents within the support milieus that helped Yousef evade capture and plan subsequent terror attacks. The CIA was unable to provide actionable intelligence on Yousef to facilitate his capture. The FBI's Legal Attaché scheme, though commendable, was severely understaffed. For example, the Legal Attaché for Pakistan was based in Bangkok, where he was responsible for several other countries.[59] Second, despite the international search operation, Yousef still managed to travel to several countries in Asia using false passports. The relative ease with which Yousef traveled across Asia, especially Southeast Asia, reveals the lack of coordination in circulating terrorism watch lists among countries.

LESSONS FOR COUNTERTERRORISM

Yousef's activities and the corresponding manhunt offer several important lessons that can be applied to current and future counterterrorism efforts. To a certain extent, the planning and execution of the WTC bombing by Ramzi Yousef and his associates can be likened to the threat posed by self-radicalized cells that are inspired by al Qaeda's ideology, which conceivably makes any lessons particularly relevant in present day circumstances.

First, the search for Yousef revealed the difficulty of tracking and apprehending terrorists ensconced in widespread clandestine networks that cross several national borders. Although Yousef was a relatively independent terrorist "entrepreneur," he received support from a sizable logistical network that was largely unknown to investigators. Reliance on such a large logistical network is a double-edged sword, since it also provides opportunities for investigators to track an individual.

Second, the United States—in order to elicit better international cooperation—must make other countries aware of the transnational nature of the terrorist threat and the risks associated with inaction in disrupting terrorist cells and operatives operating within their borders. Understandably, countries that have been directly targeted by terrorists have generally shown much greater interest in capturing or killing terrorists. However, other countries that have not been attacked by terrorists must be equally involved in counterterrorism efforts, since terrorists might be using those countries for raising funds, propaganda, and recruiting members; moreover, the absence or near absence of terrorist attacks in a country's past is not an assurance that it will never occur in the future.

Third, the security agencies, working closely with the media, researchers, and the public should develop mechanisms to ensure the functioning of an open society, while making sure that certain types of information that can be misused by terrorists are properly protected. For instance, Yousef told his captors that he learned from a CNN special report about airport screening techniques, information that he used for the Bojinka plot, including details that enabled him to devise methods to transport explosives and batteries undetected through the screening machines.[60]

Fourth, in instances of search operations, the rewards for providing information should be widely publicized in the relevant communities. In addition to financial rewards, security incentives should also be announced and widely publicized.

Fifth, Yousef was an extremely determined and innovative adversary—neither the presence of his wife and children in Pakistan, nor the fact that there was a massive counterterrorist effort arrayed against him had much effect on his willingness to plan and launch further attacks. In this case, at least, law enforcement efforts may have complicated the terrorist's operations, but did not do much to prevent further attacks by such a dedicated opponent.

Sixth, the case of Yousef indicates that even where the primary suspect is intelligent and a consummate professional, there can still be interdiction opportunities provided by less competent accomplices. While Yousef was generally extremely careful in his operations, the incompetence of cohorts like Salama or the driver of the truck in the Bangkok plot can provide law enforcement and intelligence with tangible early warning indicators, if these sometimes weak signals are detected against the pervasive background noise. Furthermore, even the very professionalism that makes a particular terrorist like Yousef so difficult to apprehend can provide distinct signals. For example, Yousef was meticulous about testing his devices and conducting dry runs, which might have provided indicators of his activities, were counterterrorism officials paying sufficiently close attention.

Last, but not least, the case of Ramzi Yousef highlights the inevitable role played by luck in counterterrorism operations, and confirms the dictum that in the long run, fortune falls equally on all sides. On the one hand, Yousef repeatedly benefited from good luck, such as when he succeeded in passing through U.S. customs while his companion Ajaj did not, or when he escaped several accidents relatively unscathed. At the same time, counterterrorism officials benefited from the coincident good fortune of identifying the van used in the WTC bombing and Salama's return to the rental company, as well as the Manila apartment fire that scuttled the Bojinka plot, and Ishtiaque Parker's decision to turn in Yousef.

CONCLUSION

In many respects, Ramzi Yousef was unique, an outlier, a terrorist with the independence of action, the ambition and the charisma of Carlos the Jackal, combined with an all-consuming hatred and desire to cause mass fatalities. In this light, one must draw any lessons from his exploits and capture with some degree of caution. However, in other ways, Yousef served as the harbinger of certain novel aspects of terrorism that counterterrorism officials would increasingly have to deal with at the beginning of the twenty-first century. His lust for revenge on a large scale would become the norm amongst the strain of jihadist terrorism most prominently represented by al Qaeda, while the diffuse, transnational nature of his support network and multinational contacts would continue to hamper counterterrorist efforts when these were used on a larger scale by groups like al Qaeda. Thus, while differing somewhat from the typical religious fanatic, Yousef displayed many of the operational characteristics that would come to be successfully employed by a generation of violent jihadists, especially self-starting terrorist entrepreneurs. This makes a careful study of his strengths and weaknesses—as well as the successes and failures of the counterterrorist effort against him—particularly instructive, as counterterrorism forces struggle to find answers to the multitude of current terrorist threats.

NOTES

1. See Dwyer et al. describing the moniker applied to Yousef by the Federal Bureau of Investigation—Jim Dwyer, David Kocieniewski, Deidre Murphy, and Peg Tyre, *Two Seconds Under the World* (New York: Ballantine Books, 1994) 76.

2. Simon Reeve, *The New Jackals: Ramzi Yousef, Osama bin Laden and the Future of Terrorism* (Boston, MA: Northeastern University, 1999) 254.

3. The obscurity surrounding Yousef's identity has led to a host of alternative, if tenuous, theories about his origins, including that he was an Iraqi intelligence

and inadequate preparation used in the attempt on the USS *The Sullivans*, the group was most likely an affiliate that ventured out on its own without strong support from al Qaeda.

For years, al Qaeda has recognized the potential of Yemen in both recruiting operatives and for staging operations. According to one estimate, Yemenis are the third largest national group represented in al Qaeda.[7] However, Ambassador Bodine notes that although Yemenis are numerous in al Qaeda, they rarely assume leading roles in the operations. Yemen's connection to al Qaeda stems, in part, from its relationship to the jihad in Afghanistan. During the 1980s, jihadists from Yemen joined the mujahideen's struggle in Afghanistan against Soviet occupation.[8] Numerous Yemenis volunteered to fight, and analysts contend that it was in Afghanistan that Yemenis and others formed the embryonic al Qaeda movement. Osama bin Laden's father was born in Yemen, and this historical tie may have inspired bin Laden to contact Yemenis who fought in Afghanistan, in order to plan and execute attacks against Western targets. In 1992, bin Laden provided Tariq al Fadhi with financial support to bomb the Gold Mahur Hotel in Aden, with the intention of killing U.S. military personnel serving in Somalia.[9]

According to some reports, after the Soviet withdrawal from Afghanistan in 1989, returning jihadists—both Yemeni and Arab Afghans—were incorporated into Yemeni President Ali Abdullah Saleh's security apparatus.[10] The rationale behind this action was to employ them, give them a stake in the status quo, and retain the ability to surveil them.[11] Yemeni jihadis were enlisted to fight against the rebel south during the 1994 civil war. Some jihadis joined the conservative Salafi movement that espoused a literal interpretation and application of Islamic law. The Salafis in Yemen have particularly strong ties with Saudi Arabia due to their similar beliefs. A very small element of these Yemeni jihadis formed the Islamic Army of Aden (IAA), also known as the Aden-Abyan Islamic Army (AAIA), and was responsible for several bombings in Yemen as well as the 1998 kidnapping of 16 tourists.[12] The group also utilized training camps in Yemen.[13] In 1997, Yemeni sheikhs met with al Qaeda operatives, and supposedly bin Laden considered transferring his base of operations to his ancestral homeland.[14] After Yemen's government captured and executed the group's leader, Zein al-Abidine al-Midhar in October 1999, the organization's appeal diminished; however, the IAA, along with two previously unknown offshoot groups—Muhammad's Army and the Islamic Deterrence Forces—later claimed responsibility for the *Cole* bombing.

One other reason that Yemen appeals to al Qaeda as a base of operations is related to its interconnection with Saudi Arabia and the kingdom's influence on Yemen's education system. During the oil boom of the 1970s, many Yemenis found work in Saudi Arabia's oil and construction industries, and when they returned home they brought with them Salafi teachings. Islamic schools in Yemen began to teach this more radical version of Islam.[15]

A result of Yemen's decentralized government structure that clearly appealed to al Qaeda was the almost unimpeded stream of weapons into the state. Investigators have traced weapons used in attacks against Western interests in Saudi Arabia to Yemen.[16] Due to the years of internal warfare and ensuing chaos in Yemen between 1967 and 1994, significant numbers of weapons entered the country. According to some estimates, there are three weapons for every one person in Yemen.[17]

Part of Yemen's appeal for terrorists is its forbidding geography and the tribal networks that have frequently shielded al Qaeda operatives. When al Qaeda militants fled Afghanistan after the U.S. attack on the Taliban in October 2001, many sought refuge in Yemen.[18] Although bin Laden's historical ties to Yemen partially explain why Yemenis play a large role in al Qaeda, another account holds that bin Laden is able to provide financial incentives to tribal leaders in order to secure their support of al Qaeda operatives in the country. Some tribes that shield al Qaeda members resist the authority of the government in Sanaa. They prefer to remain independent from a central authority and keep Sanaa's control out of the tribal regions. According to Mark Katz, many tribal leaders are motivated more by mercenary concerns than ideological ones when it comes to supporting al Qaeda.[19] Katz contends that some tribes support al Qaeda in order to pressure Sanaa to counter al Qaeda's influence by providing resources to their tribes as well.[20]

Al Qaeda has frequently used Yemen as a base of operations or as a point of transit in its war against the West. Investigators have linked the 1998 East Africa embassy bombings with both the *Cole* bombings and the attacks of September 11, 2001. During a meeting between U.S. President Bill Clinton and Yemeni President Saleh in April 2000, terrorism was high on the list of topics, with President Saleh requesting enhanced support from the United States to counter foreign jihadis.[21] Several members of the group that conducted the East Africa embassy bombings made lengthy visits to Yemen—including Muhammad Reshed Daoud al-Ahwali, who was a passenger in the truck delivering the bomb to the U.S. embassy in Nairobi, Kenya, on August 7, 1998.[22] Some members of the embassy bombing cell also held false Yemeni passports and had spent time in Yemen.[23]

THE *COLE* BOMBING

U.S. naval commanders are required to file force protection plans detailing the security measures being undertaken to secure the vessel while refueling or making port calls. The *Cole*'s plan was approved at high levels in the government and the ship was placed at threat condition Bravo (the second lowest level of four).[24] However, some reports indicate that the United States had received a warning of a terrorist threat 12 hours prior to the *Cole* bombing. According to Walter Slocombe, then Undersecretary of Defense for Policy, the warning was not specific enough for the military to take appropriate action.[25] A day after the *Cole* bombing, a defense intelligence agency analyst resigned, citing that his warnings of terrorist plots against U.S. targets in the Middle East went unheeded.[26]

Despite the failure by terrorists in Yemen to bomb the USS *The Sullivans*, the idea of conducting a maritime attack clearly appealed to al Qaeda operatives. Reportedly, a suspect later arrested for participation in the *Cole* bombing set the idea in motion to use boat bombs as early as 1996. Abd al Rahim al Nashiri allegedly received approval from bin Laden in 1998 to prepare for a maritime assault in Yemen.[27] On the morning of October 12, 2000, as the *Cole* was refueling, a small boat approached the ship. According to witnesses, two men on the small boat stood up, waved or saluted, and then detonated their explosives, leaving 17 sailors dead and inflicting $250 million worth of damage on the destroyer.

THE INVESTIGATION

From previous al Qaeda operations, it is clear that the terror network was meticulous in its planning process, and thus expectedly sent advance teams to gather intelligence for the *Cole* operation. In Yemen, expatriates with ties to al Qaeda returned to their country of origin in order to recruit operatives for the *Cole* operation. According to a Rand study, the terrorist cell that conducted the *Cole* operation was comprised of 16 members, 11 of whom were Yemeni.[28] Yet as the RAND study concludes, the impetus for the attack did not appear to come from local militants, though several were used for logistics inside Yemen.[29] The *Cole* plot was part of a global network of terror operations that had been implemented over the past several years against Western targets.

Investigators have determined that local Yemeni groups did not have the level of technological sophistication that was evident in the *Cole* attack. Therefore, early into the investigation, terrorism experts concluded that al Qaeda directed the operation. Furthermore, the technology and long-term planning bore the fingerprints of bin Laden. The bombers used a shaped explosive charge, a clear indication of increasing sophistication.[30] Some reports claimed that Osama bin Laden used expert bombers from the Shia Lebanese group Hizbollah to build the huge bomb that incapacitated the *Cole*.[31]

A day after the *Cole* bombing, seven U.S. planes landed in Aden's airport carrying representatives from numerous U.S. government agencies charged with a variety of missions. Under the direction of the Ambassador and the Embassy, based on instructions from the Secretary of State, the missions were: recover the ship and her crew, provide force protection, establish a joint investigation with the Yemenis, and maintain a strong bilateral relationship with the Yemeni government.[32] Included among the groups was the Foreign Emergency Support Team (FEST)—a rapid response, interagency group that is deployed when U.S. interests abroad have been attacked.[33] From its base in Aden, the team, led by a senior Department of State officer with Yemen experience, supported the Ambassador and members of her staff now working from Aden with communications equipment, interagency liaison staff, and crisis management expertise.[34]

Two agents from the FBI's Washington Field Office had established a working relationship with Yemeni investigators in the aftermath of the 1998 Mudiyah kidnappings. These agents immediately deployed to Aden along with legal attachés assigned to a number of U.S. embassies in the region. The Navy Criminal Investigative Services (NCIS), which also had a preexisting relationship with the Yemenis, deployed a small, language-competent team to Aden. FBI Head Advisory Agent John O'Neill arrived in Aden several days after the bombing and stated that he intended to deploy 150 agents to Aden. The Ambassador countered that there was only room for 50 agents at that time and suggested that the remaining agents could be staged out of Cairo until there was a clearer delineation of investigative requirements. Despite this decision, O'Neill brought the entire 150 agents into the country and sent away all regionally based legal attachés and Washington Field Office agents who had already established working relationships with the Yemeni government.[35]

According to several American investigators, some Yemeni authorities in Aden—in contravention of their government's stated policy—were uncooperative and refused to allow FBI investigators to directly interview alleged suspects in the *Cole* bombing.[36] Initially, Brigadier General Mohammad Ali Ibraheem, the commander of the naval base at Aden, claimed that the explosion came from inside the ship and did not appear deliberate.[37] The day after the explosion, however, at the request of the U.S. Ambassador, President Saleh sent his own ranking military advisor and a team of experts to the ship, who determined that the attack on the ship was clearly terrorism.[38] A week after the explosion, President Saleh publicly referred to the bombing as an act of terrorism.[39]

One crucial problem in the investigation was that the FBI decided to rotate their senior advisory agent every 30 days, hindering the development of effective continuity in the relationships among U.S. agencies and between the FBI and the Yemenis. The FBI did not develop an efficient handover from one agent to the next, leaving some agents with only a minimal grasp of the situation. Many of the agents lacked a background in counterterrorism, further impeding progress in the investigation. Although several agents were qualified for the position, many came with the attitude that they would get through their 30-day deployment and return to their "real job."[40] This attitude filtered down to other agents, and was also recognized by the Yemenis.

In November, because of difficulties between senior members of the FBI and local Yemeni investigators, Ambassador Bodine—along with the new senior supervisory agent, Patrick Paterson, and a senior Yemeni judge—negotiated and concluded a memorandum of agreement setting the terms and parameters for both Yemeni and American investigators. Although this was a significant step in fostering a better working relationship between the FBI and Yemeni investigators, some agents remained dissatisfied with their inability to question suspects directly, a situation that was ameliorated when the FBI sent agents who were native Arabic speakers to work with the Yemenis.[41]

Some agents from the New York Field Office alleged that the Aden investigators impeded the investigation in order to sanitize records and conceal senior Yemeni officials' involvement in the plot.[42] The allegation that government personnel were somehow implicated in the attack stemmed from the previously mentioned fact that during the 1980s numerous volunteers from Yemen joined jihadists in Afghanistan to battle the Soviet occupation.[43] Clearly, there is an undisputable connection between the government and jihadist fighters, but not necessarily between the government and those involved in the *Cole* attack. During the USS *Cole* investigation, FBI Director Louis Freeh insisted upon a broad investigation that he asserted had the potential to lead to powerful officials in the President Saleh's government.[44]

The investigation into the *Cole* bombing was initially hampered by several key factors that Ambassador Bodine describes as "some inevitable, some avoidable and some unacceptable."[45] The inevitable factors included the resentment that any law enforcement perceives toward an outside entity arriving to investigate an event that took place within their jurisdiction. The resentment was amplified by Yemen's extremely unsophisticated investigative services, lacking even fingerprint powder to process crime scenes colliding with a state-of-the-art service such as the FBI. As Ambassador Bodine succinctly put it, "coming from two different planets couldn't have been more of a shock to both sides."[46] In terms of avoidable issues, the Ambassador had requested in a meeting with Director Freeh a legal attaché at the embassy months earlier, in order to increase ties with the Yemenis. Additionally, the Ambassador believed that the U.S. Navy could have stationed a representative full-time in Aden to manage the refueling program. The creation of networks and interrelationships could have facilitated the investigation during its early phases. Furthermore, Ambassador Bodine had advocated the reopening of the consulate in Aden, which would have increased networks with Adeni officials.

Information on the *Cole* bombing was difficult to obtain due, in part, to the reluctance of Yemeni officials to share intelligence with American investigators and the unwillingness of the FBI to share the results of their forensic work with the Yemenis. For Ambassador Bodine, the manner in which some senior agents handled the investigation was unacceptable, and led to some of the Yemeni reluctance to share information. She recounts that the Yemenis up to and including the President "had long advocated a more robust and formal cooperative relationship on counterterrorism and were rebuffed by the United States on a number of occasions."[47] From her perspective, the Yemenis were interested in cooperating with the U.S. investigation, but the FBI's heavy-handed and culturally insensitive approach threatened to derail the investigation—in fact, she notes, President Saleh and members of his cabinet, military, and investigative services made it very clear to his government that they would work with the Americans.[48] Yemeni officials agreed that the FBI's arrogant and culturally insensitive style hampered cooperation from the outset.[49] In fact, Ambassador Bodine denied a request for John O'Neill's return in January 2001.

There are, however, several other explanations as to why the Yemenis appeared or were reluctant to cooperate with U.S. investigators. Some members of the Yemeni security services did not like the Americans and were "probably sympathetic to the jihadi worldview, even if not supportive of their tactics."[50] Other Yemeni officials, although ambivalent about their feelings toward the United States, supported a solid relationship with the United States. When the FBI arrived with their culturally insensitive attitude, those ambivalent Yemenis were put in an awkward and embarrassing position.

Additionally, cultural misunderstandings led the FBI to perceive the Yemenis as uncooperative. For example, occasionally, when the FBI Americans asked the Yemenis for particular evidence, the Yemenis had no idea why they needed it. For example, since DNA testing is a foreign concept in a poverty-stricken developing country such as Yemen, a request for collecting fiber or hair samples was inexplicable to the Yemenis. Ambassador Bodine reiterated to her investigators that if they could explain to her why they needed particular evidence and she understood its purpose, she would then relay the significance of the request to the appropriate Yemeni official.[51]

Moreover, the issue of "pure pride" emerged as a factor in Yemen's occasional reluctance to work with the Americans. For example, Yemenis were embarrassed when the FBI requested their passport or immigration records. They had no computer records; it was all piles of handwritten paper. Thus, in some cases, Yemeni officials—in an effort to defer humiliation—dragged their feet. Ambassador Bodine worked directly with the FBI to clarify, on a case-by-case basis, whether the Yemenis were unaccommodating because they did not have the evidence requested, because they did not understand the request due to "bureaucratic incompetence," or because they were actually being obstructionist. The distinction among these is significant, as it reflects the intent of the Yemenis.[52]

One other impediment to the investigation concerned the relationship among American agencies. Organizational cultural clashes between the FBI and the Central Intelligence Agency (CIA) are legendary, and these battles were played out in the *Cole* case as well. The CIA and FBI not only "put up firewalls, but they suffered from low-intensity warfare."[53] As the agencies retained different mandates, they guarded their intelligence. The FBI's key concern is to acquire evidence that they can use to prosecute the perpetrators of the attack. For the CIA, the crucial nature of the intelligence is to prevent another attack. In one instance, Ambassador Bodine and an FBI agent paid a visit to a Yemeni official to request a particular piece of information. When they made the inquiry, the Yemeni official revealed that he had already given the information to the Americans. When the Ambassador requested clarification as to whom the information had been given, it was revealed that her CIA station chief had received the data but did not share it with the FBI.[54]

In June 2001, the FBI announced that it had identified credible threats against its agents, and decided to remove its remaining agents from Yemen. Much to the dismay of the Department of State and the other agencies resident at the American Embassy in Sanaa, the FBI refused to share its threat intelligence with anyone "despite its legal and moral obligation to do so."[55] Ambassador Bodine asserted that since an attack would not differentiate between various players, all Americans were potentially in danger. The CIA, on the other hand, did not find evidence of any particular threat against the FBI and was rebuffed when the agency requested to see on what evidence the FBI based its position. Therefore, there was no draw down of embassy personnel or their dependents. Senior officials involved in the interagency process were also not convinced that the FBI had to leave in June. At the very least, members of the interagency believed that the FBI should have left a core group of language-qualified agents behind to continue the investigation. But despite ongoing interagency discussions, "the FBI unilaterally and without notice" removed its agents in the middle of June, taking a reluctant NCIS with them.[56] Ambassador Bodine believed that 3 months of work were lost, although she continued to pursue the investigation with the CIA station chief and others in the embassy.[57]

Following the attacks, the Yemeni government quickly rounded up several low-level suspects including Fahd al Quso and Jamal al Badawi. Badawi is alleged to have rented safe houses in Aden and to have brought the boat from Saudi Arabia that was used in the attack. Al Quso was supposed to film the attack, presumably to be used for recruitment and motivation, though the tape was never recovered.[58] Some Yemenis were interested in closing the case quickly by trying the six Yemenis that they had in custody.[59] Ambassador Bodine disputes this and explained that the Yemenis were interested in a full investigation to prove that the attack was a Saudi, not Yemeni-based attack. The Ambassador, working with President Saleh, assured that the suspects' trials would be delayed as long as possible to allow the investigation to continue. U.S. officials wanted to complete additional investigations and connect the suspects to al Qaeda. FBI officials were concerned that the Yemeni legal system would quickly try the suspects and execute them before all the evidence was collected. Ambassador Bodine explained to the investigators that the Yemeni legal system did not work that way and that "the possibility of summary justice in the Saudi style was remote, if not impossible."[60]

In November 2000, al Quso told investigators about his dealings with a man named Khallid. He said that he traveled to Bangkok in January 2000 with one of the *Cole* suicide bombers, Ibrahim al Thawwar, and met Khallid, bringing him $36,000 in cash.[61] Both the CIA and FBI were familiar with Khallid, also known as Tawfiq Attash Khallad, since they had tracked him prior to the *Cole* bombing. According to U.S. officials, Khallad met with two of the eventual September 11 hijackers, Khalid al-Midhar and Nawaf al-Hazmi in Kuala Lumpur in January 2000.[62] This meeting was crucial in that it linked the *Cole* bombing with the September 11 plot, but this interconnection was not unearthed until after the attacks on the United States in 2001. After the *Cole* bombing, the FBI connected Khallid to that plot, asserting that he delivered a letter to the suicide bombers approving the assault on the ship. It was only after the *Cole* bombing that the CIA and FBI reassessed the dangerous threat posed by al Midhar and al Hazmi. By the time they were put on a terrorism watch list in August 2001, both men were already residing in the United States.[63]

Eventually, the United States also gathered information about the *Cole* bombing from al Qaeda prisoners captured in Afghanistan after the U.S. invasion in October 2001.[64] In September 2002, Pakistani officials arrested nine Yemenis including Ramzi bin al Shibh, who was a high-level planner in the September 11 attacks and was implicated in planning the *Cole* bombing. In November 2002, the United States—with the reticent acquiescence of the Yemeni government—assassinated Qaed Salim Sunian al-Harethi, one of the *Cole* attack's planners, using an unmanned U.S. predator drone.[65] At the end of April 2003, Pakistani officials arrested Khallad in the port city of Karachi, along with a cache of weapons and explosives.[66] Information collected in Afghanistan also led to the capture of Muhammad Hamdi al Ahdal, who was a known member of al Qaeda and was responsible for finances and operational planning for the *Cole* bombing as well as a subsequent attack in Yemen's Gulf of Hadhamut on a French ship, the *Limburg*.[67] In November 2003, Yemeni forces arrested al Ahdal outside of the capital city of Sanaa. According to Yemeni sources, al Ahdal was one of Osama bin Laden's key al Qaeda leaders in Yemen.[68] Undoubtedly, progress on capturing some key players in the *Cole* operation was advancing.

COUNTERTERRORISM AND LESSONS LEARNED

Aside from developing strong bilateral relationships with host nations in order to fulfill a variety of political, economic, and security purposes, resilient bilateral relationships are a crucial element in fostering effective counterterrorism links. In the late 1990s, under the direction of Ambassador Barbara Bodine, Yemen and America renewed their relationship in earnest and increased their ties in several important realms. In 1998, the United States began a modest, yet active police-training program carried out by the Department of State's Diplomatic Security Service, which included activities such as rudimentary crime scene collection and processing.[69] To further strengthen ties with Yemen, also in 1998, the United States implemented a program to remove landmines that littered Yemen as a result of conflicts spanning 30 years. Instead of bringing in a private company to remove landmines, the United States opted to assist the Yemenis in creating an indigenous capacity to do this work. Eventually, the Yemenis were able to train their own demining force.[70]

As part of the demining program, the U.S. Embassy signed a mass casualty agreement with a hospital in Aden. When the *Cole* was hit, the Yemeni deminers used the fleet of vehicles supplied by the United States to evacuate the wounded to the regional hospital. The preexisting mass casualty agreement—although anticipating an operation different than the one resulting from the *Cole* bombing—provided an important service for the United States and strengthened the goodwill and friendship between the two countries.[71]

Following the attacks in New York and Washington on September 11, Yemeni President Saleh's resolve to cooperate with the United States increased. Some analysts suspect that Yemen feared it would become a target in the global war on terror. Clearly President George W. Bush's statement that "you are either with us or against us" resonated sharply in Sanaa.[72] The Yemeni government, however, had been improving its counterterrorism capabilities prior to the attacks on the United States—for example, Yemen's police academy graduated its first class of antiterrorist police in September 2001.[73]

During President Saleh's November 2001 visit to the United States, President Bush discussed aid packages for Yemen along with Special Forces training. Additionally, the leaders discussed U.S. assistance in helping Yemen receive International Monetary Fund loans.[74] When President Saleh declared his intention to cooperate more fully with the United States in the war on terror, teams from the 5th Special Forces Group were sent to train Yemenis in counterterrorism.[75]

President Saleh supported increased collaboration with the West in order to deter terrorists from using Yemen as a base for their operations. The suicide attack against the *Limburg* in October 2002 was costly for the Yemenis, both in terms of the environmental effects of the oil spill caused by the attack and in the loss of potential trade and investment. As such, when pressure from the United States to join the West in the global war on terror intensified, President Saleh implemented several steps to counter terrorism in Yemen. He increased cooperation with the British and American Special Forces, monitored mosques, and broadened a program dating to 1997 to deport suspected terrorists.[76] Additionally, Yemen—with assistance from the United States and others—improved its surveillance of those entering Yemen from both Afghanistan and Pakistan, which provided increased intelligence on potential terrorists. Many visitors from those countries were interrogated more intensely than they had been in the past. When people requested visas in Pakistan, consular officials allowed them to complete the paperwork, then denied their visas and shared the information with American intelligence agencies.[77]

Another effort by President Saleh's government to fight terrorism and violence has been the implementation of a plan to buy back weapons from the population; however, cultural constraints have hampered the effort.[78] Yemeni men wear the traditional curved Yemeni dagger, but this tradition fosters Western misperceptions of Yemeni extremism. Additionally, in October 2003, President Saleh implemented a controversial counterterrorism program granting amnesty to low-level militants despite their suspected links to al Qaeda.[79] President Saleh was under pressure from human rights organizations for Yemen's treatment of detainees, and Amnesty International accused the Yemeni government of torturing prisoners. In November 2003, 96 prisoners who had "repented" to an Islamic cleric were released, although they continued to be closely monitored by the government.[80] This program has caused some American officials concern, although the State Department does not believe that any suspects with direct links to terrorist attacks in Yemen have been released.[81]

Although Yemeni officials have been more aggressive in their hunt for al Qaeda operatives within Yemen, questions continue to arise as to the Yemeni government's dedication to this pursuit. In April 2003, ten suspects in the *Cole* bombing escaped from prison in Yemen, including Badawi, who was subsequently recaptured. Further, in February 2006, 23 al Qaeda operatives—13 of whom had been convicted in the USS *Cole* bombing—tunneled their way out of their cells in Sanaa. Some analysts contend that without assistance from high-ranking Yemeni officials, escapes of these magnitudes would have been virtually impossible.[82] As mentioned previously, some fighters who returned from

Afghanistan were employed by the security services, thereby enhancing the plausibility of the explanation that the escapees received inside assistance. In fact, in May 2006, 12 military officers were tried in Yemen for negligence that led to the escape of prisoners in February.[83]

Despite some key obstacles and some skepticism as to the reliability of the Yemenis, the United States worked with Yemen to establish an elite Counterterrorism Unit in 2002 and continues to provide support in that operation. Additionally, in another security cooperation program that predated the attack on the *Cole,* the United States assisted Yemen in the creation of a Coast Guard to patrol its long and treacherous coastline. Situated across the Gulf of Aden from the unstable states of Sudan, Somalia, Eritrea, Ethiopia, and Djibouti, the waters here are some of the most dangerous in the world.[84] Yet the growing problem of corruption in Yemen has led donors to cut aid programs, an essential component in funding counterterrorism operations.[85]

The investigation into the *Cole* bombing led Ambassador Bodine to several conclusions that impacted the ability of the United States to carry out effective investigations in the future. First, she is adamant that U.S. agencies need to "work with, not in spite of, the host government."[86] The United States cannot enter a country and expect to transform or ignore the host government, especially one with a 4,000-year history. American investigators need to work within a particular cultural milieu and act in a respectful manner. Second, investigators must recognize not only that the ambassador is the senior U.S. government representative in the country and technically in charge of any investigation, but also that embassy personnel have "well-honed tools" for both collaboration and cooperation. The embassy role is to facilitate the investigators' ability to do their job, utilizing its cultural knowledge and established networks. Implementing tactics that are effective in the United States might not yield positive results overseas. According to Ambassador Bodine, the FBI "never asked, but always demanded" during their investigation into the attack on the *Cole.*[87] Third, constant rotation of the FBI senior advisory agent seriously hampered the continuity and effectiveness of the investigation. This problem has since been corrected with the establishment of a permanent legal attaché office in Sanaa.

Some other key lessons learned relate to maritime force protection and a reassessment of security measures. In a U.S. Department of the Navy report released on January 19, 2001, it was found that many procedures in the ship's security plan were not followed.[88] Although one cannot say with certainty whether or not different measures might have prevented the *Cole* attack, the Navy has implemented new guidelines for protecting its vessels. The Navy has recognized that bolstered security measures are required in a region as volatile as the Middle East, and has revamped its antiterrorist and force protection plans accordingly. The Navy is also updating its technology and access to intelligence, along with enhancing its use of the NCIS agents in ports to give the commanding officers intelligence assessments.[89]

CONCLUSION

The investigation into the bombing of the USS *Cole* indicated clear shortcomings on a variety of levels. First, agencies within the United States must work together to increase the effectiveness of the investigations. Issues regarding intelligence sharing between agencies such as the CIA and FBI have been addressed in earnest since September 11, and progress has been made. Second, the United States must recognize the indigenous capability of a host nation, such as Yemen, and capitalize on those areas where the host nation retains a clear advantage over American investigators. Despite the fact that Yemeni officials initially would not allow U.S. agents to interview suspects, the host nation has the distinct advantage in human intelligence.[90] Clearly, had a mutually beneficial joint investigation occurred initially, with each group exploiting its comparative advantage—U.S. technology and Yemeni human intelligence—more expedient progress could have been made. Third, the U.S. government must grasp the flexible and ever-changing tactics utilized by al Qaeda. Finally, although it is nearly impossible to anticipate new modes of attacks, the government must remain forward thinking and vigilant.

NOTES

1. Christopher Cooper and Neil King, Jr., "Why Was the U.S. in Yemen Anyway: Some think Washington Planned Staging Area for Regional Crises," *Wall Street Journal*, October 27, 2000: A.15.

2. "Terrorism against the USS *Cole* and the Context in Yemen," Policy Watch #499, The Washington Institute for Near East Policy, http://www.washingtoninstitute.org (accessed June 15, 2006).

3. Ibid.

4. Ambassador Barbara Bodine, phone interview with author, June 26, 2006.

5. Cooper and King: p. A.15.

6. Bodine, phone interview.

7. Jonathan Schanzer, "Yemen's War on Terror," *Orbis* (Summer 2004): 522.

8. Michael Knights, "Internal Politics Complicate Counterterrorism in Yemen," *Jane's Intelligence Review* (February 1, 2006), http://www4.janes.com (accessed June 7, 2006).

9. Schanzer: p. 522; see also, Knights.

10. Knights, Arab Afghans refer to those non-Yemeni Arabs who trained with Islamic militant groups in Afghanistan. Yemeni Jihadis refer to those Yemenis who fought in Afghanistan.

11. Bodine, e-mail correspondence with author, July 6, 2006.

12. Jillian Schwedler, "Yemen's Aborted Opening," *Journal of Democracy* 13, no. 4 (October 2002): 53.

13. According to Ambassador Bodine, the instigator of the AAIA was a British cleric, Abu Hamza al-Misri, who financed the group and established the first team made up of his Egyptian and Pakistani relatives and not Yemenis. Additionally, training camps existed in Yemen since the time of the Marxist People's Democratic Republic of Yemen.

14. Schanzer: p. 522.

15. Kim Cragin and Scott Gerwehr, *Dissuading Terror: Strategic Influence and the Struggle against Terror* (Santa Monica, CA: RAND Corporation, 2005) 44, http://www.rand.org. Ambassador Bodine vehemently disagrees with the idea that the Yemenis returned home and fostered Salafi teachings. She argues that the Yemenis dislike most aspects of the Saudis. For Ambassador Bodine, Yemen's appeal to terrorist groups remains in its large and young population along with its rugged and uncontrolled territory. Bodine, e-mail correspondence.

16. Knights.

17. James Brandon, "Yemen Attempts to Rein in Outlaw Tribes," *Christian Science Monitor*, January 24, 2006: 6. Ambassador Bodine remains skeptical about this estimate of the number of weapons in Yemen and believes it is "urban legend." Bodine, e-mail correspondence.

18. Dana Priest and Susan Schmidt, "Hunt Grows in Yemen for Al Qaida: Persian Gulf Nation's Links to Terror Fuel U.S. Resolve," *Washington Post*, September 15, 2002: A1.

19. Mark N. Katz, "Breaking the Yemen-Al Qaida Connection," *Current History* (January 2003): 41.

20. Ibid.

21. Bodine, e-mail correspondence.

22. Richard Shultz, Jr., and Ruth Margolies Beitler, "Tactical Deception and Strategic Surprise in Al Qai'ida's Operations," *Middle East Review of International Affairs* 8, no. 2 (June 2004): 63.

23. Scott Peterson, "Is Yemen a Conduit for Global Terrorism?" *Christian Science Monitor*, March 31, 2000: 1.

24. Raphael Perl and Ronald O'Rourke, "Terrorist Attack on the USS *Cole*: Background and Issues for Congress," CRS Report for Congress # RS20721, p. 2, http://www.fas.org/sgp/crs/index.html.

25. John Diamond, "U.S. had Warning 12 Hours before *Cole* Blast, Pentagon Official Says," *Chicago Tribune*, October 25, 2000. Ambassador Bodine recalls that the report of a threat against U.S. naval vessels was too vague to be actionable. Bodine, e-mail correspondence.

26. Rowan Scarborough, "Pentagon Analyst Resigns over Ignored Warnings," *Washington Times*, October 26, 2000: A1.

27. "The Enemy's Patient Plotting," *Newsweek*, August 16, 2004: 26.

28. Cragin and Gerwehr: p. 42.

29. Ibid.

30. "Terrorism against the USS *Cole*."

31. Richard Sale, "USS *Cole* Update: Hezbollah Built Bomb," *United Press International*, May 20, 2001, http://web.lexis-nexis.com (accessed June 6, 2006).

32. Ambassador Barbara Bodine, e-mail correspondence with author, June 25, 2006.

33. For more on the responsibilities of the FEST, see http://www.state.gov/s/ct/rls/fs/2002/13045.htm#5.

34. Bodine, phone interview.

35. Ibid.

36. Charles Schmitz, "Investigating the *Cole* Bombing," *Middle East Report Online*, September 6, 2001, http://www.merip.org/mero/mero090601.html (accessed June 12, 2006).

37. Walter Pincus, "Yemen Hears Benefits of Joining U.S. Fight," *Washington Post*, November 28, 2001: A8.

38. Bodine, e-mail correspondence.

39. Ibid.

40. Ibid.

41. Bodine, phone interview.

42. Knights.

43. However, Ambassador Bodine argues that it was "a leap" to connect anti-Soviet mujahideen from Afghanistan to the Cole attack. Bodine, e-mail correspondence.

44. "FBI, U.S. Ambassador Clash over *Cole* Probe," *United Press International*, November 12, 2000, http://web.lexis-nexis.com (accessed June 14, 2006).

45. Bodine, e-mail correspondence.

46. Ibid.

47. Bodine, e-mail correspondence.

48. Bodine, phone interview.

49. Danna Harman, "Yemen Slowly Warms to U.S." p. 6.

50. Bodine, phone interview.

51. Ibid.

52. Ibid.

53. Ibid.

54. Ibid.

55. Ibid.

56. Bodine, e-mail correspondence.

57. Ibid.

58. Michelle Mittelstadt, "U.S. Government Indicts Two Fugitives in 2000 Attack on USS *Cole*," *Knight Ridder*, May 16, 2003: 1. Ambassador Bodine explained that al Quso claimed to have slept through the attack. Bodine, e-mail correspondence.

59. John F. Burns, "FBI's Inquiry in *Cole* Attack is Nearing Halt," *New York Times*, August 21, 2001: A1.

60. Bodine, phone interview and e-mail correspondence.

61. David Johnston and James Risen, "Inquiry into Attack on the *Cole* in 2000 Missed Clues to 9/11," *New York Times*, April 11, 2006: 1.

62. Zahid Hussain, "Pakistan Arrests Yemeni with Ties to *Cole*, Sept.11," *Wall Street Journal*, May 1, 2003: A16.

63. Johnston and Risen: p. 1.

64. Harman, "Yemen Slowly Warms to U.S." : p. 6.

65. David Cloud and Greg Jaffe, "U.S. Kills al Qaida Suspect in Yemen," *Wall Street Journal*, November 5, 2002: A8.

66. Zahid Hussain, "Pakistan Arrests Yemeni with Ties to *Cole*, September 11,": p. A16.

67. Ibid. See also, "Suspect in USS *Cole* Bombing is Arrested," *Houston Chronicle*, November 26, 2003: 20.

68. Ibid.

69. Bodine, phone interview.

70. Ibid.

71. Ibid.

72. Scott Peterson, "Yemen Quakes in *Cole*'s Shadow," *Christian Science Monitor*, September 21, 2001: 6.

73. Nabil Sultan, "Yemen: Fatal U.S. Chopper Crash May be Tied to Al Qaida Escape," *Global Information Network*, February 20, 2006: 1.

74. Pincus: p. A8.

75. Priest and Schmidt: p. A1.

76. Schanzer: p. 527.

77. Karl Vick, "Yemen Walks Tightrope in Terrorism Stance," *Washington Post*, September 29, 2001: A 20.

78. Schanzer: p. 521.

79. Bodine, e-mail correspondence.

80. "Yemen Pardons Al Qaida Suspects," *United Press International*, November 16, 2003, http://lexis-nexi.com (accessed June 28, 2006).

81. Jonathan Schanzer, "Yemen's Al Qaida Amnesty: Revolving Door or Evolving Strategy?" Policy Watch #808 *Washington Institute for Near East Policy*, November 26, 2003, http://www.washingtoninstitute.org.

82. Sultan: p. 1.

83. "Yemen puts officers on military trial over al Qaida Jailbreak," *Duetche Press Agenur*, May 25, 2006, http://lexis-nexis.com (accessed June 28, 2006).

84. Kevin Whitelaw, "On a Dagger's Edge: Yemen has Become America's Surprise Ally in Fighting Terrorism," *U.S. News and World Report*, March 13, 2006, http://proquest.umi.com (accessed June 12, 2006).

85. Whitelaw.

86. Bodine, phone interview.

87. Ibid.

88. Raphael Perl and Ronald O'Rourke, "Terrorist Attack on the USS *Cole*: Background and Issues for Congress," CRS Report for Congress # RS20721, p. 2, http://www.fas.org/sgp/crs/index.html.

89. Richard Scott, "USN Ups Tempo for Anti-Terrorist Force Protection," *Janes Defence Weekly*, January 4, 2002, http://www4.janes.com (accessed June 7, 2006).

90. Bodine, phone interview.

CHAPTER 10

CAPTURING KHALID SHEIKH MOHAMMAD

Robert N. Wesley

The fight against al Qaeda and its affiliates has produced a mixture of successes and frustrated efforts since its post-9/11 reinvigoration. One of the highest priorities of the United States' counterterrorism strategy is the capture or killing of the movement's traditional leadership. Although, as of this writing, al Qaeda's Osama bin Laden and Ayman al-Zawahiri continue to elude concerted efforts by allied intelligence and security forces, the organization's other top ranks have been in perpetual need of replenishing. Some of these achievements have been in the form of assassination strikes on difficult targets. More significantly, though, are successes where U.S. officers—working with local security services—have been able to actually capture high-ranking al Qaeda operatives alive.

One such success involved a March 3, 2003, raid in the Pakistani city of Rawalpindi. Acting on intelligence generated from a string of raids stretching over a year, scores of Pakistani paramilitaries raided an apartment building in an upscale section of Rawalpindi, awakening the mastermind of the September 11, 2001, attacks on the United States. Khalid Sheikh Mohammad (widely referred to by his initials KSM), the most important catch thus far in the fight against al Qaeda-inspired terrorism, was taken without a fight, carrying with him the details of the inner workings, history, and future operations of the network.

The most significant capture of an al Qaeda operational leader deserves to be detailed, not only for the strategic importance of the individual involved, but for delineating the complex process that led to his detainment and the lessons underlined by this process. His capture serves to emphasize how the United States will be operating in the future to ensure continued progress in disrupting both the traditional leadership and those who replace them.

Mohammad's case study allows for reflection on several counterterrorism issues likely to have an impact on the future of this conflict. These include, *inter alia*, the importance of: developing strong international partnering relationships; harnessing the core competencies of joint operations involving United States and host-country organizations; creating and exploiting actionable intelligence; identifying and provoking security mistakes by al Qaeda operatives; and targeting "partner organizations" of al Qaeda.

THE MASTERMIND

Although this case study will focus on the lessons learned from the counterterrorism perspective, the content of Khalid Sheikh Mohammad's background is significant enough to merit further elaboration. Mohammad was not an ordinary operative; nor was he a mediocre leader. He had a hand in so many of the most significant attacks preceding his arrest, including both World Trade Center attacks, that some counterterrorism officials gibingly referred to him as the "Forrest Gump" of al Qaeda. His insatiable appetite for the spectacular, and being the most experienced executor of attacks, elevated his detainment to the highest priority. Hence his capture on March 3, 2003, put al Qaeda's most accomplished operational leader out of business. As al Qaeda and its broader movement the Global Jihad have become more laterally structured and loosely coordinated, such capable independent-minded leaders are of the utmost importance in terms of executing complex terrorist attacks.

Mohammad is thought to have been born in 1964 or 1965 in Kuwait to parents likely from Baluchistan, an area covering parts of Pakistan and Iran.[1] Mohammad's experiences and natural attributes made him an exceptionally well-endowed operative. His mixed heritage, along with his Western education and traveling, account for his being fluent in at least Arabic, English, Urdu, and Baluchi. These languages allowed him to operate in disparate environments, freely moving about under multiple covers.

One of the common denominators of al Qaeda's core leadership is that most grew up in what can be considered religious families.[2] Mohammad is no exception, and it is believed that he joined a sect of the Muslim Brotherhood in Kuwait around age 16.[3] From this foundation, he was inculcated in violent jihad from an early age, even participating in desert training encampments. After finishing his secondary schooling, Mohammad decided to venture to the United States for a Western university education and enrolled in a small Baptist college in North Carolina in 1983.[4] After pursuing mechanical engineering, he transferred to North Carolina Agriculture and Technology University and finished his degree in 1986.[5] His religious fervor never seems to have weakened over the years, as he was constantly engaged in jihadi activities, even while simultaneously pursuing nonrelated objectives. His radicalization was further galvanized after traveling to Afghanistan to fight the Soviets in 1987.[6]

In Afghanistan, Mohammad confided in Abdul Rasul Sayyaf, a leading Afghan resistance figure and head of the Islamic Union Party (Hizbul-Ittihad al-Islami). From 1988 to 1992, Mohammad was engaged in, among other hobbies, helping to run a nongovernmental organization (NGO) in Peshawar, Pakistan. The NGO was sponsored by his mentor Sayyaf and was involved in facilitating travel and other support to mujahideen wishing to join the Afghan jihad. During this period, Mohammad's network of associates grew significantly. After leaving the NGO, Mohammad—like many career mujahideen—spent some time fighting and supporting the Bosnia jihad. Mohammad's nephew, Ramzi Yousef, was at this time planning the first World Trade Center (WTC) bombing. The two relatives were in communication, and indeed Mohammad wired Yousef $660 for the operation.[7]

By the time of the first WTC bombing in 1993, Mohammad had moved to Qatar and taken a position as an engineer at the Qatari Ministry of Electricity and Water, following the advice of Sheikh Abdallah bin Khalid bin Hamad al-Thani, the former Qatari minister of Islamic affairs.[8] This was not a "settling-down" period for Mohammad; rather, it was a time for realigning his path of jihad. Apparently inspired by the near success of the WTC attack, Mohammad moved with its mastermind, his nephew Yousef, to the Philippines to plan further grandiose attacks.[9] While in Manila, a plan was hatched that would be the inspiration for the 9/11 attacks.

The widely known but failed Yousef-Mohammad plot to blow up 11–12 airliners over the Pacific Ocean [a plot they referred to as "Oplan Bojinka"] was in the final planning stages when it was disrupted.[10] An explosives accident in Manila, along with investigations of other attack plans, led to the disruption of the cell and the subsequent return of Mohammad to Qatar, where he regained his government position while clandestinely globetrotting to meet with associates in Sudan, Malaysia, Brazil, and Yemen.[11]

Simultaneously, a U.S. court indicted Mohammad in January 1996 for his involvement in the first WTC bombing. U.S. authorities were also tracking Mohammad during this period and were hoping to arrest him and transport him to face trial. After learning of his residence in Qatar, U.S. officials debated where or not to snatch Mohammad by force, eventually deciding to request permission from the Qatari government. Unfortunately, however, the response from Qatar came too late, as Mohammad had already fled to Pakistan to seek refuge with brothers in the region.[12]

Later in 1996, Mohammad, needing financing and operatives, was able to meet with Osama bin Laden, where he proposed to train pilots for a plan that involved crashing airplanes into buildings on the east and west coasts of the United States. Bin Laden reportedly was not particularly interested in pursuing the plan at the time as he had recently moved from the Sudan to Afghanistan and was assumedly more concerned with reorganizing and consolidating his position in the chaotic region.[13]

The roaming Mohammad was also trying to find his jihadi nitch, and thus became enamored with jihadi training camps and supporting groups operating in the region and beyond. Mohammad moved his family to Karachi, Pakistan, in 1997. Later the same year, he tried to join Ibn al-Khattab, the famous Saudi militant leader in Chechnya, but failed to transit through Azerbaijan. During this period, Mohammad maintained his ties to al Qaeda's operatives, including Mohammad Atef and Sayf al-Adl, assisting them in various projects. These relationships flourished until bin Laden in late 1998 or early 1999 gave Mohammad the go-ahead for the "planes operation," and the September 11 plot began in earnest.[14]

As the September 11, 2001, attacks have been detailed in other publications, this study will only emphasize that Mohammad was the operational leader, the strategic guide, and the overall commander of the operation. It is also important to note that Mohammad had not sworn an official oath of allegiance, *bayat*, to bin Ladin, and thus preserved his autonomy for the coming years. Mohammad, conforming to his *modus operandi*, was also engaged in simultaneous planning for further operations, as the "planes operation" was viewed as the beginning of a protracted campaign. Following the surprising success of the operation, the hunt for Mohammad, which had been initiated in the mid-1990s, accelerated.

CAPTURING THE FORREST GUMP OF AL QAEDA

Mohammad, like many al Qaeda operatives with previous knowledge of the attacks, expressed surprise at the magnitude of destruction of September 11. Correspondingly, the strength and determination of the U.S. response to the attacks seems to also have caught leaders such as Mohammad off guard. However, Mohammad's role in the attacks did not become clear until 2002, when interrogations—especially of al Qaeda senior leader Abu Zubaydah—revealed Mohammad to have been the primary organizer.[15]

Even though al Qaeda's operational environment was being constantly restricted after the U.S. intervention in Afghanistan and the strengthening of cooperation with the government of Pakistan, the network continued to plan future attacks and reevaluate existing plans. For example, the September 11 attacks were to be followed by a "second wave" of attacks in the United States by operatives such as Zacarias Moussaoui.[16] The "second wave" plans seemed to have been postponed or cancelled following intense counterterrorism operations and the arrest of Moussaoui. Nonetheless, Mohammad pushed on with multiple operations.

On September 10, 2001, the same day that the Northern Alliance leader Ahmed Massoud was assassinated by al Qaeda operates in Northern Afghanistan, Khalid Sheikh Mohammad dispatched his trusted operative Mohammad Mansor Jabarah to South East Asia to lay the groundwork for multiple suicide truck bombings in the region targeting U.S., British, and Israeli interests.[17] This operation was reportedly frustrated in December 2001 after the cell in Singapore was dismantled.[18]

A week after the September 11, 2001 attacks, Mohammad is reported to have traveled from his base in Pakistan to Afghanistan to seek out bin Laden, who congratulated Mohammad and instructed him to continue operations with increasing autonomy.[19] Mohammad responded by delegating operational authorities to subordinates and sanctioning further attacks. One such move involved giving $20,000 and a fake passport to Jemaah Islamiya senior operative Riduan Isamuddin, commonly known as Hambali, with instructions to case targets in the region for further attacks.[20] Mohammad is also believed to have had a hand in the April 2002 attack on a synagogue in Jerba, Tunisia, which claimed the lives of 19 people.[21]

In the early stages of the U.S. and allied campaign against the al Qaeda organization and its networks, both sides were caught trying to come to grips with what had happened and what the future direction of the conflict would be. Al Qaeda's cadres began to seek out refuges for regrouping and continuing operations. Mohammad seems to have decided that utilizing the numerous contacts and affiliates he had collected over the years in Pakistan's cities was the wisest method of evading capture while planning future attacks.

Pakistan's cities are teaming with numerous militant groups of all varieties, and Mohammad had connections with operatives and facilitators throughout many of them. One of the most familiar cities to him was Karachi. A huge port city with a population of over 14 million, Karachi offered Mohammad easy access to people, materials, and numerous safe houses from which to evade counterterrorism initiatives. Militant groups have long had a heavy presence in the city, and support networks sympathetic to al Qaeda and Mohammad were well entrenched. The negative side of taking refuge in Karachi, however, was that it was swarming with intelligence officers and agents. Unlike the border regions of Afghanistan and Pakistan, any neighborhood in Karachi could be easily accessed within a moment's notice. Mohammad undoubtedly weighed these advantages and disadvantages, and in the end decided that Karachi was a beneficial place from which to operate.

The city of Karachi was a primary suspect for the location of Mohammad due to his previous residencies there coupled with the known presence of al Qaeda operatives in the city. However, in late 2001 and early 2002, Mohammad's location was still unclear, and indeed the priority of his capture had not yet fully matured. Later in 2002, it became known that Mohammad, Khalid bin Atish, and probably Ramzi bin al-Shibh as well had been hiding in Karachi since at least January 2002. This information was partially based on subsequent raids where it was discovered that Atish had been giving lectures in January and February 2002 to local militants, primarily from the violent sectarian group Lashkar-e-Jhangvi.[22]

Much information is not publicly known concerning Mohammad's movements or counterterrorism activities targeting him in the early months of 2002; however, it can be assumed that since both groups were in a perpetual state of operations, there was much occurring in this respect. Indeed, the Jerba synagogue bombing occurred in April of 2002, thus emphasizing Mohammad's continued relevance. Meanwhile, the U.S. and allied intelligence agencies were in need of more specific information on Mohammad's whereabouts in order to focus their resources.

The break that investigators had been searching for occurred after al-Jazeera investigative reporter Yosri Fouda received an invitation from al Qaeda to conduct an interview in June 2002. Fouda arrived in Karachi and was escorted on a series of well-orchestrated countersurveillance procedures before reaching a residence where he met two of the primary planners of the September 11, 2001 attacks: Khalid Sheikh Mohammad and Ramzi bin al-Shibh.[23]

Eager to take credit for the attacks and to voice their justifications, opinions, and goals, the two senior operatives proceeded over the next 2 days to outline the attacks and impress their ideology upon Fouda. This was the turning point in the hunt for Khalid Sheikh Mohammad.

The importance of the interview rested not in the rhetoric of the two planners, but rather in how the circumstances of the interview were exploited. The first mistake made by Mohammad was allowing the interview to take place in the same city, regardless of its size, as where he was in "long-term" hiding. Fouda was able to identify the sequence of events of his escort to the safe house and determine that he was conducting the interview in Karachi. This enabled joint Pakistani-U.S. tracking teams to focus their immediate energies on the city where they knew he had been hiding.

After finishing the interview, Fouda was not able to return with any of the audio or video tapes that had been recording the 2-day event. Mohammad and Bin al-Shibh had claimed that they needed to black out their faces by their own technical means. Fouda was promised the videotapes but never received them. After some time, Mohammad made his second mistake by allowing an audio recoding of the interview to be sent to Fouda as documentation. This recording now allowed U.S. signals intelligence (SIGINT) technicians to develop a "voiceprint" of both al Qaeda operatives. These prints enabled U.S. agencies to monitor telecommunications transmissions for matching voice patterns with the hope of further isolating Mohammad or Bin al-Shibh's location. From this point, the manhunt began to pick up momentum.

One of the most successful ways of tracking down the location of leadership figures such as Mohammad is by producing "actionable" intelligence based on information gleaned from interrogations and clues collected in raids of individuals who could be in close proximity to the leader in question.[24] This intelligence must be exploited quickly, as al Qaeda's leaders—although making mistakes at times—tend to practice effective personal security procedures. The trail usually dries up quickly, and thus U.S. and Pakistani joint teams must work in fluid cooperation in order to harness their core competencies and maintain production of this actionable intelligence.

The period between the Fouda interview and September 2002 saw multiple low-level raids and intelligence collection activities focused on uncovering new leads in Karachi. One such raid netted Sheikh Ahmed Salim Swedan, a Kenyan national wanted for his participation in the 1998 embassy bombings. His arrest is reported to have come as the result of information retrieved from the interrogation of members of a sectarian group in Karachi, most likely from Laskar-e-Jhangvi.[25]

A series of raids conducted in September 2002 were the most considerable to date. The most significant of these began on September 9, when two foreigners and a Pakistani were arrested in a Karachi apartment. The suspects reportedly told investigators of two apartments in the Defense Housing district of Karachi that were purported to contain additional militants.[26] Investigators were also chasing down the location of a satellite phone call that was thought to have matched Mohammad's voiceprint.[27] U.S. and Pakistani teams were generating actionable intelligence that was encouragingly pointing to the location of Mohammad.

The following day on September 10, Pakistani officers raided two apartments in the Bahadurabad neighborhood. The terrorists contested the raid with automatic weapons and grenades, which led to the death of two of their comrades and the capture of five. Inside the apartments, investigators found satellite and mobile phones, laptop computers, CDs, $5,000, and other valuable materials that required immediate attention. Mohammad was apparently a frequent visitor of the raided safe houses.[28] Interrogations of suspects and individuals in and around the apartment directed the joint teams to another apartment in a run-down business district of Karachi. Pakistani Interservice Intelligence (ISI) paramilitaries raided this apartment on September 11, 2002. On the one-year anniversary of the attacks on the United States, one of the leading perpetrators was captured.[29]

Ramzi bin al-Shibh had essentially become Khalid Sheikh Mohammad's proverbial right-hand man. The former roommate of Mohammad Atta, the tactical Emir of the 9/11 attacks, bin al-Shibh, was initially meant to take part in the attacks, but could not gain the proper visa to enter the United States.[30] He thus became a primary facilitator and organizer for the 9/11 attack group. Excelling in this role, he became even closer to KSM and began taking leading positions in further operations. He even participated in refining the ideological justifications of al Qaeda's campaign.[31] Although ISI officials and U.S. intelligence officers might have been surprised to have discovered bin al-Shibh instead of KSM during the September 11, 2002 raid, they no doubt knew they had caught a substantial figure with serious implications for future operations. Indeed, KSM referred to bin al-Shibh as the "Coordinator of the Holy Tuesday Operation" in their joint interview with Fouda.

The September 11, 2002 raid not only captured bin al-Shibh, but also provided new intelligence on the activities of KSM and his associates. Authorities expected to find KSM and Khalid bin Atish at the apartment, and indeed they probably had been staying there previously, as Atish's artificial leg was found in one of the rooms.[32] Other materials indicated to investigators that some of those who were operating out of the safe house were involved in facilitating the foreign travel of al Qaeda operatives in Pakistan wishing to exit the country.[33] Also present were the usual assortment of phones, computers, documents, CDs, and money.[34]

Investigators exploited the intelligence gleaned from the previous raids to conduct yet a third raid the next day on September 12 in the Gulshan-e-Iqbal district of Karachi.[35] The raid captured seven suspects, including an Egyptian woman who reportedly told investigators that KSM had stayed in the building several times during the preceding weeks. Mohammad was clearly moving often from one safe house to another, and would receive news of the compromised refuges in very short order. However, Mohammad was still believed at this time to be in Karachi. Subsequent raids in mid-November 2002 led to the capture of eight al Qaeda suspects, although Mohammad was not among them.[36]

Joint U.S. and Pakistani teams were tracking leads generated since September all over Pakistan. In Lahore, a joint ISI and U.S. team conducted a midnight raid on the Manawan compound owned by the prominent Dr. Ahmed Javed Khawaja. The doctor was found to be harbouring al Qaeda operatives identified as Abu Yasir al-Jaziri, Assadullah Aziz, Sheikh Said al-Misri, and Abu Faraj. Khawaja was the third known Pakistani doctor to have been arrested since September 2002. Abu Faraj was reportedly also known to have been a deputy of Mohammad.[37]

The first month of 2003 brought another wave of important raids targeting Mohammad and his associates. ISI agents raided the compound of a highly visible female leader of the Jama'at-e-Islami (JeI) political party in the Gulshan-e-Maymar neighborhood of Karachi on January 9.[38] She was the wife of the famous Pakistani field hockey player Shahid Ali Khan. In addition, the raid led to the arrest of two Arab members of al Qaeda and information that could be exploited for future operations.[39] After a gun battle the next day in Gulshan-e-Maima district, another raid netted suspected al Qaeda operatives Abu Omar and Abu Hamza.[40] Investigators also uncovered weapons, mobile phones, computers, and $25,000 in cash.[41]

On January 17, 2003, investigators identified four safe houses and captured four suspected al Qaeda operatives with links to Mohammad and the banned group Lashkar-e-Jhangvi.[42] An Australian citizen was also arrested during January and questioned regarding his links to Mohammad.[43] Investigators had started slowly identifying the network of supporters that was facilitating Mohammad's movements or who was otherwise linked to him. They were getting the kind of actionable intelligence that was necessary for breaking up a network and capturing its members.

The arduous process of pursuing leads and finding dead ends, frustrated near misses, big catches, and sleepless hours came to a climax starting in February 2003, when a combination of investigative techniques and intelligence collection methods—and possibly the reward money offered by the United States—resulted in the arrest of Mohammad Abd al-Rahman, son of the infamous Omar Abd al-Rahman imprisoned in the United States.[44] Al-Rahman was arrested on February 14 in the Pakistani city of Quetta. It is reported that al-Rahman divulged valuable details of KSM, with whom he had purportedly been hiding.[45] U.S. technicians were also able to exploit the materials that were left behind in the Quetta compound to trace previous communications to individuals with whom KSM might have sought refuge.

Khalid Sheikh Mohammad's trail was picked up again in Rawalpindi, and the ISI—with the support of the United States—employed surveillance and stalking techniques to arrest at least seven individuals associated with Mohammad. Mohammad had apparently been staying for 10 days with Ahmed Abdul Qadus, the son of an eminent microbiologist in the city with links to the Jama'at-e-Islami political group.[46] Mohammad was caught sleeping when officers raided the house in the early morning of March 3, 2003.

Arrested along with Mohammad and Qadus was Mustafa Ahmed al-Hawsawi, a trusted associate of Mohammad who had, among other activities, facilitated finances for the 9/11 operation.[47] Mohammad was quickly interrogated for more actionable intelligence and then handed over to U.S. officials to be flown out of the country for more extensive, long-term interrogations. After an arduous process, less than a year after the Fouda interview, the mastermind of the 9/11 attacks was captured along with dozens of other highly experienced associates.

LESSONS LEARNED

Such a robust and protracted counterterrorism project can provide insights as to how counterterrorism has been practiced in the past, and how it could be effectively practiced in the future. This chapter focuses on five of these lessons. These lessons are in many respects interdependent of one another, since the failure to accomplish one can lead to the marginal benefits of another. A successful counterterrorism campaign, as demonstrated by the KSM case study, will display a positive incorporation of these lessons.

International Partnering Relationships

Probably the most glaring lesson that this case study of KSM illuminates is the necessity of building strong, trusting relationships between the country hosting the operations—in this case Pakistan—and the other involved parties, such as the United States. This cooperation must be comprehensive, affecting all levels of government from the policymakers to the working-level operators collecting intelligence and conducting raids.

Al Qaeda and those following a similar philosophy and terrorist strategy are a danger to all states. Most major counterterrorism operations that have involved targeting leadership have been the result of bilateral or multilateral cooperation. Mohammad would have continued to elude capture if the vested countries had pursued the hunt unilaterally. The necessity of close cooperation cannot be understated.

Synergy and Core Competencies

Closely connected to the development of international partnering relationships is defining and exploiting the core competencies of working-level officers and agencies. Developing a synergy of strengths is crucial to breaking highly adaptive and loosely connected networks such as al Qaeda. Capturing the leadership, which is even more evasive, requires the optimizing of joint operations to develop the necessary actionable intelligence.

Pakistan exhibited strengths, or core competencies, in the area of human intelligence (HUMINT); local knowledge; human capital; national and local police capabilities; and the authority to raid, detain, and interrogate suspects. The United States brought to the team refined investigative techniques such as surveillance and stalking; advanced analytical tools; additional HUMINT resources; and unique SIGINT capabilities, all of which complemented the core competencies of its Pakistani partner.

Creating and Exploiting Actionable Intelligence

Mohammad did not suffer the same fate as his nephew Ramzi Yousef, who was captured as a result of one of his associates walking into the U.S. Embassy and leading U.S. and Pakistani officers to his location. Rather, Mohammad was captured as a direct result of months of the tireless joint efforts of Pakistani and U.S. intelligence and police officers who created their own "lucky breaks" by exploiting one piece of intelligence information to cause another to appear. Although joint operations are usually far from displaying perfect synergy, the competencies harnessed by the teams involved in the hunt for Khalid Sheikh Mohammad allowed for a continual production of actionable intelligence.

Terrorist groups under the strain of counterterrorism operations continuously adjust their security procedures. They also learn to compartmentalize information in order to insulate themselves when colleagues are detained and safe houses raided. Although this tradecraft is becoming highly advanced, it is permeable, and thus synergetic exploitation teams are necessary to maintain production of actionable intelligence.

Need to Identify and Provoke Mistakes

Most terrorist leaders are well practiced in covert tradecraft, and have proven to be adept at insulating themselves from detection and capture. Intelligence collection and counterterrorism operations can place significant pressures on leaders, which in turn constricts their operational capabilities, but may not necessarily lead to capture. However, terrorists cannot solely concentrate on evading detection as they must remain relevant by interacting with their audiences and continuing operations. Terrorists can make mistakes when they engage in these necessary activities, and these mistakes can be exploited.

In this case study, Khalid Sheikh Mohammad was an operational commander who tragically decided to dabble in public relations. Mohammad exposed his location and later his voice to an exogenous source. Al Qaeda leaders have since learned of the danger of inviting journalists for interviews and thus now produce their propaganda indigenously in order to maintain full control of the information released. After unnecessarily exposing himself, U.S. and Pakistani intelligence was able to pick up his trail. Since KSM was the chief operational commander, he had to maintain active communications and access to personnel, which further exposed him to SIGNIT activities and Karachi-focused counterterrorism operations.

Such mistakes will eventually occur when pressure is applied, but they can also happen by chance, as this case depicts. An intimate understanding of the necessary activities and objectives of terrorist leadership can allow pressure to be applied more effectively to induce more mistakes.

Targeting Partner Organizations

The idea of targeting organizations that support or are otherwise connected to terrorist groups is not a novel concept. This case study serves to underline the fact that rolling up complex and amorphous networks such as al Qaeda requires targeting the groups that can provide an actionable intelligence "cascade" or a piece of information that leads to another, thus developing a trail that can be followed toward more significant targets.

An example of this is the tangential relationships between al Qaeda members and Lashkar-e-Jhangvi (LeJ). The two groups shared resources and facilitated movement for each other in Karachi, and indeed vital information gathered in the KSM case came from LeJ. Jama'at-e-Islami, another group in this case study with links to al Qaeda, is a bit more difficult to target due to the size of the political party and the backlash major investigations might have. However, directly targeting groups with less potential political backlash such as the LeJ, with the goal of obtaining information on al Qaeda in Karachi, can produce real results.

NOTES

1. "Profile: Al-Qaeda 'Kingpin'," *BBC News Online*, March 5, 2003.

2. Marc Sageman, *Understanding Terrorist Networks* (Philadelphia, PA: University of Pennsylvania Press, 2004) 77.

3. *The 9/11 Commission Report*, National Commission on Terrorist Attacks Upon the United States, 2004, Chapter 5. Available at http://www.911commission.gov.

4. "Profile: Al-Qaeda 'Kingpin'".

5. Ibid.

6. *The 9/11 Commission Report*, Chapter 5.

7. Ibid.

8. Ibid.

9. "Substitution for the Testimony of Khalid Sheikh Mohammed," Defendant's Exhibit 941, *U.S. v. Moussaoui*, 2006.

10. For a detailed analysis of this plot, see Rohan Gunaratna, "Al Qaeda's Lose and Learn Doctrine," in *Teaching Terror: Strategic and Tactical Learning in the Terrorist World*, ed. James J. F. Forest (Lanham, MD: Rowman & Littlefield, 2006) 171–188.

11. "Profile: Al-Qaeda 'Kingpin',"; *The 9/11 Commission Report,* Chapter 5.

12. Niles Lathem, "Neighbors Sold out 9/11 Fiend: Reward-Seekers Gave Cops Tip that Ended 8-Year Hunt," *New York Post*, March 3, 2003.

13. *The 9/11 Commission Report,* Chapter 5.

14. "Substitution for the Testimony of Khalid Sheikh Mohammed," Defendant's Exhibit 941, U.S. v. Moussaoui, 2006; *The 9/11 Commission Report,* Chapter 5.

15. Yosri Fouda, "War on Terror: The Masterminds," *The Sunday Times*, September 8, 2002.

16. "Substitution for the Testimony of Khalid Sheikh Mohammed," Defendant's Exhibit 941, U.S. v. Moussaoui, 2006.

17. "Khalid Shaikh Mohammed: Life of Terror," *CNN.com*, March 5, 2003.

18. Yoram Schweitzer, "The Capture of Khalid Sheikh Mohammad," Jaffee Center for Strategic Studies, March 5, 2003; Robert MacPherson, "Al-Qaeda Initially Planned to Hit Nuclear Plants," *Agence France-Presse*, September 8, 2002.

19. Paul Martin, "Chicago, L.A. Towers Were Next Targets," *The Washington Times*, March 30, 2004; Christina Lamb, "Focus: The Confessions of Khalid Sheikh Mohammed," *The Sunday Times*, March 28, 2004.

20. Lamb, "Focus: The Confessions of Khalid Sheikh Mohammed."

21. Schweitzer, "The Capture of Khalid Sheikh Mohammad."

22. Mazhar Abbas, "Al-Qaeda Terror Mastermind Gives Pakistani Security the Slip," *Agence France-Presse*, November 14, 2002; Rana Jawad, "Arrest of Top al-Qaeda Suspect a Lucky Break," *Agence France-Presse*, September 18, 2002.

23. Fouda, "War on Terror: The Masterminds."

24. For more analysis on intelligence gathering and best practices in manhunting, please see several chapters in Volume One of this book.

25. "Two al-Qaeda Leaders Allegedly Arrested in Karachi," *Xinhua News Agency*, September 9, 2002.

26. Jawad, "Arrest of Top al-Qaeda Suspect a Lucky Break."

27. Rory McCarthy, "Al-Qaeda Linchpin Eludes His Pursuers, Most Wanted is Elusive Quarry," *The Guardian*, September 23, 2002.

28. Abbas, "Al-Qaeda Terror Mastermind Gives Pakistani Security the Slip."

29. Rana Jawad, "Alleged 9/11 Mastermind in U.S. Custody," *Agence France-Presse*, March 2, 2003.

30. "Substitution for the Testimony of Khalid Sheikh Mohammed," Defendant's Exhibit 941, *U.S. v. Moussaoui*, 2006.

31. Fouda, "War on Terror: The Masterminds."

32. Jawad, "Arrest of Top al-Qaeda Suspect a Lucky Break."

33. Nick Fielding, "Phone Call Gave Away al-Qaeda Hideout," *The Sunday Times*, September 15, 2002.

34. Abbas, "Al-Qaeda Terror Mastermind Gives Pakistani Security the Slip."

35. McCarthy, "Al-Qaida Linchpin Eludes His Pursuers, Most Wanted is Elusive Quarry."

36. Abbas, "Al-Qaeda Terror Mastermind Gives Pakistani Security the Slip."

37. "Informant to be Paid Millions over Al-Qaeda 'Big Fish' Arrest," *Agence France-Presse*, March 4, 2003.

38. Azfar-ul-Ashfaque: "Two Arabs among Nine Held in Karachi," *The News* (Islamabad), January 10, 2003.

39. "Four Al-Qaeda Suspects Arrested," *The Nation* (Islamabad), January 18, 2003.

40. Aamir Ashraf, "Pakistani Officials Question Two al Qaeda Suspects," *Reuters*, January 11, 2003.

41. "Captured Al Qaeda Suspects Questioned by Pakistani Intelligence," *EFE*, January 10, 2003.

42. "Four Al-Qaeda Suspects Arrested," *The Nation* (Islamabad), January 18, 2003; Ghulam Rabbani, "Clash between Government, Religious Parties Imminent," *Pakistan Observer*, January 11, 2003.

43. "Four Al-Qaeda Suspects Arrested," *The Nation* (Islamabad), January 18, 2003.

44. Phillip Smucker, "Al-Qa'eda Chief Betrayed by Bin Laden's Friend," *The Daily Telegraph*, March 5, 2003; Azfar-ul-Ashfaque, "Two Arabs among Nine Held in Karachi."

45. Lathem, "Neighbors Sold out 9/11 Fiend: Reward-Seekers Gave Cops Tip that Ended 8-Year Hunt."

46. Ibid.

47. "Bin Laden Financier Among Detained in Pakistan Raids," *Agence France-Presse*, March 4, 2003.

CHAPTER 11

THE SIEGE OF BESLAN'S SCHOOL NO. 1

Adam Dolnik

On September 1, 2004, a group of terrorists took more then 1,200 hostages on the first day of school in the North Ossetian town of Beslan. The deadliest hostage crisis, and at the same time the third deadliest terrorist attack in history, was about to unfold. After a 52-hour standoff, the detonation of explosive devices inside the school triggered a chaotic rescue operation, in which 31 terrorists and 331 victims were killed, 176 of them children. The Beslan school hostage crisis was an unprecedented terrorist attack, both in its scale and targeting. It is clear that understanding the lessons of Beslan is one of the key prerequisites of designing counterterrorism strategies for the twenty-first century.

Despite its global notoriety, the Beslan school tragedy still remains an incredibly misunderstood phenomenon, and many questions are yet to be satisfactorily answered. Based on exhaustive open source research in three languages, examination of thousands of pages of witness testimonies and court transcripts, analysis of available video footage, and extensive field research in Beslan, Chechnya, and Ingushetia, including the examination of evidence left behind in the school, visits to the perpetrators' home villages, reconstruction of their trip from their training camp to Beslan, and dozens of interviews with hostages, witnesses, relatives, negotiators, and investigators, this chapter will analyze the myths and facts of the attack, with the clear purpose of identifying the lessons learned. The central focus will be devoted to the Russian response—namely, the crisis negotiation approach and management of the tactical assault. In addition, the chapter will examine events that occurred before Beslan that in retrospect could have provided an intelligence picture concrete enough to prevent the attack, as well as the media management and investigation aspects of the incident.

The greatest limitation of this chapter stems from the fact that most available accounts of the hostage crisis differ significantly in their description of virtually every aspect of the incident. This is further complicated by government secrecy, vested interests, and media censorship, as well as the fact that even eyewitness accounts are often contradictory. Some details are still being disputed, and therefore some aspects of the crisis cannot be determined with absolute certainty. For the sake of completeness, alternative interpretations of events (or author's comments on the uncertainty of certain pieces of information) are included as notes. For a complete picture, it is important to pay particular attention to these.

The first part of the chapter will provide a short chronology of the crisis. The second part will examine the alleged "intelligence failure" associated with Beslan, and will provide some details on what information was available prior to the attack. The third part will focus on the operational management of the incident, including an assessment of the negotiation efforts as well as some of the success and failures of the rescue operation. The fourth part will look at media management during the crisis, followed by an exploration of some mind-boggling questions that are yet to be answered about Beslan. And finally, the conclusion will summarize the implications and lessons learned for crafting effective counterterrorism policies in the twenty-first century.

INCIDENT PROGRESSION

This section will provide a basic chronology of the events that unfolded in Beslan. Given the limited space of this chapter, it is impossible to include many fascinating details of the crisis. However, other excellent and highly detailed descriptive accounts exist and an interested reader is strongly encouraged to consult them for additional information.[1]

Day 1

On September 1, 2004, just after 9 A.M., a group of terrorists arrived at School No. 1 in Beslan, Russia, and with swift action took over 1,200 people hostage, also deploying 127 homemade explosive devices around the school building. The initial response to the incident consisted of a brief shootout of armed parents with the hostage takers. An hour and a half after the takeover, soldiers and policemen finally started arriving at the scene. This is amazing considering the fact that the main police station is located a mere 200 meters from the school.[2] The initial telephone contact was reportedly handled by a local Federal Security Service of the Russian

Federation (FSB) negotiator, Vitalii Zangionov.[3] He spoke to a man who on the inside was known as Ali, but for the negotiations used the name "Sheikhu." From the very start, it was clear the terrorists were instructed by their leadership to speak only to high-level officials. According to hostages who sat close to Ali, he spoke with someone on the phone ending a conversation by saying: "I will only talk to the president." His phone rang again in 15–20 minutes. "President?" "No, his aide." Ali interrupted the talk at once.[4] In the meantime, the authorities compiled their first list of hostages and publicly announced that there were only 120 of them.

Around this time, doctor Larisa Mamitova was treating two of the hostage takers who were injured in the initial takeover. Mamitova offered her help in communicating with the authorities, and was eventually sent outside by the leader of the group, Ruslan Khuchbarov (a.k.a. "Polkovnik") with the following hand-written message:

8-928-738-33-374[5]
We demand for negotiations President of the Republic Dzhosokhov, Zaizikov, president of Ingushetia, Roshal, children's doctor. If they kill any one of us, we will shoot 50 people to pieces. If they injure any one of us, we will kill 20 people. If they kill 5 of us, we will blow up everything. If they turn off the light, even for a minute, we will shoot to pieces 10 people.[6]

From early on, the terrorists selected out two groups of men and led them outside the gym. One group had the task of barricading windows, while the other was forced to kneel in the corridor with hands behind their backs facing the wall. The first group never returned. Once its job was finished, they were led to a classroom on the second floor, lined up against the wall, and shot. Their bodies were thrown out of the window.

As the incident progressed, tensions grew even higher. In the afternoon, the hostages overheard an argument between the terrorists and their leader, in which particularly the two female attackers present expressed their displeasure with holding children hostage. Around four o'clock in the afternoon one of the suicide bombers detonated, killing five or six of the men lined up in the hallway and injuring many more.[7] Those injured were later sprayed with gunfire, and their dead bodies were thrown out of the window. At this point, the number of dead hostages already reached 21.

In the meantime, negotiations continued. According to the now former President of Ossetia, Alexander Dzasohov, a deal to exchange the children for the release of 31 terrorists arrested in an earlier raid in Nazran had almost been made, but at the last moment the terrorists backed out. When Mikhail Gutseriev—the former speaker of the Russian State Duma and president of the "Rusneft'" oil company—asked the terrorists about specific demands, Sheikhu suggested that they be handed over in writing.[8]

After 7 P.M., one of the men demanded by the terrorists for negotiations, Dr. Leonid Roshal, entered the picture. Never requested by the authorities, he flew to Beslan on his own initiative after being informed of the situation by journalists. Once he reached the school, Roshal called the terrorists expressing his readiness to enter with water and medicines, but was told that he could only enter the school with the other three men demanded earlier; if he approached alone he would be shot.

Day 2

In the early the morning of September 2, Mamitova overheard a radio broadcast reporting that only 354 hostages were held inside the school, and that the telephone number provided by the terrorists was nonoperational. She asked to see Polkovnik and informed him of the report, also suggesting to send another note with a new telephone number. Polkovnik tore a piece of paper from a notebook and handed it over to Mamitova. "Write again," he said. "Our nerves are at a breaking point . . ."

As the day progressed, the terrorists were becoming increasingly angry and frustrated, mainly due to the repeated government claims made in the media that the number of hostages was 354, and that the hostage takers had not presented any demands. The hostage takers saw this as a deliberate attempt to obstruct negotiations and to justify the launching of an armed assault on the school. Infuriated, around noon of the second day, the terrorists called a "dry strike" and stopped giving the hostages water. From this point on, the hostages really started to suffer from the lack of food, water, and deteriorating conditions inside.

Just before 2 P.M., the terrorists' mood suddenly changed and they became visibly excited. From the top floor they announced on a megaphone that "big person" was coming in for the negotiations. This "big person" turned out to be Ruslan Aushev, Afghan war general and former Ingushetian president. Aushev and Khuchbarov held a discussion in the teachers' room,[9] and at the end of the meeting, Aushev was handed a handwritten note dated on August 30, 2004, addressed to President Putin "from Allah's slave Shamil Basayev":

Vladimir Putin, you were not the one to start the war, but you could be the one to end it, that is if you find the courage and resolve to act like de Gaulle. We are offering you peace on a mutually beneficial basis in line with the principle "independence for security." We can guarantee that if you withdraw the troops and recognize Chechen independence, then: We will not strike any political, military or economic deals with anyone against Russia; We will not have any foreign military bases even temporary ones, we will not support

or finance groups fighting the Russian Federation, we will join the Commonwealth of Independent States, we will stay in the ruble zone, we could
sign the Collective Security Treaty, although we would prefer the status of a
neutral state; we can guarantee that all of Russia's Muslims will refrain from
armed methods of struggle against the Russian Federation, at least for 10–15
years, on condition that freedom of religion be respected. . . . The Chechen
nation is involved in the national liberation struggle for its Freedom and Independence and for its preservation. It is not fighting to humiliate Russia or
destroy it. As a free nation, we are interested in a strong neighbor. We are
offering you peace and the choice is yours.[10]

The terrorists set a deadline for the Kremlin to respond by the morning of September 4.[11] Aushev promised to hand over the letter and asked
for the release of children.[12] Khuchbarov agreed, and the nursing mothers
were released along with one baby each, some of them having to leave
their other children behind. After leaving the school with the 26 released
hostages, Aushev immediately transmitted the text of the letter to the
Kremlin with an urgent plea for negotiations. In addition, a list of specific
demands was also handed over in writing. These demands were never
made public, but available evidence suggests that the list corresponded to
the one later provided by Basayev himself:

– We demand that the war in Chechnya be stopped immediately and that the
  withdrawal of forces be carried out;
– We insist that Putin immediately resigns from his post as president of the Russian Federation; and
– We insist that all hostages, be it children or adults, go on hunger strike in support of our demands.

In the evening of the second day, Aslanbek Aslakhanov, Putin's advisor who was one of the negotiators demanded by the terrorist, called the
school. He was informed that he could come to Beslan to negotiate only
if he had the authority to do so granted by Putin. Aslakhanov answered
affirmatively and added "some demands are unrealistic and you know it.
Some we will fulfill. I'll talk to the president." Sheikhu replied: "If you do,
then see you tomorrow at 3 P.M., we'll hold an official meeting." According to his own account, Alsakhanov then spoke to President Putin, who
allegedly stated that "the children's lives must be saved at all costs. Agree
to everything. But the first two demands cannot be met."[13] This is an extremely interesting point. If Aslakhanov did indeed talk about the possibility of satisfying some of the terrorists' demands, it clearly contradicts
the official claim that no demands were made. Similarly, Putin's comment
about the unacceptability of the "first two demands" confirms their existence. It is not clear, however, what the president meant by "agree to

everything"; if the first two demands—withdrawing of troops from Chechnya and his own resignation—were unacceptable, then there was nothing else to agree to but the demand that hostages go on a hunger strike. So while the statement "agree to everything but the first two demands" by itself may be interpreted as evidence of the Russian leadership's willingness to offer almost any concession in order to save the lives of the hostages, in the context of the actual list of demands it translated into agreeing to absolutely nothing.

The terrorists' desperation to speak to the authorities was evident inside the school. Polkovnik even sought out Mamitova and told her that if there were any members of parliament or other politicians that she knew, she should call them. Mamitova remembered hearing from someone in the gym that the children of the North Ossetian Parliament speaker Mamsurov were also among the hostages. Before they were summoned to the teachers' room, Ali took aside the boy, hugged him, and kissed him on the head. "Don't worry. Nothing bad is going to happen to you. We just need you to help us jumpstart the negotiations. Talk with your daddy and tell him what's going on."[14]

When Mamitova and the children finally managed to get through to Mamsurov, he replied: "The government has ordered me to leave my parental emotions at home." Visibly upset, Khuchbarov then turned on the TV, where the government media were still reporting that there were only 354 hostages, and where Dr. Roshal was claiming that kids were not in immediate danger, and that they could survive 8–9 days without water. Khuchbarov then send Mamitova and the kids back to the gym. "Go, nobody needs you."

On the evening of September 2, Ali came into the gym visibly distressed. When asked by Larisa Kudzyeva what had happened, he replied: "I don't want to lift my foot from the trigger,[15] but I'm forced to do it. They don't want to talk. The answer is no. They told me that Russia will never talk to terrorists. That the problem does not exist." When she asked what that meant, Ali replied: "I don't know what that means. They told me I have a day and a half to sort it out." Kudzyeva countered: "That can't be, maybe you didn't understand." "No, I understood. I understood everything."[16]

The authorities have a different story. According to official sources, Roshal called the terrorists in the evening of the second day and offered them free passage. The offer was allegedly bluntly refused.[17] In the evening of the second day, Aushev suggested to engage Aslan Maskhadov, the last elected president of the separatist government, for negotiations. Maskhadov had publicly condemned the attack and this gave a glimpse of hope.[18] By midnight, among the civilian segment of the local crisis staff, an agreement was allegedly drafted, containing key components oscillating around negotiations between Russian leaders and Maskhadov, a plan for Chechen autonomy, and a gradual troop withdrawal.[19]

Day 3

The morning of September 3 brought some optimistic news: Maskhadov had sent a message confirming that he was ready to fly to Beslan to negotiate. The local authorities responded by announcing: "Important new faces are about to enter the negotiation process, they will arrive soon." Only an hour after this announcement the storming started, leading some sources to speculate that the explosions that triggered the mayhem were no accident, and that their purpose was to deny Maskhadov the chance to come in and save the day.[20] The federal authorities in turn, categorically denied Maskhadov's willingness to come to Beslan to negotiate.[21]

The small glimpse of optimism that was present outside following the morning announcement, however, was not shared by the people inside the gym. Conditions were increasingly deteriorating, with some of the children resorting to drinking urine to survive, and at least two of the kids already reaching the verge of death. The terrorists acted increasingly aggressive, became even less responsive to hostages' anxious pleas for water, and their anger grew with their inability to quiet the hostages down.

At 1:02 P.M., following a morning agreement with the terrorists to allow the collection of bodies of the hostages killed on the first day, a lorry approached the school and suddenly, several shots were fired. Almost simultaneously, the first explosion inside the school ensued, followed by a large explosion exactly 22 seconds later. Shortly thereafter, all hell broke lose. By this point the firefight had become irreversible. At 6:13 P.M., there was one last contact with the hostage takers. "Its all your fault. Say hi to you Putin!" Around 2 A.M., more then 12 hours since the initial explosions, the last shots were fired.

INTELLIGENCE FAILURE

Even several months before the Beslan tragedy, there were a number of indications of a heightened level of terrorist activity in the region, as well as some specific indications of an impeding attack. Ossetia itself had been the site of several recent attacks, most of which had specific links to the attackers later found in Beslan. On June 5, 2003, a woman dressed in a white overcoat killed 18 people when she detonated her explosive belt while trying to board a bus carrying Russian airmen to their base in Mozdok. Two months later, that same base became the site of another attack, when two suicide bombers drove an explosive-laden truck into the 58th Army military hospital, killing 50 people and injuring many others.[22] At this time, the authorities in Moscow were already in possession of a suspected suicide bomber named Zarema Muzhakhoyeva. According to Muzhakohyeva's interrogation reports, she was supposed to be the original bomber during the first Mozdok attack, but lost her nerve and pretended to be ill and thus unable to participate. She was then sent to Moscow with two other women, and on July 5, 2003, she witnessed the demise of her two colleagues during the twin suicide bombings at a rock concert in Moscow's Tushino Airfield, in which 18 people died. Five days later, she herself had been arrested and accused of attempting to commit a suicide attack near the Mon-Café restaurant in the heart of Moscow. A police officer died while trying to defuse the device.

Muzhakhoyeva's interrogation following her arrest led to the apprehension of Rustam Ganiev, who was accused of recruiting and training suicide bombers for Basayev's *Riyadus-Salikhin* (RAS, a.k.a. *Riyadh-as-Saliheen*, The Reconnaissance and Sabotage Battalion of Chechen Martyrs), and whose two sisters had died in the attack on Dubrovka theater in Moscow during October 2002. Ganiev had very close links to a number of the Beslan terrorists. For instance, the one person who was arrested along with Ganiev was Mayrbek Shaybekhanov (who would however under mysterious circumstances later be freed).[23] In September 2004, Shaybekhanov was one of the terrorists holding 1,200 people hostage in the Beslan school along with his wife (who was allegedly one of the suicide bombers).[24] Another Beslan terrorist with close links to Muzhakoyeva and Ganiev was Khanpashi Kulayev, who coincidentally was also supposed to be sitting in jail at the time of the Beslan attack.[25] According to Muzhakoyeva's testimony, she and Khanpashi not only belonged to the same division, but also "practically lived together" though officially never married.[26] Similarly, one of the Beslan leaders—Vladimir Khodov—was also not unknown to authorities, having been previously wanted on charges of rape, and was also publicly sought for the February 2, 2004, bombing in the center of Vladikavkaz in which three military cadets died.[27] Although a wanted man, Khodov freely moved around and even visited his home village of Elkhotovo in Ossetia several times.

The fact that at least two of the Beslan terrorists were supposed to be in jail at the time of the attack, and that another one moved around freely in his home village despite being a wanted man, is highly disturbing. In addition, more indications of heightened terrorist violence were visible in neighboring Ingushetia, where the presence of the Beslan attackers was felt even more. On September 15, 2003, a suicide bomber detonated a 600-pound truck bomb 16 feet short of the newly constructed FSB building in Magas, killing three people.[28] One of the key organizers of the attack was Ruslan Khuchbarov—the same man whom the authorities accused of training suicide bombers for the operations in Dubrovka and Mozdok, and who would later lead the Beslan commando team.[29] Khuchbarov was also one of the leading figures in the June 21, 2004, attack on the now former Ingushetian capitol of Nazran,[30] in which 200 attackers wearing local police uniforms set up roadblocks intercepting and killing real policemen and interior troops who raced to reinforce their colleagues. The attack followed a statement by Basayev that RAS was ready to launch a series of special operations that would be "very painful for the Putin regime and [would] take [Russia] by surprise."[31] Nearly 100 people, including several ministers, died before the fighters withdrew and disappeared in the largest Chechen operation since 1999.

Besides Khuchbarov, at least six other Beslan attackers participated in this earlier attack. In addition, 31 of the attackers who were arrested during the Nazran raid later became an object of Beslan negotiations. And finally, it has now been reliably established that among the weapons found in the possession of the terrorists in Beslan were seven Kalashnikov assault rifles and three pistols that had been stolen during the attack on Ingushetia. During the month of July, a number of additional incidents related to the Nazran raid and Beslan took place in Ingushetia. These included the death of the deputy police chief of Malgobek and the deputy head of the Malgobek crime police, who were killed in a shootout with suspected terrorists on the city's outskirts; the discovery of a large stockpile of weapons from Nazran in the woods near Sagopshi; and two shootouts near the same village, in which one militant was killed and another escaped.[32] Little did anyone know that in the forest on the hill overlooking Sagophsi and Psedakh was a training camp in which the Beslan team was preparing for the operation, and that the man who escaped from the shootout was Musa Tsechoev, whose body would later be found among the 31 corpses of Beslan terrorists.[33] Apparently, the terrorists from the camp were able to move around freely in their home villages. This is not too surprising given then fact that the small village of Psedakh officially has one policeman, who is supposed to be on duty in the village only during daylight. In practice none of the Psedakh residents consulted have ever even seen him.[34]

All of these activities in the region should have had the local authorities on high alert. And indeed, just 12 days before the Beslan attack, the Russian Ministry of Internal Affairs allegedly had sent a telegram to all regional police commanders, warning about a possible "Budyonnovsk style operation" in Northern Ossetia. This information apparently became even more specific several days later. One Beslan resident, Baliko Margiev, asked a traffic policeman just 4 days before the attack why his car was being so unusually carefully inspected, and was told that "a group of militants had penetrated Beslan."[35] In retrospect, this intelligence was accurate, as one of the terrorists was spotted by two Beslan residents in the local marketplace a week before the attack. Similarly, Beslan residents reported several unknown men sitting on boxes in the courtyard of the school during the week leading up to the incident.[36] And finally, according to a report to Interior Minister Rashid Nurgaliev, at 5 A.M. on September 1, 2004, police in the Chechen town of Shali detained a man named Arsamikov who told them that there was a plot to seize schools in Beslan on the very same day.[37] Considering the fact that there are only four schools in Beslan, and that School Number 1 was by far the biggest and most prominent one, it is incredible that even after receiving this intelligence, the school was guarded by just one unarmed female police officer who did not even have a mobile phone.[38] Even more disturbingly, despite elevated threat levels, the local traffic police who guard major intersections near the school every day were not present on September 1. According to officials, the two officers who were supposed to have served as armed security at the school had been sent off to the Caucasus Highway, allegedly to provide extra protection for a high-ranking official who was supposed to pass through. As of this writing, nobody is able to explain who that official was supposed to be.[39] With all of these early warning signs, concrete intelligence, elevated risk levels, and thereby associated increased security measures, how is it possible that a large group of armed militants was able to travel all the way to Beslan? There are still considerable doubts and many conspiracy theories floating around in Beslan.[40] Police corruption is certainly one feasible explanation. But more importantly, the government's reactions in the wake of Beslan have directly contributed to the terrorists' goal of undermining government authority in the eyes of its own citizens.

It also does not help that the only police officer who actually stood up to the terrorists on their way to Beslan and tried to stop them received less then a hero's welcome—the fact that he was not killed was enough for the police to accuse him of being a terrorist accomplice, and torture him during an interrogation.[41] This is not a good precedent for any police officer that finds himself in a similar situation in the future. The message is: if you do something heroic such as single-handedly stand up to a group of terrorists on their way to the target, you will end up being fired from your job with lacerations on your face and crushed testicles.[42] Looking at Gurashev's fate, can anyone really expect an average police officer to go out of his way and risk his life to prevent another Beslan in the future?

OPERATIONAL MANAGEMENT

Even more pressing and disturbing than the intelligence failure is the bleak picture surrounding the storming of the school, and the contradictory statements of various officials with regards to the negotiation efforts. This section will focus on some of the discrepancies and mistakes associated with operational management.

Negotiations: Missed Opportunities

The negotiability or nonnegotiability of the Beslan crisis will always be an issue of much contention. It is not possible to provide a fully detailed analysis of the negotiation aspect in this short chapter, but the author has elaborated on this topic in much greater detail elsewhere.[43]

The official Russian position is that a maximum negotiation effort was undertaken but with no result. Throughout the crisis, the federal authorities kept denying the existence of any demands whatsoever on behalf of the hostage takers, implying that there was nothing more that could have been done to save the lives of the hostages but to storm the location. However, these statements are an evident manipulation of the reality. Throughout the crisis the terrorists presented a clear set of demands and were eager to speak to the authorities, but according to hostages, no one would talk to them.[44] Yes, it is true that the terrorists also kept repeating that they came to Beslan to die, that the hostages were "not needed by anyone," that "no one will leave alive." But it is beyond reasonable doubt that the terrorists' primary objective was to achieve a specific set of political concessions. Yes, their stated demands were by themselves difficult to achieve, both logistically and politically.[45] However, the fact that their proposal included multiple demands and specific conditions provided much room for discussions without necessarily giving in.[46]

Beslan was, of course, an extremely challenging situation with huge stakes, a number of executed hostages, and extremely well-prepared terrorists who seemed to be holding all the cards and who had an obvious knowledge of the hostage negotiation playbook. However, this by itself was not a sufficient reason to give up on the possibility of a negotiated settlement altogether. This is especially true when the terrorists have taken many preventive measures such as fortifying the location, placing a large number of explosive devices throughout the school, booby trapping possible entrances and monitoring them with remote control surveillance cameras,[47] deploying snipers in strategic positions, using gas masks and sentry dogs in order to prevent the use of anesthetic gas, and employing other protective measures designed to make a possible rescue attempt as costly in terms of loss of human life as possible. Under such conditions, is a full breach really the preferable option? Or even a plausible worst case alternative? Do other, less costly means of resolving the situation exist?

The terrorists' demands should have been broken up into smaller pieces, which would then be discussed in more detail. For instance, consider the demand that the president declare an end to the war in Chechnya. The negotiators should have focused on asking about the specific language and semantics of the text. Further, on day two it was clear that the number one priority of the negotiations had to be the improvement of the conditions inside the school to improve the survivability of hostages. Clearly, the situation in which the hostages were not being given water could not have lasted much longer. The authorities should have worked step by step to offer some small concession to facilitate the improvement of the conditions inside, and then work toward the prolongation of the incident in an attempt to wear out the hostage takers, while at the same time working to get as many hostages as possible out of the school in the process. The terrorists stopped giving water to the hostages on the second day, after the officials repeated their claim that there were only 354 people held in the in the gym. Perhaps publicly admitting the actual number of hostages could have been exchanged for water for them?

In the end, it would be difficult to argue that Beslan could have been solved without the loss of life. Nevertheless, even if the incident was bound to end in bloodshed, maximum effort should have been made to get as many hostages out of the school as possible before resorting to a violent solution. Not only did the federal authorities fail in this task, they failed to even seriously try. Even more disturbingly, the official re-actions and statements on television—such as the deliberate and clearly false downplaying of the number of hostages inside—added even more fuel to the fire. As in past hostage crises in Russia, the Kremlin seems to have had only one goal in mind: to discredit the separatist leadership and to teach Basayev a lesson. Many people may applaud Putin's "courage" and argue that the "no negations with terrorists" policy should be upheld at all costs, and that the "national interest" should come before the fate of individual hostages no matter how painful the decision. It is not the issue here to debate the pros and cons of this argument. The point is to recognize that in the handling of the Beslan crisis, political realities played the main part, and that the lives of hostages inside the gym were considered only secondary to the "national interest." As a result, the *worst* possible lesson we could learn from Beslan is that it is impossible to negotiate with the "new terrorists."

Rescue Operation

From the beginning, the response management of Beslan was highly disorganized. The incident was handled by two different command centers with little cooperation among them. The first one was the "civilian" command center manned by local politicians such as Ossetian president Dzosokhov, while the other one was a command center set up by two FSB Deputy Directors (Vladimir Pronichev and Vladimir Anisimov) several hours after the takeover.[48] There was a well-built man standing in front of the door of the federal command center, who would not let any-one in, including local officials.[49] According to Russian newspaper *Novaya Gazeta*, shortly after Russian commandos began to storm the school "the group of FSB employees quickly packed up their equipment and left the administration building in an unknown direction."[50]

The chaotic nature of the setup was underlined by the number of agencies that were present at the site, including the elite Alfa and Vympel units, Military Intelligence troops, Interior Army, Local FSB division, Center of Special Purpose, local police, Army Secret Police, Special Purpose Detachment of Militsiya, Rapid Deployment Special Troops, and regular Russian Army.[51] All of these had their own chain of command, and mutual communication among them was limited. Two principal perimeters existed, with the external perimeter set up by the 58th Army about 3 hours into the attack, who were joined by some local policemen who took up positions on their own initiative without any specific orders or instructions. In the inner perimeter, there were a number of different operational teams and local civilians with guns. This presented a major problem, as this perimeter was too close to the school, and exchanges of sniper fire with the terrorists were common. On the second day, the terrorists even fired a rocket-propelled grenade at a car to force the armed men outside to keep their distance. In addition, the armed locals, with vivid images of the 129 dead hostages in the Moscow theater hostage crisis in mind, threatened to shoot the federal troops in their backs if they started storming the school. Throughout the incident, these local volunteers were never disarmed and neutralized, adding a high level of instability to the already bad situation. An additional mistake was the fact that the double perimeter, despite the large number of troops present, was far from secure. For instance, Russian journalist Madina Shavlokhova—who arrived several hours into the crises and was looking for the school—accidentally found herself right in the courtyard without ever running into a single police or Army barrier.[52]

In short, the entire setup of the operation was highly chaotic. There was no clear idea of who was in charge, too many bodies without sufficient communications and coordination, and armed civilians who were not instructed or controlled in any way. In other words, the operational scene was a disaster waiting to happen. Given these circumstances, it is no surprise that the origin of the explosion that triggered the storming is a subject of speculation rivaling that of the JFK assassination. No less then 14 different versions of what allegedly caused the initial explosion have been uncovered thus far. About four of them appear to be plausible, but in each case there are many other pieces of evidence that do not seem to fit. The two versions with the highest level of plausibility include an accidental detonation of the first bomb and the "sniper theory." The former is essentially the official version, which claims that one of the bombs that was attached to a basketball hoop by adhesive tape detonated accidentally, after it slipped off the hoop following the meltdown of the glue in the tape in the unbearable heat of the gym. The second explosion was then allegedly triggered deliberately by the terrorists who thought they

were being stormed. However, this version has many holes. First is the fact that it was not the bomb in the hoop that actually exploded first, but one that was hanging on a string connecting the two hoops. Second, according to hostages, the bomb exploded in the air, suggesting that it was triggered by something other then impact with the floor. Third, according to Andrei Gagloyev, the commander of the engineering troops of the 58th Army, "such explosive devices cannot be triggered by hitting the floor."[53] Fourth, the fact that the explosion took place at the very same moment that a truck pulled up to collect the bodies of the 21 men who were killed earlier suggests a likely connection between these two events.

The sniper theory received a lot of publicity after the testimony of the sole surviving terrorist, Nur-Pashi Kulayev, in which he claimed that the detonation occurred as a result of a sniper killing the terrorist whose foot was constantly on the detonation pedal preventing the circuit from closing. But in Beslan it was the story of Fatima Dudiyeva, the local policewoman who later became a hostage, which introduced the sniper theory long before Kulayev's testimony. Right before the detonation, she was sitting next to the window trying to stretch her back and her arms came upward. At that moment she "heard a sound like a stone being thrown through the window. And then there was pain." She looked at her right hand and it was bleeding out of a hole in her palm.[54] Shortly thereafter, there was an explosion. Ala Ramonova, another hostage confirms this: "Right before the first explosion, something flew into the gym with a whistling sound, and the terrorist standing on the switch clutched his side and fell over."[55] Not surprisingly, the federal commission in Moscow was extremely quick to discredit the sniper theory. Head of the commission, Alexander Torshin explained that the glass in the windows of the gym was coated with a special plastic called "lexan" that made it impossible for a sniper to see anything that was going on inside. "Besides," said Torshin "this terrorist [with the foot on the switch] was standing in a 'dead zone' where he could not have been in the line of fire. Terrorists are not idiots."[56] However, even if lexan was used to coat the glass, as early as the first day, the terrorists had broken the top parts of the windows, fearing the use of gas as in the Moscow Theater, thus effectively removing any obstacle in visibility. In addition, from the upper floors and the roof of one of the two five-story apartment buildings near the school where snipers were positioned, it is not only possible to see inside the gym through the top parts of the windows, but even the spot where the terrorist was standing is in a clear line of fire. In addition, the fact that the blast took place as the lorry pulled up to collect the bodies does suggest a level of coordination, as the distraction provided a good opportunity to strike.

Another point of controversy, besides the initiation of the storm, was its course. From the very outset, the officials were claiming that no storm was ever even considered as a possibility. For instance, from the very beginning FSB First Deputy Director Vladimir Pronichev spoke categorically against any military scenario, claiming that as a matter of principle, the FSB did not develop plans to attack the school.[57] This, of course, is nonsense. Having a rescue operation plan in place as an option of last resort, should the hostage takers start killing hostages, is one of the basic components of any response to a situation involving hostages. Even in cases where negotiation takes absolute priority, having a rescue operation plan in place (and therefore posing a plausible threat to the hostage takers) is an indispensable part of the negotiations strategy. A rescue operation plan was certainly in place.

According to witnesses, tanks and armored vehicles pulled up to the school on the evening of the second day.[58] These were not only later used as a cover for the advancing Spetsnaz troops, but also used to fire tank shells at the school during the later stages of the rescue operation. According to testimony given by Sergeant Godovalov, the commander of one of the T-72 tanks in question, the tank fired on the school at the orders of an officer of Alpha, the elite antiterrorist unit. According to the testimony, the tank "fired four times at a spot where one of the terrorists was believed to be located, and then was moved to another area, where, again on the Alpha officer's orders, it fired three "antipersonnel rounds at three outermost windows on the school building's second floor."[59] Whether the tank fire took place while hostages were still at the gym is a point of much controversy. For instance, Andrei Gagloyev, commander of the engineering troops of the 58th Army, testified at the Kulayev trial that the tanks fired when the gym did not contain any more hostages.[60] However, First Deputy Chairman of the Parliament of North Ossetia Izrail Totoonti disagrees, claiming that he first heard the tanks fire at about 2:00 p.m. in the day. "That was before we began bringing hostages out of the school."[61] Totoonti's version is in concert with the testimonies of hostages, and a source of much anger on behalf of Beslan residents who have lost their loved ones in the siege.

Tanks were not the only equipment not exactly suitable for hostage rescue operations that were brought to Beslan. Even more controversial is the issue of the use of Shmel flamethrowers, given the fact that according to the Beslan Mothers Committee, in the case of 218 of the 331 fatalities, burns were established as the cause of death.[62] The issue of Shmels first came up after residents of Beslan found several launchers and passed them over for investigation. Originally, the authorities denied the use of these weapons, claiming that the discovered launchers belonged to the terrorists. However, two of the used launchers were discovered on the roof of an adjacent building, suggesting that the Shmels were fired from the outside. This is consistent with the testimonies of hostages who claimed that even after the initial explosions there was only a small fire inside the gym. At the same time, melting plastic was dripping on them from the ceiling, long before any fire was visible from the inside. Eventually, an aide to the military prosecutor of the Vladikavkaz garrison, identified as Major of Justice Eminov, confirmed that Shmel flamethrowers were used, saying that they may have "possibly killed hostages or caused them bodily injuries of various degrees of severity."[63] It did not help that the fire trucks that arrived at the scene ran out of water almost immediately.

Overall, the rescue operation was a huge blunder. That is not to say that hostage rescue teams in other countries would have necessarily come out with a significantly lower death toll in such difficult circumstances.[64] But even if one considers the possibility that the security services might not have been the ones initiating the storming, the use of tanks and flamethrowers to fire at the school while it still contained hostages is mind boggling. Everything suggests that the lives of hostages were again considered secondary to the punishment and elimination of the terrorists in order to teach them a lesson. The main problem (other then the tragic deaths of so many hostages, of course) is the fact that this heavy-handedness of the Russian authorities actually played into Basayev's strategy. Basayev has learned in Budyonnovsk, Kizlyar, and Dubrovka that the Russian leadership can *always* be expected to launch a rescue operation—typically around the end of the third day of the crisis—and that these actions produce on average more than 130 deaths among the hostages. He has learned to use this fact to his advantage. Consider Basayev's claim of responsibility for Beslan in which he stated: "We came there not to kill people but to stop the war, and if it works out that way, to force the Russian leadership to kill its own civilians, if only through this to force the lying and vain world to understand what is really going on, to lay bare our wound and pain, because people don't see what is happening in Chechnya. They see it only when huge actions like this one occur on the territory of Russia itself."[65] The disturbing predictability of the Russian response clearly has played into Basayev's hands, and also provides a lesson for other countries that may face similar situations in the future. Even though our instinct may be to violently strike back at the terrorists, we should realize that by doing so we are likely to be playing right into the hands of their strategic calculus.

MEDIA MANAGEMENT

Since media coverage can directly influence the outcome of a hostage crisis, media management is an absolutely crucial part of the response strategy. First, the media picture shapes perceptions among the general population in terms of what is going on, thereby directly impacting the perception of the most effective course of action, as well as the level of perceived urgency of that action. Second, media coverage also influences the perceptions of the hostage takers, as it serves as one of the main sources of information for the people on the inside. In moments when the negotiations hit a roadblock, televised coverage of public statements can be used to communicate massages to the hostage takers indirectly. This is especially the case in the aforementioned hostage crises in Russia, where the hostage takers always followed the reporting on television and radio in order to gain knowledge about what was going on the outside. And third, media coverage has always been one of the most important tools in resolving hostage crises, especially ones motivated by political or ideological grievances. In such cases, the hostage takers are typically interested in conveying their point of view to the highest number of viewers possible. In such a setting, the access to media has historically been used as a valuable bargaining chip to obtain the release of hostages or some other concessions on behalf of the hostage takers. On the other hand, the media's impact on the outcome can also be a very negative one. In the past, a number of hostage crises have been complicated by irresponsible reporting such as the airing of live footage of rescue teams moving into position and therefore ruining the element of surprise, or the revealing of the identity of the hostages passing information from the inside, thereby leading to their execution. As a result, media management is one of the key issues that need to be handled with utmost attention in any hostage situation. This requires a mutual understanding of media and government interests.

From this perspective, Beslan was again a colossal failure. The information that was released to the media was manipulated, moreover, in such a blatant and obvious way that everyone in Beslan knew that this could not have been a mistake, including the terrorists. On the first day, Lev Dzugayev,[66] the spokesman of the North Ossetian President, identified the number of hostages inside the school as 150, later correcting this number to an implausible final figure of 354. This was School Number 1, the largest school in Beslan, housing nearly 1,000 students. Moreover, it was September 1, a day when many parents and family members accompany the younger children to school for a special celebration known as the Day of Knowledge. In addition, the fact that the number of hostages was over 1,200 was conveyed by the terrorists in telephone conversations with officials and to Ruslan Aushev who personally visited the gym. Aushev was even handed a videotape that featured the scenes from the gym, where it was obvious that there were at least 1,000 hostages present. The authorities immediately and stubbornly claimed the tape was blank, even when it was later shown on the NTV station. Mamitova, the doctor who on two occasions brought out the terrorist demands on a piece of paper, also conveyed the real number of hostages on both occasions. In short, it is beyond reasonable doubt that the actual number of hostages in the gym was known to every person in the region, as demonstrated by the fact that 1,045 hospital beds in four Beslan and Vladikavkaz hospitals were being freed in preparation for the worst. And yet, the authorities continued to insist that the number of hostages was 354. This approach not only angered the local residents and undermined public confidence in the government statements; it was also directly responsible for escalating the tensions in the crisis. The terrorists knew immediately that the government was purposefully downplaying the number of hostages, and interpreted this move as public relations preparations for the aftermath of an inevitable rescue operation. Immediately after the number 354 was announced, the terrorists started to run around the gym screaming: "They say that there are 354 of you. Nobody needs you. Maybe we will just reduce you to that number!" In addition, when this number was consistently repeated even on the second day, the terrorists stopped giving the children water. Overall, the government's insistence on the unrealistically low number of hostages made a bad situation much worse.

INVESTIGATION

The confidence in the authorities' handling of the Beslan crisis was by no means strengthened in the aftermath of the attack and the subsequent investigation. Many questions still remain unanswered. The first such question concerns the issue of the number of terrorists involved. Official figures indicate that 31 terrorists were killed, and 1 captured alive. Since the authorities claim that not a single terrorist escaped, the number of terrorists participating in the attack is officially 32. However, there is a consensus among hostages and residents of Beslan that the number of terrorists was much higher, with most estimates falling into the range between 50 and 70 attackers. And while the authorities dispute even the possibility that anyone got away, numerous pieces of evidence seem to point in this direction. First, there are specific terrorists that "disappeared" after the second day, never to be seen again even among the dead terrorists. Amongst them was Ali, one of the leaders and the main negotiator. Hostages also report the disappearance of a number of Slavic-looking terrorists, including a woman with fair hair tied in a pony tale, in black camouflage overalls, holding a sniper rifle and smoking a cigarette,[67] and a mysterious "big, red-haired man with a red face who spoke Russian without an accent, and whom the hostages were specifically forbidden to look at."[68] In addition, a number of hostages recognized three militants that are currently at large and on the most wanted list in Dagestan, including Omar Sheykhulayev, Shamil Abidov, and Gadzhi Melikov.[69] The hostages consulted when gathering research for this chapter all agreed, after being shown the pictures of these men, that Sheykhulayev was there; about half of them remember seeing Abidov, though only two pointed to Melikov.

Their absence on the list of identified terrorists has, of course, other explanations as well. Only 19 of the bodies have been actually identified,[70] while the rest are so dismembered that their faces are not recognizable, 5 of them so badly that it was not even possible to obtain fingerprints.[71] As a result, it is possible that at least some of the terrorists that are "missing" could be among these unidentifiable bodies. Nevertheless, this does not explain the fact that the federal troops reported having a shootout with Sheikhulayev and several of his men in Dagestan on January 5, 2005.[72] Similarly, Iznaur Kodzoyev—whose wife was summoned to the school on the second day to try to convince her husband to release the children—was killed not in September 2004 in Beslan, but instead, in his native village of Al'tievo in April 2005.[73]

Overall, it is more then probable that a number of terrorists did actually get away from the school, which is hardly surprising given the chaos at the scene and the fact that the terrorists were equipped with civilian clothing and other items to help them get away. The greater issue than the fact that not all terrorists were caught or killed is the failure of the authorities to acknowledge this possibility, which results in the further upsurge of conspiracy theories and in the declining faith in the government's honesty.

Overall, the investigation of Beslan has been a blunder, to the point that one even has to wonder about the sincerity of the federal attempts to achieve a productive result. The school itself was never sealed off for a forensic examination of any kind. Many items that ended up being critical pieces of evidence only entered the investigation after they were collected directly by the people in Beslan and handed to the authorities. The authorities keep releasing so many controversial and contradictory pieces of "evidence" that no one can be sure about what is true anymore. For example, the body of Vladimir Khodov (who, as described earlier, was already wanted by the Russian authorities) has clearly and unanimously been identified among the dead terrorists by the hostages and investigators alike.[74] However, a North Ossetian police spokesman claimed that Khodov had been captured alive but committed suicide the next day. "You understand," he added, "that is the official version."[75]

CONCLUSIONS

In the aftermath of Beslan, Basayev—in his typical fashion—tried to put all the blame on Moscow by stating that he regretted that "so many children died at the hands of the Russians," but also emphasizing that he did not regret the seizure of the school itself.[76] Unlike in the aftermath of Dubrovka, however, he did not make an attempt to plead for international sympathy; on the contrary, Basayev threatened to attack "citizens of states whose leaders support Putin's Chechen policy," also proclaiming that "this world will sooner be set on fire than we refuse to fight for our freedom and independence!"[77] In another interview conducted in January 2005, Basayev confirmed his intention to launch more "Beslan-style" operations in the future.[78] However, on July 10, 2006, Shamil Basayev was killed by an explosive-laden truck in a small Ingush village of Ekhazhevo, making the fulfillment of his threats uncertain.

What are the key lessons we can learn from Beslan? The first lesson is that we can certainly expect the resolution of future hostage incidents to be extremely challenging due the hostage takers' extensive knowledge of our operational procedures, security precautions designed to make a rescue operation as costly in terms of human life as possible, and a high level of distrust in the authorities' intentions. Another lesson is that despite all of these challenges, the room for a negotiated settlement is likely to exist, and that it may in fact be the only realistic option for solving the incident without a massive loss of life among the hostages. Whether we will succeed in this endeavor in the future will largely depend on the political sanction of the use of negotiations as the preferred means to resolve terrorist hostage situations, as well as on our ability to think outside the box and adapt to the different circumstance and requirements of situations involving ideologically inspired hostage takers. For the lack of a better option, we will need to redefine our own measures of success and increase our tolerance for casualties in terms of not giving up on negotiations based solely on the fact that hostages have died during the incident. At the same time, it is quite possible that some situations will ultimately need to be addressed by a tactical resolution. But even in such situations, the negotiation element will still be crucial, as it can be used to get the maximum number of people out of the target location before the storming.

Another key lesson of Beslan has to do with management of the scene. In hostage situations all of the elements need to be communicating with each other under a clear chain of command. Any disruptive elements such as armed outsiders need to controlled, disarmed, and moved behind a secured perimeter. Given the extreme level of emotion involved, this will require a skilled negotiation effort of its own. Further, effective consequence management will be critical to reducing the negative impact of a possible rescue operation. Quite simply, a timely response saves lives.

Perhaps the most important lesson is that while in some cases secretiveness and temporary spin-doctoring of information can have short-term benefits in helping to solve a hostage crisis, applying such a strategy in the long term will ultimately be counterproductive. When governments are caught covering up and manipulating evidence in the aftermath of a failed counterterrorism effort, it only benefits the terrorists for whom the embarrassment of a government and the undermining of its authority is a critical component of their grand strategy. The key point to realize is that we need to not only avoid feeding into this strategy, but we also must learn to effectively counter it. Perhaps the best defense is to provide a comprehensive public investigation that will release as much detailed information as possible to dispel any doubts among the public. Examples of this effort are the *9/11 Commission Report* published by the U.S. Congress or the White Paper about the activities of the *Jeemah Islamiyah* cell in Singapore published by the city state's home ministry. Both of these reports reveal in great detail the involvement and activities of the individuals responsible, and do not hide anything with the exception of very specific sensitive information that would endanger the security of human intelligence sources. Even more importantly, they facilitate the identification of mistakes and the drawing of lessons learned, with the goal of ensuring that the same mistakes do not occur in the future. The Russian government, despite originally dismissing the idea, also finally agreed to conduct a similar open investigation into the events of Beslan. Unfortunately, the report that was prepared by the (federal) Torshin Commission differs sharply in many of the descriptions of events and conclusions form report compiled by the (local) Kesaev Commission. The inability or unwillingness to admit and identify the flaws in the response to Beslan does more than just protect the individuals responsible for these mistakes; it effectively inhibits the learning process, which means that Beslan is bound to repeat itself.

NOTES

1. The best works on the Beslan events include: Uwe Buse, Ullrich Fichtner, Mario Kaiser, Uwe Klussmann, Walter Mayr, and Christian Neef, "Putin's Ground Zero," *Der Spiegel*, December 27, 2004: 65–101; Dunlop. John B., "Beslan: Russia's 9/11?" The American Committee for Peace in Chechnya; and The Jamestown Foundation, October 2005; C. J. Chivers, "The School: The inside story of the 2004 attack in Beslan," *Esquire* 145, Issue 6 (June 2006), available at http://www.esquire.com/features/articles/2006/060512_mfe_beslan.html; Dolnik, Adam, "Beslan and Beyond: Negotiating with the 'New' Terrorists," presented at the Processes of International Negotiation workshop titled *Negotiating with Terrorists*, International Institute for Applied Systems Analysis, Luxemburg, Austria, June 9–10, 2006. Publication forthcoming.

2. It was later reported that the late arrival of policemen on the scene was caused by the fact that the duty officer with the key to the weapons locker could not be located for a full 40 minutes.

3. Interview with Stanislav Kesaev, Vladikavkaz, July 2005.

4. Chief Beslan gunman described, *Caucasian Knot*, August 4, 2005.

5. A mobile phone number.

6. Xeroxcopy of original, author's collection.

7. According to one version, the woman was detonated remotely by Khuchbarov because of her disobedience. But, since the bomber detonated in a doorway, also killing the other suicide bomber and another terrorist in the process, it

seems more likely that the detonation was an accident. Further, the other terrorists immediately afterwards prayed by the bodied of their dead colleagues, which is something that wouldn't happen if they were considered traitors.

8. Uwe Buse, Ullrich Fichtner, Mario Kaiser, Uwe Klussmann, Walter Mayr, and Christian Neef, "Putin's Ground Zero," *Der Spiegel*, December 27, 2004: 65–101.

9. RIA: Inquiry Finds Chechen Separatist Leader Was Given Chance To Intervene at Beslan, March 3, 2005.

10. Xeroxcopy of Basayev's note, author's collection.

11. Plater-Zyberk, Henry, "Beslan–Lessons Learned?" Conflict Studies Research Centre, November 2004.

12. Interview with Ruslan Aushev, Moscow, November 2005.

13. Aslanbek Aslakhanov interviewed in Kevin Sim's documentary "Beslan: Siege of School No. 1," Wide Angle, 2005.

14. Interview with Larisa Kudzyeva, Beslan, November 2005.

15. The terrorists had a book that was rigged as a switch to the explosive daisy chain. One terrorist always had his foot on this book. If he lifted the foot, detonation would occur.

16. Interview with Larisa Kudzyeva, Beslan, November 2005.

17. Uwe Buse, Ullrich Fichtner, Mario Kaiser, Uwe Klussmann, Walter Mayr, and Christian Neef, "Putin's Ground Zero," *Der Spiegel*, December 27, 2004: 65–101.

18. On the other hand, the Kremlin has tried to implicate Maskhadov in previous acts of terrorism, and providing him an opportunity to appear as a savior by engaging him in this crucial role, was hardly going to be acceptable to the Kremlin. Nevertheless, both Dzosokhov and Aushev contacted Maskhadov's envoy Zakayev in London. The reply was that Maskhadov was ready to assume the negotiating role, but asked for a guarantee that he would be provided unhindered access to the school and that the Russians would not kill him.

19. Uwe Buse, Ullrich Fichtner, Mario Kaiser, Uwe Klussmann, Walter Mayr, and Christian Neef, "Putin's Ground Zero," *Der Spiegel*, December 27, 2004: 65–101.

20. "New Details Emerge on Maschadov's Bid to Mediate in Beslan," *Chechnya Weekly* VII, Issue 1 (January 5, 2006), available at http://www.jamestown.org/publications_details.php?volume_id=416&issue_id=3576&article_id=2370636

21. Further, after Beslan the federal authorities accused him of actually planning the attack and put a $10 million bounty on his head. Maschadov was then killed on March 8, 2005, in the village of Tolstoy-Yurt, near Grozny.

22. Paul Murphy, *Wolves Of Islam: Russia and the Faces of Chechen Terror* (Washington, DC: Potomac Books, 2005) p. 231.

23. School hostage-takers released from prison. *The Russia Journal*, September 7, 2004.

24. Shvarev Aleksander, "'Man With a Gun' From Engenoy," *Moscow Vremya Novostey*, September 16, 2004.

25. Yekaterina Blinova and Anton Trofimov, "Beslan Hostage Takers May Have Included Arrested Terrorist, Basayev Link Likely." *Nezavisimaya Gazeta*, September 8, 2004.

26. Farniev, Zaur, "Who Should We Kill Now, Zarema?" *Kommersant*, December 24, 2005.

27. "Professional Terrorists" *Moscow Vremya Novostey*, September 17, 2004.

28. Murphy (2005): p. 232.

29. *Vremya Novostey*: Russian Law Enforcement Identifies Beslan Ringleader as Chechen Ruslan 'The Colonel' Khuchbarov. FBIS ID#: CEP20040910000096.

30. RFE/RL Fact Box: Major terrorist Incidents tied to Russian-Chechen War, http://www.rferl.org/featuresarticle/2004/09/d981dd2d-8b08-41ff-a2e2-ada25338093c.html.

31. *Kavkaz-Tsentr News Agency*: Basayev Says 'Special Operations' Prepared for 'Occupying Forces' FBIS ID#: CEP20040617000031.

32. Uwe Buse, Ullrich Fichtner, Mario Kaiser, Uwe Klussmann, Walter Mayr, and Christian Neef, "Putin's Ground Zero," *Der Spiegel*, December 27, 2004.

33. In an informal chat, several policemen who were also Sagopshi residents denied the existence of the camp, as well as the discovery of the weapons and shootout with Tsechoyev. But the body language and inconsistency in their story have led the author to conclude that they were lying. This is no surprising as some of the Beslan terrorists were their childhood friends and fellow policemen.

34. Conversations with residents of Psedakh, November 2004.

35. "Newspaper Provides Fresh Beslan Details," Jamestown Foundation, *Chechnya Weekly* 6, Issue 21 (June 01, 2005), available at http://www.jamestown.org/publications_details.php?volume_id=409&issue_id=3352&article_id=2369825

36. "Kulayev Trial: The Missing Slavic Snipers," Jamestown Foundation, *Chechnya Weekly* 6, Issue 30 (August 03, 2005), available at http://www.jamestown.org/publications_details.php?volume_id=409&issue_id=3424&article_id=2370105

37. "Newspaper Provides Fresh Beslan Details," Jamestown Foundation, *Chechnya Weekly* 6, Issue 21 (June 01, 2005), available at http://www.jamestown.org/publications_details.php?volume_id=409&issue_id=3352&article_id=2369825

38. Interview with Fatima Dudiyeva, the sole police officer present at the school during the takeover, who later became a hostage.

39. Dunlop. John B., "Beslan: Russia's 9/11?" The American Committee for Peace in Chechnya and The Jamestown Foundation, October 2005.

40. For instance, Khodov told Larissa Mamitova: "Doctor, you will not believe it if you knew how we ended up here. Just wait till I tell you the story." Khodov also mocked the authorities, boasting aloud to a number of hostages: "Nobody cares about you. Your police sold you out for $20,000." According to hostages, Ali also claimed that getting to Beslan did not cause any problems whatsoever, and that at every [police] post they paid money and passed through. It seems that the hostage takers were eager to capitalize on the doubts for propaganda reasons, as documented by the recorded message that they left behind in the school. It said: "There is small puddle. There's nothing here, no lakes no rivers. No sources of water at all. Just trees, leaves, animals and that puddle. One question really interests me: Where did the frogs come from?"

41. When Major Sultan Gurashev, an Ingush police officer that encountered and single-handedly tried to stop the suspicious vehicles near the village of Khurakao, he was disarmed and tied up in one of the cars. The terrorists left him there as they stormed to school.

42. Conversations with Sultan Gurashev's close relatives, Khurikau, July 2005.

43. Adam Dolnik, "Beslan and Beyond: Negotiating with the 'New' Terrorists," Presented at the Processes of International Negotiation workshop titled "Negotiating with Terrorists," International Institute for Applied Systems Analysis, Laxenburg, Austria, June 9–10, 2006. Publication forthcoming.

44. Kulayev Trial provides New Beslan Details, *Chechnya Weekly* 6, Issue 23 (June 16, 2005), available at http://www.jamestown.org/publications_details. php?volume_id=409&issue_id=3370&article_id=2369896

45. Putin who had won his first presidency based solely on a tough stance on Chechnya, could hardly afford being seen as negotiating with terrorists. Allowing Maskhadov to enter the negotiations and perhaps succeed would also have been a huge political and personal blow to Putin.

46. For more details on possible approaches see Adam Dolnik, "Beslan and Beyond: Negotiating with the 'New' Terrorists," Presented at the Processes of International Negotiation workshop titled "Negotiating with Terrorists," International Institute for Applied Systems Analysis, Laxenburg, Austria, June 9–10, 2006. Publication forthcoming.

47. Henry Plater-Zyberk, "Beslan – Lessons Learned?" Conflict Studies Research Centre, November 2004.

48. "Documents Suggest that the Feds Were in Charge During Beslan," Jamestown Foundation, *Chechnya Weekly* 6, Issue 15 (April 20, 2005), available at http://www.jamestown.org/publications_details.php?volume_id=409&issue_id=3305&article_id=2369625

49. Interview with Stanislav Kesaev, Vladikavakaz, November 2005.

50. "Documents Suggest that the Feds Were in Charge During Beslan," Jamestown Foundation, *Chechnya Weekly* 6, Issue 15 (April 20, 2005), available at http://www.jamestown.org/publications_details.php?volume_id=409&issue_id=3305&article_id=2369625

51. Interview with Andrei Soldatov, Moscow, July 2005.

52. Interview with Madina Shavlokhova, Beslan, July 2005.

53. Controversial evidence in Kulayev case, *Caucasian Knot*, January 17, 2006.

54. Interview with Fatima Dudiyeva, Beslan, November 2005.

55. Interview with Ala Ramonova, Beslan, July 2005.

56. Снайперам мешало специальное остекление в бесланской школе, August 12, 2005, http://lenta.ru/news/2005/08/12/sniper/.

57. Lawrence Uzzell, "Reporter Puts Forward Another Version of Events." Jamestown Foundation, *Chechnya Weekly* 5, Issue 35 (September 15, 2004), available at http://www.jamestown.org/publications_details.php?volume_id=396&issue_id=3071&article_id=2368508

58. Elena Milashina, "Eyewitnesses: 'The roof caught fire when they began shooting shells at it'" *Novaya Gazeta*, October 7, 2004.

59. "Newspaper Provides Fresh Beslan Details," Jamestown Foundation, *Chechnya weekly* 6, Issue 21 (June 01, 2005), available at http://www.jamestown.org/publications_details.php?volume_id=409&issue_id=3352&article_id=2369825

60. Controversial evidence in Kulayev case, *Caucasian Knot*, January 17, 2006.

61. Interview with Israil Ttoonti, Beslan, November 2005.

62. Interview with the head of the Beslan Mother's Committee Susanna Duadyieva and local journalist and witness Murag Kaboev, Beslan, July 2005.

63. "Newspaper Provides Fresh Beslan Details," Jamestown Foundation, *Chechnya weekly* 6, Issue 21 (June 01, 2005), available at http://www.jamestown.org/publications_details.php?volume_id=409&issue_id=3352&article_id=2369825

64. The author is aware of several simulations in Western countries that resulted in even greater number of casualties in a similar setting.

65. Basayev Interview for *Channel 4 News*, February 04, 2005.

66. Lev Dzugayev's father passed away several days prior to the incident, so this was a very difficult time period for him.

67. "Kulayev Trial: The Missing Slavic Snipers," Jamestown Foundation, *Chechnya Weekly* 6, Issue 30 (August 03, 2005), available at http://www.jamestown.org/publications_details.php?volume_id=409&issue_id=3424&article_id=2370105

68. "Kulayev Trial: The Missing Slavic Snipers," Jamestown Foundation, *Chechnya Weekly* 6, Issue 30 (August 03, 2005), available at http://www.jamestown.org/publications_details.php?volume_id=409&issue_id=3424&article_id=2370105

69. Madina Shavlokhova, "Beslan Gunmen Recognized Among Living," *Izvestiya* (November 21, 2005).

70. This identification problem extended to the hostages as well. At least five bodies had to be exhumed due to false identification. A large number of bodies has still not been identified. Those parents that were not sure whether the bodies are really the one of their children were told that they can have DNA tests run at Rostov on Don for 300 Euros, an large sum for most Beslan residents. Similarly, many parents were not allowed to keep their children's bodies in the morgue due to insufficient space, and were force to rent space in refrigerated trucks for 300 rubles per night.

71. Sergey Dyupin, "The Investigation is Hitting it on the Head," *Kommersant*, September 15, 2004.

72. "Federal Forces Battle Handful of Dagestani Militants," Jamestown Foundation. *Chechnya Weekly* VII, Issue 1 (January 6, 2006), available at http://www.jamestown.org/publications_details.php?volume_id=416&&issue_id=3576

73. PRESS-RELEASE #1251: Special operation in Al'tievo http://friendly.narod.ru/2005-2e/info1251e.htm, April 14, 2005.

74. *MosNews*: Russian Commando Says Officials Concealing Truth Behind Beslan, November 04, 2004, http://www.mosnews.com/news/2004/11/04/vasskp1.shtml.

75. Mark Franchetti and Matthew Campbell, "How a repressed village misfit became the butcher of Beslan," The Sunday Times, September 12, 2004, http://www.timesonline.co.uk/article/0,,2089-1257953_1,00.html.

76. Statement of Chief of the Military Council of State Defense Council ⟨⟨Majlis al-Shura⟩⟩ of Chechen Republic of Ichkeria Abdullah Shamil Abu-Idris concerning the events of October 23–26, 2002, in Moscow, http://62.212.121.113/www.kavkazcenter.com/eng/articlebe27.html?id=605.

77. Ibid.

78. Kavkaz Center: Transcript of Shamil Basayev Interview for *Channel 4 News*, http://kavkazcenter.com/eng/article.php?id=3500 (accessed on April 8, 2005).

CHAPTER 12

THE MADRID ATTACKS ON MARCH 11: AN ANALYSIS OF THE JIHADIST THREAT IN SPAIN AND MAIN COUNTERTERRORIST MEASURES

Rogelio Alonso

This chapter will analyze the worst terrorist attack ever suffered by Spain on March 11, 2004. On that day, ten bombs planted in four different trains filled with thousands of commuters on their way to Madrid were detonated between 7:37 and 7:40 A.M., killing 191 people. Although Spain had been constantly targeted by various types of terrorism since the late 1960s, violence from the ethno-nationalist Basque terrorist group *Euskadi Ta Askatasuna* (ETA, or Basque Fatherland and Freedom) being by far the most intense, never before had a terrorist attack in the country been so indiscriminate and lethal. Both characteristics showed that the way in which the terrorist attack was perpetrated did not represent the traditional modus operandi of ETA. As it would soon emerge, the killings on March 11 were carried out by a group of Islamist terrorists, some of whom were closely linked to individuals who were also part of the al Qaeda network. The chapter will look at the events that led to this terrorist attack, analyzing how and why such an atrocity was perpetrated, as well as its implications for counterterrorism in the country. The main measures implemented as a response to this tragedy will also be described and assessed.

THE BACKGROUND AND AFTERMATH
OF THE MARCH 11 ATTACKS

The terrorist attacks perpetrated in Madrid on that day and the collective suicide of seven of those responsible for them weeks later, on April 3, 2004—when Spanish police surrounded the apartment where some of the men involved in the March 11 explosions were hiding—exposed the prominence that the jihadist movement had reached in the country. Spain, which as far back as 2001 had been described by Italian judicial authorities as the "main base of al Qaeda in Europe"[1] as a result of the activities of Islamist radicals during the previous decade, had also become a target of violence. The evolution of jihadism demonstrated the extent to which the country had become a hub for the recruitment and radicalization of individuals prepared to commit terrorist attacks in Spain and further away. In order to understand the rationale of an attack like the one perpetrated in Madrid it is important to stress that the al Qaeda network in Spain had been involved in different terrorist activities since the mid- and late 1990s that were mainly oriented toward other countries. Spain was initially regarded as a valuable base for logistical and infrastructure support, to the point of being described as "one of the favorite sanctuaries" of Islamist terrorists,[2] but not as a target of violence itself. It was during that period that different activists, some of whom would be later sentenced for membership and collaboration with a terrorist organization, engaged in the indoctrination and radicalization of other individuals, as well as in the financing of terrorist cells in several countries throughout the world, and the recruiting of mujahideen in order to send them to conflict spots such as Bosnia, Chechnya, Indonesia, and Afghanistan. Therefore, March 11 exposed a significant shift in the terrorist strategy, since Spain itself had for the first time become a target.

Some observers find a direct cause-effect relation between the Iraq conflict and this change in the scene. The fact that the terrorist attacks took place three days before a general election in the country has led to speculation about the likely intentions of the terrorists. Contrary to extended opinion, however, no evidence has emerged yet to prove that those responsible for the March 11 attack aimed at destabilizing the government or even influencing the nation's vote in order to damage the party in power at the time, which had supported the military intervention in Iraq. In fact, the relationship between electoral processes and terrorism is not uncommon, with previous experiences demonstrating that very often the outcome of terrorists attacks does not fulfill the expectations of those behind them since violence can be—and sometimes is—counterproductive for those who perpetrate it.[3] It is reasonable to argue that if the Spanish government at the time of the March 11 attacks had responded in a different way, avoiding certain mistakes made in the management of the crisis, the electoral results could have been different.[4] Therefore, two points can be made. First of all, it is not possible to establish that the terrorists' main motivation was to punish the Spanish government for its involvement in the Iraq war. Secondly, even if this had been the terrorists' intention, the final outcome was determined not only by the attack itself, but also by the government's response to it. In other words, the fact that a different response could have strengthened the Spanish government at such a critical time, puts into question that the terrorist intention was to change the sign of the election.[5]

Instead of Iraq, another issue may have acted as a stronger motivational factor for those behind the terrorist acts described here and the ones—some of them of a suicide type—that were to follow but did not materialize as a result of subsequent police successes. The major setback suffered by the network of Islamist terrorists in Spain, when at the end of 2001 key figures were arrested by Spanish police, was probably a decisive variable. Such a strike against the infrastructure of the terrorist network may have triggered a strong feeling of revenge that would have materialized in the terrorist campaign initiated in 2004.[6] It should be stressed that the March 11 attack was not a "one off" from the terrorist's point of view. The bombs on that day constituted the beginning of a campaign that was going to continue weeks afterward and that was cut short as a result of the security forces' successes that led to the siege of seven of the terrorists in the suburb of Leganés, located in the outskirts of Madrid, and their collective suicide. The fact that the socialist José Luis Rodríguez Zapatero, the new Spanish prime minister elected at the polls on March 14, had decided to pull out the troops from Iraq, did not deter the terrorists from planning more attacks after his election victory. In fact, as police and judicial investigations have confirmed, the arrest of several relatives of some of those directly involved in organizing and perpetrating the attacks two weeks later led the terrorists to threaten the government with more attacks. The threats issued by the terrorist cell in the aftermath of these detentions are seen by investigators as directly related to those arrests which were explicitly mentioned and criticized in a video recording. The contents of the tape proved quite revealing of the fanatical rationale of the terrorists, as the following extract demonstrates:

> Two weeks after our blessed incursion in *Mayrit*[7] and following your new ruler's declaration of intent to inaugurate his mandate maintaining his combat against Muslims by sending more of the soldiers of the cross to Afghanistan, the death brigade of Al Ansar al Qaeda (the supporters of al Qaeda) announces that we are continuing the path of our blessed jihad until the defeat of all of those who may consider following Bush's example of combating Muslims in the name of the war against terrorism. Therefore, the brigade in the land of Al Andalus has decided not to leave the territory until

their soldiers have been taken from the lands of Muslims immediately and unconditionally. If they didn't do it in a week's time from today we well keep our jihad until we fall as martyrs in the land of Tareq ben Ziad.[8] You must know that you will never be safe and that Bush and his administration will only bring you destruction. We will kill you at any time and place. We will not distinguish between the military and civilians. Thousands of our innocents die in Afghanistan and Iraq. Is your blood more valuable than ours?[9]

Directly addressing those Muslims that would also die in the indiscriminate attacks contemplated in such a threat, the terrorists went on to justify their killings as follows: "You know the grudge that the Spain of the crusades holds against Muslims. The history of Al Andalus and the inquisition is not far. We are very sorry for the injustices you suffer but our jihad is above anything else because our brothers suffer death and destruction. Those who are afraid of being killed or involved must leave before the week's deadline set before the truce expires."[10]

The threats did materialize, and on April 2, 2004, an explosive device was found at the railway line in the province of Toledo, near Madrid. As it would be later revealed, the fingerprints of Anwar Asrih Rifaat, one of the suicide terrorists, were found in the plastic bag that contained the explosives that seemed aimed at derailing one of the high-speed trains on the Madrid-Seville route. The finding confirmed that, as police feared, the cell responsible for March 11 had planned more attacks. Other discoveries would confirm, too, that suicide attacks in the country were also contemplated by the terrorists. In the meantime, Spanish police had managed to locate some of the terrorist suspects. One of the bags that failed to explode on March 11 proved decisive in the police investigations, leading to some arrests two days after the attacks. Jamal Zougan was the first person to be detained. A Moroccan born in Tangier in 1974, he had lived in Spain for 20 years, where he had caught the attention of Spanish police. His name appeared in the judicial report written by Judge Baltasar Garzón in 2002 after the arrest of Imad Eddin Barakat Yarkas, alias *Abu Dahdah*, regarded as the leader of al Qaeda in Spain.[11] As a result of the investigations conducted at that time, Zougam's surveillance demonstrated he had regularly offered assistance to al Qaeda individuals.

Jamal Zougam was the person who bought the phone cards used in the terrorist attack on March 11, and that would allow Spanish police to track down the rest of the members of the operational cell, most of whom were hidden in an apartment located in Leganés. On Saturday April 3, 2004, one day after the explosive device had been found at the railway line, police surrounded the building. One of the terrorists identified police officers outside the apartment, alerting the rest of the group before managing to escape from the scene. The terrorists initiated a shoot-out and the GEO (*Grupo Especial de Operaciones*), the special unit of the Spanish police trained for siege situations, was deployed. Two hours later, and after carefully assessing the situation, some members of the unit entered the building taking positions right outside the apartment. As a member of the police squad who led the operation explained later, a small amount of explosives was placed outside the door by officers. Once the door was blown off, the police attempted to negotiate with the terrorists, but to no avail, since they continued shooting from inside while challenging the officers to come into the apartment. While the police outside were considering the use of tear gas, one of the terrorists announced they were sending an emissary who the police feared could be carrying explosives.[12] It was at that point that a huge explosion was heard, resulting in the death of seven terrorists in the apartment, and killing one of the members of the special police squad. According to the attorney in charge of the case at the Spanish National Court, the terrorists only decided to kill themselves after realizing they were besieged with no prospect of escaping. As it was revealed by the search of the house in the aftermath of the explosion, the terrorists had detailed plans for future attacks that they were going to carry out beginning April 4, 2004. This was the deadline established in a statement written by one of the suicide terrorists, Sarhane Ben Abdelmajid Fakhet, nicknamed *the Tunisian*, that was sent to the Spanish daily *Abc*. The communiqué, signed by Abu Dujan Al Afgani in the name of "The Death Battalion," demanded the withdrawal of Spanish troops from Iraq and Afghanistan and threatened with more attacks.[13] As it was also found later on, the targets included two recreational centers frequented by Jewish families, and a British school, all in the Madrid area. Once again, the terrorists had opted for soft targets.

Religious Dimensions

The manner in which the terrorists claimed responsibility for the attacks on March 11, using a video recording released two days later, led the police and intelligence services to believe that a suicide attack was definitely contemplated. The video showed a man dressed in a white gown with his face covered by a white sheet, wearing dark glasses and a hat with a banner behind his back in which some Arab words could be read: "There is no other God than Allah and Mohammad is his prophet." Armed with a 9-mm pistol, the terrorist read a statement that he claimed was "a warning from al Qaida's spokesperson in Europe, Abud Dujan Al Afgani." The terrorist, who was later identified as Rachid Oulad Akcha, one of the seven men who committed suicide on April 3, 2004, said: "This is a response to the crimes you have committed in the world, and particularly in Iraq and Afghanistan, and there will be more if God so desires....You want life and we want death....If you don't stop your injustices there will be more and more blood. These attacks are very little compared to what may happen."[14] According to Jorge Dezcallar, the director of the Spanish Center for National Intelligence (CNI, *Centro Nacional de Inteligencia*) at the time of the attack, the dressing of the male terrorist who claimed responsibility for March 11 was quite revealing. In his testimony to the Commission of Inquiry on March 11, Dezcallar emphasized that the video showed that the terrorist regarded himself as if he was already dead and, in his opinion, so it was with the rest of the group. "The problem is that if they haven't killed themselves yet, they are going to do it. They already regard themselves purified and on their way to paradise," Dezcallar added.[15] As it has already been mentioned, only days before the suicide, on March 27, the group had recorded another video full of threats that was found after the explosion in Leganés. In this case, the video footage showed three terrorists who some sources have identified as three of the suicide terrorists, heavily armed, dressed in white gowns and with their faces covered by balaclavas. The three members of the self-named "Company of Death" appeared holding what resembled detonators connected to explosive devices that were attached to their bodies.

The radical neosalafist religious ideology of the seven men who killed themselves in Madrid was most certainly of great relevance to their behavior, since they were individuals already predisposed to suicide terrorism. This course of action was finally precipitated by factors such as the police siege of the apartment where they were hiding. According to the judiciary investigation, the terrorists intended to prevent the police from conducting future investigations that could result from their arrests and interrogations, and decided to end their lives while trying to kill as many policemen as possible. Some sources argue that their intention to kill policemen or other individuals was motivated by the fact that Islam prohibits suicide and, therefore, their act would be seen in a different light if those whom they regarded as infidels also died in the explosion. This point also illustrates the rational and utilitarian nature of the reasoning behind their decision to kill themselves. The telephone conversations that some of them kept with their relatives minutes before committing suicide, informing their families of their decision to kill themselves, demonstrates that their death was a deliberate act, revealing a combination of religious fanaticism and rational choice. The farewell letters left by some of the terrorists also strengthens this argument confirming their willingness to die.

One of the seven suicide terrorists, Abdennabi Kounjaa, nicknamed *Abdallah*, born in the Moroccan city of Taourit in 1975, wrote a "farewell letter" days before his suicide in which he thanked God for guiding him through the path he followed and assured his family that he had left them behind in Morocco because it was "a decision made by God almighty." He demanded that his daughters not emigrate to "infidel" countries like Spain, which he described as "hell." While addressing his daughters, Kounjaa asked them to follow the "*mujahideen* brothers throughout the world." He went on to say: "I can't put up with this life living like a weak and humiliated person under the scrutiny of the infidels and tyrants." He also added that "this life is the path towards death," thus preferring "death rather than life." The letter concluded: "I hope you follow the words and deeds, the jihad in Islam, since it's a full religion. Make Westerners your enemies. May God punish the tyrants."[16] Another letter found at the bomb site constitutes another "testament" by one of the suicide terrorists, in which he says goodbye to his "beloved mother, father, brothers, and sisters" and to all his "dearest comrades and Muslims in general." He added: "I have chosen this path by my own will, the path of the prophets and those sent by Allah, because the time of humiliation and dishonor has reached its conclusion. To me, it's more honorable to die dignified than to live humiliated while I see my brothers being slaughtered, murdered and arrested throughout the world while we survive like beasts."[17] Another unfinished letter—bearing similarities with the ones previously described—was also found at the Madrid apartment of Said Berraj, a terrorist suspect allegedly involved in the March 11 attacks who managed to escape police arrest.[18]

The Investigation and Trial

In April 2006, Judge Juan del Olmo, the magistrate in charge of one of the most complicated cases in the protracted history of Spain's fight against terrorism, was able to present charges against 29 suspects in relation to their involvement in March 11. Many of these men had already been under investigation prior to the massacre in Madrid, as part of other investigations related to Islamist terrorism and criminality. In fact, the judicial investigation contained detailed transcriptions of telephone conversations of some of the suspects that were taped by Spanish police only days before the terrorist attack. Jamal Ahmidan (nicknamed *the Chinese*), born in Tetuan, Morocco, in October 28, 1970, was one of the activists under surveillance and the person who acquired the explosives used on March 11, exchanging them for drugs and a considerable amount of money. He also managed to acquire weapons and ammunition through his contacts in the Spanish criminal world developed since he got involved in petty crime and drug smuggling shortly after he entered Spain illegally in 1990. Police informants were able to provide information on some of the terrorists' movements prior to March 11, although limited human and material resources as well as important gaps in the coordination of different agencies prevented security forces at the time from conducting more intense and efficient surveillance of the suspects. In fact—as was acknowledged by leading figures in the Spanish government in charge of security at the time of the terrorist attacks—"mistakes" were definitely made,[19] lapses that, as will be further analyzed later in this chapter, needed to be addressed in order to improve the country's capacity to prevent future terrorist attacks.

Internal notes produced by Spanish police reveal that their knowledge of some of the activities of the cell involved in the attack went as far back as October 2002.[20] Up to 30 individuals involved in the attacks had been investigated separately by the Spanish intelligence service and police forces in advance of the attacks. Twenty of them had already been investigated in the course of investigations that led to the detention of key figures in the so-called "Spanish cell of al Qaeda" in November 2001. Jamal Zougam, Sarhane Ben Abdelmagid Fakhet and Allekema Lamari were among those investigated at that time. Lamari, one of the seven suicide terrorists, was considered a highly dangerous individual, to the point that the Spanish intelligence service warned four months before March 11 of the likelihood of him perpetrating an attack. In September 2003, a reliable source had informed the Spanish intelligence service that Lamari could be organizing a suicide terrorist attack. Lamari's willingness to perpetrate terrorist actions aimed at derailing trains or setting a forest on fire had already been mentioned months earlier by informers.[21] The Spanish Civil Guard (*Guardia Civil*) had two informers closely linked to members of the plot responsible for stealing considerable amounts of explosives in a mine located in Asturias, a northern Spanish region. This intelligence background allowed investigators to make significant progress in the immediate aftermath of the March 11 attacks, rapidly uncovering and dismantling the network of terrorists who took part in the attacks as well as those who collaborated in their preparation. The analysis of phone conversations was one of the most useful pieces of the complex investigation that would finally enable investigators to explain in considerable detail how the terrorist attack was planned and perpetrated.

Paradoxically, although in 2002 the United States praised Spanish police successes against al Qaeda, describing the country as a "champion" in the fight against Islamist terrorism,[22] security forces were in the end unable to prevent an attack whose overall cost has been estimated by police to be around 100,000 Euros (US$126,380).[23] Although the country's antiterrorist framework against ETA had been improved over the years reaching a high degree of efficiency that managed to extremely weaken the Basque terrorist group, the same could not be said of the structures needed to properly combat the threat of Islamist terrorism, as acknowledged by one of the most prominent police authorities at the time who admitted that Spain was aware of a serious threat but lacked the resources to confront it successfully.[24] Such an awareness was complemented by José María Aznar's statement in 2002 in which the then prime minister stressed the importance of the threat faced by the country, warning that "We all have to be prepared because we can all be targets since there are sleeping cells in all of our nations."[25] These were not the only warnings *vis-à-vis* Islamist terrorism, as corroborated by Europol's assessment of the situation in Spain, produced in October 2003, in which they indicated: "The various terrorist groups comprising the so-called 'Islamic World Front' (under the leadership of al Qaida), as well as the advocates of internationalization of Jihad on a global scale, continue to pose the greatest threat to our interests as well as to the interests of the other EU Member States. The Spanish Government's support of the military intervention in Iraq by the United States and its Allies constitutes without doubt a further risk factor for Spain, even though it might not be the most decisive or dangerous one."[26]

THE GOVERNMENT'S RESPONSES TO MARCH 11

Spain's protracted history of confronting violence perpetrated by the Basque nationalist terrorist group ETA has enabled the country to reach a high level of efficiency against this type of terrorism. Different measures implemented over the years provided ample experience that would be used in order to improve Spain's capacities against a new brand of terrorism for which the country was not so well prepared by March 11. As mentioned earlier, the origins of jihadism in the country can be traced back to the previous decade when the first networks—composed mainly of Algerian and Syrian individuals—started to settle down in Spain. Although police surveillance led to important successes at the turn of the century, efforts directed to counter Islamist terrorism at the time were considerably restricted given the limited amount of human and material resources available. The emergence and development of the threat since the 1990s raised concerns among the main security agencies—that is, the National Police (*Policía Nacional*), Civil Guard (*Guardia Civil*), and the Intelligence Service (*Centro Nacional de Inteligencia, CNI*). Nonetheless, the commitment to confront Islamist terrorism became stronger as a result of the terrorist attacks in the United States in September 2001, and most definitely after the atrocity perpetrated in Madrid in 2004. In fact, the attacks in the United States led to a slight increase in police personnel, followed by another small boost after the 2003 Casablanca terrorists' attacks in neighboring Morocco. In these few years, the Spanish National Police increased its capacities by 25 percent, forming up to 70 specialists on Islamist terrorism and doubling those who concentrated on the Maghreb region, which was regarded as the main area of threat.[27] At the same time, the Civil Guard also increased its specialists on the subject, although the 60 experts available then were still regarded as insufficient. Despite these efforts, police and intelligence personnel, including translators, could always benefit from a more generous increase, with initiatives aimed at preventing the radicalization and terror group recruitment still scarce. It was only after Spain had suffered the loss of almost 200 people on March 11 that a broader counterterrorist framework was put into place. In the aftermath of the terrorist attacks, different measures were announced by the newly elected Spanish government. The scope of these initiatives coincides with the objectives set out by the European Union's strategy for combating terrorism and the radicalization and recruitment of individuals: Disrupt the activities of the networks and individuals who draw people into terrorism; ensure that voices of mainstream opinion prevail over those of extremism; and more vigorously promote security, justice, democracy, and opportunity for all.[28] The measures implemented by the Spanish authorities in order to fulfill these objectives can be divided into five different sections, which will be now examined.

Increase in Intelligence Capabilities

The fact that previous to the massacre perpetrated in Madrid, many of the terrorist suspects involved in the March 11 attacks had already been under investigation in the course of other investigations, exposed serious shortfalls that had to be confronted. In fact, the judicial investigation contained detailed transcriptions of telephone conversations of some of the suspects that were taped by Spanish police only days before the terrorist attack. Undoubtedly, "mistakes" were made, as the security minister at the time of the attacks acknowledged shortly after. The limited human and material resources available seriously constrained the work of the main security agencies, thus a significant increase was announced immediately after the attacks. The increase in translators was particularly relevant in the aftermath of the atrocity, given the surprising small number of professionals who were devoted to such an important part of the investigation process. The limited number of translators had considerably hampered previous investigations to the extent that in a few occasions, some recordings of terrorist suspects were not translated because of the lack of a professional who could speak the particular language required. The vast amount of dialects and unfamiliar cultural and social codes constitute important barriers for a better understanding of the current terrorist phenomenon and the activities of individuals under investigation, thus the absolute necessity of incorporating not only translators but also police and agents who are capable of working within the communities of concern. The complex access to what are already very closed clusters remains a daunting task that will require a coherent policy for the recruitment of translators, subject specialists and security personnel qualified to work in such an environment, as well as members of minority groups, preferably from a second generation.

Between 2004 and 2005, 600 new policemen have been allocated to the fight against Islamist terrorism, and 300 more are currently being trained with the intention of having over 1,000 specialists in this particular area, which requires important expertise and specific knowledge that has not been traditionally available. This increase is aimed at improving the quantity and the quality of intelligence; requiring more informers, under-cover, and infiltration agents; and better technical means for intercept-ing communications and conducting surveillance and scientific investi-gations. Intelligence gathering and the exploitation of a wide variety of sources—with the intention of providing accurate threat assessments and a fruitful response analysis—require vast and efficient resources. Coun-terterrorism requires a huge amount of information to be processed and carefully analyzed by competent staff.

The Spanish intelligence service began recruiting 300 new members, with the view of having 1,000 new agents within the next few years. How-ever, several challenges remain. First, the new agents will have to be fil-tered and properly selected before recruitment, and later will have to be trained through a slow process that requires existing members to devote some of their time and energy to the newcomers, thus stretching already limited resources until new ones are made fully available. The limited presence of police and intelligence personnel abroad was also a problem that the authorities began to address in the period after the March 2004 terrorist attacks. Police representatives have been dispatched to key areas such as Pakistan, Syria, Libya, Algeria, Jordan, Indonesia, Philippines, and Saudi Arabia. However, such a welcomed display cannot obscure the fact that the presence abroad of the Spanish intelligence service still consists of only 10 percent of its resources.

Judicial and police investigations before and after March 11 have re-vealed strong connections between terrorism and other criminal activities such as drug trafficking, smuggling, and robbery. Such a pattern was rec-ognized in 1995 by the then head of Britain's MI5, Stella Rimmington, who expressed how worrying it was to see a marked increase of activities re-lated to organized and serious crime, indicating the need to look for coun-termeasures similar to the ones that would be required against terrorist networks, among them a narrower cooperation involving security agen-cies at a national and international level as well as better coordination and assistance among governments.[29] Such a development would also have implications for models of analysis, advising a more thorough ap-proach that would take into account the aforementioned close relationship between terrorism and crime. This is particularly relevant to the Span-ish experience, as revealed by the fact that criminal networks have been involved in the preparation and support of terrorist operations such as March 11.

Improvement and Enhancement of Coordination

Intelligence, together with coordination, constituted one of the main pillars of counterterrorism in the fight against the Basque nationalist terrorist group ETA, and remain key elements of the counterterrorist framework against Islamist terrorism. Coordination among the different security agencies involved in counterterrorism remains a very important challenge. In an attempt to improve this type of coordination, a new National Center for the Coordination of Anti-Terrorism (*Centro Nacional de Coordinación Antiterrorista, CNCA*) was created in May 2004. Following in the steps of the Joint Terrorism Analysis Center (JTAC) created in the United Kingdom, the CNCA's main aim is to receive, process, and assess strategic information available from various sources and agencies, thus integrating information from the main security forces and the intelligence service. The center is composed of representatives of the two main police forces and the intelligence service, and one of its main objectives is to provide a good exchange of information through the correct management of databases. Although progress has been made in the development of such a center during the short time since its creation, very important challenges still lay ahead. On one hand, threat assessment has become a dominant activity for the center, producing analyses that have very little impact on the operational level. As police officers acknowledge themselves, this limitation—that stems from the nature of the information handled, which usually lacks a strong operational component—prevents common investigations from becoming more frequent and effective. Traditionally, the main agencies have been very reluctant to share information, leading to mistakes that in occasions have seriously endangered the lives of personnel engaged in antiterrorist operations. So far, the CNCA has been unable to overcame this legacy, which still remains despite the efforts by institutions like this one or another one created after March 11 with the aim of improving coordination—the Executive Committee for the Unified Command (*Comité Ejecutivo para el Mando Unificado, CEMU*), whose main task is to guarantee an efficient and coordinated performance of the two main Spanish police forces, the National Police and the Civil Guard.

Coordination between security agencies is also required between different countries, given the nature of the current threat faced by our societies. The transnational and international nature of Islamist terrorism means that internal security relies heavily on good cooperation and coordination with other countries where terrorists may plan their operations or develop their support networks with the aim of dispatching individuals abroad for the commission of attacks. Therefore, the necessary cooperation between police agencies both internally and externally must be complemented with effective coordination on the political and judicial level. To this extent, the reluctance to share sensitive information raises important obstacles that are not only limited to the domestic level but very common beyond this dimension. The increasing need for better and wider cooperation (as well as coordination) on a European level has been slowed down by obvious technical difficulties which have prevented a more thorough harmonization of tools and procedures.[30] Further, the unwillingness to engage in initiatives that may entail (or be perceived as) diminishing national sovereignty, as would be the case in an area such as security, has been characteristic of the way in which many European countries have approached this issue. This attitude has prevented a more decisive collective action, which has also been hindered by different perceptions about the terrorist threat and the response to it. The seriousness of the problem is not perceived in the same way by members of the European Union, with different experiences of Islamist terrorism shaping their understanding and concern of the phenomenon in different ways. Such an acknowledgement has led a group of five European partners—Spain, United Kingdom, France, Germany, and Italy—to meet periodically with the view of seeking ways to overcome the obstacles that prevent more effective cooperation and coordination on the areas outlined. The initiatives being considered by the group (initially known as the G5, but later on referred to as the G6 after the addition of Poland in 2006) include the elaboration of a list of terrorist suspects that could be shared by the country members, exposing the legal difficulties that the implementation of such a useful measure raise and the challenges still ahead in the struggle for better coordination. The complexity around this issue is even more evident when efforts are directed toward the improvement of coordination between European and Arab countries, a necessary objective of particular relevance to Spain, given its geo-strategic situation, which has led authorities to increase various initiatives in that direction.

Legislative Reforms

The Spanish protracted fight against terrorism during the previous 30 years provided the country with a legal framework originally designed in 1977 when the National Court (*Audiencia Nacional*) was established in Madrid in order to deal with serious organized crime and terrorist offences. Various reforms of the Penal Code over the years introduced new terrorist offences to the extent that after the terrorist attacks in Madrid in 2004, political and judicial authorities concluded that the legal framework already in existence did not require further amendments in order to properly confront Islamist terrorism. This was indeed the case, with the exception of new provisions introduced with the aim of strengthening the control of explosives. The fact that ordinary criminals had been able to steal a considerable amount of explosives from a mine in the North of Spain, and subsequently sold this to the terrorists responsible for perpetrating the March 11 attacks, demonstrated worrying shortfalls in a country that should have been particularly concerned about the need to avoid such a serious break of security given the terrorist threat posed by ETA, a terrorist organization in constant search for supply of this type of material.

Other legislation amendments aimed at strengthening the control of private activities have been considered over the last few years but have failed to materialize so far. Among these new legal provisions there is particular concern about the need to develop legislation on telecommunications, with the intention of achieving better cooperation from operators and the identification of pre-pay cards for use with mobile phones in order to properly identify callers. The importance of mobile phones and phone conversations in police and judicial investigations related to Islamist terrorism has to be stressed, since the tracking down of suspects has been greatly facilitated by the monitoring of an individual's movements and location. Given the importance that the Internet has acquired as a means of communications as well as radicalization and recruitment of individuals susceptible to be involved in terrorist activities, amendments to the 1999 Data Protection Law have also been assessed so as to demand from Internet providers that data from users is held for a year. At the same time, preexisting legislation has also been reinforced and extended in order to include stricter mechanisms of control aimed at preventing financial institutions from conducting operations that may aid terrorist activities or organized crime.

Protection of Targets and Response

A response plan (*Plan Operativo de Lucha contra el Terrorismo*) has been developed after March 11, contemplating the participation of the Spanish Army (should it be required) in protecting strategic installations, ranging from communications networks to energy or nuclear facilities. The protection of big events and the monitoring of bus stations, train stations, ports, and airports is of particular relevance once the program is activated as a result of a terrorist alert or threat. This plan has been activated on various occasions during the last few years coinciding with the holiday season, when massive concentrations of civilians are more common, and in the aftermath of the terrorist attacks in London in July 7, 2005. In order to complement this program, the Army and the Civil Guard have also increased their capabilities and preparedness in advance of a nonconventional terrorist attack. Thus, the supplies of several vaccines have been considerably increased, and the Civil Guard has designed a special plan for the prevention of and reaction to threats and attacks involving nuclear, radiological, bacteriological, and/or chemical components. The measures implemented so far in this area will be soon complemented with a new plan for the protection of critical infrastructure.

Spain has also introduced regulations requesting that air companies provide the authorities with a list of passengers on international flights.[31] Moreover, a new information system is being developed with the intention of improving the quality and the amount of data on people who wish to enter the country. This is nonetheless a difficult task given the open nature of borders within the Schengen area. Spain's geographical location—acting as a bridge between Europe and North Africa, where radical Islamism is particularly strong—as well as the constant flux of immigrants from such an underdeveloped region, has demonstrated the complexity of a much necessary duty such as border control, which still remains a key challenge to the country's authorities.

Prevention of Radicalization and Recruitment

Apart from the measures previously described, there have been several more specific initiatives aimed at dealing with one of the key issues as regards counterterrorism. The awareness of the relevance that the processes of radicalization and recruitment have in the fight against terrorism has increased in the last few years, as demonstrated for instance by the European Union's growing concern for these issues as revealed in different statements on the matter since December 2004, when the European Council agreed to elaborate a strategy and action plan to address this problem.[32] The decision by the European Commission to appoint a group of experts to provide policy advice on fighting violent radicalization is in line with this concern.[33]

Spain's initiatives in relation to radicalization and recruitment can be defined as multifaceted, thus requiring the participation of different ministries in its design and implementation. Responses coordinated by the Ministry of Justice and the Ministry of Interior do share a common objective, which is the improvement of the relationship between the authorities and the Muslim community in Spain and its main representatives. Although the Spanish state and the Islamic Commission of Spain did sign a cooperation agreement in 1992, in which important aspects of the relationship between Muslims and the authorities were articulated,[34] many of the issues covered by such a text were not fully developed. The Office of Religious Affairs of the Ministry of Justice, as the body in charge of the preparation, coordination, and implementation of the government's policy on religious matters (including relations with Muslim communities) has been responsible for the assessment and development of this agreement. Thus, the office is in charge of the register of religious entities, communication with federations and bodies regarded as representatives of Muslim communities, and the judicial aspects derived from the relationship between Muslims and the state.

By way of example, in the last few years the office has managed to stabilize the situation of imams who lacked social security benefits, offering them the possibility of regularizing their situation in the country. It should be remembered that preaching is one of the factors that may influence individuals in order to embrace opinions, views, and ideas that could lead to acts of terrorism. Therefore, it is important to monitor those responsible for it, while enabling moderate preachers to fulfill their jobs by lessening the difficulties that may arise for them from a legal point of view. As part of such a process, it has been decided that permits of residence will be issued for imams as a result of their religious activity, which is considered a professional one. Such a development is seen as much more effective than the control of speeches by imams made in mosques—an approach that was contemplated at some point by the authorities, but was never implemented following the wide criticism that resulted when originally proposed shortly after the terrorist attacks in Madrid on March 11. The rejection of such a measure stems from the technical difficulties of its implementation, as well as from the restrictions to freedom of speech that it would have entailed, as corroborated by the fact that amendments to the current legislation would have been required if finally introduced.

As with other previous terrorist expressions of nationalist ideology, the role of the communities of reference is particularly relevant when confronting violence perpetrated by individuals who espouse a radical and fundamentalist interpretation of Islam. Experience demonstrates that the required de-legitimization and condemnation of violence by the majority of a community's members will prevent terrorists from increasing their social support.[35] This is a necessary but insufficient precondition for terrorism to remain a phenomenon confined to a minority. Therefore, counter terrorism also needs to include measures that encourage such condemnation and de-legitimization, which is particularly efficient when coming from political or religious leaders who are respected in the community, and are thus able to exert a positive influence on other members of that particular section of the population.[36] What has been defined as the "battle of hearts and minds" can also be regarded as part of the counterterrorist framework against Islamist terrorism, inspiring initiatives like the ones already described or the fatwa issued against Osama Bin Laden by the main Islamic religious authorities in Spain after March 11, measures which have also been complemented by some other actions on the communication front. As a result, contacts have intensified with Muslim communities as well as with Arab media and governments in the Arab world. The Spanish government has engaged in a type of public diplomacy aimed at better explaining to a wide Arab audience its foreign policy, the country's realities and its policies on issues such as immigration as well as other areas with the potential of becoming mobilization factors for certain individuals. To this extent, of particular significance remains the role played by certain Arab media whose particular coverage and interpretation of current affairs contributes to the strengthening of solidarity bonds between Muslims throughout the world by the portrayal of a globally victimized and humiliated Muslim community. Violence polarizes and forces audiences to take part by choosing either the side of the victims or that of the terrorist. Therefore, the media provide "identification mechanisms" since "the terrorist's invitation to identification is brought home to us by the public and the private media."[37] It has proved extremely difficult so far to confront that dimension as well as the increasingly powerful influence of the Internet for individuals who can easily access sites where violence in the name of Islam is not only justified but actively and strongly encouraged.

Finally, the Spanish government has also introduced some measures with the intention of preventing the radicalization and recruitment of incarcerated individuals. The dismantling of a terrorist cell inside one of Spain's prisons and the evidence of other cases where radicalization of prisoners have occurred led the authorities to opt in November 2004 for the dispersal of those inmates who were linked to jihadist terrorism, allocating them in 30 different centers. The dispersal of prisoners constitutes an important policy adopted in the mid 1980s to confront ETA's terrorism. It has been maintained since then, given its efficiency in preventing the association of members of the same organization that would strengthen the group's pressure over the individual, raising obstacles in the process of disengagement from the terrorist organization, and also increasing the chances of posing various challenges to the prison authorities. With such a background, the dispersal of prisoners associated with jihadist terrorism was also seen as a very positive initiative, although the outcome could vary as a result of the key differences between these types of terrorism. The dispersal of individuals linked to jihadist terrorism may actually enable them to contact other inmates with the potential of being radicalized and recruited. Whereas the nationalist ideology espoused by ETA's activists was unlikely to be an effective tool for the indoctrination of other prison inmates with no connection with the terrorist organization, given the sheer rejection of ETA's objectives by the majority of the Spanish prison population, the same could not be said of Islamism, when conveniently manipulated as a means of justifying extremism. The search for new recruits by jihadist terrorists has often extended to marginal groups and crime circles, where individuals are prone to accept ideological doctrines that help their criminal acts to be seen in a different light. In other words, a radical interpretation of Islam may become a useful instrument to justify previous and further transgressions, shielding the individual from his own self-questioning and criticism that usually ensues decisions that generate negative consequences. The prison environment could provide a facilitational context for such a course of action, and this requires proper management if further processes of radicalization are to be prevented. This risk has led prison authorities to apply a tight control of communications of certain inmates, in addition to the measures previously described in this chapter.

Overall, Spain's long struggle with terrorism helped prepare it for an effective response to the events of March 11. However, changes made since those attacks have clearly helped improve the country's ability to face the challenges it now confronts in the form of Islamist extremism.

NOTES

1. *El País*, March 3, 2002.
2. Javier Valenzuela, *España en el punto de mira. La amenaza del integrismo islámico* (Madrid: Temas de Hoy, 2002) 64.
3. David Rapoport and Leonard Weinberg, "Elections and Violence," *Terrorism and Political Violence* 12 (2000): 15–50.
4. Rogelio Alonso, "El nuevo terrorismo: factores de cambio y permanencia," in *Madrid 11-M. Un análisis del mal y sus consecuencias*, ed. Amalio Blanco, Rafael del Águila, and José Manuel Sabucedo (Madrid: Editorial Trotta, 2005) 143–146.
5. In fact some authors argue that opinion polls held in advance of the terrorist attack already indicated that the difference between the party in power and the socialist party was narrowing to the extent that a victory for the latter did not look unlikely. See Julián Santamaría, "El azar y el contexto," *Claves de Razón Práctica* 146 (2004): 28–40; and Ignacio Lago Peñas y José Ramón Montero, "Los mecanismos del cambio electoral. Del 11-M al 14-M," *Claves de Razón Práctica* 149 (2005): 36–45.
6. Fernando Reinares, "Al Qaeda, neosalafistas magrebíes y 11-M: sobre el nuevo terrorismo islamista en España," in *El nuevo terrorismo islamista. Del 11-S al 11-M*, ed. Fernando Reinares and Antonio Elorza (Madrid: Temas de Hoy, 2004) 36–37.
7. *Mayrit*, the term used by the terrorist in the recording, is the old Arab name used to refer to Madrid.
8. Tareq ben Ziad is the name of the Muslim leader who crossed the strait of Gibraltar when centuries ago Spain was conquered by the Arabs.
9. Juzgado Central de Instrucción Número 6, Audiencia Nacional, Madrid, Sumario N° 20/2004, Madrid, Auto, April 10, 2006, p. 336.
10. Ibid.
11. Juzgado Central de Instrucción N° 005, Madrid, Sumario (Proc. Ordinario) 0000035/2001 E, September 17, 2003. In September 2005 a total of 18 men were sentenced by the Spanish National Court after magistrates found them guilty of membership and collaboration with Al Qaeda. Abu Dahdah was sentenced to 27 years in prison accused of leading a terrorist organisation and conspiring to perpetrate the $9/11$ attacks in the United States in 2001. In June 2006 the Spanish Supreme Court reduced to 12 years this sentence after qualifying that although Abu Dahdah was definitely a member of a terrorist organization he did not take part in the preparation of the terrorist attacks perpetrated in the United States in 2001. The 2005 judicial verdict stated that the men found guilty had engaged over a prolonged period of time, which in some cases went back as far as 1995, in activities of indoctrination and proselytising, financing terrorist cells in different countries all over the world, as well as recruiting mujahideen in order to send them to conflict spots abroad.
12. *Abc*, March 6, 2005.

13. Juzgado Central de Instrucción Número 6, Audiencia Nacional, Madrid, Sumario N° 20/2004, Madrid, Auto, April 10, 2006, pp. 284–285.

14. Ibid., pp. 339–340.

15. Cortes Generales, Diario de Sesiones del Congreso de los Diputados, Comisión de Investigación, Año 2004 VIII, Legislatura Núm. 7, Sesión núm. 13, July 19, 2004.

16. Juzgado Central de Instrucción Número 6, Audiencia Nacional, Madrid, Sumario N° 20/2004, Madrid, Auto, April 10, 2006, pp. 230–231.

17. Ibid., p. 516. These letters are very similar to letters written by suicide terrorists in other regions of the world in advance of their deaths.

18. In the aftermath of the terrorist attacks on March 11, security personnel at the U.S. embassy in Spain realized that Berraj had been seen in the surroundings of the building located in the centre of Madrid, fearing that he had been scouting in preparation for a terrorist attack against such a significant and symbolic target.

19. See for example the testimony of Ignacio Astarloa before the Commission set up by the Spanish Parliament to investigate the March 11 attacks. Astarloa was at the time of the attacks a minister in charge of security. Cortes Generales, Diario de Sesiones del Congreso de los Diputados, Comisiones de Investigación, Año 2004, VIII Legislatura Núm. 18, Sesión Núm. 31, November 18, 2004.

20. *El Mundo*, June 21, 2005.

21. Juzgado Central de Instrucción Número 6, Audiencia Nacional, Madrid, Sumario N° 20/2004, Madrid, Auto, April 10, 2006, pp. 1206–1207.

22. *El País*, June 9, 2002.

23. It is believed that the cost of the explosives may not have exceeded 45,000 Euros (56,870 USD). In addition to this, terrorists incurred other expenses in the purchase of different properties used for the preparation of the attacks and with the intention of providing refugee, as well as the acquisition of mobile phones and cards to activate them. Juzgado Central de Instrucción Número 6, Audiencia Nacional, Madrid, Sumario N° 20/2004, Madrid, Auto, April 10, 2006, p. 1137.

24. José María Irujo, *El agujero. España invadida por la yihad* (Madrid: Aguilar, 2005) 195.

25. Ibid.: p. 164.

26. *Terrorist Activity in the European Union: Situation and Trends Report (TE-SAT) October 2002–15 October 2003*, p. 37.

27. Testimony by Jesús de la Morena, senior police officer responsible for counterterrorism, given before the Commission of Enquiry set up by the Spanish Parliament to investigate the March 11 attacks. Cortes Generales. Diario de Sesiones del Congreso de los Diputados. Comisiones de Investigación, Año 2004, VIII Legislatura Núm. 3, Sesión núm. 7, July 7, 2004.

28. "The European Union Strategy for Combating Radicalisation and Recruitment to Terrorism," Council of the European Union, Brussels, November 24, 2005, 14781/1/05 REV 1, JAI 452 ENFOPOL 164, COTER 81.

29. Quoted in Ronald D. Crelinsten and Iffet Özkut, "Counterterrorism Policy in Fortress Europe: Implications for Human Rights," in *European Democracies Against Terrorism. Governmental policies and intergovernmental cooperation*, ed. Fernando Reinares (Aldershot: Ashgate, 2000) 249.

30. For more on the challenges of European intelligence collaboration, please see the chapter by Magnus Norell in volume of this publication.

31. "Batería de medidas," Jorge Rodríguez, *El País*, January 8, 2006.

32. Council of the European Union, 14894/04 (Presse 332), Press Release, 26th Council Meeting, Justice and Home Affairs, Brussels, December 2, 2004. See also on this issue "Communication from the Commission to the European Parliament and the Council concerning Terrorist recruitment: addressing the factors contributing to violent radicalisation," Commission of the European Communities, Brussels, September 21, 2005, COM (2005) 313 final.

33. "Commission Decision of 19 April 2006 setting up a group of experts to provide policy advice to the Commission on fighting violent radicalisation" (2006/299/EC), *Official Journal of the European Union* April 25, 2006, L 111/9.

34. *Acuerdo de Cooperación del Estado Español con la Comisión Islámica de España*, approved by Law 26/1992, of November 10, 1992, *Boletín Oficial del Estado de 12 de noviembre de 1999*, http://www.mju.es/asuntos_religiosos/ar_n08_e.htm.

35. On these issues see Alex P. Schmid, "Terrorism and Democracy," in Alex P. Schmid and Ronald D. Crelinsten, *Western Responses to Terrorism* (Londres: Frank Cass, 1993) 14–25; and Alex Schmid, "Towards Joint Political Strategies for Delegitimising the use of Terrorism," in *Countering Terrorism through International Cooperation*, ISPAC, International Scientific and Professional Advisory Council of the United Nations Crime Prevention and Criminal Justice Programme, Proceedings of the International Conference on "Countering Terrorism Through Enhanced International Cooperation," Courmayeur, Mont Blanc, Italy, September 22–24, 2000, pp. 260–265.

36. See for example *Muslim Youth in Europe: Addressing Alienation and Extremism. Report on Wilton Park Conference*, WPSO5/3, February 7–10, 2005.

37. Alex Schmid, "Terrorism and the Media: The Ethics of Publicity," *Terrorism and Political Violence* 1 (1989): 539–565, p. 545.

CHAPTER 13

THE LONDON TERRORIST ATTACKS OF JULY 7, 2005

Tom Maley

On the morning of July 7, 2005, Londoners were in an optimistic mood. The day before, the announcement by Jacques Rogge, International Olympic Committee President, that the Games of the XXX Olympiad in 2012 were awarded to London, had been received joyously by thousands of people gathered in Trafalgar Square and at other locations across the capital. There was also an expectation that the G8 Summit, hosted by the United Kingdom (UK) and opening later that morning at Gleneagles in Scotland, would address issues of poverty in Africa highlighted so clearly by the Live 8 concerts held across the world a few days earlier. The fact that previous G8 Summits had been targeted by anarchists led the authorities to throw a ring of steel around the Gleneagles hotel in order to protect the world leaders gathered there. Because of the possibility that the Summit venue might be the target of a terrorist attack, local police had been reinforced by some 1,400 Metropolitan Police Service officers from London, many of them antiterrorist specialists; a fact that was to cause consternation later that morning.[1]

In London, Thursday July 7 was a normal day and, like every weekday morning, tens of thousands of commuters were making their way to work by public transport. The first indication that July 7 might not be a normal day came at 8:51 A.M., when staff working at London Underground's Network Control Center—which monitors all 12 underground railway lines and the 275 stations that serve them—received a report that a loss of traction current or a power surge had occurred on the electrical system. What Network Control Center staff did not immediately realize was that this report was the result of a bomb explosion that occurred at 8:50 A.M. on an eastbound Circle Line train traveling from Liverpool Street station to

Aldgate station in the heart of the financial district. Within a minute, a second bomb detonated on another Circle Line train traveling westbound, just moments after it had left Edgware Road station for Paddington station, and then a third, approximately 2 minutes later, on a southbound Piccadilly Line train traveling from King's Cross station to Russell Square station. All three explosions occurred while the Underground trains were in transit in the tunnels connecting the various stations, and passengers were immediately plunged into total darkness as the internal carriage lights failed. Additionally, internal communications between the driver and passengers on each train were not working, and drivers were unable to communicate with their line control centers.[2] This meant that passengers had no idea whether the driver of their train had been killed, whether anyone knew they were there, or if emergency help was on its way. However, what they did know was that they were involved in a very serious incident where people had been killed and seriously injured, that there was a risk of fire, and that they were unable to summon help because their mobile phones would not work in the underground tunnels.

The situation from 8:50 A.M. until about 9:15 A.M. was inevitably chaotic. Many reports were being made to London Underground's Network Control Center, to the emergency services, and to the media, and because of the often conflicting nature of some of these reports and the fact that the explosions had occurred underground and out of sight, it took some time to establish exactly what had happened and where. Initially, it was thought that there may have been up to five separate incidents on the Underground because, with the exception of Paddington, reports were coming in from the stations at both ends of each of the tunnels where the explosions had occurred and from nearby locations where smoke had been seen issuing from tunnels and grids at street level.[3] This led to the emergency services being deployed to six separate Underground stations, including Euston Square station, which turned out not to be involved in any of the incidents. The effects of the explosions and the subsequent actions of London Underground staff, in conjunction with British Transport Police officers, soon led to sections of the Underground network becoming inoperable. Indeed, at 9:15 A.M., the decision was taken to declare a network emergency and to evacuate the entire Underground train network.[4] This resulted in many thousands of commuters having to abandon their journeys on the London Underground and switch to surface transport instead, although travel by bus and taxi was becoming increasingly difficult. Meanwhile, the emergency services realized that they were dealing with a series of explosions, and declared "major incident" status at the several London Underground stations to which they had been called.

At 9:40 A.M. (or a little after), a No. 30 double-decker, London bus traveling eastwards from Marble Arch and crowded with passengers (following the closures on the Underground), diverted from its normal route because of the traffic congestion. At 9:47 A.M., as the bus entered Tavistock Square, a bomb exploded on the upper deck toward the back, which ripped the roof off the bus almost in its entirety. Unlike the three explosions that had occurred on the Underground an hour earlier, it was immediately obvious what had happened. By chance, the Metropolitan Police Service happened to have an officer at the scene, and the fact that the incident occurred outside the headquarters of the British Medical Association meant that several doctors and trained first-aid providers were very quickly on the scene and able to provide immediate medical help to the bus passengers that had been badly injured. If there was any doubt previously as to the cause of the explosions, this fourth, highly visible incident persuaded many that London was being hit by a series of near simultaneous terrorist attacks, and that al Qaeda was most likely to be responsible.

SUBSEQUENT POLICE INVESTIGATIONS

Over the following days, forensic investigations carried out by the police proved that all four explosions were the work of suicide bombers, who had carried their bombs in rucksacks. In relation to the sequence of bomb detonations, the attackers have been identified respectively as Shehzad Tanweer, Mohammad Sidique Khan, Jermaine Lindsay, and Hasib Hussein.[5] In the explosions on the Underground, 7 members of the general public were killed and 171 were injured in the first explosion; 6 were killed and 163 were injured in the second explosion; and in the third explosion, which was in the deepest and most inaccessible of the tunnels, 26 were killed and over 340 were injured. On the crowded bus in Tavistock Square, 13 were killed and over 110 were injured. In total, this meant that 52 innocent people from many different backgrounds had lost their lives in the attacks and over 784 were injured, some so seriously that they would require medical treatment for many months.[6] In addition, hundreds more were caught up in the July 7 (7/7) attacks and, although physically uninjured, many were traumatized by their experiences.

Subsequent investigations by the police have shown that, on the day of the attacks, Tanweer, Khan, and Hussein traveled from Leeds in West Yorkshire to Luton, some 35 miles north of London, in a light blue Nissan Micra that had been rented by Tanweer. At 6:49 A.M. they arrived in the parking lot of Luton mainline railway station where they met up with Lindsay, who had traveled from Aylesbury in Buckinghamshire in a red Fiat Brava, arriving some 90 minutes earlier. The four of them then got out of their respective cars, appeared to move items between the trunks of both cars, shouldered their rucksacks, which closed circuit television

(CCTV) showed to be large and full, and then made their way to the station entrance where they were again captured on CCTV.[7] It has been estimated that the bombs in each rucksack contained between 2–5 kilograms of hexamethylene triperoxide diamine (HMTD) explosive, a homemade organic peroxide-based substance, relatively straightforward to develop, although dangerous to manufacture because of its instability.[8] A number of smaller homemade explosive devices and some other items consistent with explosives, together with a 9-mm handgun, were left in the two cars. The reason for this is unclear, but it is possible that these items were for self-defense or diversion during the journeys to Luton.[9] The four bombers left Luton station at 7:40 A.M. on the train to London King's Cross, where they arrived at 8:23 A.M., slightly late due to delays on the line. Shortly thereafter, they were seen hugging each other before splitting up to carry out their deadly suicide missions.

For some time after the attacks, it was unclear why the three bomb explosions on the Underground had all occurred within about 3 minutes of each other, whereas the fourth bomb explosion had occurred on a red London bus almost an hour later. As the police investigations into the attacks proceeded in succeeding days and evidence of what had happened slowly emerged, it seems probable that Hussein, the fourth bomber, had also intended to attack an Underground train at about 8:50 A.M., but was unable to achieve this and therefore switched his attack to a target of opportunity, and this target happened to be a crowded No. 30 bus. Most of the evidence for this explanation comes from CCTV coverage of the area in and around King's Cross main railway station. The first such CCTV coverage of the four terrorist bombers was at 8:26 A.M. on the station concourse, which captured them heading in the direction of the Underground train system. At 8:55 A.M., telephone call records show that Hussein tried unsuccessfully to contact the three other bombers on his mobile phone over the next few minutes, but, of course, they were already dead by this time. Further CCTV coverage then shows Hussein returning to the station concourse where he visited a W. H. Smith's store and, apparently, bought a 9-volt battery. At 9:06 A.M., he entered a McDonald's restaurant on Euston Road, leaving about 10 minutes later, and was then seen at 9:19 A.M. on Grays Inn Road. Subsequently, a man fitting Hussein's description may have been seen on a No. 91 bus before apparently transferring to the ill-fated No. 30 bus from Marble Arch.[10] The fact that Hussein needed to buy a battery when the attacks were already underway indicates that, initially, he had difficulty setting off his device and then could not reaccess or chose not to reaccess the Underground as the station closures began to take effect. This sequence of events illustrates well how chance plays a part in the way that terrorist attacks unfold, and emphasizes the wholly indiscriminate nature of terrorism.

THE BOMBERS AND THEIR MOTIVATIONS

So what is known about Shehzad Tanweer, Mohammad Sidique Khan, Jermaine Lindsay, and Hasib Hussein? Police established their identities through DNA and documents recovered from the scenes of the attacks, and it is now clear that all apart from Lindsay were British nationals of Pakistani origin, who were born and brought up in the UK and were living in the Leeds and Dewsbury area of West Yorkshire at the time. By contrast, Lindsay was a British national of West Indian origin, born in Jamaica, brought up in Huddersfield in West Yorkshire, but who moved to Aylesbury in Buckinghamshire in September 2003, following his marriage to a white British convert to Islam a year previously. Like his wife, he had converted to Islam, although this had been very strongly influenced by his mother's conversion to Islam in 2000.[11] By all accounts, the backgrounds of the four men were largely unexceptional, although by virtue of his different ethnicity and late conversion to Islam, Lindsay was somewhat of an outsider to the group. It is not known exactly when Lindsay first met Khan, the acknowledged ringleader of the group, but this was likely to have been in 2002 or early 2003, probably through his local mosque or other Islamic groups in the Huddersfield and Dewsbury area. By contrast, Tanweer, Khan, and Hussein had known each other for longer, but it was probably at about this same period of 2002–2003 that they began to form a closer relationship through their shared and developing religious beliefs and their mutual participation in the social life around the mosques, youth clubs, gyms, and the Islamic bookshop in Beeston, Leeds, that would eventually lead them with Lindsay to commit the 7/7 suicide attacks in London.[12]

It is now apparent that Khan visited Pakistan, and possibly Afghanistan, on a number of occasions from the late 1990s onwards. He certainly visited Pakistan in July 2003, and then spent almost 4 months there with Tanweer between November 19, 2004 and February 8, 2005, during which it is considered likely that they had some contact with al Qaeda figures.[13] Pakistani intelligence sources have gone further in suggesting that Khan and Tanweer might have met with Ayman al-Zawahiri, al Qaeda's number two, in Pakistan's tribal areas sometime in January 2005.[14] This suggests that the 7/7 attacks were to some extent planned and directed, although maybe not controlled, by contacts in Pakistan or elsewhere. The intelligence and security agencies also believe that some form of operational training is likely to have taken place while Khan and Tanweer were in Pakistan, and contacts in the lead-up to the attacks suggest that they may have received some advice or direction from individuals there.[15] That this might be the case is also supported by the nature, style, and broad timing of the attacks; the video message from Khan, which was aired by Al Jazeera on September 1, 2005, during which he praised Osama bin Laden and Ayman al-Zawahiri as heroes; the very fact that he and Tanweer had prepared video messages in advance of the attacks, most probably during their visit to Pakistan; and the subsequent claim of responsibility for the attacks by al-Zawahiri in another video message aired by Al Jazeera on September 19, 2005.

So what exactly motivated Khan and his coconspirators to carry out the 7/7 attacks? It seems very unlikely that there was a single cause or reason that led these four young men to resort to terrorist violence on July 7. Much more plausible is the view that they became radicalized over a period of time as a result of exposure to a number of malevolent influences, which might have included individuals, groups, places, schools, institutions, training camps, and information sources such as extremist literature, videos, and Internet Web sites. How long such a process of radicalization might take will vary from individual to individual, but there seems to be some evidence that it can happen relatively quickly if the malevolent influences are recognized as authoritative, credible, and commanding of obedience. There may also be an acceleration toward the desire to commit violent terrorist acts in the later stages of radicalization as individuals become more convinced of the "rightness" of the arguments and causes to which they have been exposed. The lack of countervailing influences within societies, communities, families, and other institutions to which individuals belong will also have an impact on how quickly an individual makes the journey toward radicalization and extremism, including the desire for martyrdom through suicide attacks. A key characteristic of so-called "new" terrorism is that violent acts are seen as being legitimized by and through religious belief. Of course, such legitimization of violence will be open to much argument and, regardless of the religion, a significant majority of "believers" will not take such a view. That Khan, Tanweer, Hussein, and Lindsay were all Muslims will have helped not only to forge strong bonds of "brotherhood" between them, bonds that transcended their different ethnicities, but also led to their exposure to the extremist interpretations of Islam that are implicit in al Qaeda's ideology and used to justify the group's terrorist methods. That this actually occurred seems clear from the historical record and from Khan's video message of September 1, 2005, in which he said:

> I and thousands like me are forsaking everything for what we believe. Our driving motivation doesn't come from tangible commodities that this world has to offer. Our religion is Islam—obedience to the one true God, Allah, and following the footsteps of the final prophet and messenger Muhammad ... Your democratically elected governments continuously perpetuate atrocities against my people all over the world. And your support of them makes you directly responsible, just as I am directly responsible for protecting and avenging my Muslim brothers and sisters. Until we feel security, you will be our targets. And until you stop the bombing, gassing,

imprisonment and torture of my people we will not stop this fight. We are at war and I am a soldier.[16]

What comes through strongly from Khan's message is his alienation from the British way of life and modern society in general; his perception that the UK in particular, and the West in general, are at war with Muslims the world over; and his obedience to his deeply held religious beliefs that obligate him to undertake global jihad on behalf of all Muslims. The perceived sense of grievance and injustice in places such as Palestine and Iraq, and apparent universal Muslim disadvantage, underachievement and underrepresentation at the hands of Western influence and policies would seem to have been key motivational themes for Khan and his fellow terrorists; so much so, that they sought martyrdom operations in their quest to right these wrongs.

THE 7/7 BOMBERS IN CONTEXT

Following the first attack on the World Trade Center in February 1993; the near simultaneous attacks on the U.S. Embassies in Kenya and Tanzania in August 1998, which had the effect of bringing al Qaeda to prominence among the wider public across the Western world; and the highly significant 9/11 attacks on the World Trade Center and the Pentagon in 2001, it was clear beyond any doubt that the nature of the terrorist threat had changed. In essence, the terrorist threat had become international, emanating from new, religiously motivated groups, networks and individuals across the globe that were now operating in a different way than what had gone before. Al Qaeda and its affiliate organizations espoused a violent and extremist ideology that was based upon a particular interpretation of Islamism called Salafi or Salafist. Unlike terrorism of the past, mass casualties were now seen as a necessary prerequisite for a successful attack, and terrorist targets ranged from the United States and other Western nations, both at home and abroad, to Muslim states whose governments were branded as apostate for the secular and often pro-Western policies that they adopted and pursued.

After 9/11, the "new" terrorism of al Qaeda and its affiliate organizations supplanted the Northern Ireland Troubles as the main dimension of the terrorist threat in the United Kingdom, although the latter continued, albeit at a lower level of intensity, despite the Belfast or "Good Friday" Agreement having been signed in April 1998. This occurred not only because the UK was active militarily in Afghanistan (in pursuit of al Qaeda and the Taliban) and more recently in Iraq, but also because the global jihadists found that they could not easily topple the apostate Muslim regimes that they so despised in their own regions due to Western support. There was therefore a need to switch their terrorist attacks to the

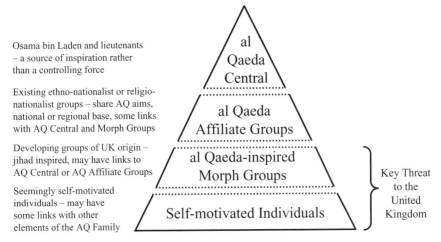

Figure 13.1   The al Qaeda "Family" at the time of the 7/7 Attacks.
Source: **Author.**

"far enemy"—the United States and Europe. A further factor was that the UK was conducive to international terrorist activities by virtue of the cosmopolitan nature of its population, made up of many second and third generation immigrants; significant numbers of foreign students in many of its larger cities; and converts to Islam from among its indigenous population, who might well sympathize (at the very least) with the salafist ideology. Taken together, all these factors combined to produce a fertile terrorist recruiting ground in the UK, which has spawned the development of what might be described as al Qaeda-inspired "morph" groups and seemingly "self-motivated individuals" as two additional dimensions of the al Qaeda threat. The international terrorist threat to the UK from al Qaeda "family" at the time of 7/7 may therefore be summarized as shown in Figure 13.1.

In Figure 13.1, al Qaeda "central"—also known as the al Qaeda "core"—represents Osama bin Laden and his immediate lieutenants, a somewhat depleted grouping since the invasion of Afghanistan post-9/11, but nevertheless a continuing source of inspiration rather than a controlling force. The al Qaeda affiliate groups represent a range of existing ethno-nationalist or religio-nationalist terrorist groups that subscribe to al Qaeda's ideology and broadly share Osama bin Laden's aims, although each organization will also tailor its aims to its own local, national, or regional situation. These groups will be nationally or regionally based and will have some links with al Qaeda "central," most probably through personal acquaintances and shared experiences in the al Qaeda training camps or in the conflicts in Afghanistan, Bosnia, Chechnya, or Iraq. Typically, such groups will attack British interests in their local areas, although those with significant ethnic links to communities in the UK may also support terrorist operations there. The UK Home Office Web site lists all the al Qaeda affiliate groups of concern and at the time of 7/7 listed some 25 international terrorist groups (defined as such under the *Terrorism Act 2000*).[17] The al Qaeda-inspired morph groups represent a range of developing terrorist groups of UK origin, typically made up of second or third generation immigrants holding British passports or recent legal or illegal immigrants from a range of countries. They will be inspired by the salafist interpretation of jihad, and may or may not have links to al Qaeda "central" or al Qaeda affiliate groups. Khan, Tanweer, Hussein, and Lindsay epitomized such an al Qaeda-inspired morph group, although it is clear that there have been (and continue to be) others, not least the group that planned (but failed) to mount suicide terrorist attacks in London on July 21, 2005.

Self-motivated individuals represent a fourth dimension of the al Qaeda threat to the UK, and typically comprise British citizens that appear initially to have acted alone, albeit aligned with the al Qaeda ideology. Examples of British self-motivated individuals include Richard Reid, the so-called "shoe bomber" who attempted unsuccessfully to blow up American Airlines Flight 63 from Paris to Miami on December 22, 2001; Saajid Badat, who similarly planned to blow up a passenger jet flying to the United States in December 2001, but found that he could not go through with the attack; and Asif Mohammed Hanif and Omar Khan Sharif, who mounted successful and unsuccessful suicide bombing attacks (respectively) in Tel Aviv, Israel, in April 2003. In most cases, police and security agency investigations have revealed that such individuals probably received some direction, guidance, or support from others in the planning and execution of their attacks, although this is often very difficult to prove. However, what is clear is that the al Qaeda-inspired morph groups and the self-motivated individuals represented a severe and substantial threat to the UK at the time of 7/7, and are likely to continue to remain a threat for some time into the future.

THE COUNTERTERRORISM RESPONSE TO THE 7/7 ATTACKS

The counterterrorism response to the 7/7 attacks in London can best be analyzed in the context of the UK's long-term counterterrorism strategy, known as CONTEST.[18] This strategy was the brainchild of Sir David Omand, the former Security and Intelligence Coordinator at the Cabinet Office, and was adopted by the UK government in early 2003 in response to the post-9/11 terrorist threat environment, although it has recently undergone some subtle changes of emphasis. At the time of the 7/7 attacks, the strategic aim of CONTEST was to "reduce the risk from international terrorism, so that our people can go about their business freely and with confidence," and this was to be achieved by reducing both the threat of international terrorism and the UK's vulnerability to it.[19] Operationally, the strategy was based upon four pillars: Prevention, Pursuit, Protection, and Preparedness, known colloquially as the "Four Ps." The first two pillars were designed to reduce the threat, whereas the remaining two pillars focused upon the UK's vulnerabilities with respect to international terrorism. The four pillars should not be viewed as separate silos; rather, they should be seen as mutually supporting lines of action, which cut across government.

Importantly, the "Four Ps" were underpinned by intelligence and public communications, a critical duo that aimed to provide a solid base for the strategy as a whole. It can be argued that intelligence is the key instrument in the fight against international terrorism, because without intelligence little else can be achieved. Moreover, intelligence needs to be shared, not only between agencies within a nation, but also between allies and partner nations. Within CONTEST, the former was achieved at the time of the attacks principally through the Joint Terrorism Analysis Center (JTAC), and this remains the case today. Formed in June 2003, JTAC provides assessment and analysis of intelligence relating to the international terrorist threat, both in the UK and abroad, by bringing together 13 different government agencies, and there is little doubt that it has proved to be a significant UK asset in the fight against international terrorism. Of course, sharing intelligence will always be a difficult business, dependent as it is upon the development of trust between agencies and nations, but in times of severe threat significant progress is often made in this regard. Much intelligence in relation to terrorism comes from the general public, and this is where the link to public communications as the other critical activity underpinning the strategy can be seen as important. Traditionally, the UK government has sought to keep the general public "alert, but not alarmed," and this has been a challenge, not least in deciding how much information should be passed on to people generally.[20] If anything, the government has erred on the side of caution in what it tells the public, yet it can be argued that public opinion is the center of gravity for the government's counterterrorism strategy as a whole and therefore it needs the public's support in all that it does, if it is to be successful. A schematic representation of CONTEST at the time of the 7/7 attacks is shown in Figure 13.2. Subsequent sections of this chapter will examine the "Four Ps" in the context of 7/7, as well as trace some of the important initiatives and actions that have resulted from the attacks.

Prevention: Preventing Terrorism by Addressing Its Underlying Causes at Home and Abroad

Prevention, as the first pillar of the strategy, was mainly concerned at the time of the 7/7 attacks with addressing the causes of terrorism at home and abroad. Subsequently, it has become more narrowly focused

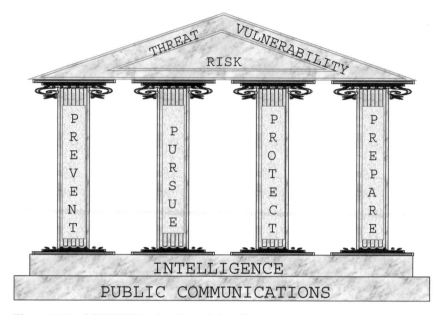

Figure 13.2 CONTEST at the time of the 7/7 Attacks.
Source: **Detective Chief Superintendent Keith Weston/Author.**

upon tackling the radicalization of individuals.[21] It can be argued that prevention is both the most important and the most challenging of the four lines of action, because successful action in this area not only saves lives, but also largely renders action under the other three pillars as unnecessary. It is also the most challenging, because it is the most difficult to achieve. There is considerable debate surrounding the causes of terrorism and radicalization, and even when consensus emerges as to the causes, developing action plans is more problematic than in the other pillars. More generally, addressing the causes of terrorism and radicalization is a long-term challenge for governments, and progress is often difficult to discern. Consequently, there is a tendency for governments to focus their efforts on the more immediate challenges implicit in the other lines of action, and the UK government has not been immune to this tendency.

Clearly, neither the UK government nor any of its agencies were able to prevent the 7/7 attacks, and 52 people lost their lives and over 700 were injured in the four explosions. This was a tragedy for all those involved as well as for their families and friends. Subsequent to the attacks, it became clear from a "restricted" report leaked to the *New York Times* that, on May 26, 2005, JTAC had judged that "... at present there is not a group with both the current intent AND the capability to attack the UK," and that, as a result, they had reduced the overall threat level for the UK from

"Severe General" to "Substantial."[22] After the 7/7 attacks, JTAC was heavily criticized in the media for this apparent error of judgment, but further reading of JTAC's report makes clear that "Substantial" indicates a continued high level of threat and that "an attack might well be mounted without warning," a point not well covered by the media at the time. Clearly, JTAC was completely unaware that, by late May 2005, Khan and his coconspirators were well advanced in both their planning and their preparations for the July attacks, but in reducing the overall threat level to "Substantial" they were acting within the agreed threat level definitions, and agency staff who read their report would (or should) have been aware that JTAC were simply saying that, at the time, there was no firm intelligence of attack planning, not that plans to attack did not exist.[23] To avoid any ambiguity on this score, a new, simplified system of threat levels for the UK has been introduced.[24] More importantly, however, the 7/7 attacks have made the whole counterterrorism community in the UK much more aware of the nature of the terrorist threat now facing the country, in particular the threat from homegrown al Qaeda-inspired morph groups and self-motivated individuals—a threat that can develop quickly and virtually unnoticed in disparate communities across the nation. Prevention has suddenly become more urgent and more difficult.

In line with this new awareness, there has been a more determined effort to prevent terrorism by tackling the issue of radicalization within British society, principally within the Muslim community. This reflects a realization that not enough was done in this area prior to 7/7. By tackling radicalization, the UK government hopes to be able to prevent the formation of the next generation of Islamist terrorists. The government seeks to achieve this by tackling disadvantage and supporting reform; deterring those who facilitate terrorism; and engaging in the battle of ideas—essentially, challenging the ideologies that extremists believe can be used to justify violence.

In tackling disadvantage and supporting reform, the main effort has been in addressing structural problems in the UK and elsewhere that may contribute to radicalization. There are many initiatives that work toward this end, but of considerable importance is the government's broad based "Improving Opportunities, Strengthening Society" strategy, which aims to reduce inequalities, especially those associated with race and faith, and to increase community cohesion, and which predates 7/7. The "Commission on Integration and Cohesion," established in June 2006, is a more focused effort along similar lines to consider how local areas themselves can play a role in forging cohesive and resilient communities. Crucially, this initiative will examine how local communities can be empowered to tackle extremist ideologies in their midst. The intention is that the Commission will report its findings to the Secretary of State for Communities and Local Government in June 2007 for implementation by the UK government shortly thereafter. Abroad, the Foreign and Commonwealth Office's "Global Opportunities Fund" has supported numerous projects in the Middle East, North Africa, Afghanistan, and key countries in South and Southeast Asia and Africa to support the development of effective, accountable governments, democratic institutions, and the promotion of human rights. In trying to deter those who facilitate terrorism, the main effort has been legislative. The *Terrorism Act 2006* made it a criminal offence to encourage the commission, preparation, or instigation of acts of terrorism or to distribute terrorist literature, including material that glorifies terrorism—a somewhat controversial measure. The same Act also widened the basis set out in the *Terrorism Act 2000* for proscribing international terrorist groups—to include organizations that promote or encourage terrorism—and this has had the effect of increasing the number of proscribed groups and organizations, thereby prohibiting those who belong to such groups from entering the UK. The government has also devised and published a list of "Unacceptable Behaviors" likely to lead to an individual being deported or banned from the UK. It covers any non-UK citizen, who uses any medium to express views that foment, justify, or glorify terrorist violence in furtherance of particular beliefs; seek to provoke others to terrorist acts; foment other serious criminal activity or seek to provoke others to serious criminal acts; or foster hatred which might lead to intercommunity violence in the UK. By the first anniversary of 7/7, some 36 foreign nationals had been banned from the UK on grounds of unacceptable behavior, and other cases were under active consideration. In the battle of ideas, the UK government is working with communities across the country to help them discourage susceptible individuals from turning toward extremism. Notable among the initiatives in this area are those trying to empower Muslim women to play a greater role in countering extremism within their communities, but success in this area will require significant cultural changes, and is likely to be a long-term endeavor.[25]

Pursuit: Pursuing Terrorists and Those That Sponsor Them

Pursuit, as the second pillar of the strategy, was mainly concerned at the time of 7/7 with pursuing terrorists and those that sponsor them, and this remains the case today. In a sense, this line of action is the most time-urgent and is very central to the whole UK counterterrorism effort. The key requirement is to identify terrorists and their sponsors, although this is very difficult given the covert ways in which they operate. This line of action requires gathering intelligence, in particular a deep understanding of the capabilities and intentions of terrorist organizations, so that their operations in the UK and abroad can be disrupted. International cooperation is vital since working with allies and partners abroad helps to strengthen the intelligence-gathering effort and to achieve disruption of terrorist activities overseas, a task that may involve British military forces.

In the UK, the intelligence and security agencies and the police are mainly responsible for the pursuit of terrorists and the disruption of their attack plans. Clearly, all were unaware of Khan's plan for attacking London on July 7, 2005 and, ultimately, they were unable to disrupt it, with disastrous consequences. The question then arises as to why this intelligence failure occurred. Indeed, this was a key question addressed by the cross-party, Parliamentary Intelligence and Security Committee in their investigation into the 7/7 attacks.[26] From their report, it is clear that Khan was the subject of detainee reporting of which the Security Service was aware prior to July 2005, but his true identity was not revealed in this reporting and it was only after the 7/7 attacks that the Security Service was able to identify Khan as the subject of the reports. It is also clear that the Security Service had come across both Khan and Tanweer on the peripheries of other operations prior to the 7/7 attacks, but again their identities were unknown and their significance was not appreciated. The Security Service told the Intelligence and Security Committee that there were more pressing priorities at the time, including the need to disrupt known plans to attack the UK, and so the decision was taken not to investigate them further or seek to identify them.[27] Of course, had different priorities been agreed in 2003–2005, or had the agencies had more resources available to conduct investigations, then the chances of identifying the attack planning and of actually preventing the 7/7 attacks might have been greater, but, even so, the attacks might still have occurred. However, what is clear is that the UK government began to increase the resources available to the intelligence and security agencies well before the 7/7 attacks, and increases in funding will continue through to at least the 2007–2008 financial year, thereby allowing all the agencies to recruit yet more staff.[28] There is also a determination among the agencies to work smarter and faster and to develop further their relationships with the police Special Branches across the UK in order to build a "richer" picture of the al Qaeda-inspired morph groups and self-motivated individuals operating within the UK who, more than likely, have links with others abroad.

The failure to disrupt the 7/7 attacks should be seen in context. As explained earlier, the nature of the terrorist threat to the UK changed markedly after 9/11, and homegrown terrorists—inspired by salafist Islamic jihad ideology—progressively became the key concern. Since 9/11, the intelligence and security agencies and the police have disrupted many planned terrorist attacks against the UK, including four in the year since 7/7 alone. With the threat at such a scale, it is perhaps inevitable that an attack would succeed sooner or later. Disruption followed by prosecution of those involved in terrorist activity remains the preferred UK government approach, and on the first anniversary of 7/7, there were over 60 individuals in the UK awaiting trial on terrorist charges. Other options for taking disruptive action include deportation on grounds of national security or unacceptable behavior, control orders made under the *Prevention of Terrorism Act 2005*, the freezing and seizure of financial assets, and the proscription of terrorist organizations mentioned previously.[29] The operation of control orders has been subject to significant controversy, in that the legislation and its operation have been challenged in the courts. The UK High Court ruled on April 12, 2006 that the legislation was incompatible with Article 6 of the *European Convention on Human Rights* (the right to a fair hearing), and again on June 28, 2006 that the obligations (a curfew or travel restrictions) imposed in six specific cases amounted to a deprivation of liberty under Article 5 of the same convention. The UK government is appealing both judgments in the Court of Appeal and decisions are expected in Fall 2006, but if the government fails in its appeals, then use of this counterterrorism tool will have to be discontinued. For democracies, getting the right balance between security and the human rights of citizens is clearly an enduring challenge.

Protection: Protecting the Public and UK Interests

Protection, as the third pillar of the strategy, was mainly concerned at the time of 7/7 with protecting the public and UK interests, the latter now being more precisely defined as key national services and UK interests overseas.[30] As such, protection involves reducing the UK's vulnerability to terrorist attacks—essentially, trying to make the UK a harder target, both at home and overseas. Open democracies have a particularly difficult task in this regard, since there are many assets to protect and the essence of a free society demands that they be made easily accessible to the general public. Limited resources also mandate that prioritization—based upon a sound understanding of the threat—must be a key principle in deciding what to protect. Additionally, a multilayered approach that makes appropriate use of modern technologies will provide protection in depth in a cost-effective manner.

On 7/7, Khan and his coconspirators attacked the London transport system (specifically London Underground), which can be described as a "soft target" where people gather in large numbers, particularly in the morning and evening rush hours. Trying to protect the transport infrastructure is a complex challenge for large cities such as London and Madrid, but one that must be tackled in the current threat environment. The introduction of a new, simplified system of threat levels for the UK has already been mentioned, and this will go some way toward ensuring that the security professionals involved in making London's transport infrastructure as safe as it can be post-7/7 have a clearer understanding of the terrorist threat. Of more practical importance, however, the UK government is now working with the transport sector to examine and test various methods of screening people and their baggage on both the mainline Rail network and the London Underground. The air transport sector has considerable experience in this area, but typically this sector does not deal with the volume of passengers that use London Underground on a daily basis, and so the real challenge will be to find a solution that is effective without slowing passenger flow network-wide.

In addition to enhanced protection of the critical national infrastructure, particularly within the transport sector, the UK government is also doing much post-7/7 to strengthen the UK's border security and people tracking systems, an area that undoubtedly needs major repair. The "Border Management Program" (BMP) is a cross-government initiative aimed at strengthening border security while minimizing the impact on legitimate traffic. Key strategic objectives of the BMP are to improve intelligence sharing in support of border operations, as well as to provide more effective border control. Clearly, for counterterrorism purposes, it is essential to know the identities of those entering and leaving the country, and the "e-Borders" initiative aims to revolutionize the UK's capability in this regard. By gathering passenger information and checking this against various agency watch-lists, the British intelligence and security agencies and the police will be in a better position to pursue those involved in terrorist activities. Knowledge that the UK is adopting a much more comprehensive approach to border security will also have a deterrent effect on individuals or groups thinking of entering the UK for terrorist purposes, as well as narrowing their travel options if they wish to avoid the enhanced surveillance now being put in place.[31]

Preparedness: Preparing for the Consequences of a Terrorist Attack

Preparedness, as the fourth pillar of the strategy, was mainly concerned at the time of 7/7 with preparing for the consequences of a terrorist attack, and this remains the case today. This pillar recognizes the possibility that, despite everyone's best counterterrorism efforts, prevention, pursuit, and protection may fail, and the UK will need to deal with the aftermath of a successful terrorist attack such as occurred on 7/7. This means that the UK must develop the necessary resilience to withstand such attacks by improving its ability to respond effectively to the direct harm caused during an attack; to recover quickly those essential services that are disrupted by an attack; and to absorb and minimize wider indirect disruption. It is important to realize that there are multiple stakeholders involved in the development of resilience, who are spread across the public, private, and voluntary sectors, and that all of them need to work together if a truly effective response to an emergency is to be achieved.

In practical terms, the UK government sees the key elements of this pillar of the CONTEST strategy as identifying the potential risks that the UK faces from terrorism and assessing potential impact; building the capabilities to respond to them; and regularly evaluating and testing the UK's preparedness through exercises. Learning lessons from actual events such as 7/7 will also be enormously valuable.[32]

When the nature and scale of the attacks on London became clear during the morning of July 7, a decision was taken to airlift many of the Metropolitan Police Service antiterrorist specialists from the G8 Summit at Gleneagles in Scotland back to London, a task undertaken by British military forces. Prime Minister Blair also returned to London from the Summit and immediately chaired a meeting of the Cabinet Office Briefing Rooms (COBR), the UK government's national crisis management facility, which had been activated in response to the explosions earlier in the day. This body provided strategic level coordination of the response to the attacks, although the Metropolitan Police Service commanded the incidents onsite. In many respects, the response to the 7/7 bombings—by the emergency, transport, health and other services, as well as by Londoners themselves—has been described as outstanding, with many individual acts of strength, initiative, and courage reported. Stoicism in the face of the attacks was observed by many and was widely reported in the media. Indeed, in updating Parliament on the situation on July 11, 2005, Prime Minister Blair indicated that:

> 7 July will always be remembered as a day of terrible sadness for our country and for London. Yet it is true that, just four days later, London's buses, trains and as much of its underground as possible are back on normal schedules; its businesses, shops and schools are open; its millions of people are coming to work with a steely determination that is genuinely remarkable.[33]

Whether, this steely determination was born out of the necessity to endure previous terrorist attacks on the capital launched by Irish republican terrorists, or whether it is more deep-seated in the British psyche, is difficult to know, but clearly it was an asset to the nation's resilience at such a challenging time.

While the overall response to the 7/7 bombings has been described as outstanding, a number of significant concerns or "failings" have been identified. A London Assembly report has drawn attention to a lack of consideration for the individuals caught up in the attacks, pointing out that London's emergency plans tend to cater for the needs of the emergency and other responding services, rather than explicitly addressing the needs and priorities of the people involved.[34] The same report also noted the significant communication problems that beset the response at many levels—in particular, the difficulties experienced by those caught up in the underground incidents in trying to communicate with the train drivers; by the drivers themselves, seeking to inform their network control rooms as to what had happened; and by the emergency services, trying to communicate with their control rooms while underground and, more generally, to talk to each other both above and below ground to ensure essential coordination of effort.[35] Concern has also been raised regarding the capacity of the Casualty Bureau and its ability to handle the huge volume of calls that were experienced on the day.

From the police perspective, the scale of the 7/7 investigation has proved enormously challenging, with some 39 different crime scenes being declared. Dealing with the media was also difficult. Clearly the public need to be told what has happened, but equally the police cannot speculate, they can only work from certainties, and even then they must be conscious that public enquiries, coroner's courts, and criminal prosecutions may well follow. The importance of coordinating a consistent public message is a lesson learned, not only by the police, but more generally by all the emergency services involved. In terms of preparedness, the 7/7 attacks have further galvanized the UK government and over a year later, the cross-government Capabilities Program, managed by the Civil Contingencies Secretariat within the Cabinet Office, is developing enhanced capability to deal with emergencies, including terrorist attacks, under 17 different workstreams. Some are essentially structural, dealing respectively with national, regional, and local response capabilities; others are concerned with the maintenance of essential services; and yet others focus on specific issues such as responding to chemical, biological, radiological, and nuclear attacks.[36]

CONCLUSION

All successful terrorist attacks come as a shock, but the 7/7 attacks were anticipated. Indeed, were it not for the efforts of the intelligence and security services and the police, the UK would undoubtedly have been attacked by a similar morph group or self-motivated individual at an earlier stage. To this extent, CONTEST was successful; but on 7/7 it failed to prevent Khan and his coconspirators from killing 52 innocent people and injuring over 700 others, all going about their business on London's transport system. On that day, the preparedness pillar of the strategy demonstrated its value, and the UK proved remarkably resilient in the face of the attacks. Lessons have been learned from 7/7 and, yes, the UK will be stronger next time, but it still might not be able to prevent further attacks from succeeding.

NOTES

1. David Lister and Shirley English, "Anarchists' weapon is 90 gallons of cooking oil," *The Times,* July 8, 2005.

2. London Assembly, *Report of the 7 July Review Committee* (London: Greater London Authority, 2006), p. 12.

3. Ibid.: 13.

4. Ibid.: 38.

5. Intelligence and Security Committee, UK Parliament, *Report into the London Terrorist Attacks on 7 July 2005*, Cm 6785 (London: The Stationery Office, 2006), p. 2.

6. House of Commons, *Report of the Official Account of the Bombings in London on 7th July 2005*, HC 1087, (London: The Stationery Office, 2006), pp. 5–6.

7. Ibid.: 2–4.

8. Greg McNeal, "London casts long shadow in New York," *New York Times,* August 3, 2005. See also Intelligence and Security Committee, UK Parliament, *Report into the London Terrorist Attacks on 7 July 2005*: 11.

9. House of Commons, *Report of the Official Account of the Bombings in London on 7th July 2005*: 3.

10. Ibid.: 4–5.

11. Ibid.: 18.

12. Ibid.: 15–17.

13. Intelligence and Security Committee, UK Parliament, *Report into the London Terrorist Attacks on 7 July 2005*: 12.

14. Gordon Corera, "Were bombers linked to al-Qaida?" *BBC News on the Web,* 6 July 2006, http://news.bbc.co.uk/1/hi/uk/5156592.stm (accessed July 7, 2006).

15. Intelligence and Security Committee, UK Parliament, *Report into the London Terrorist Attacks on 7 July 2005*: 12.

16. Ibid.

17. At the time of 7/7, the UK Government, Home Office, listed on its website 25 international terrorist organizations proscribed under the *Terrorism Act 2000,* http://www.homeoffice.gov.uk/terrorism/threat/groups/index.html (accessed July 28, 2005). Just over one year later, the Home Office list had grown to 44 international terrorist organizations proscribed under the *Terrorism Act 2000,* including two organizations proscribed under powers introduced in the *Terrorism Act 2006,* as glorifying terrorism, http://www.homeoffice.gov.uk/security/terrorism-and-the-law/terrorism-act/proscribed-groups?version=1 (accessed September 6, 2006).

18. The name CONTEST is not a direct acronym, but may be loosely based on "COuNter-TErrorism STrategy."

19. See for example Hazel Blears, "The Tools to Combat Terrorism," Speech to the Royal United Services Institute, February 24, 2005, http://press.homeoffice.gov.uk/Speeches/02-05-sp-tools-combat-terrorism (accessed September 6, 2006).

20. See for example Hazel Blears, "Homeland Security—Opening Address," Speech to Cityforum 'Second Extraordinary Round Table on Homeland Security', October 28, 2004, http://security.homeoffice.gov.uk/news-and-publications1/speeches-statements/Speech_homeland_security1.pdf?view=Binary (accessed September 6, 2006).

21. Her Majesty's Government, *Countering International Terrorism: The United Kingdom's Strategy*, Cm 6888 (London, UK: The Stationery Office, July 2006), p. 1.

22. Elaine Sciolino and Don van Natta, Jr., "June report led Britain to lower its terror alert," *New York Times,* July 19, 2005, Section A, Late edition—Final.

23. Intelligence and Security Committee, UK Parliament, *Report into the London Terrorist Attacks on 7 July 2005*: pp. 20–24.

24. Her Majesty's Government, *Threat Levels: The System to Assess the Threat from International Terrorism*, Issued with Cm 6888 (London: The Stationery Office, July 2006).

25. Her Majesty's Government, *Countering International Terrorism: The United Kingdom's Strategy*: pp. 11–15.

26. Intelligence and Security Committee, UK Parliament, *Report into the London Terrorist Attacks on 7 July 2005*: p. 13.

27. Ibid.: pp. 14–16.

28. Ibid.: pp. 33–35.

29. Her Majesty's Government, *Countering International Terrorism: The United Kingdom's Strategy*: pp. 17–21.

30. Ibid.: p. 2.

31. Ibid.: pp. 23–24.

32. Ibid.: p. 25.

33. Prime Minister Blair, "London Attacks," *House of Commons Hansard Debates* 436, part 31, col 567 (July 11, 2005).

34. London Assembly, *Report of the 7 July Review Committee*: p. 124.

35. Ibid.: pp. 124–130.

36. Her Majesty's Government, *Countering International Terrorism: The United Kingdom's Strategy*: pp. 25–26.

CHAPTER 14

THE APRIL 1995 BOMBING OF THE MURRAH FEDERAL BUILDING IN OKLAHOMA CITY

Daniel Baracskay

Terrorism has an altogether destabilizing effect on society. It psychologically distraughts the average person and instills anxiety and an atmosphere of ambivalence. Governments (including state and local entities) are temporarily confounded by the resultant chaos, and are forced to balance the distribution of emergency resources to effected area(s), reaffirm the misgivings of the citizenry, and refocus attention toward researching and developing a workable premise for repairing the breach in the system. These functions are in addition to the more symbolic role of restoring feelings of domestic tranquility. As Martha Crenshaw argues, "terrorist violence communicates a political message; its ends go beyond damaging an enemy's material resources. The victims or objects of terrorist attack have little intrinsic value to the terrorist group but represent a larger human audience whose reaction the terrorists seek."[1]

The Alfred P. Murrah Federal Building was located in the center of Oklahoma City. The building, which housed several federal agencies and bureaus, was constructed in 1997 and named after federal judge Alfred P. Murrah.[2] The sprawling Oklahoma City metropolitan area serves as the state's capital. Numerous industrial hubs and corporate headquarters are located within the 608 square-mile boundaries of the city, and the largest single employer is the Tinker Air Force Base, which is positioned in the southeastern suburb of Midwest City.[3] The population for the Oklahoma metropolitan statistical area was slightly more than one million people in 1995, ranking it forty-sixth in terms of metropolitan size.[4]

The bombing of the Murrah Federal Building in Oklahoma City was the second of the three most impressionable and violent terrorist attacks to affect the United States in recent history. The first incident occurred in 1993 with the bombing of the World Trade Center's north tower in New York City. That attack was a political statement by Islamic extremists from the Middle East, who wanted to demonstrate their discontent with U.S. foreign policy in the region, which they deemed as oppressive and intrusive. Two years later, the bombing of the Murrah Building continued what appeared to be anti-American rhetoric. This second attack occurred on U.S. soil, but was a domestically spawned plot to instigate an antigovernment and antilaw movement by radical militants. The third attack on 9/11 was the most recent. It not only collapsed the north and south World Trade Center towers, but also caused the deaths of scores of Americans.

The Oklahoma City bombing in 1995 was a significant event for three principle reasons. First, the bombing established that American cities are not just vulnerable to the threats of external terrorist groups, but also to the impulses of internal extremists that are willing to use violence to advance their objectives. Second, the Oklahoma City bombing was the second large-scale assault on a public building in a 2-year period. The use of terrorism as an instrument of destruction is becoming more pervasive, if not expected. Finally, trends have shown that terror groups purposefully identify large and densely populated urban centers for targets in the United States, and intentionally use violence in these cities to gain media coverage. This chapter will analyze the Oklahoma City bombing incident in greater detail and examine several implications and lessons that have surfaced in the decade following the event.

EXAMINING THE OKLAHOMA CITY BOMBING OF 1995

The Murrah Federal Building in Oklahoma City was a hub of employment for more than 500 federal workers. It also housed a daycare center on the second floor of the building for children of federal employees.[5] On April 19, 1995, a truck containing nearly 5,000 pounds of explosive chemicals detonated at 9:02 A.M. in front of the northern section of the building. The attack killed a total of 168 people and wounded over 800 others (see Table 14.1 below). Originally constructed of reinforced concrete, the front and middle portions of the nine-floor building crumbled without the support of a steel frame.[6] The blast was felt 55 miles away and registered a 6.0 on the Richter scale, blowing out windows and doors in a 50-block area.[7] The sound waves, smoke, and debris from the explosion scattered throughout the surrounding areas. The force of the explosion damaged 324 surrounding buildings and destroyed automobiles and other nearby property.[8]

Table 14.1   Effects of the Bombing

Number of People Affected	Result
19 children	Died in the second floor daycare center
30 children	Orphaned from parents who died
219 children	Lost a parent
250 individuals	Number of visitors in the building
400 individuals	Left homeless
600 workers	Number of federal and contract workers in the building
7,000 individuals	Lost their workplace
16,000 individuals	Were downtown when the explosion occurred
360,000 Oklahoma residents	Knew someone who worked in the Murrah Building

Source: Data derived from Oklahoma Department of Mental Health and Substance Abuse Services figures referenced in: U.S. Department of Justice, *Responding to Terrorism Victims: Oklahoma City and Beyond,* (Washington, DC: Office of Justice Programs, October 2000) 1.

Prior to September 11, 2001, the Oklahoma City bombing had the distinction of being the largest act of terrorist aggression to transpire within U.S. borders. With the incident occurring just 2 years after the first World Trade Center bombing, the immediate reaction by the mass media was to assert the blame on recognized terrorist organizations. Pictures of conspirators of Middle Eastern origin were dispatched in the event that an observer had witnessed the attacker's profile at the scene.

But within 90 minutes of the incident, Gulf War veteran Timothy McVeigh was arrested on an Oklahoma state highway after a state trooper cited him for driving a motor vehicle without a license plate and for carrying a loaded firearm. Some speculation has arisen on whether McVeigh consciously wanted to be captured and credited with the attack. An automobile traveling without a license plate draws the attention of law enforcement officers, particularly when there is a heightened sense of alert after a major terrorist attack. This was reinforced by the possession of other incriminating evidence found on his person at the time of arrest.[9] Interrogation of McVeigh revealed his antigovernment, extremist, and libertarian philosophy. Portions of the radical 1978 novel by William Luther Pierce (whose pen name was Andrew Macdonald) entitled *The Turner Diaries* were found in McVeigh's vehicle. Macdonald's narrative provided a violent portrayal of a racially based revolutionary movement that declares genocide against all individuals not of Caucasian origin.[10] A segment of the book describes a fictitious attack scenario against the FBI building in Washington, DC, analogous to what McVeigh had instigated in Oklahoma City.

Law enforcement officers quickly determined that McVeigh had the primary role in the bombing incident, with help from an accomplice, Terry Nichols. Both men had been acquainted during their service in the U.S. Army when stationed with the 1st Infantry Division headquartered at Fort Riley, Kansas. Nichols was not present during the actual event, but was detained in connection with the bombing after McVeigh's arrest. The motivations behind the actions of the two offenders were divulged during the course of investigation. Both shared a strong disdain for government. Nichols' scorn for government came after he had failed in a number of jobs and subsequent business ventures. He later lost his small farm and had to appear in court. To create a new start and build security for his retirement through a military pension, Nichols joined the U.S. Army at a Michigan recruiting office. During his military service, Nichols progressed through the ranks to become a senior platoon leader. Being older than the traditional recruit, Nichols was admired by younger members in his squadron, including McVeigh. His contempt of the federal government's gun laws and the financial problems faced by American farmers each year seemed to entice great resentment in him.[11]

McVeigh was an extremely passionate adherent of firearms and gun collections. He perceived any laws implemented by the federal government to limit possession as an encroachment of the second amendment. It is ironic that this cause compelled him to oppose the same government he had served under during his years in the military. His animosity toward the government was further exacerbated by a letter McVeigh received in 1993 by the Finance and Accounting Office of the U.S. Department of Defense, which claimed that he had been overpaid by $1,058 while serving in the Army, and required that repayment commence immediately. McVeigh had allegedly known about the overpayment in his paychecks at the time, but had never reported it. The incident outraged him and further reinforced his antigovernment thinking. McVeigh responded by accusing the government of purposefully forcing him out of work, since his only asset at the time was a car that he expected would be seized.[12] Two weeks after receiving this letter, McVeigh watched, with millions of other Americans, the confrontation in Waco, Texas, unfold (see below). The Department of Alcohol, Tobacco, and Firearms (ATF) and Federal Bureau of Investigation's (FBI) joint handling of this incident furthered McVeigh's belief that the U.S. government was slowly becoming a socialist regime. McVeigh left his Florida job at the time and traveled to Waco and other regions of the West, where he purportedly encountered other people and groups who were displeased with the federal government's policies, and who fueled his cause and antigovernmental temperament.[13]

Substantive evidence gathered in the course of the investigation indicated that McVeigh and Nichols were guided by a right-wing militia movement that renounced the policies of the federal government as hostile and antagonistic.[14] Members of these private "citizen militias" typically embrace a subculture of resistance and violence. The existence of private militias has been more perceptible in recent decades, with the protest activities of Gordon Wendell Kahl over the federal government's taxation policies and collection mandate of the U.S. Department of Taxation's Internal Revenue Service (IRS), the confrontation in Ruby Ridge in Northern Idaho between a group of racially motivated white supremacists and the federal government, and the highly publicized Waco incident. In particular, the raid by federal agents of the religiously inspired Branch Davidian Group (from the Seventh-Day Adventist Church) at a rural location near Waco, Texas, signaled the persistence of militant groups in American culture, and their willingness to use violence and standoffs to promote their causes.

In this instance, four agents from the ATF and six Davidian group members were killed during a raid on February 28, 1993. The event instigated a 51-day standoff that ended on April 19 after the FBI and ATF sought closure to the confrontation, and the complex was consumed by a fire that killed the movement's leader, David Koresh, along with many of his followers. Official governmental inquiries suggest that the fire was started inside the complex by the Davidians.[15] McVeigh later asserted that the principal raison d'être for his own conspiracy plan to bomb the Oklahoma City federal building was in fact retaliation for the outcomes of the Ruby Ridge and Waco incidents, particularly the latter.[16] As Lou Michel and Dan Herbeck note, "Timothy McVeigh was preparing to teach the government a lesson. He was preparing to strike back for Waco, for Ruby Ridge, for U.S. military actions against smaller nations, for no-knock search warrants. It was a list of grievances he'd been amassing for years: crooked politicians, overzealous government agents, high taxes, political correctness, and gun laws."[17]

The bombing became the largest criminal case in U.S. history. Directed by FBI agents, 28,000 interviews were conducted and 3.5 tons of evidence gathered.[18] McVeigh and Nichols were indicted and convicted of the crime in separate cases. Terrorist acts of aggression fall under federal jurisdiction, and perpetrators are investigated and prosecuted by federal law enforcement officials. The rights and restitution of the victims are administered by federal criminal justice agencies that possess the corresponding statutory responsibilities.[19] Overall responsibility for prosecuting the McVeigh case and protecting victims' rights was given to the U.S. Attorney's Office for the Western District of Oklahoma, which was later supplemented by the U.S. Attorney's Office for the District of Colorado. The location for the trial (Denver, Colorado) was decided upon after a change of venue hearing was held in January of 1996. However, this produced extensive controversy and concern that out-of-state travel would be an obstacle for the victims and their families. Congressional legislation and efforts by

Attorney General Janet Reno worked to make the trial proceedings more easily accessible, namely through the use of closed-circuit television. In the case of *United States v. Timothy McVeigh,* the courts found McVeigh guilty of the terrorist crime. He was convicted on June 2, 1997, and sentenced to death by the jury 11 days later. Despite numerous court appeals, one of which made it to the U.S. Supreme Court but was denied, McVeigh was executed by lethal injection at a federal penitentiary in Indiana on June 11, 2001.

His accomplice, Terry Nichols, was tried in McAlester, Oklahoma. In *United States v. Terry Nichols,* Nichols was convicted of both manslaughter and conspiring with McVeigh. A U.S. District Court first convicted Nichols of eight counts of manslaughter on December 23, 1997. The jury rendered a guilty verdict on the conspiracy charges to bomb a federal building, along with eight counts of involuntary manslaughter for the deaths of eight federal law enforcement officers. The jury sentenced Nichols to life in prison without the possibility of parole. Another acquaintance, Michael Fortier, was also detained for questioning and eventually pleaded guilty to failing to inform authorities in advance about the plot. He testified against both McVeigh and Nichols, and was sentenced to 12 years in prison. He was released early in January 2006 for good behavior. A second trial began on March 1, 2004, in Oklahoma, charging Nichols with 160 counts of first-degree murder and one count for each of the crimes of first-degree manslaughter, conspiracy to commit murder, and of aiding and counseling with the bombing of a public building. The jury in the second case found him guilty on all charges, most particularly 161 counts of first-degree murder. The jury deadlocked over the issue of whether Nichols should have been given the death penalty, and he was subsequently sentenced by Judge Steven Taylor to 160 consecutive life sentences in prison without the possibility of parole. Judge Taylor also asserted during the Nichols case that no additional evidence existed to implicate involvement by any persons other than McVeigh and Nichols.[20]

THE RESPONSE TO THE ATTACK

The response to the Oklahoma City bombing consisted of three tiers. The first tier was the immediate reaction that civil society and federal, state, and local agencies of government had to the incident. It was represented by the individuals and professionals who arrived first on the scene. The second tier, which was enmeshed with the first, involved a search and rescue strategy and efforts to provide relief through emergency management and assistance for victims and their families. This became a short- to medium-term endeavor. The third tier was a long-term response. It involved passing new antiterror legislation, conducting investigations, reforming counterterrorism measures, and using attributes of the criminal justice system to seek restitution for the incident. Each of these tiers of response will be considered below.

Civil society responds atypically in disaster situations, both in terms of perceptions and expectations, than what is routinely demonstrated in the course of normal daily circumstances. The criminal nature of a terror attack and the use of lethal force engender a public expectation that the government will respond. At the same time, the public also assigns blame on the government and associated political institutions for the breach in public security. Even the most expedient response times by federal, state, and local officials tend to be discernibly prolonged in the aftermath of such an event. The inclination for not-for-profit organizations and private citizens to assist with immediate action becomes noticeably higher. Individuals act for the betterment of society and accept roles that they are not specifically trained or recompensed for under the ethos of moral civic virtue. This became the first tier of response to the attack.

First-hand accounts of the incident acknowledged that initial response came from nearby individuals already present, and those marginally wounded survivors who were still able to provide assistance despite their bewildered states.[21] These untrained civilians had no formal or professional obligation to assist, but nevertheless willingly offered their support. The subsequent deluge of police officers, firefighters, and other law enforcement personnel to the scene constituted the initial "governmental" response to the crisis. The sound waves of the blast and the visual acuity in which observers miles away could see the smoke and debris solicited a large number of emergency calls for both departments. This grouping of professionals assumed the initial lead and logistically began coordinating the rescue efforts. The Oklahoma City Fire Department established an Incident Command System (ICS) to manage the search-and-rescue mission and coordinate federal, state, and local human and agency resources. The State Emergency Operations Center was operational by 9:25 A.M. State-level agencies in the fields of public safety, human services, military, health, and education sent cohorts of representatives to join the center.[22]

Other agencies likewise responded to the crisis. Local health care workers and not-for-profit organizations such as the Salvation Army, American Red Cross, and United Way pledged human and financial resources. Medical care by local hospitals was particularly imperative given the number of fatalities and wounded individuals, both of which were unknown statistics prior to analyzing the site. Pertinent in-state and county agencies sent their own employees to examine and analyze the scene. For instance, the Oklahoma Department of Human Services and Oklahoma County Sheriff's Office were involved with some of the logistical and safety concerns that surfaced immediately after the incident.

Also on the afternoon of the bombing, the Office of the Chief Medical Examiner and the Oklahoma Funeral Directors Association established the Compassion Center to help victims and their families deal with the psychological and physical effects of the bombing. The American Red Cross assumed operation of the center the next day. Support from the community in terms of workers and volunteers from across the nation, along with financial contributions, demonstrated the generous nature of the private, public, and not-for-profit sectors' responses to the disaster. Members of the business community joined nonprofit personnel from the American Red Cross, local churches, health care organizations, and other organizations driven by similar missions to assist public sector personnel from the federal, state, and local levels of government.[23]

This initial reaction was reinforced by a second tier of response. This tier involved search-and-rescue efforts and emergency management. Explosions or natural disasters that collapse building structures bury inhabitants and present a perceptible challenge for rescue workers to accurately ascertain survival rates. The overall search-and-recovery effort lasted through May 4 and focused on generating the identity and status of affected victims of the blast.[24] An out-of-state search-and-rescue team reinforced local efforts within 24 hours of the explosion. This team added additional public sector and civilian aid in a time-sensitive setting that urged expedient medical care for the injured.

The Federal Emergency Management Agency (FEMA) sent ten teams to assess the damage. These teams were experienced in various types of natural disasters but had to adapt their skills to an artificially induced catastrophe that was no less destructive. Ironically, Oklahoma City has historically implemented an efficient emergency management response system since the city is geographically situated in the center of "tornado ally" and falls victim to higher than average rates of tornado-spawned damage nationwide each year. FEMA's deployment of various response teams tactically addressed salient matters like search and rescue, medical care, and technical support (equipment and hazardous materials).[25] These teams were led by an operations chief who coordinated efforts at the federal level with the local police and fire departments. Military personnel from Tinker Air Force base offered additional specialized expertise. The FBI and CIA likewise sent agents to conduct criminal investigations of the scene. The detainment and questioning of McVeigh and Nichols indicated that the incident was a product of domestic origin rather than international. This signified the third tier of response to the attack.

The principal political actor that the American public looks toward in times of crisis is the president.[26] President Clinton's rapid response to the attack was one of reproach, assurance, and resolution. Clinton's reproach of the bombing rebuked the attackers for a crime that killed and wounded hundreds of individuals of all ages, races, and demographic backgrounds. Clinton stated that "the bombing in Oklahoma City was an attack on innocent children and defenseless citizens. It was an act of cowardice, and it was evil."[27] His symbolic role as president was exemplified through presidential speeches that assured the public that assistance was en route and the federal government would have a fundamental role in seeking justice. The president's resolution was evident with the signing of the Emergency Declaration FEMA-3114-EM-OK under the title V provisions of the Robert T. Stafford Disaster Relief and Emergency Assistance Act [PL 93-288], which gave the federal government the lead in responding to the catastrophe. This was signed within 90 minutes of the incident.[28]

The bombing was also a challenge for then-Governor of Oklahoma, Frank Keating. Keating, who had assumed his gubernatorial seat just 4 months earlier, responded with a strong commitment of state personnel and financial resources. His resolute leadership style during the crisis helped him win reelection for a second term as governor, which he completed in 2003. The legislature worked closely with the governor throughout the recovery process and helped establish the Murrah Fund, which solicited donations for the Crime Victim Compensation Program. Approximately $14 million was donated to the Oklahoma City Disaster Relief Fund. The Oklahoma Department of Mental Health and Substance Abuse Services created Project Heartland on May 15. The program was the first of its kind to respond to a large-scale terrorist attack. Initial funding for the program was provided by the federal government to provide counseling, intervention, outreach, and education.[29]

These critical responses by private, not-for-profit, and public sector organizations in the civic sphere addressed the pressing need for immediate disaster relief and emergency responsiveness. Longer-term relief efforts revolved around rebuilding the affected downtown area and returning life to a state of normalcy. The federal, state, and local levels of government implemented plans for emergency preparedness and then examined how to reform counterterrorism measures to deter or better respond to further incidents. One noteworthy legislative endeavor that followed the Oklahoma City bombing was the Antiterrorism and Effective Death Penalty Act of 1996 (AEDPA). Passed by both houses of the Republican-controlled 104th Congress, and signed into law on April 24, 1996 by President Clinton, the AEDPA provided bipartisan reassurance that acts of terror were intolerable and would be met with utmost severity.

The act imposed discernible limitations to court appeals falling under the right to writ of habeas corpus for capital cases, and reduced the length of the appeals process, thus curtailing the authority of federal courts.[30] It also provided for the effective use of the death penalty for those found guilty of terrorist acts, and dealt with the issue of victims' rights and the restitution process. Despite these provisions, the act fell short of President

Clinton's initial proposition, which would have provided some of the very elements that are being contested in today's recent debate over the USA PATRIOT Act. Clinton's proposal would have increased the government's authority to wiretap phone lines, sanctioned greater access to various records (including phone), and expanded security at airports.[31] The integrity of the act remained intact despite the challenge later raised in the U.S. Supreme Court case *Felker v. Turpin* (1996). That case questioned the constitutionality of the act on the grounds that it limited the filing of successive writ of habeas corpus petitions, and thus violated Section 9, Clause 2 of Article I of the U.S. Constitution. Chief Justice William Rehnquist wrote the decision of the court, which unanimously concurred that the act did not violate the Constitution's suspension clause.

As mentioned in the above section, the criminal justice and investigatory aspects of the incident occurred rapidly. The arrests and convictions of McVeigh and Nichols brought relatively swift justice to the perpetrators of the crime. The ramifications for reforming counterterrorism measures are discussed more thoroughly below. These reforms are more time-consuming and incessant, meaning that institutional and procedural changes must be evaluated, updated, and implemented consistently to ensure that the system is in fact adapting to an unpredictable environment.

IMPLICATIONS AND LESSONS OF THE OKLAHOMA CITY BOMBING

The 1995 terrorist attack in Oklahoma City effectively achieved three primary but interconnected objectives. First, the densely populated nature of the federal building provided a forum for the terrorists to fatally and/or severely injure a large number of people. The incident consequently became recognized as a "mass" bombing. Second, the act occurred in an urban center of national and international standing. This attracted worldwide attention as the mass media deluged the vicinity with reporters and analysts. Media coverage transmitted the event over airwaves and satisfied one of the primary aims that terror groups seek to achieve through violent acts—publicity and exposure. Third, the secretive and covert means used to deploy the plan created a sense of fear, as citizens worried over what appeared to be an unseen aggressor.[32] The perception that terrorists could be comprised of average, everyday citizens who may plausibly be a neighbor or resident inhabiting the same geographic region is psychologically unsettling. As with all unanticipated attacks of a similar nature, the motive behind the incident was not immediately known. Nor was there an indication of whether the act was one of foreign or domestic origin. This section will build upon these implications by further examining salient lessons learned in the decade following the attack.

American Perceptions and the Scope of Terror Activities

The threat of terrorism is obviously not constrained to overseas—nor is it solely a characteristic of clandestine organizations operating in destabilized countries. Both foreign and domestic terrorists pose a significant threat to U.S. security. However, prior to the escalated interval of terrorist activity that occurred throughout the 1990s, Americans largely perceived the threat to be an external one. The bombing of the U.S. Embassy in Beirut, Lebanon, in 1983, the truck bombs that killed U.S. Marines and French paratroopers in Beirut in 1985, the explosion of Pan Am Flight 103 over Lockerbie, Scotland, in 1988, and the French U.T.A. jet explosion over Niger provided Americans with perceptible evidence that the 1980s were turbulent times for international terrorism. The hijacking and crash of a Xiamen Airlines plane at a Chinese airport in 1990, and the bombing that destroyed the Israeli Embassy in Buenos Aires, Argentina, in 1992 provided further verification that foreign terror networks were growing in number.[33] These incidents concerned Americans, but still did not present a significant cause for alarm domestically.

Lynn Kuzma's analysis of public opinion data collected during the 1980s revealed that Americans perceived terrorist acts around the world as an "extreme" or "very serious threat" between 68 percent and 84 percent of the time. This was in contrast to poll figures from the mid-1990s, which suggested that 50 percent of the respondents perceived terrorism as a "very serious" threat inside the United States.[34] Kuzma also found that after 1993, when respondents were asked how worried they were that either they or someone in their family will become victims of a terrorist attack like the one in Oklahoma City, the data showed that only 10 to 14 percent responded with the "very worried" category, and between 22 and 28 percent with the "somewhat worried" category. This indicates that the Oklahoma City bombing alerted citizens, but did not significantly induce widespread feelings of panic. It is also important to note that changes in American culture and perceptions are incremental. Two isolated but significant terror incidents in 1993 and 1995 altered people's perceptions, but terror attacks abroad still reinforced the tendency of Americans to perceive terrorism through an international rather than domestic lens.

National Security and Criminal Justice Are Interrelated

One lesson from previous terrorist attacks is that while the motivations driving various terrorist groups may be distinct (particularly when distinguishing between secular and nonsecular groups), the use of violence and projected level of destruction are still analogous. Measures for counterterrorism are designed to prevent both internationally and domestically spawned acts of terror. While the main difference in the two spheres rests in the geographic location where the terrorists originate (externally versus internally), their use of violence to inflict damage is shared. This negates the notion that there could be a posture of mutual exclusivity in the manner in which policies are developed for the two spheres. A shared propensity for violence by terrorists from both spheres inherently forces counterterrorist agencies to adopt a cooperative and universal approach to treating the existence of threats within the system. Cohesiveness in preventing acts of terrorism fundamentally relies upon cross-jurisdictional cooperation and a unified system of codes and procedures. The process is in some ways complicated, but still complemented by the system of federalism that decentralizes most criminal justice functions of domestic jurisdiction to state and local governments. Nevertheless, breaches present significant concerns to all levels of government, and have forced greater communication between the top and bottom layers of the system.

The relatively porous nature of U.S. borders, and the traditional culture that has valued American individualism, have both presented challenges to maintaining the security of the nation. No layer of government within the system presented a significant challenge to the ease in which McVeigh and Nichols successfully implemented their plan. The plan was not very technologically complex or expensive, and demonstrated—as CIA veteran Paul Pillar recently observed—"that even the infliction of mass casualties does not always require much capacity. That horror was accomplished with two men, a truck, and homemade fertilizer-based explosives."[35]

The entire plot by McVeigh and Nichols was relatively inexpensive. From September 30 to October 18, 1994, Nichols purchased a combined total of 4,000 pounds of ammonium nitrate using the alias Mike Havens. McVeigh had also purchased smaller quantities of the chemical. Both men made roughly eight purchases to accumulate the necessary amount for their plan.[36] They funded the plot from personal savings, spending approximately $5,000. This amount covered a rental truck ($250), fertilizer ($500), the ammonium nitrate ($2,780), and a vehicle to flee the scene ($1400).[37] Their military training, fascination with firearms, and nominal research on chemical reactions easily allowed them to execute the plan. Yet, very little notice was taken throughout the purchase of these volatile and unstable substances. This questions whether further safeguards are necessary to prevent both internal and external assailants from gaining easy access to materials that can be used in an assault of similar magnitude.

Further, lessons learned from breaches in national security show that emergency response plans are essential components for all cities, particularly larger ones. This function goes hand-in-hand with crime prevention efforts and is as essential as policies that are geared toward maintaining economic development, transportation, and infrastructure. Emergency response plans are more difficult to execute in populated environments, since there are practical limitations to channeling people into or out of an area. Yet the dense nature of highly populated cities makes them a more attractive target for terrorists than suburban locations, since terrorists seek maximum damage and exposure for their actions.

Consequently, as former U.S. Attorney General Edwin Meese argues, governments must effectively cultivate five tiers of counterterrorism measures. The first tier is the preparation stage, where agencies formulate policies to combat terrorism. This stage addresses the nature of federalism by delineating responsibility and lines of authority. It balances opposing objectives and develops guidelines for the use of force. The second tier is prevention. This stage relies upon intelligence gathering, and works to successfully deny terrorists access to the system and an opportunity for attack. This stage relies upon successfully sharing intelligence information across jurisdictions and levels of government. It also has a significant role in corresponding American agencies with international entities that have the same mission, thus recognizing the interconnected nature of national security and local criminal justice efforts. For instance, the international police organization INTERPOL gathers large amounts of information related to criminal activity, and offers intelligence to foreign countries that use the information in their counterterrorism strategies. This helps to improve the chances of capturing terrorists who span the globe in their use of acts of violence, and seek solitude in terror-friendly states.

The third tier in an effective counterterrorism strategy is operation. For this stage, governments must demonstrate resolution and decisiveness after an incident has occurred. This was exemplified after the Murrah Building was bombed and President Clinton televised a series of speeches to reassure the American public. As mentioned above, the president also signed the Emergency Declaration FEMA-3114-EM-OK to focus the federal government's response, and passed the Antiterrorism and Effective Death Penalty Act in 1996. Elected officials and bureaucrats endeavor to prevent terrorists from spreading fear throughout society and forcing overreaction. The fourth phase—adjudication—is initiated when the terrorists are apprehended, and the final tier involves an educational process which helps to demystify the act and inform citizens of the perils that both domestic and foreign terrorists pose to society.[38] It is also partially designed to build national cohesion by involving civilians in the fight against terrorism, thus diffusing the gap and consequential negativity that exists between citizens and their perceptions of government.

Understanding and Responding to the Motivations of Domestic Terrorists

The supposition that terrorists use violence to try and achieve their objectives is assumed. However, there is a certain ambiguity in the restitution they seek for perceived grievances. Terrorists identify targets (both human and physical) that are "representative" of the institutions or groups they seek to avenge. Victims of terror attacks are not selected on the basis of personal guilt or a specific infraction committed against the assailants.[39] However, they are the closest artifact that the terrorists can associate with. For the Oklahoma City bombing, McVeigh's anger grew cumulatively as Congress passed various gun control laws during the 1990s, and the ATF and FBI's conduct during the Waco incident presented a threat to his way of thinking. And yet, neither McVeigh nor Nichols were targeting specific members of Congress or the corresponding bureaucratic agencies they held in such contempt. Rather, they used the Murrah Building to symbolize their disdain for governmental policies, and because the site contained a large number of federal workers.

Agreement that the Murrah Building would be the target was reached after McVeigh and Nichols had considered numerous other urban centers for the bombing. McVeigh had toured federal buildings in Arkansas, Missouri, Arizona, and Texas. In addition, he considered the J. Edgar Hoover FBI building in Washington, DC, which would have paralleled the scenario in *The Turner Diaries*. Nichols scoped federal buildings located in Kansas and Missouri. Ultimately, the decision to select the Murrah Federal Building in Oklahoma City was made after considering two primary and interconnected issues. First, it was the supposed location where the orders had originated for the Waco raid. Second, the building housed numerous federal workers and several federal law enforcement agencies. McVeigh in particular wanted to target the FBI, ATF, and U.S. Drug Enforcement Agency (DEA) after their roles in the Waco incident. He intentionally chose a glass-framed building that shattered under the force of the blast, causing extensive damage. Unlike some of the other federal buildings they toured that had nongovernmental workers on the site (i.e., restaurants, floral shops, etc.), the Murrah building presented the fewest number of lay citizens from all the alternatives.[40] This indicated that McVeigh and Nichols may have been somewhat selective in their use of violence, targeting federal employees and excluding nongovernmental civilians. However, their attack murdered dozens of innocent children who were playing in the daycare center on the second floor, negating any intent to avoid nongovernmental casualties.

Terrorist groups (aside from those propagating the large revolutions of transitionary states) are typically small and cohesive entities. The tightness of the group is a function of how closely the members share each others' values and beliefs. Hence, a tight-knit group is assumed to share perceptions and a reality that is alien to those from outside of the group. McVeigh and Nichols were both linked to the Michigan Militia, a paramilitary group with an estimated 12,000 members, who share the view that the U.S. government is gravitating toward the left of the political ideological spectrum. It sees government policies as coercive and controlling facets in the lives of Americans.[41] There are an estimated 800 militia groups in existence in the United States that fall into one of two categories. The first are "talking militias," which use rhetoric to entice their members to protest antigun legislation. These groups are not particularly violent in nature. The second type is "marching militias," which use violence to advance a revolutionary ideology that is often racist and anti-Semitic. This is the type that most closely encapsulates the activities of McVeigh and Nichols. Both types prove that there is "difficulty in gauging even the rough dimensions of the American militia movement [given] its geographical pervasiveness and its unimpeded growth in years."[42]

CONCLUSION

The remnants of the destroyed Murrah building were subsequently demolished in 1995. Today, the site of the building is occupied by a large memorial that stands in remembrance of the many fallen victims of that day. A new federal building opened in Oklahoma City in 2004, one block from the site of the original federal building.

The shortcomings of homeland security are still apparent. Americans do not profess a positive attitude for political institutions, or for the ability of government to prevent a future terrorist attack. The consequence is "a loss of confidence on the part of the ordinary citizen in the resolve and competence of his government . . . the initial shock is transformed into criticism and anger at the government for not acting to prevent or curb such attacks. People instinctively agree with Churchill's dictum that a government's first obligation is to protect its citizens."[43] In light of this, what challenge can be more testing than a government's quest to win back the confidence of its citizenry?

NOTES

1. Martha Crenshaw, "The Causes of Terrorism," *Comparative Politics* 13, no. 4 (July 1981): 379.

2. Alfred P. Murrah lived from 1904 to 1975. He was appointed to the U.S. District Court for Oklahoma in 1937, and the 10th Circuit Court of Appeals in 1940. He retired from the bench in 1970 after a long and distinguished judicial career.

3. Clive Irving, ed., *In Their Name* (New York: Random House, 1995) 20.

4. The Metropolitan Statistical Area (MSA) population for Oklahoma City in 1995 was calculated at 1,013,000 people. Despite the 1995 attack, the rate of population growth continued in the MSA to 1,039,000 (1998). See: U.S. Census Bureau, *Statistical Abstract of the United States: 2000*, 120th edition (Washington, DC: U.S. Government Printing Office, 2000) Table no. 34.

5. Irving, ed., *In Their Name*.

6. S. A. Pressley, "Bomb Kills Dozens in Oklahoma Federal Building," *Washington Post* (April 20, 1995) Section A: 1.

7. U.S. Department of Justice, *Responding to Terrorism Victims: Oklahoma City and Beyond* (Washington, DC: Office of Justice Programs, October 2000).

8. Ibid.

9. Lou Michel and Dan Herbeck, *American Terrorist: Timothy McVeigh & the Oklahoma City Bombing* (New York: Regan Books, 2001) 248.

10. Brian L. Keeley, "Of Conspiracy Theories," *The Journal of Philosophy* 96, no. 3 (March 1999): 109–126.

11. Michel and Herbeck, *American Terrorist.*

12. Ibid.

13. Ibid.: see p. 121 in particular.

14. For more on this topic, please see the chapter by Eric Shibuya in this volume.

15. Clifford E. Simonsen and Jeremy R. Spindlove, *Terrorism Today: The Past, the Players, the Future* (NJ: Prentice Hall, 2000) 276.

16. Keeley, "Of Conspiracy Theories."

17. Michel and Herbeck, *American Terrorist:* p. 2.

18. Tim Talley, "Experts fear Oklahoma City bombing lessons forgotten," in *The San Diego Union Tribune*, April 17, 2006.

19. U.S. Department of Justice, *Responding to Terrorism Victims: Oklahoma City and Beyond* (Washington, DC: Office of Justice Programs, October 2000).

20. Michel and Herbeck, *American Terrorist.*

21. Irving, ed., *In Their Name.*

22. U.S. Department of Justice, *Responding to Terrorism Victims.*

23. Ibid.

24. Ibid.

25. Irving, ed., *In Their Name.*

26. Norman Thomas, Joseph Pika, and John Maltese, *Politics of the Presidency,* 5th ed. (Washington, DC: Congressional Quarterly Press, 2002).

27. U.S. Department of Justice, *Responding to Terrorism Victims.*

28. Ibid.

29. Ibid.

30. Writ of habeas corpus is a Latin term that orders court officials to explain the reasons of confinement to any person who is being held in custody, and to bring that person into court to explain the reasons for confinement. It is a protected right under Article I of the U.S. Constitution.

31. Lynn M. Kuzma, "Trends: Terrorism in the United States," *The Public Opinion Quarterly* 64, no.1 (Spring 2000): 90–105.

32. Paul R. Pillar, *Terrorism and U.S. Foreign Policy* (Washington, DC: Brookings Institution Press, 2001).

33. Thomas R. Dye, *Politics in America* (Upper Saddle River, New Jersey, NJ: Prentice Hall, 2005) 649, Table 18.2.

34. Kuzma, "Trends: Terrorism in the United States," pp. 90, 98.

35. Pillar, *Terrorism and U.S. Foreign Policy.* p. 33.

36. Michel and Herbeck, *American Terrorist.*

37. In an interview with reporters, McVeigh allegedly stated that the robbery he had committed months earlier against Roger Moore on an Arkansas ranch was not for money to finance his plot, but rather for revenge. See: Michel and Herbeck, *American Terrorist:* pp. 172–176.

38. Edwin Meesse III, "The Five Tiers of Domestic Action," in *Terrorism: How the West Can Win*, ed. Benjamin Netanyahu (New York: The Jonathan Institute, 1986) 165–167.

39. Cindy C. Combs, *Terrorism in the Twenty-First Century*, 2nd ed. (Upper Saddle River, New Jersey, NJ: Prentice Hall, 2000).

40. Michel and Herbeck, *American Terrorist*.

41. Bruce Hoffman, *Inside Terrorism* (New York: Columbia University Press, 1998).

42. Ibid.: p. 107. For more on these groups, please see the chapters by James Aho, Cindy Combs, and Eugenia Guilmartin in *The Making of a Terrorist: Recruitment, Training and Root Causes*, ed. James Forest (Westport, CT: Praeger, 2005).

43. Benjamin Netanyahu, "Terrorism: How the West Can Win," in *Terrorism: How the West Can Win*, ed. Benjamin Netanyahu (New York: The Jonathan Institute, 1986) 200.

Part II

CASE STUDIES OF THE LONG-TERM FIGHT AGAINST TERRORISM AND INSURGENCY

CHAPTER 15

STATE RESPONSE TO TERRORISM IN SRI LANKA

Thomas A. Marks

Sri Lanka has for decades been forced to deal with the violence now faced by states worldwide.[1] The target of a ruthless insurgent movement that has utilized terror as a strategy for insurgency, Colombo has fielded a series of responses which, though not altogether successful, nevertheless have prevented political and economic collapse.

The complexity of the threat faced is significant. Liberation Tigers of Tamil Eelam (LTTE) is labeled "terrorist" by any number of governments, but in reality, it is an insurgency in intent and methodology. It has, however, gone from using terror as a tool for mass mobilization to using it as a strategy for insurgency.[2]

The problem for security forces is that, early on, armed challenges to the government's authority appear more or less the same. A systemic response to these challenges that is centered around the use of force, to the near exclusion of other facets, is inappropriate. Most commonly, abuse of the populace creates a new dynamic that allows an operationally astute insurgent challenger for state power to mobilize additional support.

INITIAL REACTION TO THE "TERRORIST" CHALLENGE

In the decades after achieving independence from Britain in 1948, Sri Lanka was a state remarkably unprepared to deal with even substantial overt protest action much less subversion and its challenges, whether terrorism or guerrilla action. Only 10,605 policemen were scattered in small stations amidst a population of 12.5 million. The military was in a similar state: small (the army numbered but 6,578 and had only five infantry battalions) and minimally equipped.

These forces grew little in the decades that followed, even as the population reached 18 million. Political efforts to raise the societal position of the majority that was Sinhala-speaking Buddhists (80 percent of the population) clashed with the efforts of the minority (17 percent) who were Tamil (overwhelmingly Hindu, speaking Tamil) and sought to retain their position. Small groups of radical Tamil youth formed, both at home and abroad, strongly influenced by Marxism. Their solution to their "oppression" was to call for "liberation"—that is, the formation of a separate socialist or Marxist Tamil state, *Tamil Eelam*. The early strength of this movement was no more than 200. The Tamil people, whatever their plight, did not readily give their support to "coffee house revolutionaries."

Without a mass base, these groups could do little more than to plan future terror actions. Police and intelligence documents speak of small, isolated groups of a half dozen or so would-be liberationists meeting in forest gatherings in Sri Lanka to plot their moves. Actions that occurred, bombings and small-scale attacks upon government supporters and police positions, were irritating but dismissed as the logical consequence of radicalism.[3]

There was method to the upstart schemes, though. By 1975, according to interrogations of captured Tamil insurgents, contacts had been made between these groups and the Palestine Liberation Organization (PLO) through PLO representatives in London. Shortly thereafter, Tamils began to train in the Middle East. At home, LTTE initiated its armed struggle with a reported April 7, 1978 ambush, when four members of a police party were killed and their weapons captured. This was followed by a series of hit and run attacks, which led to the banning of the "Liberation Tigers" on May 19, 1978 by Parliament. Though the police bore the brunt of LTTE activities, the army was also committed early on. This was carried out through the normal, legal procedures of representative government. The burden for implementation of very correct dictates and prohibitions, modeled after those of the former British colonial power, fell upon a post-colonial security apparatus that proved inadequate to the task. The difficulty was that the substance did not match the form.

Thus the advantage lay with the insurgents. That they should be described as such at this point in time stems from the key definitional element: they desired and sought to form a counter-state. By July 11, 1979, the government claimed 14 policemen had been killed by LTTE. Hence a state of emergency was declared on that date in Jaffna and at the two airports located in the Colombo vicinity. A week later, Parliament passed a "Prevention of Terrorism Act" that made murder, kidnapping, and abduction punishable by life imprisonment.[4]

In Jaffna, LTTE "military wing" commander, Charles Anton, was killed in a firefight with Sri Lankan military personnel on July 15, 1983. In retaliation, on July 23, an ambush executed by an LTTE element left 13 soldiers dead. Their subsequent funeral in Colombo ignited widespread rioting and looting directed against Tamils. At least 400 persons were killed and 100,000 left homeless; another 200–250,000 fled to India. The police stood by, and in many cases members of the armed forces participated in the violence.

This spasm of communal terror served to traumatize the Tamil community and provided LTTE with an influx of new manpower. The ascendancy of radical leadership in the struggle for *Tamil Eelam* was complete. Though there may at one point have been as many as 42 different active groups, they were dominated by just five: Liberation Tigers of Tamil Eelam (LTTE); People's Liberation Organisation of Thamileelam (PLOT, also frequently rendered as PLOTE in the Western press, a variance caused by use of Tamil Eelam rather than Thamileelam as adopted by the group itself for its formal communications); Tamil Eelam Liberation Organisation (TELO); Eelam People's Revolutionary Liberation Front (EPRLF); and Eelam Revolutionary Organisation (EROS). LTTE emerged as the dominant force by ruthless application of terror against its rivals.[5]

Clearly a product of Sri Lankan internal contradictions, these groups nevertheless existed within the larger strategic realities of the Cold War. Sri Lanka was, at least under the United National Party (UNP) administration so central to events described in this chapter, a Western-oriented democracy with a market economy. In contrast, neighboring India, closely linked to the Soviet Union, was a democracy with a socialist economic approach and had a geo-strategic view that called for absolute domination of its smaller South Asian neighbors.

Apparently to gain information on developments concerning the Sri Lankan port of Trincomalee, which New Delhi feared was coveted by the West as a military base, Indian Prime Minister Indira Gandhi agreed in 1982 to a plan by the Research and Analysis Wing (RAW, India's equivalent of the CIA) to establish links with a number of the Tamil terrorist organizations above.[6] India was not interested in the ideology of those who received its training. It sought to safeguard its regional position while calming pro-Tamil communal passions within its own borders.

Consequently, an extensive network of bases in Tamil Nadu, the 55 million Tamil-majority Indian state directly across the narrow Palk Strait from Sri Lanka, was allowed to support the clandestine counter-state that was formed within Sri Lanka itself. This facilitated a dramatic expansion of insurgent actions, and by the end of 1984, insurgent activity had grown to the point that it threatened government control of Tamil majority areas in northern Sri Lanka. The security forces had increased in size and quality of weaponry, but a national concept of operations was lacking.

The extent to which insurgent capabilities had developed was amply demonstrated in a well-coordinated and executed attack on November 20, 1984, in which a Tamil force of company size used overwhelming firepower and explosives to demolish the Chavakachcheri police station on the Jaffna peninsula and kill at least 27 policemen defending it. There followed continued ambushes of security forces, as well as several large massacres of Sinhalese civilians living in areas deemed by the insurgents to be "traditional Tamil homelands." The use of automatic weapons, mortars, and RPG-7 rocket launchers by the insurgents was reported during this time.

Even as these developments took place, it became clear to the authorities that a drastic upgrading of security force capabilities was needed, a task that was accomplished in remarkably short order. Oxford-educated Lalith Athulathmudalai, a possible successor to President Junius R. Jayewardene, was named head of a newly created Ministry of National Security, as well as Deputy Defense Minister (Jayewardene himself was Defense Minister). This effectively placed control of the armed services and counterinsurgency operations under one man. The armed forces grew substantially, with the army ultimately reaching 76 battalions in strength (each with roughly 800 men). Interservice coordination improved under a Joint Operations Center (JOC), as did military discipline and force disposition.

To relieve pressure on the military, a new police field unit, Special Task Force (STF), was raised under the tutelage of ex-SAS (Special Air Services) personnel employed by KMS Ltd. STF took over primary responsibility for security in the Eastern Province in late 1984, freeing the army to concentrate on areas of the Northern Province (which included Jaffna). The army itself stood up new special forces and commando units. Such changes were reasonably effective. Government response to the insurgency, though, was crippled by the state's inability to set forth a viable political solution within which stability operations could proceed. Focusing on "terrorism" rather than on an insurgency that used terror as but one weapon, Colombo ordered its military leaders to go after the militants and to stamp out the violence. There was little movement toward the kind of political accommodation that would have isolated the insurgent hardcore from the bulk of the movement, the followers.

TRANSFORMATION OF THREAT

Though it did not put together the necessary *national* campaign plan, Colombo did come up with an approach for the *military* domination of insurgent-affected areas. Pacification in the east and near-north left only Jaffna as an insurgent stronghold as 1987 began. As their position in Jaffna peninsula collapsed, the Tigers became more fanatical. They adopted the suicide tactics favored by radical Islamic movements. Individual combatants had previously been issued with cyanide capsules to use rather than be captured. Suicide attacks began, both using both individuals and vehicles. A "Black Tigers" suicide commando unit was formed to carry these out.

There remains considerable debate as to the precise inspiration for this shift in tactics, but the result was not in doubt—the character of LTTE's terror and its level of violence became much more lethal.[7] Ironically, it was not these tactics that rescued LTTE from destruction but democratic India. New Delhi, responding to domestic pressure, entered the conflict directly in the form of an "Indian Peacekeeping Force" (IPKF). Sri Lankan forces returned to their barracks, and India assumed directly responsibility for overseeing implementation of a to-be-agreed-upon cessation of hostilities.

The Indian presence, while having some tactical advantages, was strategically disastrous. It not only reinforced the nationalist aspects of the *Eelam* appeal amongst the Tamil mass base but also provoked a Sinhalese nationalist reaction in the south that absorbed virtually all of security force attention. As the Indians attempted to deal with the Tamil insurgents, the Sri Lankans were forced to move troops south to deal with Sinhalese Maoist insurgents of the *Janatha Vimukthi Peramuna* (JVP, People's Liberation Front), a body that had led a 1971 insurgency, which was crushed at considerable cost to the population.

By exploiting nationalist passions and using terror to murder those who did not comply with their demands, the JVP insurgents gained influence far beyond their numbers. The industrial sector, thoroughly cowed by a spate of well-selected assassinations, was functioning at a mere 20 percent capacity. Such economic paralysis, in turn, fed the JVP cause, while Sri Lanka's government staggered. A change in leadership, with Ranasinghe Premadasa replacing the retiring President Jayewardene, brought a new government approach that again turned the tide. Crucial to this was the employment of the very techniques that had gradually come to be standard in dealing with the Tamil insurgency.

Particularly salient was the command and control structure that had evolved. A prerequisite for everything was the continuing evolution of the military, especially the army. Having become a more effective, powerful organization, its 76 battalions were now deployed to areas where, among other things, it spoke the language of the inhabitants and had an excellent intelligence apparatus. Superimposed upon the tactical organization of the army was the counterinsurgency structure itself. Administratively, Sri Lanka's nine provinces were already divided into 22 districts, each headed by a Government Agent (GA) who saw to it that services and programs were carried out.

To deal with the insurgency, these GAs were paired with Coordinating Officers (COs), whose responsibility it became to handle the security effort in the district. Often, to simplify the chain of command, the CO would be the commander of the battalion in the district. Only as the conflict progressed did the army place its battalions under permanent, numbered brigades—though these remained continually changing in composition—and its brigades under divisions. In theory, there was a brigade for each of Sri Lanka's nine provinces. These were grouped under three division headquarters, only two of which were operational at this point in time, because the third was designated for the area under Indian occupation. The brigade commanders acted as Chief Coordinating Officers (CCO) for their provinces, and each reported to one of three division commanders, who were also Area Commanders. Areas 1 and 2 divided the Sinhalese heartland into southern and northern sectors, respectively; Area 3 was the Tamil-populated zone under IPKF control.

Used historically with considerable effect by any number of security forces, particularly the British, this system had the advantage of setting in place security personnel whose mission was to win back their areas. They could be assigned assets, military and civil, as circumstances dictated. COs controlled all security forces deployed in their districts; they were to work closely with the GAs to develop plans for the protection of normal civilian administrative and area development functions. For these tasks, they were aided by a permanent staff whose job it was to know intimately the area. In particular, intelligence assets remained assigned to the CO headquarters and guided the employment of operational personnel. They did not constantly rotate as combat units came and went.

The framework culminated in the Joint Operations Center. This, however, never really hit its stride as a coordinating body. Instead, manned by senior serving officers, it usurped actual command functions to such an extent that it *became* the military. The service headquarters, in particular the army, were reduced to little more than administrative centers.

Though often lacking precise guidance from above, local military authorities nonetheless fashioned increasingly effective responses to the JVP insurgency. This was possible because the CO and operational commanders, older and wiser after their tours in the Tamil areas, proved more than capable of planning their own local campaigns. Decentralization in a state lacking communications and oversight capabilities led some individuals and units to dispense with the tedious business of legal process. Those suspected of subversion were simply eliminated. Under the combined authorized and unauthorized onslaught, the JVP collapsed.

Having ended the second Sinhalese insurgency, the security forces were able to return their attention again to the Tamil campaign when India withdrew in January–March 1990 (almost 3 years and several thousand IPKF casualties later). Ominously, it was a greatly strengthened LTTE that awaited the Sri Lankan military. Its power grew during a round of post-IPKF negotiations, which the Tigers used to eliminate their Tamil insurgent rivals. When LTTE abrogated the talks, renewed hostilities left the security forces facing mobile warfare, the insurgents attacking in massed units, often of multiple battalion strength, supported by a variety of heavy weapons. Deaths numbered in the thousands, reaching a peak in July–August 1991 in a series of large battles around Jaffna. The 25 days of fighting at Elephant Pass, the land bridge that connects the Jaffna peninsula with the rest of Sri Lanka, saw the first insurgent use of armor, which was supported by artillery.

Elsewhere, terror bombings and assassinations became routine. Even national leaders, such as Rajiv Gandhi of India and Sri Lanka's President Premadasa, were casualties of LTTE bomb attacks (on May 21, 1991 and May 1, 1993, respectively), as were numerous other important figures, such as Lalith Athulathmudalai and members of the JOC upper echelons. Heavy fighting in Jaffna in early 1994, as the security forces attempted to tighten their grip around Jaffna City, resulted in government casualties approaching those suffered by LTTE in the Elephant Pass action. The conflict had been reduced to a tropical replay of the World War I trenches.

Only with the election of a coalition headed by the Sri Lanka Freedom Party in August 1994, followed by the November presidential victory of Sri Lanka Freedom Party (SLFP) leader Chandrika Bandaranaike Kumaratunga, was politics again introduced into the debate over the state's response to the insurgent challenge. The SLFP political victories ended 17 years of UNP power and led to a 3-month ceasefire, during which Colombo sought to frame a solution acceptable to the warring sides. The effort came to an abrupt halt when LTTE again, as it had in each previous instance, unilaterally ended the talks by a surprise attack on government forces.

Significantly, the ensuing wave of assaults highlighted the military side of the conflict. New LTTE techniques included the use of underwater assets to destroy navy ships, as well as the introduction of SA-7 surface-to-surface missiles into the conflict. What had begun as a campaign by terrorists had grown to main force warfare augmented by terror and guerrilla action.

Much more had changed, as well. With the end of the Cold War, LTTE quietly dropped all talk of Marxism,[8] though it continued to portray itself as socialist.[9] New Delhi, though still closely linked to Moscow, had seen its patron collapse and cautiously reached out to establish more normal relations with the United States and other supporters of Colombo. There was no objection raised when the United States agreed, in mid-1994, to begin a series of direct training missions conducted by special operations elements.[10]

New circumstances, in particular a new administration in Colombo, dictated a review of the counterinsurgency approach. In mid-1995, therefore, the government held a series of meetings designed to settle upon a revised national strategy for ending the conflict. A political plan was articulated for devolution that came close, in all but name, to abandoning the unitary state in favor of a federal system.

While all official bodies basically agreed that LTTE would have to be dealt with militarily in order for the political solution to be implemented, there was considerable disagreement on the plan of operations. On the one side were those who favored a *military-dominated* response. Opposed were those who favored a *counterinsurgency* campaign that would systematically dominate areas using force as the shield behind which restoration of government authority and the rule of law would be secured. This is what had worked successfully in the south. It was the military approach that won out, initiated by a successful (but unfortunately, "bridge too far") multibrigade seizure of Jaffna.

It was a conventional response to an unconventional problem. LTTE adroitly used a combination of main force and guerrilla units, together with special operations, to isolate exposed government units and then overrun them. These included headquarters elements, with even brigade and division headquarters being battered. In the rear area, LTTE used a suicide truck bomb to decimate the financial heart of Colombo in February 1996, killing at least 75 and wounding more than 1,500.

Much worse was to come, as overextension of forces and an inability to handle the complexities of main force operations left the Sri Lankan military badly deployed. Debacle was not long in coming, and on July 17, 1996, estimated 3,000–4,000 LTTE combatants isolated and then overwhelmed an under-strength brigade camp at Mullaitivu in the northeast, resulting in at least 1,520 deaths among the security forces.[11] This exceeded the 1,454 total death toll for 1994 and shattered army morale. Desertion, already a problem in Sri Lanka's military, rapidly escalated. There followed stalemate.

LTTE, needing only to exist as a rump counter-state that mobilized its young for combat, had demonstrated the ability to construct mechanisms for human and fiscal resource generation that defied the coercive capacity of the state. Linkages extended abroad, from whence virtually all funding came (US$20–30 million per year); and diasphoric commercial linkages allowed the obtaining of necessary weapons, ammunition, and supplies. Though the security forces could hold key positions and even dominate much of the east, they simply could not advance upon the well-prepared and fortified LTTE positions in the north and northeast, which, in any case, were guarded by a veritable carpet of mines.

Political disillusionment again followed and increased as LTTE continued to conduct spectacular attacks: the most sacred Buddhist shrine in the country, the Temple of the Tooth in Kandy, was attacked by suicide bomb in 1998; Chandrika herself narrowly missed following Premadasa as a presidential victim, surviving a 1999 LTTE bomb attack but losing an eye; the Elephant Pass camp that had previously held out against severe odds fell in 2000; and in July 2001, a sapper attack on the international airport in Colombo left 11 aircraft destroyed.

It was not altogether surprising that in the December 2001 parliamentary elections, the UNP, led by Ranil Wickremasinghe, was returned to power. This left the political landscape badly fractured between the majority UNP (and its leader, the prime minister), and the SLFP's Chandrika, still the powerful president in Sri Lanka's hybrid system of governance similar to that of France. That the two figures were longtime rivals, with considerable personal animosity, did not ease the situation.

Again, it was changes in the international arena that dealt a wild-card. The September 11, 2001 terrorist attacks in the United States and the resulting "Global War on Terrorism" (GWOT) caused Western countries finally to pass legislation banning LTTE fundraising activities on their soil. In February 2002, for reasons that remain unclear, LTTE suddenly offered to negotiate with the new UNP government. The government accepted the offer, and an uneasy truce commenced that has held to the present.

The cessation of hostilities was a very mixed bag. LTTE used the restrictions on Sri Lankan security forces to move aggressively into Tamil areas from which it had hitherto been denied and to eliminate rival Tamil politicians. Throughout Tamil-populated areas, Tamil-language psychological operations continued to denounce the state. Chandrika watched uneasily and then asserted her power, in early November 2003, while Wickremasinghe was in Washington meeting with U.S. President George W. Bush. Claiming that the UNP approach was threatening the "the sovereignty of the state of Sri Lanka, its territorial integrity, and the security of the nation," she ousted the three UNP cabinet ministers most closely associated with the talks, dismissed Parliament, and ordered the army into Colombo's streets.

LTTE bided its time, but in the April 2004 parliamentary elections that were held as a consequence of talks between the dueling Sinhalese parties, SLFP unexpectedly swept back into power at the head of a United People's Freedom Alliance (UPFA). The Tigers withdrew from negotiations but did not at first renew active hostilities. There was no need to: the "ceasefire" served as the ideal cover for the elimination of all whom the group saw as standing in its way. These included even the Sri Lankan Foreign Minister, Lakshman Kadirgamar, an ethnic Tamil, Sarath Ambepitiya, the judge who had sentenced Prabhakaran to 200 years in jail *in absentia* for the 1996 bombing of Colombo, and literally hundreds of Tamil politicians and activists opposed to LTTE (as well as those who were misidentified). The latter remained committed to *Eelam*, whatever the verbiage connected with the peace process, and behaved as such. Unable or unwilling to fight back, Colombo dithered as its citizens were murdered, in ones and small numbers. Finally, in May–June 2006, LTTE violations—which included an effort to assassinate the head of the army by a suicide bomber—reached such a point that an inexorable slide back to general hostilities seemed likely. There was the sate of affairs when this chapter was completed.

LESSONS FOR THE COUNTERTERRORIST STATE

Assessing this two-decade chain of events, the defining thread is mistakes of strategic approach and operational implementation. These began with a persistent failure to assess the insurgency in terms appropriate to framing a correct response. In this, Colombo's experience foreshadows what we see happening in the GWOT: attacking the symptoms to the near-exclusion of the causes of the violence; and the misinterpretation of that violence once it has appeared.

In Sri Lanka's case, insurgency was the goal of the militants all along. Terror, though used extensively, was never intended as an end unto itself. From its use as one weapon among many in the effort to form a counter-state, terror became a strategy for insurgency—to inflict so much pain upon the "occupying force" that it would have to quit the field. This is essentially what happened. What could have arrested this process, of course, was addressing the grievances of the mass base early on. Leaders and followers, though thrown up by the same injustice, occupied different positions in the struggle. Leaders sought structural change, revolution, as the route to liberation; followers looked to redress of immediate issues. Had the state driven a wedge between the two, what became a profound security threat would likely have remained a law and order problem.

Indeed, it was the very scale of state abuses that galvanized both India and the diasphoric Tamil communities to open their hearts and their wallets to the insurgent groups.[12] Even as the LTTE and other groups transformed, becoming ever more violent and divorced from any sense of compromise, their identity as avenging angels was maintained as a powerful motivating force by alienated Tamils abroad. To focus upon the tactical acts of terror, then, was precisely the wrong approach. Certainly repression was a necessary element of state response, but the security forces should only have been the instrument for the accomplishment of the political solution. This was realized by any number of actors within the conflict, but they were rarely in the right spot at the right time, hence unable to alter the course once set.

Still, it is noteworthy that a Third World state, with very limited capacity and resources, was able to put together a response that came within a whisker of delivering a knockout punch. Learning and adaptation were constant features of an approach that—even if imbalanced, tilted toward repression as opposed to accommodation—produced favorable results. The counterinsurgency structure and procedures utilized through 1987 (and thereafter in JVP-affected areas), emphasizing unity of command and long-term presence in affected areas, proved capable of dealing with the situation—but the test was not completed.

The Indian military invasion ended the greatest chance Sri Lanka had for victory on its terms. Subsequently, it was the 3-year IPKF interlude that allowed LTTE not only to recover from its desperate situation in July 1987 but to move to the mobile warfare stage of insurgency. Fielding main force units in conjunction with guerrilla and terror actions, the insurgents emerged in 1990 as a truly formidable, multidimensional force.

Most frightening about LTTE success is what it tells us about the ability of a radical, institutionally totalitarian movement to recruit, socialize, and deploy manpower so rigidly indoctrinated that combatants prefer death by cyanide or self-destruction to capture. Having gained control of certain areas early on, LTTE was able to recruit manpower at young ages and then guide them in ways that produced entire units comprised of young boys and girls who had never known alternative modes of existence.

In the world created by LTTE leadership, Sinhalese were demons, and a reality beyond the insurgent camps did not exist. Even sex lives were rigidly controlled by draconian penalties. Combatants knew only their camps and each other, and behaved accordingly when unleashed upon targets. As relative moderates passed from the insurgent leadership scene, those who knew other worlds vanished, their places taken by a new group of hardcore members who had risen within the movement. They generally spoke no language other than Tamil and had limited life experiences. Brutality was to them simply a weapons system to be deployed against all enemies.

To what, then, was owed LTTE participation in the now defunct ceasefire? It may have been a simple matter of tactics, a need to repair the fundraising apparatus. Or LTTE may have sensed that a Sri Lanka in disarray as to its own course was ripe for an appeal to a "political solution." The two are not mutually exclusive, and the ceasefire certainly gave LTTE all that it had been unable to acquire through its campaign of political violence: nearly complete control over the Tamil population in the area delimited as *Eelam*.

It has used the hunger for normalcy to make the state complicit in meeting LTTE's own ends. Nothing could better illustrate the essence of terror as politics by other means.

ACKNOWLEDGMENTS

The views expressed in this chapter are those of the author and do not reflect the official policy or position of the National Defense University, the Department of Defense, or the U.S. Government.

NOTES

1. An earlier version of this chapter appeared as Thomas A. Marks, "At the Frontlines of the GWOT: State Response to Insurgency in Sri Lanka," *Journal of Counterterrorism & Homeland Security International* 10, no. 3 (2004): 34–46 (w/photos by author).

2. For discussion of this topic, see Thomas A. Marks, "Counterinsurgency and Operational Art," *Low Intensity Conflict & Law Enforcement* 13, no. 3 (Winter 2005): 168–211 (Appendix 1).

3. Data summarized in *Terrorist Groups Fighting for Tamil Eelam (Top Secret)*, working document of Intelligence Wing, Counter-Terrorism Branch, National Intelligence Bureau (NIB); undated but mid-1985. See also M.R. Narayan Swamy, *Tigers of Lanka: From Boys to Guerrillas*, 3rd ed. (Delhi: Konark, 2002) 97–101. The latter remains the premier reference for the formative years of the Tamil insurgency.

4. Text may be accessed at: http://www.peacebrigades.org/lanka/slppta 1979.html.

5. Number of groups fluctuated constantly; lists contained in Intelligence Wing files (see n. 3 above) fluctuated. Further discussion, to include personalities, may be found in Thomas A. Marks, *Maoist Insurgency since Vietnam* (London: Frank Cass, 1996) Ch. 4, 174–252.

6. This effort continues to be denied officially by India but has been fairly well documented. Swamy, *Tigers of Lanka* deals with the subject in his Ch. 5, "Tamils Get Training" 93–114. See also the entire volume by Rohan Gunaratna, *Indian Intervention in Sri Lanka: The Role of India's Intelligence Agencies*, 2nd ed. (Colombo: South Asian Network on Conflict Research (SANCOR), 1994). For my own contributions, based upon field work at the time, see "India is the Key to Peace in Sri Lanka," *Asian Wall Street Journal* (September 19–20, 1986): 8 (reproduced under the same title in *The Island* [Colombo] (October 5, 1986): 8; abridged under the same title in *Asian Wall Street Journal Weekly* (September 22, 1986): 25; and "Peace in Sri Lanka," *Daily News* [Colombo], 3 parts, July 6–7–8, 1987: "I. India Acts in its Own Interests," July 6: 6; "II. Bengali Solution: India Trained Personnel for Invasion of Sri Lanka," July7: 8; "III. India's Political Solution Narrow and Impossible," July8: 6 (published under the same titles in *Sri Lanka News*, July 15, 1987: 6–7; in *The Island* as "India's Covert Involvements," June 28, 1987: 8,10).

7. I am not aware of any scholarly work that explicitly addresses the origins of all facets of LTTE suicide tactics. Even the introduction of suicide capsules is a source of conflicting accounts from LTTE figures from whom one would expect "first hand" accounts. Most useful, however, are the contributions of Peter Schalk, particularly "The Revival of Martyr Cults Among Havar," *Temenos* 33 (1997): 151–90, http://tamilnation.org/ideology/schalk01.htm; as well as his "Resistance and Martyrdom in the Process of State Formation of Tamil Eelam," excerpt from Joyce Pettigrew, ed., *Martyrdom and Political Resistance: Essays From Asia and Europe* (Amsterdam: Centre for Asian Studies/Vu University Press, 1997), http://www.tamilnation.org/ideology/schalkthiyagam.htm. These highlight the salience of Tamil and South Asian elements in the continuing evolution of what

Schalk terms "a political movement with religious aspirations" ("The Revival of Martyr Cults among Havar").

8. Even LTTE, though Prabhakaran himself initially held ideology as of little value, required that its recruits undergo political training. "Desmond," for instance, a militant captured in March 1985, spoke of 1981 training at a base in Tamil Nadu that included instruction by three different instructors on "the various wars of the world," on "communism" [*sic*], and "about politics." A fourth instructor taught "firearms." See the NIB file, "Interrogation of Terrorist Suspect Soosaiha Rathnarajah @ 'Desmond'," SF Headquarters, Vavuniya, April 2, 1985 (Secret). NIB/INT/89. A 19-year old LTTE guerrilla, following his capture in August 1986, offered the following brief description of such sessions, "The leaders always spoke about Marxism. They wanted a Marxist *Eelam*. That was their main idea." An older, higher-ranking captive, in another discussion, observed, "We were hoping to establish a Tamil socialist state in the north and east." *Field work*, Sri Lanka, summer 1986 (both discussions conducted using translators).

9. The precise position of Marxism within LTTE has in many respects been driven by the personal relationship between undisputed LTTE leader Prabhakaran and the decade-older penultimate figure, Balasingham, a relationship sources have variously characterized as son/father or pupil/teacher. That Balasingham (now deceased) was a committed Marxist is beyond dispute; that Prabhakaran continues to find ideology tedious but perhaps useful up to a point, as long as secondary to combat, seems to be a position that evolved over time. In the early years of the movement, as indicated above in n. 8, LTTE combatants were required to undergo instruction in Marxism as part of the daily training schedule, but this practice apparently lapsed as the military elements of the struggle became more salient. In my discussions with LTTE combatants and prisoners (who became scarce once suicide became the movement-facilitated alternative to capture), I found not a single insurgent who knew the first thing about Marxism, though they could relate the physical particulars of indoctrination sessions. This was in stark contrast to, for instance, at least some PLOT combatants (and all of the PLOT leadership figures), as well individuals within the other main insurgent groups.

10. These were initially scheduled in advance, two per year, as a part of the normal training cycle of the U.S. special operations units concerned. As Sri Lankan needs were further clarified, both individuals and teams returned as dictated by circumstances. Interestingly, these trainers were never threatened by LTTE, much less attacked. Evidence indicates that a decision was made by the insurgents not to risk an aggressive U.S. response to an overreaction by LTTE. When all was said and done, went the insurgent logic, U.S. aid would have, at most, minor tactical impact; while a lashing out by Washington, even if only in the form of increased aid, could have operational or even strategic impact.

11. LTTE filmed the entire operation, which featured suicide personnel clearing defensive minefields by blowing themselves up, and the defenders overwhelmed by repeated "human wave" assaults. Indeed, the LTTE name for the assault was Operation Oyada Alaikhal, or "Endless Waves." Details in Paul Harris, "Bitter Lessons for the SLA," *Jane's Intelligence Review* (October 1996): 466–468.

12. Though written a considerable time after the events under discussion, best single sources are Anthony Davis, "Tamil Tiger International," *Jane's Intelligence Review* (October 1996): 469–473; and Daniel Byman, Peter Chalk, Bruce Hoffman, William Rosenau, and David Brannan, *Trends in Outside Support for Insurgent Movements* (Santa Monica, CA: RAND, 2001), *passim*.

CHAPTER 16

COUNTERING WEST GERMANY'S RED ARMY FACTION: WHAT CAN WE LEARN?

Joanne Wright

On September 5, 1977, the Red Army Faction (RAF) kidnapped Hans Martin Schleyer, President of the Employers' Association of the Federal Republic of Germany. In exchange for his safe return, the kidnappers demanded the release of several of their members being held in Stammheim prison, including founder members Andreas Baader, Gudrun Ensslin, Jan-Carl Rapse, and Irmgard Möller. For over a month the West German security services searched in vain for Schleyer and the kidnappers continued to demand the release of their imprisoned comrades.

On October 13, 1977, two men and two women hijacked Lufthansa Flight 181 headed from Palma de Mallorca to Frankfurt with 86 passengers and 5 crew on board. The hijacked plane first landed in Rome where the hijackers made it clear that their demands also included the release of the same RAF prisoners being demanded by the kidnappers of Schleyer. Despite pleas from the West German government that the hijacked plane should not be allowed to leave, the Italian authorities chose to ensure that any ensuing drama would not be played out on Italian soil, and they refueled the plane and allowed it to leave. After a brief stop at Larnaca in Cyprus the hijacked plane flew on to Dubai. Two things of note happened while the plane was in Dubai. The first was the arrival of a contingent of the elite West German counterterrorist unit, GSG9. Unfortunately, the Dubai authorities refused to countenance any GSG9 storming of the plane, but they did offer to use their own British-trained forces. The second was that the Dubai authorities revealed in a radio interview that the captain of the hijacked plane, Jürgen Schumann, had been passing on details about the hijackers. This was overheard by the hijackers and they forced Captain Schumann to put the plane back in the air.

The plane then landed in Aden, where the hijackers shot Captain Schumann dead in front of the passengers and crew. By October 17, the hijacked plane (flown by the copilot) had relocated to Mogadishu, Somalia. At this point, the West German government told the hijackers that the prisoners in Stammheim would be flown to Mogadishu. However, this was only to give GSG9 time to position itself for an attempt to storm the plane. Under the cover of darkness, members of GSG9 successfully stormed the plane, recovering all the hostages and shooting dead three of the four hijackers.

Before news of this successful rescue operation could be digested by the West German government and people, the authorities at Stammheim announced that they had found the bodies of Baader and Ensslin, the mortally wounded body of Raspe and seriously injured body of Möller in their cells. It emerged that Baader and Raspe had shot themselves, Ensslin had hung herself, and Möller had stabbed herself repeatedly in the chest. The following day, October 19, the RAF revealed that it had murdered the kidnapped Hans Martin Schleyer.

So ended 44 days that have entered twentieth-century terrorist fact and fiction. The murder of Schleyer also symbolized the end of the "first generation" of the RAF. The organization continued with a "second generation" in the early and mid-1980s, and it attempted to capitalize on widespread anti-United States and anti-NATO sentiment surrounding the deployment of short and intermediate range nuclear weapons. However this second generation, although it was responsible for a number of high-profile attacks, failed to attract the same degree of support or concern as the original Baader-Meinhof Gang.[1] The fall of the Berlin Wall in 1989, and the subsequent confirmation of links between the RAF and the East German secret police pushed the organization even further to the margins of relevance and acceptability.

In April 1998, the RAF announced that it had formally disbanded, having carried out its last active operation in 1993 when it bombed a prison. Since then it has essentially disappeared from the twenty-first-century lexicology of terrorism and threat analysis. Yet the RAF, its motivating ideology and particularly the West German government's counterterrorism policies can provide valuable lessons and insights into twenty-first-century terrorism. It can show, for example, how a relatively small and seemingly irrational group[2] can create a physical and psychological impact way out of proportion to size and threat. Perhaps even more usefully it can illustrate that whatever sympathy terrorist groups do manage to generate among national and international audiences is largely derived from government responses to terrorism. In the case of West Germany, these responses can be grouped into three categories:

security force behavior, prisoners and prison conditions, and legislative changes. All of these responses remain as critical today as they were in West Germany during the 1970s.

HISTORICAL BACKGROUND AND IDEOLOGY

All terrorist groups emerge from distinctive historical contexts and ideological analyses. In the case of West Germany's RAF there are a number of interwoven themes to be considered. Firstly and perhaps most obviously, there was the legacy of the Nazi era and the process of de-Nazification. Added to this was the development of an essentially capitalist economy and the acceptance of this by the mainstream political left in West Germany—the Social Democratic Party (SPD). This, in turn, alienated those on the more extreme left, who began to organize what was known as the Extra Parliamentary Opposition (APO). The APO both influenced and was influenced by radical theorizing in West Germany's universities and the Cold War international environment. All this combined to produce an RAF ideology that glorified action over intellect and defined students as the key revolutionary actors.

In the days and months immediately after the defeat of Nazi Germany there was much soul searching about what characteristics had produced Nazism and how they could be avoided in the new German state. One analysis that was prominent among many was that a combination of selfish materialism and aggressive nationalism had played major roles in the development of the Nazi state. However, before any real German notions of the new state could be consolidated, the reality of economic chaos and Cold War tensions predominated. This led the center-right of Germany's political spectrum, the Christian Democratic Union (CDU), to embrace both a market-driven economy and strong foreign policy alignment with the United States and NATO (including rearmament in 1955) as the main characteristics of the new West German state.

Initially, the SPD opposed both a market-driven economy and a clear foreign policy alignment, but after poor federal election results it undertook an assessment of its socialist economic policies and its support for a united, neutral Germany. In 1959, it formally shifted its platform to embrace a social market economy and West Germany's integration into both NATO and the developing European Economic Community. In electoral terms, this was a success for the SPD and in 1966 it entered a governing coalition with the CDU. However, it left those to its left on the political spectrum disillusioned and increasingly isolated from the political process. With the CDU and SPD together controlling more than 90 percent of the seats in the parliament, the radicals turned their attention to extra-parliamentary opposition.

The APO movement was very much associated with radical theorizing that had begun in several West German universities in the mid and late 1950s, especially Frankfurt and Berlin. Students in West Germany, and indeed elsewhere in the industrialized world, came to see themselves as in possession of a superior moral theory, and felt justified in taking direct action against an unresponsive and morally corrupt parliamentary system. What was peculiar about the West German situation was the positions of influence that were occupied by ex-Nazis.

Events in the international arena also played a part in motivating the APO. Students identified with the various national liberation struggles being played out in South East Asia, Africa, and the Middle East. Their heroes were people like Mao, Che Guevara, and Frantz Fanon. They were critical of the evolution and conduct of the Cold War and especially U.S. policy in Vietnam. When the Shah of Iran visited Berlin in 1967, there was open confrontation and a young student was shot dead by the police. This prompted the West German authorities to introduce much-needed reform into the archaic and overcrowded university system, which served to dissipate much of the student anger. But it also served to alienate the radicals even further, and it was at this point that the RAF emerged.[3]

The RAF's ideology was eclectic and largely secondhand, and it is certainly much easier to identify what it opposed than what it advocated. Broadly speaking, the RAF saw itself as part of a global communist struggle against capitalism and imperialism. Thus, it is not surprising that its ideology contains elements of Marxism and Leninism. It also contains elements from the thinking of many of the post-1945 guerrilla war theorists such as Mao, Guevara, and Marighella. The critical analyses of parliamentary democracy by thinkers such as Marcuse and Sartre were also (mis)used by the RAF to provide ideological justifications for their attack on the West German state and its representatives.

While RAF ideology generally accepted Marxist views on the ills of capitalism and that terrorism could ultimately be part of the revolution, it did not accept Marx's strong views that there were objective conditions that needed to be met before a proletariat revolution could be successful. Another person who could not accept that capitalism would inevitably produce a politically conscious working class that would rise to overthrow capitalism was Lenin. Rather than wait for these objective conditions to be created by crises in capitalism, Lenin believed that these conditions could be hastened by the actions of a politically enlightened vanguard. The RAF certainly saw itself as such a vanguard, but much else of Lenin's analysis—while it may have had some relevance to early twentieth-century nonindustrialized Russia—had little to do with mid-twentieth-century industrialized West Germany.

While the conditions in agrarian China were also a marked contrast to 1960s West Germany, Mao's theory of guerrilla warfare is also something to note in the development of the RAF's ideology. Mao, in adapting Marxism-Leninism to suit the conditions of China, introduced an element of "voluntarism" into the revolutionary process. This idea of "voluntarism" was taken much further by Che Guevara in his thinking and actions in Cuba and various other parts of South America. And Che Guevara was an immense influence not only on the RAF but also on a whole generation of radicals throughout the industrialized world.

There were two modifications that Guevara made to Marxism-Leninism that were to influence the RAF and other European terrorist groups that emerged in the late 1960s, such as Action Direct in France or the Red Brigades in Italy. The first was his analysis of how the revolution could be brought about. Guevara argued that the Cuban revolution proved not only that popular forces can win a war against a repressive regime, but also that it refuted those who feel the need to wait until, in some perfect way all the required objective and subjective conditions are at hand, instead of hastening to bring these conditions about by their own efforts.[4]

Second, Guevara took Lenin's notion of a revolutionary vanguard and applied it to active guerrillas rather than a political elite:

> The essence of guerrilla warfare is the miracle by which a small nucleus of men—looking beyond their immediate tactical objective—becomes the vanguard of a mass movement, achieving its ideals, establishing a new society, ending the ways of the old, and winning social justice.[5]

Although these aspects of Guevara's thoughts appealed to the RAF, there were other elements of his thinking that were less attractive. Guevara, although he recognized a role for urban environments, stressed that his ideas were only applicable to rural environments that were replete with "land-hunger." He also stressed that the people need to see clearly "the futility of maintaining a fight for social goals within the framework of civil debate."[6]

So the RAF needed to recontextualize Guevara in a way that gave primacy to an urban environment and stressed the futility of parliamentary democracy. As regards the former, the RAF was helped by the Brazilian theorist Carlos Marighella, who developed a strategy of urban guerrilla warfare based around "firing groups."[7] As regards the latter, the RAF was helped by the radical theorists of the 1960s "New Left" movement and APO, as described above. While the contexts and motivations are very different, there are some striking similarities in the ideological justifications offered in support of violence by the RAF and by more modern groups such as al Qaeda.

One of the key figures of the New Left Movement of the 1960s was Herbert Marcuse. While his own views on violence were ambivalent and he did condemn RAF terrorism, his analysis of parliamentary democracy, the special position he gave students, the links he made between repression in the industrialized and nonindustrialized worlds, and the privileging of action over intellect were clearly picked up by the RAF. Marcuse's characterization of liberal democracies as repressive was based on his view that the capitalist mode of production had so subsumed the proletariat (and others) that the revolution could not be achieved through its mass action. As Marcuse explains:

> the basic idea is: how can slaves who do not even know they are slaves free themselves? How can they liberate themselves by their own power, by their own faculties? They must be taught and they must be led to be free, and this is the more so the more the society in which they live uses all available means in order to shape their consciousness and to make it immune against possible alternatives. This idea of an educational, preparatory dictatorship has today become an integral element of revolution and of the justification of the revolutionary oppression.[8]

Because they are not fully integrated into the capitalist mode of production, students are able to take on this educational function and develop and lead the revolutionary consciousness. In an interview published in the *New York Times Magazine*, Marcuse says of students that they are "militant minorities who can articulate the needs and aspirations of the silent masses ... the students can truly be called spokesmen" (sic).[9] This was certainly taken up by the RAF's principal ideologues Ulrike Meinhof and Horst Mahler. Mahler, for example, claimed "it is not the organization of the industrial working class, but the revolutionary sections of the student body that are today the bearers of the contemporary conscience."[10]

Marcuse's concept of revolution was not limited to industrialized societies. He argued that capitalism had global effects and that a successful revolution required an alliance between forces within industrial societies and forces in the Third World. Marcuse saw these two forces as being interdependent, neither being able to succeed without the other.[11] This idea of fighting the same battle as revolutionaries in the Third World is very prominent in RAF ideology and propaganda. In a letter to the Labor Party of the Peoples' Republic of North Korea, Ulrike Meinhof claimed:

> We think the organization of armed operations in the big cities of the Federal Republic is the right way to support the liberations movements in Africa, Asia and Latin America, the correct contribution of West German and West Berlin communists to the strategy of the international socialist movement in splitting the powers of imperialism by attacking them from all sides, and striking once they are split.[12]

Marcuse also helped the RAF provide ideological justifications for taking violent action by defining the revolutionary avant garde—the students—

as both an objective and subjective element in the revolutionary process. It was part of the function of the avant garde to raise the revolutionary consciousness of those oppressed by capitalism who are unable to see their oppressed or repressed situations. Therefore, according to Horst Mahler, it "would be wrong to engage in armed struggle only when the 'consent of the masses' is assured, for this would mean to … renounce this struggle altogether."[13] Mahler goes on to claim that when the RAF throw bombs "aimed at the apparatus of oppression" it is also aiming at the "consciousness of the masses."[14]

Marcuse did not, however, condone the view that violence was itself positive. A positive view of violence was provided by another famous New Left Philosopher, Jean Paul Sartre. Sartre's vision of society was undoubtedly a bleak one, where people competed with each other for scarce resources in a system underpinned with terror. By according violence a positive role, a new system could be created. This positive view of violence is best seen in Sartre's preface to Frantz Fanon's widely read text, *The Wretched of the Earth*.[15] In it he says "[t]he rebel's weapon is proof of his humanity. For in the first days of the revolt you must kill: to shoot down a European is to kill two birds with one stone, to destroy an oppressor and the man he oppresses at the same time." In this way society can recover because violence "like the Achilles' lance can heal the wounds that it has inflicted."[16] Mahler echoes this when he argues that to overcome the habits of obedience that the bourgeois order has instilled in the oppressed of West Germany, "*repeated* violation of norms in *deeds* is required."[17]

While the secular ideology of the extreme left in the late 1960s and 1970s might seem diametrically opposed to the claimed theological ideology of those terrorist groups most prominent 30 years later, there are quite striking similarities that might suggest that the "newness" of today's terrorism is somewhat overstated. For example, it is noteworthy that many of the suicide bombers that have been associated with al Qaeda have been students—marginalized in both home countries and those in which they study.[18] There is no doubt that al Qaeda sees itself as part of a global struggle against the non-Muslim world and that it is the vanguard of this struggle.[19] Finally, al Qaeda has justified its violence as both right in itself and in terms of raising the consciousness of others.[20]

According to the RAF, one further function of its violence was to force the West German state to reveal openly its repressiveness and fascism. Indeed, RAF claimed some success in this. By 1975, it was declaring that "many changed their attitudes towards this State because of the measure of the government against us."[21] Given that forcing governments to react in ways that will increase its support is also a stated aim of al Qaeda,[22] is there anything that can be learned from the West German government's attempts to counter the RAF?

SECURITY FORCE BEHAVIOR

The security services—civilian and military, overt and covert—are a major part of any government's counterterrorism strategy, and thus it is critical that they are utilized in a proper and efficient manner. It is also true that attacking the security services is a major part of most terrorist groups' strategy, either directly or indirectly. Terrorist groups generally aim to invoke in governments and citizens some sense of crisis. The government's response to this crisis is then presented as evidence of an increasingly repressive and aggressive state. If this is even to a degree successful, terrorists can present their violence as defensive and transfer all guilt to the state. The RAF certainly had some degree of success in doing this.

Members of the security services were undoubtedly physical targets of the RAF. The rationale for this, according to Mahler, was to make it increasingly difficult for the state to recruit new members of the security forces, thereby applying further pressure on the state and hastening its downfall. As he explained "those who see a cushy job in being a policeman or a soldier will increasingly understand the risk which this profession entails under the changed circumstances" making it difficult for the state to "find the tens of thousands of heroes ready to fight under such anxiety."[23] It would, however, be difficult to claim that the RAF's violent actions had any impact on recruitment to the West German security services. Where it did have more success was in a more indirect strategy of attacking the credibility of the security forces. Attacking the credibility of the security services is most commonly done by accusing them of adopting "shoot-to-kill" policies and other illegal behavior. (Accusing them of torturing prisoners is another key area that will be dealt with later in this chapter.)

The student demonstrations that began in the late 1960s resulted in the first time that the West German police had to confront unrest on the streets. Between 1967 and 1971, the police had shot dead two demonstrators and injured several more in what were heavy-handed and clumsy responses. After the death of the first student in 1967, RAF founder Gudrun Ensslin is reported to have claimed that the "fascist state means to kill us all. We must organize resistance. Violence is the only way to answer violence."[24] In mid-1971, the respected Allensbacher Institute of Public Opinion conducted a survey that suggested that one in four young West Germans admitted "a certain sympathy" with the RAF. According to one study of these events, the actions of the police in countering student demonstrations and in searching for perceived radicals only drove people "further towards" the RAF.[25]

A further strand of this sort of ideological success was to accuse the state's security services of engaging in all sorts of illegal behavior. In the RAF's case, much of this was centered on the treatment of RAF prisoners and their lawyers that will be discussed below. But another illuminating example in the case of the RAF concerned Peter Urbach. Urbach worked for the West German intelligence agencies and penetrated the increasingly radical student movement. This also put him on the fringes of the RAF and in 1971 he was called to give evidence at a trial of RAF members. However, it was announced to the press that Urbach's evidence would be limited, and this caused speculation as to the reason. According to the RAF this was because he might have been obliged to shed light on state involvement in the bombing of a Jewish synagogue in 1969.[26] Such cases, even if they are completely untrue, do allow for speculation, and have played an important part in creating a reservoir of tolerance (if not sympathy) for many terrorists among people like Otto Schily, who was a lawyer representing some RAF prisoners and who ultimately became the German foreign minister.

PRISONERS AND PRISON CONDITIONS

The trial and imprisoning of terrorists presents a number of challenges for governments, and many governments have had to adapt both their judicial and penal systems to cope with terrorism. For example, the British government had to introduce special nonjury courts in response to threats to potential jurors and witnesses from terrorist organizations, and both the British and West German governments built special purpose terrorist prisons to house convicted and suspected terrorists. For terrorist organizations too, prisoners are important, as can be gauged from the large numbers of operations and resources terrorist groups often devote toward freeing their comrades in custody. For example, in West Germany in 1975, members of RAF-affiliate group 2 June Movement kidnapped a Berlin politician and succeeded in exchanging him for five of their imprisoned colleagues. The fact that the West German government agreed to release the terrorists undoubtedly inspired members of the RAF to seize the West German Embassy in Stockholm just 2 months later demanding the release of Baader, Meinhof, Ensslin, and Raspe. When the West German government refused this demand two embassy personnel were shot dead by the assailants. However, before any further negotiations could take place, the terrorists accidentally set off their own explosives, thus bringing the siege to an end. But it is likely that this "premature end" of the siege encouraged the RAF to try again, leading to the kidnapping of Hanns Martin Schleyer and the subsequent events of the "German autumn" described at the beginning of this chapter.

While governments around the world have become more united in their refusal to release terrorist prisoners in response to kidnappings or seizures, this has to be recognized as a continuing possibility, although perhaps an unlikely one. Where the RAF had more success—and caused the West German government some acute international embarrassment—was in focusing attention on the government's treatment of imprisoned RAF members. This can be seen in two related areas: first, the RAF's campaign to have the conditions they were held under defined as torture; and second, the various hunger strikes they engaged in to support this campaign.

Complaints by the RAF about the conditions under which they were held centered on the practice of keeping the prisoners in total isolation from each other and from other non-RAF prisoners. Undoubtedly, these conditions were very harsh, and one of the first—and indeed best known—attempts to bring this to both West German and international public attention involved a visit to Stammheim prison by the French philosopher Jean Paul Sartre. Sartre described the conditions of custody as "torture"—the white painted cells, with no natural light and no other sound than the sound of the warders' footsteps, he claimed, was likely to cause "psychological disturbances."[27] This was a claim supported by the RAF's lawyers, even the state-appointed ones, who argued that the health of the prisoners had been detrimentally affected by the years in isolation. Amnesty International also stated its belief that these sorts of custody conditions were likely to lead to physical and mental disorders.[28]

The prison conditions also led to the creation of several support groups both within West Germany and elsewhere. Within West Germany, two such groups were formed under the names Red Aid and the Committee Against Torture. The function of these groups was to prepare publicity statements for the press, organize demonstrations in support of the prisoners, and meet the requests of the prisoners themselves for books and information. Demonstrations in support of the prisoners took place frequently in West Germany, such as in March 1981 when police had to evict protestors from the canteen of a leading German newspaper, *Der Spiegel*, in Hamburg. In the Netherlands, a Dutch support group seized Amnesty International offices in 1978 and demanded better treatment for RAF prisoners in Dutch prisons, and the following year, also in Amsterdam, another group attempted to take over the offices of the Swiss national airline demanding better treatment for RAF prisoners in Swiss gaols. The West German authorities did ease the conditions of custody in response to these protests, but they found the protests even more difficult to deal with when they were accompanied by hunger strikes.

The hunger strike is a tactic that has been used with varying degrees of success by several terrorist groups' prisoners, perhaps most notably by the Irish Republican Army. The hunger strike can be a particularly effective weapon for terrorist groups as the state can be presented as barbaric if it lets the prisoner die and barbaric if it intervenes to force feed. The RAF engaged in a series of hunger strikes that were to result in the deaths of two people, Holger Meins in November 1974, and Sigurd Debus in April

1981. The death of prisoners on hunger strike had an effect on members of the RAF still at liberty. After the death of Meins, for example, RAF member Hans Joachim Klein reported that the death had acted like "a trigger: I had to put an end to the impotence of legality ... For a while I kept the horrendous photograph of Holger's autopsy with me, so as not to dull the edge of my hatred."[29] But it is possibly the effect on wider national and international audiences that is of more import.

The West German authorities did initially force feed RAF prisoners on hunger strike. This led to two of their lawyers, Otto Schilly and Klaus Criossant, bringing charges against the doctors responsible, accusing them of mistreatment and torture. The West German authorities, who had tried to create a criminal justice system free from the baggage of the past, especially the Nazi past, were thus unable to escape the accusation that their system-endorsed torture. Another criticism that the West German state was unable to escape was that it had introduced legislation that was at odds with its image as a modern liberal democratic state. These changes to legislation also helped generate sympathy for the RAF.

LEGISLATIVE CHANGES

The terrorist threat presents all governments with challenges to their legislative and judicial systems. The need for security services to have power relating to surveillance, intelligence collection, data storage, and data access can conflict with cherished notions of civil liberties and individual rights to privacy. Putting suspected terrorists on trial also presents difficult and challenging problems for the authorities. Witnesses and judges are particularly subject to intimidation and physical attack, and it is a common terrorist tactic not to recognize the jurisdiction of the court or cooperate with its proceedings. The need to gather information, especially in times of emergency, can put immense stress on the rights of prisoners, including those on remand—as well as on the relationship between prisoners and their lawyers. All these issues can be seen in the West German government's response to terrorism, but perhaps the most difficult and controversial was the relationship between RAF members and their lawyers. There is clear evidence that the RAF used lawyers both to communicate and to circumvent prison security systems. For example, it is most likely that the guns used in the Stammheim suicides were smuggled in via lawyers, and ultimately around 30 lawyers were arrested for assisting the RAF.

In general terms, the most controversial of the West German government's legislative responses to the RAF was the Radicals Edict, which was introduced in January 1972 at the height of the hunt for the RAF's leaders. The purpose of this edict was to ban from public employment or tenured status people whose loyalty to the constitution was in question. In the first 4 years of its existence, nearly half a million people were subjected to the screening processes of the Radicals Edict, even though their actual behavior might have been quite legal. Another problem was that potential terrorist connections were not the only criteria used; people were screened for what might be more generally termed "political reliability."[30] The Radicals Edict, popularly known as the "jobs ban," was extremely unpopular in West Germany and attracted international criticism as well. It was certainly used by the RAF to try and attach credibility to its claims of a repressive state, and it did help arouse some degree of sympathy for the group.

In terms of the criminal code, the West German government introduced two changes that became effective in January 1975 and were aimed at defending lawyers. The first defined conditions under which a lawyer could be excluded from the defense. These included:

- Suspicion that the defending lawyer may abuse contacts with defendants in prison for the purpose of putting the security of an institution in jeopardy;
- Suspicion that the defense lawyer is likely to abuse the privileges of personal contact with defendants; and
- Suspicion of personal involvement by the defending lawyer in the commission of crime or benefiting from the proceeds of crime or frustrating the apprehension, processing and disposition of the perpetrators of crime.

The second law prohibited lawyers from representing more than one defendant and limited the number of counsel available to the defendant to three.

At the end of September 1975, in response to hunger strikes and refusals by RAF members to cooperate with trial proceedings, the West German government introduced a further legislative amendment to allow trials to continue in the absence of the defendant if that absence is self-inflicted. This measure also attracted a lot of national and international criticism. As Fetscher pointed out, these "in absentia trials break with a legal tradition that, with the exception of the Nazi era, has been followed in Germany since 1877."[31]

But as mentioned earlier, the most controversial measure was the Contact Ban introduced in 1977 as a direct response to the Schleyer kidnapping. As soon as the kidnappers' demands became known, RAF prisoners were subject to a contact ban that not only prevented them from having any contact with each other, but also prevented contact between them and their lawyers. Preventing contact between prisoners and their lawyers was a serious and unconstitutional act, and several of the defending lawyers appealed to the Constitutional Court for a ruling. However, before the court could give its ruling, the West German government introduced legislation to create a legal basis for the ban.

This package of measures, and especially the contact ban, was widely criticized by the West German legal community and outside observers. For example, the *London Times* claimed in 1978 that the lawyers that were put on trial in West Germany accused of assisting the RAF most were doing no more than "the normal fulfilling of a defense lawyer's duties." The same article reported international legal concern because:

> the political pressure for a conviction is now considerable, and what better way is there to intimidate other lawyers, and crush opposition . . . The mass of ordinary German lawyers is ashamed by what is happening. But they are also frightened. To practice in Germany, every law student must do a period of training in a public office; if at the end of it his attitude is deemed unsuitable for defending the constitution, he will be kept from office.[32]

The combination of prison conditions and these changes to the criminal code certainly provoked a number of accounts more sympathetic to the RAF than they might otherwise have been. The deaths of Baader, Ensslin, and Raspe in Stammheim led many people to question how they had been treated by the state and how this treatment measured up to West Germany's claims to be a model, modern liberal democratic state, even if this did not translate into overall support for the RAF's violence or its vague ideological aim of world communist revolution. The deaths and behavior of the West German government also helped produce the second generation of RAF, who continued to mount terrorist attacks well into the 1980s—although this campaign focused more on anti-NATO targets than the "repressive" West German state.

Of course, it is impossible to say that if the West German government had reacted any differently, the path and ultimate withering of the RAF would have been any different. It is also important to remember that the RAF was always a very small group whose ideology and violence was rejected by the overwhelming majority of West German citizens. In this sense, it is most definitely a "failed" terrorist organization. But are there any lessons that governments today can learn as they face the threat posed by al Qaeda and others?

CONCLUSIONS

While the success (or otherwise) of terrorist groups is ultimately linked to their ideology and operating environment, government responses also play a key role in determining tactical successes and giving some credibility to terrorist propaganda. This chapter has suggested that the RAF was able to generate some degree of success and attach some degree of credibility to its analysis of a repressive state (although not its objective of some vaguely defined communist new world order) in three areas:

security force behavior, prisoners and prison conditions, and legislative changes. Heavy-handed police reaction to student demonstrations in the late 1960s was one of the key triggers in provoking the emergence of the RAF. Its members argued, with some degree of credibility, that their actions were defensive. Accusations of illegal security force behavior—such as the use of *agents provocateur* or the illegal taping of conversations between prisoners and between prisoners and the lawyers in Stammheim—were also used to give credibility the argument of an aggressive and oppressive security force behavior. Prison conditions were another at least partially successful propaganda theme for the RAF, as members accused the state of torture and illegality. The legislative changes introduced by the West German government were also used by the RAF to add evidence to its thesis of a dangerous state intent on subverting the constitution in order to protect its repressive powers.

It may well be true, as some have argued, that the terrorist threat faced by governments today is qualitatively and quantitatively different from terrorism in the 1970s and 1980s. But what should also be noted is that security force action, prisons, and legislative changes remain at the center of government responses. Security force action against terrorists and their bases in the first decade of the twenty-first century includes much more conventional military action, as the military services of (predominantly, but not exclusively) the U.S. attempt to deal with terrorist organizations in Afghanistan and Iraq, which has included some very questionable techniques.[33] The need for security forces to deal with street demonstrations, such as the recent protests in Europe against the publication of cartoons in a Danish magazine and the need to collect intelligence data, have also provided propaganda opportunities.

Prisoners and prison conditions are another area where both the U.S. and British governments in particular are very vulnerable. There have been well-documented cases of abuse of prisoners, and there are many issues surrounding the legality of—and conditions in—the U.S. military detention facility at Guantanamo Bay, Cuba. There are many groups of concerned citizens and professional groups inside and outside the United States who—while they have no sympathy with al Qaeda's ideology and strategy of violence—find these sorts of seemingly government-condoned reactions at variance with claims of "civilized" democratic governance. Much the same can be said about legislative responses introduced in both the United States and the United Kingdom. For example, the USA PATRIOT Act and the United Kingdom's Prevention of Terrorism Act have both been subject to extreme criticism both within the judiciary and from civil liberties groups.

All of these themes appeared in a tape recording, supposedly from bin Laden, that was played and translated by the *al Jazeera* news organization in April 2006. According to the transcript, bin Laden first of all urges Muslims to "punish the perpetrators of the horrible crime committed by some Crusader-journalists and apostates against . . . our prophet Muhammad." He goes on to place this within a continuing and extensive "crusade" against Muslims that can be seen in Palestine, the Sudan, Bosnia, Indonesia, Kashmir, Pakistan, Chechnya, Somalia, France, and of course Iraq. He accuses the infidel of using "murder, destruction, detention, torture" urges all Muslims to use themselves and their material possessions ~port of the jihad.[34] Al Qaeda, however, remains a small group and efined ideological goal of some sort of caliphate is rejected by an lming majority of Muslims (as well as by non-Muslims). In this as similarities to the RAF. However, governments should be out allowing al Qaeda to create credible propaganda oppor- which it can generate a degree of success. The West German gests perhaps, that current policies in relation to security especially military), prisoners and prison conditions, and es should be reviewed.

1. The first generation RAF was also called the Baader-Meinhof Gang after its two most famous founders, Andreas Baader and Ulrike Mienhof who also killed herself in Stammheim in May 1976.

2. The RAF never had a hard core membership of more than 20 or so.

3. For a fuller and somewhat contemporaneous account of these events see Kurt Shell, "Extraparliamentary Opposition in Postwar Germany," *Comparative Politics* 2, No. 4, (July 1970) 653–680; and Richard. Merritt, "The Student Protest Movement in West Berlin," *Comparative Politics* 1, No. 4, (July 1969) 516–533.

4. Che Guevara, "Guerrilla Warfare," in *Mao Tse-Tung and Che Guevara, Guerrilla Warfare*, translated by F. A. Praeger Inc. (London: Cassell, 1962).

5. Che Guevara: p. 114.

6. Che Guevara quoted in Robert Taber, *The War of the Flea* (London: Paladin, 1970) 31.

7. See Carlos Marighella, "Minimanual of the Urban Guerrilla," reprinted as an appendix to R. Moss, "Urban Guerrilla Warfare," *Adelphi Paper* 79 (London: IISS, 1971).

8. Herbert Marcuse, "Ethics and Revolution," in *Ethics and Society*, ed. R.T. De George (New York: Doubleday, 1968) 137–138.

9. "Marcuse Defends His New Left Line," *New York Times Magazine*, 27 October 1968: 298–299.

10. Horst Mahler quoted in Hans Horchem, "West Germany's Red Army Anarchists," *Conflict Studies* (June 1974): 8–9.

11. Herbert Marcuse, "Re-examination of the Concept of Revolution," *New Left Review* 56 (1969), 17–25

12. Ulrike Meinhof, quoted in Stefan Aust, *The Baader-Meinhof Group*, translated by Anthea Bell (London: The Bodley Head, 1987) 183.

13. Horst Mahler, *Kollectiv RAF: über den bewaffneten Kampf in Westeuropa* (West Berlin: Wagenbuch-Rotbuch, 1971) 43.

14. Mahler: p. 59.

15. Frantz Fanon, *The Wretched of the Earth* (Harmondsworth: Penguin, 1967).

16. Jean Paul Sartre, "Preface" in Frantz Fanon, *The Wretched of the Earth* (Harmondsworth: Penguin, 1967) 19, 25.

17. Mahler: p. 46 (emphasis in the original).

18. See *BBC News* on 19 August 2005, http://newsvote.bbc.co.uk/mpapps/pagetools/print/news.bbc.co.uk/1/hi/world/europe where reference is made to the Hamburg-based al Qaeda cell with four of its members being science students (retrieved May 12, 2006).

19. Christopher Blanchard, "Al Qaeda: Statements and Evolving Ideology," *CRS Report in Congress* (RS 21973, November 16, 2004): 3.

20. For example bin Laden has claimed that to "kill the Americans and their allies, both civil and military, is an individual duty for every Muslim who is able, in any country where this is possible until the al-Aqsa Mosque and the Haram Mosque are freed from their grip and until their armies, shattered and broken winged, depart from all the lands of Islam," quoted in Benjamin Orbach, "Usama Bin Ladin and Al-Qa'ida: Origins and Doctrines," *Middle East Review of International Affairs* 5, no. 4 (2001): 60. Ayman Zawahiri, the deputy leader of al Qaeda has talked of the role of violence in rallying ordinary Muslims to the cause. See for example Christopher Henzel, "The Origins of al Qaeda's Ideology: Implication for US Strategy," *Parameters* 35, no. 1 (2005): 76.

21. RAF statement, *Der Spiegel*, January 2, 1975.

22. Zawahiri claims that attacking the United States will force Americans to personally wage battle against Muslims. See Henzel: p. 76.

23. Mahler: pp. 33–34, 42.

24. Gudrun Ensslin quoted in Aust: p. 44.

25. Aust: p. 150.

26. Aust: p. 145.

27. *The Times* (London), December 5, 1974.

28. *The Times* (London), November 2, 1980.

29. Hans Joachim Klein in Jean Bougereau, *Memoirs of an International Terrorist. Conversations with Hans Joachim Klein* (Orkney: Cienfuegos Press, c1981) 19–21.

30. See Martin Oppenheimer, "The Criminalization of Political Dissent in the Federal Republic of Germany," *Contemporary Crises* 2 (1978): 97–103.

31. Iring Fetscher, "Terrorism and Reaction," *International Summaries—A Collection of Selected Translations in Law Enforcement and Criminal Justice* (Washington DC, U.S. Department of Justice, National Criminal Justice Reference Service, 1979) 45–51.

32. *The Times* (London), May 26, 1978.

33. One of the most distasteful of these practices is "extraordinary rendition." According to a former CIA agent Robert Baer "if you want a serious interrogation, you send a prisoner to Jordan. If you want them to be tortured, you send

them to Syria. If you want someone to disappear— never to be seen again—you send them to Egypt." See http://www.aclu.org/safefree/extraordinaryrendition/22203res20051206.html (retrieved May 12, 2006).

34. See http://english.aljazeera.net?NR/exeres/554FAF3A-B267-427A-B9EC-54881BDE0A2 (retrieved May 12, 2006).

Chapter 17

COUNTERING TERRORISM IN LATIN AMERICA: THE CASE OF SHINING PATH IN PERU

David Scott Palmer

Beginning in May 1980, the government of Peru faced the first attacks from a Maoist insurgency originating in the Andean highlands known as Shining Path, attacks that expanded dramatically over the decade.[1] By 1990, more than 20,000 Peruvians had been killed, $10 billion of infrastructure had been damaged or destroyed, and some 900,000 internal refugees and emigrants had fled their homes.[2] However, with a series of changes in counterinsurgency strategy and tactics, beginning in 1989, the government finally began to gain the upper hand in this conflict. The turning point came with the capture of the movement's leader, Abimael Guzmán Reynoso in September 1992; within three years, the insurgency ceased to pose a serious threat to the Peruvian state.

This chapter offers an abbreviated account of the rise and fall of Shining Path. It discusses the conditions contributing to the initial formation and growth of the insurgency, the largely counterproductive responses by the Peruvian government and its security forces, and the key elements of the major strategic and tactical overhaul that turned the tables on the insurgents. The conclusion draws together the lessons to be learned as to how a guerrilla movement could come close to succeeding and how a besieged government could overcome the threat, lessons of possible use to other governments in the formulation of their own counterterrorism policies.

EXPLAINING THE RISE OF SHINING PATH

Since Peru's independence in the 1820s, the military has played a central role in politics and government. Civilian-led democracy has been the exception, and most political parties have been personalist, populist, and poorly institutionalized. Between 1968 and 1980, a reformist military regime attempted to transform Peru through major social, economic, and political reform.[3] The self-titled Revolutionary Military Government (RMG) was ultimately unsuccessful, most importantly because it attempted too much with too few resources. By the time military officials, chastened by their experience with long-term rule, agreed to turn power back to the civilians between 1978 and 1980, the multiple parties of the Marxist left were major political players, particularly in unions and universities.[4] With Peru's first presidential elections in 17 years in 1980, also the first ever with universal suffrage, the political landscape dramatically changed.

Into this unlikely political context the radical Maoist guerrillas of the *Partido Comunista del Perú-Sendero Luminoso* (the Communist Party of Peru-Shining Path, or PCP-SL) also emerged.[5] In what seemed a quixotic folly at the time, Shining Path launched its self-declared "peoples' war" on the eve of the most open and democratic elections in Peru's political history.[6] A decade later, however, the guerrillas had Peru's democracy on the verge of collapse.

How can we explain such a development? Of the multiple forces and factors in play, one set of explanations relates to the origins, nature, and dynamics of Shining Path itself; another, to the policies and mindset of various Peruvian governments from the 1960s through the 1980s.

How Shining Path Formed and Grew

One important element is that the group that eventually became known as Shining Path began and took root in the early 1960s, largely out of public view in Ayacucho, a remote and isolated department (state) of highland Peru. While a very important region historically, there had been only sporadic and limited central government attention to the area for many years. As a result, the group and its leadership could operate and expand almost unperceived by the outside world for close to two decades before launching military operations.[7]

Secondly, the original ancestor of Shining Path started at the National University of San Cristóbal de Huamanga (UNSCH) in this department's capital. While the university dated from the 1670s, it had been closed for almost 80 years before being refounded in 1959 with a mission then unique to Peruvian institutions of higher education—the promotion of development in the region.[8]

Thirdly, the opportunity to carry out such a mission attracted a number of Peru's best scholars, as well as a few with a more political agenda. Among the latter was the young Communist Party militant Abimael Guzmán Reynoso, later to become the head of Shining Path. Within a few months of his arrival in 1962, he revitalized the almost moribund local Communist party organization and established his presence in the still small university (about 400 students and 40 faculty). As a committed and charismatic professor of the left, he was able, over the next few years, to build a powerful Marxist student organization that gained control of the university in 1968 elections. The UNSCH, with over 5,000 students by 1970, then served even more than before as a forum, incubator, and launching platform for the expansion of Guzmán's increasingly radical organization and ideology.[9]

Fourth, given the extreme poverty and the indigenous peasant-dominated nature of Ayacucho, it is no surprise that Guzmán sided with China after the Sino-Soviet split of 1963–1964. With this new ideological commitment, he successfully built a strong Maoist party both within the university and in the countryside, especially among primary school teachers.[10]

A fifth important factor revolved around Guzmán's relationship with the Chinese. He and his principal lieutenants made extended trips to China between 1965 and 1975, in the midst of the Cultural Revolution, and became adherents of the most radical faction in that struggle, the Gang of Four. When their Chinese mentors lost out in 1976 PCP-SL was cast adrift. Totally radicalized by his Chinese experience, Guzmán concluded that only a properly directed people's war in Peru could bring about a true revolution.[11]

A sixth element was voluntarism. Although objective conditions for the armed struggle did not exist in Peru in early 1980, Guzmán concluded that Lenin's voluntarist dictum could be appropriately applied. By launching the people's war at this moment, he believed, its actions would create over time more favorable objective conditions for revolutionary expansion.[12]

A seventh factor related to Shining Path's quest for the military resources to sustain its peoples' war. In the early years, Shining Path secured guns, ammunition, and dynamite through raids on isolated police stations and the mines that dot the slopes of the highlands. As the movement gathered strength, its needs increased correspondingly.[13] By the mid-1980s, it had found a new source of local support and funding in the coca producers and drug trafficking of the Upper Huallaga Valley in north central Peru. Although it had to compete there at first with its smaller and less radical guerrilla rival, the *Movimiento Revolucionario Tupac Amaru* (Tupac Amaru Revolutionary Movement—MRTA),[14] Shining Path soon achieved a dominant position in the valley. By the late 1980s it is estimated that the guerrillas were extracting at least 10 million dollars a year from the "taxes" paid by Colombian traffickers operating there.[15]

Shining Path set up a finance committee to distribute the funds to the organization's central and regional committees to buy weapons, bribe local officials, and pay cadre. The guerrillas also enlisted the support of local coca growers by forcing buyers to pay higher prices for their production. Thus, having decided to go it alone, Shining Path was able to garner substantial internal resources to fund its operations and maintain its autonomy.[16]

How Peru's Government Aided Shining Path's Growth

Assisting the PCP-SL in its quest were the efforts by the RMG between 1969 and 1975 to effect major change in economic and political organization, particularly a comprehensive agrarian reform. The private land redistribution model applied, however, was not well suited to highland community-based agriculture, particularly in Ayacucho, where only a few productive private estates operated. Its implementation further degraded the already precarious position of indigenous peasants, opening up opportunities the radical Maoists were able to exploit.[17]

Contributing to Shining Path's ability to expand its operations in the 1980s was a second consideration—the reluctance of the new democratic government to recognize the presence of an insurgency. President Fernando Belaúnde Terry (1980–1985), ousted by a coup during his previous term of office (1963–1968), was so fearful of renewed military influence in his second administration that he downplayed the problem for over 2 years. Although he did order specialized police forces, the *sinchis*, into Ayacucho in 1981, their extraordinarily bad comportment forced him to withdraw them within a few months. In addition, throughout his second term he resisted calls to provide complementary economic support, resulting in a government response that focused almost exclusively on military operations.[18]

The *sinchis'* actions highlighted a significant third factor, the long history of misunderstanding and exploitation in Peru between the white and *mestizo* center, based in Lima, and the largely indigenous highland periphery.[19] This contributed to a racist mindset among police and military that often produced, once they intervened, inappropriate responses amounting to state terrorism. Such actions not only served to drive indigenous peasants into the arms of Shining Path, but also provided insurgents with further justification for their armed struggle.[20]

With the historic 1985 electoral victory of Peru's longest standing and best institutionalized party, the reformist *Alianza Popular Revolucionaria Americana* (American Popular Revolutionary Alliance—APRA), the initial policies of President Alan García Pérez (1985–1990) suggested a shift in counterinsurgency strategy that included economic as well as military initiatives in the highlands. However, his misguided macroeconomic policies produced hyperinflation and a virtual economic implosion over the last half of his administration, not only forcing the abandonment of the highland strategy but also creating a serious erosion in both civil government and military institutional capacity.[21]

One result was a sharp decline in military and police morale, as defense budgets were cut by more than 50 percent in the late 1980s and inflation reduced salaries to less than 10 percent of mid-1980s levels.[22] Exacerbating the problem was the growing number of police and armed forces casualties at the hands of Shining Path—a total of 1,196 deaths over the first 10 years of the conflict.[23] These developments provoked mass resignations and contributed to a decline in the armed forces' readiness status from 75 percent in 1985 to 30 percent by 1990.[24]

Such corrosive dynamics played out in the field in a loss of discipline, increased corruption, and, all too often, virtually complete operational ineffectiveness. Although the García government undertook an organizational overhaul of the armed forces, police, and eight separate intelligence agencies by consolidating and renaming them, the lack of resources, both human and material, insured that no effective change would be immediately forthcoming.

In summary, the insurgents were able to initiate and expand their people's war through long preparation, charismatic leadership, a remote base, a radicalized ideology, and voluntarism. They were aided in their efforts by government inaction, a belated response, massive human rights violations, and economic crisis. This combination produced a set of conditions favorable for revolution that had not existed at the outset of the people's war, and enabled Shining Path to make major advances toward its goal of revolutionary victory.

REBEL FAILURE ON THE BRINK OF SUCCESS

This set of considerations raises a second fundamental question. If Shining Path was poised for victory by the early 1990s, why did its revolution not succeed? Within 5 years, the revolutionaries were a spent force, dead, in jail, or rehabilitated, the remnants scattered and no longer a threat to the state. Part of the explanation has to do with ways in which Shining Path contributed to its own collapse and part, with major shifts in official strategies and policies.

Rebel Mistakes

One of Shining Path's problems came to be overconfidence bordering on hubris. Although the organization's leadership envisioned a long-term struggle at the outset of its peoples' war, their successes against a government almost pathologically unwilling to mount effective responses gave rise to the belief that they were on the brink of victory. Such overconfidence led the leadership to exercise less caution in their security and in tracking the rural support structures that had long provided their core cadre.[25]

Another could be characterized as ideological myopia. While Shining Path's radical and uncompromising Maoist ideology served for years as a potent unifying force for militants, over time it also served to alienate the revolution's presumed beneficiaries, the indigenous peasantry. Initially attracted by the promise of a change in status, peasants within Shining Path's orbit had imposed on them an organizational structure completely at odds with their heritage and needs, and were subjected to terrorism and intimidation as cadre tried to maintain their "support."[26]

A third was the hydrocephalic nature of Shining Path's organization. Although the guerrillas developed a set of national, regional, and local organizations and central and regional party committees, all power flowed from a single individual, President Gonzalo (Guzmán's *nom de guerre*). He was the group's founder, ideologist, strategist, and internal contradiction synthesizer, and explicitly fostered a "cult of personality" within the membership. As a result, Shining Path was particularly vulnerable as a guerrilla organization should he be removed.[27]

Fourth was Guzmán's decision to initiate more systematic urban terrorism in the late 1980s, particularly in Lima. Operations in the capital city sowed havoc and panic, but also brought the peoples' war to the doorsteps of the political elites for the first time. It helped them realize that the very survival of the nation was at stake, and strengthened the resolve of central government to find solutions. These operations also made the guerrillas more vulnerable due to intelligence services' greater familiarity with urban than with highland surroundings.[28]

In short, just as much of the explanation for the ability of Shining Path to advance its revolutionary project can be attributed to government errors over the decade of the 1980s, the guerrillas' own mistakes contributed to their failure in the early 1990s.

Government Successes

Whatever Shining Path's errors, it is unlikely that the threat would have been overcome without major adjustments in the government's approach to counterinsurgency. These occurred over a period of several years in the late 1980s and early 1990s, as Shining Path was gaining the upper hand in the conflict in a rapidly deteriorating socioeconomic context. The cumulative effect of these changes was to turn the tide decisively in the government's favor.

A New Approach to Counterinsurgency

One significant change was the military's top to bottom review of its counterinsurgency strategy in 1988–1989. It compiled a

"Countersubversive Manual" that systematically analyzed the anti-guerrilla campaign to that point and developed a new strategy to include political, economic, and psychosocial aspects of counterinsurgency.[29] This manual became the guide for the progressive introduction of a new approach by the Peruvian armed forces to deal with Shining Path.

One innovation following from this review, beginning in 1990, was a military "hearts and minds" civic action campaign in a number of the urban neighborhoods and communities most susceptible to Shining Path influence. The initiatives were modest, from free haircuts to health clinics, but quite quickly turned local indifference, fear, or hostility to support. With carefully coordinated publicity for these initiatives, the media began to convey a more positive image of the military that helped to change public perceptions as well.[30]

A second adjustment was to attach a soldier or two native to the area to the unit conducting operations in that locality. The individuals involved knew the community, spoke the local language or dialect, and often could help the military unit communicate with locals and gather better information on Shining Path sympathizers and operations. The military's reluctance to use such personnel stemmed from a deeply held view in a highly centralized political system that these individuals would be likely to have a greater allegiance to their friends and relatives in the community than to the organization for which they worked. With the looming specter of failure and possible government collapse, however, this change produced positive results—better communication with the locals and the collection of previously unavailable intelligence.[31]

In a third significant adjustment, the military began to be much more sensitive to the negative effects of indiscriminate attacks on local populations, and began training its operational units to carry out missions with fewer human rights violations. As their counterinsurgency activities became more precisely targeted and less repressive, they began to gain the support of local populations. This shift in approach contrasted sharply with Shining Path's increasingly violent operations as it tried to retain local control through force and intimidation.[32]

A fourth shift in counterinsurgency strategy involved 1991 congressional legislation sponsored by the Fujimori government to support training and arming peasant organizations (called *rondas campesinas* locally, or Civil Defense Committees—CDCs by the army) as a first line of defense against rebel attacks. Over many decades, when local highland communities found themselves threatened by cattle rustlers or attempts by neighboring communities to forcibly take some of their land, they would organize community members into *rondas* to overcome such threats to their livelihood or well being.[33]

Shining Path's activities in the 1980s represented to many communities one more threat that had to be resisted. Often, however, their primitive weapons of stones, slingshots, and sharpened sticks were no match for

Shining Path's superior arms. Even so, for years Peru's military resisted any initiative to support the *rondas*, both out of fear that training and arms could be turned against the government and from a lack of confidence, rooted in long-standing racist views, in the ability of indigenous populations to use the assistance properly.[34]

After the army began its program of limited military training and even more limited arming of the *rondas*, by 1993 their numbers grew to more than 4,200 across the highlands, with almost 236,000 members.[35] They often proved able to fend off Shining Path attacks long enough to give army units time to arrive on the scene and rout the rebels. This was a crucial shift in the government's counterinsurgency strategy because it provided local populations most affected by the guerrillas and with the greatest stake in overcoming threats with the capacity to resist them.[36]

A fifth significant change in the Peruvian government's counterinsurgency approach was the late 1989 decision by APRA administration interior minister, Augustín Mantilla, to create a small, autonomous police intelligence unit, the *Grupo Especial de Inteligencia* (Special Intelligence Group—GEIN) with the sole mission of tracking the Shining Path leadership. After a shaky beginning, with only five members and outdated equipment, the unit received infusions of new resources and personnel.[37] Although unsuccessful in its early efforts due to intense political pressure to show results in the waning weeks of the discredited García government, incoming President Fujimori chose to leave GEIN in place.

Given virtually complete autonomy, the intelligence group slowly progressed in its capacity to identify and follow the guerrilla leadership. Over the course of 1991, GEIN operatives were able to round up a number of second-level Shining Path leaders, even as the organization was carrying out ever more brazen and violent terrorist acts. The breakthrough occurred on September 12, 1992, when some 35 GEIN personnel burst into a Lima safe house and captured without violence a startled and security escort-less Guzmán, along with several other PCP-SL Central Committee members and key files.[38]

With this dramatic success, soon followed by the round up of several hundred other militants and cadre, the government delivered a mortal psychological and tactical blow to the Shining Path organization. The Fujimori government milked the moment to its full extent by publicly displaying Guzmán to the media in a cage especially constructed for the occasion, and then quickly tried him in a military court under new procedures that kept the identities of the judges hidden. Predictably, the court sentenced him to life imprisonment.[39] In addition, President Fujimori himself handed over to GEIN members the million-dollar reward offered for Guzmán.

Although violent incidents declined only slightly over the 6 months following Guzmán's capture and then increased over 7 months in 1993, these proved to be the last gasps of a dying movement.[40] By the end of 1994, Shining Path, while still a nuisance in some parts of the country, had ceased to pose a threat to the Peruvian state. Clearly, the new counterinsurgency strategy played a major role in such a dramatic turn of events.

Other Significant Policy Adjustments

The Fujimori government also undertook four other important initiatives in its efforts to gain the upper hand over Shining Path. One was the 1992 establishment of a military and civilian court procedure of "faceless" judges to ensure rapid trials of insurgents and protection from reprisals. A major problem successive Peruvian governments experienced to this point had been the long delay in bringing prisoners accused of subversion to court, with time in jail awaiting trial averaging over 7 years. Another was the systematic intimidation and even assassination of judges assigned to the trials, which had a chilling effect on their willingness to convict as well as a tendency to find legal excuses to justify release from prison of already convicted terrorists.[41]

This new trial procedure was controversial from the outset because of the courts' short-circuiting of due process (Peruvian judicial authorities subsequently determined that several hundred convictions had been secured without legal justification).[42] However, its positive effects were to quickly overcome both the backlog of pending cases and to process new ones, which helped restore public confidence in government efficacy and its own sense of security.

A second important initiative of the Peruvian government was the implementation of a "repentance law" in early 1993, in effect until late 1994. This law was designed to allow Shining Path cadre and sympathizers to turn themselves in with weapons and/or information in exchange for their progressive reintegration into society. Over 5,000 individuals availed themselves of this opportunity, although most were lower level supporters and sympathizers rather than regional or national leaders. Even so, the government gained additional intelligence in the process, and the law also offered a way out for those who had chosen to support Shining Path. In the context of the capture of Guzmán, the timing of the repentance law was ideal, as it came when the incentive for sympathizers and militants to turn themselves in had increased markedly.[43]

A third government initiative, simultaneously a component of the new approach to counterinsurgency and a response to the economic crisis that had gutted government bureaucracy and left millions of Peruvians in desperate poverty, was to create a new set of small official microdevelopment organizations for districts where extreme poverty was the most severe, almost all rural. Many of these were also centers of Shining Path activity.[44]

The new agencies were small (about 300 employees each nation-wide), and the employees were highly trained specialists, often engineers, recruited on merit criteria, paid high salaries, and given significant regional autonomy. The agencies were also focused on small development programs that would have significant and rapid local impact, and included irrigation, potable water, reforestation, soil conservation, electrification, school building, and access roads.[45]

Most projects were $2,000 or less, with labor provided by the communities themselves and technical oversight by the agencies. In many, the requirement to begin a project was for the community to decide what it most needed and to elect a small committee to oversee the project. Between 1993 and 1998, these agencies expended about a billion dollars on these projects and succeeded in reducing extreme poverty by one-half (from 31 percent to 15 percent). The agencies significantly improved citizen well being in many districts affected by political violence and demonstrated that government cared about them enough to extend its reach once again to even the most isolated parts of Peru. They also fostered new local organizations that helped to recreate a measure of institutional capacity within civil society at the grassroots.[46]

Finally, a government response not directly related to the counterinsurgency but which played a significant role in addressing the larger context of deepening economic crisis that contributed to Shining Path expansion was the effort to restore economic stability and growth. When President Fujimori took office in July 1990, he faced hyperinflation, loss of international credit, severe economic decline, and high unemployment. Without immediate and drastic measures to turn the national economy around, it is doubtful that counterinsurgency initiatives alone could have stemmed the growing threat posed by Shining Path.[47] Almost immediately the new government instituted a drastic economic shock program to break the inflationary cycle, soon restored payments on the foreign debt, created a new tax collection agency, revamped the bloated government bureaucracy, and introduced major neoliberal economic reforms.

The Fujimori government's draconian measures reversed the downward economic spiral within a year; broke hyperinflation and regained Peru's good standing in the international economic system within 2 years; and restored economic growth, foreign investment, and effective governance by the end of its third year in office. In spite of the multiple problems the country was facing and the strong medicine the administration was administering to try to overcome them, the president's public approval ratings remained high. The general popular perception was that Peru now had a head of state willing to take action rather than play politics and thinking about the public interest rather than personal gain.[48]

However dramatic the turnaround during these first years of the Fujimori administrations, the peoples' war exacted a high cost for the country and its citizens. Over the 15-year trajectory of Shining Path's revolutionary terrorism and the government's efforts to combat it, close to a million Peruvians, mostly humble highland peasants, were displaced from their homes and became internal refugees. Roughly an equal number emigrated out of fear for their safety and despair of ever finding secure opportunities in their homeland. The dollar estimates of the total damage caused by Shining Path operations between 1980 and 1995 were over $15 billion to infrastructure and $10 billion in lost production, or about half of Peru's 1990 GDP. The previous official estimates of 35,000 deaths and disappearances turned out to be significantly underestimated. A careful study by Peru's Truth and Reconciliation Commission, mostly in rural highland areas, concluded that the correct total was close to 70,000.[49]

Sadly, democracy was also a casualty, with President Fujimori's self coup (*autogolpe*) in 1992. While pressured to restore democratic forms a year later by the Organization of American States (OAS), following his 1995 reelection, Fujimori and his advisors progressively constrained democratic procedures with a set of provisions of dubious legality. Though forced from office in a spectacular set of developments in 2000, shortly after his fraudulent reelection, the path to democratic reconstruction has been a difficult one.[50]

Although a transition government led by Valentín Paniagua (2000–2001) righted the democratic ship, his elected successor, President Alejandro Toledo (2001–2006), proved unable to sustain the political momentum, even with significant economic growth, due to vacillation and improvisation. Shining Path has shown new signs of life, with recruitment efforts in universities and peasant communities, incidents of political violence, renewed activity in coca growing areas, and utilization of a more transparent and human rights respecting government to renew contacts from prisons and bring back members completing their jail terms. Even so, Shining Path no longer represents a threat to the Peruvian state or to most of the population. Whatever the continuing difficulties of Peru's democracy, and they are many, it is unlikely that Shining Path will be in any position to exploit them for the foreseeable future.

CONCLUSIONS: LESSONS LEARNED FROM THE PERUVIAN EXPERIENCE

Peru eventually overcame the threat posed by the radical Maoist Shining Path, but at great human and institutional cost. What does this major example of a government's struggle against a determined guerrilla adversary reveal about the best ways to deal with the challenge and about what should be avoided?

1. Respond promptly. Looking back, had the government taken the threat seriously as soon as Shining Path began to carry out armed operations after publicly declaring its peoples' war, it would very likely have nipped the insurgency in the bud.[51] However, the government's initial response was to withdraw from more isolated police posts as soon as they were attacked or threatened. The result was to open up additional space for Shining Path to build popular support groups in the indigenous communities and to strengthen its military capacity.

2. Conduct counterinsurgent operations that balance military force with economic incentives and that treat local noncombatants with respect. When the government finally did begin to take the guerrillas seriously, it responded almost exclusively with military force, often directed indiscriminately and in a racist manner against the local indigenous population. Field commanders who requested an economic development component to support their military activities were ignored or dismissed. By such operations, the military, however unwittingly, helped to create the very conditions conducive to the expansion of local support for Shining Path that had not existed at the outset of the conflict. Once the government, with disaster looming, undertook a comprehensive overhaul of its counterinsurgency strategy and the military began to conduct operations that were more sensitive to the needs of the local population, it was able to undercut Shining Path's presence and regain the advantage in the countryside.

3. Maintain responsible macroeconomic policies. The APRA government that came to power in 1985, after a promising start, pursued an economic policy that increased poverty dramatically and virtually bankrupted the country. By the end of the decade, Peru faced its most serious economic crisis in over one hundred years, a situation that provoked a legitimacy crisis for the government and enabled Shining Path to advance its revolutionary project much more rapidly than its leaders had originally anticipated. Once APRA's successor, the Fujimori regime, adopted major economic restructuring, ended hyperinflation, and began to generate renewed economic growth, it was able to reestablish the Peruvian government's legitimacy with the wider public and reduce the sense of inevitability of an imminent Shining Path victory.

4. Develop a comprehensive counterinsurgency strategy that includes tracking the leadership. Although long delayed and pursued only in a context of great duress, Peruvian governments eventually put together a multifaceted approach to cope with the growing guerrilla threat. This new strategy included the creation of a specialized police intelligence unit to identify and find the insurgent leadership, the implementation of multiple approaches designed to garner local support, and the decision to train and arm the *rondas*. While each component of the new strategy played an important role in restoring authorities' ability to deal more effectively with Shining Path, the work of the specialized police intelligence unit in tracking down and capturing the organization's leader proved to be the decisive blow. Once these measures enabled the government to regain the initiative, the repentance law offering Shining Path sympathizers rehabilitation and reinsertion into society became a critical instrument of pacification.

Along with such specific and significant adjustments in the government's approach to counterinsurgency, the Fujimori administration also established of a set of new official agencies to carry out a range of small development programs in the poorest districts of Peru, often where Shining Path had a significant presence. These provided significant benefits in a short period of time to two to four million of the country's most needy citizens, while simultaneously reestablishing the government's presence and legitimacy in the periphery.

5. *Take advantage of carefully targeted external counterinsurgency support.* External actors, particularly the U.S. government, became sufficiently concerned about Shining Path's advances against the beleaguered Peruvian democracy to provide significant military and intelligence support in 1991 and 1992. With Fujimori's April 1992 *autogolpe*, however, the United States immediately suspended military assistance and training. However, the U.S. government did not end specialized intelligence aid. It is believed that such support was critical in locating the safe house occupied by Guzmán, support that enabled the Peruvian police intelligence unit to conduct its successful raid and capture Shining Path's leader.[52] The conclusion of Peruvian authorities that the snaring of the head of the insurgent organization would be a devastating psychological and organizational blow turned out to be correct. In an organization where a single individual held most of the power, removing that person would be the group's death knell.

6. *Understand the enemy and exploit its weaknesses.* Unlike the government, the insurgents did not learn or adapt. From the outset, Shining Path pursued the single objective of overthrowing the regime through the peoples' war. Negotiation was never an option. Convinced of the ideological correctness of its approach, which included the complete reorganization of civil society along Maoist lines, the Shining Path leaders tried to impose a model in its areas of operation that in no way reflected the traditions, patterns, and needs of those they said were to be the beneficiaries of their revolution. Their ideological fervor and their successes against the government for a number of years blinded them to the possibility that they could be defeated. While they often learned from failures in field operations and adjusted their military strategy accordingly, they did not do so in their relations with the civilian populations under their influence. But their greatest failure was to underestimate the capacity of government to learn from its own mistakes and to develop a new set of counterinsurgency initiatives that exploited Shining Path's weaknesses.

7. *Retain democracy for the internal and external legitimacy it conveys.* Beyond the physical and human destruction wrought by the insurgency and the government's response, another casualty was Peru's democracy. Although President Fujimori defended his *autogolpe* as necessary to prevail against Shining Path, most observers conclude that success occurred in spite of the suspension of the constitution, congress, and the judiciary, not because of it. The military, frustrated by the failures of the elected governments of the 1980s to stem the insurgency or to govern effectively, amidst the chaos of the last months of the García government put together a plan for gaining greater control over the process, the so-called *Libro Verde*, or Green Book. This plan envisioned stronger executive control, a comprehensive counterinsurgency strategy, and the implementation of free market principles to restore the economy.[53]

With Fujimori's 1990 election, the military saw an opportunity to accomplish the *Libro Verde* objectives through civilian rule. Since Fujimori did not have a strong party apparatus to support him, the military became his major pillar of institutional support and backed his 1992 suspension of constitutional government. However, through patronage and careful cultivation of some top military officials, Fujimori and his close advisors, particularly Vlademiro Montesinos, not the military, became the controlling force in government policy.

While it is not clear that Fujimori planned a coup from the outset of his administration, he certainly had no patience for the give and take of democratic politics with the opposition majority in congress. On balance, the 1992 democratic breakdown can be attributed not only to the president's personal proclivities, but also to the corrosive forces of the people's war and counterinsurgency that were at work over more than a decade and to the multiple errors of elected civilian authority in other areas of governance, most particularly economic mismanagement.

As subsequent events were to demonstrate, nevertheless, even after the threat of Shining Path had passed, the Fujimori government continued to manipulate the system to shut off dissent and to ensure that it would continue to run the country. So instead of receiving acclaim for the success of the counterinsurgency effort and for the significant improvement in the economic and personal security of much of the citizenry, the former president was pilloried for the abuses of power that he and his closest advisors committed while in office.

Democracy has been reestablished in Peru, though still fraught with problems and challenges. While the country still faces many difficulties, the generalized terrorism of Shining Path is no longer one of them. Nevertheless, the continuing fragility of democratic process and procedures, the erosion of confidence by most Peruvians in their government, and the inability of the Toledo administration to channel constructively the almost constant local and regional protest movements provide a context within which another insurgency, perhaps even one led by Shining Path, could again emerge.

NOTES

1. This chapter draws from a longer and more detailed study, "Revolution in the Name of Mao: Revolution and Response in Peru," in *Democracy and Counterterrorism: Lessons from the Past*, ed. Robert Art and Louise Richardson (Washington: United Institute of Peace Press, 2007), a project supported by the United States Institute of Peace.

2. David Scott Palmer, "Peru's Persistent Problems," *Current History* 89, no. 543 (January 1990): 6–7. The casualty figures cited here have been revised sharply upward by Peru's Comisión de la Verdad y Reconciliación (Truth and Reconciliation Commission) in its 2003 report, noted below in footnote 49.

3. Carol Graham, *Peru's APRA: Parties, Politics, and the Elusive Quest for Democracy* (Boulder, CO: Lynne Rienner, 1992) 37–39.

4. Philip Mauceri, *State under Siege: Development and Policy Making in Peru* (Boulder, CO: Westview, 1996) 21–25.

5. Gustavo Gorriti Ellenbogen, *Sendero: La historia de la guerra milenaria en el Perú* (Lima: Editorial Apoyo, 1990).

6. David Scott Palmer, "Rebellion in Rural Peru: The Origins and Evolution of Sendero Luminoso," *Comparative Politics* 18, no. 2 (January 1986): 128–129.

7. Carlos Iván Degregori, *Ayacucho 1969–1979: El surgimiento de Sendero Luminoso* (Lima: Instituto de Estudios Peruanos, 1990).

8. Fernando Romero Pintado, "New Design for an Old University: San Cristóbal de Huamanga," *Américas* (December 1961) np.

9. Gustavo Gorriti Ellenbogen, "Shining Path's Stalin and Trotsky," in *Shining Path of Peru*, 2nd editon, ed. David Scott Palmer (New York: St. Martin's, 1994) 167–177.

10. Degregori, *Ayacucho 1969-1979*: pp. 41–47.

11. Ellenbogen, *Sendero*.

12. Peter Flindell Klarén, *Peru: Society and Nationhood in the Andes* (New York: Oxford University Press, 2000) 369–370.

13. Simon Strong, *Sendero Luminoso: El movimiento subversivo más letal del mundo* (Lima: Peru Reporting, 1992) 106.

14. For a comprehensive overview of the MRTA, see Gordon H. McCormick, *Sharp Dressed Men: Peru's Tupac Amaru Revolutionary Movement* (Santa Monica, CA: Rand, 1993). It should be noted, however, that the MRTA was responsible for only a small proportion of incidents of political violence (less than 3 percent), and even fewer of the deaths attributed to guerrilla activity in Peru through the early 1990s (less than 1 percent).

15. José E. Gonzales, "Guerrillas and Coca in the Upper Huallaga Valley," in *Shining Path of Peru*, ed. Palmer: pp. 123–144.

16. Gabriela Tarazona Sevillano, *Sendero Luminoso and the Threat of Narcoterrorism*, Center for Strategic and International Studies, Washington Papers 144 (New York: Praeger, 1990).

17. David Scott Palmer, *Revolution from Above: Military Government and Popular Participation in Peru, 1968–1972* (Ithaca, NY: Cornell University Latin American Studies Program, 1973) 230–237.

18. Gen. Roberto C. Noel Moral, *Ayacucho: Testimonio de un soldado* (Lima: Publinor, 1989).

19. Julio Cotler, "La mecánica de la dominación interna y del cambio social en el Perú," *Peru Problema* (Lima: Instituto de Estudios Peruanos, 1969) 145–188.

20. Carlos Tapia, *Las Fuerzas Armadas y Sendero Luminoso: Dos estratégias y un final* (Lima: Instituto de Estudios Peruanos, 1997) 27–43.

21. Philip Mauceri, "Military Politics and Counter-Insurgency in Peru," *Journal of Interamerican Studies and World Affairs* 33, no. 4 (Winter 1991): 100.

22. David Scott Palmer, "National Security," in *Peru: A Country Study*, Area Handbook Series, 4th Edition, ed. Rex A. Hudson (Washington D.C.: Federal Research Division, Library of Congress, 1993) 289, 292.

23. Palmer, "The Revolutionary Terrorism of Peru's Shining Path," in *Terrorism in Context*, ed. Martha Crenshaw (University Park, PA: Pennsylvania State University Press, 1995) Table 7.1, 271.

24. Palmer, "National Security": p. 292.

25. Carlos Iván Degregori, "After the Fall of Abimael Guzmán: The Limits of Sendero Luminoso," in *The Peruvian Labyrinth: Polity, Society, Economy*, eds. Maxwell A. Cameron and Philip Mauceri (University Park, PA: Pennsylvania State University Press, 1997) 179–191.

26. Carlos Iván Degregori, "Harvesting Storms: Peasant Rondas and the Defeat of Sendero Luminoso in Ayacucho," in *Shining and Other Paths: War and Society in Peru, 1980–1995*, ed. Steve J. Stern (Durham, NC: Duke University Press, 1998) 131–140; Billy Jean Isbell, "Shining Path and Peasant Responses in Rural Ayacucho," in *Shining Path of Peru*, ed. Palmer: pp. 77–100; Tapia, *Las Fuerzas Armadas y Sendero Luminoso*: pp. 103–104.

27. See the revealing interview given by Guzmán to Luis Borje Arce and Janet Talavera Sánchez in *El Diario*, a sympathetic Lima weekly, which they titled, "La entrevista del siglo: El Presidente Gonzalo rompe el silencio," July 24, 1988: 2–48. Also, the organizational structure and its vulnerabilities, in Benedicto Jiménez Bacca, *Inicio, desarrollo, y ocaso del terrorismo en el Perú* (Lima: SANKI, 2000), Tomo 1.

28. Tapia, *Las Fuerzas Armadas y Sendero Luminoso*: pp. 133–152.

29. Tapia, *Las Fuerzas Armadas y Sendero Luminoso*: pp. 43–55.

30. Orin Starn, "Sendero, soldados y ronderos en el Mantaro," *Quehacer* 74 (noviembre-diciembre 1991): 64–65; Lewis Taylor, "La estratégia contrainsurgente: El PCP-SL y la guerra civil en el Perú, 1980–1996," *Debate Agrario* 26 (julio 1997): 105–106.

31. Palmer, Interviews with military personnel in Ayacucho, July–August, 1998.

32. Starn, "Sendero, soldados, y ronderos": p. 64; Tapia, *Las Fuerzas Armadas y Sendero Luminoso*: pp. 47–48.

33. Orin Starn, ed., *Hablan los ronderos: La búsqueda por la paz en los Andes*, Documento de Trabajo No. 45 (Lima: Instituto de Estudios Peruanos, 1993) 11–28.

34. José Coronel, "Violencia política y respuestas campesinas en Huanta," in *Las rondas campesinas y la derrota de Sendero Luminoso,* Carlos Iván Degregori, et al. (Lima: Instituto de Estudios Peruanos, 1996): 48–56.

35. Ponciano del Pino, "Tiempos de guerra y de dioses: Ronderos, evangélicos y senderistas en el valle del río Apurímac," in *Las Rondas campesinas y la Derrota de Sendero Luminoso,* Carlos Iván Degregori, et al.: p. 181.

36. Orin Starn, "Villagers at Arms: War and Counterrevolution in the Central-South Andes": p. 232.

37. GEIN personnel increased to about 35 by 1990, and 50 a year later. Gustavo Gorriti, "El día que cayó Sendero Luminoso," *Selecciones de Reader's Digest* (deciembre 1996): 121, 123, 127.

38. Gorriti, "El día que cayó Sendero Luminoso": pp. 136–142; Benedicto Jiménez Bacca, *Inicio, desarrollo y ocaso del Terrorismo en el Perú,* Tomo II, 740–756.

39. Sally Bowen, *The Fujimori File: Peru and its President, 1990–2000* (Lima: Peru Monitor, 2000) 137–143.

40. Violent incidents declined by less than 10 percent in late 1992 and early 1993 and then increased by over 15 percent during the following 7 months. David Scott Palmer, "The Revolutionary Terrorism of Peru's Shining Path": pp. 284, 304.

41. Comisión de Juristas Internacionales, *Informe sobre la administración de justicia en el Perú,* 30 de noviembre de 1993, typescript, *passim.*

42. In 1999, the Inter-American Human Rights Court (IAHRC), of which Peru was a signatory, declared that the faceless judge procedure was an unconstitutional violation of due process. Though rejected by the Fujimori government, its successor accepted the IAHRC decision and set up new trials for those convicted under the unconstitutional arrangement.

43. Tapia, *Las Fuerzas Armadas y Sendero Luminoso*: pp. 80–81; Bowen, *The Fujimori File*: pp. 155–157. Ponciano del Pino, "Family, Culture, and 'Revolution',": pp.171, 177.

44. David Scott Palmer, "Soluciones ciudadanas y crisis política: El caso de Ayacucho," in *El juego politico: Fujimori, la oposición y las reglas,* ed. Fernando Tuesta Soldevilla (Lima: Fundación Fredrich Ebert, 1999) 285–290.

45. David Scott Palmer, "FONCODES y su impacto en la pacificación en el Perú: Observaciones generales y el caso de Ayacucho," in Fondo Nacional de Compensación y Desarrollo Nacional (FONCODES), *Concertando para el desarrollo: Lecciones aprendidas del FONCODES en sus estratégias de intervención* (Lima: Gráfica Medelius, 2001) 147–177.

46. David Scott Palmer, "Citizen Responses to Conflict and Political Crisis in Peru: Informal Politics in Ayacucho," in *What Justice? Whose Justice? Fighting for Fairness in Latin America,* eds. Susan Eva Eckstein and Timothy P. Wickham-Crowley (Berkeley, CA: University of California Press, 2003) 233–254.

47. Javier Iguíñiz, "La estrategia económica del gobierno de Fujimori: Una visión global," in *El Perú de Fujimori,* eds. John Crabtree and Jim Thomas (Lima: Universidad del Pacífico y el Instituto de Estudios Peruanos, 2000) 15–43.

48. John Crabtree, "Neopopulismo y el fenómeno Fujimori": pp. 45–71.

49. Comisión de la Verdad y Reconciliación Perú, *Informe Final: Tomo I: Primera parte: El proceso, los hechos, las víctimas* (Lima: Navarrete, 2003) 169. But also see

other sections of this volume for basic information and analysis of Peru's political violence.

50. Among others, Carmen Rosa Balbi and David Scott Palmer, "'Reinventing' Democracy in Peru," *Current History* 100, no. 643 (February 2001): 65–72.

51. There are precedents. In 1959, the military responded quickly to a Trotskyite-organized rebellion in the La Convención valley of Cuzco, and again in 1965 to a Castro-inspired attempt to establish *focos* in three isolated locations in the central Andean highlands. For La Convención, Wesley W. Craig, Jr., "Peru: The Peasant Movement of La Convención," in *Latin American Peasant Movements*, ed. Henry A. Landsberger (Ithaca, NY: Cornell University Press, 1969) 274–296; for the Andean highlands, Luis de la Puente Uceda, "The Peruvian Revolution: Concepts and Perspectives," *Monthly Review* 17 (November 1965): 12–28. The failure of the Peruvian government to respond quickly to this new rural insurgency is puzzling, given its earlier successes. The explanation rests in part on President Belaúnde's aversion to deploy the military again, as he had in 1965, because he feared another coup as in 1968, and in part on the military's own reluctance, having been weakened as an institution by 12 years in power.

52. For this and other information on the U.S. role, Cynthia McClintock and Fabian Vallas, *The United States and Peru: Cooperation at a Cost* (New York: Routledge, 2003) 69–73. Also Cynthia McClintock, *Revolutionary Movements in Latin America: El Salvador's FMLN and Peru's Shining Path* (Washington, DC: U.S. Institute of Peace Press, 1998) 145, 238, and *passim*. While not the focus of this study, the United States also contributed to the Peruvian military's preparations to end the dramatic December 1995 takeover of the Japanese ambassador's residence by the MRTA. When extensive and drawn out negotiations faltered, in mid-April 1996 Peru's counterterrorism unit mounted a spectacular and successful operation. It freed 42 hostages, killed all 14 MRTA guerrillas, and demonstrated the effectiveness of the counterterrorism capacity originally developed to deal with the Shining Path threat.

53. Enrique Obando, "Fujimori y las Fuerzas Armada": pp. 361–362.

CHAPTER 18

A LONG ROAD TO VICTORY: DEVELOPING COUNTERINSURGENCY STRATEGY IN COLOMBIA

Román D. Ortíz and Nicolás Urrutia

Colombia's force structure and counterinsurgency doctrine have largely been shaped by the military's tactical and operational interaction with a host of insurgent groups that have come into existence and, to an appreciable degree, thrived over the past five decades. However, understanding the military's strategic evolution over the past half century requires a brief review of the country's prior legacy of political violence and military history. With this in mind, the present chapter analyzes the evolution of Colombian counterinsurgency over the past half-century. First, the Colombian military's nineteenth- and early twentieth-century legacies are summarily reviewed. Second, a quick look is given to the outburst of sectarian violence that shook the country during the 1950s, followed by a third section that highlights the long-term consequences of a peculiar civil-military relations doctrine instituted toward the 1960s. A fourth section reviews the rise of modern insurgent movements across the country during the 1970s and 1980s. This is followed by a more detailed look into the causes of Colombia's precarious security scenario in the early 1990s. Sixth, the military's broad reforms and their impact on the strategic balance toward the late 1990s are analyzed. Finally, a seventh section summarizes some of the shortcomings of Colombia's current strategy, and the last draws broad lessons for counterinsurgency theory and practice.

THE ROOTS OF MODERN COLOMBIAN MILITARY TRADITION

When mass political violence erupted in 1948, the Colombian military had several things in common with other Latin American forces, as well as significant differences. Like others in the region, the Army had some experience in matters of domestic security, particularly in dealing with mass worker mobilization by groups associated with communism. Such was the case, for instance, of its participation in the dissolution of a 1928 strike of banana workers that turned violent and came to be known as the *masacre de las bananeras* (massacre of the banana plantations).[1] It should be noted that, to a significant degree, the military's role in internal security had much to do with the lack of an alternative security force capable of performing such a role. In this sense, though a police force did exist in the early twentieth century, it suffered from four sources of organizational weakness. First, it was a decentralized, regional force, subject to the whims of local governors. Second, it was, by any conceivable measure, too small for the task at hand. Third, it was systematically underfinanced and therefore underequipped; and fourth, it was highly politicized by the partisan confrontation between the main political parties in Colombia: liberals and conservatives.[2] That being said, the Colombian military also shared with its regional counterparts some experience in the conduct of external defense, particularly as it pertained to matters of border disputes. Such was the case of Colombia's war with Perú in 1932, initiated when Peruvian forces took de facto control of the Colombian southernmost town of Leticia. Colombia won in a series of engagements that forced the military to confront the operational difficulties inherent to a tropical jungle environment and made it realize the advantages of small-unit tactics and of exercising control over river-based communications.[3]

Unlike other militaries in Latin America, however, Colombia's forces were distinctly young institutions during the early twentieth century. Though officially the Republic's armed services had been formed in the 1830s, when the *Gran Colombia* was split into modern Venezuela, Ecuador, and Colombia, the military was not a organized as professional organization from the start. Instead, it emerged as a highly politicized body, frequently employed by both liberal and conservative governments against political opponents.[4] In fact, it could be said that there was no such thing as a national army until the beginning of the twentieth century, since even at the end of the nineteenth century the country served as battleground for a civil war fought between two quasiregular armies. One was the officially sanctioned army, commanded and manned by conservative militants. The other was a liberal force, similarly constructed along partisan lines, but lacking official recognition. At the turn of the century, these two forces clashed in the *Guerra de los Mil Días* (the

Thousand-Day War: 1899–1901), the last episode of military confrontation between liberals and conservatives conducted along the lines of regular warfare.[5] Only after the war was it possible to create a truly National Army, trained at a unified War College (*Escuela Superior de Guerra*) and commanded by a General Staff (*Estado Mayor*) independent from partisan manipulation.[6] Said process was carried out under the auspices of various foreign military missions, notably a number of Chilean advisory groups that imprinted a strong Prussian tradition on the Army's organizational culture.[7]

Thus, when the period of mass political violence known as *La Violencia* ("the Violence") erupted in 1948, Colombia's modern military was barely three decades old and, given the circumstances described above, it held both a number of advantages as well as a number of disadvantages for accomplishing the task at hand. In its favor, the military could count on existing knowledge regarding the conduct of internal security operations. Likewise, the organization's relative youth and incomplete establishment as a conventional force made it quite malleable to change in the face of need. However, these factors also stood as organizational limitations, since the Army's scarce time and operational experience as a unified structure, as well as its new and relatively untested officer corps, hindered its capability to design long-term strategies and conduct large-scale operations.

CONFRONTING *LA VIOLENCIA*: THE ROOTS OF COUNTERINSURGENCY IN COLOMBIA (THE 1950s)

The period of intense sectarian violence known as *La Violencia* began with a wave of popular uprisings resulting from the assassination of liberal party leader and presidential candidate Jorge Eliécer Gaitán on May 9, 1948.[8] Upon lynching his assassin, a mob set out to pillage and destroy downtown Bogotá, setting off regional uprisings and street violence throughout wide areas of the country under liberal control. Faced with a general breakdown of public order, the conservative government launched a series of operations to restore order. These efforts began by reasserting military control of Bogotá, where the meager 2,000-strong police force had disintegrated and joined the rioting, and continued outwards, into towns and villages throughout the country.[9] Though successful in urban centers, the military operations drove a number of radical liberal militants to the countryside, where they were able to organize into guerrilla units based mainly out of the *Llanos Orientales* (the western plains), and the Tolima and Sumapaz regions. Allowing them to regroup and establish base camps in these areas, relatively undisturbed by government forces, would later prove to be a major strategic mistake.[10]

While over the course of the following years, the liberal guerrillas launched a harassment campaign against official forces from their safe havens in the Llanos and Tolima camps, they never managed to organize their efforts around a strategic plan to overthrow government. Despite the guerrillas' limited impact on the strategic scenario, however, the inability of both liberal and conservative politicians to bring an end to political violence did set the stage for a bloodless "coup of opinion" by General Gustavo Rojas Pinilla in 1953.[11] Upon seizing power, Rojas launched a pacification campaign markedly more sophisticated than the efforts of his predecessors, particularly in two aspects. First, his decision to appoint the Army as the primary force charged with the campaign was fairly well-received, largely because the military's apolitical character since the early twentieth century constituted a guarantee of neutrality that both liberal and conservative militias—or even the police—lacked. Second, Colombia's participation in the Korean War, through the deployment of an infantry battalion embedded within U.S. forces, allowed the military to capitalize on the freshly acquired operational expertise of its officers in operational intelligence, general staff organization, and infantry maneuvers. The latter circumstance was amplified by the fact the U.S. government integrated the Colombian pacification effort into the larger campaign to contain the spread of communism in Latin America in the context of the early Cold War, thus opening the door to American military assistance.[12] In this context, Rojas seized the opportunity warranted by this increase in available resources and set forth an effort that, for the first time in Colombia, combined the political and military elements of a modern counterinsurgency campaign: an amnesty offering and a simultaneous dose of military pressure aimed at promoting the demobilization or, if necessary, destruction of the guerrillas.

In the conduct of the campaign, Rojas introduced a number of relevant tactical innovations, among which is the Army's still used "cordon and search" concept of operation. Likewise, the military's newly available air and ground equipment, fruit of U.S. cooperation, was rapidly deployed and integrated into the Army's and the Air Force's operational repertoire. Innovations were also made with respect to combat unit structure, including the introduction of irregular warfare training, a process that culminated in the founding of the *Escuela de Lanceros* ("Lancers School") in 1955, an irregular warfare training center inspired by that of the U.S. Army Rangers, and the first of its kind in Latin America. At higher levels of the military echelon, Rojas' innovations included the creation of the *Comando General de las Fuerzas Militares* ("General Command of the Military Forces"), home to the *Estado Mayor Conjunto* ("Joint General Staff").[13]

Besides changes made to the military's structure proper, the Army's standing force was increased from 15,000 in 1950 to 36,000 in 1955, and support forces were assembled under various formats. Thus, former guerrilla fighters and defectors were inserted into units that, while not embedded in the military, did serve in support and intelligence-collecting roles. More importantly, the military unified and centralized the existing police force into a national structure and placed it under the command of the Joint General Staff, manning much of its officer corps with military personnel. In parallel with the above, the existing intelligence structure, up to then consisting of a small office attached to the Interior Ministry and largely used as a political police, was reformed into an agency directly responsible to the Presidency, the *Servicio de Inteligencia Colombiano—SIC* ("Colombian Intelligence Service"). The new agency was given a broad intelligence mandate, along with judicial police capabilities. Simultaneously, the recently reformed National Police created an intelligence directorate know as the F-2, and the military capitalized on its Korean experience to modernize its intelligence structure.[14]

Beyond its military component, however, the Rojas era also marked the beginning of the government's civic action efforts. Through the *Secretaría Nacional de Asistencia Social—SENDAS* ("National Secretariat for Social Action") program, economic assistance was directed toward those regions where military operations were conducted, serving a dual purpose: eroding the guerrilla groups' social base and strengthening the military government's.[15] It is worth noting that this program was under direct control and oversight of the Presidency, though Rojas' appointment of his daughter to the post of program director led to a propensity for directing public funds for rather short-lived, populist initiatives.

As a consequence of these government reforms, sectarian violence decreased significantly during the Rojas era. The government's amnesty caused an internal split among the guerrillas, so that while "pure liberals" demobilized, "common liberals"—connected with the Communist Party—refused to do so. At any rate, these results were made possible by the inclusion of two elements of modern counterinsurgency theory into the security effort: a political-social program aimed at dissolving the guerrillas' social support base and promoting desertion, and sustained military pressure through the strengthening of intelligence capabilities and the adoption of irregular warfare tactics.[16] It must be noted, however, that these key elements were implemented in relative isolation from each other, so that while tactical innovations led to better tactical results and improved intelligence capabilities permitted greater efficiency in the use of force, political-social programs debilitated the guerrillas' support, but no institutional structure was put in place to oversee their coordinated implementation, nor was there any grand strategy designed to bring together the various elements into a coherent, integrated effort. Thus, despite the fact that the guerrillas needed to be dealt with militarily at the tactical level and their vindications needed to be resolved at the strategic level through amnesties and social programs, the Rojas government did not understand the need for a long-term strategic plan to do both things. Thus, military operations were conducted autonomously, without any coordination or integration with efforts made in the socio-political arena.

COUNTERINSURGENCY AND THE *LLERAS* DOCTRINE
OF CIVIL-MILITARY RELATIONS (THE 1960s)

Five years after his rise to power, the political establishment had grown weary of Rojas, leading to his removal from office in 1958. By that time, the level of political violence throughout the country had decreased significantly, yet two problems remained: first, despite broad demobilization initiatives, a number of guerrilla fighters turned to common banditry; and second, a number of disaffected guerrilla leaders associated with the Colombian Communist Party refused to give up arms and secluded themselves in remote strongholds called *Repúblicas Independientes* ("Independent Republics").

At the time, Colombia's institutional framework in general and its security establishment in particular were undergoing a transition phase, designed by the newly elected civilian government and aimed at preventing the military from regaining power. Thus, in a speech given before the military general staff and a wide audience in May 1958, President Alberto Lleras Camargo laid the foundations of what came to be known as the *Lleras* doctrine. Therein, he defined two independent spheres of government: civilians were to become the sole decision-makers in matters of general policy, with no military interference, and in return the military was granted broad autonomy in the conduct of external defense and internal security policy.[17] Laying down this sharp division was instrumental in distancing the military from the general affairs of government, a top priority for the newly elected administration that was emphasized by a failed coup aimed at returning Rojas to power just 2 weeks before President Lleras' speech. The doctrine, however, also signified an immense difficulty for the successful conduct of a counterinsurgency campaign since, as exponents of British counterinsurgency doctrine have observed, counterinsurgency is an integrated governmental effort, wherein military operations are but one element of a broader government effort. Or, in the words of General Sir Gerald Templer: "The shooting side of this business is only 25 percent of the trouble and the other 75 percent lies in getting the people of this country behind us."[18]

Alongside the Lleras doctrine, two other reforms were made during the late 1950s with significant effects for the conduct of the counterinsurgency effort. First, the National Police was separated from the Joint General Staff, albeit it remained attached to the Ministry of National Defense. Second, the existing *Servicio de Inteligencia Colombiano (SIC)* was transformed into the *Department Administrativo de Seguridad* (DAS), a predominantly civilian agency and kept under direct supervision of the Presidency.[19] In general, the reforms introduced during the Lleras era served to democratize civil-military relations and to shield civilian governance from military interference, but at the same time they increased the number of independent actors in charge of security policy without providing an institutional structure capable of directing and coordinating their efforts. Inasmuch as institutional resources could not be coordinated by any single instrument of government, a significant obstacle emerged for the conduct of any counterinsurgency campaign.[20]

The Lleras doctrine was put to the test not long after its public announcement, curtailing the first comprehensive attempt at implementing an integrated counterinsurgency strategy in Colombia. As Commander of the Army, General Alberto Ruiz Noboa designed the blueprint for a national-level counterinsurgency strategy named *Plan Lazo*, which he effectively began to implement upon reaching the post of defense minister. The plan's origins owed much to the combination of three factors: the broadly accepted value of implementing social initiatives aimed at resolving the grievances from which the guerrillas drew their support; the military's ready acceptance of operational concepts of counterinsurgency warfare promoted by the United States throughout Latin America during the late 1950s and early 1960s, and a broad conception of the military's role as an institution called to be a leading actor in the nation's economic development processes. Based on these broad ideas, the plan called for an integration of the military's combat-proven tactics from past counter-guerrilla operations with an extended social development program aimed at pacifying the country once and for all. That is to say, the idea was putting together in a coordinated fashion a number of policy tools already used in the past.[21]

With respect to the military component of the campaign, the Army's existing concept of "area control" was put in practice to separate the guerrillas from the civilian population so as to locate the armed groups and neutralize them. For this purpose, a number of tactical instruments were perfected, such as small units specifically charged with the task of penetrating enemy territory to locate and destroy guerrilla units. Operational intelligence capabilities were strengthened, particularly with respect to the development of local intelligence networks, an effort that was articulated through the creation of the *Batallón de Inteligencia y Contrainteligencia* in 1962, a battalion-level unit charged exclusively with intelligence and counterintelligence operations. Most notably, special light infantry units were created specifically for counter-guerrilla operations, starting with companies *Arpón* ("Harpoon") and *Flecha* ("Arrow") as pilot programs.[22] Their operational performance was so well received that the program was soon broadened, leading to the creation of battalion-size counter-guerrilla units called *Batallones de Orden Público—BATOPs* ("Public Order Battalions").[23] Support for the military's regular units was also broadened through a greater emphasis on psychological operations and, more importantly, the establishment of local self-defense units and the formal adoption of the "operational control" mechanism, through which National Police units in a given area of operations were subject to military command.

In parallel with these military measures, the Plan Lazo put in motion a number of rural development programs under the coordination of the *Comité Nacional de Acción Cívico-Militar* ("National Civic-Military Action Committee") an organization created within the central government specifically for the purpose of implementing civic action programs, which included regional branches that allowed coordination procedures to be replicated regionally. This institutional structure initiated a broad and ambitious public works program, along with social programs in those areas where military operations were concentrated.[24]

The plan's overall outcome was favorable, as the government gradually regained control of the Independent Republics between 1964 and 1965. Yet, General Ruiz Noboa and his staff believed that far broader reforms were needed in order to consolidate and complete the pacification process. These ambitions led Ruiz Noboa to clash with then-President Guillermo León Valencia, resulting in his demotion from active duty and, in the process, the military's abandonment of any attempt to design a national-level grand strategy for pacification. In this manner, General Ruiz Noboa's removal from office became the first tangible demonstration of the Lleras doctrine, just as it foreshadowed the near-impossibility of implementing a comprehensive counterinsurgency strategy for years to come. The military, on one hand, was not allowed to design or participate in matters of public policy—particularly social policy—beyond the strict limits set by security operations, since doing so was perceived as a breach of the civil-military rules set forth under the Lleras doctrine. Civilian leaders of government, on the other hand, lacked the institutional tools and professional expertise necessary to appropriately guide the use of military force as an element of a comprehensive counterinsurgency strategy.[25] Thus, from this point onwards it became practically impossible to design—let alone implement—a comprehensive counterinsurgency strategy. In this manner, until the early 1990s, government efforts to pacify the country were marked by a sort of schizophrenia: while the military developed tactical instruments to obtain tactical victories over the guerrillas, civilians pushed forth reforms aimed at managing the political and social grievances used by the guerrillas to gather support. However, both types of efforts were carried out in isolation from each other, thereby making it impossible to achieve a strategic outcome favorable to the State. Thus, the government's inability to develop a national-scale, integrated counterinsurgency plan caused it to lose the strategic initiative, a loss that would later prove to entail enormous costs.

While the aforementioned circumstances hindered the Colombian government's ability to design and implement a comprehensive counterinsurgency strategy, the guerrillas appropriated a range of strategic concepts that allowed them to put in motion broad war plans. Thus, in 1966 the *Fuerzas Armadas Revolucionarias de Colombia—FARC* ("Revolutionary Armed Forces of Colombia") was founded by a mixed group of former liberal guerrillas and communist militants expelled from the Independent Republics. An insurgent organization whose ideology combined agrarianism and pro-Soviet Marxism, the FARC embraced the Vietnamese version of People's Warfare, known as Interlocking Warfare.[26] Two years earlier, a group of radical Marxist students, former liberal militants and popular Christian movement activists had already formed the *Ejército de Liberación Nacional—ELN* ("National Liberation Army"), inspired on Ernesto Guevara's Foco strategy.[27] A few years later, in 1968, a number of pro-Chinese dissidents from the Colombian Communist Party established the *Ejército de Liberación Popular—EPL* ("Popular Liberation Army") and followed the orthodox Maoist concept of People's War.[28] Finally, in 1973 another group of former Communist Party militants came together with leftist members of the populist *Alianza Nacional Popular—ANAPO* ("National Popular Aliance") party and give birth to the *Movimiento 19 de Abril—M-19A* ("April 19th Movement"), an organization based on Carlos Marighella's concept of urban guerrillas.[29] Hence, by the early 1970s the Colombian government was confronted by a broad range of insurgent organizations drawing their organizational and strategic orientation from the entire spectrum of revolutionary doctrines existent in Latin America: People's War, both in its classical Maoist conception and its Vietnamese version, Guevara's Foco strategy and Marighella's Urban Guerrilla.

INSURGENT STRATEGIES VERSUS GOVERNMENT TACTICS (THE 1970s AND 1980s)

Given the difficulties in implementing a comprehensive strategic plan due to the Lleras doctrine, the military opted for the pursuit of tactical victories with strategic implications, that is to say, operations aimed at the insurgents' military annihilation. This was the objective of an operation launched against ELN in 1974, when the insurgent group concentrated the bulk of its rural units in the municipality of Anorí and the Army devised an operation to destroy it. Based on massive troop deployments and intelligence-gathering, the Army initiated a prolonged "search and destroy" operation, integrating helicopters into troop movements. The operation's significant success was in good measure due to ELN's Foco strategy, since it tended to concentrate its forces in such a way that made them vulnerable if located and cordoned by the military. Government forces came close to the complete annihilation of ELN, through the deployment of a unit named *Comando Operativo No. 10* ("Operative Command No. 10"), which brought together five light infantry battalions, an air support component from the Air Force and another unit from the Naval Infantry, in what later was to become the conceptual basis for Mobile Brigades. At the end of the operation, ELN was reduced from its initial 150 combatants to 23,[30] but the lack of a national-level plan for exploiting operational success limited Anorí's strategic impact, since the few ELN militants left standing were allowed to disperse and regroup in the western plains. They remained there awaiting a new opportunity, which presented itself in the early 1980s when oil extraction began in the western department of Arauca, and the group soon found a way to profit from extortion. These shortcomings were explained by the absence of a national-level strategy which, in turn, was the result of two factors. First and foremost was the legacy of the Lleras doctrine, and second, the military's lack of sufficient resources to conduct a sustained, national-level campaign. Anorí thus made it clear that strategic plans could only be designed and thoroughly implemented when sufficient military resources were available; the lack thereof limited implementation to local or, at best, regional levels.

Since the early 1970s, the M-19A group set forth a strategy for developing a rural and an urban foco simultaneously. The urban structures were mostly dismantled by government forces by the early 1980s, based on the combination of military and police efforts in response to a series of spectacular operations carried out by the insurgents, including a massive arms theft operation from a military base and the seizure of the Dominican Republic's Embassy in Bogotá. Under intense pressure, M-19A moved the bulk of its operatives to its rural units, particularly in the Caquetá, Cauca, and Valle del Cauca departments.[31] In 1982, President Belisario Betancur initiated negotiations with M-19A while simultaneously strengthening the Army's presence in Caquetá, including the establishment of the 12th Brigade in the departmental capital, Florencia, alongside a more generalized use of helicopter support.[32] Once again, the Lleras doctrine entailed difficulties for the articulation of government efforts: as the civilian government was in the midst of negotiations, the military exercised increasing pressure in both the Caquetá and Cauca departments, yet neither did civilian negotiators use military pressure to their advantage, nor did the military carry out its operations in support of ongoing negotiations.[33] At the end of the day, M-19A was forced to the negotiating table due to the gradual loss of its military options as a consequence of the Army's operations in the Cauca region. Nonetheless, the group's near-defeat was not seized by the government as a strategic negotiating advantage, even as the group's remaining urban structures were neutralized after its infamous assault on the *Palacio de Justicia* in 1985 ("Palace of Justice," the Colombian judiciary's headquarters).

Once again, the government's campaign against M-19A insurgent group demonstrated the two main limitations of Colombia's counterinsurgency efforts: the lack of an integrated political-military strategy and the military forces' inability to carry out sustained, national-level operations. In this manner, the military struggle against ELN and M-19A bore results in good measure because, in both cases, the insurgents were concentrated in limited geographical areas. In fact, when the insurgents chose to concentrate their forces in relatively small areas, the military was able to locate them, surround them, and destroy them. However, when the insurgents were able to spread their resources across the territory and put into practice a nationwide strategy, the military proved unable to deliver significant successes.

ON THE BRINK: CHANGES IN THE STRATEGIC BALANCE (THE EARLY 1990s)

At the beginning of the 1990s the strategic context had changed both for the government and for the insurgents, due to a new Constitution drafted in 1991 with the participation of recently demobilized militants from the M-19A. The Constitution mandated a number of significant reforms in government structure, including broader controls on executive power, mandatory earmarking of a portion of the public budget to social programs and a new wave of administrative decentralization, all of which limited the government's ability to develop an integrated security strategy. These reforms, however, also served to restore government legitimacy and democratic credibility, thereby decreasing support for the insurgents' political agenda. The winds of change also brought about a significant innovation in terms of the counterinsurgency campaign: by appointing a civilian to the post of minister of national defense in 1991, President César Gaviria Trujillo signaled an effective break with the Lleras doctrine.[34] It seems difficult to overemphasize the importance of this reform for three reasons. For starters, a civilian in charge of the nation's defense policy could effectively integrate the political and military elements necessary in any counterinsurgent campaign, as he could transmit the military's needs to the political establishment as well as oversee the integration of military efforts into a broader plan. Likewise, the arrival of a civilian to the post bore an improvement in resource management to a large, complex, inertia-ridden bureaucracy. Finally, a civilian minister could push forth progress in joint military capabilities, as he was better able than his uniformed predecessors to act as a neutral mediator between the services, particularly given the Navy's and the Air Force's embedded suspicion of a far larger, powerful and budget-hoarding Army.[35]

In the meantime, various efforts had been made to augment the military's capacity to develop strategic-level operations. Thus, the 20th Army

Brigade had been created in 1986, effectively upgrading this service's intelligence structure from a battalion-level organization to larger, better-equipped system. With regard to combat units, a new type of counter-guerrilla formation was created, named the "Mobile Brigade" and composed entirely of professional soldiers organized in light infantry units, equipped with a light support structure and high mobility assets. These improvements in military capabilities were accompanied by the launch of the *Estrategia Nacional Contra la Violencia—ENCV* ("National Strategy against Violence"), a policy framework that integrated political measures, civic action programs, counterfinance measures, and military efforts into a comprehensive effort to pacify the country.[36] The ENCV succeeded in the northern state of Córdoba, when political and military efforts were combined to fight the EPL. In 1991, the newly formed Mobile Brigade No. 1 was deployed to the area in an operation that confirmed the military's augmented ability to conduct effective, sustained regional operations.[37] The following year negotiations were initiated and soon thereafter concluded with the Maoist group's demobilization.

As in the cases of ELN in Anorí and M-19A in Cauca, EPL was given a fatal blow, in no small measure due to the fact that it had concentrated its forces in an area where the military could deploy with overwhelming force. However, two major problems persisted in terms of counterinsurgency strategy. First, just as the military had gradually improved its ability to conduct regional operations, it still lacked the ability to conduct a sustained, national-level campaign against guerrilla forces that, while spread out across the country, had the ability to conduct large-scale operations (that was the case of FARC and ELN in the mid-1990s, as shall be seen later). Second, the government was still unable to consolidate its tactical gains into permanent ones, thereby avoiding fleeting victories and prohibiting the insurgents' return to any given area once government forces had left. This was the case of the campaign against EPL in Córdoba, where once the Maoist insurgents were expelled by the Army, FARC and illegal self-defense groups closely associated with narcotics trafficking rapidly stepped in to take control of the area. This lack of follow-up efforts in both time and space was aggravated when National Police Director, General Rosso José Serrano, initiated a plan in the mid-1990s to transform the police into a predominantly urban security and counter-narcotics force. This caused a functional vacuum, which became evident when numerous police units under increasing insurgent pressure retreated into large urban areas, leaving scores of small-town rural areas unprotected from the guerrillas.[38] At any rate, the ENCV did not live up to expectations, in good part because just a few years into the 1990s, the Colombian government had to confront the growing threat of narco-terrorism, led by Pablo Escobar and the Medellín cartel, who organized an armed group named *Los Extraditables* dedicated to reversing an extradition treaty signed by Colombia and the United States.[39] The ENCV's shortcomings also had to do with the military's still latent inability to conduct large-scale, national operations.

While the government forces' resource limitations became evident, FARC and ELN managed not only to survive through the past decade, but indeed thrived on the exploitation of three types of resources that became increasingly available between the late 1980s and the early 1990s. First was the widespread growth of the illegal narcotics business, supported by the growth of large-scale coca leaf plantations across Colombia's southern border. Second, though kidnapping for ransom had been an accepted tactic by guerrilla forces for quite a while, a wave of economic liberalization measures during the late 1980s permitted an unprecedented inflow of foreign investment into Colombia, making it possible for the insurgents to systematically target large multinational corporations for extortion and thereby develop a multimillion dollar business. Third, as part of successive civilian governments' attempts to promote democracy and social justice, in the late 1980s Colombia began a process of political and administrative decentralization. The end result was strategically disastrous, as the measures adopted meant the transfer of political, social and economic power to the lowest levels of local public administration which, given the already-mentioned limitations of Colombia's security forces, the government was incapable of protecting and thereby shielding from insurgent extortion or cooptation.[40]

Given this newfound availability of political, social, and financial resources, both FARC and the ELN embarked on broad strategies for expansion. Hence, during the course of its *VII Conferencia* ("Seventh Conference"), FARC designed a strategic plan for the overthrow of government and the seizure of power, which called for a 30,000 strong guerrilla army, the expansion of its structure, and the conduction of armed actions throughout the country. Following this plan, the group's militants increased from roughly 1,000 in 1982 to an estimated 7,000 by 1989.[41] ELN also pursued expansion plans, though not as ambitious as those of FARC. The *elenos* (ELN militants) did make a concerted effort to project the group's actions and expansion from the western Llanos toward the pacific coast and the south, leading it to grow from 190 militants in 1978 to 2,600 by 1990.[42] Beyond their numerical growth, both groups developed increasingly sophisticated methods of operation, as well as new tactical recipes. Most notably, FARC prepared to make the leap from guerrilla warfare to mobile warfare, including operations like large area ambushes and assaults on military bases. These strategic innovations were supported by newly created battalion-type combat units called *Columnas Móviles* ("Mobile Columns") and special operations forces, such as the *Columna Móvil Teófilo Forero*.[43] Meanwhile, ELN's attempt to emulate this strategic leap failed due to its more limited access to resources and problems with organizational cohesion.

In light of the above combination of the military's operational limitations, the insurgents' strategic leap, and the general deterioration of security conditions due to narco-terrorism, the stage was set for a broad security crisis. This was evidenced by the FARC's success in a series of large-scale operations launched against military bases and combat units between 1994 and 1998, as was the case of its attack on Las Delicias military base (August 1996), its seizure of the Cerro Patascoy military outpost (December 1997), its ambush of an entire counterguerilla company in El Billar (March 1998) and its assault on the National Police's Miraflores counter-narcotics base (August 1998).[44] Further complicating the scenario, the Colombian government's need to concentrate its efforts on combating FARC opened a window of opportunity for ELN growth, making it a strategic freerider. At the same time, the deteriorating security situation and the expansion of narco-trafficking stimulated the emergence of powerful illegal self-defense groups. This development brought about two negative consequences for the conduct of the counterinsurgency campaign: an erosion of government legitimacy among certain population groups and the involvement of a minority portion of the military in the activities of the self-defense groups. Thus, by the end of the 1990s the Colombian conflict had evolved into a three-sided war, wherein the democratic government was pitted against, on one end, two groups of determined, well-financed insurgents and, on the other end, an array equally well-financed and brutal self-defense groups.

TURNING THE TIDE: CONFRONTING THE CRISIS AND MILITARY REFORMS (THE LATE 1990s)

The widespread perception of a security crisis instilled strong reactions across the Colombian political spectrum. This was particularly true within the military, leading to a number of reforms that would permit a dramatic shift in the strategic scenario years later. Based on the premise that FARC was the premier threat to national security, correcting the military's inability to anticipate and counter the insurgents' concentration of forces prior to launching an attack was established as the first order of business. This amounted to acknowledging that the FARC had developed a superior ability to concentrate and project its military resources in remote areas of the country, thereby allowing it to seize removed military outposts by surprise with overwhelming force superiority, in a manner that was both more agile and speedy than the military's response capabilities.

In this context, reforms were initiated to provide the military with better instruments to anticipate large guerrilla concentrations and counter them, thus denying the insurgents the ability to conduct large-scale operations. This was done by procuring significant upgrades in the military's existing intelligence, mobility, and firepower assets, as well as by restructuring its personnel system. With regard to the latter, measures were taken to build a professional fighting force, increasing the number of volunteer soldiers from a few thousand in the mid-1990s to 55,000 by 2002.[45] This growth in professional personnel allowed the Mobile Brigade model, successfully tested against the EPL in Córdoba, to be significantly expanded. This increase in the number of available Mobile Brigades, in turn, allowed for the creation of the *Fuerza de Despliegue Rápido—FUDRA* ("Rapid Deployment Force"), a division-level force made up of three Mobile Brigades and a Special Forces Brigade. Personnel reforms were accompanied by the creation of the Army's own airlift unit, the *Brigada de Aviación* ("Aviation Brigade") in 1995, a unit equipped primarily with transport helicopters aimed at providing the Army with its own airmobile capability, thus sidestepping traditional interservice rivalries between it and the Air Force, upon whom ground units had traditionally depended for such capabilities.[46] It is worth noting that because this capability was initially built up with a combination of Colombian and U.S. funds, until 2002 the American-funded share of the fleet was restricted to missions directly tied to the United States-led counter-narcotics effort in Colombia. Despite these restrictions, the helicopters' availability for counter-narcotics missions allowed Colombian aerial assets to be freed for counterinsurgency operations. With respect to the military's intelligence capabilities, following a series of human rights violation accusations, the 20th Brigade was dissolved and the *Centro de Inteligencia Militar de Ejército—CIME* ("Army Military Intelligence Center") was created in its place, with a renewed emphasis on the use of technical intelligence resources.[47] Finally, a crucial reform was made throughout the personnel education and training programs, with a new emphasis on counterinsurgency operations, exemplified by the Army's publication of its first-ever field manual dedicated exclusively to irregular warfare in 1999.[48] Though slower than other reforms in reaping visible benefits, changes made in education and training contributed to a slow but steady improvement of the Colombian military's battlefield performance.

The military's reforms were first battle-tested in 1998, when FARC concentrated more than 1,000 combatants and launched an attack on the town of Mitú, capital of Vaupés, a western border department deep inside the Amazon basin. Though the guerrillas managed to take hold of the town for a period of 24 hours, the military was able to drive out the insurgents and cause significant casualties before they were able to disperse their forces.[49] After the iconic battle, FARC was never again able to successfully launch equivalent large-scale operations, characteristic of mobile warfare. At any rate, though Mitú marked a turning point in the counterinsurgency campaign, its impact on the strategic scenario was not immediately felt, due to the beginning of peace conversations between President Andrés Pastrana Arango and FARC later that same year. Part of the government's concessions so that dialogue could begin was the establishment of a 42,000-kilometer demilitarized zone (DMZ), which FARC subsequently used to store and accumulate weapons, train new units, and launch nationwide operations. This opportunity for resource accumulation allowed the insurgents to deploy in 2001 four battalion-size mobile combat units, which were put into operation using the DMZ as a strategic rearguard.[50]

The schizophrenia between the military modernization process and the government's pursuit of peace negotiations amounted to the resurrection of the Lleras doctrine, wherein civilian leaders in government pursued peace while the military waged war, with little or no coordination between the two. The final outcome was doubly frustrating: on one hand, military operations were handicapped by the group's ability to use the DMZ as a safe haven; on the other hand, government negotiators failed to capitalize the State's military superiority to their advantage. At any rate, the failed peace process came to an end in February 2002, when President Pastrana ordered the military occupation of the DMZ by means of Operation *Tanatos*. Though massive and well-executed, Tanatos did not represent a relevant blow to FARC, as the group's commanders had been anticipating the negotiations' breakdown and had ordered the area's gradual evacuation prior to the military's offensive.

Following the failed peace talks, the election of Álvaro Uribe Vélez to the presidency in 2002 marked a new phase in the evolution of Colombian counterinsurgency practice. Soon after reaching office, Uribe Vélez set down the guiding principles of the *Política de Defensa y Seguridad Democrática—PDSD* ("Democratic Security and Defense Policy"), an institutional heir of the ENCV launched by the Gaviria government a decade earlier. Based on the priority accorded by the Uribe administration to the resolution of the Colombian conflict, the PDSD delineated a comprehensive effort aimed at exerting military pressure on the country's illegal armed groups simultaneously with a standing offer for demobilization.[51] Thus, the PDSD set the basis for increased budgetary support of the military effort and for direct coordination of all political and military elements of the campaign. In fact, these two fundamental policy instruments— military pressure and political concessions for demobilization—were used in a variety of stick-and-carrot combinations with regard to each of the main armed groups. While FARC's refusal to negotiate with the Uribe Vélez government made it the primary target of a sustained military campaign, the ELN began negotiations in late 2005, following a slow but steady process of attrition. The illegal self-defense forces, in turn, began negotiating as early as 2003, a process that culminated with their complete demobilization in 2005.

In military terms, the PDSD did not incorporate many conceptual innovations per se, but it did bring together, organize into a coherent whole, and secure proper financial support for a number of existing ideas. Thus, the campaign's primary objective reflected a traditional strategic principle of counterinsurgency called "area control" or "territorial control." This concept emphasized the importance of reasserting military control over territory and population, based on the premise that if the insurgents where cut off from their civilian support bases, they could be located, pressured and, if necessary, destroyed with relative ease. Therefore, the campaign incorporated an operational concept whereby counter-guerrilla forces grouped into Mobile Brigades were tasked with sweeping insurgent territory and clearing it from guerrilla combat forces. Once the task was completed, police and locally recruited security forces were deployed in lieu of the counter-guerrilla units, to consolidate government presence and authority. The effort was complemented by limiting the insurgent's freedom of movement, through the deployment of High Mountain Battalions across the passes used by guerrillas in the Andean mountain chain as well as the implementation of a road-protection program named *Plan Meteoro* ("Meteor Plan").[52] At the same time, a number of Naval Infantry units were tasked with controlling river transit, protecting local commerce from insurgent raids and denying the guerrillas freedom of movement in the densely interconnected river systems of Colombia.[53] The simultaneous, articulated, and sustained execution of the above efforts amounted to the military's first strategic campaign plan since General Ruiz Noboa's Plan Lazo decades earlier. The magnitude and geographical scope of the programs carried out under the PDSD, however, had no comparable precedent in Colombian military history.

It is difficult to overstate the strategic impact of the PDSD. Not only did it bring about a significant reduction in violence levels across the country, but it also dealt significant blows to the insurgent forces, such as the destruction of FARC's forces deployed around the capital, by means of operation *Libertad I* ("Freedom I").[54] As the campaign developed, however, some of its shortcomings made themselves known, as explained below.

First, it seems increasingly clear that the military's concept of operation against FARC was to a large degree based on its past successes against ELN in Anorí, M-19A in Cauca, and EPL in Córdoba. Thus, the basic operational concept called for encircling the area where the enemy's main force was concentrated and overwhelming it with superior troop numbers and firepower. In the case of FARC, for this purpose, an 18,000-strong task force named *Fuerza de Tarea Omega—FTO* was put together by joining the FUDRA with large Air and Naval Infantry units. In the hope of dealing a definitive blow to FARC, this force was deployed in the sparsely populated southern part of the country, where the insurgents kept their main combat units and logistical infrastructure.[55] The operation, however, had mixed results: on one hand, large quantities of equipment and infrastructure were destroyed, yet on the other hand, guerrilla casualties and captures were limited. Explaining these results requires a look at FARC's strategic tradition. Because the group's military behavior follows the dictates of People's War, time is considered a strategic asset that plays in their favor, and large-scale battle is shied away from unless optimal conditions are met. Therefore, FARC avoided a direct confrontation with a potentially catastrophic impact on its survival, and chose to redeploy its main units to various regions in Nariño and Putumayo. For these reasons, the end result of FTO's deployment was the destruction of FARC's physical support infrastructure in the Caquetá and Guaviare departments but, contrary to military plans, no decisive victory was achieved. The operation was a relevant success, but not a total victory.

A second increasingly visible limitation is that the PDSD's implementation has strained personnel and financial resources near their limits. In this sense, the policy seems to have become a victim of its own success, since steady improvements in general security conditions have made a greater share of the public reluctant to invest additional resources in consolidating a campaign already deemed "successful." Likewise, the military's rapid increase in troop levels was largely done at the expense of shorter training cycles and further pressure on an officer corps already too small for the size of the force under its command.[56] In fact, by early 2006 the officers-to-troops ratio was the lowest in 15 years, with obvious negative effects for troop performance in the context of decentralized, politically sensitive operations, typical of any counterinsurgency campaign.

A third issue that limited PDSD's effectiveness has to do with FARC's proven ability to adapt to changing strategic circumstances. The group's abandonment of mobile warfare and its return to guerrilla warfare operations after 2002 meant the reduction of its force exposure, combat contact, and attrition rates. Therefore, the PDSD's military campaign had to face the challenge of sustainability. FARC's return to guerrilla warfare put a strain on the security forces, whose limited resources did not permit decreasing marginal returns in operational efficiency. Given the above circumstances, it seems clear that the PDSD brought about major improvements in the recent conduct of Colombia's counterinsurgency campaign, but it should also be understood that, 4 years after being put into practice, this policy demands a strategic review.

LOOKING AHEAD: TOWARD A STRATEGIC REVIEW OF CURRENT COUNTERINSURGENCY EFFORTS

In light of the above analysis, the current status of Colombia's counterinsurgency efforts appear to demand a careful review aimed at adapting the military's strategy to the evolving security environment. This section brings together a number of policy recommendations for said purpose.

For starters, it seems worthwhile to differentiate geographical areas in terms of their relative political and economic relevance as well as the varying degrees of insurgent presence therein. This should serve to maximize the operational impact of military resources, by discriminating and prioritizing areas of operations based on prior assessments of the government's objectives and observed threat levels. In particular, areas recently "cleared" of guerrilla presence demand specialized treatment, focusing on the effective consolidation of government presence and authority. Without proper consolidation, insurgents may return to old territories, so the government must devise a strategy that denies the guerrillas this possibility. Colombia is, however, a vast and geographically fragmented country, so whatever structure is put forth must be both robust and financially viable. Furthermore, strategic differentiation of the territories should entail efforts to restructure of the military's current deployment. This process should take into account insurgent redeployment patterns across different areas of the country, adjusting the security forces' structure based on the increase or decrease of insurgent presence and activity.

In a related matter, the military's accelerated growth has caused an imbalance in the officers-to-troops ratio, an issue of particular importance in counterinsurgency if one keeps in mind the long-established principle of centralized decision-making and decentralized execution. This becomes ever more relevant given an operational context defined by the internal nature of the conflict and the high density of civilian presence in most operational theaters. At the same time, the current trend of diminishing operational efficiency as a consequence of the insurgents' return to guerrilla-type operations requires increasingly flexible close air support as well as changes in infantry units' tactics, equipment, and organization. All of these factors constitute sufficient grounds for a careful review of the military's current growth rates and the adoption of measures aimed at consolidating force professionalism.

One final aspect that ought to be included in a strategic review is a reformulation of the campaign's evaluation metrics. The long-lived and much criticized system of body counting remains stubbornly embedded as the cornerstone of the campaign's evaluation system, despite the fact that it has been discarded as unsatisfactory by most modern counterinsurgency theorists and practitioners. More so, given Colombian insurgents' return to guerrilla warfare and their intentional avoidance of frontal engagement with government forces, the body counting system on its own has become pointedly inadequate. Naturally, it will remain necessary to measure the number of enemy combatants killed and captured, but complementary metrics such as local threat levels and the mid-term impact of operations should be integrated as common measures of campaign progress.

11. For a thorough look into the events that led *Rojas* to power, see: Silvia Galvis y Alberto Donadio, *El Jefe Supremo: Rojas Pinilla en la Violencia y en el poder* (Bogotá: Planeta, 1988) 249–256.

12. A comprehensive account of the impact of US military cooperation on the Colombian military during the 1950s can be found in: Saúl Mauricio Rodríguez Hernández, *La influencia de los Estados Unidos en el Ejército colombiano: 1951–1959* (Bogotá: La Carreta Editores, 2005).

13. Eduardo Pizarro Leongómez, "La profesionalización militar en Colombia (III): Los regímenes militares (1953–958)" in *Análisis Político*, no. 3 (Enero-Abril 1988): 20–39.

14. Pardo (2004): 407–411.

15. Ramsey: p. 239.

16. See, for instance: Robert Thompson, *Defeating Communist Insurgency: Experiences from Malaya and Vietnam*, (London: Chatto & Windus, 1966).

17. Francisco Leal Buitrago, *La seguridad nacional a la deriva. Del Frente Nacional a la Posguerra Fría* (Bogotá: AlfoOmega, CESO–UNIANDES, FLACSO, 2002).

18. Gerald Templer, cited by Simon Smith, "General Templer and Counter-Insurgency in Malaya: Hearts and Minds, Intelligence and Propaganda" in *Intelligence and National Security* 16, no. 3 (Autumn 2001): 60–78, p. 65.

19. Pardo (2004).

20. On the importance and utility of coordinated command authority in counterinsurgency operations, see: John Deverell, "Seguridad rural: la experiencia Británica en Irlanda del Norte" in *El rol de la Policía Nacional de Colombia en escenarios de conflicto y posconflicto—Documentos de trabajo 2: Seguridad rural, algunas experiencias internacionales*, comp. Nicolás Urrutia (Bogotá: Fundación Ideas para la Paz—Grupo Editorial Semana, forthcoming).

21. César Torres del Río, *Fuerzas Armadas y Seguridad Nacional* (Bogotá: Planeta, 2000).

22. Fuerzas Militares de Colombia—Ejército Nacional, "Apuntamientos y experiencias contra bandoleros", *Revista de infantería* 7 (1964).

23. Rigoberto Rueda Santos, *De la guardia de fronteras a la contrainsurgencia: elementos de la evolución política e institucional del Ejército Colombiano, 1958-1965* (Bogotá: Instituto Colombiano de Fomento a la Educación Superior, 2000).

24. Ramsey: p. 235.

25. In the view of Francisco Leal, the design and implementation of defense policy came to be regarded by elected officials as a strictly technical matter, thus making it unnecessary and even counterproductive for them to have an active role in the process. In this sense, just as macroeconomic policy was largely left to the hands of nonsectarian technocrats, defense and security were left to uniformed men. See: Francisco Leal Buitrago, *El oficio de la Guerra – La seguridad nacional en Colombia* (Bogotá: TM Editores, 1994) 91.

26. See: Román D. Ortiz, "La guerrilla mutante" in *En la encrucijada: Colombia en el siglo XXI*, ed. Francisco Leal Buitrago (Bogotá: CESO—UniAndes—Grupo Editorial Norma, 2006) 323–356.

27. See: Carlos Medina Gallego, *ELN: una historia contada a dos voces* (Bogotá: Rodríguez Quito Editores, 1996).

28. See: Pardo (2004): pp. 441–444.

29. Ibíd.: pp. 459–465.

30. Hernán Hurtado Vallejo, "Operación Anorí: golpe al corazón del ELN" in *Hablan los generales*, comp. Glenda Martínez Osorio (Bogotá: Norma, 2006) 145–174.

31. In Colombia, a "state" in the sense of Texas or California is called a "department."

32. Pardo (2004).

33. For an insider's account of the process' coordination difficulties, see: Rafael Pardo, *De primera mano. Colombia 1986-1994: Entre conflictos y esperanzas* (Bogotá: CEREC—Grupo Editorial Norma, 1996) 93–146.

34. See: Pardo (1996): pp. 311–350.

35. Insufficient attention has been paid to budget-related interservice rivalries in Colombia. However, preliminary research seems to indicate a complex dynamic of bureaucratic interests. See: Nicolás Urrutia, "Una segunda mirada al presupuesto militar: ciclos de adquisiciones y desarrollo tecnológico" in *Documentos de coyuntura GESED*, 2006, http://seguridadydefensa.uniandes.edu.co.

36. For a summary review of the early 1990's reforms, see: Leal (1994): pp. 127–162.

37. Hugo Tovar, "Operación final contra el EPL" in *Hablan los generales*, comp. Glenda Martínez Osorio (Bogotá: Norma, 2006) 191–203.

38. For a look into the Police's internal debates on this matter, see: Llorente: pp. 457–460.

39. See: Pardo (1996): Chapters 7, 13, 14.

40. This argument is thoroughly presented in Ortíz: pp. 326–330. Also, empirical research on the strategic effects of decentralization can be found in: Fabio Sánchez y Mario Chacón, "Conflicto, Estado y descentralización: del progreso social a la disputa armada por el control local" in *Documentos CEDE*, 2005-33 (Bogotá: CEDE-UniAndes, 2005).

41. Paul E. Saskiewicz, *The Revolutionary Armed Forces of Colombia People's Army (FARC-EP): Marxist-Leninist Insurgency or Criminal Enterprise?* (Monterey, CA: Naval Postgraduate School, 2005) 32–33. It is worth noting that, according to official figures, FARC would grow to have approximately 17,000 men-in-arms by the late-1990s. See: Centro de Información Estadística–Ministerio de Defensa Nacional, *Logros y retos de la Política de Defensa y Seguridad Democrática*, 2006, Agosto, http://www.mindefensa.gov.co.

42. According to some analysts, this growth allowed ELN to augment its "combatant fronts" from 7 in 1978 to 38 by 1989. See Peñate: p. 86.

43. See, for instante: Román D. Ortíz, "Revolutionary Strategies in the Post-Cold War: The Case of the Revolutionary Armed Forces of Colombia" in *Studies in Conflict and Terrorism* 25, no. 2 (March–April 2002): 127–144.

44. Andrés Villamizar, *Fuerzas Militares para la Guerra. La agenda pendiente de la reforma militar* (Bogotá: Fundación Seguridad y Democracia, 2003) 21–24.

45. Centro de Información Estadística–Ministerio de Defensa Nacional.

46. For a detailed account of reforms carried out during this period by the Colombian military, see: Thomas Marks, *Colombian army adaptation to FARC insurgency* (Carlyle, PA: Strategic Studies Institute—U.S. Army War College, 2002).

47. See: Andrés Villamizar, *La reforma de la inteligencia: un imperativo democrático* (Bogotá: Fundación Seguridad y Democracia, 2004).

48. Fuerzas Militares de Colombia—Ejército Nacional, *Reglamento de operaciones en combate irregular* (Bogotá: Primera División, 1999).

49. Villamizar (2003): p. 25.

50. Ortiz (2006): p. 339.

51. Presidencia de la República–Ministerio de Defensa Nacional, *Política de Defensa y Seguridad Democrática* (Bogotá: Ministerio de Defensa Nacional, 2003).

52. Ministerio de Defensa Nacional, policy briefing, April 2003.

53. Informal interview with RA Luis Alfredo Yance Villamil, Commander, Colombian Naval Infantry, February 2004.

54. For an insider's account of the operation, see: Reinaldo Castellanos, "Operación Libertad Uno: la política de Seguridad Democrática en acción" in *Hablan los generales*, comp. Glenda Martínez Osorio (Bogotá: Norma, 2006) 311–334.

55. A summary overview of the military's findings of significant support infrastructure in the south can be seen in: Carlos Alberto Ospina, "El Plan Patriota como Estrategia Militar" in *Sostenibilidad de la Seguridad Democrática* (Bogotá: Fundación Seguridad y Democracia, 2005) 41–50.

56. For a recent analysis of the negative effects brought about by the Colombian military's rapid growth, see: Fundación Ideas para la Paz, "Las condiciones de la tortura" in *Siguiendo el conflicto*, no. 41 (March 3, 2006): 6–10, http://www.ideaspaz.org.

CHAPTER 19

THE WARS IN CHECHNYA AND THE DECAY OF RUSSIAN DEMOCRATIZATION

Thomas Sherlock

Chechen separatism and terrorism, which have deeply scarred the political landscape of post-Soviet Russia, both reflect and accelerate the withering of Russian democratization.[1] This chapter explains the origins of the Chechen crisis, assesses the costs to Russian pluralism of the Kremlin's efforts to pacify Chechnya, and suggests what the West might do to help resolve one of Russia's most important political problems.

It is not surprising that the most unstable region in post-Soviet Russia is the North Caucasus, which had been a fiercely contested outpost of tsarist expansion in the nineteenth century. Over a period of four decades (1816–1856), the Russian state encountered strong resistance from the mountain nationalities of the region, particularly the Chechens. The Chechens, who are a distinct ethnic group (but closely related to the neighboring Ingush), are the largest group in the North Caucasus (with around 1 million inhabitants, according to the 1989 census), and the second largest ethnic group in the Caucasus as a whole (after the Georgians).

In this initial, brutal encounter with Russia, Chechen civilian casualties were high, and forced, mass deportations from the Caucasus to the interior of Russia were common. Hundreds of thousands of members of these communities fled to Turkey and other regional states. This pattern of extreme violence by the Russian state against the Chechens occurred again in early 1944, when the Chechen nation—now part of the Soviet Union—was accused by Stalin's regime of mass collaboration with the Nazi invaders. The Chechens were deported en masse to Siberia, Kazakhstan, and Kyrgyzstan. The collective memories of these calamitous events have shaped Chechen identity and the Chechen "Othering" of the Russian state and the Russian people.

At no point in the post-Soviet period has Russian policy toward Chechnya been guided by a consistent recognition that the Chechen people suffered greater political, physical, cultural, and economic repression under the tsars and Communists than perhaps any other ethnic or religious group in the Russian empire or the Soviet Union. This legacy of almost two centuries of historical grievances against Russia largely accounts for Chechen secessionism in the 1990s and for the ferocity of Chechen resistance to Russian attempts to quell the Chechen rebellion.

Although memories of tsarist and Soviet oppression fueled the Chechen bid for independence from Russia, it was the weakness of the Russian state as it emerged from the collapse of the Soviet Union that permitted Chechen separatists to calculate that secession had good prospects for success. This movement had gathered strength in 1990 and 1991 under former Soviet Air Force General Dzhokhar Dudaev, although it is unclear precisely how widespread the support for secession was in the republic. Dudaev refused to negotiate a federal treaty with Yeltsin's administration that would have provided Chechnya full autonomy within the Russian Federation similar to arrangements negotiated with Tatarstan.

In late 1993, the Russian government under Yeltsin launched the first of two invasions of Chechnya. It is likely that the first conflict was a case of "diversionary war," motivated more by political considerations than concerns for territorial integrity.[2] According to the literature on diversionary war, embattled leaders and elites may instigate hypernationalist programs and perhaps initiate war to attract elite and popular support. For example, Sergei Witte remarked on the eve of the Russo-Japanese War that what the tsar needed was "a short, victorious war" to restore his prestige and weaken the growing revolutionary movement in Russia.

Edward Mansfield and Jack Snyder suggest that similar political motives were at work in Russia's First Chechen War (1994–1995). In their discussion of "Weimar Russia," Mansfield and Snyder argue that recently empowered voters injured by Yeltsin's market reforms and privatization cast their ballots in droves for ultranationalists like Vladimir Zhirinovsky, putting ostensible liberals like Yeltsin and Foreign Minister Andrey Kozyrev on the defensive and contributing "to the climate that led to the [first] war in Chechnya [1994–1996]."[3] At the same time, embattled old elites, particularly from the Army and the security forces, saw an invasion of Chechnya as a means to restore their sagging legitimacy and advance their standing in the budgetary struggles of the post-Soviet period.[4] Other factors doubtless also played a role in the decision to invade, including Moscow's desire to reclaim the significant oil resources of the region.

Expecting a quick victory, the Russian Army entered Chechnya over-confident and unprepared both in terms of planning and provisions. Chechen fighters inflicted a series of humiliating defeats on Russian forces,[5] eventually leading to a political settlement in August 1996. That agreement, signed for the Chechens by Aslan Maskhadov, the most famous of the Chechen generals, stipulated the withdrawal of Russian troops, followed by long-term negotiations as to the future status of relations between Russia and Chechnya. Chechnya's status was not to be determined before December 31, 2001.

THE SECOND CHECHEN CONFLICT: JUST WAR OR DIVERSIONARY CONFLICT?

For the Chechens, the price of their victory over Russia was high. The war caused widespread devastation and social dislocation in Chechnya, and the reparations for reconstruction promised by Russia never materialized, not least because Moscow had difficulty keeping its own fiscal house in order. Although the Chechens elected Maskhadov as president in a free and fair election in 1997, he was unable to govern the territory with any effectiveness. The collapse of civil order in Chechnya was evident in rampant smuggling operations, trade in white slavery, and ransom kidnapping of Russian citizens and journalists by numerous Chechen gangs. During the period 1996 to 1999, over 1,300 Russian citizens, mostly from neighboring Dagestan, were abducted.[6]

The primary source of instability was the struggle among Chechen political elites over the future of Chechnya. Prominent Chechens who were commanders in the first Chechen War, including Shamil Basayev, increasingly denounced Maskhadov—who envisioned a nominally independent Chechnya but with close political and economic ties to Russia—as a traitor to the Chechen cause. The wave of kidnappings was partly due to the efforts of radical Chechens to undermine Maskhadov's efforts at cooperation with Russia and with Western aid organizations. Twenty-two humanitarian workers were assassinated and over twenty were kidnapped during this period. These attacks culminated on March 5, 1999, when General Gennady Shpigun—the Russian Interior Ministry representative in Chechnya—was seized at the Grozny airport by masked gunmen. As NGOs began to leave Chechnya in fear and disillusionment, President Maskhadov failed to restore order.

Conviction, as well as political expedience, led many of Maskhadov's opponents to embrace Muslim fundamentalism at this time and form alliances with the numerous mujahideen from Afghanistan and elsewhere who were drawn to Chechnya by the Russian invasion of 1994 and the prospect of a holy war against Russia and the West. In 1998, a political and military union was struck between three forces: Basayev and his Chechen followers; Ibn-ul-Khattab, the Arab leader of international mujahideen in Chechnya; and Islamic radicals from neighboring Dagestan. The Arab mujahideen were primarily of Saudi Wahhabi background, and many were also veterans of the Afghan war against the Soviet Union. They had financial resources, battle experience, and a fervent commitment to undermining Russian rule throughout the Caucasus. Although Maskhadov attempted to counter the spread of radicalism by more publicly embracing Islamism himself, this defensive measure promoted an unintended spiral of political outbidding that ultimately strengthened Islamic radicalism, while also alienating the West and moderates in Russia. For example, after his election Maskhadov introduced Islamic law (sharia), leading to widespread and public corporal punishment and even to executions broadcast on local television.[7]

Islamic militancy in Chechnya was also buoyed by the tentative spread of Islamic radicalism among ordinary Chechens made desperate by the socioeconomic and political disorder that followed the war with Russia. Their search for security led some of them to embrace the idea of an "Islamic order," weakening Chechnya's strong traditions of secularism and moderate Sufism. Yet another source of destabilization was the growth of radical Wahhabism in a number of villages in neighboring Dagestan. In April 1998, these extremists formed the Congress of Peoples of Chechnya and Dagestan for the purpose of joining the two Russian republics in an Islamic state.

Border skirmishes beginning in April 1999 between Russian and Chechen forces culminated in early August 1999 with the invasion of neighboring Dagestan by several hundred Chechen, Dagestani Wahhabis, and other Muslim fighters who seized several villages. Yeltsin dispatched Vladimir Putin, his newly appointed Prime Minister, to restore order in Dagestan.[8] On September 5, it was reported that 2,000 additional Chechen fighters had crossed the Dagestani border to support the initial invasion. However, by mid-September all of the invaders had been dislodged from Dagestan by massive Russian air and ground assaults, which laid waste to much of the contested area.

Amid the crisis in Dagestan, a terrorist bombing campaign was launched against civilian targets in Russian cities. On August 31, a bomb exploded in the Manezh shopping area near Red Square. On September 9 and September 13, powerful bombs destroyed two apartment buildings in Moscow. And on September 16, another bomb exploded near an apartment building in the city of Volgodonsk. Almost 300 people died in these explosions.

Although no group claimed responsibility for these terrorist acts, the bombings served as the proximate cause for Russia's second invasion of Chechnya. Russian authorities blamed Chechen rebels for the explosions, and declared they would wipe out the source of terrorism in Chechnya.

Military operations commenced against Chechnya, and aerial attacks on Grozny occurred on September 23. Nevertheless, Russian journalists and Western analysts remained unconvinced by the Kremlin's accusations and blamed the government itself for the blasts, which were viewed as efforts to provoke popular outrage and justify a second invasion of Chechnya.[9]

Did the Second Chechen War begin as a just war or as a diversionary conflict? The bombings *did* galvanize Russian public opinion for military action and the invasion of Chechnya *did* serve the political interests of the Kremlin. Most important, the invasion provided Yeltsin with an exit strategy from his failing presidency. Allegations of corruption had dogged Yeltsin in 1999, and members of his family and circle of advisors were placed under investigation abroad. In May 1999, the Duma started impeachment proceedings against Yeltsin, accusing him of high treason and other crimes. Although Yeltsin survived this ordeal, only 12 percent of Russians were happy with the outcome.[10]

On New Year's Eve 2000, Yeltsin resigned his office, making Putin—his appointee as Prime Minister—the acting president according to the provisions of the Russian constitution. Within 24 hours, Putin extended immunity to Yeltsin and his family, who had been threatened with corruption investigations both at home and abroad.[11] By this time, the war in Chechnya had made Putin enormously popular and the ideal shield for Yeltsin. A former lieutenant colonel of the *Federalnaya Sluzhba Bezopasnosti* (FSB)—the Federal Security Service, the domestic successor to the *Komitet Gosudarstvennoy Bezopasnosti* (KGB) or Committee for State Security—Putin had been plucked from obscurity to head that agency in 1998 and was then appointed prime minister in 1999. The surprise of Yeltsin's resignation also made it unlikely that Russian political society would have sufficient time to field a viable challenge to Putin in the presidential elections that were now rescheduled for March 2000. Thus, the Second Chechen War created conditions that protected Yeltsin from criminal investigations and all but ensured the election of Putin, his protégé and presumed protector, as president.

Despite the continued belief of many Russians and Western analysts in a government conspiracy, it is more likely that the terror bombings were set off by Islamic militants, such as Basayev and Khattab, to advance their campaign to create a united Chechen-Dagestani Muslim state.[12] Convinced that Russia was a paper tiger after its defeats in Afghanistan and in the First Chechen War, the Chechen militants believed that a second war with Russia would destroy the political center in Chechen politics and propel them to power at the head of an independent trans-Caucasus Islamic state.

The steady descent of Chechnya into anarchy over the preceding 2 years, and the dramatic incursions into Dagestan from Chechnya (followed by the terror bombings) were ample justifications for a military response from Moscow to curb Chechen radicalism and bring a semblance of order to a region still legally part of the Russian state (the only states to recognize Chechen independence were Afghanistan under the Taliban and the Turkish Republic of Northern Cyprus, which itself was recognized only by Turkey).

However, Russia's conduct in the second Chechen conflict was strongly influenced by domestic politics. Yeltsin and Putin abandoned the initial goal of fighting terrorism soon after the beginning of the invasion. Moscow refused to exploit the deep political rifts in Chechen ranks or to join forces with President Maskhadov against the Chechen militants, despite Maskhadov's repeated entreaties to the Kremlin for support in his struggle with radicals like Basayev. Nor did Moscow demonstrate any interest in tapping the war-weariness of the average Chechen, who was either indifferent or hostile to Muslim radicalism—the proclaimed target of the Russian invasion. Instead, the Kremlin prosecuted a war of unrestrained brutality, which it justified by the demonization of the Chechen people in the state-controlled media. Putin refused to rein in the Russian Army, whose rampage in Chechnya was clearly retribution for its humiliating defeats in the First Chechen War. Putin personally encouraged the brutality of the army by coarsening public discourse ("We will kill them all in the shit house") and by placing strict limitations on Russian and foreign press coverage. In the words of Sergey Parkhomenki, the editor-in-chief of the Russian magazine *Itogi*, "The wonder and triumph of Putin rest not only on the blood of innocent people who have perished in Chechnya . . . but on a cold-blooded policy aimed at exploiting the gloomy shadows residing in the hidden corners . . . of 'everyday' nationalism."[13] Thus, the launching of Second Chechen War was justified as a response to significant military provocations, particularly the invasion of Dagestan from Chechnya by Chechen radicals led by Shamil Basayev and his jihadist allies. But the unrestrained prosecution of the war, which led to widespread loss of life and homelessness among the Chechen population, subsequently undermined the Kremlin's claim that it was engaged in a just conflict.

The political interests of Yeltsin and Putin and the prestige considerations of the Russian Army best explain the dramatically broadened scope and objectives of the war. Just as the terror bombings in Moscow and the incursions of Chechen and Dagestani radicals into Dagestan in 1999 helped Yeltsin to hand-pick Putin as his successor at a time when all other political options appeared exhausted, the launching of the Second Chechen War by the Kremlin enabled Putin as president to use Russia's "war on terror" to legitimate the Kremlin's attacks on democratic institutions and freedoms in Russia.

Russian civil society, including the independent media, suffered significant losses during this period and remains under constant political pressure. One of the notable features of the First Chechen War was the determination of Russian journalists to expose the Kremlin's lies and misinformation on the course of the war as well as the vast cost of the conflict in blood and treasure.[14] By contrast, the Second Chechen War has seen a much higher degree of support among the Russian media. This support is partly due to the widespread belief—after the apartment bombings in September 1999 in Moscow and elsewhere—that Chechnya now poses a serious threat to the national security and territorial integrity of Russia. But direct and indirect government pressure on the media has also played an important role in marginalizing criticism of the Kremlin in its efforts to use the war in Chechnya to generate political support. Although the evidence does not support the accusation that Yeltsin and Putin manufactured pretexts for the invasion of Chechnya in September 1999, it is clear that the Kremlin seized the opportunity for war once it presented itself in the form of the terror bombings the previous month. Kremlin spokesman, Sergei Yastrzhembsky, spelled out the politicized nature of the war: "When the nation mobilizes its forces to achieve some task, this condition imposes obligations on everyone, including the media."[15]

The Russian state has used the cover of antiterrorism to attack other segments of Russian civil society in order to curb potential political opposition and dissent. In December 2005, the Duma (legislature) approved a bill that places strict controls on nongovernmental organizations in Russia. The bill, which was signed into law by Putin the following month, provides for a new state agency to oversee the registration, financing, and activities of thousands of foreign and domestic NGOs. The new agency, not the courts, will determine the legal status of an NGO. Supporters of the proposed law, which requires NGOs to continually account for their activities to the government, argue that the measure is necessary to identify groups that support terrorism and extremism. But opponents say the law will further cripple Russian civil society. They maintain that the legislation stems from the Kremlin's hostility to NGOs that criticize Putin's authoritarianism and might support a Russian "color revolution," recalling the mobilizing role of indigenous and foreign NGOs in Ukraine, Georgia, and Kyrgyzstan.[16] Pro-government commentators openly admit that the law was meant to forestall efforts to establish a "Western version of democracy in Russia."[17]

ONE STEP FORWARD, ONE STEP BACK: PUTIN'S CHECHENIZATION STRATEGY

Using overwhelming and often indiscriminate firepower in the Second Chechen War against a Chechen force that was internally divided (unlike the First Chechen War), the Kremlin eventually achieved a measure of success in its struggle to re-conquer the breakaway republic. By 2001, a harsh militarized peace had been imposed: Government or pro-government republican forces controlled the urban areas of Chechnya and a pro-Kremlin Chechen administration was installed in Grozny, the capital.

Although the shrinking numbers of Chechen insurgents were forced into the rugged countryside, they often ranged freely after nightfall, attacking the Russian "occupiers" and the militias of the Chechen "puppet" government and its supporters. Underlining the fragility of the occupation, Akhmad Kadyrov—the Chechen mufti who was appointed by Putin in 2000 to head the interim civilian administration, and was later elected president of the Chechnya in October 2003—was assassinated in May 2004. Equally important, the radical wing of the Chechen insurgents continued to launch spectacular and gruesome terror assaults against Russian civilian targets, not only in neighboring regions but also in Moscow.

The worst episode of terrorism was the attack by Shamil Basayev, the most effective and brutal of the Chechen rebels, on the schoolhouse in the town of Beslan, in the Russian republic of North Ossetia. The ensuing battle between the rebels and government forces led to the deaths of over 350 adults and children.[18] Ruslan Aushev, the former president of the neighboring republic of Ingushetia, served as an intermediary during the siege of the schoolhouse and later provided a sobering assessment of the prospects for peace in the region. According to Aushev, the continued mistreatment of the Chechen population by Russian forces and their proxies was constantly replenishing the insurgency with new, increasingly fanatical recruits. Only if the Kremlin was willing to negotiate in good faith with moderate insurgents could the new "fanatics" be isolated and the cycle of violence be arrested. Otherwise, political unrest and terrorism would continue to spread to other parts of the Caucasus, and perhaps beyond.[19] Similarly, other Russian observers argue that revenge—not radical Islamism—is the primary source of terrorism (and support for terrorism) in the Caucasus. Oleg Orlov of the *Memorial Society*, Russia's leading human rights organization, followed this line of thinking in his explanation for why Chechen women were becoming suicide bombers, detonating their explosives on Russian commercial airliners and in Moscow's subway and on its streets.

Orlov places much of the blame on the *zachistki*, the violent operations conducted by Russian forces and their Chechen allies searching for rebel forces, which have inflicted widespread murder, rape, and torture on the local population. Another important catalyst for rebellion are the undocumented kidnappings of suspected Chechen rebels or sympathizers by security forces, which according to Orlov now equal the number of similar abuses committed at the peak of the Stalinist repression in 1937–1938. These intolerable conditions have left Chechen society "completely unprotected.... People are angry. Some of them start sympathizing with terrorists; others... start helping them. There is a mass of insulted, humiliated, and desperate people." Increasing numbers of Chechen women who had lost their husbands, parents, or children to "state terror" often see suicide bombing as the "only recourse."[20]

Khassan Baiev, a Chechen physician who risked his life treating both insurgent and Russian casualties in the Second Chechen War and who later received political asylum in the United States, provides a more complete picture of the losses suffered by Chechen society since the first Chechen War:

> About one-quarter of our population has been killed since 1994. Fifty percent of the Chechen nation now live outside Chechnya... Estimates claim that 75 percent of the Chechen environment is contaminated.... Pediatricians report that one-third of children are born with birth defects.[21]

Despite its support for the inhumane conduct of the Russian Army in the Second Chechen War, Putin's government has gradually moved closer to understanding that brutality breeds extremism and that a political solution—not simply fear and violence—must be part of any plan to pacify Chechnya. To that end, the Kremlin inaugurated a policy of "Chechenization" in 2001 with the purpose of drawing Chechens into Moscow-supported institutions that would govern the republic and direct its reconstruction. Elections for a new president were held in 2003 and parliamentary elections took place in December 2005. To support this process, Putin criticized the gross mistreatment of the Chechen nation by the Soviet and then post-Soviet Russian state, and has suggested that such abuse was partly to explain for the extreme hostility of many Chechens toward Russia. Most important, in an address before Chechnya's newly elected republican parliament, Putin publicly deplored Stalin's deportation of the Chechen nation to the steppes of Central Asia in 1944.[22] Shortly after the tragedy at Beslan, Putin also admitted to a group of journalists that the First Chechen War "was probably a mistake," and seemed to grasp the importance of political compromise in resolving the problem of Chechen separatism.

For some Chechens, Putin's willingness to tell the truth about the deportations of 1944 seemed to open to the door to authentic political reconciliation. Indeed, Moscow's greatest potential asset in finding a political solution in Chechnya is the Chechen people, who have been traumatized by more than a decade of conflict, insecurity, and deprivation. Understanding the hard choices before them, most Chechens now reject secession and the goal of an independent Chechnya. In a recent authoritative survey, 78 percent of Chechens said that Chechnya should remain one of the 89 regions of Russia.[23] Only 19 percent of those polled felt that Chechnya should pursue independence.

The complication for the Kremlin is that 61 percent of the respondents would support Chechnya remaining part of Russia only if Chechnya was given "more freedom" than any other constituent part of Russia. Responding to this widespread opinion, Putin has promised that a policy of "Chechenization" would establish genuine autonomy based on electoral legitimation as well as the devolution from the center of significant powers to the republic, even to the point of "violating the Russian constitution."[24]

Despite the extensive publicity given to Chechenization by the Kremlin, it is doubtful that Putin's plan will bring lasting stability to the region. While it is true that the new Chechen constitution sponsored by the Kremlin in 2003 provides more autonomy to Chechnya than to any other regional government in Russia, many Chechens question the durability of such powers at a time when the federal center has been aggressively reducing the rights of the other federal "subjects." Skeptics in Chechnya need look no further than next door, to the Russian Republic of Ingushetia, where Ruslan Aushev—the republic's popular and independent-minded president—had demonstrated considerable skill in weakening local radical Islamism and more generally keeping the potentially explosive multiethnic republic at peace through effective socioeconomic and cultural policies. Despite his impressive performance, the Kremlin forced Aushev to resign in December 2001, and engineered the election of Murat Ziazikov—a general in the FSB—as the new president of Ingushetia. Ziazikov has relied on coercion and intimidation to neutralize Islamic radicalism in the republic, which has inadvertently worked to inflame extremism. Although Putin has installed other leaders in the North Caucasus who are genuinely popular, competent, and apparently honest (such as Mukhu Aliyev, the President of Dagestan), the Kremlin's record of appointments in the region reveals a preoccupation with maintaining above all else political loyalty to Moscow.

Even if Chechnya is exempted from Putin's efforts to recentralize power in the Kremlin and reduce Russian federalism to window-dressing, there is much else that is flawed in his plan for stabilizing Chechnya. The essential missing ingredient in this political process is inclusiveness: not only rebels but also peaceful advocates of separatism have been excluded from participation in the elections. Yet as the experience of the Irish Republican Army and other separatist movements has shown, progress becomes possible only when the staunchest opponents of compromise are offered a role in the political process.

To make matters worse, by all accounts the presidential and parliamentary elections that Russia supervised in Chechnya were not free and fair, even in terms of the limited field of candidates who were permitted to run. The Kremlin threw its weight behind Alu Alkhanov and Ramzan Kadyrov, the son of the assassinated president. After the apparently fraudulent electoral victory of Alkhanov, Kadyrov was appointed his deputy prime minister. Although Alkhanov has earned the respect of many Chechens for his commitment to economic recovery and stability in Chechnya, Kadryov is widely feared. Within the government, Kadyrov has wielded significant and independent power, not least because he commands perhaps the largest of the private militias that now vie with Russian forces and other Chechen militias for control of key sectors of Grozny and other parts of Chechnya.

Appointed prime minister in March 2006, Kadyrov has tightened his grip on Chechen politics. His militia (the "kadyrovtsy") is held responsible by Chechens and knowledgeable Russian and foreign observers for widespread kidnapping, torture, murder, extortion, and other crimes. Kadyrov, who is a vocal supporter of governing Chechnya by Sharia law, has been accused by human rights groups of personally torturing his victims. Although such lawlessness and atrocities cripple the prospects for reconciliation between Chechnya and Russia and among Chechens themselves, Kadyrov operates with impunity in part because the Kremlin has strongly supported his leadership.

The death of Aslan Maskhadov in Chechnya at the hands of Russian security forces in March 2005 marked the loss of another opportunity to work for a durable peace in Chechnya. The killing of Maskhadov, who was elected president of Chechnya in 1997 and had led Chechnya's underground separatist government after 1999, was dramatic evidence that the Kremlin held fast to imposing a political settlement on Chechnya on Russia's terms. Although Maskhadov's death was hailed by the Kremlin as a victory in the war against terrorism, Russian human rights groups pointed out that Maskhadov had consistently opposed the use of terrorism as a political tool and had never abandoned his efforts to negotiate with the Kremlin. Although Maskhadov had fought a losing battle with Chechen extremists such as Basayev from 1997 to 1999, and did not possess sufficient authority to speak for all of the rebel factions fighting Russian forces after the outbreak of the Second Chechen War in August 1999, he did represent authentic moderation and still commanded widespread respect among the Chechen population. While in office, Maskhadov had spoken in favor of secular education in Chechnya and against Islamic fundamentalism. With the rise of Muslim radicalism and terrorism in 1999, Maskhadov sought Russian help to defeat the alliance of religious fundamentalists and radical secular separatists, but Moscow rejected his appeals.

A brief window of opportunity to broker a peace deal between Russia and Chechnya opened in August 2001, when delegations from the Russian Duma and Maskhadov's underground government met for secret talks in Caux, Switzerland, and the following year in Liechtenstein. The meetings were sponsored by the American Committee for Peace in Chechnya

(ACPC), an American NGO chaired by former National Security Advisor Zbigniew Brzezinski, former Secretary of State Alexander M. Haig, Jr., and former Congressman Stephen J. Solarz. The organization is dedicated to finding a peaceful solution to the Chechen conflict, but nevertheless remains extremely critical of Russia.

The ACPC-sponsored talks produced a draft agreement that stipulated that Chechnya would remain legally a part of Russia, but would enjoy a maximum degree of authentic self-rule. Although plans were made to present the draft formally to the Kremlin, Putin suddenly and inexplicably disowned the plan as the work of Boris Berezovsky, the rogue Russian oligarch living in self-exile in the United Kingdom.[25]

The Kremlin's unwillingness to negotiate with the Chechen resistance has been strengthened by the killing of key Chechen leaders in 2006 by Russian security forces. Abdul-Khalim Sadulayev, Maskhadov's successor as Chechen president, was killed in June 2006. In July 2006, Russian forces killed Basayev himself in an operation southeast of Nazran, the capital of Ingushetia. Despite these events, it is still too early to predict an end to the secessionist movement in Chechnya. Although clearly weakened by the loss of its top leaders, and suffering from increased fragmentation as well as significant defections to the pro-Russian government in Grozny, the Chechen resistance still appears to attract sufficient recruits to remain a threat to stability in the North Caucasus.[26]

The consequences of Russian brutality and the Kremlin's refusal to implement an inclusive political settlement are compounded by the Kremlin's failure to address adequately the disastrous social and economic conditions that beset Chechnya. Disease is rampant, and the lack of basic necessities is a chronic and widespread problem. Alkhanov, the pro-Russian president of Chechnya, openly complained that the "70% jobless rate [in Chechnya] drives young men desperate to earn money into the arms of rebels fighting Russia."[27]

Andreas Gross, the Swiss representative of the Parliamentary Assembly of the Council of Europe (PACE), traveled to Chechnya in November 2005 to observe unofficially the Chechen parliamentary elections. Gross was not surprised that the elections were "not free or fair." Observing that the ordinary voters he spoke to on election-day were wracked by constant fear for their lives, Gross traced the multiple problems facing Chechnya to Russia's wrong-headed policies and to the unrestrained power of Kadyrov and his followers:

> The absence of security can undermine any election. That is why it is so important to include opponents in the process and to take over the control of security forces that do not obey the elected government and are not under the jurisdiction of the Courts. Moreover, a majority of the population is unemployed. That is why it is so important to restore the economy, the village,

and the spirit of the people. There is money for these goals, but . . . it is stolen by corrupt officials.[28]

WHAT IS TO BE DONE?

Promoting democratization in Russia and working to resolve the crisis in Chechnya are important goals for the West. Yet the West must recognize the limits of its influence in both areas. Russia is too large and also geo-graphically too distant for the democratic international community to play a decisive role. If a state is self-sufficient, or nearly so (as is Russia), and possesses a vast base of natural resources, its rulers can more easily refuse to consider political reforms that might improve state capacity but may also weaken their rule. Such rulers can also skillfully exploit the reliance of external actors on trade or strategic cooperation with their country (in Russia's case, European reliance on its energy resources or America's de-sire for Russian acceptance of U.S. bases in Central Asia) to moderate or fend off international demands for internal reforms. A dramatic illustra-tion of this point was the decision of Gerhard Schroeder, the recently de-feated German chancellor, to take a high position with GAZPROM, the huge Russian gas conglomerate.

Furthermore, location matters, even in the era of globalization. The con-siderable distance of Russia from Europe's institutionalized democracies reduces the ability of the West to pressure or encourage Russia to change. It must also be doubted whether core Western institutions such as the EU and NATO have the capacity to absorb a country as large as Russia into their ranks.

Finally, the recent, unexpected and tumultuous "revolutions" on Rus-sia's borders are viewed as threats by Russia's ruling elites, who are in-creasingly drawn from the security services since Putin's accession to power, and who worry that Russian influence is yet again receding in post-Soviet space. Democratization in Ukraine, Georgia, and Kyrgyzstan may very well be the harbinger of new, stable democracies on Russia's borders—with the potential one day for powerful, positive demonstration effects on domestic politics in Russia itself. That would be an historical irony indeed, as the former subservient republics of the Soviet empire help advance political change in the former metropole. But for now the "color revolutions" are stark reminders to Russia's rulers of the inability of the Russian state to control events in contiguous states that were recently constituent parts of the Russian and Soviet empires. Such perceptions of vulnerability strengthen the desire to treat the problem of Chechnya as a completely "internal" matter.

Given the realities noted above, the Kremlin is unlikely to heed Western calls to explicitly "internationalize" the Chechen problem, either through the United Nations or another international body that might supply peacekeepers and police.[29] This is especially so given the altered configuration of elites under Putin and the installation of officials who are deeply suspicious of the West. Although the Russian leadership was particularly sensitive to Western pressures and preferences in the early years of the Yeltsin administration, under Putin that proclivity no longer exists.

Dedicated human rights advocates in both Russia and the West respond that the West has never adopted a consistent hard-line toward Russia on the question of Chechnya, and that sustained pressure and threats of ostracism from Western institutions stand a good chance of yielding results. Yet even sympathetic policymakers in the West must weight the potential costs and benefits of such a strategy, and may fear that Russia will weaken its support for global security norms, particularly the prohibition of the spread of weapons of mass destruction (WMD). Specifically, Russia might complicate Western efforts to pressure North Korea or Iran to abide by international nonproliferation regimes.

This does not mean that no useful policies or leverage are available to the West, but it does mean that the West should have a balanced and consistent approach to the twin problems of Russian democratization and Chechnya. The West should not oscillate between condemnation and approval of Russian behavior in Chechnya, even in the face of dramatic intervening events, such as the terror attacks of 9/11, which led Washington to adopt generally supportive language regarding Kremlin policies in Chechnya.

While holding Russia publicly and privately accountable for atrocities committed in Chechnya by Russian and pro-Russian Chechen forces, the West should reassure the Kremlin of its support for Russia's territorial integrity. Although Putin has politicized and "instrumentalized" the crisis in Chechnya, it is also clear that Putin and Russia's political elites—already shaken by the "color revolutions"—fear that instability in Chechnya will spread throughout the Caucasus. As noted above, these fears are not unfounded, given the increased political unrest and violence that is spreading beyond Chechnya to the North Caucasus as a whole.

Clear support for Russia's territorial integrity is in the interest of the West and the vast majority of Chechens. Chechnya is far from possessing the political, civic, or administrative institutions to support an independent state. An independent Chechnya would quickly descend further into the anarchy that marked the period 1996–1999, but with a difference. The stillborn Chechen state would be home to even larger numbers of criminals, traffickers, and predatory politicians and bureaucrats. Perhaps most important, radical Islamists—both Chechen and non-Chechen—would have a secure base from which to spread the gospel of jihad throughout the Caucasus.

The policy options available to the West are familiar but nevertheless important. The expansion of NATO and the European Union eastward since the fall of communism has fostered political stability and democratization in their new and prospective members. NATO should continue this advance and step up negotiations with Ukraine and Georgia over the terms for entry into the organization. Entry into NATO will not only help anchor both countries to the West, but also bring the West and its democratic culture closer to Russia.

Although NATO is not an ideal vehicle for spreading Western democratic culture, its further expansion to Georgia and Ukraine, if done with care and transparency, is likely to be accepted, however grudgingly, by Russia's political elites. Nevertheless, it is clear that Russia's relations with the West, particularly the United States, have deteriorated significantly over the course of 2006. Engaging in "soft balancing," Russia has increasingly attempted to counter American influence in former Soviet space, particularly Central Asia. Flush with oil wealth and emboldened by American difficulties in Iraq and Afghanistan, the Kremlin has strongly criticized Washington for pursuing a hegemonic foreign policy thinly disguised by the rhetoric of democracy promotion. In order to counter such reactions, the United States must take care as it presses Russia to democratize in order to avoid being perceived as "hypercritical, hypocritical, or excessively meddlesome."[30] To this end, NATO enlargement should be accompanied by serious efforts on the part of the West to empower more fully institutions, such as the NATO-Russia Council, that provide Moscow with increased visibility on NATO decision making as well as opportunities to cooperate on a range of important issues, including terrorism and proliferation.

The West must also relearn the importance of human-to-human contacts between Russia and the West as an important measure to further develop a democratic culture in Russia. The West should also step up its business investments in Russia for two important reasons. First, investments will help nurture the Russian middle class and hopefully stimulate the growth of a democratic political culture. Second, investment is important for its injection of Western managerial expertise and its attendant emphasis on transparency and good governance in the marketplace.

Western pressure on Russia over Chechnya, which has never been strong, has visibly weakened as Russia has asserted its role as a leading energy supplier but also as the insurgency in Chechnya has lost the support of most Chechens, leading to a significant reduction in political violence in the republic. Yet it seems likely that political stabilization in Chechnya has struck only shallow roots, and that popular support in Chechnya for secession will reignite if Razman Kadyrov, Moscow's anointed leader in the republic, fails to alleviate the profound socioeconomic problems that continue to beset the republic. Also of concern is the fact that as insurgency has waned in Chechnya, it has waxed in neighboring republics. Although Chechen militants have assisted in this development, it is clear that local Islamic radicals are taking the lead in North Ossetia, Ingushetia, and Kabardino-Balkaria. In the North Caucasus as a whole, Russian federal and local authorities have contributed significantly to this development by persecuting observant Muslims as likely insurgents, by failing to address endemic poverty and joblessness, and by promoting widespread corruption.

Given the nationalistic and increasingly anti-American tenor of the Kremlin's official discourse, the United States by itself could not change Russian policy in Chechnya and in the North Caucasus as a whole even if Washington decided to push strongly in that direction. Policies such as the careful expansion of NATO and an increase in economic ties with Russia will improve conditions in the North Caucasus only indirectly and only if they help move Russia toward authentic democratization over time. Yet it remains the responsibility of the West to forcefully remind Russia that the establishment of representative and legitimate political institutions in the North Caucasus would constitute the most effective and just response to the rise of ethnic and religious violence in the region.

ACKNOWLEDGMENTS

The views expressed herein are those of the author and do not purport to reflect the position of the United States Military Academy, the Department of the Army, or the Department of Defense.

NOTES

1. This chapter draws on the author's chapter 4 in Cindy R. Jebb, P.H. Liotta, Thomas Sherlock, and Ruth Margolies Beitler, *The Fight for Legitimacy: Democracy vs. Terrorism* (Westport, CT: Praeger, 2006).

2. On diversionary war, see Jack Levy, "The Diversionary Theory of War: A Critique," in *Handbook of War Studies*, Manus I. Midlarsky, ed. (Boston, MA: Unwin Hyman, 1989) 259–288.

3. Edward Mansfield and Jack Snyder, "Democratization and War," *Foreign Affairs* 74, no. 3 (May/Jun 1995): 79–97.

4. For an informed alternative argument for the First Chechen War as a political diversion, see Peter Reddaway, "Desperation Time for Yeltsin's Clique," *New York Times*, January 13, 1995: 29.

5. For example, please see the chapter on the Chechen siege of Grozny, by James Robbins, in this volume.

6. See Robert Bruce Ware and Ira Straus, "Media Bias on Chechnya," *Christian Science Monitor*, March 15, 2000.

7. For a balanced assessment of conditions in Chechnya at that time, see Sergei Kovalev, "Putin's War," *The New York Review of Books*, February 10, 2000. On Stephasin's statement, see Andrew Jack and John Thornhill, "Chechnya Assault 'A Long-Term Plan,'" *Financial Times*, January 31, 2000. Stepashin elsewhere argued that planning for a limited invasion of Chechnya began after the Russian

general, Gennady Shpigun, was kidnapped by Chechen rebels. See Jamie Dettmer, "Stepashin Joins Putin Bandwagon," *Insight*, February 25, 2000.

8. Matthew Evangelista, *The Chechen Wars: Will Russia Go the Way of the Soviet Union?* (Washington, DC: Brookings, 2003) 62–64.

9. Yelena Skvortsova, "Blown Up Space," *Obshchaya Gazeta*, March 16, 2000. Translated and reproduced in *Johnson's Russia List*, no. 4189.

10. "Fund of Public Opinion," *Bulletin*, May 26, 1999.

11. For Putin's decree, see *Johnson's Russia List*, January 8, 2000.

12. Alexander Lebed accused the then Prime Minister Putin and President Yeltsin of engineering the incursion into Russian Dagestan by Chechen militants. As for the apartment bombings, Alexander Korzhakov, Yeltsin's former body-guard, accused oligarch Boris Berezovsky, who was closely connected to Yeltsin, of responsibility for the bombings. See Julie Corwin, "Lebed Posits Secret Agreement between Basayev and Russian Leadership," *RFE/RL Caucasus Report* (September 30, 1999); and Natalya Shuyakovskaya, "Korzhakov Says Bombings Were Bere-zovsky's Doing," *The Moscow Times*, October 28, 1999: 1. It should be recalled that the Russian press had accused Korzhakov of instigating the First Chechen War. For another account that blames the Kremlin for orchestrating the incursion into Dagestan and the urban bombings, see Igor Oleinuk, "Vlast Ostaiotsia v Rukakh 'Sem'i,'" *Novaya Gazeta*, January 10, 2000.

13. As quoted by Roy Medevedev in "Getting to Know Putin," *Rossiyskaya Gazeta*, March 11, 2000. Reproduced in *Johnson's Russia List*, no. 4188.

14. On the First Chechen War, see Stephen J. Blank and Earl H. Tilford, Jr., *Russia's Invasion of Chechnya: A Preliminary Assessment* (Carlisle Barracks, PA: U.S. Army War College, 1995).

15. See Masha Gessen, "Lockstep to Putin's New Military Order," *New York Times*, February 29, 2000.

16. "Russian Parliament Approves NGO Bill in Final Reading despite Criti-cism," *Mosnews*, December 23, 2005.

17. Vladimir Simonov, "Russia Devises Protection against Color Revolutions," *RIA Novosti*, November 24, 2005.

18 Please see the chapter on the Beslan attack, by Adam Dolnik, in this volume.

19. As recounted in Mark Kramer, "The Perils of Insurgency," *International Se-curity* 29, no. 3 (Winter 2004–2005): 61.

20. *Mosnews.com* at http://www.mosnews.com/feature/2004/09/01/terror. shtml. For Orlov's account of Russia's inhumane prosecution of the First Chechen War, see O.P. Orlov and A.V. Cherkasov, *Rossiia—Chechnya: Tsep' Oshibok i Prestu-plenii* (Moscow: Zveni'ia, 1998).

21. Khassan Baiev, "A History Written in Chechen Blood," *Washington Post*, February 24, 2004: A21. Also see his *The Oath. Surgeon under Fire* (New York: Walker and Co., 2004). Baiev's book provides a valuable account of growing up as a Soviet Chechen and of life in wartime Chechnya, where he treated scores of Chechen and Russian combatants, including Shamil Basayev.

22. "Putin Makes a Lightning Visit to Chechnya's Capital," *Chechnya Weekly* 6, no. 47 (December 15, 2005). Available at http://www.jamestown.org/ publications_details.php?volume_id=409&issue_id=3567.

23. POLL: Validata.ru/e_e/Chechnya (August 2003); *Validata* "Public Opinion of the Chechen Population on the Actual Issues of the Republic" (March–August

2003),   http://www.validata.ru/e_e/chechnya/eng/chechnya_details_21.html (September 1, 2003).

24. For Putin's comments, see Fiona Hill, "Stop Blaming Putin and Start Helping Him," *New York Times*, September 10, 2004: A25.

25. S. Frederick Starr, "A Solution for Chechnya," *Washington Post*, September 17, 2004.

26. Liz Fuller, "Chechnya: Basayev's Death Poses Fateful Choice for Moscow," *RFE/RL*, July 10, 2006.

27. "Alkhanov: Poverty Helps Rebels," *Moscow Times*, November 2, 2004: 2.

28. "Chechnya Parliamentary Vote Goes as Planned," *Chechnya Weekly* 6, no. 45 (December 1, 2005). Available at http://www.jamestown.org/ publications_details.php?volume_id=409&issue_id=3554.

29. For a similar proposal see Leon Aron, "Responding to Terrorism," *AEI Online*, September 1, 2004.

30. For a discussion of recommended changes in U.S. policy toward Russia, see John Edwards and Jack Kemp, chairs, *Russia's Wrong Direction: What the United States Can and Should Do* (New York: Council on Foreign Relations, 2006).

CHAPTER 20

ITALY AND THE RED BRIGADES: THE SUCCESS OF REPENTANCE POLICY IN COUNTERTERRORISM

Erica Chenoweth

Many different forms of terrorism have troubled Italy over the past four decades. The grievances against the Italian government in the postwar period have generated political violence ranging from nationalist-separatist terrorism near the Austrian border in the South Tyrol area, to right-wing terrorism with neofascist tendencies, left-wing Marxist and anarchist terrorism, foreign Middle Eastern terrorism emanating from the Palestinian territories and other Arab lands, and Mafioso violence that has often contained quasipolitical elements. This chapter examines one terrorist group in particular—the Red Brigades—since it represents one of the most durable and evasive terrorist groups of the 1970s and 1980s in Italy. An investigation of the history of the Red Brigades illuminates the successes and failures of the Italian government in confronting the Red Brigades, providing several observations that should inform current U.S. policy in fighting terrorism and insurgency.

PROFILE OF THE RED BRIGADES: HISTORY OF A LEFT-WING TERRORIST GROUP

The second half of the 1960s was a period of great social unrest in Italy. The country was home to the largest Communist party in Western Europe, with a wide membership of students and workers. However, the postwar parliament had been dominated by the center-right Christian Democrat (DC) party, with left-wing parties such as the Italian Communist

Party (PCI) in virtually permanent opposition. The lack of alternation in government is the oft-cited reason why the Italian system gave rise to violent political extremism within the student movements of the period.

Origin and Early Activities: 1970–1976

Left-wing terrorism originated out of the declining social protest movements existing in Italy during the 1960s. Sidney Tarrow describes the common encounters that created the atmosphere out of which terrorism emerged:

> Violence occurred most often when left-wing students encountered right-wing students in the schools or on the streets. The pattern was set up as early as April 1966.... Typically, a group of leftist students would occupy a school; subsequently, fascist youth groups would attack them, defending the "right to study" and bashing heads in the process. These groups would later encounter each other on the streets, disrupt each others' public meetings, or lie in wait for one another outside their parents' homes. Violence between competing social movements made the streets dangerous and provided a background in violence for many future terrorists.[1]

The continual tit-for-tat exchange between right- and left-wing radicals soon earned the phrase "strategy of tension." This phrase refers to the way that the extreme right and extreme left interacted, adopting a "strategy of tension" to prevent one another from obtaining too much influence in public opinion and forcing an electoral outcome. In truth, however, the neofascist groups enjoyed sympathy within the repressive bodies of the government as well as from external supporters, such as the United States, which were interested in preventing a Soviet infiltration of the Italian polity. Indeed, in 1948–1949 several neofascists within Italy had formed a secret program called "Gladio," a NATO-supported band of paramilitary units, which was unknown even to the Italian parliament until four decades later.[2] Gladio was to be deployed in the event of a communist revolt within Italy, during which NATO would hypothetically support Gladio operatives in a military coup that would restore Italy to its democratic path. Such was the political atmosphere in which the left-wing terrorist groups, including the Red Brigades, would eventually take form.

However, there were more immediate events that led to the decision by leftist groups to use violence. On December 12, 1969, a bomb exploded on the Piazza Fontana in Milan, killing 14 and injuring 80 people. The government initially assigned blame to leftist student groups, which were widespread in Milan and in other industrial cities throughout Italy. However, later revelations confirmed that the bombing was actually the work of neofascist groups who were intending to provoke a reaction within the government to resort to more repressive means vis-à-vis communists within Italy. Even more shocking was the discovery that Italian officials—particularly in the law enforcement and secret services—were conspirators in the bombing, suggesting shadowy forces at work. This theme of government complicity in neofascist violence was to arise repeatedly throughout the history of the Red Brigades, often legitimating their battle in their own eyes.

The PCI, expected by its communist members to react to the Piazza Fontana incident with outrage, instead became increasingly more moderate as a response to the coalition dynamics and a need to attract new members with less extreme persuasions. While the PCI moved toward the center and the DC persisted in dominating parliament, left-wing protest groups became more radical. Mention of the Piazza Fontana bombing appeared in numerous documents of left-wing extremist groups for the next several years.[3] Hostility toward both the DC and the PCI increased among left-wing groups during this time, who argued that the DC was defending right-wing terrorist groups and sponsoring repressive police tactics in quieting student demonstrations, while the PCI was useless in preventing such transgressions.[4]

The *Brigate Rosse* (Red Brigades, hereafter BR) arose out of this milieu, forming among discontented PCI members and radical students in 1970. The *brigatisti* (as BR members called themselves) who made the decision to use violence as a means of political expression were apparently disillusioned by the continual immobility of the parliamentary system, which was often engaged in policy gridlock due to the fragility of the ruling coalitions.[5] Bonds of solidarity formed within networks of social and political activity appeared to influence the individual and collective decisions to resort to terrorist violence, rather than conventional political means of expression.[6]

The pronounced goal of the BR was "to provoke a fascist takeover of power in Italy that in turn would bring Italian communism back to its revolutionary stance betrayed by the historical compromise" between the PCI and the DC.[7] In a 1971 publication entitled *Classe contro classe, guerra di classe* ("Class against class, class war"), the BR described their self-proclaimed purpose as: "groups of armed propaganda whose fundamental task is to gain the solidarity and support of the proletarian masses for the Communist revolution . . . to reveal the most hidden power structures and the conniving between power groups and/or apparently separate institutions."[8]

Terrorist activities began in 1972, as the BR grew from a small faction to a large organization with a wide external support base. Within 4 years, the BR consisted of more than 600 full-time terrorists operating in city columns in Milan, Rome, Naples, Genoa, and Turin, which were subdivided into "brigades" with three- to five-members "cells."[9] This organization into independent cells, combined with groups of people performing auxiliary operations and large groups of sympathizers within society, shaped the BR into a "serious challenge" to Italian society over the next 15 years.[10]

Initially, the BR primarily targeted managers of industrial concerns, right-wing trade unions, and right-wing interest groups.[11] Interestingly, however, the BR were regarded as a mere nuisance among politicians, and little notice was given to them by the elites who were occupied by the struggle to maintain the unity of coalitions in government.

By 1974, the BR decided that the group's objective was no longer the mere "exposure" of the hidden maneuverings of power or the "punishment" of enemies of the collective movements; the terrorist organization set itself the task of attacking and destroying capitalist power itself.[12] Thus, in 1974–1975, the BR began to attack and kidnap government officials in an attempt to draw more attention to the group and its grievances.

The BR adopted a two-fold strategy in selecting its targets during this period. On one hand, the BR decided to "strike one to educate a hundred" by injuring dozens of local and regional DC officials, which reflected the desire of the BR to dislocate the state by intimidating intermediate-level political personnel. The second tactic was to adopt a more "direct confrontation" in order to eliminate the political opponents whom they considered to pose the greatest threat to the BR's plans.[13] During the same period, there was a subsequent escalation of violent attacks, especially in light of increased activities by right-wing terrorist groups.

In fact, an intense dynamic of competition between terrorist groups in outbidding one another for new recruits, resources, and attention drove the terrorists to escalate their activities throughout the life of the BR.[14] This competition existed not only between groups on the left and right, but also between groups of similar ideologies. For instance, one of the most fearsome rivalries existed between Prima Linea and the BR, both of whom were left-wing terrorist groups with similar objectives. It is vital to note that regardless of ideological and strategic similarities, terrorist groups operating within democracies are likely to compete with one another for recruits, financial support, and attention. This competition creates a constant incentive to monitor, anticipate, and counteract one another's activities, which often leads to an escalation of propaganda and attacks—in frequency and in lethality.[15]

From 1970–1974, the Italian government underestimated the BR and the problem of terrorism in general, despite several high-profile attacks conducted by right-wing terrorist groups during this period. These attacks sometimes implicated police and secret services members, and to make matters worse, investigations into these events were often stymied by cover-ups and corruption within the justice system. Thus, while the Italian government was generally ignorant of the destructive potential of the BR, elements of the state were involved in perpetrating terrorist attacks that fueled the anger of the BR. Subsequently, the BR scaled up their activities. Only after the BR began to focus on political personnel, such as a Genoan judge, did Rome begin to focus more on countering this terrorist group. By that time, however, the BR had already developed organizational capacity and momentum.

"The Years of Lead": 1977–1981

Members of the BR have referred to the period between 1977 and 1981 as "the years of lead." During this time, the BR was unified, active, and growing in strength. Furthermore, during this period, the BR carried out its most high-profile attacks.[16]

Between 1974 and 1979, the Italian government began to steadily increase its attention to the Red Brigades and other left-wing terrorist groups. There were two police groups involved: the Pubblica Sicurezza (PS) and the Armata dei Carabinieri (CC).[17] Within the secret services, two new specialized institutions developed: the General Inspectorate for Action Against Terrorism (*Ispettorato Generale per la Lotta contro i terrorismo*), and the Special Group of Judiciary Police (*Nucleo Speciale di Polizia Guardiziaria*).[18] The Ispettorato antiterrorismo was created by the home minister in 1974 to deal with the growing problem of internal political violence. Despite its name, however, the Ispettorato was not exclusively concerned with terrorism.[19]

The joint efforts of the Nucleo and the Ispettorato resulted in the first massive police offensive against terrorist groups around 1974–1975. This offensive resulted in the demise of several left-wing terrorist groups and the arrests of BR founders Renato Curcio and Alberto Franceschini.[20] It appeared that the first wave of left-wing terrorism had come to an end.

However, from 1974–1978, the government continued to underestimate the motives and capacity of the BR. In fact, after the successful raids of 1974–1975, both the Nucleo and the Ispettorato were dissolved in 1976 without explanation, and attention to terrorism subsequently decreased.[21] In the meantime, the BR had regrouped around fugitive militants and other left-wing sympathizers. Its operational capacity restored, the BR resumed its activity, pursuing high-profile targets.

In 1977, criminal legislation demonstrated a degree of political attention to terrorism. However, this attention was more focused on a so-called "general increase of criminal violence" rather than on terrorism in particular.[22] Moreover, the security system was "characterized by a very low level of control over security agencies by representative political bodies, such as the Parliament."[23] What security apparatus did exist was therefore unconstrained by normal democratic checks and balances, as it was fraught with corruption and mismanagement from within.

In fact, the entire intelligence system was modified in 1977 through legislation mainly intended to ensure stable political oversight over Italian intelligence services. This reform was put in place in response to revelations of police complicity in right-wing terrorist activities and other criminal endeavors—particularly the arrest of Vito Micelli, chief of the army intelligence service since 1969 and head of the secret service from 1970–1974, who was charged with conspiracy. The secret service was dissolved and replaced by two agencies with distinct responsibilities: the Servizio Informazioni Sicurezza Militare (SISMI), which was assigned to protect military security, and the Servizio Informazioni Sicurezza Democratica (SISDE), which was designated to oversee internal security. These agencies united under new rules that defined responsibilities, control, and coordination.[24] They were also placed under the direct oversight of Italy's interior ministry and the prime minister in 1980.[25]

Unfortunately, however, during the installation of these reforms, the operational abilities of this intelligence system were quite weak—especially due to a lack of coordination and sharing of information. Notably, this period of weakness in intelligence coincided with the height of the BR's terrorist activities. Certainly, the shifting of the bureaucracy contributed to vulnerabilities, which the BR exploited.

The lack of preparation and foresight experienced by the intelligence community at that time had its greatest consequence in the abduction of the president of the DC, Aldo Moro, in March 1978—an event that the intelligence system neither predicted nor prevented. The BR abducted Aldo Moro in a crowded Rome street, killing five of his bodyguards in the process. The Italian government refused to negotiate with the BR or pay a ransom on Moro's behalf. After the lengthy and dramatic crisis in which the BR held Moro hostage for several months, the former prime minister was executed and dumped into the streets of Rome. Indeed, the Moro case was a virtual disaster for Italian politics. It was especially disturbing that the government refused to negotiate for Moro's release, yet it conceded to the BR later for the release of another captive, Ciro Cirillo, in 1981. This mid-level official apparently possessed potentially damaging personal information about some high-level politicians that, if discovered, might mean ruin for their political careers. So a large ransom was paid for his release, igniting wide debate as to the neutrality of the government in waging a successful campaign against the BR and illuminating the endemic corruption within the political system.[26]

Terrorism scholars Gian Carlo Caselli and Donatella Della Porta argue that Moro's abduction "had a double objective: to mobilize the various armed groups working in Italy, pushing them to intensify their actions and to 'raise the level of attack,' and to provoke a climate of civil war that would facilitate some form of legitimation of the underground organization by the state institutions."[27] However, the abduction ultimately had the opposite effect on both fronts: not only did it cause many terrorists to become introspective concerning the armed struggle, but also it induced the national government to take the terrorist threat seriously and adopt appropriate counterterrorist measures that would ultimately lead to the downfall of the BR.

Thus, as Caselli and Della Porta observe, "in the period beginning in 1979, we see a series of internal splits and divisions, with long-lasting reciprocal antagonisms that sometimes ended in death threats and in the rather pathetic invitation to adopt a sort of federalism of armed groups that was not followed up."[28] In addition to the internal splits, there arose tension within the groups that resulted from living underground. Despite the increase in activity, BR terrorists were growing weary of the criminal lifestyle, and this weariness produced anxiety and frustration in addition to the ideological disagreements that tormented the BR. Such conflicts resulted in the first split of the BR in 1979.

This split constituted a severe risk for the militaristic hierarchy of the BR. Indeed, the leaders of the BR responded to such insubordination by releasing a document directed at the mutinous terrorists, entitled "Beat liquidationist opportunism and defeatist ideology."[29] In addition to internal tensions, according to Caselli and Della Porta, "the collapse of the web of solidarity within the organization had a deleterious effect on the network of external supporters who had in the past supplied the important logistic support."[30] The number of attacks by the BR during this time declined, but the severity of the attacks increased. Some argue, however, that the "real motivation for many of the terrorist crimes carried out during this period can be traced to the struggle among the various factions fighting over the hegemony of the leftovers of the organization."[31]

The weakness of the state intelligence system as a result of the 1977 reorganization lasted about 2 years.[32] However, the shift in attitude following the political kidnappings of 1978 generated several pieces of legislation that finally addressed the terrorist threat in a direct way. Stortini-Wortmann suggests that the "widening of police powers was considerable and a general shift of power from the judiciary to the police was introduced, even if for a limited time and restricted to particular crimes."[33] Moreover, new preventive measures came into effect in 1978. First, the home minister obtained the authority to ask for copies of legal proceedings and transcripts to prevent future crimes or to assemble them into a database. Second, the same decree declared that the police could collect limited information from suspects and detainees without requiring the presence of a defending attorney.[34] These decrees were enacted without much political discussion, deliberation, or consensus due to their urgency.

In a more repressive response, the government created the second Nucleo Dalla Chiesa, which was "directed to fill the operational gap in the existing police structures and to cope with terrorist organizations by tactics used by terrorists, first of all surprise and secrecy."[35] The Nucleo was quite efficient in its performance—it was mainly composed of CC members and had few bureaucratic constraints, since it responded directly to the home minister.[36] Its strength lay in its attempts to directly connect information, analysis, and operations.[37] Despite its immediate efficacy, however, Stortini-Wortmann argues that the Nucleo was quite undemocratic in its organization and methods, noting that there was little accountability or transparency concerning its tactics, and its creation was no more than "a response to citizens' emotional need to be reassured to the active response of the state."[38] This sort of response is common in crisis situations—to give a "non-elected figure large amounts of free rein and to pay little attention to the less satisfactory aspects of his approach."[39] In hindsight, some may rightly condemn the participation of secret police, the use of decrees, and few restrictions on such forces as undemocratic, since they lacked the transparency and accountability usually required of democratic institutions.

The Italian state also created groups to evaluate intelligence coming in from regional units and to develop profiles of the terrorists' ideological positions. One particularly informative practice was to compare different groups, their hierarchies, goals, tactics, and resource bases.[40] Moreover, special secret commandos—which were created between 1978 and 1979 inside both the CC and the PS—were deployed to terrorist emergencies and achieved some significant success, as with the liberation of U.S. Army General James Dozier in 1981.[41] Moreover, the flow of intelligence improved beginning in 1979.

Interestingly, Della Porta finds that the state's extra-judicial or more violent repressive activities produced an *increase* in terrorist recruitment during this period until 1980.[42] However, two vital pieces of legislation came into effect in 1980 and 1982: the *pentiti* laws. The *pentiti* policy, commonly referred to as "repentance policy," provided sentence reductions for terrorists who collaborated with police and special treatment for those who publicly denounced the use of violence to pursue political goals.[43] In fact, Della Porta records that before 1980, only 20 percent of terrorists had been arrested; however, 42 percent were arrested in 1980 alone, with 37.2 percent arrested in the following years.[44]

As a result of numerous defections from the BR, followed by confessions and an inflow of intelligence, police were able to apprehend terrorists and thwart some potentially deadly attacks. For instance, in 1981, the BR kidnapped U.S. General Dozier. Based upon experience from the Moro abduction and the confessions of several terrorist informants, however, the police were able to mount a successful rescue effort to free Dozier from terrorist captivity. This successful event was followed by a wave of arrests at the end of 1982, which demolished the infrastructure of the BR.

In effect, the *pentiti* laws directly and indirectly hastened the disintegration of the BR, creating numerous splinter groups.[45] The terrorist groups themselves launched numerous campaigns to find and punish the *pentito*.[46] Moreover, from 1981 the number and severity of BR attacks declined and were mainly focused on Rome, with some attacks taking place in Naples.[47] Pluchinsky argues that three key elements must exist for a left-wing terrorist group to survive the arrests of its main leadership cadre: "(1) an active prison front, (2) a dedicated circle of supporters and sympathizers who will not be discouraged when top leaders are arrested, and (3) ideological unity within the group."[48] While the BR maintained a somewhat active prison membership and the potential for a large body of external sympathizers, it became engulfed in a devastating ideological debate during this period from which it never recovered.[49]

Schism and Decline: 1982–1988

Especially following the *pentiti* legislation in 1980 and 1982, the BR was in crisis. Those terrorists remaining loyal to the BR were under constant threat of discovery by police, especially since informants were cooperating fully with state officials. Moreover, the legislation produced a constant suspicion between group members that undermined the effectiveness of the group. The need to go further underground only exacerbated the already-existing ideological tensions within the group. The most serious organizational schism occurred toward the end of 1984, when the BR split into two factions: the Communist Combatant Party (BR/PCC) and the Union of Fighting Communists (BR/UCC).

The BR/PCC was the main military faction, believing that the armed struggle must be conducted by a revolutionary body. This faction rejected the importance of grassroots political action. The BR/UCC, on the other hand, was considered the "movementalist" faction of the mainline BR, maintaining that the armed struggle should include both a revolutionary vanguard and an informed proletariat that was actively engaged in the process of revolution.[50]

In 1986, the Italian government passed a further *pentiti* law, which reduced the penalties for those terrorists who abandoned the armed struggle even without collaborating or informing on other terrorists. Prison laws were adopted providing concessions for imprisoned terrorists, including preparation for reentry into society, professional training, and the ability to fraternize with other former terrorists.[51] These acts of good faith not only removed the incentives for weary terrorists to continue clandestine activity within the terrorist group, but also began to restore faith in the democratic system among some former militants.[52]

Among those *brigatisti* still active in the armed struggle, evidence of their decline was discovered in June 1988 during a police raid. Police found notes from a series of secret meetings in January 1988 between the BR/PCC and the Red Armee Faktion (RAF), a German left-wing terrorist group.[53] Strangely, the terrorists had maintained full transcripts of the meetings. It was clear that the BR and the RAF had attempted to find some common ideological ground in order to unify forces. However, they could not firmly overcome disagreements about strategy and ideology, and therefore were unable to avail themselves of organizational or tactical assistance.[54]

This last-gasp attempt to incorporate the assistance of a foreign terrorist group is indicative of the struggle for survival experienced by the BR at this time. Information gained as a result of interrogations of defectors led to several key raids that resulted in the arrest of the remaining active militants. Indeed, the end of the BR was soon to come—police raided several BR hideouts in mid-1988, and the group was effectively destroyed at that time.

All told, the Red Brigades were responsible for approximately 400 deaths, 5,000 injuries, and 12,500 attacks on property over the course of their 18-year existence.[55] Like many terrorist groups, however, the BR could withstand neither the internal challenges of ideological and organizational disunity, nor the external pressures of a dwindling support base and a well-timed government response. In the long term, several groups have "reincarnated" the tradition of the BR—namely, the BR/PCC, which persists in attacking Italian society even at the writing of this chapter. However, this group is sporadic in its operations and represents a lesser threat to Italian politics and society.

THE GOVERNMENT RESPONSE: SUCCESSES AND FAILURES

As noted previously, the Italian government pursued a response to terrorism in several important phases. In the first phase, which occurred from 1970–1974, the government was fairly negligent of the Red Brigades' activity. In the second phase, from 1974–1979, the government took greater notice of terrorism, endorsing the creation of several special units devoted to undermining terrorist activities despite enduring bureaucratic problems within the state apparatus. And finally, from 1980–1988, successful counterterrorist measures enacted by the government led to the demise of the Red Brigades. An assessment of the various tactics adopted to combat terrorism, especially identifying failures and successes, offers useful lessons for responding to the challenges of contemporary terrorist threats.

First, there were two obvious failures of the Italian government in dealing with terrorism: its negligence of the left-wing terrorism groups, and its failure to purge the government of neofascists who sympathized with the right-wing terrorists. The Italian government was very slow to respond with effectiveness to the terrorist crises of the 1970s and 1980s. It is difficult to discern whether this was more a function of the policy gridlock and sensitivity to coalition dynamics, or whether it was more indicative of sympathy with the neofascist groups; it was most likely a function of both, to varying degrees within different levels of the bureaucracy. However, what is clear is that conspirators within the government were quite a hindrance to pursuing justice vis-à-vis the right-wing groups, which in turn fueled the grievances on the left. Moreover, the lack of a unified effort against the left further reduced the government's efficacy in responding to and anticipating the devastation that the BR would inflict.

Second, a natural response by the government was the adoption of specialized antiterrorist units, such as the Nucleo Dalla Chiesa and the Ispetoratto. While these units certainly coordinated the counterterrorism effort within Italy and gave the public a sense of safety, they lacked sufficient oversight necessary for a democratic system. In effect, police raids were often accompanied by broad sweeps of nonviolent left-wing groups that failed to discriminate between suspects and ordinary activists.[56] Not only did this state behavior raise ethical concerns, but also ultimately aided in the recruitment of terrorists due to a desire for retaliation among angered individuals.

The final failure of the Italian government in pursuing a proper counterterrorist response was its inattention to the competitive dynamics between existing terrorist groups. The state was either unaware of, or unable to confront, the constant tit-for-tat attacks that occurred as a result of competition between terrorist groups on both the right and the left. Indeed, few governments have ever found a way to defuse such competition. The Italians may have come closest, in fact, by changing the rules of the game through the adoption of *pentiti* legislation.

Notably, from 1980–1988, the Italian government put into place the *pentiti* reforms, which effectively destroyed the already struggling BR. The adoption of *pentiti* legislation provides a model for other governments. It is likely that *pentiti* was successful because the BR were experiencing a period of internal struggle—a condition that may be a prerequisite for the success of such policies in other contexts. Terrorist groups are most vulnerable to internal struggles when they have been underground for an extended period, when there are ideological divisions within the group concerning strategy and tactics, or when there are incentives offered to terrorists for exit from the group, such as decreased sentences in exchange for information.[57] It was particularly important that the Catholic Church provided a venue by which such repentant terrorists were able to reenter society following their defections. This experience suggests that nongovernmental organizations can be helpful in aiding the implementation of counterterrorist policies.[58]

In sum, there are several failures and successes to learn from this Italian counterterrorism experience. Initially, Italian counterterrorism failed because of shadowy complicity between elements of the state and right-wing terrorism; refusal of the government to acknowledge the destructive potential of the BR; knee-jerk reactions resulting in undemocratic policies, which raised some ethical considerations; and a failure to appreciate the escalatory effects of intergroup rivalries among terrorist groups. However, the successes of Italian counterterrorism included a unification of intelligence units and a coordination of their activities; creation of special commando forces with training in hostage crises; and, finally, the introduction of *pentiti* policies that exploited internal divisions within the BR and led to the defection of many members.

CONCLUSION

As with any other liberal democracy, Italy struggled with the balance between freedom and security—the Nucleo units and the Ispettorato pushed the boundaries of democracy in terms of method and operation. However, Italy ultimately found a strong and effective counterterrorist response that destroyed the BR terrorist group while preserving civil liberties and respect for human rights. This balance was struck as Italy pursued a vigorous criminal justice approach, arresting and trying BR terrorists, while providing incentives for militants to surrender their arms and join the fight against their former comrades. Persistent internal troubles within the BR, an attempt to reform the intelligence system to purge it of its neofascist conspirators, the proper coordination of police action, and the introduction of *pentiti* laws all combined to end the major threat of the BR once and for all.

NOTES

1. Sidney Tarrow, "Violence and institutionalization after the Italian protest cycle," in *The Red Brigades and Left Wing Terrorism in Italy*, ed. Raimondo Catanzaro (New York: St. Martin's Press, 1991) 41–69, p. 52.

2. Dennis Mack Smith, *Modern Italy: A Political History* (Ann Arbor, MI: University of Michigan Press, 1997) 448.

3. Gian Carlo Caselli and Donatella Della Porta, "The history of the Red Brigades: organizational structures and strategies of action (1970–82)," in *The Red Brigades and Left Wing Terrorism in Italy*, ed. Raimondo Catanzaro. (New York: St. Martin's Press, 1991) 70–114, p. 79.

4. Jan Oskar Engene, *Terrorism in Western Europe: Explaining the Trends since 1950*. (Cheltenham, UK: Edward Elgar, 2004) 138–139.

5. For a description, see Mack Smith: pp. 443–466.

6. Raimondo Catanzaro, ed., *The Red Brigades and Left Wing Terrorism in Italy* (New York: St. Martin's Press, 1991) 5; Caselli and Della Porta: p. 74.

7. Engene: p. 139.

8. Caselli and Della Porta: p. 75.

9. Yonah Alexander and Dennis Pluchinsky, *Europe's Red Terrorists: The Fighting Communist Organizations* (London: Frank Cass, 1992) 194.

10. Engene: p. 139.

11. Caselli and Della Porta: p. 76.

12. Ibid.: p. 90.

13. Ibid.: p. 91.

14. Sidney Tarrow, *Democracy and Disorder* (Oxford: Clarendon, 1989); see also Erica Chenoweth, *The Inadvertent Effects of Democracy on Terrorist Group Proliferation*, Ph.D. Dissertation, University of Colorado (2007).

15. See Chenoweth 2007; see also Mia Bloom, *Dying to Kill: The Allure of Suicide Terror* (New York: Columbia University Press, 2005) for a discussion of these dynamics in Palestinian, Sri Lankan, Chechen, and Turkish groups.

16. Dennis A. Pluchinsky, "Western Europe's Red Terrorists: The Fighting Communist Organizations," in *Europe's Red Terrorists: The Fighting Communist Organizations*, eds. Yonah Alexander and Dennis Pluchinsky (London: Frank Cass. Pluchinsky and Alexander, 1992) 16–54, p. 46.

17. Luciana Stortoni-Wortmann, "The Political Response to Terrorism in Italy from 1969 to 1983," in *European Democracies against Terrorism: Governmental policies and intergovernmental cooperation*, ed. Fernando Reinares (Burlington, VT: Ashgate, 2000) 147–171, p. 153.

18. Donatella Della Porta, "Left-Wing Terrorism in Italy," in *Terrorism in Context*, ed. Martha Crenshaw (State College, PA: Pennsylvania State University Press, 1995) 105–159, p. 114.

19. Stortini-Wortmann: p. 157.

20. Ibid.: p. 158.

21. Della Porta: p. 117.

22. Stortini-Wortmann: p. 153.

23. Ibid.: p. 155.

24. Ibid.: p. 157.

25. Della Porta: p. 117.

26. Smith: p. 467.

27. Caselli and Della Porta: p. 91.

28. Ibid.: p. 97.

29. Ibid.: p. 98.

30. Ibid.: p. 99.

31. Ibid.: p. 102.

32. Stortini-Wortmann: p. 148.

33. Ibid.: p. 153.

34. Ibid.: p. 153.

35. Ibid.: p. 163.

36. Ibid.: p. 159.

37. Ibid.: p. 159.

38. Ibid.: p. 163.

39. Paul Furlong, "Political terrorism in Italy: responses, reaction, and immobilism," in *Terrorism, a Challenge to the State*, ed. Juliet Lodge (Oxford: Martin Robertson, 1981) 61–62. Excerpted in David J. Whittaker, *The Terrorism Reader*, 2nd ed. (New York and London: Routledge, 2004) 228.

40. Stortini-Wortmann: p. 160.

41. Ibid.: p. 160.

42. Della Porta: p. 118.

43. Caselli and Della Porta: p. 105

44. Della Porta: p. 117.

45. Ibid.: p. 119.

46. Caselli and Della Porta: p. 102.

47. Ibid.: p. 104.

48. Pluchinsky: p. 42.

49. Ibid.

50. Alexander and Pluchinsky: p. 194.

51. Della Porta: p. 154.

52. Ibid.

53. For more on this group, please see the chapter by Joanne Wright in this volume.

54. Alexander and Pluchinsky: p. 222.

55. David Moss, "Politics, Violence, Writing: the Rituals of 'Armed Struggle' in Italy," in *The Legitimization of Violence*, ed. D.E. Apter (New York: New York University Press, 1997) 85. Excerpted in David J. Whittaker, *The Terrorism Reader*, 2nd ed. (London and New York: Routledge, 2004) 223.

56. Tarrow (1990); p. 45.

57. Martha Crenshaw, Paul Wilkinson, Jon B. Alterman, and Teresita Schaffer "How Terrorism Ends," United States Institute for Peace Special Report (Washington, DC: USIP, 1997); see also Della Porta.

58. Martha Crenshaw, *Terrorism in Context* (State College, PA: Pennsylvania State University Press, 1995) 24.

CHAPTER 21

LEBANON, HIZBOLLAH, AND THE PATRONS OF TERRORISM

Richard M. Wrona, Jr.

Less than a year after the September 11 attacks of 2001 by operatives of al Qaeda, senior American officials pointed to another organization, the Lebanese Hizbollah,[1] as the true "A-Team" of terrorists.[2] In the wake of the most devastating terrorist attacks against American targets, many observers wondered whether these comments demonstrated an appreciation for a significantly more dangerous threat to the United States or a continuing animosity resulting from events of the 1980s. Recent history points to an organization that is both a more dangerous and a less immediate threat than al Qaeda to American interests. In studying Hizbollah, an observer gains insight into a case study that exemplifies some of the critical questions tied to terrorism studies. How do groups balance domestic interests with international interests? What are the impacts of state sponsorship of terrorist groups? Can integrating them into the political process mollify terrorist organizations? As a tightly controlled hierarchical organization with an enduring ideology, international recognition, and international reach, Hizbollah demonstrates the efficacy that terrorist operations lend to organizations facing more powerful international opponents.

HIZBOLLAH'S ORIGINS

It is impossible to comprehend the development and maturation of Hizbollah (or "Party of God") apart from the organization's domestic, regional, and temporal contexts. Hizbollah's origin is best understood in terms of the organization's impetus being reinforced by an example and, finally, sparked by a catalyst. Many variables weighed into the group's formation, but no variable can be pointed to as the single decisive factor.

While certain international actors recognize Hizbollah as a Foreign Terror-ist Organization (FTO), the overwhelming majority of states and intergov-ernmental organizations perceive a far different entity. Without exploring Hizbollah's development, it is impossible to either understand this differ-ence of perceptions or to develop a coherent strategy for dealing with the organization.

Impetus: The Lebanese Context

Lebanon is a state that has faced nearly insurmountable obstacles since its origin. Of all its difficulties, Lebanon's demographics and resulting sys-tem of government acted as the bedrock for Hizbollah's development.

Formed by the National Pact of 1943, Lebanon is a state built upon a deeply fragmented social structure. With over 18 recognized religious sects, the state's history revolves around the interaction of Maronite Chris-tian, Sunni Muslim, Shi'a Muslim, and (to a lesser extent) Druze ethno-religious groups. Because of their monopoly of economic and political power in the 1940s (and the patronage of outside actors), Lebanon's Ma-ronite and Sunni factions established the National Pact in such a way as to maintain their shared hold on power. To achieve this goal and simulta-neously gain the acquiescence of other factions, Lebanese national leaders decided upon a confessional system of government in which power was allocated based upon the size of each religious confession/sect, as deter-mined by the results of a 1932 national census. Patronage was determined by the ruling semifeudal families (zu'ama) of each sect. The resulting gov-ernment was built upon an agreement (without codification) that entailed a 6–5 split of the Lebanese parliament between Christian and Muslims representatives, a similar split between the factions in the bureaucracy, and the allocation of key leadership positions (the presidency, the prime ministry, and the position of speaker of the parliament) to the major sec-tarian groups.

The inflexibility of such a system, reinforced by the strong desire of the Maronites and the Sunnis to maintain their preeminent positions, could not endure changing Lebanese demographics. In particular, the system could not account for the changing numbers, strength, and political ac-tivism of Lebanon's Shi'a population. In 1950, Shi'a Lebanese comprised approximately 19 percent of the population.[3] Moreover, the Shi'a were the rural poor in Lebanon—largely illiterate, relying predominantly on subsistence farming, and concentrated in communities in the southern and eastern regions of the country. Like most rural populations, the Shi'a growth rate in Lebanon soon outpaced that of the Maronite and Sunni urban populations. Three mutually reinforcing dynamics then came into consideration. First, because of the increasing birth rate, more Shi'a began to relocate to Lebanon's urban centers, placing them in closer proximity to the more prosperous Sunnis and Maronites. Second, those prominent Shi'a families that were affluent at the time of the National Pact saw no need to champion changes for the poor Shi'a masses. Finally, because of increasing Shi'a numbers, their increasing interaction with the more prosperous sects, and the lack of effective representation by the Shi'a *zu'ama*, grassroots Shi'a leaders surfaced with increasingly clamorous calls for greater Shi'a allocations of political and economic power.

In 1970, an already-tenuous social structure was burdened with yet another complication. As a result of Jordan's "Black September" and its resulting civil war, the Palestinian Liberation Organization (PLO) relocated to southern Lebanon, in order to persevere in its fight against Israel. In doing so, the PLO soon formed a state-within-a-state (popularly recognized as "Fatahland") in southern Lebanon. As if this incursion was not enough of an imposition upon the Lebanese Shi'a, the indigenous population soon faced Israeli military attacks meant to counter the PLO's cross-border actions into northern Israel.

With so many stressors on such a fragmented society, Lebanon's disintegration into civil war seemed almost preordained. As the society splintered along sectarian lines, the Shi'a were, once again, at a disadvantage. While the other ethno-religious groups had armed militias with which to defend themselves and their interests, the Shi'a had no such protection. In this atmosphere, Musa al-Sadr—a youthful, vibrant Shi'a cleric who had studied in the great centers of Shi'a religious education in Iraq—stepped to the fore to lead his community. After forming the Movement of the Deprived in 1974 in an effort to better represent Shi'a interests, al-Sadr developed the militant *Afwaj al-Muqawama al-Lubnaniyya* (Lebanese Resistance Brigades), better known by the acronym AMAL, in order to protect the Shi'a population and its interests.[4] Unfortunately, AMAL faced significant disadvantages in trying to build its military power when competing against the developed militias of the other Lebanese factions. While its framework provided a structure on which to build, AMAL was relatively ineffective during the early years of the war. This factor, combined with popular disenchantment with the secular leaders who succeeded Musa al-Sadr (after his mysterious disappearance in Libya in 1978), allowed the space necessary for more radical Shi'a organizations to develop.[5]

Lebanon's domestic situation provided fertile ground for the Shi'a radicalization that blossomed in the 1980s and coalesced into what would become Hizbollah. Already facing an historical legacy of oppression because of their minority status in the Muslim community (the *umma*), the Lebanese Shi'a faced an inflexible political system that could not represent their increasing demands for greater political and social power. In effect, the Shi'a faced *de jure* oppression from the other Lebanese sectarian groups because of the system instituted by the National Pact, and *de facto* oppression from the strong Shi'a families that were unwilling to fight for the interests of the larger Shi'a community. Added to this foundation were the consequences of foreign occupation by the PLO and the Israeli military actions stemming from Palestinian attacks. Religiously, domestically, and regionally, the Lebanese Shi'a faced reinforcing patterns of domination and subjugation that strongly supported the radicalization of the community.

Example: The Iranian Revolution

The 1970s were a tumultuous decade for not only the Lebanese, but for the greater Near East. Of the decade's regional highlights, however, no single event had as great an impact as the Islamic Revolution in Iran in 1979. For the Lebanese Shi'a, particularly those who had studied in Najaf during the 1960s and 1970s, the successful overthrow of Shah Reza Pahlavi and the introduction of an Islamic regime provided ideological and tangible benefits. Moreover, it resulted in an organizational relationship that continues to influence regional politics.

The overthrow of the autocratic and secular Shah brought to power the Iranian clerical establishment under the leadership of Ayatollah Ruhollah Khomeini. Khomeini, triumphantly returning from exile in Iraq and Paris, immediately moved to implement a form of government centered upon Islam. Specifically, *sharia* (Islamic law) was instituted under the *wilayet al-faqih*, or rule of the Jurisprudent. Khomeini, departing radically from Shi'a tradition, believed that clerics were to form the core of the ruling political establishment. In an equally important departure from the same tradition, he held that one cleric (the *faqih*) should be recognized by his peers as the supreme head of the regime.[6]

The Iranian Revolution had an electrifying effect upon the Lebanese Shi'a for a host of reasons. First, the Lebanese Shi'a, while not a majority of the population like their Persian coreligionists, certainly viewed the Islamic Revolution as a grand departure from the Shi'a tradition of oppression by other groups. Iran's example provided the possibility that the Shi'a plurality in Lebanon might someday also come into its own in terms of political power. Second, the Islamic Revolution demonstrated the viability of a regime governed by *sharia*. Given the Lebanese Maronites' and Sunnis' disproportionate shares of power in Lebanon's political system, the idea of an Islamic republic seemingly promised the Lebanese Shi'a a greater hope of social justice.[7] Finally, Iran's self-imposed isolation from outside influences, particularly influences from the West, offered the Lebanese Shi'a the promise of a break from their subjugation by international sources—sources either directly imposing themselves upon the Shi'a (the PLO and the Israelis) or indirectly imposing themselves upon the community (by supporting the other sectarian groups of Lebanese society).

Beyond simple example and ideological mentorship, Iran's revolution also provided tangible benefits to the Lebanese Shi'a. Soon after the revolution, Iran deployed members of the *Pasdaran* (Iran's Revolutionary Guard) to Lebanon to aid the Shi'a militias in training and planning for operations against the other sectarian groups and (in the near future) Israeli adversaries. In addition to military training and hardware, Iran also began to devote significant financial resources to the Lebanese Shi'a, which would act as the initial capital required to develop many of Hizbollah's future formidable social services.

Catalyst: Israel's Invasion of Lebanon

Lebanon's civil war had implications beyond the country's borders. Once thought to be the most modern of Near Eastern countries, the civil war's instability soon drove foreign investment from Lebanon's shores, further impoverishing the state. More important, however, were the war's exports. As noted above, the large influx of Palestinians after the PLO's expulsion from Jordan in 1970 significantly contributed to Lebanese instability. The PLO's international actions also had important Lebanese ramifications. Its continuing efforts against Israel resulted in multiple Israeli cross-border attacks, culminating in full-scale invasions of Lebanon in 1978 and 1982. While the former invasion was temporary in nature, the latter was of longer duration. 1982's invasion resulted in the ouster of the PLO from Lebanese territory, but it also resulted in an extended Israeli occupation that was the final catalyst for Hizbollah's formation.

Two aspects of this invasion were germane concerning Hizbollah's origin. First, as was the case with the overwhelming majority of the Arab population in the region, Hizbollah's forefathers denied not only the legitimacy of the Israeli occupation, but also the legitimacy of Israel's existence. The Jewish state had no basis other than that of an illegal occupier of stolen (Palestinian) land. Thus, any actions by the entity were corrupted by this "original illegitimacy." Second, while privately celebrating the incursion in its early stages (because it ousted the PLO from Shi'a areas in Lebanon,) the Lebanese Shi'a soon realized that they had simply traded one occupying power for another. As the Israelis were unwilling to revert to the *status quo ante* (that had allowed the conditions for the PLO's attacks), they established an Israeli "security zone" in southern/Shi'a Lebanon, complete with an imported militia, the South Lebanon Army (SLA). Thus, rather than experiencing an eagerly anticipated liberation, the Lebanese Shi'a instead faced occupation by their foremost enemy.

The breaking point had been met. Example reinforced impetus, and the catalyst sparked Hizbollah's formation. According to Middle East scholar Eyal Zisser, "The Lebanon War of 1982, coming close upon the heels of the Islamic revolution in Iran in 1979-80, hence found at least a portion of the

Shi'a community on the threshold of extremism which would characterize it in the years to come."[8] Without a formal declaration (until 1985) of its existence, Hizbollah gained minimal recognition until the 1983 attacks that catapulted it to its preeminent position in both Lebanese politics and world recognition.

HIZBOLLAH'S IDEOLOGY[9]

As with its origins, Hizbollah's ideology was (and continues to be) greatly influenced by both Shi'a history and the success of the Iranian revolution. Based on four key foundations, the ideology is both enduring (in that, philosophically, Hizbollah has hardly deviated from the tenets), and controlling (in that political realities, while sometimes accommodated, are consistently subservient to the ideology). The group's consistent maintenance of the ideology and adherence to its principles have set Hizbollah apart from many of its contemporaries participating in Near Eastern conflicts.

First, as the group claimed in its "Open Letter Addressed to the Downtrodden in Lebanon and the World" of February 16, 1985, "we stress that we are convinced of Islam as a faith, system, thought, and rule and we urge all to recognize it and to resort to its law. We also urge them to adopt it and abide by its teachings at the individual, political, and social levels."[10] In short, "the cornerstone of Hizbu'llah's intellectual structure is the Islamic state ideal."[11] Hizbollah aspires to the establishment of a Lebanese theocracy both modeled after and tied to the Iranian example.[12] As with other Islamic theories, there is no separation between the secular and the spiritual. Rather, clerical leaders act as both religious and political leaders in a society that, while not based on popular sovereignty, does require a high amount of popular legitimacy for rulers to maintain power.

The adoption of this ideal as the fundamental foundation of Hizbollah's ideology can be attributed to two major influences. As with other tenets of its philosophy, the success of the Iranian revolution established, in Hizbollah's mind, the feasibility of a functioning modern-day Islamic state. The overthrow of the Shah and installment of Ayatollah Khomeini, followed by the (relatively) smooth transition of power to Khameini upon Khomeini's death, support the model's feasibility. Moreover, the perceived ability of Iran to segregate itself from outside (Western) influences and follow an independent and Islamic path reinforced the model's desirability.

The Shi'a role in the failed Lebanese political system (as represented by the efforts of AMAL) reinforced the need for an Islamic state. Whether being taken advantage of by the economically dominant Christians or Sunnis or by their own familial leaders, the confessional system of governance consistently placed the Shi'a in a position from which they could not hope to gain political or economic power. The initial forays of AMAL into the political arena and the resulting compromises[13] only reinforced these disadvantages and the hopelessness of the Shi'a situation. Thus, the siren's call of the equality and advantages of an Islamic state greatly appealed to Hizbollah's future followers.

The second core tenet of Hizbollah's ideology involves the constant tension between "the oppressors" and "the oppressed."[14] Although heavily influenced by the Shi'a historical record of being a disadvantaged minority in most of the Sunni-dominated near East, this ideological principle also has its basis in the philosophy of Ayatollah Khomeini and the Iranian revolution. However, unlike certain dichotomies found in the Sunni tradition, Saad-Ghorayeb notes that in Hizbollah's ideology "the oppressors do not represent the non-Muslims and the oppressed Muslims, but rather those who are socially and economically deprived, politically oppressed and culturally repressed vis-à-vis those who practise this oppression, regardless of their religious identity."[15] This distinction has two important implications. First, it results in a degree of tension between competing near Eastern philosophies and regimes. For example, the Kingdom of Saudi Arabia is one of Hizbollah's largest regional opponents,[16] partially due to Saudi messianic efforts tied to the Wahhabi interpretation of Islam. More important, however, is the fact that the "oppressor vs. oppressed" ideological tenet creates the potential for common cause between Hizbollah and many other national liberation organizations—organizations not necessarily based in the Near East or Islamic in nature.

As Sami G. Hajjar observes, the totality of the "oppression tenet" also has important implications for Hizbollah's overall ideology and subsequent interactions in that it allows "little room for compromise. [A] conflicting relationship cannot be resolved by some mechanism leading to a win-win situation."[17] This absolute ideological certainty, combined with an ability to focus on long-term strategic objectives rather than tactical measures and accomplishments, gives Hizbollah an uncommon resilience when compared to similar national liberation efforts.

The third core tenet of Hizbollah's ideology involves the extermination of Israel. While the catalyst for Hizbollah's rise (the 1982 Israeli invasion of Lebanon) certainly falls in this realm, the ideological principle runs deeper in that "the conflict with Israel is portrayed as 'an existential struggle' as opposed to 'a conflict over land' ... there can be no prospect of reconciliation with Israel whose very existence is called into question and whose eradication is pursued."[18] This conflict results from the confluence of a number of different influences. First, one must consider the strong case made for an inherent anti-Judaic strain in the Islamic tradition.[19] Although Jews are considered "People of the Book," Hizbollah (and other regional actors) consistently refer to key Koranic verses as justification for an underlying antipathy against Judaism as a religion, rather than Israelis as national or regional actors.[20] Second, the illegitimate formation of

Israel in 1947 on what is considered occupied Palestinian land continues to influence Hizbollah's ideology. The Israeli occupation of Jerusalem since the Six Day War (1967) further exacerbates this illegitimacy. Finally, Hizbollah's perception of Israeli regional expansionism (resulting from Israel's occupations after the 1967 war of the West Bank, Gaza Strip, and Golan Heights; as well as the 1982 invasion of Lebanon) fuels a hatred of the Jewish state, as the latter is seen to be not only illegitimate, but a threat to its Arab neighbors.[21]

Like the "oppression tenet," hatred of Israel imbues Hizbollah with a longevity not specific to successes or failures in Lebanon. Since the very existence of Israel is deemed illegitimate, even a complete withdrawal of Israeli forces from all Lebanese territory will do little to placate Hizbollah. In the purely theoretical realm, the extreme measure of returning to the 1947 borders still will not end Hizbollah's animosity, as only the complete eradication of the Jewish state in Palestine, the liberation of Jerusalem, and the acquiescence of the remaining Jews to an Islamic Arab/Palestinian regime will suffice. As the recent writings of Hizbollah's Deputy Secretary General indicate, the movement's anti-Israeli fervor has not been quenched by the 2000 withdrawal and continues to serve as a *raison d'etre* for the organization:

> Let us not forget our responsibility of supporting the Palestinian people, the association between the Palestinian cause and our own daily realities and how the Palestinian issue reflects on Lebanon and the entire region. This makes belief in liberation a unified, common cause ... The Israeli entity represents a grave peril to Palestine and to the entire region, one that should be countered, confronted, and resisted ... The basis is to refuse the legitimacy of occupation and to *adopt the persistence of resistance as a core pillar*.[22] [Emphasis added.]

Hizbollah's belief in an inherent conflict between Islam and "the West" (principally identified by the United States) serves as the group's final core ideological tenet. The basis for this conflict is two-fold. First, as Saad-Ghorayeb notes, "Hizbu'llah is engaged in a 'civilisational' struggle with the West, inherent in which is a rejection of the 'values, beliefs, institutions, and social structures' of western society."[23] Western culture and influences are doubly damaging, in that they are corruptive and expansive. Thus, Hizbollah, while not seeking the eradication of Western states or Western culture, does desire their exclusion from the Near East. Although not nearly as encompassing as Hizbollah's antipathy for Israel (for example, Western [specifically American] education is viewed as superior and desirable),[24] Hizbollah does maintain a core belief that Islamic and Western cultures are not compatible. However, these different and conflicting cultures do have the ability to maintain parallel, separate existences.

Consistent Western support for Israel in the ongoing Middle Eastern struggle reinforces Hizbollah's belief in this inherent conflict. Through political, ideological, and material support of the Jewish state, Western states remain at odds with Hizbollah's strategic goals. Hizbollah's perceptions of Western-Israeli collusion, at times, become so extreme as to consider the different states a single entity.[25]

THE PATRONS—IRAN AND SYRIA

Just as it is doubtful whether Hizbollah would have developed without the example of the Iranian Revolution,[26] the organization's continuing success relies heavily on the aid and acquiescence of two state actors—Iran and Syria. While both states proved essential to Hizbollah's achievements, the organization's religious foundations tie it more closely to the Iranian regime.

Iran

Since the Islamic Revolution, Iran's aid to Hizbollah has been critical in every aspect—political, military, and economic. From Hizbollah's early recognition of Khomeini as the *faqih* of the organization (to whom all unresolved matters of import were to be taken), to military equipment and training over a 25-year period, to financial aid, Hizbollah has married itself closely to Iran.[27] On both sides, this relationship is based on ideological and strategic considerations.

Ideologically, Hizbollah views Iran as benefactor and example when striving toward the long-term goal of a Lebanese Islamic republic. This ideological affinity can be attributed to a number of variables. First, one must consider the lasting personal relationships between Lebanese and Iranian clerics. As A. Nizar Hamzeh, a professor at the American University of Beirut and longtime analyst of Hizbollah, notes, "[t]he relationship between the Lebanese Shi'ite clergy and Khomeini and [Muhammad Baqir] al-Sadr before and after Iran's revolution helped to establish an effective network that would subsequently facilitate Iran's demonstration effect in the Lebanese political arena and be the godfather of Hizbullah's future leaders."[28] Likewise, the appeal of the social justice promised by an Islamic regime continues to energize Lebanese Shi'a, particularly given the uncertain political and economic atmosphere in Lebanon. Iran, ideologically, clings to Lebanon as an example of the successful export of the revolution, especially given the lack of successful revolutions by the Shi'a populations of the Gulf States. Moreover, Lebanon provides proof that Iranian influence is not curtailed by the ethnic divide (Persian versus Arab) that has been used to explain Iran's lack of influence in other aspects of regional politics.

Strategically, Hizbollah and Iran have a continuing relationship predicated first and foremost on their joint perception of American and Israeli threats in the region. Hizbollah, while gaining a large amount of autonomy and influence after Israel's 2000 withdrawal from Lebanon, still relies on Iran for the supply of military armament and for financial aid, which is estimated to exceed $100 million a year. Although the organization has been able to generate additional sources of income, funding from Iran remains central to Hizbollah's ability to maintain its social programs in Lebanon and its military footing against Israel.[29] On the opposite side of the strategic coin, Iran counts Hizbollah and the organization's ability to strike Israel's northern border as a significant variable upon which to be called.[30] In response to the strategic military imbalance in the region (since Israel is the only regional actor known to have nuclear weapons), this relationship effectively provides Iran with some preemptive and/or retaliatory insurance, should Israel strike the nascent Iranian nuclear program. Also, a relationship with Hizbollah provides Iran a critical point from which to operate in its ongoing efforts to export the Islamic revolution and build regional alliances. This latter strategic calculation has proved beneficial in establishing and developing Iranian relationships with militant Palestinian factions in the occupied territories.

Syria

The Syria-Hizbollah relationship is more tenuous.[31] In 1976, Syrian troops occupied Lebanon under the auspices of an Arab League mandate. While ostensibly in Lebanon as the head of a multinational force deployed to quell the intersectarian violence, the Syrian army soon focused on achieving two strategic goals of the Assad regime. First, the occupation of Lebanon reinforced Hafez al-Assad's hand in subsuming Lebanon into a "Greater Syria." Second, Syrian occupation of southern Lebanon and the Bekaa Valley provided Syria's allies (the Palestinian factions) protected territory from which to attack Israel. From Assad's perspective, this Palestinian pressure on Israel from Lebanon might provide the variable necessary to negotiate a return of the Golan Heights (lost to Israel in the 1967 Six Day War.) Initially, these goals did not place Syria and Hizbollah on the same side of the Lebanese equation. With Syria initially entering Lebanon to bolster the Maronite Christians, and then the Syrians fighting on the side of the Palestinians against the other factions (particularly after the 1982 Israeli invasion,) a future alliance with Hizbollah did not become readily apparent. Even with Hizbollah's emergence in 1982, there were no initial indications of the alliance that holds even after the Syrian withdrawal from Lebanon in 2005.

Instead, the Syria-Hizbollah alliance results from the proximity of the actors in question and their mutual antipathy for Israel. Three aspects of this relationship indicate why it endures, even in the free-flowing environment of alliances that is the Lebanese political culture. First, Syria provides the transportation route for Iranian military supplies and other hardware to reach Hizbollah.[32] Given Hizbollah's continued reliance on Iranian hardware, it must maintain a modicum of peaceful relations with the Assad regime. Second, Hizbollah's ability to maintain arms in the wake of the 1989 Taif Accord, when every other Lebanese militia was forced to disarm, was due in large part to the influence of the Syrian regime. This recognition of Hizbollah as a "national resistance" movement, rather than yet another sectarian militia, allowed the organization to continue its military operations against Israel and subsequently gain its exalted status in the wake of the 2000 Israeli withdrawal. Third, Hizbollah's and Syria's joint desire to maintain pressure on Israel, albeit for different strategic reasons, gives them common cause for a continuing relationship.

HIZBOLLAH IN THE 21ST CENTURY

Capabilities

Hizbollah of the modern day is a far cry from the loose band of Shi'a militias that developed in the late 1970s and coalesced after the 1982 Israeli invasion of Lebanon. Today, the organization acts as a political, economic, social, and military leader in Lebanese society. Politically, Hizbollah has become one of the foremost participants in Lebanese elections. Since its initial forays into the electoral process in 1992, Hizbollah has consistently gained legislative seats and executive positions at the municipal and national levels. In the elections of 2005, Hizbollah made its greatest political gains ever, winning 14 seats in the Lebanese parliament, virtually sweeping the elections of south Lebanon and the Bekaa Valley, and having one of its members, Muhammed Fneish, appointed as the Lebanese Energy and Water Minister. Hizbollah's Secretary-General, Hassan Nasrallah, meets regularly with national and international leaders, including the Secretary-General of the United Nations and ambassadors and foreign ministers of European states. Hizbollah is one of the Near East's strongest political actors, commonly recognized by state and nonstate entities alike as the *single* entity to defeat Israel and force unilateral Israeli concessions.

Economically and socially, Hizbollah has been the leading nonstate provider of social services to the Lebanese—regardless of religious affiliation. One of the foremost reasons for Musa al-Sadr's development of the Movement of the Deprived (1974) was to combat Maronite and Sunni largesse and gain a just share of social services and benefits for the Lebanese Shi'a. With the civil war, even the meager share of public services that the Shi'a had enjoyed disappeared. Into this void stepped Hizbollah. Through a centrally controlled hierarchy known for its lack of corruption, the members of Hizbollah set to providing the social services necessary to ameliorate the plight of the not only the Lebanese Shi'a, but also those in the south displaced or harmed by the Israeli occupation. From basic sewage and water services to collegiate scholarships, from construction and reconstruction firms to satellite television services, and from legal/judicial services to the protection of widows and orphans of "martyred" members, Hizbollah moved to fill the gap left by a failed state and continuing internecine warfare. With a budget estimated in excess of a billion dollars,[33] Hizbollah acts as the sole social provider for an ever-increasing percentage of the Lebanese population.

Militarily, Hizbollah's modern capabilities are a far cry from the lightly armed militias and suicide truck bombers that the organization employed in the early 1980s against Israeli and Western targets. Particularly after the 2000 Israeli withdrawal from southern Lebanon, Hizbollah has been able to significantly expand its military arsenal. While still maintaining a contingent of martyrs (*istishadiyyun*) to conduct suicide operations, the organization now counts unmanned aerial vehicles (UAVs), advanced surface-to-air missiles, and over 12,000 surface-to-surface missiles in its arsenal.[34]

Strategy

Mirroring the development of its capabilities, Hizbollah has developed a coherent and detailed strategy to achieve its domestic and regional goals and to combat its threats. Its strategy, calculated and measured, allows the organization to prosper and expand in the face of great political upheavals. Such abilities denote an organization that, while still quite willing to use terrorist methods, cannot be considered a terrorist organization in the traditional mold.

The organization's strategy is steered by three primary variables. First, as noted earlier, Hizbollah's ideological tenets and goals remain the lodestone[35] of the organization. Thus, while Hizbollah has had to make tactical concessions and alliances in order to deal with contemporary affairs, it has retained foremost on its agenda the objectives of an Islamic Lebanese state, the elimination of Israel, and the separation of the Lebanese population (particularly the Shi'a population) from Western influences. Second, Hizbollah has become adept at adjusting to the fluid system of alliances in Lebanon and in the region. Particularly in the wake of the 2005 assassination of former Lebanese Prime Minister Rafik Hariri and the withdrawal of Syrian military forces from Lebanon, Hizbollah has played the political game to its advantage. While the organization has come under increasing pressure to disarm, Hizbollah has successfully maintained its status as the only armed Lebanese nonstate/substate entity. It has done so by selling itself both as a national (rather than Shi'a) resistance/protection force and by being perceived as relatively free of corruption. Third, Hizbollah has successfully employed the tactical and strategic use of measured force to further its political and ideological objectives.

Since the end of the civil war in 1990, the organization's force has been used almost exclusively against Israel, rather than against other domestic actors.[36] Moreover, the use of force against Israel has been generally discriminate, measured, and calculated. Hizbollah has executed conventional operations (including light infantry attacks, rocket/artillery/mortar attacks, and UAV overflights) and unconventional operations (including kidnappings and providing financial, training, and planning support to Palestinian factions in the occupied territories) to support its ideological objectives and to achieve other interim or tactical objectives. For example, in support of maintaining its political position in Lebanon and arresting Israel's perceived expansion, Hizbollah has aimed to achieve a "balance of terror" with Israel, in order to limit the latter's regional force-projection capabilities.[37] Thus, Hizbollah officials have intimated on numerous occasions that attacks can be undertaken not only in response to Israeli attacks, but also in response to Israeli violations of Lebanese air and maritime spaces. Likewise, Hizbollah has undertaken specific missions to capture/kidnap Israeli military members, in order to use them in bargaining for the release of imprisoned Lebanese and Palestinians in Israel.[38] Analysts have also speculated that Hizbollah is willing to use force in responding to increased international pressure.[39] Finally, in its continuing bid to not only curb Israeli offensive action but also place Israel on a defensive footing, Hizbollah has provided exceptional support to both the Palestinian population in the occupied territories and to the Palestinian factions conducting regular terrorist attacks against Israelis in those same areas.[40]

In addition to its regional importance, Hizbollah has successfully demonstrated an ability to operate globally in support of its objectives. Militarily, the organization has conducted numerous operations outside of the Near East, to include successful attacks against Israeli and Jewish targets in Argentina in 1992 and 1994. Financially, it has developed income and materiel flows throughout the world.[41] Because of its quarter-century development, the size and international dispersion of the Lebanese diaspora, and its close affiliation with Iran, Hizbollah is thought to have significant financial, operational, and intelligence-gathering capabilities in North America, South America, Africa (particularly West Africa), Europe, and Southeast Asia.

LEBANESE RESPONSES

As an organization that successfully weds the appeals of nationalism and Shi'a Islam, Hizbollah places increasing importance on its position and credibility within Lebanon's domestic sphere. Particularly since its recognition after the 1990 Ta'if Agreement as the country's only accepted armed faction, the organization treads a thin line between representing Lebanese Shi'a interests and, simultaneously, assuaging the doubts and fears of the state's other ethno-religious factions. While striking such a balance might be difficult in any context, Hizbollah's ability to do so among the constantly shifting alliances of Lebanon proves the organization's ability to adapt and to seize new instruments with which to forward its ideological agenda. Even though Lebanon's political elites consistently demonstrate a schizophrenic love-hate opinion of Hizbollah, the movement has gained widespread popular support across sectarian lines. As a result, the organization has become the preeminent Lebanese faction and acts as the object of other entities' balancing or bandwagoning strategies.

While the Ta'if Agreement ended the bloody sectarian fighting of the Lebanese civil war, it failed to remedy the sectarian divisions between Lebanon's ethno-religious groups. Almost immediately after the signing of the agreement, the national elites of the different groups renewed the bartering for political power that has been a constant theme of the country's political culture. In a new development, however, the brokering was not wholly constrained by religious divisions. With the ascent of the Shi'a, particularly as a result of Hizbollah's increased stature and Syria's tacit alliance with the organization, Lebanon's former power-brokers eschewed former alliances in their efforts to maintain personal and sectarian influence. After the assassination of Sunni leader and former Prime Minister Rafik Hariri in February 2005, the increasing complexity of Lebanon's internal dynamics became even more apparent. Examples of such complexity include the division of the Christian community and the political flexibility of the Druze community. Before and during the civil war, the Christian community could generally be counted upon to coalesce around a few key leaders in attempts to maintain power at the expense of the Sunni and Shi'a groups. Now, Christian leaders have divided between those in complete alliance with Hizbollah (like President Emile Lahoud), those in an alliance of temporary convenience (including General Michel Aoun and his Free Patriotic Movement), and those who attempt to maintain the old Christian-Sunni dominance (like Samir Geagea and Samir Franjieh.) Likewise, the Druze leader Walid Jumblatt has proved to be the most flexible of Lebanese political actors. Casting his lot with Hizbollah and the Syrians until the autumn of 2004, Jumblatt used the turmoil surrounding the extension of Lahoud's term as president to switch gears and ally the Druze with Hariri's Future Movement and certain Christian elements.

In the autumn of 2006, Lebanon's political environment is more fragile than at any other time in the last 20 years. While endemic corruption and sectarian in-fighting prevent the government from developing effective institutions, Hizbollah's valuable mechanisms provide social services and effectively supplant the state.[42] While sectarian leaders maneuver to maintain and gain power, Lebanon's ethno-religious groups increasingly identify with some of Hizbollah's objectives and, simultaneously, are increasingly wary of the Shi'a organization's growing power.[43] As Anthony Shadid, a *Washington Post* reporter and close follower of the Lebanese situation, observed "[d]ivisions between the Shiite Muslims and the country's other sects—Druze, Sunni Muslim, and Christian—have grown deeper than at any time in perhaps a generation. To an unprecedented degree, Lebanese speculate whether the government can remain viable, or even survive."[44]

REGIONAL RESPONSES

Hizbollah's power and influence cause concerns regionally as well as domestically. A variety of actors view Hizbollah as a threat to both regional stability and the stability of individual Arab regimes. As such, certain actors have moved to check Hizbollah's growing stature. The summer 2006 conflict between Israel and Hizbollah provided an appropriate lens through which to view the regional unease concerning this Shi'a organization.

Hizbollah's contemporary threat to the Jewish state is worth revisiting. With conventional and unconventional military capabilities (including rockets with ranges in excess of 100 km and a robust information warfare effort), a close alliance with Iran, and an important association with Assad's regime in Syria, Hizbollah acts as a proximate and strategic threat to Israel. Many analysts point to this threat as the foundation for Israel's seemingly disproportionate response to Hizbollah's capture of two Israeli soldiers on July 12, 2006. Immediately after the soldiers' capture, Israel opened a wide-scale campaign against targets throughout Lebanon. While the safe return of the Israeli soldiers was certainly one of the political aims, prominent Israeli political and military leaders also specified the destruction of Hizbollah and the reduction of the organization's military capabilities as the core objectives of the conflict. First, Israel sought to limit Hizbollah's deterrent capabilities that give Hizbollah a stronger hand in supporting Palestinian factions.[45] More importantly, Israel sought to reduce Hizbollah's ability to respond to an Israeli preemptive attack against Iran's nascent nuclear capabilities. However, when hostilities ceased and Israel's blockade of Lebanon was lifted in early September, none of those objectives had been achieved, and the two soldiers were still in Hizbollah's possession.

Regional actors other than Israel are also increasingly concerned about Hizbollah's growing political stature. In particular, some autocratic regimes (such as Saudi Arabia, Egypt, and the United Arab Emirates) have consistently moved to check Hizbollah's growing power. These regimes worry not only about Hizbollah's example to their Shi'a populations (some of which are quite significant), but also about the possibility of increasing coordination between these communities. These fears are founded upon history and the Shiites' religious bonds. In most cases, the senior religious leaders of the Shi'a communities lived and learned together in the same *hawzah* (religious centers of learning) in Iraq during the 1960s and 1970s. Therefore, enduring personal relationships have the possibility of reinforcing religious affinities. Moreover, historical cases demonstrate that Iran has effectively influenced Arab Shiites to support each other and work together in attempting to form Islamic republics throughout the Middle East. One prominent example of such cooperation concerned the attempted assassination of Kuwaiti royalty by the "Dawa 17" (a radical Shi'a organization) and the subsequent regional responses to gain the freedom of the would-be assassins after their capture.[46]

Again, regional responses to the July–August 2006 conflict prove instructive. Soon after the conflict's start, the Saudi Foreign Ministry and Egypt's President Mubarak separately castigated Hizbollah for its "reckless adventures" and "exterior adventures."[47] Saeb Erekat, the chief negotiator of the PLO, viewed the conflict as a victory for regional extremists at the expense of moderates.[48] Saudi and Kuwaiti efforts at the start of the war to provide the Sunni-dominated Lebanese government with sufficient funds for emergency and humanitarian aid were made, in part, to preempt and dilute Iranian financial support for Hizbollah. After the conflict, one Saudi analyst lauded the Kingdom's desire and ability to "leverage its economic might and religious authority to build the conditions for long-term peace and stability in Lebanon"—partially in an effort to contain growing Iranian regional influence through Hizbollah.[49]

As in Lebanon, the regional responses to Hizbollah are governed by a disparity between leaders' anxieties and popular support for the organization. While Arab leaders worry about Hizbollah's growing influence, Arab populations overwhelmingly support the organization's efforts against Israel and praise its success in providing social services to a needy Lebanese population. These vastly different perceptions of the organization increase Hizbollah's political stature internationally and bode ill for Arab states with populations that look to Hizbollah as the example of an Islamic alternative to their autocratic and dysfunctional regimes.

AMERICAN RESPONSES

The United States' responses to Hizbollah have historically been ineffective, inconsistent, and marked by rhetoric rather than action. The paucity of an American response has been founded upon decision-makers' continuing lack of familiarity with Hizbollah, an inability to successfully develop an international consensus concerning Hizbollah's status, and—perhaps most importantly—an inability to consider the second- and third-order effects of American foreign policy in the Near East.

Since Hizbollah's explosion onto the international scene in 1983 with its suicide bombings against American and French targets in Lebanon, the United States has failed to effectively respond to or preempt the organization's attacks against the United States. After the 1983 bombings of U.S. diplomatic facilities (twice) and the Marine barracks in Beirut, the United States quickly withdrew from Lebanon without a credible military response to the attacks. When Americans—to include government and military officials—were taken hostage by elements of Hizbollah throughout the 1980s, the United States failed to respond. When terrorists from Hizbollah (or from one of the organizations that fell under its wide umbrella) hijacked TWA 847 in 1985, killing one American sailor and holding 39 Americans hostage for over 2 weeks, the United States failed to respond. When one of the TWA hijackers was released from a German prison in December of 2005, the United States unsuccessfully demanded his extradition by the Lebanese government. In each and every instance, a lack of American action has conveyed two parallel messages not only to Hizbollah, but to other groups and organizations amenable to the use of terrorist tactics. First, the precedent of American inaction, particularly before 2001, established beliefs among members of these organizations that American interests could be attacked without serious repercussions. Second, the United States' 1984 withdrawal from Lebanon combined with these beliefs to give terrorist organizations the opinion that not only could the United States be attacked with impunity, but that attacking the United States would cause that country to withdraw. In the twenty-first century, the ramifications of historical inaction became devastating, when al Qaeda drew on the lessons of Beirut (in part) to plan and carry out the devastating attacks of September 11, 2001.

As a case study, Hizbollah also demonstrates the lack of American consistency when dealing with organizations that resort to terrorism. American focus on Hizbollah has been sporadic and, in many instances, poorly timed. Throughout the 1990s, when Hizbollah was solidifying its position in Lebanon as a social provider and as Lebanon's protector against Israel, the United States demonstrated little interest in the organization, even though these years witnessed several devastating and traumatic terrorist events. Then, in the aftermath of the September 11 attacks, the United States government reenergized its focus on (and antipathy for) Hizbollah. After the level of disregard demonstrated during the 1990s, Hizbollah was again in the spotlight, even though no recent attacks could be attributed to the organization. Paradoxically, this renewal of focus came after Hizbollah's ability to coalesce, centralize authority, develop as a national leader with international regard, and implement restraint and calculation in the use of its military power. It was as if the United States sought to reengage with a foe that had been long forgotten, and after that foe had been allowed to dramatically improve its capabilities.

Finally, Hizbollah starkly reveals an American inability to recognize and plan for the indirect effects of American foreign policy. American support of the Lebanese regime in the early 1980s had the unintended consequence of turning the Shi'a population against the United States, because support of the regime equated to support of the Maronite factions controlling the government. Likewise, American support of Israel, particularly after the 1973 Yom Kippur/Ramadan War, came to be viewed by Hizbollah as both an indirect attack on the Lebanese people and direct support for Israeli regional expansion. In neither case could the resulting perceptions be remotely tied to what the American government was actually trying to achieve.[50] However, because of a lack of understanding of the domestic, regional, cultural, and religious considerations in question, and because of an overwhelming emphasis on immediate solutions without considering the long-term ramifications of immediate actions, the United States sowed seeds of discontent, and hate that give Hizbollah a portion of its lasting role in Lebanese and regional politics.

CONCLUSION

Hizbollah, while more than a terrorist group, is certainly an organization comfortable with resorting to terrorist methods. Its ideology, maturation, and contemporary standing in the Near East leave the student of terrorism with a number of observations. Hizbollah's origins point to the fact that terrorist organizations require both underlying causes and a catalyst to spark radicalization and violent action. Its example also weighs heavily against the theory that the integration of radical groups into the political process will cause the groups to forego radicalization and militant action in favor of political action. Hizbollah's history demonstrates that integration into the political process has simply given the organization more tools by which to achieve its goals. Finally, the example of Hizbollah demonstrates the power of organizations that combine national, religious, and class appeal successfully. While some terrorist organizations (most notably the European groups of the 1970s) have been unable to expand beyond a small core of radicalized supporters, Hizbollah is the textbook case of an organization that has built a constituency that guarantees the group's longevity and importance for the foreseeable future.

ACKNOWLEDGMENTS

The views expressed herein are those of the author and do not purport to reflect the position of the United States Military Academy, the Department of the Army, or the Department of Defense.

NOTES

1. The "correct" English spelling of the group's Arabic name is Hizb'Allah or Hizbu'llah; however, it is more usually spelled "Hizbollah," "Hizbullah," or "Hezbollah." For purposes of standardization across all three volumes, the editor has chosen "Hizbollah" because that is the spelling employed in the URL designating the group's official homepage. However, where I have employed quotation I have retained the original spelling used by the author.

2. Richard L. Armitage, Remarks at the United Institute of Peace Conference (Washington, DC: Sep. 5, 2002); "Hezbollah: 'A-Team of Terrorists,'" CBSNews.com, Apr. 18, 2003, http://www.cbsnews.com/stories/2003/04/18/60minutes/printable 550000.shtml (accessed Feb. 14, 2005).

3. Eyal Zisser, "Hizbollah in Lebanon-at the Crossroads," in *Religious Radicalism in the Greater Middle East*, eds. Bruce Maddy-Weitzman and Efraim Inbar (London: Frank Cass, 1997) 94.

4. Ahmad N. Hamzeh, *In the Path of Hizbullah* (Syracuse, NY: Syracuse University Press, 2004) 20–21.

5. Hamzeh: p. 23; Amal Saad-Ghorayeb, *Hizbu'llah: Politics and Religion* (Sterling: Pluto Press, 2002) 15.

6. Hamzeh: pp. 30–33.

7. Augustus Richard Norton, *AMAL and the Shi'a, Struggle for the Soul of Lebanon* (United States: University of Texas Press, 1987) 56–58.

8. Zisser: p. 96.

9. Excerpted in part from Richard M. Wrona, Jr., "A Deafening Silence: Hizbollah after the American Invasion of Iraq," paper presented at the 2005 US Air Force Institute for National Security Studies Research Results Conference, Nov. 8, 2005.

10. "Open Letter Addressed by Hizb Allah to the Downtrodden in Lebanon and in the World," in Norton: pp. 174–175; Hamzeh: pp. 28, 30.

11. Saad-Ghorayeb: p. 16.

12. Sami G. Hajjar, "Hizbollah: Terrorism, National Liberation, or Menace," Monograph for the Strategic Studies Institute (Carlisle, PA: US Army War College, Aug. 2002) 8.

13. Hajjar: p. 5.

14. "Open Letter . . ." in Norton: pp. 183–184.

15. Saad-Ghorayeb: p. 17.

16. Saad-Ghorayeb: p. 79.

17. Hajjar: p. 11.

18. Saad-Ghorayeb: p. 135.

19. For a thorough development of this argument, see Saad-Ghorayeb: pp. 168–186.

20. "Open Letter . . ." in Norton: p. 171; Verse 5:82, as quoted in Saad-Ghorayeb: p. 175.

21. "Open Letter . . ." in Norton: pp. 179–180.

22. Naim Kassem, "Hizbullah's Future," http://www.naimkassem.org/materials/books/hizbullah/Hizbullah's%20Future.htm (accessed January 28, 2005).

23. Saad-Ghorayeb: p. 88; "Open Letter . . ." in Norton: p. 170; Hamzeh: p. 69.

24. Hajjar: pp. 14–15.

25. "Above all," he [Sayyed Mohammad Hussein Fadlallah] said, "we must not forget that the nation's problems started with the American-Israeli occupation of Arab states." Karine Raad, "Fadlallah calls for Sunni-Shiite unity."*The Daily Star*, Aug. 04, 2005, http://www.dailystar.com.lb.

26. Saad-Ghorayeb: p. 14; Norton: p. 56.

27. Hamzeh: pp. 25, 33, 63; Avi Jorisch, *Beacon of Hatred: Inside Hezbollah's al-Manar Television* (Washington, DC: The Washington Institute for Near East Policy, 2004) page unknown, as quoted by Matthew A. Levitt in testimony before the House of Representatives International Relations Committee (Middle East and Central Asia Subcommittee), Feb. 16, 2005.

28. Hamzeh: p. 19.

29. Hamzeh: p. 63.

30. Huda al-Husayni, "Hizbollah—Iran's First Line of Defense against Israel," *Al-Sharq al-Awsat*, May 11, 2006 (translation provided by US Government's Open Source Center, document number GMP2006051100006).

31. "These [Syrian-Hizbollahi] relations have passed through several stages. They developed from a not so clear and ambiguous relationship in 1982–1985 to confrontational and tense relations in 1985–1989, calm and positive relations in 1989–1992 and strategic and stable relations from 1992 until now." Qasim Qaysar, "Strategic Reading of Options, Challenges, Repercussions; What Future Awaits Hizbollah Following Syria's Withdrawal?" *Al-Mustaqbal*, Mar. 02, 2005 (translation provided by US Government's Open Source Center, document number GMP20050302000252).

32. "Kuwaiti Daily: Iran Delivered Missiles to Hizbullah in Lebanon via Syria," *MEMRI Special Dispatch Series-No. 765* (Washington DC: The Middle East Media Research Institute) Aug. 19, 2004, http://www.memri.org/bin/opener.cgi?Page=archives&ID=SP76504 (accessed Sep. 24, 2004); Shlomi Stein, "Mofaz: Hizbollah Has Missiles that Can Hit Tel Aviv," *Tel Aviv Ma'ariv*, Jan. 27, 2005 (translation provided by US Government's Open Source Center, document number GMP20050127000202).

33. Hamzeh: p. 63. For obvious reasons, the finances of Hizbollah are opaque, and estimates of budget amounts (and funding sources) vary considerably.

34. Hamzeh: pp. 70–72; Hadi Khatib, "Israel believes Hizbullah has Hi-tech missiles: SAMs could threaten Israeli overflights," *The Daily Star*, Feb. 01, 2005, http://www.dailystar.com.lb (accessed Feb. 01, 2005).

35. While a cornerstone provides foundation, a lodestone provides direction.

36. "Domestic" is used rather than "Lebanese" to denote the importance of the Palestinian camps that are still in existence in southern Lebanon and the Bekaa Valley. These camps include not only Palestinian refugees, but also armed factions of Palestinian rejectionist groups, to include the PLO and the PFLP-GC. As an example, see Lusi Barsikhyan, "More Than 10,000 Donums under Ahmad Jibril's Control. The Four Positions of Al-Biqa—Areas, Elements, and Dangers," *Sada al-Balad*, May 19, 2006 (translation provided by US Government's Open Source Center, document number GMP20060519511005).

37. "Shaykh Qawuq: The Lebanese People Are Too Intelligent To Believe That America Is Ready To Help Them," *Lebanese National News Agency*, Apr. 21, 2006 (translation provided by US Government's Open Source Center – http://www.opensource.gov-document   number   GMP20060421511001); Saad   Hamiye,

"Islamic Resistance Restabilizes [sic] Equation 'Balance of Terror': Hostile Out-posts of Command & Control Within Range of Freedom Fighters' Fire," *Al-Intiqad* (online newspaper) Jun. 02, 2006, http://intiqad.com/english/mainnews/newsdetails.php?id=371 (accessed Jun. 8, 2006).

38. Adnan El-Ghoul, "Nasrallah won't rule out kidnapping more Israelis: Denies claims of plans to assassinate Abbas," *The Daily Star*, Jan. 31, 2005, http://www.dailystar.com.lb(accessed Jan. 31, 2005).

39. Nicholas Blanford, "Attack in Shebaa Farms may be a sign of more to come," *The Daily Star*, Jan. 11, 2005, http://www.dailystar.com.lb (accessed Jan. 12, 2005).

40. Sa'di Ulwah, "Hizbollah, Coalition of Benevolence, and Islamic Group continuing their campaigns to aid the Palestinians. Conditions in Lebanon are difficult 'but nothing is too dear for Palestine'," *Al-Safir*, Jun. 08, 2006 (translation provided by US Government's Open Source Center, document number GMP20060612611001); Special Information Bulletin, *Herzliyya International Policy Institute for Counterterrorism,* Jan. 12, 2005 (translation provided by US Government's Open Source Center – http://www.opensource.gov – document number GMP20050120000226).

41. Maggy Ayala Samaniego, "Drug trafficking ring that financed Lebanese extremist group Hizbollah dismantled," *El Tiempo*, June 22, 2005, (translation provided by US Government's Open Source Center – http://www.opensource.gov – document number GMP20040820000204); "Highlights: Argentina-Brazil-Paraguay Triborder Press 3 Aug 05," *Open Source Center/Foreign Broadcasting Information Service Report*, Open Source Center/FBIS Document number-LAP20050803000094, accessed 04 Aug. 2005; "Head of Canadian Shipping Company Charged With Attempting to Export Night-Vision Goggles to Hezbollah," *US Department of Justice Press Release* (online) May 25, 2004, http://newyork.fbi.gov/dojpressrel04/khali052504.htm (accessed Jun. 14, 2006); Matthew A. Levitt, The Washington Institute for Near East Policy, in testimony before the Senate Committee on Homeland Security and Governmental Affairs, May 25, 2005.

42. Osama Habib, "Hizbullah deluges economy in dollars," *The Daily Star*, Aug. 24, 2006, http://www.dailystar.com.lb (accessed Aug. 24, 2006).

43. For example, over 86 percent of those polled (and over 80 percent in each ethno-religious group) supported Hizbollah's continuing actions against Israel after the group's capture of two Israeli soldiers on July 12, 2006. Over 70 percent of the population (and at least 54 percent in each ethno-religious group) supported the capture/kidnapping itself. See these and other applicable poll results from a July 24–26, 2006 Beirut Center for Research and Information survey at http://www.beirutcenter.info/default.asp?contentid=692&MenuID=46 (accessed Aug. 25, 2006).

44. Anthony Shadid, "What Next, Lebanon?" *The Washington Post*, July 30, 2006: A1.

45. From this perspective, Hizbollah had a relatively free hand to support the Palestinian factions because of its ability to launch rockets into the northern third of Israel. This "balance of terror" limited an Israeli response to Hizbollah and, by extension, prevented Israel from fighting HAMAS and the Palestinian Islamic Jihad as effectively as it might have been able to.

46. See Chapter 13 ("Beginning of a War: The United States and the Hijacking of TWA Flight 847") of this volume for a brief description of events surrounding the Dawa 17.

47. Nawaf Obaid, "The Saudis and containing Iran in Lebanon," *The Daily Star*, Aug. 30, 2006, http://www.dailystar.com.lb (accessed Aug. 30, 2006); "Egypt rules out intervention in Lebanon," *The Daily Star*, July 27, 2006, http://www.dailystar.com.lb (accessed July 27, 2006).

48. Benjamin Barthe, "Only Extremists Will Emerge Winners from this Latest War," *Le Monde*, Aug. 1, 2006, pages unknown, (translation provided by US Government's Open Source Center, document number EUP20060801029006.)

49. Obaid, online edition.

50. For more on this topic, please see Ruth Margolies Beitler, "The Complex Relationship between Global Terrorism and U.S. Support for Israel," in *The Making of a Terrorist (Vol. 3)*, ed. James J. F. Forest (Westport, CT: Praeger, 2005).

CHAPTER 22

TURKEY AND THE PKK

Lydia Khalil

Since 1978, Turkey has been battling the Partia Karkaren Kurdistan, or the Kurdistan Workers Party, a Kurdish separatist movement better known as the PKK. Turkey's struggle against the PKK has spanned many years and undergone many iterations. Many times the Turkish government believed it had defeated the PKK and every time, the PKK has resurrected itself.

Turkey achieved a form of military victory over the Kurdish insurgent group after what effectively amounted to a scorched earth campaign in Turkey's southern region and the capture of its charismatic leader, Abdullah Ocalan in 1999. Turkey truly believed that it had finally put the reign of terror wrought by the PKK behind it, and began efforts to reconcile with its Kurdish population. This ushered a hopeful era among Kurdish political activists and ordinary citizens. It seemed as if the Turkish government was finally able to discuss the status of Turkey's Kurds outside the paradigm of the PKK.

However, proposed reforms did not go far enough or were never implemented, leaving Turkey's Kurdish population disenchanted. The PKK, sensing an opening due to increasing Kurdish dissatisfaction, as well as Iraqi Kurdish success in Northern Iraq, turned again to armed struggle. In 2004 attacks by the PKK were on the rise after a 4-year lull. In June 2004, the PKK withdrew the unilateral ceasefire it declared in 1999 after Ocalan's capture, citing the Turkish government's refusal to enter into a negotiated settlement. The PKK, now also operating under the name KADEK (Kurdistan Freedom and Democracy Congress), grew more forceful in its attacks against Turkish interests in the summer of 2006.

This has left Turkey once again feeling insecure and vulnerable; and once again it has set its military sights on the PKK. In response to the

withdrawn ceasefire, Turkish forces launched fresh
suspected targets in southeast Turkey. Turkey is ever
border action into northern Iraq.

A great deal of Turkey's domestic and foreign policy
to the Kurdish question. The Turkish government has
solve the problem once and for all.[1] The Kurdish ques
this—Where do Turkey's minority Kurds fit in a state an ̶ ̶, ̶ ̶that has
been largely defined as exclusively ethnic Turkish and has rejected the existence of an exclusive Kurdish identity? After many decades of forced
assimilation, Kurdish identity has not been erased, and has in fact grown
over the years.

Turkey's Kurdish citizens are dismayed that Kurdish issues are once
again viewed through the prism of PKK violence, upending the hopes of
a political solution and stifling moderate Kurdish activists. Has Turkey
squandered its initial victory over the PKK, or could it ever have claimed
victory in the first place? With so many unresolved political and cultural
issues between the Turkish government and its Kurdish population, the
PKK remains a violent factor in Kurdish struggle for greater political and
cultural recognition.

In light of renewed PKK violence and potential military operations into
Northern Iraq, Turkey would do well to learn from its past history dealing
with the PKK, as the Turkish government attempts, once again, to eradicate PKK terrorism once and for all. This analysis will discuss the arch
of Turkey's struggle against the PKK, a struggle that can be roughly divided into four categories: Failure to Acknowledge (1978–1985), Conventional Military Strategy (1985–1991), Transition to Counterterrorism Operations (1991–1999), and Post-Ocalan Arrest (1999–present). After a study
of Turkey's different counterterrorism policies this analysis extrapolates
lessons learned from Turkey's successes and failures in dealing with the
PKK.

A FAILURE TO ACKNOWLEDGE (1978 TO 1985)

With over 25–30 million people living in the same geographic area for
thousands of years, the Kurds are the largest ethnic group in the world
without a state to call their own. There are Kurds living in Syria, Iraq, Iran,
as well as Turkey; more than half of them (over 15 million) live within
Turkey's borders. When Turkey was consolidated out of the remains of
the Ottoman Empire, the Kurds were unable to form their own state and
were forcibly assimilated into Kamal Ataturk's vision of a single Turkish
identity after the empire's fall. Kurdish language and cultural expressions
such as music and dress, associations, and newspapers were banned. In
fact, the very concept of Kurdish identity, let alone nationality, was not
recognized until as recently as 1991.[2]

The PKK certainly was not the only Kurdish political movement brewing in Turkey, but it quickly established a reputation as the most violent. Instead of initially attacking the institutions of the Turkish state and its interests, it began by going after the traditional Kurdish elite who were believed to be loyal to the Turkish government, and muscled out more moderate Kurdish political associations. The PKK became known for its violent and fearless tactics, impressing or terrifying the local population into cooperation. By the late 1970s, the PKK had eradicated its political rivals and became the most important Kurdish political organization in Turkey, with a dedicated cadre of insurgents and supporters.[3]

By avoiding initial confrontation with the Turkish government and focusing their efforts on consolidating political control among the Kurdish community, the PKK avoided the scrutiny of the Turkish state while also demonstrating that it could challenge the status quo and state authority. The PKK did not directly attack Turkish interests until 1984. Meanwhile, the PKK had put in place all of the necessary elements and conditions for a guerilla war—a cadre of trained recruits, external funding and support, and at least the tacit support of Kurdish civilians.[4] When the PKK finally launched its first attack, the Turkish military, although aware of the PKK activities, was left unprepared, preoccupied as it was with regional conflicts.

Turkish inattention continued for the first 6 years of PKK activity. Turkish forces did not realize the extent of the PKK military threat and respond adequately.[5] Turkish military intelligence did not have a complete understanding of its enemy or its goals, therefore, it often miscalculated and wrongly assessed PKK strategic maneuvers. For example, Turkish security forces assumed that PKK militants would only use the Iraqi border as a base of operations to attack Turkey. They did not set up enough security along the Iranian border as they did not think Iran, with a restive Kurdish population of its own, would support the PKK. However, the PKK did receive Iranian support and acquiescence to set up operations along its border in exchange for intelligence information on Turkey and the promise not to establish contacts with Iranian Kurds.[6]

While Turkey was caught up in regional disputes, the PKK adeptly manipulated regional conflict to its advantage. Between 1979 and 1982, the PKK benefited from intelligence contacts with Syria, training facilities in Lebanon, and rear basing in Northern Iraq, as well as support from Iran, Greece, Cyprus, and the Soviet Union. All the while, the Turkish military was embroiled in the Turkish-Greek dispute. Its most effective forces, elite commando brigades, were stationed in the Aegean Sea and unavailable to fight against the PKK.[7]

More broadly, the Turkish government was not able to develop a comprehensive strategy for addressing the PKK threat. It could not come to a cohesive understanding of the problem among its military and political figures because there was considerable rivalry between civilian officials and military elements in the Turkish government. Civilian officials struggled to gain the upper hand over Turkey's national security strategy, while military leaders dismissed the civilian politicians as inexperienced in security matters. The military considered itself to be the traditional guardians of the Turkish state. Consequently, there was little dialogue or cooperation among the various elements of the government. Since they could not come to an agreement, the default response was to dismiss the PKK as a nuisance.

Although the PKK eventually became a force to be reckoned with, active popular support for the organization was still lacking in the early years. Most Kurdish villagers only wished to live and farm in peace. They may not have been completely satisfied with Turkey's treatment of their people, but they were not willing to disrupt their relatively peaceful existence and fight for abstract principles such as socialism or Kurdish nationalism. To remedy this, the PKK established ERNK, the National Liberation Front for Kurdistan, a political wing they used to manage its political and popular activities, in 1985.

The PKK did not rely solely on mass meetings and propaganda campaigns. They also used more aggressive methods to coerce Kurdish participation. The PKK began attacking Kurdish villages that did not support the PKK or were loyal to the Turkish state. By attacking villages, the PKK reasoned that Kurds would eventually conclude that Turkey could not protect its own citizens and it was therefore futile to fight against the PKK and cooperate with the Turkish military.[8] The PKK also began abducting young people from villages, instead of recruiting them, in order to solve the immediate problem of speedily increasing the PKK's ranks. They reasoned it would ultimately increase support for the organization, as families of abducted recruits would provide food and shelter to the militants.[9]

The PKK's aggressive and coercive tactics against Kurdish villagers began to backfire, but the Turkish military did not recognize its own advantage. The Turkish security establishment could have effectively taken advantage of Kurdish apathy or active derision toward the PKK by eradicating ERNK as soon as was established or offering incentives to Kurdish villagers. But because the Turkish government did not acknowledge the extent of the PKK threat, they and missed a key opportunity to nip PKK terrorism in the bud while it was still lacking popular backing and employing questionable tactics that alienated its potential base of support.

CONVENTIONAL MILITARY STRATEGY (1985–1991)

By the mid-1980s, the Turkish military began to internalize the threat posed by the PKK. By this point, the Turkish government viewed the PKK and Kurdish nationalist aspirations solely as a security issue, not a problem manifested from deeper political injustices against the Kurds.

Because Turkey could not muster the political imagination to deal with the Kurdish question and the PKK politically, it concentrated on fighting the PKK militarily. But instead of mounting a counterinsurgency and intelligence operation, they chose to respond through conventional military tactics. By the late 1980s, Turkey was undergoing greater democratization, but the military was still at the forefront of Turkish national security policy. The military regarded the PKK as it would any other conventional military threat, and embarked on a conventional military campaign to fight against it. It did not make use of the various political, economic, and intelligence tools necessary for fighting an effective counter-insurgency.

It was a mostly misguided military effort, complicated by internal struggles among civilian and military elements of the government. In 1987, the Turkish parliament lifted martial law and declared a state of emergency in the southeastern provinces. The hierarchy under the state of emergency was complicated and did not allow Turkish military troops freedom and flexibility to carry out operations. Furthermore, the army units that had been fighting the PKK for a number of years were recalled and replaced with gendarmerie units that had little combat experience.[10]

The military campaign against the PKK was also very defensive in posture. According to a study by Ersel Aydinly and Umit Ozdag, "The main aim of the commanders at this point became a defensive one of trying to stop and primarily avoid the attacks. The extra security measures included closing down some gendarmerie stations, halting nighttime operations and leaving smaller villages virtually on their own …"[11] In other words, force protection became more important that stopping the insurgency.

Mimicking the PKK's strategy of forced recruitment, Turkish forces made use of Kurdish villagers in their battle against the PKK through the village guard program, where Kurdish villagers became the Turkish military's fighting proxies. This solved two problems for the Turkish military. One, Turkish forces were not the ones on the front lines, so they could continue to maintain their defensive posture. Two, Kurdish village guards had more indigenous knowledge, thus they were naturally better combatants. Village guards were useful because they knew the PKK trails and the terrain, and they served as scouts for Turkish soldiers in search of rebel camps.

Villagers were co-opted before the PKK could get to them. If they fought on the side of the Turkish troops, they couldn't spend their time (directly or indirectly) supporting the PKK. However, these benefits were tempered by the fact that most village guards did not join this service out of any conviction. Even though they may have not supported the PKK,

Kurdish villagers in PKK territory were coerced or forcibly recruited into the village guard program. Kurdish villagers cooperated with Turkish forces because they had no choice. Furthermore, they were poorly equipped and poorly trained. This had the lasting effect of engendering more resentment towards the government.

Although the PKK often outwitted the lumbering Turkish military, they still did not have the level of popular support they needed to realize their goals. Turkey could have taken advantage of the PKK's lack of popular support; instead, brutal military tactics drew more Kurdish civilians to support the PKK. In their efforts to eradicate the PKK, Turkish forces destroyed entire Kurdish villages. The Turkish government resorted to the deportation and destruction of entire villages, and widespread use of brutality and torture.[12] According to one account, "Villagers suspected of sheltering guerillas or charged with refusing to participate in the officially promoted village guard system were forced to leave their homes and farms, which then are often burned to the ground to deprive guerillas of shelter."[13]

The PKK adeptly used Turkey's misguided military strategy to its advantage. Turkey's harsh and indiscriminate response to attacks allowed the PKK to rally popular support. Kurdish civilians came to view the PKK as the lesser of two evils. As the Turkish government became more indiscriminate in carrying out their scorched earth campaign, the PKK reconsidered its previous strategy of village raids and soft target attacks against uncooperative Kurds. They capitalized on Turkey's alienation of its Kurdish population and went one step further to bring more Kurds to their cause. The PKK offered a general amnesty to former village guard members who came over to their side. By 1991, the PKK's ranks had ballooned to 12,000.[14] While Turkey seemed to be doing everything to alienate popular support, the PKK proved increasingly adept, learning from its past mistakes and capitalizing on Turkish missteps.

The PKK was also able to take advantage of its relatively small size to outmaneuver the Turkish military. Observing total secrecy, the highly mobile PKK forces operated mostly at night. Even though the Turkish military was large, it was not large enough to control the entire Kurdish region and patrol every village. While, somewhat successful, the village guard system ultimately did more harm than good in terms of isolating popular support for the Kurdish cause.

TRANSITION TO COUNTERTERRORISM OPERATIONS (1991–1999)

Turkey's conventional military strategy failed on two fronts. Not only was it not effective in stopping PKK attacks, it also increased popular support for the PKK through its indiscriminant nature. Conventional forces and conventional military tactics were fundamentally ill equipped to battle a mountain insurgency.

The political-military leadership began to understand it needed a change. The civilian establishment had unwittingly limited the use of its own military against the PKK through democratization efforts. This stemmed from a misunderstanding of the nature of the conflict, as well as power struggles between civilians and military elements. The military establishment realized it needed a more offensive strategy.

Turkey fundamentally changed its threat perception toward the PKK. Although the Turkish government had gradually come to realize the extent of danger the PKK posed, it wasn't until the early 1990s that Turkey designated the PKK as the number one threat to the state, above Greece.

In 1991, the General Staff decided to give up on its defensive posture and adopt a "battlefield domination concept." The Turkish military was finally on the offensive. Army units were reorganized and retrained for counterinsurgency. The army purchased new equipment so it could better fight against the PKK at night and in the winter. They began adapting to guerilla tactics by laying ambushes and constantly patrolling areas of operations. According to one study of Turkey's counterterrorism tactics, "security forces ... in a sense lived and fought like the PKK members themselves."[15]

Turkish troops also launched cross-border operations into Northern Iraq, targeting PKK bases of operations. Turkey secured the support of Iraqi Kurdish groups like the Kurdish Democratic Party (KDP), successfully exploiting rivalry and tension between the PKK and the KDP. In 1995, the KDP began full cooperation with Turkey after the PKK overextended itself and attacked KDP installations. This time, Turkey was in a position to fully take advantage of this PKK mistake.[16]

The Turkish government also began working to turn Turkish and Kurdish popular opinion in their favor by using the media to broadcast their message discrediting the PKK and suppressing PKK propaganda. PKK publications were officially banned and the government recruited the mainstream media to voice their support for the new war policy against the PKK.[17]

The PKK, realizing that it was rapidly losing the military fight, began to concentrate on political activities. But the Turkish military also moved against ERNK and disrupted the large network the PKK had put in place.

Turkish propaganda against the PKK was beginning to show results. Kurds began to grow weary of the PKK. They grew tired of the violence and believed it was the result of misguided PKK objectives, strategy, and tactics, not Turkish brutality. This was an important turnaround for the Turkish government. They dulled the PKK's political edge by casting the blame for Kurdish suffering on the PKK, not their own policies.

Thus, the PKK began to moderate its political goals. It no longer called for separation or regional socialism, but greater cultural and civil rights for Kurds as well as for all Turks. As Michael Gunter, a leading expert on Kurdish issues, has noted, "Over the years his ideas evolved, so that by the early 1990s, Ocalan was asking only for Kurdish political and cultural rights within the preexisting Turkish borders. In part he had mellowed in the face of the hard realities imposed by the Turkish military and the outside world, hostile to any independent Kurdish state which might destabilize the volatile but geo-strategically important Middle East ... Ocalan has come to believe that both the Turks and Kurds would be better off living together in a Turkey that has become fully democratic."[18]

As a result of Turkey's shift in threat perception, offensive military posture and counterinsurgency (rather than conventional military) campaign, 1995 was the last year of intensive military clashes between the Turkish forces and the PKK. Despite the PKK's efforts to expand the area of engagement, recruit suicide bombers, and revert back to hitting soft targets, the PKK was unsuccessful in recovering momentum. The Turkish military successfully controlled PKK strongholds in northern Iraq, and by the summer of 1998, had wiped out of all its ranks from the Black Sea area. Remaining units fled to Iran and Iraq.[19]

The final blow was the arrest of PKK supreme leader Abdullah Ocalan and the PKK's second in command, Semdin Sakik, in April 1998. The arrests effectively destroyed the PKK's top-heavy hierarchy. Syria had harbored Ocalan for years, shielding him from Turkey's reach. Turkey became fed up with the situation and seriously threatened Syria with war if it did not expel him. Syria, sensing Turkey was serious in its threat, expelled Ocalan and the PKK leader roamed from Russia to Italy searching for safe haven. No country would have him, and in November 1998 he was detained in Italy. Ocalan was also forced out of Italy and was eventually captured by Turkish and Kenyan forces (with the help of U.S. intelligence) at the Greek embassy in Kenya.

Ocalan's capture was an especially significant event in the fight against the PKK because the group was a personality-driven, hierarchal organization that depended on his leadership to function. He made all the strategic decisions and was responsible for the political vision and military strategy. His arrest caused the PKK to fall apart due to dissent within the ranks and lack of political direction.

To the amazement of his supporters and government officials alike, Ocalan declared after his arrest that "The armed struggle was a mistake ... We are going to find a peaceful solution through dialogue within the framework of a democratic republic."[20] Since his arrest, Ocalan has repeatedly contradicted the ideological position he has advocated since the founding of the PKK. He effectively acknowledged that Kurdish society in Turkey did not support his long-held objectives and strategy.

He even acknowledged that the PKK's pursuit of a separate Kurdish state "could not be maintained and was not necessary either."[21]

Some viewed Ocalan's recounting as cowardly, others as a true change of heart on the issue of Kurdish independence. Either way, it discredited years of struggle of the PKK by its very founder. This was an unbelievable opportunity for the Turkish government to turn the conflict into a positive political prospect.[22] Ocalan did all of the work for the Turkish government; all the state had to do was capitalize on his statements. He de-legitimized himself as a leader and the decades-long struggle and goals of the PKK. He even called for the symbolic surrender of PKK forces.

Many found his stance unbelievable or intolerable, as many PKK senior commanders were quick to come out against the statements he made after his capture. However, his capture and declarations afterwards still paralyzed and destabilized the PKK.

POST-OCALAN ARREST (1999–PRESENT)

Throughout the conflict, Turkey has mostly focused on the military rather than political side of the counterterrorism equation. Turkey adapted its military strategy to effectively fight a mountain insurgency; however, it was much slower to incorporate and adapt an effective political strategy to deal with the PKK and curb its support among Turkey's Kurdish population.

Turkey's military strategy, while ultimately effective, was at times brutal and indiscriminate. It did not differentiate between the PKK and Kurdish civilians living in their area of operation. This seriously hindered Turkey's efforts to win the hearts and minds of its Kurdish citizens, whose cultural identity they did not even acknowledge. Abdullah Ocalan's capture and subsequent recanting of the Kurdish nationalist cause was the perfect opportunity to reconcile with its Kurdish population by recognizing their identity and granting them greater rights within the Turkish state. Turkey could engage with more moderate Kurdish political forces now that it had defeated the PKK insurgency.

But Turkey's views on Kurdish aspirations were tainted by the violent strategies of the PKK. After Ocalan's capture, and even prior to it, the PKK realized that it could not win the battle militarily and made overtures to the Turkish for political dialogue. However, the Turkish government refused to be seen negotiating with the PKK, even after it was defeated.

Just as Turkish forces had failed to see that a conventional defensive military posture would not defeat the PKK, Turkish forces once again failed to see that the PKK was a broken organization and that it could (and should) enter into dialogue with the group as a means to neutralize or eradicate the organization once and for all. Instead, the general staff declared that the PKK's peace offers were "propaganda spread by the terrorist organization in order to maneuver itself out of the dead end it has reached ... for this reason, the Turkish armed forces are determined to continue the battle until the last terrorist has been neutralized."[23]

Turkey's intransigence toward incorporating a political solution into its successful counterinsurgency strategy was finally reversed in August 2005 by Prime Minister Erdogan, who traveled to Diyarbakir and gave a groundbreaking speech in which he admitted to past mistakes of the Turkish government in the treatment of its Kurdish population. This was the first time a Turkish officials publicly declared that there was a "Kurdish problem." This gave new hope to Turkey's Kurds. The government was finally acknowledging their grievances.[24] This was an extremely important step for the Turkish government. It was difficult for the government to separate the terrorist insurgency perpetrated by the PKK from the legitimate concerns of its Kurdish population.

This is partly due to the fact that the PKK has been allowed to monopolize the discourse on the status of Kurds in Turkey. Up until Erdogan's 2005 speech, Turkey had proactively avoided resolving the Kurdish problem, effectively allowing the PKK to set the agenda and terms of debate. The PKK has dominated over all other Kurdish.

Now that Turkey had put democratization and EU accession on the top of its agenda, as opposed to regime survival, this afforded Turkey the opportunity to deal with the status of its Kurds outside the framework of the PKK and the insurgency. Turkey's Kurds no longer relied on the PKK to set the discourse and represent them.

Unfortunately, Erdogan's Justice and Development Party (JDP) created expectations that fell far short of Kurdish aspirations. Although Turkey—apparently determined to meet EU human rights standards—lifted the state of emergency in the southeast, and Kurdish villages are beginning to be resettled, there has been little implementation of reform laws. Local government officials continue to detain peaceful Kurdish activists and there has been little economic development in Turkey's poorest region.[25]

The JDP government took some important but fundamentally insufficient steps to legislate reforms that would guarantee Kurds greater cultural rights. Due to EU pressure, Turkey had previously allowed limited broadcasts in Kurdish on the state-run television channels. However Kurdish programming was not allowed on private television or radio stations. In December 2005, the Supreme Board of Radio and Television allowed private media companies to *apply* to be able to broadcast only 45 minutes a day in Kurdish. This was a positive, but very limited step.[26]

Although they address important cultural concerns, the reforms were still insufficient and inconsistent. The government allowed more Kurdish

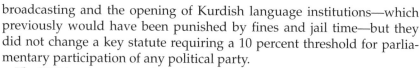

broadcasting and the opening of Kurdish language institutions—which previously would have been punished by fines and jail time—but they did not change a key statute requiring a 10 percent threshold for parliamentary participation of any political party.

The JDP is adamant against changing the 10 percent threshold because they benefit from the status quo. In the most recent elections, the JDP received 34 percent of the total vote but wound up with 66 percent of the seats in parliament because of the 10 percent rule. Smaller parties who received votes but fell short of the 10 percent threshold—like the Kurdish parties—were not allowed seats in parliament and the JDP reaped the benefits. The restructuring of this statute would be a truly significant reform that would open up political space for Kurdish and other minority representation in parliament, but the government is hesitant to do so.

Additionally, the JDP has used the Kurdish issue to fight secularism in Turkey instead of dealing with the Kurdish issue on its own merits. The JDP has identified secularism, not history and deep-seated political injustice, as the cause of Kurdish grievances and division between ethnic Turks and Kurds.[27] The JDP argued that Islamists had also suffered like the ethnic Kurds under the Kemalist ideology of previous Turkish governments. It set itself up as the opposition party, opposing state ideology and the military presence in the Kurdish regions, and garnered a great deal of the Kurdish vote. The JDP fears that the Kurdish issue could split the party and possibly undermine its support in certain provinces.

In a positive development, the JDP-led government finally approved a counterterrorism law in June 2006 that widens the definition of terrorism and gives additional powers to counterterrorism officials. This comes after years of inaction by the JDP because the party feared an expanded counterterrorism law could also be used against Turkish Islamist parties. The new law includes a number of provisions, including increased prison time for those who support terrorist organizations. The law also criminalizes financial and propaganda support of terrorist organizations.[28]

But Turkey may still be depending too much on military solutions. In late April 2006, the Turkish government deployed over 30,000 additional troops in the Kurdish southeast area to prevent the PKK from entering the border area between Turkey and Iraq. Recent reports suggest that the additional troop deployment is 250,000 strong, a considerable force to fight PKK troops that are not more than a few thousand in number.[29]

Is Turkey really doing everything it can? The passage of the counterterrorism law is an important step in the right direction. But Turkey is also contemplating crossborder operations into northern Iraq that could widen the conflict by upsetting an already fragile and hesitatingly cooperative neighbor by invading its territory.[30]

But with the PKK recently gaining renewed strength, the Turkish government has no choice but to be proactive politically, as well as militarily, lest the recent terrorist acts should increase and threaten to reopen Kurdish nationalist aspirations. The Turkish government must take care not to let knee-jerk military action overpower good political judgment. Potential gains from the counterterrorism law could be undermined by hasty military action or indiscriminate targeting of Kurdish politicians. Despite its recent passage, the counterterrorism law has already been used to stifle Kurdish political activity rather than fight the PKK.[31]

LESSONS LEARNED

In the age of international terrorism, all countries could learn from Turkey's struggle against the PKK. Turkey's experience also has important similarities with other high-profile insurgencies in the world today, among the many lessons that can be drawn, seven are highlighted here.

Acknowledging the Problem

This may seen like an obvious point, but it is critical for governments to acknowledge the true extent of an insurgent or terrorist threat before they can begin to remedy the problem. As in Turkey's case, the PKK did not begin by immediately attacking state institutions. This is why it is important to pay attention not only to the actions, but to the rhetoric and propaganda of terrorist insurgent organizations, and how they are interacting with other groups.

Not only must government officials realize the extent of the threat, but they must correctly diagnose the source of the problem. Terrorism and insurgencies are violent responses to political problems. All too often, governments characterize terrorist groups as psychopathic or pathological when there are political roots beneath their violent actions.

Throughout much of the conflict with the PKK, the Turkish government has maintained that citizens of Kurdish origin enjoyed full and equal rights. It has persistently denied that there was a "Kurdish problem"—admitting only that it had a terrorism problem. But according to historical researchers, an increasing number of Turkey's Kurds have demanded greater cultural and political rights over the years precisely because they were not there.[32]

Turkey's failure to acknowledge Kurdish grievances or Kurdish identity stems from deep-seated fears over the integrity of Turkish state. The Turkish government viewed the Kurdish issue as a zero sum game. If any other identity other than exclusively Turkish was recognized, the government feared it would lead to the disintegration of the state. Once Turkey had fully realized the extent of the PKK threat, officials came to believe that if they relented even slightly on any issue, it could escalate to the break-up of the country.[33]

Propaganda Is Paramount

A war against a violent political insurgency has two components. One is defeating the opponent militarily through effective counterinsurgency, counterterrorism, and intelligence measures. The other component is a propaganda/IO campaign. Unfortunately, terrorists and insurgents are typically more adept at the propaganda game than state governments.

The PKK perfected its propaganda war against Turkey over the years, highlighting Turkey's abuses against the Kurds, indiscriminant attacks against civilians and entire villages, and stagnant democratization measures. They waged the propaganda war as far away as Europe, and did so quite effectively, striking at a key Turkish aspiration (EU membership) and galvanizing the expatriate Kurdish community.

Early on, Turkey was not as successful in the propaganda war. They buckled under (many times accurate) depictions of the Turkish military and government treating its Kurdish population unjustly, fueling sympathy for the PKK cause. Although public opinion in Turkey is largely against the PKK, the global debate has been blurred. Ocalan embodied the axiom that one man's terrorist is another man's freedom fighter.

But over time, Turkey revved up its public relations campaign against the PKK, and it was able to discredit Ocalan and the PKK in the eyes of many at home and abroad. People were less willing to acknowledge the ambiguity of Ocalan's standing and the PKK's modus operendi—not only against Turkish forces and the Turkish official interests, but against the people whose lot they are purported to improve through their war against Turkey. Turkey drew attention to the fact that the PKK's military campaign centered on attacking and weakening the village guard system, essentially attacking their fellow Kurds.[34]

Turkey also had a lot of ammunition to discredit the PKK's claim as the premier representatives of the Kurdish nationalist cause. While this claim is often taken for granted by outside observers, it is not entirely true. The PKK began as a Marxist-socialist organization, and its primary aim was not Kurdish nationalism. Rather, the PKK envisioned a Kurdish socialist state primarily to promote socialism in the region. Furthermore, the PKK often had conflicting and adversarial relationships with other Kurdish groups in the Middle East, such as the KDP and PUK. For the most part, the PKK has not brought the region's Kurds together; rather it has fueled internecine conflict.[35]

One valuable tool Turkey used was the very words of PKK members. After Ocalan's capture, close lieutenants articulated serious criticisms of Ocalan and the organization. They claim he ordered the murder of rivals and dissidents, and declared his despotism on par with Hitler and Stalin. One commander stated, "I went to the mountains to liberate my country and for the independence of Kurdistan, but realized it was not possible to fight against [Turkey] in this organization."[36]

It is important to diminish the PKK's credibility as a nationalist organization as part of any ongoing IO/campaign. The PKK claims that Turkey is not representative of the Kurdish people, but it is equally important to point out that neither is the PKK. According to one analyst, "By virtue of its being considered a nationalist organization, the PKK seems to have inoculated itself against at least some of the damage that might be expected to result from reports of its murders, insurgent attacks, and collaboration with dictators."[37]

Counterinsurgency Is a Protracted Effort

Perhaps one of the most important lessons to be learned from Turkey's struggle against the PKK is that fighting an insurgency or terrorist movement is a protracted effort and there is no such thing as rapid or immediate success. By definition, insurgent terrorist groups are diffuse and flexible, making it easy for them to disappear in the face of a setback and reemerge when the time is right—usually when the government's forces are least ready.

In addition to anticipating a quick defeat, not matter how disheveled the insurgent forces seem, it is equally detrimental to declare victory too soon. The Turkish military repeatedly declared that the PKK was destroyed. Every time it declared victory, the PKK would attack, while the military would lose credibility and PKK would gain it. When Ocalan was captured, Turkey declared the end of the PKK. When Turkey adopted counterinsurgency tactics and successfully eliminated PKK fighters through helicopter attacks, Turkey declared the end of the PKK. Yet there is still no end to the PKK.[38]

States are eager to show progress against insurgents and demonstrate that they are taking strides to quickly defeat insurgent terrorist groups. Each major military campaign Turkey publicizes is a repeat of a previous effort it labeled decisive. During a major military offensive in the spring of 1997, journalists reported, "We've had figures from 30,000–50,000 troops involved ... So this seems perhaps to be on a scale of an operation two years ago, March 1995, when 35,000 troops were involved in a six week operation against PKK bases in northern Iraq. Many times the Turkish military has told us that the PKK is finished.

And, lo and behold, every springtime the PKK pops up again and we have attacks, and we have reports of clashes. And it never seems to happen."[39]

Insurgent groups are not easily deterred and tend to take the long view when it comes to their struggle. Steady, rapid progress is not easy to come by and this is a key lesson that government officials and military forces must realize and communicate to the public.

Insurgencies Are Targeted Not Total Wars

While it is important to pay attention to the concentric circles of support that sustain insurgent activity militaries will not be able to quell support from noncombatants through blunt military measures. Turkey at first battled indiscriminately through a scorched earth campaign that did not differentiate between civilians and fighters in its attempt to suppress support of the PKK. This achieved the opposite effect, compelling citizens to support the insurgents in the face of brutal military tactics.

Turkey's total war strategy did not help in their overall battle to defeat the PKK because they alienated hearts and minds and expanded the conflict unintentionally. Every Kurd had to choose a side. They either became actively involved against the PKK, came to resent the Turkish government (if they were forced into cooperating) or began to actively support the PKK. No one could remain neutral and because more personal stakes were involved, the fighting carried on. Everyone faced retaliation no matter what course they chose. The PKK could now justify its attacks against villages, attacks that had previously seemed indiscriminate in nature, giving them greater legitimacy.

Turkey's indiscriminate and brutal military campaign drew unfavorable comparisons with the PKK. One Kurdish villager perceived the situation this way when asked if the PKK also attacks and brutalizes civilians, "[The PKK] kill the village guards because they are looking for food and if the villagers don't give it they take it by force. But they don't destroy villages, they just kill the guards."[40] Turkey's total war policy was so out of control that a terrorist insurgency was viewed as more restrained in its tactics. It also depicted Turkish forces as weak instead of all- powerful, emboldening the PKK and its supporters further. One teenager from Yamac stated, "The soldiers can't find the guerrillas so instead they shoot us ... The soldiers were here a few days ago, and they told us to move out or else they would come back, burn our homes and kills us.... There is no life here, at least with the guerillas I will have a chance to defend myself."[41]

All Elements of Government Must Come Together

As researchers Aydinly and Ozdag have noted, "In a conventional war all the elements of national power are present to support the military, whereas in a low intensity conflict, the military is only one of the elements in the political, economic, cultural and social campaign . . ."[42] Cooperation and cohesion of all elements of government is required for an effective counterterrorism policy.

Over the years Turkey has moved further away from military rule. This shift is driven by Turkey's desire for greater democratization and EU accession, and has helped create opportunities for alternative solutions to the PKK problem. During periods of greater civil military cooperation and civilian control of the military, Turkey has had its greatest success against the PKK. When there have been clashes between civilian and military elements, counterterrorism policy is the least effective.

When former President and Prime Minister Turgut Ozal came to power in 1989, he originally took a very hard-line on the Kurdish issue and the PKK. However, he came to promote political dialogue on the Kurdish issue as an alternative to military action. He initiated efforts to remove the military from politics and decrease their policy role.[43]

The military's influence on policy is both direct and indirect. Many times, Turkey's political leaders have abdicated their responsibility for Turkey's security and role in providing a solution to the PKK problem, leaving the military to come up with its own solutions within its own paradigms. According to one report, "The military's influence on politicians is not always direct: Very often, politicians will simply fail to act, or take an initiative precisely because they fear alienating the commanders . . . in part because it indirectly absolves them from assuming responsibility for what generally is a failed policy."[44]

After Ozal's death in 1993, Tansu Ciller came to power as Prime Minister and tried to continue the political dialogue that had begun on the Kurdish issue. However, she could not overcome the hard-line position of other key officials, and underestimated the military's strength in influencing Turkey's policy toward the PKK. Chastised by the generals, she backed down from promoting dialogue and understanding on the Kurdish issue in favor of the military's line—"no concessions to Kurdish demands."[45] As this example shows, noncooperation between civilian and military leadership led to inconsistent and unimaginative policies.

Recognize the Time for Political Dialogue

It is also important for governments to realize that military defeat of an insurgency force is the first, not final, step. It needs to be coupled with a political solution, or else military victory is lost. This has been a difficult lesson for the Turkish government to learn. Turkey has been fearful of political dialogue with certain Kurdish elements and mostly refuses to deal with the PKK on a political level.

Officials fear dialogue will give the PKK greater legitimacy. This is certainly a justifiable concern of all governments, but there can be appropriate times to deal with an insurgent organization on a political level. The PKK has been crushed as a robust military organization, but in order to completely eradicate its military activities, it will be necessary to take political rather than military measures.

It is important to realize when it is time for political negotiations. This usually comes when an organization has been militarily defeated and its leadership is humbled. This is when the government has the upper hand. If no political dialogue is offered after military defeat, especially when the defeated have legitimate grievances (as in the case of the Kurds), it could spur continued fighting. An opportunity that offers a conclusion to the conflict instead becomes a period of lull and regrouping of insurgent elements. Ocalan's capture and denunciation of the PKK's cause was a tremendous opportunity Turkey could have taken further.

Regional Support Is Necessary

The world's Kurdish population is not confined to Turkey's borders. Kurds live in neighboring Iraq, Iran, and Syria and all three countries struggle with a Kurdish problem of their own. Dealing with their own Kurdish population's desire for greater representation and displays of identity, while conducting geopolitical rivalries among themselves, has led to a tangle of foreign and domestic policies on Kurdish issues and the PKK in particular.

For example, Syria had given safe haven and allowed Abdullah Ocalan to operate out of Damascus in order to keep Turkey distracted in a prolonged counterinsurgency against the PKK. Meanwhile, Syria was also violently repressing its own Kurdish population, whose aspirations they feared would weaken the Syrian state. Iraqi Kurdish groups are allowing PKK remnants to operate out of northern Iraq despite their commitment to better relations with Turkey. The PKK has taken advantage of regional rivalries to conduct operations and regroup during periods of intense military response.

Turkey needs the support and cooperation of its neighbors if it is to eradicate PKK violence once and for all. In seeking the support of its neighbors, Turkey should also take the opportunity to explore joint political solutions for the region's Kurds. Much of the anxiety over Kurdish political aspirations stems from the fear of spillover and insecurity over territorial integrity. All of the neighboring countries fear the establishment of a Kurdish nation-state carved out of their respective territories, and actively suppress their Kurdish populations so that this will never occur.

The Kurdish question is at its essence a regional issue. Expanding the political dialogue on a regional level will lead to a number of positive outcomes. One, the PKK will lose its monopoly over the dialogue on Kurdish issues. Two, if successful, it will relieve regional tensions and suspicions between countries who have historically used the Kurdish issue to influence neighboring countries' policies. And three, it could prevent the PKK from expanding its regional ties by keeping regional Kurdish leaders, especially Iraqi Kurds, engaged with nation-states instead of insurgent groups. Whatever political steps it takes must not be undermined by regional states who may be threatened by greater political freedoms afforded Kurds in Turkey.

Since Turkey has taken steps to deal with the Kurdish question politically and has strong ties to Iraq's Kurdish leaders—who now have considerable autonomy and control of territories—Turkey can and should begin to initiate regional dialogue on this topic so that whatever military victories it gains against PKK terrorism will not be undercut by PKK sanctuary or haven in other countries of the region. To its credit Turkey has been aggressively seeking Iraqi and U.S. cooperation on the PKK, but both have been intransigent. Turkish officials have become frustrated and are now threatening military action inside Iraq. Erdogan has publicly stated that he expects Iraq to remove the PKK presence in the northern mountains, otherwise "we will do what has to be done."[46] The danger is that Turkey's impatience to eradicate a few thousand PKK fighters could lead to a regional war.

The PKK has once again been brought to the regional fore. Angered by stepped up attacks against Turkey by the PKK from bases in Iraq and Iran, Turkey has called on the United States and its neighbors to take action and is threatening cross-broder operations. Turkey also rejected the PKK's offer for a renewed ceasefire and open talks.

It appears as if Turkey is reverting back to its old ways of doing things, while the PKK itself has fundamentally changed. Over the years, the PKK has adapted itself to changing circumstances. It altered its tactics, base of operations, its leadership—even its ideology. Turkey must also confront new realities and adopt lessons learned from its past experiences with the PKK.

NOTES

1. Nihat Ali Ozcan and M Hakan Yavuz, "The Kurdish Question and Turkey's Justice and Development Party," *Middle East Policy* 13, Issue 1 (Spring 2006): 102–119.

2. Kevin McKiernan, "Turkey's War on the Kurds," *The Bulletin of Atomic Scientists* 55, Issue 2 (March/ April, 1999): 26–37.

3. Roddy Scott, "PKK is down but not out as leaders talk of three front war," *Jane's Defense Weekly* 11, Issue 5 (May 1, 1999): 1.

4. Ersel Aydinly and Umit Ozdag, "Winning a Low Intensity Conflict: Drawing Lessons from the Turkish Case," *Review of International Affairs* 2 (2003): 101–121.

5. Michael Radu, "The Rise and Fall of the PKK." *Orbis* 45, Issue 1 (Winter 2001): 147.

6. Aydinly and Ozdag, "Winning a Low Intensity Conflict: pp. 101–121.

7. Ibid.

8. Ibid.

9. Kevin McKiernan, "Turkey's War on the Kurds," *The Bulletin of Atomic Scientists* 55, Issue 2 (March/April 1999): 26–37.

10. Ersel Aydinly and Umit Ozdag, "Winning a Low Intensity Conflict: Drawing Lessons from the Turkish Case," *Review of International Affairs* 2 (2003): 101–121.

11. Ibid.

12. Chris Kutschera, "Abdullah Ocalan: The End of a myth," *Middle East*, Issue 298 (February 2000): 12.

13. Marvine Howe, "As Generals Seek Military Solution, Kurdish Problem Poisons Turkish Life," *The Washington Report on Middle East Affairs*, 15, no. 4 (October 1996): 8.

14. Ersel Aydinly and Umit Ozdag, "Winning a Low Intensity Conflict: Drawing Lessons from the Turkish Case," *Review of International Affairs* 2 (2003): 101–121.

15. Ibid.

16. Roddy Scott, "Ankara's PKK hunt leaves regional conflict cycle intact," *Jane's Intelligence Review*, August 1, 1997: 355.

17. Ersel Aydinly and Umit Ozdag, "Winning a Low Intensity Conflict: Drawing Lessons from the Turkish Case," *Review of International Affairs* 2 (2003): 101–121.

18. Michael M. Gunter, "The continuing Kurdish problem in Turkey after Ocalan's capture," *Third World Quarterly* 21, no. 5 (2000): 849.

19. Ibid.

20. Chris Kutschera, "Abdullah Ocalan: The End of a myth," *Middle East*, no. 298 (February 2000): 12.

21. Michael Radu, "The Rise and Fall of the PKK," *Orbis* 45, no. 1 (Winter 2001): 147.

22. Michael Gunter, "The continuing Kurdish problem in Turkey after Ocalan's capture," *Third World Quarterly* 21, no. 5 (2000): 894–869.

23. Ibid.

24. Jon Gorvett, "Erdogan Speak Out," *Middle East*, no. 360 (October, 2005): 32–33.

25. "Hope versus fear; Turkey's Kurds," *The Economists* 368, no. 8335 (August 2, 2003): 40.

26. Ibid.

27. Nihat Ali Ozcan and M Hakan Yavuz, "The Kurdish Question and Turkey's Justice and Development Party," *Middle East Policy* 13, no. 1 (Spring 2006): 102–119.

28. "Anti-terror law toughened despite protests," *Turkish Daily News*, July 1, 2006, www.turishdailynews.com.tr.

29. "Turkey Deploys More Troops to Contain Kurdish Guerillas," *Associated Press*, April 28, 2006.

30. "Turkish premier expects Iraq to remove 'terrorist PKK groups,'"*TRT Television*, July 24, 2006.

31. "Pro Kurdish regional leader sentenced to two years in prison." *TRT Television*, July 26, 2006.

32. Ibid.

33. Ibid.

34. Mark Burgess, "In the Spotlight: PKK (aka KADEK)- Kurdish Workers Party (aka Kurdish Freedom and Democracy Congress)" *Center for Defense Information*, www.cdi.org/terrorism/pkk.cfm.

35. Michael Radu, "The Rise and Fall of the PKK." *Orbis* 45, no. 1 (Winter 2001): 147.

36. Chris Kutschera, "PKK dissidents urge a descent from the mountains." *Middle East*, no. 358 (July 2005): 12–15.

37. Ibid.

38. Roddy Scott, "PKK is down but not out as leaders talk of three front war," *Jane's Defense Weekly* 11, no. 5 (May 1, 1999): 1.

39. "Turkish Military Moves against PKK," *All Things Considered*, May 14, 1997: 1.

40. Richard Dowden, "The war that cannot speak its name." *The Economist* 339, no. 7969 (June 8, 1996): 13.

41. "Turkey's Kurds fight on alone," *The Nation* 258, no. 1 (January 3, 1994): 8.

42. Ersel Aydinly and Umit Ozdag, "Winning a Low Intensity Conflict: Drawing Lessons from the Turkish Case," *Review of International Affairs* 2 (2003): 101–121.

43. Henri J. Barkey and Graham E. Fuller, *Turkey's Kurdish Question* (Maryland: Roman Littlefield, 1998)

44. Ibid.

45. "Turkey's Kurds fight on alone," *The Nation* 258, no. 1 (January 3, 1994): 8.

46. "Turkish premier expects Iraq to remove 'terrorist PKK groups,'" *TRT Television*, July 24, 2006.

47. James Brandon, "The Evolution of the PKK: New Faces, New Challenges," *Terrorism Monitor* 4, no. 23 (November 30, 2006).

CHAPTER 23

ISRAEL'S STRUGGLE AGAINST PALESTINIAN TERRORIST ORGANIZATIONS

Joshua L. Gleis

Former U.S. Secretary of Defense Donald Rumsfeld put it best when he described Israel at the Munich Conference on Security Policy on February 7, 2004. In response to a question about America's policies toward Israel, he described the Jewish State as follows:

> We take the world like you find it; and Israel is a small state with a small population. It's a democracy and it exists in a neighborhood that in many— over a period of time has opined from time to time that they'd prefer it not be there and they'd like it to be put in the sea. And Israel has opined that it would prefer not to get put in the sea, and as a result, over a period of decades, it has arranged itself so it hasn't been put in the sea.[1]

The State of Israel views itself as a state under constant risk of annihilation, and as a result the country has always contributed a considerable amount of its GDP toward its defense.[2] Following the peace agreements with Egypt and Jordan, the risk of a full-scale ground assault on the scale of the 1973 Arab-Israeli War diminished considerably. However, with peace agreements not yet reached with the Palestinians and other Arab powers as well as Iran, Israel still remains vulnerable to both conventional and unconventional attacks. It is susceptible to terrorist attacks at home and abroad, and particularly low-intensity urban warfare in the West Bank and Gaza Strip as well as guerilla insurgencies from southern Lebanon. For this reason, Israel has classified terrorism as a tier-one threat to its security for quite some time. While the threats are not new, the lethality and number of attacks have increased significantly following the signing of the Oslo Accords in 1994 and later with the "Al Aqsa" Intifada in

2000.[3] Consequently, Israel has adopted many innovative policies, tactics, and technologies to counter these and other types of fourth-generation warfare.[4] As a result of these innovations, Israel's unparalleled experience with fighting terrorism makes it an important case study which the U.S. government and academics alike can learn from and apply to their own counterterrorism strategies.

Prior to the terrorist attacks of September 11, 2001, the United States' security apparatus had assumed a predominantly reactive role. Terrorism was viewed as a legal matter for the U.S. Justice Department to handle, with cooperation from other law enforcement agencies. U.S. intelligence collection was constrained by law and a fear of change that could disturb the status quo. Senior military officials in the Department of Defense were reluctant to take on a more active role.[5] Following the September 11 attacks, this began to change. The U.S. population demanded that more be done to protect the nation and new laws such as the USA PATRIOT Act were rushed through Congress. The necessity of a proactive approach led to an important revision of U.S. counterterrorism policies and a revamping of U.S. intelligence and military capacities to better meet the threat posed by terrorism.

The terrorist attacks also ushered in an initial increase in cooperation between the United States and its allies. Cooperation took many forms, with a special focus on additional conventional and unconventional military operations, and specifically on preemption against non-state actors and the states that assist them. While global cooperation has waned, Israel has continued to play a quiet but significant role in supporting the United States in boosting American domestic and international security.[6] With a substantial counterterrorism apparatus that is under constant international scrutiny, Israel is one country that the United States should look to in order to better understand and prepare against terrorist attacks.[7] This chapter will examine Israeli counterterrorism measures that it has incorporated in its fight against Palestinian terrorist organizations.

BACKGROUND

Under constant scrutiny and with few allies in the international community, Israel has been forced to take actions to protect itself while preserving its democratic principles. Its ability to adapt has allowed it to survive and thrive as a regional economic and military superpower, even while under the constant threat of attack. As Michael Goodspeed explains, the Israeli Defense Force (IDF) has been "Determined, brassy, bold and decisive. This characteristic doubtless stems from the sense of *En Brera* (no choice) ... The IDF in most of its numerous campaigns and countless counterterrorist operations has been dynamic and mentally adaptable."[8]

These characteristics are not just limited to the IDF but apply to the Israeli intelligence and counterterrorism communities as well. Two of the world's leading terrorist organizations, al Qaeda and Hizbollah, have attacked Israeli targets on separate occasions and have also cooperated with one another in developing terrorist tactics.[9] There are a number of reasons why this is the case.[10] Despite these enemies, Israel's flexibility and initiative has allowed it to remain in its current position of power in the world today—even in the face of continued terrorist threats and attacks. Israel has been forced to adopt a number of inventive methods that have allowed it to remain one step ahead of its adversaries. The following analysis will review the critical counterterrorism measures Israel has taken to better prepare for, as well as respond to, terrorist attacks on her own soil and abroad.

ORGANIZATION

Israel's ability to collect intelligence data on neighboring militaries, terrorist cells, and enemy activities is arguably its most effective and critical counterterrorism tool. The 1973 Arab-Israeli War was but one example of how dangerous a situation can quickly become when intelligence data is not properly collected, analyzed, and assessed. While many hear of the successful suicide bombings, rocket attacks, and other terrorist attacks on Israeli civilian targets, few are aware of the numerous terrorist attempts Israel foils every day.[11] When a terrorist cell is mobilized and has entered Israel proper, the country has already lost half the battle. It must then scramble its military and police forces to try to stop the terrorists before they can successfully strike—a high stakes gamble to say the least. The country has learned, therefore, the importance of procuring hard intelligence of a terrorist organization, cell, or even individual. This ability to acquire good intelligence in areas that it occupies, known as "intelligence dominance," has become a hallmark of Israeli intelligence agencies.[12] Intelligence allows Israel to better prepare for, as well as prevent, terrorist attacks. Below is a brief review of the security organizations in Israel that are responsible for preventing and reacting to terrorist attacks.

Shin Bet

Israel's "*Shin Bet*"[13] is the country's primary security wing responsible for protecting politicians and other dignitaries, providing counterintelligence, and collecting intelligence both domestically as well as in the West Bank and Gaza Strip. It has been highly successful in detecting terrorist threats because of its ability to successfully penetrate terrorist cells and interrogate its enemies. This has been done primarily by securing informants who will notify the Shin Bet of terrorists' movements, activities, and plans.[14] The Shin Bet then has the option of launching a military operation to arrest the terrorist cell and interrogate the terrorists, launch a targeted strike to eliminate the terrorists if the risk of arrest is too high or too late, or reconnoiter in order to acquire more information on the terrorist cell, its financiers, and sympathizers. If a terrorist cell has already been dispatched to launch a strike, it is the Shin Bet's responsibility to mobilize the necessary security forces to hunt the cell down, issue relevant security alerts to the public, and interrogate potential followers to obtain more information.[15] As a result, its cooperation with the Israel Defense Forces is of critical importance.

The Shin Bet is often inaccurately compared to the Federal Bureau of Investigation (FBI). A more precise comparison would be to that of Great Britain's Security Service (MI5).[16] While the FBI investigates white-collar crimes, violent crimes, criminal organizations, and combating public corruption under its priorities, the Shin Bet and MI5 do not.[17] As a result, the Shin Bet can devote more of its resources to combating terrorism.

Mossad

The *Mossad* (also known as the Institute for Intelligence and Special Operations or *ha-Mossad le-Modiin ule-Tafkidim Meyuhadim*) is Israel's primary foreign intelligence collection agency. On its web site, the Mossad states that it "has been appointed by the State of Israel to collect information, analyze intelligence and perform special covert operations beyond its borders."[18] In order to recruit Israel's best and brightest, both for electronics and programming as well as clandestine operations, the Mossad offers salaries competitive with the private sector.[19] It tends to focus on longer-term global projects and analyses than other Israeli intelligence agencies.

Directorate of Military Intelligence

The Directorate of Military Intelligence (more commonly known as *Aman*, an acronym for *"Agaf Hamodi'in"*) is believed to be one of the largest branches of the IDF, and is responsible for creating the National Intelligence Estimate (NIE) as well as provide early warning of approaching wars and other threats to the state.[20] Consisting of intelligence collection,[21] analysis, operations, counterintelligence, and assessment, *Aman* is the main intelligence arm of the IDF, and shares along with the Shin Bet and Mossad the intelligence responsibilities for the State of Israel. The three organizations work together and harmonize activities through a coordinating committee known as the Heads of Intelligence Services (or the Hebrew acronym VARASH).[22] While the heads of the Shin Bet and Mossad operate out of the Office of the Prime Minister (and thus report directly to the Prime Minister), the head of Aman reports to the Chief of Staff of the IDF, who then reports to the Minister of Defense. Following the intelligence failures of the 1973 Arab-Israeli War, the government decided to separate one of Aman's main collection divisions, known as Unit 8200 (responsible for signals intelligence, among other things) from the rest of the organization, in order to create better discipline and assessments, as well as spur competition, while still ensuring the organization works together overall.[23]

Civilian Aviation

While Israeli intelligence is widely known for its focus on human intelligence collection (HUMINT), the emphasis on human factors is seen throughout the Israeli counterterrorism security apparatus and in the security of its civilian aviation in particular. Israel's national airline El Al was successful for this reason in flagging the now infamous "shoe bomber" Richard Reid on his flight to Israel. He was subject to additional security checks, including x-raying his shoes and having an undercover armed marshal seated next to him.[24] This scrutiny was made possible by Israel's focus on the human factors for selecting suspicious people. A series of questions are asked of passengers prior to ticketing on El Al. Depending on the answers given and the appearance of the passenger (whether they look nervous, for example), about 1 percent of the passengers will be held for additional extensive security checks. The Shin Bet will also carry out surprise drills with dummy explosives to keep the level of vigilance high amongst screeners.[25]

Counterterrorism Teams

Israel has a number of police and military counterterrorism forces. Due to the relatively small size of the country,[26] these units can be deployed to most of Israel's cities fairly quickly. Some of these units can operate both domestically and abroad, depending on the type of mission or the threat posed. Three different types of counterterrorism units exist: *takeover units* have counterterrorism as their primary specialty; *engagement units* have counterterrorism as a secondary specialty; and *assisting units* help engagement and takeover units in their counterterrorism missions. There is also a designated counterterrorism unit that operates in Israel's southernmost, isolated city, Eilat.[27] During peacetime, at least two takeover units and one engagement and assist unit are on alert at any given time. This means they are in full gear and ready to be deployed to any location in less than an hour. Each assisting unit has a different specialty, such as hostage rescue, tracking, K-9, operating in snow and mountainous terrains, and bomb disposal.[28]

When time is of critical importance, an overlap of counterterrorism teams available becomes essential. For example, on April 7, 1980, terrorists took over the sleeping quarters of children at a *kibbutz* called *"Misgav Ham,"* taking seven children and one adult hostage, and killing one adult and one infant in the ordeal. The IDF's *Sayeret Matkal*,[29] the only "takeover" hostage rescue unit at the time, was on another mission and not available for immediate action. As a result, a secondary unit that was based in the region—*PALSAR Golani*—was chosen for the initial assault. Unfortunately, *Golani*'s assault failed, but *Sayeret Matkal*, which was en route to Misgav Ham at the time, eventually led a successful rescue operation that killed all of the terrorists and freed the remaining hostages, with no soldiers or hostages killed or injured.[30] The operation was the first in Israel to use attack dogs from the specialized *Oketz* unit (also known as "Unit 7142") for the assault. The lessons for U.S. forces from this operation are:

1. Overlapping counterterrorism units are essential.
2. The use of attack dogs both in rescue operations as well as in arrests and assaults on terrorists is very useful. Using dogs helps prevent the loss of human life, as the animals have a better sense of smell, and can reach and access places that soldiers cannot (and do so faster).

SECURITY VERSUS CIVIL LIBERTIES

Balancing a democracy's security while upholding civil liberties can be a difficult task. Western nations such as the United Kingdom, Spain, and France have all encountered such dilemmas over the years to varying degrees, and the United States is certainly dealing with these issues today. Yet what makes the Israeli case particularly extraordinary is threefold: First, Israel is looked at more vigilantly by the international community than are most other nations in the world.[31] Second, the extended period of time and frequency under which Israel has suffered from terrorism has provided Israel with a wealth of time to explore different legal alternatives, and these changes continue to evolve. Third, unlike other conflicts where fourth-generation warfare is used to liberate a part of a given territory in order to claim an autonomous state, in the Israeli case the situation is different:[32] "liberation" according to the majority of terrorist groups currently engaged in activities against Israel, is not just the liberation *from* Israel, but instead the "liberation" of the entire country *of* Israel through its destruction. As a result of these three factors, Israel's level of balancing security against serious threats of terrorism makes it a quintessential example of a country experiencing the "democratic dilemma." This predicament pits a democratic society's counterterrorism policy against preserving liberal and democratic values.[33]

Interrogations

Interrogations are an important aspect of intelligence gathering, and are critical to a successful counterterrorism policy. The methods of interrogation, though, can be highly controversial, depending on the techniques used. Torture, for instance, is a common interrogation tool used by nations and organizations around the world. According to Michael Koubi, the chief interrogator for the Shin Bet from 1987 to 1993, the Israeli security service does not focus on torture to get information from terrorists. Instead, interrogations are conducted using psychology, mind games, tricks, and an understanding of the adversary.[34] Regarding the importance of mastering the language of the person he is interrogating, Koubi explains,

> At school I learned Arabic better than other students, even the small nuances....I can speak Arabic better than most Arabs. I learned the Egyptian, Lebanese and Jordanian dialects as well as Palestinian....So when I'm interrogating someone who lived in Egypt they'll think I was actually there ... Language is the key.

He continued:

> It's about making them think they cannot hide anything from you. If they live in a certain neighborhood in Cairo, I will learn everything about that neighborhood. I will know it like the back of my hand....You have to learn everything about him and his background....You have to be better than him, wiser than him.[35]

Concerning the incident in the Abu Ghraib prison, Koubi was reluctant to criticize U.S. actions, but explained that while Israel has one member of a security service for every 1,000 people in the Gaza Strip, U.S. forces have one security person for every 100,000 people. He further observed that when interrogators do not understand those they are interrogating—their culture, their language, and their behavior—then incidents such as Abu Ghraib may be expected to occur.[36]

While the usefulness of torture is debatable, its violation of international law is not.[37] As Israel has signed and ratified the United Nations Convention against Torture and Other Cruel, Inhuman or Degrading Treatment or Punishment, and whereas torture is outlawed under the Israeli Penal Code, accusations by detainees and human rights groups of torture prevalent throughout the 1980s and 1990s, were taken seriously.[38]

Consequently, the Landau Commission of Inquiry was set up in 1987 to review the interrogation methods of the Shin Bet.[39] According to an Israeli document submitted to the United Nations Convention against Torture and Other Cruel, Inhuman or Degrading Treatment or Punishment:

The Landau Commission recognized the danger posed to the democratic values of the State of Israel should its agents abuse their power by using unnecessary or unduly harsh forms of pressure. As a result, the Commission recommended that [among other points] psychological forms of pressure be used predominantly and that only 'moderate physical pressure' (not unknown in other democratic countries) be sanctioned in limited cases where the degree of anticipated danger is considerable.[40]

The Commission further established that in dealing with terrorists that have information vital to the security of the State of Israel, "moderate degree[s] of pressure, including physical pressure, in order to obtain crucial information, is unavoidable under certain circumstances."[41] The commission recognized the danger as a democracy for making such guidelines, and as a result, included several additional principles in order to ensure the preservation of human dignity. These included:

1. Disproportionate exertion of pressure on the suspect is not permissible—pressure must never reach the level of physical torture or maltreatment of the suspect, or grievous harm to his honor that deprives him of his human dignity.
2. The use of less serious measures must be weighed against the degree of anticipated danger, according to the information in the possession of the interrogator.
3. The physical and psychological means of pressure permitted for use by an interrogator must be defined and limited in advance, by issuing binding directives.
4. There must be strict supervision of the implementation in practice of the directives given to Shin Bet interrogators.
5. The interrogators' supervisors must react firmly and without hesitation to every deviation from the permissible, imposing disciplinary punishment, and in serious cases, causing criminal proceedings to be instituted against the offending interrogator.[42]

Following the decision of the Landau Commission, human rights groups continued to argue that while the Israeli interrogation methods had changed, the Shin Bet was still committing torture. At the time, the State of Israel received little sympathy for this dilemma from its allies.[43] Once again, the Supreme Court of Israel (High Court of Israel) heard arguments by human rights groups against Shin Bet's interrogation methods.

On September 6, 1999, the Supreme Court ruled unanimously that, while it recognized Israel's "unique security problems," the Shin Bet would no longer be able to perform even moderate forms of torture and instead would be required to employ the same methods as the police.[44] The ruling banned shaking, placing prisoners in contorted positions, and all other forms of physical abuse that had been cited by human rights groups and the United Nations Committee on Torture.[45] The Supreme

Court did leave open an exemption to the law, but only with regard to immediate threats (i.e., "ticking bombs"). Such cases would require the torturer to later be put on trial and justify his actions before the court.[46] This was a landmark decision for a democratic state constantly under the threat of terrorism, and one that the United States' government, human rights organizations, the United Nations, and other nongovernmental organizations (NGOs) should study.[47]

TACTICS, DOCTRINE, AND TRAINING

Proper military doctrine and training is essential for carrying out effective counterterrorism measures. Israel has recognized for many years the need to adapt its training and doctrines to better deal with its own war on terrorism. As U.S. Marine Lt. Col. Dave Booth—who oversaw recent Marine Corps-Israeli Defense Force exchanges—stated, "We're interested in what they're developing [in Israel], especially since September 11 . . . we're interested in their past experience in fighting terrorism. So there's a lot of things we could learn from them."[48]

Iraq, in particular, is one place where many similarities can be drawn between Israeli and American efforts. Battles often take place in densely populated refugee camps in the West Bank and Gaza Strip, where the IDF is under severe media scrutiny that holds sway over world opinion. As a result, the IDF has to be extra careful not to cause many civilian casualties that could result in a successful military victory becoming a diplomatic defeat. While fighting an asymmetrical war, Israel's adversaries quite rationally employ unconventional tactics, since they are aware of the fact that they cannot challenge the IDF in a conventional manner. As a result, they use tactics to inflict damage that also risk interfering and even killing their own civilian population, with the knowledge that these deaths can and will be used in the future as a propaganda tool. As an Islamic Jihad bomb-maker during a battle in Jenin described to the Egyptian *Al-Ahram Weekly*:

> We had more than 50 houses booby-trapped . . . We chose old and empty buildings and the houses of men who were wanted by Israel because we knew the soldiers would search for them . . . We cut off lengths of main water pipes and packed them with explosives and nails. Then we placed them about four meters apart . . . in cupboards, under sinks, in sofas.[49]

Due to these measures taken by terrorists and militants, Israeli forces have been forced to adopt methods to avoid such successful defenses. Narrow alleys require infantry to move house to house, blowing holes through walls in order to limit the danger to them from snipers and explosives planted in the entrances.[50] While these tactics are criticized by some as being unnecessarily harsh, one must take into account the reality in which the Israeli security forces are operating, and these counterinsurgency tactics should be kept in perspective. Israel has the capability to use its Air Force and artillery to strike at targets without risking the lives of its infantry soldiers. Yet it chooses to send in infantry in order to avoid unnecessary harm to civilians. Counterterrorism actions are not pretty, and the IDF is not perfect; however, none of the Palestinian cities remotely resemble Grozny following the Russian offenses or Dresden in 1945.[51]

Education

Sustaining the morale of the public is considered essential, according to counterterrorism experts such as Dr. Boaz Ganor, the Executive Director of the International Policy Institute for Counterterrorism (ICT) in Herzliya, Israel. A crucial element of terrorism is the psychological effect it has on the target's population. To counter this, Israel has enacted educational policies in its schools to combat this "morale warfare."[52] The ICT is one of the country's leaders in these educational programs. They include seminars for teachers, civic leaders, and students, as well as training courses for teachers, all of which focus on countering the psychological effects of terrorism.[53]

Due to the measures taken by these Israeli educational programs, the level of vigilance of the average Israeli plays an important role in the counterterrorism campaign. As Jonathan Tucker explained in his *Strategies for Countering Terrorism: Lessons from the Israeli Experience*, "the average Israeli is highly aware of suspicious packages, individuals, and actions that could pose a threat to public safety, and does not hesitate to notify the police. As a result, ordinary citizens foil more than 80% of attempted terrorist attacks in Israel, including time bombs left by terrorists."[54]

Preemption

Israel is famous today for its preemptive attack in the 1967 "Six Day" War. As the 1973 Arab-Israeli War would later prove, the preemptive gamble was a wise move. However, Israel has used other techniques at its disposal to defend itself, including prevention. For example, Israel's bombing of the Osirak reactor was a preventive action that it took to prevent Iraq from developing nuclear weapons.[55] While it was condemned by the United Nations and the United States at the time, Israel's actions were later recognized by many in the United States and others countries to have been a great service to the region; especially considering that if Saddam Hussein had nuclear weapons when it invaded Kuwait, the outcome would likely have been very different than what actually occurred.

Diplomacy

Diplomacy was used to help achieve peace agreements with Egypt and Jordan. Clearly, ending hostilities with both nations could never have been achieved through preemption or other uses of force. Recognizing that military force can only achieve so much, Israel has attempted to use diplomacy throughout its history, often times secretly, and not always successfully. Nonetheless, it is a critical tool that should not be abandoned in these difficult times.

Targeted Assassinations

Can a democratic society kill a terrorist without bringing them to trial first? Israel has argued that due to the relative ease and effectiveness of dispatching a suicide bomber, compounded with the fact that deterrence or prevention by the time of dispatch is ineffective, targeted assassinations are a necessary counterterrorism action that saves lives.[56] Israel has contended that the policy of targeted assassination works. For example, following the assassinations of Hamas chiefs Sheikh Ahmed Yassin and (later) Abdel Aziz Rantitisi, Hamas vowed massive retaliations against Israeli targets. Political commentators and politicians around the world condemned the attacks and stated that it would just inflame the "cycle of violence." The "boomerang effect" would surely take place once again.[57] Yet no such attacks took place in the aftermath of the bombings. In fact, it took nearly 6 months for any successful Hamas attack to be inflicted upon Israel.[58] The assassinations left Hamas without their number one or number two leaders in the West Bank or Gaza Strip, and caused other leaders to go into hiding. Thus, the infrastructure and activity of Hamas was badly damaged by the fact that terrorists were suddenly too preoccupied with their own personal safety to focus on orchestrating attacks against Israel. As Tucker and others have observed, Israel views terrorism as warfare and therefore the laws of war as applying to it, including preemption.[59]

One reason for Israel's ability to carry out targeted assassinations effectively is its excellent intelligence in the region. While there are those who argue that all assassinations, including targeting heads of state, are not only moral but essential,[60] in this context targeted assassinations refers to the targeting only of terrorists and other members of nonstate armed groups who cannot be otherwise apprehended. With this said, Israelis have argued that assassinations should not necessarily be limited just to "ticking bombs," but to the leaders and other members of the organizations that uphold the day-to-day operations. Limiting it to just "ticking bombs"—i.e., terrorists who are on their way to carry out an attack—would in fact leave open the possibility of the "boomerang effect."

Deterrence

On July 12, 2006, after firing katyusha rockets on Israeli towns along Israel's northern border, Hizbollah operatives kidnapped two Israeli soldiers and brought them to Lebanon. By day's end eight Israelis were killed, dozens more wounded, and two soldiers kidnapped. Hizbollah had committed a similar kidnapping operation on October 7, 2000, shortly after Israel's withdrawal from southern Lebanon in May 2000 in compliance with United Nations resolutions. After the October 2000 kidnapping, Israel agreed in 2004 to release over 400 Palestinian and Lebanese prisoners for one Israeli businessman (who was a reserve IDF colonel) and the corpses of the three kidnapped Israeli soldiers. The hope by Hizbollah was that Israel would act again in a similar fashion,[61] especially considering that Prime Minister Ehud Olmert and Defense Minister Amir Peretz did not come from military backgrounds, and that the IDF was in the midst of a campaign to release another Israeli soldier who had been kidnapped by Hamas right outside of the Gaza Strip on June 25, 2006.[62] The Hizbollah kidnapping in 2000, along with Israel's withdrawal from southern Lebanon due to what was interpreted by much of the world as caused by pressure from Hizbollah, decreased Israel's deterrence capability—a critical weapon in its arsenal.

As groups such as Hizbollah and Hamas (as well as their sponsors Iran and Syria) continued to target Israelis without facing repercussions, their operations and aims grew bolder. Whereas in the past enemy countries and terrorist organizations knew that if they crossed certain "red lines" Israel would respond with its characteristic massive counterattack, following Israel's 2000 withdrawal from southern Lebanon this began to change. As a result, after the Hizbollah kidnapping operation in the summer of 2006, the Israeli government decided to reengage Hizbollah in battle, not only to get back its kidnapped soldiers but more importantly, to regain its deterrent capability in the eyes of the enemy; in the hopes of preventing attacks in the future. It was critical to show the enemy that attacks against Israel would not go unanswered. While there is argument over whether Israel performed as well as it should have against Hizbollah, it is certain that Israel's actions privately helped it regain its deterrence capabilities and will give pause to terrorist organizations and their sponsors when deciding how and whether to attack Israel in the future.

Psychological Warfare

The fighting with Hizbollah in southern Lebanon in the summer of 2006 provided a rare glimpse into Israel's psychological operations. In August of 2006 it was reported that Israel was interrupting Hizbollah's television and radio station news reports with pictures of dead Hizbollah fighters and other Israeli propaganda, in order to show the Lebanese that while Hizbollah was not reporting their casualties, its death toll was mounting. Israel also sent messages to Lebanese land and mobile phones, e-mail messages and notes dropped from airplanes to provide similar information, in another effort to convince the Lebanese public opinion that Hizbollah was not invincible and that Israel was capable of reaching everyone, everywhere.[63]

Risk Aversion

Finally, the issue of risk aversion must be addressed. As counterterrorism expert Paul Pillar noted, "while Israeli counterterrorist commando forces are second to none," success still comes at a price.[64] Many Israeli counter-hostage and counterterrorist missions have led to the deaths of both rescuers and hostages. However, despite these setbacks, Israel continues to dispatch counterterrorist forces for hostage rescue missions.[65] It can ill afford to withdraw from conflicts where there are initial setbacks or loss of life.[66] This is not to say that Israel has no concern for the lives of its citizens; quite the contrary. Groups such as Hizbollah and Islamic Jihad have actually pointed to Israel's almost obsessive desire to protect its soldiers and citizens as a weakness.[67] However, despite this "obsession," the use of Special Forces, counterinsurgency, and specific counterterrorist methods discussed above are essential to winning the fight against terrorist groups, sometimes in the face of criticisms from the international community, and even its own pubic opinion.

TECHNOLOGY

Technology is another critical element of counterterrorism measures employed by Israel to protect its civilian population and members of its armed forces. Israel is one of the world's leading exporters of weapons today, with many of these extensive technologies having been incorporated into U.S. military hardware as well.[68] It is responsible for many innovations, from the world's fastest supercomputer to new tools for disinfecting water.[69] Furthermore, Israel has developed a number of specific technologies for use in the counterterrorism arena. These include technologies for protecting both its civilian population and security apparatuses.[70] For example, Israelis have developed an anti-suicide bomber bus, an aircraft anti-missile system, a flying rescue car, and a robotic rescue spider for the civilian sector, while in the military sector new technologies include an anti-ballistic missile, bulletproof wall covering, and a long-range explosives detector. Each of these is described in the following section of this chapter.

Counterterrorism Bus

Israeli authorities recognize that a security guard cannot be in all places at all times. Since Israeli buses are constantly targeted by terrorists, one technology currently in a pilot program in high-risk cities in Israel is a new anti-terror bus that reduces the risk of suicide bombers successfully entering a bus and blowing himself/herself up. According to reports, the bus includes:

> An explosives-detection device at the front of the bus; a turnstile through which passengers enter but which can be locked by the driver to prevent entry of suspicious persons; a device to protect the driver and passengers in the front of the bus; another turnstile at the back of the bus to allow passengers to exit but to prevent bombers from entering; and a two-way communication system between the driver and the people outside waiting to board the bus.[71]

Civilian Aircraft Anti-Missile System

"Flight Guard" is an anti-missile airborne system designed for protecting civilian aircraft. The system has radar that automatically responds to incoming missiles or rocket attacks by laser tracking the incoming projectiles and releasing invisible flares to destroy them.[72] Following the attempt by al Qaeda elements to shoot down an Israeli airliner during takeoff from Mombasa, Kenya, using a shoulder-fired missile, the Israeli government has made the development and implementation of this system a priority.[73] The system, which currently costs approximately $1 million, has already been purchased by Israel's national airliner "El Al."[74]

"Rotorless" Vertical Takeoff and Landing Vehicle

An Israeli company called Urban Aeronautics has designed a vertical takeoff and landing (VTOL) vehicle called the "X-Hawk" that does not have rotors and whose engines are internal.[75] With fly-by-wire technology and engines that are currently in use in helicopters, this vehicle is able to fly and land in places where other aircraft cannot. For example, it can park inside a building or latch onto the window of a skyscraper.[76] The significance of this vehicle is that it can be used for ferrying firefighters and law enforcement agents to the top of skyscrapers as well as rescuing civilians stranded on top floors. Israel's skyscrapers in Tel Aviv have been targeted by terrorists before, and there is serious concern about a 9/11-type of attack taking place on Israeli soil.[77] As a result, there are a number of new technologies that are in development; however, the X-Hawk has recently received the most attention.[78]

Robotic Spider

Led by the "Homefront Command," the IDF has an excellent reputation around the world for saving lives. IDF Search and Rescue (SAR) teams have been dispatched literally all over the world, including to the U.S. Embassy bombings in Nairobi, Kenya, and Dar es Salaam, Tanzania, on August 7, 1998. As the first foreign SAR team to arrive on the scene, the Israelis were responsible for rescuing three people, recovering 95 bodies, and performing surgeries on embassy staff.[79] To assist future rescue efforts, a team of researchers at Israel's Institute of Technology (or "*Technion*") have developed a new robotic spider that can crawl into tunnels, airways, and pipes to help locate survivors and repair infrastructure in locations that are difficult or dangerous for a person to approach. This spider is the most maneuverable robot ever created.[80]

Arrow Weapons System (AWS)

Following the 1991 Gulf War, when 39 Scud missiles were launched at Israel from Iraq, Israel and the United States began developing a missile defense system to protect against medium and short-range missiles.[81] According to the Israeli Ministry of Defense website, the main objective of the Arrow system is to "protect Israel against [a] Theater Ballistic Missiles (TBM) threat."[82] Having completed a number of successful tests, the Arrow is currently operational, making Israel the first nation in the world to have a functioning theater missile defense program.[83]

Bulletproof Wall Covering

Achidatex, a company that produces bulletproof vests and armor for vehicles, has developed a bulletproof wall covering. Made of a "special weave of cotton and Kevlar—the material in the manufacturing of bulletproof vests—[it] can be applied to a structure's interior walls like wallpaper and can be painted over."[84] Explosive blasts and aftershocks cause nearby buildings' walls to collapse, resulting in flying projectiles. These projectiles are responsible for the majority of deaths and injuries from nearby attacks.[85] This ballistic wall covering can serve as another form of protection for personnel in embassies, consulates, and military barracks, especially in locations that cannot establish ideal security perimeters.

Long-Range Explosives Detector

In order to better implement and protect lives when setting up perimeters, road blocks, and other methods for detecting and preventing suicide bombers and other terrorists, a new Israeli laser has been developed to serve as a long-range explosives detector. Using laser spectroscopy, the device can detect different explosives by the unique reflection of light that each substance emits, with a special focus on explosive materials.[86] While older versions require the device to be no farther than 2.5 meters away from the target, and its use was potentially harmful to the person targeted,[87] newer models have allowed for detection from "dozens of meters away," thus making it possible to be used both for detecting car bombs as well as suicide bombers from a safe distance.[88] Once in service, this laser can help prevent the need for inconveniencing innocent travelers who may currently have to pass through metal detectors, have their clothing swabbed, or be physically patted down.[89] Additionally, the device will enable troops to detect potential threats from safe distances, without the need to send dogs or even soldiers to verify a threat. As a result, it may become a significant addition to a soldier's defense.

CONCLUSION

Since declaring independence on May 14, 1948, Israel has enjoyed a warm relationship with the United States based on shared values, interests, and democratic principles. The United States was first to recognize the new Jewish state, and since that time, ties and cooperation between the two nations have increased significantly. The two countries are tied economically, militarily, diplomatically, and ideologically. Following the September 11 terrorist attacks, Israel's ability to support the United States in its war on terrorism, as well as its interest in offering assistance, became more apparent to American security officials, politicians, and civilians. The U.S. armed forces, and particularly the Marine Corps, have advanced their joint training exercises with Israeli forces, paying close attention to Israel's urban warfare tactics.[90] However, in the intelligence field there is still an extreme lack of trust toward the Israeli intelligence and security agencies. Regardless of this distrust, Israeli public and private organizations have consulted and trained American forces on a number of tactical and strategic missions in Iraq, and supplied Israeli know-how and technology (often developed with the help of American funding) to the United States.[91] Such cooperation is also taking place outside the military sphere, at local, state, and national levels.[92]

As religious and ethnic strife continues around the world, the use of terrorism will likely continue to expand, with targets reaching beyond the immediate borders of the conflicted regions. As a result, the United States must be prepared to continue developing its counterterrorism security apparatus to better defend itself and its interests in a proactive manner. There are few countries in the world today that can recognize and understand the predicament of the American people today. Israel is one of those nations. As President John F. Kennedy put it:

> This nation, from the time of President Woodrow Wilson, has established and continued a tradition of friendship with Israel because we are committed to all free societies that seek a path to peace and honor individual right. We seek peace and prosperity for all of the Middle East firm in our belief that a new spirit of comity in that important part of the world would serve the highest aspirations and interests of all nations.[93]

NOTES

1. *Secretary Rumsfeld Availability at the Munich Conference on Security Policy,* http://www.defenselink.mil/transcripts/2004/tr20040207-0432.html (accessed May 24, 2006).

2. *Defense Spending Fell in 2003,* http://www.globes.co.il/DocsEn/did=842906.htm (accessed May 24, 2006).

3. More recently the number of attacks against Israel has reduced dramatically. Reasons for this will be discussed in following chapter.

4. Martin van Creveld, *The Transformation of War* (New York: The Free Press, 1991) chap. VII; and *The Changing Face of War: Into the Fourth Generation,* http://www.d-n-i.net/fcs/4th_gen_war_gazette.htm (accessed May 24, 2006).

5. "Showstoppers," *Weekly Standard,* January 26, 2004: 27.

6. As will be discussed later in the chapter, Iraq in particular is a theater in which the United States can adopt many initiatives from Israel.

7. Israeli counterterrorism measures include tactics, doctrine, technology, education, and civil liberties.

8. Michael Goodspeed, *When Reasons Fail* (London: Praeger, 2002), p. 141.

9. Rohan Gunaratna, *Inside Al Qaeda* (New York: Berkley Books, 2003), p. 16.

10. Paul Wilkinson, *Terrorism Versus Democracy* (London: Frank Cass Publishers, 2000), p. 35.

11. *Chronology of thwarted terrorist attacks in Israel,* http://www.adl.org/Israel/israel_thwarted_attacks.asp (accessed December 17, 2004).

12. "Intelligence Dominance; A better way forward in Iraq," *Weekly Standard,* July 31, 2006.

13. The Shin Bet is also commonly referred to as the *"Shabak"* in Hebrew and the *"GSS"* in English. The *Shin Bet, Shabak* and GSS are all acronyms for *Sherut ha-bitachon ha-Klali,* or in English, the General Security Service.

14. *Shabak,* http://www.fas.org/irp/world/israel/shin_bet/ (accessed August 1, 2006).

15. *Shabak,* http://www.intelligence.org.il/department/secret.htm (accessed July 2, 2006) (in Hebrew).

16. *MI5 The Security Service,* http://www.mi5.gov.uk/ (accessed August 10, 2006).

17. *Facts and Figures 2003*, http://www.fbi.gov/priorities/priorities.htm (accessed December 14, 2004).

18. *About Us*, http://www.mohr.gov.il/Mohr/MohrTopNav/MohrEnglish/MohrAboutUs/ (accessed August 3, 2006).

19. *"James Bond, No Big Deal": Technological Aspects of Mosad Operations Viewed*, http://www.fas.org/irp/world/israel/mossad/techops.htm (accessed December 17, 2004).

20. Zeev Maoz, *Defending the Holy Land* (Ann Arbor, MI: University of Michigan Press, 2006), p. 503.

21. Falling under the rubric of intelligence collection are: HUMINT or human intelligence, SIGINT or signals intelligence, OPINT or open source intelligence, ELINT or electronics intelligence, VISINT or visual intelligence, as well as intelligence collection of various types from the air force and navy and other branches of the military.

22. Zeev Maoz, *Defending the Holy Land* (Ann Arbor: University of Michigan Press, 2006), p. 19.

23. Zeev Maoz, *Defending the Holy Land*, 503, and also through interviews conducted with former and current members of the military and intelligence establishments, during the summer of 2006 in Israel.

24. R. Reid and Keith B. Richburg, "Shoe Bomb Suspect's Journey Into Al Qaeda," *Washington Post*, March 31, 2002, A09. Also see: *Strategies for Countering Terrorism: Lessons from the Israeli Experience*; available from http://www.homelandsecurity.org/journal/articles/tucker-israel.html (accessed May 26, 2006).

25. This entire section was based on readings from: *Strategies for Countering Terrorism: Lessons from the Israeli Experience*; available from http://www.homeland security.org/journal/articles/tucker-israel.html (accessed May 26, 2006).

26. Including land and water, Israel is 20, 770 sq km. *The World Factbook*; available from http://www.cia.gov/cia/publications/factbook/geos/is.html (accessed May 26, 2006).

27. *Kapap*; available from http://www.answers.com/topic/kapap (accessed August 10, 2006). See also, *Israeli Security Forces*; http://experts.about.com/e/i/is/Israeli_Security_Forces.htm (accessed August 10, 2006). And: *Israeli Death Squads*; http://forum.atimes.com/topic.asp?ARCHIVE=true&TOPIC_ID=69 (accessed August 10, 2006). This information was also confirmed and expanded on in an interview with a former member of Sayeret Matkal in Israel in August of 2004, as well as through interviews conducted with former and current members of the military and intelligence establishments, during the summer of 2006 in Israel. For security purposes these people cannot be named.

28. Nathaniel Rosen And Max Kitaj, "Some of the IDF's best," *Jerusalem Post*, August 3, 2006, 5. See also, *Israeli Death Squads*; http://forum.atimes.com/topic.asp?ARCHIVE=true&TOPIC_ID=69 (accessed August 10, 2006). Some of this information was also obtained through interviews conducted with former and current members of the military and intelligence establishments, during the summer of 2006 in Israel as well as an interview with a former member of Sayeret Matkal that took place in Israel in August of 2004. For security purposes these people cannot be named.

29. Also known as the "General Staff Reconnaissance Unit", or "The Unit."

30. The majority of this information is taken from an interview with a former member of Sayeret Matkal, who participated in the *Misgav Ham* rescue operation. The interview took place in Israel in August of 2004. For security purposes this person cannot be named. Information on many of Israel's counterterrorism units can be found on the pages below. In April of 1980 the police Takeover unit *YAMAM* did not yet exist in its current form. Today it would most likely be responsible for conducting a similar raid on Israeli soil. Further information on this raid is from *Israeli Special Forces History*, http://www.jewishvirtuallibrary.org/jsource/Society_&_Culture/special.html (accessed May 24, 2006).

31. For example, Israel has been condemned more than any other nation in the world, including being the only country to ever be condemned for the act of one man (Baruch Goldstein, following the massacre in a Hebron Mosque where 29 Muslim worshippers were killed in 1994)—this despite the fact that the act was condemned by Israel and the government was in no way connected to the attack. Yet a country such as Syria was not condemned by the United Nations even after the massacre in Hama, Syria, where an entire city was destroyed by Syrian forces and an estimated 20,000 to 40,000 civilians were killed. Similarly, the United States is also viewed more critically in the world, in part due to its superpower status. *The Massacre of Hama (1982) ... Law application requires accountability*, http://www.shrc.org.uk/data/aspx/d1/1121.aspx (accessed May 24, 2006).

32. See for example, the Tamil Tigers in Sri Lanka or the Basques in Spain.

33. *Efficacy Versus Liberal Democratic Values*, http://www.ict.org.il/articles/articledet.cfm?articleid=447 (accessed May 24, 2006).

34. *Psychology and Sometimes a Slap: The Man Who Made Prisoners Talk*, http://www.nytimes.com/2004/12/12/weekinreview/12word.html?oref=login&oref=login&hp (accessed December 13, 2004).

35. "The Enforcer," *New Scientist*, November 20, 2004: 46.

36. Ibid.: pp. 35, "The Enforcer," *New Scientist*, November 20, 2004: 46.

37. *Convention against Torture and Other Cruel, Inhuman or Degrading Treatment or Punishment*, http://www.ohchr.org/english/law/cat.htm (accessed May 24, 2006).

38. It should be noted that these court rulings refer to interrogations that take place by the Shin Bet against non-citizens of Israel. Israeli police have very different guidelines for dealing with citizens.

39. On May 31, 1987, the Government of Israel resolved: "That the matter of the GSS methods of interrogation regarding the Hostile Terrorist Activity (HTA) is—in the wake of Criminal Appeal 124/98 (Nafsu)—a subject of vital public importance at this time which requires elucidation." As a result, Israel decided: "To establish a Commission of Inquiry ... [that] will make recommendations and proposals, as it sees fit, also regarding the appropriate methods and procedures concerning the unique needs of the struggle against Hostile Terrorist Activity." *Commission of Inquiry into the Methods of Investigation of the General Security Service Regarding Hostile Terrorist Activity, Report One* (Jerusalem: Government Press Office, 1987) 1.

40. Israel is the only signatory to the UN CTOCIDTP ever to argue that its interrogation methods did not constitute torture, instead of other signatories accused of torture who simply denied the claims. The cited information is derived from an Israeli claim submitted to the UN CTOCIDTP on February 18, 1997, and can be found at the Web site of the Committee Against Torture,

http://www.unhchr.ch/tbs/doc.nsf/0/653f6da51dc104d68025646400568ed6? OpenDocument (accessed May 24, 2006).

41. Ibid., p. 40.

42. Ibid., p. 41.

43. In a sign of changing times, the United States recently attempted to block a new UN treaty designed to prevent torture. *U.S. fails to block torture treaty*, http://news.bbc.co.uk/1/hi/world/americas/2150302.stm (accessed May 24, 2006).

44. Since the Landau Commission had allowed for "moderate physical pressure," it was argued that the Shin Bet had used that stipulation as a legal loophole to continue the torture of security prisoners. *Israeli 'torture' methods illegal*, http://news.bbc.co.uk/1/hi/world/middle_east/439554.stm (accessed May 24, 2006).

45. *Supreme Court Judgment Concerning the Legality of the GSS- Interrogation Methods* http://www.mfa.gov.il/MFA/Government/Law/Legal%20Issues%20and% 20Rulings/Supreme%20Court%20Judgment%20Concerning%20the%20Legality% 20of (accessed May 24, 2006).

46. *Israeli Supreme Court bans interrogation abuse of Palestinians*, http://www. cnn.com/WORLD/meast/9909/06/israel.torture/#2 (accessed May 24, 2006).

47. *Israeli ruling on torture claims*, http://news.bbc.co.uk/1/hi/despatches/ 97029.stm (accessed May 24, 2006).

48. *US Marines Studying Israeli Urban Warfare Methods at Jeninom*, http://www. rense.com/general25/usmar.htm (accessed May 24, 2006).

49. *The phantom massacre*, http://www.freerepublic.com/focus/news/672761/ posts (accessed May 24, 2006).

50. *U.S. takes pointers from Israel*, http://www.charleston.net/stories/033103/ ter_21westbank.shtml (accessed December 17, 2004).

51. "Center Right—Israel's Unexpected Victory over Terrorism," *New Republic*, September 27, 2004: 19.

52. *A New Strategy Against the New Terror*, www.ict.org.il/articles/articledet. cfm?articleid=4 (accessed May 24, 2006).

53. Paul Pillar, *Terrorism and US Foreign Policy* (Washington, DC: Brookings Institution Press, 2001), p. 216.

54. *Strategies for Countering Terrorism: Lessons from the Israeli Experience*, http://www.homelandsecurity.org/journal/articles/tucker-israel.html (accessed May 24, 2006). Also, see *Israel: Iran 'months' from making nukes*, http://edition.cnn. com/2006/WORLD/meast/05/21/iran.nuclear/ (accessed May 24, 2006).

55. Ian Lesser, Bruce Hoffman, John Arquilla, David Ronfeldt, and Michele Zanini. *Countering the New Terrorism* (Washington DC: Rand, 1999), p. 79.

56. *Supra note* 54.

57. *Supra note* 51.

58. *Supra note* 51.

59. "In early 2002, an IDF judge advocate-general ruled that the assassination of terrorists is legal when (1) well-supported information exists that the suspect has organized terror attacks in the past and is planning to carry out another one in the near future; (2) appeals to the Palestinian Authority to arrest the terrorist have been ignored; (3) attempts by Israeli troops to arrest the suspect have failed; and (4) the killing is not intended as retribution for past acts of terror

but is designed to prevent an incipient attack that is likely to inflict multiple casualties." *Strategies for Countering Terrorism: Lessons from the Israeli Experience*, http://www.homelandsecurity.org/journal/articles/tucker-israel.html (accessed May 24, 2006). This issue was also discussed with Dr. Richard Shultz during the fall of 2004.

60. Ward Thomas, "Norms and Security: The Case of International Assassination," *International Security* 25, no. 1 (Summer 2000): 105–133.

61. *Nasrallah: Hostages in secure location, far away*, http: //www.ynetnews.com /Ext /Comp /ArticleLayout/CdaArticlePrintPreview /1,2506,L-3274616,00 .html (accessed August 9, 2006).

62. Manya A. Brachear, "Kin of kidnapped soldier seek help in waiting game," *Chicago Tribune*, August 7, 2006.

63. *IDF broadcasts Hizbullah's dead on al-Manar* http://www.ynetnews.com/ articles/0,7340,L-3288442,00.html (accessed August 10, 2006); and *Psychological warfare on phone*, http://www.newsday.com/news/nationworld/world/ny-wocell094845200aug09,0,2834253.story?coll=ny-worldnews-print (accessed August 10, 2006).

64. Paul Pillar, *Terrorism and US Foreign Policy*, 98–99.

65. Israel, like the United States, has still negotiated with terrorists despite their "no negotiation" policy, and does not always follow its doctrine of preemption and prompt retaliation. As discussed in: Ian Lesser, et al., *Countering the New Terrorism*, 120.

66. Paul Pillar, *Terrorism and US Foreign Policy*, 99.

67. Hizbollah leader Hassan Nasrallah and Chief Palestinian Authority cleric Mufti Sheikh Ikrimeh Sabri have made such statements about Jews and Israel, as is explained in: *Dealing in Death*, http://www.nationalreview. com /script /printpage.p?ref = /comment /stalinsky200405240846.asp (accessed May 26, 2006).

68. *Israel Ranked as World's Third Largest Weapons Exporter*, http://www. ishitech.co.il/0303ar5.htm (accessed May 24, 2006).

69. 2005—The Year in Science & *Technology in Israel*, http://www.isracast.com/ tech_news/301205_tech_2005.htm (accessed May 24, 2006).

70. Some of the technologies are dual-use for both military and civilian purposes.

71. *Israel Unveils Unique Anti-Terror System for Buses*, http://www.cnsnews. ;om/ViewForeignBureaus.asp?Page=%5C%5CForeignBureaus%5C%5Carchive% C%5C200401%5C%5CFOR20040123c.html (accessed May 26, 2006).

72. "Flight Guard passes missile test," *Jerusalem Post*, July 14, 2004: 17.

73. *Israel plans missile protection for civilian aircraft*, http://www.janes.com/ onal_news/africa_middle_east/news/jar/jar030516_1_n.shtml (accessed May)06).

Charles Starmer-Smith, "Passenger jet gets anti-missile technology," *Daily vh* (London), November 27, 2004, Travel 04.

The placement of these engines not only helps reduce the size of the ve-t also has a considerably lower noise level. These characteristics help in he X Hawk significantly more accessible and useful than helicopters or ˉaft as a rescue tool.

76. *Flying Car—A Dream Come True*, http://www.isracast.com/tech_news/021104_tech.htm (accessed May 24, 2006).

77. *Bomb explodes at Israeli fuel depot*, http://www.smh.com.au/articles/2002/05/23/1022038458284.html (accessed May 24, 2006).

78. Other Israeli skyscraper rescue technologies have not been included in this paper because they either are not in as serious a development stage or have not been given as serious consideration. Information on other rescue technologies can be found at the following Web sites: *New interest in high-tech escapes from high-rises*, http://www.csmonitor.com/2001/1025/p14s1-stct.html (accessed May 24, 2006). See also: *Israeli flying car to provide revolutionary rescue tool*, http://www.israel21c.org /bin /en.jsp?enZone =Technology&enDisplay =view&enPage =BlankPage&enDispWhat =object&enDispWho =Articles^l814 (accessed May 24, 2006).

79. *IDF Rescue Operation in Kenya*, http://www1.idf.il/DOVER/site/mainpage.asp?sl=EN&id=5&from=history&docid=23042&Pos=27&bScope=false (accessed May 24, 2006).

80. *Robotic Spider Will Save Lives*, http://www.isracast.com/tech_news/robotic_spider_tech.htm (accessed May 24, 2006).

81. *Israel's New Arrow Missile Defense System*, http://www.brook.edu/views/interviews/ohanlon/20021006.htm (accessed May 24, 2006).

82. Managing the Arrow Weapons System are the Missile Defense Agency (MDA) for the USA and the Defense Research & Development Directorate (MAF'AT) for the State of Israel. *Welcome to the Arrow Weapon System Site*, http://www.mod.gov.il/pages/homa/index.html (accessed May 24, 2006).

83. *The Arrow Missile Program*, http://www.jewishvirtuallibrary.org/jsource/US-Israel/Arrow.html (accessed May 24, 2006).

84. *New Israeli Technology Detects Bombs and Deflects Rockets*,http://www.israelnationalnews.com/news.php3?id=66519 (accessed May 24, 2006).

85. This technology has been tested at the Marine Corps base in Quantico, VA. *Ballistic Wall Covering*, http://www.achidatex.co.il/balpbw.htm (accessed May 24, 2006).

86. Operational models are being developed jointly with the Israeli Police. *Supra note 84.*

87. *Israel Develops Laser To Detect Explosives*, http://mailman.io.com/pipermail/freemanlist/2003-July/000779.html (accessed May 24, 2006).

88. *Israeli Company Develops Long Range Explosive Detector*, http://www.isracast.com/tech_news/081004_tech.htm (accessed May 24, 2006).

89. *Supra note 88.*

90. *U.S. Marines studying Israeli urban warfare methods at Jenin*, http://216.26.163.62/2002/ss_military_06_06.html (accessed May 24, 2006).

91. *Israel trains US assassination squads in Iraq*, http://www.thepowerhour.com/articles/israel_trains.htm (accessed May 24, 2006).

92. *Bergen County Police Officers Train in Israel*, http://www.jewishbergen.org/israel/police.shtml (accessed May 24, 2006).

93. *U.S. Presidents on Israel*, http://www.jewishvirtuallibrary.org/jsource/US-Israel/presquote.html (accessed May 24, 2006).

CHAPTER 24

FIGHTING FIRE WITH FIRE: DESTROYING THE SYRIAN MUSLIM BROTHERHOOD

Brian Fishman

And thus ended the ordeal of military jihad in Syria. It started with Marwan Hadid and ended with the sacking of Hamah City, the destruction of the "vanguard" and the elimination of the "jihad pockets" of the Muslim Brotherhood.[1]

—Abu Mus'ab al-Suri

Counterinsurgency in an autocratic state is the struggle of an individual or party to fend off challenges to its power and legitimacy. During the 1970s and 1980s, Syrian President Hafez al-Asad fought off numerous enemies, some of whom plotted silently within the government's power structure, while others took up arms in the streets of Aleppo, Homs, Hama, and Damascus.

This chapter examines Asad's efforts to defeat the armed groups operating in the streets, many of whom were associated with the Syrian Muslim Brotherhood (Brotherhood). Although the focus is on Asad's campaign against the militant Islamic opposition, it is impossible (and would be entirely improper) to separate Syria's counterinsurgency policies from Asad's efforts to build a social and political system that would enable him to dominate the Syrian state.

Asad's strategy for defeating the Brotherhood contained four elements employed by all governments fighting counterinsurgencies:

1. strengthen and legitimize the government, in this case Asad himself;
2. target the insurgent's support networks domestically and internationally;

3. de-legitimize the insurgents; and
4. use violence to eliminate the insurgents and deter sympathizers.

In order to understand Asad's counterinsurgency, one must understand the social bases of both the Ba'th party in Syria and the Brotherhood. This chapter thus begins by reviewing the rise of Asad's Alawite-dominated Ba'athist regime in Syria and the Sunni Brotherhood-associated movement that violently challenged his authority. This leads naturally into a discussion of the struggle for legitimacy between Asad and the Brotherhood, which is followed by an explanation of the most important violent episodes, including the destruction of the Brotherhood's most important base: Hama.

BACKGROUND

Social divisions in Syria are organized around three important (and overlapping) axes. The first is religious. Approximately 69 percent of the population are Sunni Muslims, 14 percent are Christians, 12 percent are Alawites (which is a form of twelver Shiism), and the remainder are Druze and Isma'ilis.[2] Latent tension between the groups was exploited by the colonial French, who favored Druze and Alawite leaders as a means of controlling the majority Sunnis.[3] When the French left, many Alawites remained in positions of power, to the chagrin of Sunni leaders, who resented rule by a minority.

The second important axis is economic. The Muslim Brotherhood groups that led the rebellion against Hafez al-Asad had roots in the artisans and trading classes of large Syrian cities. This is partly because Syria's Imams and "men of religion" were so poorly compensated that they were forced to earn a living as part-time tradesmen.[4] In contrast to these small-scale traders, Syria's Ba'th party was based in Syria's rural peasants, who were attracted to Ba'thist socialism and promises of land redistribution.[5] Although the Muslim Brotherhood uprising is often portrayed as a religious struggle, frustration with migration into cities and declining wages bolstered the primarily urban insurgent movement and made cracking down on the Brotherhood much more difficult.

The third axis is political. After the French left their former colony in 1946, political factions that for years had hovered beneath the surface of social debate burst onto the national scene. Nationalists, Communists, Islamic parties, and Ba'thists struggled to assert control over a chaotic state that was "in many respects a state without being a nation-state."[6] The age-old question of power distribution was a critical issue during the insurgent period. The political chaos made plenty of room for Syria's two most important revolutionary parties: the Muslim Brotherhood and the Ba'th.

The Syrian Ba'th

Despite hints of Syrian democracy in the late 1940s, a series of military coups was punctuated only briefly by a union with Egypt between 1958 and 1961.[7] After the union dissolved (following another military coup), the stage was set for ambitious Ba'thists—including a young air force officer named Hafez al-Asad—to seize power. In 1963, he and a small cadre of fellow Ba'thists known as the Military Committee initiated a relatively bloodless coup that brought the party into power for the first time in Syria's history.[8]

Despite this victory, Asad would wait another 7 years before seizing full control in Syria. The Ba'th party was nearly as fragmented as Syrian society. By early 1970, Asad controlled much of the military, but his chief rival within the Ba'th, Salih Jadid, still held sway within the political establishment.[9] Asad's entrée to power was the Palestinian uprising in Jordan known as Black September. After supporting a half-hearted invasion of Jordan to defend the Palestinian militants from Jordanian reprisals, Asad used the chaos to arrest Jadid and his supporters.[10] Effectively, Asad had seized control of the Syrian state, an authority he would not relinquish until his death 30 years later.

The Muslim Brotherhood

The Muslim Brotherhood was founded in 1928 by an Egyptian schoolteacher named Hassan al-Bannah. Al-Bannah rejected what he considered Western decadence and cultural aggression, as well as the secular nationalist movements becoming prominent in the Middle East. In 1949, al-Bannah was assassinated (likely by Egyptian agents) for his views, but his successors continued to promote a return to what they considered Islam's core principals.

The Brotherhood's ideology first took hold in Syria among students studying Islamic law. Some had attended al-Azhar University in Egypt, while others were influenced by proselytizing teachers that traveled to Syria in the 1930s.[11] The ideas imported from Egypt found fertile ground in Syria's numerous Islamic social welfare societies.[12] Since these organizations were primarily based in large urban areas, the Brotherhood focused most of its recruiting and organizational efforts in large cities. In rural areas without Islamic social groups and a class of craftsman, the Brotherhood had trouble building social support.[13]

After the French abandoned Syria, the Brotherhood was one of many small parties that vied for political power in Syria. But the Brotherhood's effective organization, coupled with popular frustration over the creation of Israel in 1948, enabled it to capture three parliamentary seats in the 1949 election.[14]

The Brotherhood struggled along as a minor political party until 1958, when Egypt and Syria joined to form the United Arab Republic. Gamel Abdel al-Nasser's pan-Arab ideology was diametrically opposed to the Muslim Brotherhood, which was already banned in Egypt. Blocked from the political scene, the Brotherhood refocused on imparting education and moral values to Syrian society—Islamic *dawa* in the classical sense.

The Brotherhood continued in this capacity until the early 1970s, when a member of the Brotherhood—Marwan Hadid—decided that more direct action was necessary. Hadid, who had worked with Sayyid Qutb in Egypt during the 1960s, believed that only armed resistance could bring an Islamic authority to power in Syria.[15] The Brotherhood was torn between Hadid supporters in Aleppo and Hama and the more moderate wing in Damascus led by Issam Attar.[16] After a failed attempt to reconcile the factional differences in 1971, Hadid organized his own subgroup, *al-Tali'a al-Muqatila*—The Fighting Vanguard.[17]

ASAD'S STRUGGLE FOR LEGITIMACY

The Vanguard did not begin militant operations immediately, but it did start to build the organizational capacity to challenge the Syrian state. Even a low-level threat was dangerous to Asad because he was still consolidating power in the Syrian state—not an easy task for an Alawite in Syria.

One of Asad's early challenges was to write a constitution to legitimize his rule. The first draft, which emphasized the secular and nationalist values of the Ba'th, enraged much of Syria's Sunni population, which was already predisposed to believe that Alawites like Asad were not actually Muslims.[18] Asad quickly recognized his mistake: he first amended the constitution to require that the president be a Muslim, and then had the chief of the Higher Shi'i Council in Lebanon issue a fatwa confirming that Alawites were indeed Muslims.[19] Despite this effort, the episode highlighted sectarian divisions in Syria and hampered Asad's ability to refute the Brotherhood on religious grounds.[20]

Middle East scholar and former Dutch Ambassador to Iraq and Egypt Nikolaos Van Dam cites two reasons for Asad's failure to de-legitimize the Brotherhood:

> Firstly, as the Ba'th considered itself a secular Arab nationalist organization, it generally refused to enter into a religious debate. Secondly, official reactions to anti-Alawi sectarian polemics and propaganda in similar 'religiously

inspired' language would not only appear to confirm the allegations that the regime was dominated and inspired by the Alawis, but, even worse, would most probably stimulate sectarian controversy and antagonism.[21]

The problem was not just Alawite religious differences with Sunnis, but that a sect representing 10–12 percent of the Syrian population had come to dominate the Syrian government. This fact was not lost on the Muslim Brotherhood. In November 1980 the Brotherhood directly appealed to Alawites that "9 or 10 percent of the population cannot be allowed to dominate the majority because that is against the logic of things."[22]

Despite these missteps, Asad did attempt to blunt the Brotherhood's religious message, primarily by emphasizing his own Islamic beliefs. These efforts involved gratuitous public prayers, performing the hajj, and using Koranic verses in his speeches.[23] Some of these efforts backfired; when Asad released a Koran with his face on the cover, many Sunnis interpreted it as disrespectful to Islam.

Asad had more success using nationalism to bolster his legitimacy. Syria's relative success in the 1973 war against Israel bolstered Asad in Syria. Later in the decade, Asad appealed for Syrian unity after what he considered Egypt's betrayal by signing the Camp David accords with Israel.[24] The Camp David accords were used by both sides in Syria; for some, Egypt's betrayal de-legitimized secular governments generally and strengthened support for pan-Islamic ideologies.

Beyond gaining a sense of public legitimacy, Asad needed to ensure that he could control the Syrian state apparatus. But, Asad faced a paradox. As criticism of his regime increased, Asad consolidated control over the state by putting trusted advisors in positions of authority. But because most of those trusted advisors were Alawite, the process only amplified claims that he was a sectarian leader who lacked a mandate from the people.[25]

The most prominent example of this trend was Hafez al-Asad's younger brother Rif'at. The younger Asad was put in charge of Syria's feared Defense Companies, elite military units designed expressly to defend the regime.[26] These units were composed largely of Alawite soldiers and were considered to be Syria's most capable and loyal troops.[27]

Although many in the Syrian opposition believed that Rif'at al-Asad and the Defense Companies represented Syria's rampant corruption and sectarian government, Rif'at gave Hafez al-Asad the critical capability to effectively and consistently inflict violence on his enemies. Rif'at's importance reflects the dictator's classic creed: the consistent use of violence over time creates its own legitimacy.

Rif'at and his organization were essentially Asad's praetorian guards, capable and willing to do whatever it took to defeat the enemies of the regime. The Defense Companies were not only a powerful force to be used directly against the Muslim Brotherhood; their commitment and brutality also compelled loyalty among the rest of Syrian society. Rif'at's notoriety served one other purpose. As the mailed fist of the Syrian regime, the younger Asad became the focal point for much criticism, rather than Hafez al-Asad himself.[28]

ESCALATING VIOLENCE, MASSACRE, AND PROPAGANDA

By the mid-1970s, the stage was set for a showdown between the Muslim Brotherhood, particularly Marwan Hadid's *Fighting Vanguad,* and the Asad regime. Partly this was because the economic situation in Syria had soured dramatically. There were numerous contributing factors, including the decision of a number of Arab states to stop selling oil to Syria at reduced prices after Asad's intervention in Lebanon.[29] Refugees from the Lebanese civil war flooded into Syria's cities, creating a housing crunch that drastically increased the cost of living.[30]

Although small-scale terrorism against the Syrian state was not unheard of, the situation escalated drastically after Hadid was arrested and jailed by Syrian forces. Rather than facing trial, Hadid went on a hunger strike and died in the Harasta military hospital in June 1976.[31] His martyrdom catalyzed much of the Syrian opposition and brought an aggressive young engineer named Adnan Aqla into leadership of the *Fighting Vanguard.*[32]

Aqla began organizing small-scale attacks almost immediately after taking command of the *Vanguard.* Importantly, they were focused primarily on Alawite, rather than government or Ba'thist targets.[33] Low-level skirmishes continued until June 16, 1979, when *Vanguard* members attacked the Aleppo Field Artillery School, killing 32 cadets outright and wounding another 54.[34] True or not, rumors swirled that the vast majority of those killed were Alawites, which served to further stoke sectarian tensions.[35]

The Syrian government's response to the Aleppo massacre was swift. One of the most important innovations was arming Ba'th party members nationwide.[36] In doing so, Asad implicitly recognized that the fight was not so much the Syrian state versus a group of insurgents as it was a sectarian fight among unique social constituencies.

The violence only escalated. After an assassination attempt on Asad, his brother Rif'at and the Defense Companies retaliated by massacring hundreds of Brothers imprisoned in Palmyra.[37] These efforts to intimidate and demoralize the Brotherhood were matched by a major offensive to discredit the Brotherhood, primarily by painting them as agents of foreign governments.

The heart of Asad's argument was that the Egyptian and Israeli governments were conspiring against Syria and using the Muslim Brotherhood to disrupt the Syrian state.[38] The purpose of the media campaign was to discredit those committing the violence by appealing to Syrian nationalism.

Fundamentally, insurgencies are struggles for legitimacy. Asad could not fully establish his own sense of legitimacy, but he could deny the Brotherhood the same.

The Islamic movement in Syria based its legitimacy on its religious foundation. Asad tried to remove that sense of legitimacy by recasting the movement as a tool of foreign governments. This argument was particularly prescient following the Field Artillery massacre because the victims, Alawite or not, were young cadets presumably ready to serve their country. A Radio Damascus report broadcast a week after the killings explicitly questioned the patriotism of the attackers:

> Are we asked to believe that these criminals who killed young men in their prime (who) are training to go soon to the battlefield, to resist Israeli aggression and perhaps to be killed by the enemy in defense of our noble homeland and of our national dignity? Is it possible to imagine that they are bound to this homeland by even the weakest of ties? Is it possible to imagine that such action can be anything but a service (to) Israel and to all other enemies of our nation?[39]

One technique for embarrassing the Brotherhood was to put captured Brothers on television to publicly confess their misdeeds, apologize for misappropriating Islam, and explain their ties to foreign governments.[40] The purpose was to demonstrate the banality and weakness of the Brotherhood and eliminate their mystique.

Although this technique was probably not credible to many observers, the Asad government's argument was not mere fabrication. The Brothers were backed by Iraq and Jordan, and had close ties with several Lebanese militias that were closely related to Israel.[41] Indeed, in 1980 Syrian forces raided a Brotherhood training camp on Jordanian territory.[42] Furthermore, the Islamic movement's own After Action Report argues that domestic support for the movement was weakened because it relied too much on external support and leadership posted abroad.[43] It also argues that the Asad regime's media campaign to discredit the Brotherhood was relatively effective, in large part because the Brotherhood did not have a cohesive media strategy of its own.[44]

Besides playing on Syrian nationalism, Asad's media campaign struck directly at the heart of the Brotherhood's legitimacy by challenging their Islamic credentials. On June 30, 1979, he argued that the Brotherhood's "members want to monopolize Islam for themselves, despite the fact that no party has the right to monopolize Islam or any other religion . . . Islam is one thing and this gang is something else."[45] Simple wordplays were also employed to discredit the Brotherhood. Instead of referring to the movement as the Muslim Brotherhood (*al-Ikhwan al-Muslimun*), Ba'thist leaders referred to the Traitors of the Muslims (*Khuwwan al-Muslimun*).[46]

Asad also tightened his relationship with the fundamentalist Shi'a regime that had recently seized power in Iran. This was important for Asad—although a Shi'a movement, the Iranian revolution was hailed by Sunni fundamentalists as evidence that Islamic revolutions were possible throughout the region. Nevertheless, Asad generated Iranian support by comparing the Brotherhood to the anti-Khomeini Mujahidin-e-Khalq, and playing on concerns about their shared enemy, Iraq.[47]

Despite these efforts to de-legitimize the Brotherhood, the group appears to have increased its numerical strength during the late 1970s.[48] Although Asad had effectively gained control over the Syrian state apparatus in the decade after assuming control, he still did not have enough legitimacy of his own among the largely Sunni populace to effectively discredit the Brotherhood. As the Brotherhood grew stronger and more assertive, Asad turned to ever more oppressive measures to combat them. Following a brief uprising in the city of Hama in June 1980, Asad passed Law Number 49, which banned the Muslim Brotherhood in Syria and made membership in the organization punishable by death.[49]

Asad's decision to impose such an overtly draconian law underscores both his increased ability to control the Syrian state and his growing fear of the Brotherhood. The group had become an ever-present force in Syrian society, not only prosletyzing in mosques nationwide, but conducting small-scale bombings and ambushes against government and Alawite targets throughout Syria. Many of these attacks were actually conducted by Adnan Aqla's *Fighting Vanguard* rather than the broader Muslim Brotherhood, but Asad was unable or unwilling to make such fine distinctions.[50] After attacks, they would melt back into the physical and social labyrinths of ancient city centers, thus making them difficult to find or even measure their true strength.[51]

Many of the Brothers were extraordinarily devoted to their cause and would blow themselves up before being captured.[52] In both a tactical and strategic sense, compromise between Asad and the Brotherhood had become impossible. In September 1979, a Brother brought to trial in Damascus reflected the impasse: "Assassination is the only language with which it is possible to communicate with the state."[53]

HAMA

The city of Hama always had a special role in the Muslim Brotherhood's decades-long fight for power in Syria. Not only was it a traditionally religious city, Hama was Marwan Hadid's hometown, and the base of the movement's more radical elements. Asad's security forces were well aware of Hama's importance; impromptu searches were commonplace, and extrajudicial executions were normal.[54]

As 1981 ended, the escalating violence nationwide was punctuated by a bombing in downtown Damascus that killed 64.[55] Asad decided that he had endured enough. On February 2, Rif'at Asad infiltrated some 1,500 commandos into Hama and left another 1,500 on the city's outskirts. But when the commandos attempted to enter Hama's ancient Barudi neighborhood, the Brotherhood was ready. Under streams of machine-gun fire, Rif'at's commandos were pushed out of Barudi as mosque loudspeakers urged the entire city to fight.[56] Islamic fighters rushed into the streets, slaughtering Ba'thist officials in their beds, and overrunning police stations and armories.[57] The insurgency that had been limping along for years had come to a head. The Muslim Brotherhood controlled Hama.

The Brotherhood hoped that the Hama uprising would inspire similar revolts nationwide and lead to the end of the Ba'th government. These hopes went unfulfilled, despite national broadcasts (made possible by Iraqi transmitters) that urged Syrians to take to the streets.[58] The Brotherhood simply was not strong enough to spark a national uprising.

After the humbling lesson in Barudi, Rif'at and Hafez Asad regrouped. Alawi-dominated units were brought in for the battle of Hama, and soldiers originating from the city were moved out of critical units.[59] The final battle was protracted, but the outcome was never in doubt. Syrian armor and artillery surrounded the city and systematically pulverized it from a distance. Entire neighborhoods were flattened completely. *New York Times* reporter Thomas Friedman wrote the following about his visit to Hama several months after the battle:

> The whole neighborhood, with everything in it, had been plowed up like a cornfield in spring and then flattened. As my taxi driver and I rode off, we encountered a stoop-shouldered old man, in checkered headdress and green robe, who was shuffling along this field of death.
> "Where are all the houses that once stood here?" we stopped and asked.
> "You are driving on them," he said.
> "But where are all the people who used to live here?" I said.
> "You are probably driving on some of them, too."[60]

The systematic destruction of Hama crushed the Muslim Brotherhood. Up to 20,000 people were killed (though estimates tend to reflect author's disposition toward the Syrian regime), including numerous Brotherhood leaders.[61] But more importantly, the balance of terror had been fundamentally upended. Asad had demonstrated that he had the capability and willingness to kill with far more ruthlessness than the Brotherhood had ever been able to muster. The Fighting Vanguard's occasional bombings paled in comparison to the power of Asad's military state.

Critically, Asad did not run from claims of brutality. The city was not cordoned off and Rif'at Asad reportedly even exaggerated the number of people killed.[62] Hafez Asad's assault on Hama was not just a military attack; it was state-organized and executed terrorism: indiscriminate violence intended to demonstrate resolve and power. But that does not necessarily mean that it was unpopular; Friedman argues that "Assad's treatment of the rebellion probably would have won substantial approval, even among many Sunni Muslims. They might have said, 'Better one month of Hama than fourteen years of civil war like Lebanon.'"[63] Asad had finally earned his dictator's legitimacy—the legitimacy of stability backed by unencumbered power.

CONCLUSIONS

Asad's descent into unrepentant authoritarianism was not just about guns and artillery, though it was ultimately brute force that exacerbated the Brotherhood's divisions to the point where it ceased to be an effective military force. If there was a moment of victory for Asad, it was April 25, 1982, when Adnan Aqla, leader of the Fighting Vanguard, was officially "dismissed" from the Muslim Brotherhood.[64] The movement simply was not cohesive enough to effectively challenge the Syrian state. Abu Mus'ab al-Suri, a former Vanguard member, suggests that the lack of central organization among the numerous extremist groups was the biggest contributor to their ultimate failure.[65] Indeed, the former Deputy Commander of the Muslim Brotherhood, Ali Sadreddine Bayanouni, claimed in 2005 that Adnan Aqla had actually been thrown out of the Muslim Brotherhood years before full-scale violence erupted in 1979.[66]

Asad's ability to destroy the Muslim Brotherhood ultimately depended on his ability to dominate the Syrian state's mechanisms of power. His early efforts to discredit the movement were hampered by his own lack of legitimacy, particularly regarding his Alawite background. Asad's limited social base and Syria's history of interchangeable governments restricted his ability to completely isolate the Brotherhood in Syrian society.

Nevertheless, Asad's appeals to Syrian nationalism were likely effective, particularly in the wake of the Camp David Accords. Debunking pan-Arabism was a boon for Islamists, but Asad's portrayal of a Syria isolated after Egypt's accord with Israel likely stanched the Brotherhood's appeal.

Asad defeated the Muslim Brotherhood by effectively controlling and manipulating the most violent mechanisms of state power. Although this was possible in 1982, it may not have been 12 years earlier when he took control. In short, Asad's early steps to rebuff the Brotherhood may have been necessary because he did not feel comfortable initiating large-scale violence before dominating the halls of power.

The final crackdown in Hama reflects that dynamic. The battle pitted Brotherhood fighters against largely Alawite army units commanded by

Alawites. Hama was not just a military attack. Just as important, the Syrian population—chastened by 6 years of violence and the sobering example of Lebanon—were not enraged en masse by the brutal attack. Even many non-Alawites understood the need for the state to assert control. Hama was a political success. In this way, Asad's campaign against the Muslim Brotherhood ultimately provided him a means of achieving that most elusive of qualities for a dictator: legitimacy.

To be sure, it was not democratic legitimacy; it was a tyrant's legitimacy: a monopoly on violence, the will to use that power, and a population frightened enough by domestic and foreign enemies to tolerate the authoritarianism of their leader. As Patrick Seale wrote, "Asad was by nature solitary and authoritarian. These aspects of his temperament now grew more pronounced. In 1970 he was popular, by 1982 he was feared."[67]

Syria's campaign against the Muslim Brotherhood illustrates the central paradox for counterinsurgencies everywhere. In order to be successful, the government must generate widespread legitimacy and execute violence against organizations that are sometimes indistinguishable from society at large. Although, the legitimacy issue is more difficult in strictly authoritarian states like Syria, it is extremely prescient in pseudo and emerging democracies, such as Iraq. One major issue is that governments that are perceived—rightly or wrongly—as illegitimate often have difficulty controlling elements of state power. This was a major problem for Asad, and it is central to the new Iraqi government's struggles today.

One of Asad's most successful efforts was to appeal to Syrian nationalism and portray the Brotherhood insurgency as tied to foreign powers. Unfortunately, the new Iraqi government will have difficulty making a similar argument so long as substantial U.S. forces remain in the country. Nevertheless, Asad's ultimate sense of legitimacy was a function of his ability to bring stability to Syria. If the Iraqi government can safeguard the streets, it may generate its own sense of legitimacy. It remains to be seen, however, whether or not it is possible to bring stability to Iraq without a Hama of its own.

ACKNOWLEDGMENTS

The views expressed herein are those of the author and do not purport to reflect the position of the United States Military Academy, the Department of the Army, or the Department of Defense.

NOTES

1. Harmony AFGP-2002-600080. This document, which was recently released from a department of defense database called Harmony, is believed to have been written by Abu Mus'ab al-Suri, a leading modern salafist leader. Al-Suri

took part in the Syrian jihad against the Ba'th government; this document assesses mistakes made by the Brotherhood during the jihad. It can be accessed at www.ctc.usma.edu.

2. Nikolaos Van Dam, *The Struggle for Power in Syria* (London: I.B. Tauris, 1996) 1.

3. Ibid.

4. Hanna Batatu, "Syria's Muslim Brethren," *MERIP Reports*, No. 110, Syria's Troubles (Nov.–Dec. 1982).

5. Patrick Seale, *Asad: The Struggle for the Mideast* (Berkeley, CA: University of California Press, 1988) 320.

6. Moshe Ma'oz, "Society and State in Modern Syria" in *Society and Political Structure in the Arab World*, ed. Menahem Milson (New York: 1973) quoted in Van Dam, *The Struggle for Power in Syria*.

7. Seale: p. 54.

8. Ibid.: pp. 54–84.

9. Ibid.: pp. 142–165.

10. Ibid.: pp. 162–165.

11. Batatu: p. 14.

12. Umar Abd-Allah, "The Islamic Struggle in Syria" (Berkeley, CA: Mizan Press, 1983) 91.

13. Ibid.: p. 92.

14. Batatu: pp. 16–17.

15. Abd-Allah: pp. 104–105.

16. Harmony AFGP-2002-600080. This document, which was recently released from a department of defense database called Harmony, is believed to have been written by Abu Mus'ab al-Suri, a leading modern salafist leader. Al-Suri took part in the Syrian jihad against the Ba'th government; this document assesses mistakes made by the Brotherhood during the jihad. It can be accessed at www.ctc.usma.edu.

17. Ibid. See also, Abd-Allah: p. 108.

18. Alasdair Drysdale, "The Asad Regime and its Troubles," *MERIP Reports*, No. 110, Syria's Troubles (Nov.–Dec. 1982).

19. Seale: p. 173.

20. Ibid.

21. Van Dam: p. 109.

22. Included as appendix in Abd-Allah: p. 211.

23. Ibid. p. 8 Footnote.

24. Moshe Ma'oz, "Asad: The Sphinx of Damascus" (New York: Grove Weidenfeld, 1988) 95–97.

25. Ibid.: p. 160.

26. Van Dam: p. 70.

27. Ma'oz: pp. 159–161.

28. Michael Dunn, "Syria's Asad: Gambles at the Brink," *Defense and Foreign Affairs* (June 1981): 26.

29. Seale: p. 320.

30. Ibid.

31. Ibid.: p. 324.

32. Ibid.: p. 325.
33. Van Dam: p. 91.
34. Seale: p. 19.
35. Van Dam: p. 91.
36. Ibid.: p. 105.
37. Ibid.: p. 91–93.
38. Ibid.: p. 92.
39. In Van Dam: p. 92. Radio Damascus, June 22, 1979.
40. Drysdale: p. 10.
41. Seale: p. 336.
42. Ghada Hashem Talhami, "Syria: Islam, Arab Nationalism and the Military," *Middle East Policy* VIII, no. 4 (December 2001): 110–127.
43. Harmony AFGP-2002-600080. Believed to be authored by Abu Mus'ab al-Suri.
44. Ibid.
45. Hafez Al-Asad, in Van Dam: p. 95. Radio Damascus, June 30, 1979.
46. Van Dam: p. 96.
47. Ma'oz: p. 156.
48. Batatu: p. 20.
49. Batatu: p. 20.
50. Harmony AFGP-2002-600080. Believed to be authored by Abu Mus'ab al-Suri.
51. Seale: p. 324.
52. Ibid.
53. Al-Nadhir, No. 10, February 1, 1980, p. 12 quoted in Van Dam.
54. Thomas Friedman, "From Beirut to Jerusalem" (New York: Farrar Straus Giroux, 1989) 79–80.
55. Ibid.: pp. 80–81.
56. Ibid.: p. 81.
57. Seale: p. 332.
58. Drysdale: p. 9.
59. Van Dam: pp. 112–113.
60. Friedman: pp. 86–87.
61. Seale: p. 334.
62. Friedman: p. 90.
63. Ibid.: p. 101.
64. Abd-Allah: p. 195.
65. Harmony AFGP-2002-600080. Believed to be authored by Abu Mus'ab al-Suri.
66. "The Battle Within Syria: An Interview with Muslim Brotherhood Leader Ali Bayanouni" *Terrorism Monitor* III, 16 (August 2005). Available at http://jamestown.org/terrorism/news/article.php?articleid=2369769.
67. Seale: p. 338.

CHAPTER 25

STATE POWER AND THE PROGRESS OF MILITANT AND MODERATE ISLAMISM IN EGYPT

Sherifa Zuhur

Political Islam is one of the key components in contemporary Islamism. Islam, Islamism, and political Islam have a lengthy history in Egypt, and the radical strand of Islamism there has influenced other Islamic movements theoretically and tactically. For centuries, Cairo was a center of clerical education. Clerics (`ulama) then returned to various parts of the Sunni Islamic world. In contrast, other previously important intellectual centers waned in influence, like Baghdad, Qairaouan, and Fes. Egypt was the home base for nineteenth-century Islamic reform, and subsequently, for the emergence of modern Islamism. This, together with its leadership role in traditional, quiescent, and "educational" Islam, and in contemporary intellectual and cultural life in the Arab world, increased its importance in the nurturing of modern radical Islamist movements.

Egypt provided the lifeblood of the movements of Arab unity and nationalism in the middle of the century. At that time, President Gamal Abd al-Nasser, champion of these ideas and of Islamic and African unity, suppressed Egyptian Islamism, just as modernizing leaders like Ataturk of Turkey, Qadhdhafi in Libya, and Hafiz al-`Asad in Syria contained Islam as a political force.

Al-Azhar University in Cairo, founded in AD 972, with a current enrollment of some 90,000 students from 71 countries, was originally a teaching mosque for the Fatimid rulers. Al-Azhar became an influential school under Sultan Baybars, when the Abbasid family and scholars of Baghdad fleeing the Mongols were invited to Cairo.[1] Muslims of Spain fled the

Reconquista, some of them traveling to Cairo. Prescriptive Islam or themes of political Islam were never far from the surface in Egypt—where, historically, Turco-Circassian rulers, the Muslim clerics, and the military formed three strands of elite leadership, intermarried, and upheld public order. The rulers, clerics, and others utilized Islamic discourse for centuries for legitimizing, prescriptive and other functions. Thus, it is ahistorical to contrast a benign "traditional" Islam with the politicized ideas of modern radicals as some contemporary analysts do. Islam has always meant more than private religious practice. Ideas of Islamic governance did not represent a heresy from a presumed secularist norm as in the twentieth and twenty-first centuries. Rather, the use of religion or religious discourse for political purposes was expected.

Western imperialism made its entrance first with Napoleon's invasion of Egypt in 1798, and was furthered when the British invaded in 1882. During the nineteenth century, an Islamic reform movement manifested in Egypt and grappled with social ills, political weakness, educational stultification and the crisis of the Muslim intellectual. That movement featured individuals like Muhammad `Abduh, who modernized al-Azhar University, Qasim Amin, and Rashid Rida (of Syria), who provided the seeds of the twentieth-century Islamism. However, a very different sort of movement of Islamic reform was the catalyst for the Islamism phenomenon in Egypt: the ideas and organization of Hasan al-Banna. Though certain themes may be also found in the salafism of Rashid Rida,[2] in other respects, al-Banna's movement was more broadly based, working explicitly toward the goal of reform.

Al-Banna, a former schoolteacher, established the Muslim Brotherhood in 1928 in Isma`iliyya, a Suez Canal city greatly impacted by the British military presence.[3] The Brotherhood called for the cessation of British involvement in Egyptian affairs. The secularist political parties who had obtained a partial independence in 1922 had not been able to effect a British withdrawal. Hasan al-Banna also felt that Egyptian political and social life demanded the revival—not abandonment—of Islamic principles. His movement emphasized an Islamic solution for youth as well, contrasting with the very popular Scouts movement in the West, or the YMCA. Then, as many nationalist-fascist organizations burgeoned around the world, the Muslim Brotherhood (MB) represented just one trend in the region, alongside the Wafd's Party's blue shirts and Misr al-Fatat's green shirts in Egypt, and Dr. Shahbandar's grey shirts in Syria.

Al-Banna developed an interpretation of *hakmiyya* (God's sovereignty, as opposed to temporal sovereignty) that highlighted the need for an Islamic state and participation in politics. He wrote about *shura* (consultation) somewhat differently than al Qaeda's theorists; that it was not incompatible with parliamentary democracy, and, also highlighting the distinction between Islamic history and Islam itself.[4] To him, in an Islamic state, the most important principle is *tawhid*, or unity, implying more compromises between various factions, or even secularists and Islamists.

The MB acquired a large following divided into ten sections by the 1940s, as well as a women's wing of their movement.[5] In 1946, the Egyptian government provided funds, books, and supplies to the Brotherhood's schools, indicative of the cooperation between al-Banna and Isma'il Sidqi, the prime minister.[6] The MB in those years held conservative views on gender roles and the expansion of women's rights in the public sphere.[7]

World War II was fought on Egyptian soil, and Allied forces took their leave in Cairo. Their presence heightened tensions between the Egyptian regime and its citizens, and the Muslim Brotherhood protested the corruption, alcohol, drugs and prostitution that accompanied the Westerners. Journalist Muhammad Hassanain Haikal explained that extreme philosophies proffered different solutions to young people, who were also extreme in their enthusiasm for them. This ranged from his own leftist embrace of the Communist Manifesto[8] to the Muslim Brother's proposal of "*Islam huwwa al-hal*" (Islam is the solution).

The Muslim Brotherhood demonstrated their zeal and dedication in the war over Palestine in 1948, where they fought as volunteers. During this war, regular army troops were able to take Gaza, but the Arab forces eventually disappointed the public, and the fate of the Palestinian refugees would continue to disturb Egyptians.

The MB eventually developed an underground militant wing, its "secret apparatus," which clashed with the Egyptian government on several occasions.[9] Prime Minister Nuqrashi Pasha subsequently outlawed the Muslim Brotherhood, and in response, he was assassinated. Hasan al-Banna was in turn assassinated in 1949 at the age of 43. This period represented a relatively brief pinnacle of violence matched by state violence against the organization. The next wave of violence against the state would emerge in the 1980s and 1990s, but under the banners of new Islamic radical movements, and not the Brotherhood, which was further repressed in the era of Gamal `abd al-Nasser.

In 1952, a group within the Egyptian Army—the Free Officers, who had organized secretly—led a revolution, exiled King Faruq, and established a new government. Several of the Free Officers had ties with the Muslim Brotherhood, including Anwar al-Sadat. However, the new regime muzzled the workers' movement and then went after the Brotherhood, following an assassination attempt on President Gamal `abd al-Nasser in 1956. The suppression of the MB resulted in lengthy prison sentences for many of its members, and the emigration of some to the Arabian Gulf states, or to previously established branches in the Sudan, Syria, and Jordan.

An influential source of Islamist thought during this period was Sayyid Qutb, who was incarcerated from 1955 to 1964, then released and prisoned 8 months later, and then executed in 1966. Today's terrorism studies' literature treats Sayyid Qutb as the prime source of contemporary jihadism, rather superficially considering his ideas on jihad and martyrdom to the exclusion of his work as a whole. Sayyid Qutb explains the moderate path of da`wa and education in his work, and might have led a liberal trend within radical Islamism[10] were it not for the virulent response of the Nasser regime and his own incarceration, torture, and certainty of martyrdom. State repression radicalizes Islamist views, especially when there is no compromise. In Ma`lim fi al-tariq, Qutb wrote that jihad against un-Islamic rulers was necessary. Although this theme was not new, its application to the regime of his own time was novel. Qutb's ideas can legitimate today's global jihadists in the notion that the domain of warfare, dar al-harb, can include "any state that fights religious attitudes of Muslims,"[11] thus rendering Egypt a "near enemy." He also wrote in a different way about necessary political changes. In Ma`alim and several other books, Qutb calls for a revolution, a zalzala (earthquake) to bring down governments and build new Islamic societies.[12] However, it is not clear whether the revolution must be violent. For example, in the final chapter of his book al-`Adala al-Ijtima`iyya fi-l-Islam, the way forward involves Islamic education and the debunking of Western thought.[13] In the final chapter of Ma`alim, Qutb refers instead to the example of the martyrs of al-Akhdud in the Quran (Surah 85) who were burned and unavenged. Nevertheless, the martyrs were freed from life's enslavement.[14]

The Nasser regime contained and brutalized the Muslim Brotherhood during his tenure, among them a former student, Shoukri Mustafa, who was imprisoned for distributing the Brotherhood's flyers during a second wave of arrests in the 1960s. Some MB members moved abroad— for instance, to Saudi Arabia, where close contact with Wahhabism and Saudi religious elements influenced the group. In 1971, President Anwar Sadat released the Muslim Brotherhood from prison, encouraged Islamist student organizations in the 1970s to counteract Leftists, and yet fell to an Islamist assassin's bullet in 1981. Conservative and Islamist political debates of that era swirled around the 1979 reforms of family law. Sadat was accused of acting extra-legally to pass these controversial reforms (which, among other things, enhanced women's legal rights) because he had taken action while Parliament was in recess. The Muslim Brotherhood, the Islamist student organizations, and new radical groups—as well as many ordinary Egyptians—also criticized the peace agreement that Sadat forged with Israel, as did the Left and other political elements.

By then, several Egyptian Islamist groups had emerged, all of them more radical than the Muslim Brotherhood, which was attempting to operate in a quasilegal manner. The radical groups wanted to halt what they saw as the corrupt and Godless progress of a secularist regime, represented in Sadat's policies. The first group to alarm authorities was led by a Palestinian, Salah Siriyya, and attempted to assassinate President Sadat at the Egyptian Military Academy. Siriyya had a doctorate in education, and established a group emanating from the Tahrir movement, a Palestinian Islamist movement first set up by Taqi al-Din al-Nabhani. A triple exile (from Palestine, Jordan, in 1970, and Iraq, where Tahrir was illegal), he assembled a group of associates to carry out a coup d'etat that would establish an Islamic state in Egypt, after firing on the president. Instead, the guards at the Military Academy fired on Siriyya's group, which was then captured. Egyptian authorities blamed the plot on Libya, unwilling to admit the presence of indigenous militants.[15]

A second group, calling itself Jama`at al-Muslimin, was labeled by the Egyptian authorities as Takfir wa-l-Hijra (Flight and Repentence), the words *"takfir"* referring to the practice of excommunicating Muslims and the *"hijra"* was the Prophet's exodus from Mecca to Medina. With this name, Egyptian authorities highlighted the extremism and eccentricity of the group in secluding themselves in safe houses and rejecting Egyptian society. Takfir wa-l-Hijra (TWH) represented one of the first jihadi groups along bin Ladin's model, or possibly that of the `Utaybi movement in Saudi Arabia, which took over the Grand Mosque in 1979. Members who attempted or wished to leave TWH were threatened with death as apostates. This meant that some were easily manipulated by the Egyptian security services, who may have committed or instigated many of the group's crimes.[16] Some of the only data on the sociological profile of its members (and those of the Military Academy group) was collected and published by sociologist Sa`d Eddin Ibrahim.[17] Both groups were led by elder, more experienced, and charismatic individuals than the membership, which, at the time, represented petit bourgeoisie, or migrants to urban areas. Shoukri Mustafa, leader of TWH, had been associated with the Muslim Brotherhood, and was radicalized while in prison, where he first recruited members for his group. TWH operated secretly, yet authorities were alerted about its presence early on, not least thanks to several mysterious disappearances of young women. They simply vanished from their communities, as they moved with their men to safe houses and rural locations. TWH kidnapped a former Minister of Awqaf, held him for ransom, and then killed him, thereby bringing the wrath of the authorities down on the group. Court transcripts indicate the members' firm commitment to the cause of jihad.[18] Mustafa was executed, and 36 TWH members were imprisoned, while more than 100 were arrested in 1982 (which demonstrated that the group was still alive). Under the name al-Shawqiyin, TWH operated in Fayyum in the 1980s.[19]

In addition, there was the Gama`at Gihad (Jihad) Islami, usually known as the Jihad (Holy War) group (or Egyptian Islamic Jihad, EIJ, to distinguish it from the Palestinian Islamic Jihad), and a more amorphous group, the Gama`at (Jama`at) al-Islamiyya (GI, the Islamic Group) that had evolved from the student associations formed in Sadat's era into at least three groupings: one, a salafi movement at Alexandria University; a second, found in Cairene as well as Alexandria universities, which favored the Muslim Brotherhood, leading some members to leave and join the MB; and a third, centered in universities and colleges in Upper Egypt, which rejected the MB in favor of the activism of the EIJ.[20] The Jihad group was also at first two different organizations, one founded by Muhammad `Abd al-Salam Farag and the other founded by Muhammad Salim al-Rahal, a student of al-Azhar from Jordan, with some members joining in from organizations such as Shabab Muhammad. When Rahal was expelled from Egypt, the group's leadership was transferred to a young economics graduate of Cairo University, Kamal al-Sayid Habib. The two groups merged when Habib was introduced to Farag by Tariq al-Zumur whose brother-in-law—a major in Army intelligence, `Abbud `Abd al-Latif al-Zumur—became the strategist of the Farag group. Al-Zumur urged the overthrow of the government, and that the group set up an Islamic caliphate to replace it.

The EIJ had a clear structure and goals. It was governed by a *majlis al-shura* (council of consultation) with subcommittees for preparation, propaganda, and finances. Its goal was a state with a council of `ulama. Military *tarbiyya* (training) was detailed. A planned takeover of the government would actually mimic the 1952 revolution by seizing the Radio and Television building. *Tarbiyya* included first aid, knowledge of topography, vehicle training, defense, and physical exercises at stage one. Then at stage two, students learned techniques of attacks and ambushes, and securing strategically crucial sites. At the third stage, and under the supervision of Nabil al-Maghrabi, the use of weapons and explosives were taught, and simulations were planned and executed.[21]

Khalid al-Islambuli devised a plan to assassinate Sadat after a political crackdown in 1981. The aim was state collapse, not merely an assassination. Some members disputed this plan—for instance, `Abbud al-Zumur thought the organization needed more time before it could lead a popular revolution.[22] Sadat's assassination on October 6, 1981, brought the group global recognition, but the group's coup, or revolutionary aims, failed. The arrest and incarceration of some of the members of the Jihad group[23] provided the impetus to Sadat's assassination. His assassin, with a relatively small number of cohorts, killed the president at a military review, shooting into the stands. Sadat's assassination was followed by nearly a month of fighting in spots of Upper Egypt. Ultimately, this action and subsequent violence resulted in EIJ operatives fleeing from Egypt to escape the execution and trials of its leaders and membership.

There were a number of similarities between the "jihad groups," Takfir wa-l-Hijrah, the Military Academy group, the Gama`at al-Islamiyya, and Islamic Jihad—namely their militance, and the way they treated jihad as a sixth pillar of Islam, as urged by the author of the Missing Duty, *Jihad:*

al-Farida al-Gha'iba, Muhammad `Abd al-Salam Farag.[24] But there were also differences between them. Farag critiqued the TWH and GI groups in his treatise, as well as the modernist rebuttal provided by then-Shaykh al-Azhar, Jad al-Haqq. Farag's main point is that jihad is required, thus, TWH's *hijra* from barbarian, non-Islamic (*jahili*) society and reluctance to take up jihad is wrong. GI's use of *da`wah* to create a mass base, while postponing jihad is also wrong; it is improper to substitute "populism for jihad." Since the nearest enemy is the Egyptian government, not the Israelis, it should be first addressed. Only under true Muslims would Jerusalem be liberated, so the false Muslim rulers must be overthrown first. This argument essentially distinguishes the EIJ from the Muslim Brotherhood as well.

The government, through Jad al-Haqq, the Shaykh al-Azhar, the highest authority at that institution, provided a strong argument that the Qur'an contains verses limiting jihad, pointing to the propriety of jihad "by the heart," and "the tongue," and argued that the ruler could not be an apostate, because the true definition of an apostate is one who rejects all of the *shari`ah*, not just any part of it.[25] Farag attacked al-Haqq's refutal, explaining that the Qur'anic Sword Verses have abrogated all other verses and are as obligatory as fasting.[26] He calls Egyptian authorities agents of imperialism and notes that they had made promises to rule according to *shari`ah*, but did not. Likewise, al-Islambuli stated that he assassinated Sadat because the *shari`ah* was not applied, as well as because of the peace treaty with Israel and the unjustified arrests of the `ulama.[27] Islamists also stressed the corruption (*fasad*) in the Egyptian government, particularly the embezzlement and bribery and its encouragement of the physical display of women (*tabarruj al-nisa'*).[28]

During the 1980s, the radical and violent Islamist groups receded somewhat from the news, as Islamist moderates made gains with their strength in some professional syndicates, in the national university system, and in community and private-sector endeavors. As one of its strategies against the Islamist militants, the government trumpeted its own neoconservative message through the media, involving censorship and encouragement of certain traditional Muslim themes and attitudes. Paradoxically, by these actions, the present government has actually encouraged popular Islamic revivalism, while attempting to destroy activist Islamist power. This government's strategy against radicalism has made it impossible for it to democratize without including moderates who have played by its rules, and thus the overall presence of political Islam has been strengthened. Nearly all political parties, including the dominant National Democratic Party, give some lip service to Islamic ideals, given their growing or resurgent popularity in Egypt. Successful alliances of the Muslim Brotherhood with other groups gained them seats in Parliament in the 1980s, first with the Wafd, then with the Socialist Labor Party.

In the 1980s, the "legal" or official opposition in Egypt was comprised of the New Wafd, the Socialist Labor Party, the Nationalist Unionist Progressive Party, the Liberal Party, and the Umma Party. All were weak because major electoral changes had not been made.[29] The National Democratic Party still held 95 percent of the seats in 1999. By 2005, ever more elaborate rules governing the establishment or campaigning of political parties still excluded the Brotherhood, and continued to constrain the development of a loyal opposition.

Islamic community endeavors such as clinics, private schools, charitable associations, and Islamic teaching circles increased in the 1980s and 1990s. Islamist-owned supermarkets, shoe and clothing stores opened, as well as "investment" companies like al-Sharif (established in 1978), the Badr company (established in 1980), al-Rayan (1982), al-Huda and al-Sa`d (1983), and al-Hilal (1986),[30] each promising higher rates of return than government banks. In 1988, there were more than 100 such companies, and the assets of the 50 larger companies were estimated at $3 billion.[31] In November of that year, the government closed the al-Rayan company, and panic set in as the body of the al-Rayan CEO was discovered and his widow left the country. The timing and manner of the government's intervention left many investors penniless.[32]

President Mubarak's strategy has been to contain the moderates and uproot the radicals. While moderates were also arrested, imprisoned, censored, and mistreated, they managed to mount the first legal challenges to the constitutionality of the regime's actions, and tried to embarrass it through hunger strikes and other methods. Meanwhile the state security services arrested militants, put them on trial, and tried to deny them safe havens. Many MB, EIJ, GI, and other groups' members went to the Gulf, Afghanistan, and later Albania and Chechnya. Key individuals like Ayman Zawahiri joined forces with al Qaeda. The Gulf War, in many ways, furthered EIJ's aim to delegitimize the regime, when it suppressed popular protests against the coalition with the West.

A WAR WITH ISLAMISM

Mubarak governed the country during a prolonged crisis of violence from the late 1980s to 1997. Islamists attempted—and in several cases, succeeded—to assassinate a speaker of Parliament, ministers of the interior, a prime minister, judges, and other officials. There was an assassination attempt on Mubarak while he was in Ethiopia on June 26, 1995. Innocent bystanders were hurt and killed in Islamist attacks and counter raids. An Islamist assassinated the secularist writer Farag Foda, and even the Nobel Laureate in literature, elderly Naguib Mahfouz, was attacked.[33] Officials and foreigners employed guards for their homes. Islamists targeted tourists as another means of destabilizing the government, carrying out major attacks that discouraged that sector. For a time, they took over an area of Cairo, the poverty-stricken neighborhood of Imbaba on the western side of the Nile. The government was compelled to reconquer the area. In Upper Egypt, militant Islamists attacked police stations, officers, and even their families, travelers on trains, and Copts, who had been targeted ever since the late 1970s.

With the bombing of the World Trade Center in Manhattan in 1993, the specter of Egyptian Islamism and international terrorism burst loudly into the world press—featuring Shaykh `Umar `abd al-Rahman, a spiritual leader of the Islamist Jihad group. `Abd al-Rahman's preaching base had once been in the Fayyum. Due to his actions on behalf of the Muslim Brotherhood, he had lost his teaching position at al-Azhar University. He was put on trial following Sadat's assassination, found innocent, and released from jail in 1983.[34] Briefly arrested again in 1989, he made the pilgrimage to Saudi Arabia, then traveled to Sudan, and from there to the United States, where he preached against the secularist Egyptian government in the al-Salam mosque in Jersey City, and the al-Badr mosque in Brooklyn. The Egyptian government could not simply lock him up as a convenient villain because his spiritual inspiration to those involved in terrorism was no more than the `ulama`'s time-honored role of "commanding the good and denying the evil," the hisba.[35]

In April 1996, Islamists attacked a Greek tourist group in Giza believed to be Israelis. Then in October 1997, several Islamists who had been sentenced for a previous attack in Cairo escaped their confinement in a mental institution, and fire-bombed a bus filled with tourists parked just outside the Egyptian Museum. Worst of all was a full-scale attack on a group of European tourists at the temple of Hatshepsut at Dair al-Bahri, in the Valley of the Queens in Luxor at the end of that year. Millions of dollars in tourist revenues were lost. But the attacks also had the effect of turning the public—in whom various indicators of increasing religiosity had been noted—against extreme Islamists.

These highly publicized incidents were accompanied by less-reported attacks on police and Christians in villages in Upper Egypt, and on passengers on the train line bound for that area. Attacks on Copts continued to be a serious matter. On January 2, 2000, violence in the village of Kosheh left 20 Christians and 1 Muslim dead. The government condemned the official reports of this incident, preferring to take the ostrich approach, since sectarian problems in Upper Egypt appear difficult to eradicate.

The Mubarak government treads a middle path, opposing militant Islam without insulting increasingly heightened Islamic sensibilities. Decrees banned the niqab (the Islamist face veil) in public schools or settings, and required that girls who wore the hijab should have parental permission. Censorship over various publications continued as a means of forestalling Islamist criticism. The government never really engaged in an open dialogue with the Islamists. The regime continued to treat the Muslim Brotherhood and the Wasat Party (the next generation of Brotherhood leadership, which broke away to form their own movement) as illegal groups.

The struggle between Mubarak's government and the Islamist moderates impinged upon the election process. In 1992, the *Sha'b* newspaper, then representing the Islamic Alliance (composed of the Socialist Labor Party and the Muslim Brotherhood), protested the election fraud in which the NDP claimed to have won 50 slates that were actually won by the Alliance, as well as up to 27 independent seats.[36]

Prior to the 1995 elections, the police arrested dozens of Brotherhood candidates, as well as certain senior members. They closed Brotherhood headquarters and handed over their legal jurisdiction to a military court, citing the emergency laws. The elections were violent; 40 people were killed, and non-Islamist elements of the opposition spoke out against the government's tactics and sentences handed down to the Brotherhood members.[37] Saad Eddin Ibrahim, a prominent sociologist subsequently put on trial and then pardoned, fought to have the judiciary oversee the elections. These reforms were first implemented in the two-stage elections that took place in the fall of 2000.

Islamist leader `Adil Husayn, his nephew Magdi Ahmad Husayn, and a cartoonist for their newspaper *al-Sha`b* were arrested and given a prison sentence for criticizing the Minister of Agriculture, Youssef Wali. The Court of Cassation overturned the sentence, and they were able to bring the matter to the Constitutional Court.

The government soon accused the Brotherhood of launching a campaign against *Walima li-A`shab al-Bahr*, a book by Syrian author Haydar Haydar, which Islamists had suddenly discovered (though it was published in the 1960s) and deemed "atheistic" in tone. The furor over the book led to student demonstrations and deaths in May of 2000. The Political Parties Committee officially froze the Labor Party and closed the *al-Sha`b* newspaper,[38] thereby canceling out the fruits of the legal victory described above. Journalists engaged in hunger strikes in protest.

A further dimension of the conflicts between the government and Islamists, and between Islamists and secularists, spilled into the legal and intellectual spheres. The government has regularly censored the Muslim Brotherhood, forcing an end to its publications, such as *al-Da`wah*, *Liwa al-Islam*, and *al-Sha`b*. Islamist critics attacked many Egyptian intellectuals on the basis of their statements, writings, or even course materials— for example, Hasan Hanafi, Nasr Abu Zayd, and Nawal al-Saadawi. Abu Zayd's marriage was dissolved in a third party action because Abu Zayd's ideas were deemed "beyond the bounds of Islam," and thus he was deemed to be illegally wed to his Muslim wife. The couple was forced into exile in Europe. The president supported a legal change, so that when

Islamists attempted the same tactic against Nawal al-Saadawi, they were unsuccessful.

THE TRUCE

Following the Luxor attack, militant leaders offered an unconditional ceasefire to the Egyptian authorities. The leadership produced quite a few books denouncing the groups' own tactics and methodology, including their use of *takfir*. Numerous explanations have been given for this *volte de face*. It is likely that these Islamists, fearing the loss of support by the Muslim masses, had gone through a sincerely introspective phase, in which they realized that as a vanguard they were too far afield from the aspirations and views of ordinary Muslims, who could suffer as a result of their actions. Further, the Egyptian state's repressive capacity was quite strong. The Luxor incident truly threatened the regime, hence the response—in terms of arrests, torture, detentions, and so on—were unbearable to the radicals, who simply had to reconsider their way forward. Many believed the truce to be just about a permanent one, so the speculation was that such truces could provide a solution to Islamist-state conflicts elsewhere in the region. Then the ground was shaken by the events of September 11 in the United States.

AL QAEDA'S RELATIONSHIP WITH ISLAMIC MILITANTS IN EGYPT

Whether as a result of repression at home, or the growth of Islamic militancy throughout the region, a strong connection between radical Egyptian Islamism and the al Qaeda group emerged.[39] These connections predate 9/11. Of at least 29 Egyptians connected with the al-Jihad group or al Qaeda—such as Ayman Rabi `al-Zawahiri and Nasr Fahmi Nasr Hassanein, Rifa`i Ahmed Taha (of the Gama`at Islamiyya), and others such as `Adel Abdel-Quddus and Mustafa Hamzah—many fought in Afghanistan and the Balkans. Some of these "Afghan Arabs" found refuge in the United Kingdom, Germany, or Pakistan.

Al Qaeda benefited from al-Zawahiri and others like Muhammad Atef. They in turn gained a financial sponsor in bin Laden, and a field for operations. The estimates of EIJ and GI actively engaged with al Qaeda are low and possibly inaccurate. Their greatest significance was their ability to inspire other groups to ally with, or model themselves on al Qaeda.

When al-Gama`at al-Islamiyya agreed to nonviolence following the Luxor attack, part of EIJ swore to continue jihad.[40] Consequently, about 8,000 Gama`at prisoners were released, but not those of Islamic Jihad. Currently, much is made of a distinction between groups with international ideals and those with local goals, or those who will engage in

Lessons from the Fight against Terrorism

truces with local governments (i.e., nationalist or local jihadists) versus "global jihadists." This distinction will not help us too much in the long run for at least three reasons: First, movements—like nation-states—can define local, regional, and international goals, and vacillate from one to the other. Thus al Qaeda had local goals in Afghanistan and Pakistan, like EIJ's in Egypt, but can also inspire jihad elsewhere. Second, the now local, now global status of Islamism is a feature of contemporary life, reflected in Internet Islamist activities, text messaging, and other technologies. And third, we ought to have learned from the history of militant Islamism that groups like EIJ will emerge and reemerge from, or alongside, other more moderate Islamist organizations, and that they are affected and enhanced by any perceptible crusade on the Muslim world.

ZAWAHIRI

Ayman al-Zawahiri, a symbol of the nexus of al Qaeda and Egyptian Islamism, illustrates just how legitimate the Islamist tendency had become for Egypt's professional classes. His forbears, unlike Osama bin Laden's father (who rose from laborer to millionaire status) were educated professionals on both sides of the family, one line, the Azzams, featured a number of well-known public figures. Samir Rafaat points out to Egyptians that if the Azzam and Zawahiri families could produce this militant leader, then the "enemy is within."[41] Zawahiri went even further than Farag in his own book (*Knights under the Prophet's Banner*) that was serialized in *al-Sharq al-Awsat* and read all over the Arab world. He portrays himself as one who educates Muslim youth to recognize the enemies of Islam. He is spreading jihad, and the proof may be found among the thousands of young men in prisons. He recommends a "by any means necessary" strategy, pointing to the damage that even small numbers can exact, and suggests targeting the United Nations, multinational corporations, the media, international relief groups, because these are covers for other operations, according to him, and naturally rulers of Arab states. Further, both he and al Qaeda (as well as other groups) have now linked Palestine and Iraq to the struggle.[42]

Islamist attorney Montassir al-Zayat, who himself defended other Islamist prisoners, attacked Zawahiri, charging him with recklessness in his own book *Ayman al-Zawahiri as I Knew Him*. Apparently, various elites and intellectuals in Saudi Arabia and Egypt convinced al-Zayat to withdraw his book in 2002, presumably arguing that Zawahiri could not defend himself while under the heavy American attacks on al Qaeda.[43] The book was subsequently reprinted and translated into many languages, and suggests that it was the vicious torture by Egyptian officials of Zawahiri that set him onto a path of no return.[44]

OVERKILL AND REVENGE CELLS

Egyptian officials disagree that their stringent counterterrorist actions could encourage further jihad. Torture and imprisonment of Islamists in the 1960s produced several results in the 1970s: uncompromising radicalism and aims to immediately overthrow the state; or accommodation and commitment to a gradual Islamization of the state, this being the path of the Muslim Brotherhood. Torture and imprisonment in the late 1970s and 1980s led to further organizational development in prisons themselves, including the forming of new radical groups, and the spread of "global jihad," or the quest for sanctuary somewhere outside of Egypt.

What about oppressive tactics on Islamists as a deterrent? `Ali Muhammad `Ali, a jihad leader of the late 1980s in Minya, explained that the security forces attacked members "who prevented prayer services and pursued all of us without any apparent cause" (fulfilling the ideas of defensive jihad).[45] Torture, hostage-taking, and the abuse of Islamist family members, including sexual abuse, have been documented.[46] So the emergence of a new terror cell (or possibly more than one cell) in Egypt in 2004 and 2005 is alarming.

REEMERGENCE OF JIHAD IN EGYPT?

Several recent violent incidents have punctured the calm sustained since 1997, and raise important questions. First and foremost, is a new phase of radical activity in Egypt emerging precisely because of repressive tactics? How might better tactics against terror be effective if the Egyptian government does not provide more transparency and accountability in its communications to the public? Are there other means to employ, like promoting moderate Islam as an antidote to radical Islam, as some academics and a recent Rand report have suggested?[47]

In September of 2003, Egyptian police nabbed 23 suspected Islamist militants who intended to carry out attacks on U.S. forces in Iraq. Nineteen of them were Egyptians, but there were also three from Bangladesh, a Turk, a Malaysian, and an Indonesian, and all had studied at Al-Azhar. In October of 2004, Zawahiri issued a call for jihad (outside of Iraq) by audiotape. A week later on October 2004, car bombs were detonated at resorts in Taba and Ras Shitan in the Sinai, killing at least 34 persons (according to Egyptian sources) and injuring over 150. Some 12,000 Israeli tourists vacationing during the Sukkot holidays fled. The Brigades of `Abdullah `Azzam, a heretofore unknown al Qaeda affiliate group claimed responsibility. Immediately following the October 2004 attack, Abu al-`Abbas al-`A'edhi, a leader of al Qaeda fi Jazirat al-`Arabiyya (al Qaeda on the Arabian Peninsula) posted online a document titled "From Riyadh/East to Sinai," proclaiming a new jihad in Egypt to parallel attacks in Saudi Arabia.[48]

Another group, the Mujahidin of Egypt, also claimed responsibility. The authorities variously stated that the new extremists were home-grown, or were connected to al Qaeda, and Palestinians.

In Cairo, on March 29, 2005, an Egyptian stabbed two Hungarian tourists, citing Western policies in Iraq and Palestine. Again, this could have been an isolated incident, but on April 7, 2005, a bombing near the Khan al-Khalili bazaar killed 3 tourists and wounded 18 persons. Egyptian authorities initially announced that the bomber, Hassan Rafa`at Bashandi, acted alone, but then sought his accomplices.[49] They arrested Gamal Ahmad `Abd al-`Al and Ashraf Sa`id Yusif, as well as another suspect and cousin of Ashraf's who died in police custody. Egyptian authorities claim that Ihab Yousri Yassin (aka Ihab Yousri Mohammad of Saft) learned of these arrests shortly before carrying out his own attack. It seems security forces were pursuing him when he was either blown up, or blew himself up by launching himself from the bridge behind the Egyptian museum onto `Abd al-Mun`im Riyadh square on April 30. The Ministry of the Interior reported that Yassin jumped from the bridge and subsequently detonated a bomb.[50] However some eyewitnesses described a heavy object falling from the bridge onto a man walking near them, who was decapitated by the explosion.[51]

Soon after, Yassin's sister Nagat and his fiancée Iman Khamis—both fully veiled and in their twenties—reportedly opened fire on a tourist bus in the Sayyida `A'isha neighborhood. Again, accounts of this event conflict. Some reported that police fired on the women, killing one, while others held that one woman shot the other, and then wounded herself, dying later in hospital.[52] Some 226 individuals were arrested in the extremists' native villages, and in the Shoubra neighborhood of Cairo.[53] A scrap of paper found in one woman's purse said that "we will continue to sacrifice our lives to let others live"[54] —a typical characterization of "defensive" jihad. Libya subsequently extradited Yassin's 17-year-old brother Muhammad to Egypt in connection with the April attacks.[55]

Even if the events involving the third Cairo incident were disregarded, the next event in the Sinai was extremely disturbing and interrupted the tourist season for the year. On July 23, Egypt's national holiday commemorating the 1952 revolution, bomb blasts killed 64 people and killed 200 in Sharm al-Shaykh, a tourist sea resort in the south Sinai, popular with Europeans.[56] On April 24, 2006, three bombs were set off in Dahab, a Sinai resort a little further to the north, favored by wind-surfers, drug-users, Europeans, and Israelis. The timing of the attacks was calculated to exert maximum damage on tourists—though in fact, more Egyptians than Westerners were killed. Egyptian authorities at first denied a connection between the Sharm attacks and those in Dahab, but later gave substance to the idea that a new Bedouin terrorist cell affiliated with al Qaeda had developed, aggravated by the poor Sinai conditions and alienation of the Bedouin.

There are four ways of reading these recent events: 1) the truce with the Islamists has ended or is in jeopardy due to political changes; 2) extremists were merely on hiatus during the recent period of relative calm; 3) new actors have emerged, unbound by any prior arrangements with the regime; or 4) new actors have emerged and might have some association with *agents provocateurs* of the regime's security services.

Various bizarre incidents connected with the past two decades of terrorism most probably stem from the inefficiencies and brutality of the state security services and the government's tight control over the media. Even Egyptians, used to noting discrepancies in accounts of events, found it odd that the two women had no targets, or that there were so many versions of the two Cairo attacks circulating, and that the leader of the Dahab attacks conveniently left his identification card at home so he could be identified later on (how, then, did he drive through checkpoints in the Sinai?) and was reported killed three times. Concealing the facts of terrorist actions, and counterterrorist responses was a well-established government pattern during the 1990s, and continues today.

During the more active period of conflict with Islamist groups, the Egyptian press and government typically denied the entire phenomenon, instead describing isolated acts of "lunatics," notably the 1997 attack on a bus near the Egyptian Museum in which ten tourists were killed by Saber Abu `Ulla. `Ulla had previously attacked and killed tourists, but was placed in a mental hospital and then released (although authorities claimed he had escaped the institute). So the current lack of clarity about al Qaeda's influence with the Bedouin, or the emergence of new cells, is also obscured because these new incidents tarnish the government's success rate in containing militant Islamism.

2005–2006 saw the involvement of more women in militant actions in Jordan, Saudi Arabia, and Cairo (if that was indeed a bona fide militant incident). To date, women had not engaged in violence in Egypt.[57] Principles inhibiting women from taking part in jihad go back to classical definitions of mujahideen: male, adult, and without debts or, correspondingly, dependents. But such restrictions weren't operative during the time of the Prophet, when Nusayba Bint Ka`b—also known as Umm `Umara—fought in the battle of Uhud in 625 C.E., or when `A'isha, the Prophet's beloved wife, directed the Battle of the Camel, and Zaynab bint `Ali, the Prophet's granddaughter, fought in the Battle of Karbala (680 C.E.). Radical Islamists glorify these early Arabian warrior women, and believe that men, women, and children should respond when jihad becomes an individual duty of Muslims. Analysts have warned for some time that the "typical" profile of the suicide bomber should not be restricted to the young, desperate, uneducated, or male population.

The internal opposition questions official Egyptian tactics in the war on terror and calls for reform. Ayman Nour, leader of the Al-Ghad (Tomorrow Party), said the violence was the result of the "environment of oppression and depression."[58] Mohammed Mahdi Akef, general guide of the Muslim Brotherhood, has condemned the recent attacks and similarly expressed concerns about political reform. Al-Zayat, the Islamist lawyer who wrote the book on Zawahiri mentioned above, said that independently operating (or freelance) jihadis are now emerging due to their sympathies with al Qaeda, or the struggle in Iraq, or Palestine.[59] Islamist leader Isam al-`Aryan claimed that Egypt had reached a "boiling point," and that the involvement of women (in April 2005) was an indicator of despair.[60] Some suggested that the April 30 attacks were just acts of revenge. An editorial in *al-Quds al-`Arabi* blamed Egyptian leaders and the populace alike, declaring that the country is "sick beyond cure" and authorities are "as usual, falsifying the facts" and misleading the public while the jihadists reemerge.[61]

Just days after the April 2005 incidents, police clashed with pro-Brotherhood demonstrators in Fayyum, Mansura, and Zagazig, and demonstrations were also held in Alexandria, the Delta, and Cairo to protest parliamentary efforts to amend a constitutional reform to election procedures that would limit the Brotherhood's efforts to obtain votes. They condemned the state-owned media, called for an end to emergency laws, and for reform. Observers believe that the Brotherhood might secure up to 30 to 35 percent of parliamentary seats in a free and fair election. The key question is whether efforts by moderate Islamists to cash in on democratization efforts have any clear relationship to the suppression of radical Islam—particularly if militant Islamism is now reemerging, motivated by events and dynamics beyond Egyptian borders. Conversely, some may argue that since moderate Islamists are already present in the Egyptian government and educational system, the gradual infiltration of the state by Islamists has enabled the more hard-core and violent elements to escape censure and surveillance.

The same themes emerged after the Dahab attacks, because the government was able to obtain a majority in Parliament (which it possesses through the NDP) to vote for an extension to the emergency laws for 2 more years. It seems the 2006 attacks came just in the nick of time to prevent any pluralist expansion of the political system.

Three decades of militant Islamism have produced a truce that may have frayed at the edges, thanks to the influence of al Qaeda—or just possibly, the state has created or incited new cells on its own, in order to retain control over the government, and counteract the rise of moderate Islamism in its political form. It has accepted moderate Islamism in other dimensions (intellectual and social). I'm not a conspiracy theorist, and uncomfortable with this thesis, but it is a possibility. While moderate

Islamism is supported by many Egyptians, the sight of the Hamas government under fire in Gaza, and the all-out Israeli effort to rid Lebanon of Hizbollah has set everyone's teeth on edge. Would the Israelis attack Egypt if the Muslim Brotherhood won a *bona fide* election? If so, we might see the reconversion of moderates to militants overnight.

ACKNOWLEDGMENTS

Material produced by the U.S. Government cannot be copyrighted. However, some of the material in this chapter has been copyrighted through its inclusion in Dr. Zuhur's own publications and should not be reproduced without permission. This chapter expresses the author's views and they do not necessarily reflect the official policy or position of the Department of the Army, the Department of Defense, or the U.S. Government.

NOTES

1. For a thorough account of al-Azhar university see Malika Zghal, *Gardiens de L'Islam: Les oulémas d'Al-Azhar dans l'Égypte contemporaine* (Paris: Presses de Sciences PO, 1996).

2. The following request by an Indonesian Muslim and patriot, and *fatwa* given by Rashid Rida in the journal *Manar* (note that Lebanese Hizbollah's media outlet carries the same name) demonstrates his broader influence on issues of the day. Rashid Rida, "Patriotism, Nationalism, and Group Spirit in Islam," in *Islam in Transition: Muslim Perspectives*, eds. John L. Donohue and John L. Esposito (New York: Oxford University Press, 1982), pp. 46–59. While Rida was a Syrian, it is fair to represent him as a second generation member of the Egyptian reform movement.

3. Richard P. Mitchell, *Society of the Muslim Brother* (London: Oxford University Press, 1969).

4. Ahmad S. Moussalli, *Moderate and Radical Islamic Fundamentalism: The Quest for Modernity, Legitimacy, and the Islamic State* (Gainsville, FL: University of Florida, 1999), pp. 82–131.

5. Sherifa Zuhur, *Revealing Reveiling: Islamist Gender Ideology in Contemporary Egypt* (Albany, NY: State University of New York Press, 1992), p. 45.

6. Moussalli: 83.

7. Zuhur (1992): 45–48.

8. Muhammad Haikal in narration, in *Nasser* for Channel 4 and the BBC, c. 1989.

9. Tariq al-Bishri, *al-Haraka al-Siyasiyya fi Misr 1945–1952* (Cairo: al-Hayya al-Misriyya lil-kitab, 1972).

10. For a review of many of Qutb's ideas see Leonard Binder, *Islamic Liberalism: A Critique of Development Ideologies* (Chicago, IL: University of Chicago Press, 1988), pp. 170–205.

11. Moussalli: 151.

12. Sayyid Qutb, *Ma`rakat al-Islam wa al-ra`smaliyya* (Beirut: Dar al-Shuruq, 1975) 28; also see Sayyid Qutb, *Fi al-tarikh: Fikra wa-minhaj* (Cairo: Dar al-Shuruq, 1974), pp. 23–25.

13. Sayyid Qutb, *Social Justice in Islam*, translated by John Hardie (Washington DC: American Council of Learned Societies, 1953).

14. Sayyid Qutb, *al-Ma`alim fi tariq*, 7th ed. (Beirut: Dar al-Shuruq, 1980), pp. 173–174.

15. Giles Kepel, *Muslim Extremism in Egypt: The Prophet and the Pharaoh* (Berkeley, CA: University of California Press, 1984), pp. 93–94.

16. J. J. Jansen, "De betkenis van het Islamisitisch fundamentalisme: De Lotgevallen van de Shoukri-group in Egypte," in *Naar de letter, Beschouvingen over fundamentalisme*, ed. P. Boele, S. Koenis and P. Westerman, eds. (Utrecht: 1991), pp. 185–202; or see J. J. Jansen, "Takfir wa al-Hijrah, Jama`at al-" in *Oxford Encyclopedia of the Modern Islamic World*, ed. John Esposito (New York: Oxford University Press, 1995).

17. Saad Eddin Ibrahim, "Anatomy of Egypt's Militant Islamic Groups: Methodological Note and Preliminary Findings," *International Journal of Middle East Studies* 12, no. 4 (1980): 423–453.

18. Ibrahim (1980); also see Saad Eddin Ibrahim, "Egypt's Islamic Activism in the 1980s," *Third World Quarterly* 10, no. 2 (April 1988): 632–657.

19. Denis Sullivan and Sana Abed-Kotob, *Islam in Contemporary Egypt: Civil Society vs. the State* (Boulder, CO: Lynne Rienner, 1999), p. 78.

20. Sullivan and Abed-Kotob: 82–83.

21. Nemat Guenena, "The 'Jihad': An 'Islamic Alternative' in Egypt," *Cairo Papers in Social Science* 9 (Summer 1986): 63.

22. Guenena: 55.

23. Guenena.

24. A 27-year-old engineer executed after Sadat's assassination. The book draws heavily on the ideas of Ibn Taymiyya, a medieval writer. See Emmanuel Sivan, *Radical Islam, Medieval Theology and Modern Politics*. (New Haven, CT: Yale University Press, 1985), pp. 103–104.

25. Rudolph Peters, *Jihad in Classical and Modern Islam* (Princeton, NJ: Markus Wiener, 1996), pp. 161–167; see also Youssef Aboul-Einein and Sherifa Zuhur, *Islamic Rulings on Warfare* (Carlisle, PA: Strategic Studies Institute, 2004).

26. Aboul-Einein and Zuhur.

27. See Fawaz A.Gerges "The End of the Islamist Insurgency in Egypt?" *Middle East Journal* 53/54 (Fall 2000): 582–612.

28. Guenena: 43, 44.

29. Mona Makram Ebeid, "The Role of the Official Opposition," in Charles Tripp and Roger Owen, eds. *Egypt Under Mubarak*, (London: Routledge, 1989), pp. 21–52.

30. Abd al-Qadir al-Shahid, *al-Ikhtiraq: Qissat sharikat tawzif al-amwal* (Cairo: Sina lil-Nashr, 1989).

31. "Special Report on Egypt," *Middle East Economic Digest*, October 14, 1988.

32. Denis Sullivan, "Extra-State Actors and Privatization in Egypt" in *Privatization and Liberalization in the Middle East*, eds. Ilya Harik and Denis Sullivan

(Bloomington, IN: Indiana University Press, 1992), pp. 40–41; Said Aly, "Privatization in Egypt" in Iliya Harik and Denis Sullivan, eds., *Privatization in the Middle East* (Bloomington, IN: Indiana University Press, 1992), 53–54.

33. Mahfuz was attacked for the subject matter of his early trilogy (for which he won the Nobel Prize) *Children of Gebalawi*. The three novels critique Egyptian society. The characters carry the names of Muslims in early Islam, but of course, this is also typical of Egyptians, still, Islamists, took this authorial choice to mean a mockery of Islamic society and mores.

34. `Umar `Abd al-Rahman, *Kalimat al-haqq* (Cairo: Dar al-Itisam, 1987), pp. 177–199; Gehad Auda, "Omar Abdel-Rahman," in *Oxford Encyclopedia of the Modern Islamic World*, ed. John Esposito (New York: Oxford University Press, 1995).

35. Zghal; or for the commonly prevailing U.S. media perspective on the Islamists see Judith Miller, "Sheikh Emerges on TV to Deny Link to Bombing," *New York Times*, March 19, 1993.

36. Denis Sullivan and Sana Abed-Kotob, *Islam in Contemporary Society* (Boulder, CO: Lynne Rienner, 1999), 132–133.

37. Ibid.: p. 133.

38. Mandy McClure, "Stop the Presses" *Cairo Times*, 4 (May 25–31, 2000).

39. Ahmed Moussa, "Egypt's Most Wanted Egyptian Afghans," *Al-Ahram Weekly Online*, October 18–24, 2001.

40. Khaled Dawoud, "Concepts of Jihad," *Al-Ahram Weekly Online*, January 11–17, 2001, http://weekly.ahram.org.eg.

41. Samir Rafaat, "Ayman al-Zawahri The World's Second Most Wanted Man," November 1, 2001, http://www.egy.com/people.

42. Sherifa Zuhur, *A Hundred Osamas: The Future of Counterinsurgency* (Carlisle, PA: Strategic Studies Institute, 2006), 35, 38.

43. Philip Smucker, "Arab Elite Warms to Al Qaeda Leaders: Al Qaeda Biographer Stops Sales of Book Because It's Too Critical," *Christian Science Monitor,* July 30, 2002.

44. The book also offers details about organizational and personnel matters of the Gama`at, and subsequently, the al Qaida connection. Montasser al-Zayyat, *Ayman al-Zawahiri kama `ariftahu* (Ayman al-Zawahiri as I Knew Him) (Cairo: Dar Misr Al Mahrousa, 2002). Al-Zawahiri's own writing is important as well, particularly his *Bitter Harvest*, which is an attack on the Muslim Brotherhood, and in his efforts to combat popular mythologizing about al Qaida in Knights under the Banner. Here for instance, he is at pains to show that the United States did not fund al Qaida, and that its money came from popular Arab organizations (not Arab governments, though in fact, the Saudi government has been implicated in funding of the *mujahidin*). Zawhiri, *Knights under the Prophet's Banner*, December 3, 2001, as serialized in *al-Sharq al-Awsat*.

45. John Voll, "Fundamentalism in the Arab World: Egypt and the Sudan," in *Fundamentalisms Observed*, eds. Martin E. Marty and R. Scott Appleby (Chicago, IL: University of Chicago Press, 1991), p. 389.

46. "The Black Hole: The Fate of Islamists Rendered to Egypt," *Human Rights Watch,* May 2005, http://hrw.org/reports/2005/egypt0505/; and see "Hostage Taking and Abuse of Female Detainees," *Human Rights Watch*, http://www.hrw.org/about/projects/womrep/General-108.htm.

47. "The Muslim World After 9/11," RAND (www.rand.org), and as cited in "Generating Alternatives to Radical Islam" World Trends. *The Futurist*, May/June 2005: 15.

48. "From Riyadh/East to Sinai" 24/8/1425 h./October 8, 2004 posted on numerous Islamist sites.

49. April 29, *Al-Gumhuriyya*.

50. `Amaliyatan irhabitan ta`thiran al-faza fi Midan `Abd al-Mun`im Riyadh wa al-Sayida `A'isha," *al-Ahram*, May 1, 2005: 1.

51. His remains are depicted along with the official version of events in "al-Irahabi al-Qatil Qafaza min Min`ala Kubri Uktubir," *al-Ahram*, May 2, 2005: 5.

52. The latter version was provided by Security Chief Nabil El-Ezabi.

53. Jailan Halawi, "Terrorist Replay," *Al-Ahram Weekly*, May 2, 2005.

54. Summer Said, "226 Arrested after Cairo Attacks," *Arab News* (Saudi Arabia), May 2, 2005, www.arabnews.com.

55. *Al Jazeera*, May 8, 2005, also http://english.aljazeera.net.

56. Khairi Abaza, "Sharm al-Shaykh Bombings: The Egyptian Context," PolicyWatch #1023, Washington Institute for Near Eastern Policy, August 12, 2005.

57. Abd al-Mun`im Ibrahim, *Akhbar al-Khalij* (Bahrain).

58. *Al-Ghad* official statement, 1 May, 2005.

59. *Arab News*, May 2, 2005.

60. Doha Al-Zohairy, *Al Jazeera*, May 1, 2005.

61. Editorial, *Al-Quds al-`Arabi* (London) May 2, 2005.

CHAPTER 26

COUNTERTERRORISM POLICIES AND THE REVOLUTIONARY MOVEMENT OF TUPAC AMARU: THE UNMASKING OF PERU'S NATIONAL SECURITY STATE

Vera Eccarius-Kelly

Terrorism has plagued the modern Peruvian state throughout the twentieth century. Indeed, Latin America's most ruthless and vicious terror organization, the Maoist *Sendero Luminoso* (SL) or Shining Path, controlled considerable segments of the Peruvian countryside during the 1980s.[1] A second, notably smaller and much less violent terror group appeared in 1984 under the name *Movimiento Revolucionario Túpac Amaru* (Revolutionary Movement of Tupac Amaru, or MRTA). Its members specialized in targeted bombings of predominantly domestic economic interests; they carried out armed assaults and occupations, but also engaged in hostage taking and kidnapping for ransom schemes. In contrast to the highly orchestrated extremism of the Shining Path, which was fully ensconced in the central and southern regions of the country, the MRTA embraced a traditional Marxist-Leninist revolutionary strategy. The MRTA initiated a mainly urban campaign, claiming to represent society's dispossessed, and anticipated a wave of spontaneous popular assistance for its cause. In reality, the terror group received very limited support from radical trade union elements and among disillusioned working class communities around Lima and in the northern zones of San Martin and Lambayeque. As a result, MRTA cadres never managed to present a viable and direct military threat to the Peruvian state.

However, the MRTA engaged in a series of surprising publicity stunts that earned the organization a measure of sympathetic attention from segments of the population. Several times during the 1980s and 1990s, the MRTA carried out high-profile actions mocking the ineptitude and repressive nature of the Peruvian state and its counterterrorism tactics. This chapter examines several of the major confrontations between the Peruvian government and the MRTA, and offers a detailed analysis of the counterterrorism policies employed during the 1996–1997 hostage crisis at the Japanese Ambassador's residence in the capital city Lima. Several significant insights can be gained from investigating the counterterrorism measures utilized to defeat the MRTA during both the García and Fujimori presidencies between 1985 and 2000. To evaluate conclusively why specific anti-terror policies succeeded or failed during and after the hostage crisis in Lima, it is also necessary to examine the context of Peruvian sociopolitical factors.

THE MRTA AND THE STATE'S CREDIBILITY GAP

Even though Peruvian officials classified the MRTA as the lesser terror group in the country, the terrorists managed to embarrass, ridicule, and humiliate security forces several times. By 1997 however, the MRTA's high-profile and media-savvy strategy culminated in the organization's evisceration by Peruvian anti-terror commandos. Today, remnant MRTA forces struggle to free imprisoned comrades abroad and in Peru, including U.S. citizen Lori Berenson who remains incarcerated in Cajamarca prison in northern Peru.[2] In a mostly futile effort, MRTA combatants still try to recruit disillusioned slum dwellers to its depleted ranks and focus on rebuilding its decimated leadership. The U.S. Department of State estimates that the MRTA consists of fewer than 100 trained and experienced cadres in the country, with several former MRTA operatives residing in exile, some in Germany and France.[3]

The MRTA incensed security forces on July 9, 1990, when 47 high-level MRTA terrorists escaped from the infamous *Canto Grande* prison facility through a massive 250-meter tunnel that had been dug from the basement of a private home into the prison compound. The Miguel Castro y Castro high-security penitentiary, popularly known as *Canto Grande*, had been constructed by the Peruvian government to hold captured Shining Path and MRTA cadres as well as members of drug cartels. Media reports revealed that MRTA members utilized air compressors, engineering equipment, and electric lights over a period of several months to dig the tunnel. The large scale prison-break deeply embarrassed President Alan García

Pérez, particularly because members of the press speculated that prison authorities may have been bribed to aid in the escape. The extensive press coverage surrounding MRTA actions contributed to García's electoral defeat by strongman Alberto Fujimori in the summer of 1990.

To publicize their audacious prison-break and to ridicule the Peruvian government, some 20 MRTA escapees, including the group's leader Victor Polay Campos, invited Nicaraguan political poet and writer Claribel Alegría to interview the MRTA escapees in safe houses around Lima. Retelling the story of their escape, Alegría published a book, an inside story about the tunnel and the escape, entitled *Fuga de Canto Grande* in 1992, which infuriated the Peruvian government and humiliated state prison authorities and anti-terror units.[4] Although the MRTA's reputation as a powerful subversive organization benefited temporarily from the successful prison-break, Polay Campos was recaptured just 2 years later in Lima and has been languishing in solitary confinement in Yanomayo prison, located in the Andes mountains close to the Bolivian border, ever since.

During the increasingly violent atmosphere in the country in the 1990s the MRTA engaged in a high-stakes operation leading to its demise as an active terror group. On December 17, 1996, 14 members of the MRTA under the leadership of Néstor Cerpa Cartolini took hostage 450 high-level government officials, business executives, and numerous international dignitaries at the official residence of Japan's Ambassador to Peru. Having gained access to the residence under the guise of food service workers, the terrorists overwhelmed the attending guests of honor, who had been invited to celebrate Japan's Emperor Akihito's birthday. The MRTA terrorists held a group of 72 hostages for a period of over 4 months in the residence, and created an international and diplomatic nightmare for President Fujimori. On April 24, 1997, Peruvian anti-terror commandos raided the residence, overpowered the MRTA hostage takers, and freed the hostages.

Initially the rescue operation was hailed as a major success, since only one hostage and two of the anti-terror commandos died in the assault, along with all 14 MRTA terrorists. But disturbing details emerged in the weeks and months following the liberation of the hostages. Some 3 years after the event, the intensely unpopular Peruvian President Fujimori left the country facing accusations of corruption, human rights violations, and excessive authoritarianism. The Peruvian state's response to the MRTA's assault on the Japanese Ambassador's residence contributed to the unmasking of the country's repressive and corrupt security apparatus. International media coverage exposed shady, unseemly, and often brutal practices in the Peruvian government, and focused on totalitarian elements within secret police units and the military.[5] By voicing open dissent to the

Fujimori regime, the long-repressed democratic opposition gained political traction. Public opinion turned against Fujimori and his delegitimized security state apparatus that had driven the anti-terror campaigns in the country. The public withdrew its trust, angered over being misled to believe in the effectiveness of a military solution to the terrorism problem. The military had actually helped to create a society ruled by fear and intimidation. The result was an overwhelmingly repressive atmosphere that permitted a continual erosion of basic human rights, including the elimination of due process and free speech.

INCA MYTHS AND VISIONARY IDEOLOGY: THE MRTA'S ORIGIN

This section of the chapter examines the root causes and motivations of the MRTA's formation as a terrorist group in the early 1980s and provides the background for a critical examination of Peruvian counterterrorism measures. The MRTA emerged in the context of a lengthy tradition of Marxist-Leninist revolutionary thought in the region. Two men in particular, socialist and political philosopher José Carlos Mariátegui and polemic writer and activist Victor Raúl Haya de la Torre, set the stage in the 1920s for the Peruvian terror organization's formation six decades later.

In 1924, Haya de la Torre founded an anti-imperialist front called the *Alianza Popular Revolucionaria Americana* (APRA), today a Peruvian party known as APRA or PAP (*Partido Aprista Peruano*). His admiration for Lenin's use of vanguard forces led Haya de la Torre to pursue an insurrection modeled on the Bolsheviks in 1932. Brutally repressed, APRA was outlawed and its members suffered severe persecution until Haya de la Torre renounced his communist ideals and reshaped the organization into a populist party with a leftist orientation.[6] In 1985, for the first time in the existence of APRA as a party, its presidential candidate Alan García succeeded at the ballot box. The mass-based, reform-oriented political platform created a sense of optimism in the country, but nowhere else in Latin America according to Carol Graham, Senior Fellow at the Brookings Institution, were "hopes dashed as dramatically by the onset of an economic, social, and political crisis of unprecedented severity" as in Peru.[7] By the mid-1980s the country experienced "an increasingly agitated social and political climate, even without taking into account the actions of armed groups such as Sendero Luminoso and the Movimiento Revolucionario Túpac Amaru . . . ," stated Peruvian sociologist Rochabrun Silva.[8] Unresolved social demands, constant and prolonged strikes, and the frequent use of violent methods of protest became the norm to express a deep-seated frustration with the government's inability or unwillingness to fulfill campaign promises.

The other personality to play a significant role in the ideological formation of the second generation of Peruvian terror groups was José Carlos Mariátegui, one of Latin America's most revered socialist thinkers. He opposed Haya de la Torre's preference for vanguards, and argued that a successful socialist revolution needed to evolve organically within the context of local conditions and cultural practices. Mariátegui rejected the concept of what he considered imitating a European-based formula for revolution.[9] Openly breaking with Haya de la Torre and the *Aprista* movement, he projected that an authoritarian, elitist streak would emerge from a left that was dominated by APRA. He feared that authoritarianism would make the left easily coopted by bourgeois elements.

By the mid-1960s, APRA had indeed transformed itself into a pragmatic and legal political force willing to collaborate with conservative forces in Congress. At that time two guerrilla organizations, the Movement of the Revolutionary Left (MIR) and the National Liberation Army (ELN), initiated their armed struggle and failed within months of appearing on the political landscape.[10] Radical students, political activists, and a range of participants in the legal and authorized left, including former APRA members, expressed extreme disillusionment with APRA's willingness to cooperate with conservatives in Congress. Some were frustrated by the guerrilla movement's failure to launch a serious challenge to the conservative state. Protesting the shift to the center by APRA, many individuals joined socialists, Marxists, Trotskyites, and Maoists in the formation of a hard-core ideological and unauthorized challenge from the left.[11] Their aim was to punish, discredit, and weaken the *Apristas* for abandoning their original revolutionary principles. Out of this rift within the factions of the left and APRA after the party had moved toward the middle of the political spectrum, a second generation of Peruvian radical organizations emerged in the early 1980s.

Peruvian social forces became increasingly unwilling and unable to resolve conflict in a nonviolent manner. Accusations of rampant government corruption, elitism, and fraudulent deals undermined the credibility of all Peruvian institutions, ranging from congressional representatives to public servants in the smallest of towns. As a consequence of a generalized lack of trust in institutions, and the sense that crooked business practices and corruption were the only way to get ahead, the country experienced a significant rise in criminal conduct. Without a clear programmatic vision for a better future, Rochabrun Silva argued, bitterness led many to choose between "nihilism, delinquency, drug addiction, or Sendero Luminoso [or MRTA]."[12] The appearance of widespread cynicism and contempt for the rule of law, and the inability of social groups to resolve fundamental social disagreements characterizes a praetorian society.[13] Samuel Huntington articulated this concept in his seminal work *Political Order in Changing Societies*.[14] The power structure in such a society is extremely fragmented, leading a multitude of actors to utilize the entire range of techniques to gain more power, including manipulation and bribery, strikes, riots, assassinations and guerrilla warfare. Huntington proposed that

> In a praetorian system social forces confront each other nakedly; no political institutions, no corps of professional political leaders are recognized or accepted as the legitimate intermediaries to moderate group conflict. Equally important, no agreement exists among the groups as to the legitimate and authoritative methods for resolving conflict.[15]

Peru represented a prime example of such a praetorian society, because the country lacked legitimate institutions following the experiences with failed guerrilla warfare and disastrous military dictatorships in the 1960s. No social force, party, or institution provided the necessary framework for challenger communities to channel their demands within the existent political structures. The appearance of a second generation of terror organizations in this context is logical, in particular as challenger communities were confronted by an increasingly repressive state apparatus. This reality created an atmosphere of alarm, insecurity, and acceptance of extremes on both ideological poles, causing the complete deterioration of an already weakened democratic foundation.

According to MRTA leader Polay Campos, a former *Aprista* who was focused on undermining and weakening President García's government, people's anxiety about the future of the country incited the development for revolutionary action. Polay Campos believed that García and his *Apristas* represented the worst kind of demagoguery imaginable.[16] Polay Campos knew President García quite well from their membership in APRA's *buro de conjunciones*, a special training school for APRA youth leaders.[17] Their common experiences during political seminars intended to prepare them for future leadership roles in Peruvian society, as well as their obvious ideological differences, probably intensified Polay Campos' desire to expose the APRA government's inadequacies, weaknesses, and sociopolitical failures from 1985 to 1990.

Graham analyzed a pivotal moment in the development of the MRTA by describing a moment in November 1987 when "the MRTA entered the national limelight . . . it virtually took over the jungle department of Juanjui [Department of San Martin in northern Peru] and invited the TV news program *Panorama* to travel along with it; thus, the entire operation was aired on the news before the government knew anything about it."[18] Certainly, the MRTA presented anything but a serious military challenge to the García government at that time, but the organization effectively utilized media blitzes to ridicule APRA's disastrous anti-terror efforts and its inadequate social reforms.[19] With the assistance of historically based symbols, images, slogans, and propaganda, the MRTA placed itself firmly within a lengthy tradition of indigenous rebellions in opposition to unjust and abusive power structures.

The MRTA's effective use of propaganda included the symbolic integration of Inca mythology by referencing heroic anti-colonial struggles of national liberation led by Túpac Amaru. In fact, the MRTA referenced two separate Inca leaders who rebelled against Spanish domination; one in 1571, the other in 1781. The first Túpac Amaru, son of Manco Inca, was captured and beheaded in 1572 following a rebellion. But instead of snuffing out indigenous unrest as the Spanish had hoped, an Inca legend foretold the reincarnation of a new Inca leader out of the dismemberment of Túpac Amaru.[20] The second Túpac Amaru, a direct descendant of the first, rose in rebellion some 200 years later. By then, indigenous people had suffered tremendously under Spanish control, and as Ward Stavig has observed, "the reign of the Inca came to be looked upon . . . with increasing sympathy and nostalgia. Negative memories of the Inca conquest faded, and the reign of the Inca began to be seen as a period of benevolent and just rule."[21] The idealized Inca reign produced a more difficult and costly second rebellion for the Spaniards. But in 1781, the second Túpac Amaru suffered horrendous torture and dismemberment, and finally was beheaded like the first, leaving the indigenous populations to anticipate the reincarnation of a third Inca leader by the name Túpac Amaru. Political philosopher Mariátegui's analysis of the Inca periods prior to the arrival of the Spanish followed this same idealized perception of indigenous self-rule. According to his perspective, the structure of the Inca Empire provided all the material needs members of Inca society would have and, most importantly, assigned everyone a clearly defined role. With an unambiguous sense of purpose in society, the Incas supposedly created a fully committed and loyal populace.[22] Mariátegui advocated for a similar sense of commitment to the cause of revolutionary movements in Peru if one hoped to succeed.

The MRTA's deliberate appropriation of the indigenous Inca myth by claiming the name *Movimiento Revolutionario Túpac Amaru* evoked a powerful emotional connection to 400 years of struggle and national resistance to injustices perpetrated by occupying forces. By reframing the anti-colonial struggle through the incorporation of anti-imperialist language, the explicit goal of the MRTA was the creation of a socialist democracy. The organization intended to link a populist, mass-based movement with elements of nationalism in pursuit of the ideals of communal justice, human dignity, and social development.[23] Armed, militant action—according to the MRTA—would launch the popular revolution just as Mariátegui had advocated, building the foundation of a natural revolutionary process mindful of local conditions and indigenous heritage and customs. This ideological framework explained why the MRTA expected the Peruvian population to aid the terror group willingly and to embrace fully the righteousness of the struggle.[24]

THE PERUVIAN SECURITY STATE

Based on the assessments of Tarazona-Sevillano, a former prosecutor for the Peruvian justice ministry, the Peruvian legal establishment faced a fundamental crisis in the mid-1980s as a consequence of inadequately addressing and processing the rising number of terrorist cases brought to its attention.[25] As recently as 1979, the country had emerged from a decade of military dictatorship, during which essential civil rights had been suspended—including freedom of the press, freedom of expression, and freedom of political association, among others. But a newly promulgated constitution once again protected the basic rights of citizens in 1980. The legal community hoped to strengthen the building blocs of the frail democratic state. However, Peru's institutions did not manage to carry out this obligation, as the unexpected upsurge of the terrorism problem created a divisive response between two schools of thought within the legal establishment of how best to address the question of prosecuting terror suspects. One group pushed for the treatment of terror suspects as common criminals in order to avoid a weakening of the recently reestablished democratic structures, while the other group advocated for specialized military tribunals to deal with the terror challenge to the state.[26]

Initially, the Peruvian government chose to treat terrorists as common criminals in order to protect their constitutionally guaranteed rights. Yet the García government (1985–1990) enacted a series of anti-terror legislation that focused primarily on guarding the stability and security of the state, slowly undermining the weak democratic structures in Peru. After Fujimori's election in the summer of 1990, anti-terror policies hardened further. In April 1992, Fujimori carried out a coup that was supported by the military. Overturning the constitution and dissolving congress, he reshaped the political landscape in the country. The legal left was effectively excluded from governing. The MRTA experienced an upswing as a consequence of the coup, which had marginalized the entire left. Instead of consulting and co-opting myriad groups of political organizations to unite behind a national plan that aimed to defeat terrorism, the Fujimori regime was in cahoots with corrupt and anti-democratic elements in the armed forces. Creating new blocs of opposition, additional social groups decided on violent means to oppose the *caudillo* style of the Fujimori government. The 1992 coup in effect initiated a significant radicalization process in the country, rejuvenating groups such as the MRTA.

According to Tarazona-Sevillano, "the police and army...exercised liberal arresting procedures that...clogged the courts with state cases against people whose only crime may have been their presence in an area where . . . [terrorist] actions took place."[27] As a consequence of such blanket arrests, large numbers of suspected terrorists, their sympathizers, and innocent civilians went to trial with little evidence, which led to the release of significant numbers of suspects. At the same time, the Shining Path assassinated countless judges and magistrates in order to intimidate the legal community. Within months, the Peruvian police and military forces accused judges of leniency toward terrorist suspects, while members of the legal profession argued that the police failed to protect their physical safety. The state's response to this dilemma resulted in the establishment of special terrorism courts that became increasingly secretive and eventually were entirely managed and controlled by the military.

During the mid-1980s, the army and specialized military police asserted their roles as defenders of the state. A convoluted set of anti-terror legislation and the diminishing trust between the judicial branch and the army led to the creation of death squads and paramilitaries, so-called *búfalos*.[28] Their brutal actions, in addition to an upsurge of terrorism, created a cycle of violence that continuously escalated and victimized innocent peasants. In July 1988, information about a paramilitary group by the name of *Comando Rodrigo Franco* appeared in the media.[29] Reports connected the group to the interior ministry and the armed forces, who appeared to have ordered targeted assassinations of left-wing community leaders and journalists.[30] According to Graham, "the violence indicated a dangerous deterioration of the social situation, in which the legitimacy of judicial and political institutions was increasingly in question . . ."[31] By 1990, the García government merged all anti-terror police forces under the Office of Special Operations, which then housed the Sinchis and the Llapan Aticcs, two units trained to deal with subversive action in the countryside and later implicated in several massacres by the Peruvian Truth and Reconciliation Committee's final report.[32]

Representatives of the media were also regular targets for anti-terror units. Particularly under the Fujimori government (1990–2000), an atmosphere of repression and intimidation surrounded media independent of political affiliations. The monitoring organization Reporters Without Borders described Fujimori's Peru as a society in which freedom of expression was classified as difficult.[33] Journalists, writers, and radio personalities who expressed criticism—along with owners of media outlets, their managers, and editors who were responsible for airing investigative reports—regularly received death threats, were beaten, sued for libel, or prosecuted for crimes that they did not commit. Army intelligence agents who collaborated with journalists faced unspeakable torture, particularly those members of intelligence units suspected of having leaked critical information to the press.[34] In summary, the upsurge of terrorism in combination with the establishment of a security state managed by a small group of authoritarians from political and military circles, created a society entirely managed through tools of intimidation, repression, and fear.

FROM PUBLICITY STUNTS TO TARGETED ASSASSINATIONS: 1984 TO 1995

The MRTA leadership employed an artfully designed publicity campaign in pursuit of tactical advantages vis-à-vis the increasing pressure exerted from Peruvian authorities.[35] To the government's frustration, surprise MRTA actions created a flurry of headlines that pointed out to the Peruvian population how anti-terror units bungled their responses. Media coverage often identified the lack of basic logistical information available to anti-terror units, described poorly equipped or trained troops, and criticized the use of ineffectual counterterrorism measures throughout the 1980s. The fact that media pointed out such inadequacies proved important to the MRTA's strategic thinking and planning process, because it intensified general support. Publicity stunts carried out by the MRTA aimed to destabilize the centers of control within the Peruvian state by demonstrating its own strength and superiority in contrast with the government. Consequently, the MRTA targeted surprising locations at unexpected times to benefit fully from media attention. A rather typical example of such an action was the sudden appearance in 1984 of "*Radio Imperial*," a clandestine radio station utilized by the combatants to broadcast their initial revolutionary communiqué.[36] In 1985, the MRTA created the "*4 de Noviembre*" pirate radio station to communicate directly with the population, arguing that the general elections should be boycotted to "protest the ongoing political manipulation."[37] And again in 1987, the MRTA temporarily occupied a half dozen radio stations in the capital city Lima to broadcast a message that denounced increasing levels of militarism among Peruvian security forces.[38]

MRTA combatants continued to regularly occupy radio stations or articulate their goals from pirated stations such as "*Voz Rebelde*" (Rebel Voice). Peruvian authorities, however, failed to respond decisively and effectively to the airwave challenge. Apparently, the Peruvian government lacked the imagination to go beyond military measures to defeat the MRTA. Instead of engaging in an effort to create political counter-messages, public officials sounded defensive in interviews with media. In addition, TV crews accepted invitations from the MRTA to film "revolutionary actions" that then appeared on the evening news, unbeknownst to horrified members of the García government. Forced to process the news about an MRTA takeover of police barracks, an occupation of a radio station, or an act of economic sabotage at the same time as the general Peruvian public, government officials appeared uninformed and unprepared. The most embarrassing TV moment for President García came in 1987, when the well-known Peruvian *Panamericana* Television announced a special report on MRTA activities in the Upper Huallaga Valley, at a time when military police had been unable to track down the MRTA leadership and its columns in the same region.

Television images and in-depth reports, radio transmissions of revolutionary messages and communiqués, interviews with MRTA leader Polay Campos, and newspaper articles featuring specific details effectively assisted the MRTA in three important ways: (1) the media provided extensive coverage of MRTA actions, which in turn allowed the organization to inflate its power and number of combatants; (2) this bolstered the MRTA's opportunity to recruit new members, as the coverage was sympathetic or at least less hostile than reports related to the brutality of the Shining Path; and (3) the coverage aided the MRTA in demoralizing and even ridiculing the government's attempts to defeat the MRTA. The terror group's actions received more intensive media attention than the small organization warranted, which led to the public's perception that the MRTA could develop into a serious threat to stability. According to the U.S. Department of State, the MRTA never managed to attract more than 1,500 committed and trained combatants to its ranks.[39] A few leaders may have received specialized training in Colombia by the insurgent group *Movimiento 19 de Abril* (the 19th of April Movement, or M-19), but many combatants joined the organization as teenagers without exposure to extensive military or survival training.[40]

Gordon McCormick of the RAND Corporation and an authority on both the Shining Path and the MRTA, examined a tactic frequently used by MRTA leader Polay Campos to garner sympathetic press attention. Portraying the organization under his leadership as a friendlier guerrilla force with a conscience and willingness to respect human rights, Polay Campos clearly intended to distance the MRTA from the horrific acts carried out by Shining Path columns.[41] Through the Peruvian press, he disseminated the idea that MRTA combatants followed the regulations established by the Geneva Convention regarding internal warfare, and "that MRTA was a revolutionary organization that answers to a higher 'moral authority' and would 'prefer to avoid war.'"[42] The Peruvian government, under pressure from civil society, established a Truth and Reconciliation Commission (TRC) in 2002 to record, examine, and evaluate atrocities carried out by the two terrorist organizations and representatives of state authorities. In its August 2003 final report, the Commission stated that approximately 69,000 persons had died during the conflict between 1980 and 2000, and that the vast majority of the victims consisted of uneducated, impoverished, and indigenous peasants. Demonstrating the brutality of the conditions in the country, the Commission suggested that about 54 percent of all atrocities were committed by members of the Shining Path, 44.5 percent by the armed forces, (including the Sinchis and the Llapan Aticcs), police forces, and armed self-defense committees, and 1.5 percent by members of the MRTA. The TRC's conclusion states that

> Unlike Shining Path, and like other armed Latin American organizations with which it maintained ties, the MRTA claimed responsibility for its actions, its members used uniforms or other identifiers to differentiate themselves from the civilian population, it abstained from attacking the unarmed population and at some points showed signs of being open to peace negotiations.[43]

While there is evidence that the MRTA avoided killing random civilians or innocent bystanders and never targeted peasants or the urban poor for elimination as did the Shining Path, MRTA combatants engaged in bombings of commercial targets and carried out disturbing kidnapping operations that terrorized the economic and political elite in the country. Most actions undertaken by the MRTA served either a propagandistic or a financial purpose.[44] The majority of activities were orchestrated to create a sympathetic public reaction. An example for such an action was a Robin Hood-like stunt that earned the MRTA high praise among impoverished striking miners who demanded safer working conditions with improved pay. MRTA combatants emerged with a stolen truck of chickens that they distributed among the appreciative miners and their families. In this very simplistic yet easily grasped operation the MRTA demonstrated its commitment to a more just and communitarian social structure. They symbolically expropriated goods from the elite and redistributed them to needy and vulnerable members of the community.

Other events, however, had been planned to project power and advance the organization's cash flow in preparation of future operations. Several kidnapping schemes provided the organization with money, including the abduction for ransom of Hector Jeri, a retired air force general. After the transfer of a ransom payment estimated to have been close to $3 million and the publication of a statement related to the goals of the MRTA, the general was released unharmed.[45] But the MRTA also committed vicious killings and engaged in bloody battles. In 1989, the MRTA lost a brutal jungle-zone struggle over control of territory with the native Asháninka tribes after the MRTA kidnapped and later murdered Alejandro Calderón Espinoza, the spiritual leader and head of the tribal federation of all the Asháninka peoples. Instead of submitting to the terror threat, the tribal council sent 2,000 Asháninka warriors, who tracked MRTA columns (as well as Shining Path combatants and narco-traffickers who had invaded their land) to kill them "with bows and arrows, blowpipes, and curare-dipped darts."[46] The MRTA had to withdraw from the region. And in January 1990, an MRTA unit murdered former defense minister General Enrique López Albújar, claiming that this was justified punishment for his orders to torture and kill MRTA members.[47]

By 1990, the MRTA had suffered a series of military setbacks. The organization experienced a defeat by both Shining Path and tribal peoples in its attempt to expand into rural zones and jungle departments. Most MRTA combatants retreated to urban areas, but a remaining group was detected by the Peruvian military, encircled, and bombed from the air. Military personnel then executed all surviving MRTA members after their capture.[48] According to the MRTA, 60 combatants died in heavy fighting, excluding a dozen or more civilians.[49] At that time, the Peruvian military regularly committed human rights violations of the most serious kind, including extrajudicial executions. The massacre at Los Molinos foreshadowed what was to take place in 1997 after the raid on the Japanese Ambassador's residence. It was clear that the MRTA had suffered significant losses and would not be able to recover very easily. Although Polay Campos escaped in 1990 from *Canto Grande* prison through the spectacular tunnel his companions had constructed, his freedom was short-lived, as his recapture came in June 1992. That same year a unit of specialized police detained another MRTA leader, Peter Cárdenas Schulte. The police also found an MRTA computer center that belonged to the organization's headquarters. The discovery provided much-needed insight into the leadership structure and hierarchy of the terror group.[50] Careful observers of both terror groups in Peru, such as Gordon McCormick and Cynthia McClintock, have noted that by the early 1990s the MRTA had passed its revolutionary peak.[51]

THE HOSTAGE CRISIS AT THE JAPANESE AMBASSADOR'S RESIDENCE: 1996–1997

When the MRTA seized the Ambassador's home in Lima, both the domestic and international media became fascinated with the crisis. Fujimori prohibited and obstructed direct contact between the MRTA and media representatives, but several reporters sneaked into the compound despite stern government warnings. In fact, it was the international press that provided an early assessment of the hostages' conditions rather than the tightlipped Peruvian officials who refused to provide any statements. Koji Harada, for example, a photographer for Japan's Kyodo News Agency, delivered the first—and according to Peruvian officials, illegally obtained—images of conditions inside the residence. Harada was quickly arrested and interrogated by Peruvian forces, but his employer, Kyodo, challenged Fujimori's right to cordon off the compound and defended its photographer's approach to establish contact with the MRTA on Japanese property. Shortly thereafter, Peruvian anti-terror units detained Tsuyoshi Hitomi from Asahi TV, along with his Peruvian translator Victor Borja. They had just completed a 2-hour face-to-face meeting with the MRTA inside the Japanese Ambassador's residence. Then Miguel Real, from the

London-based Worldwide Television News (WTN), communicated with MRTA leader Néstor Cerpa by short-wave radio.[52] President Fujimori despised the uncontrollable and noncompliant foreign media, and encouraged security forces to use intimidation methods to suppress critical perspectives. Several international news crews were expelled from the country, accused of providing strategic advice and sensitive logistical information to the terrorists.[53]

Undoubtedly, the Peruvian government faced a tremendous level of international scrutiny because of the brazen act of just 14 terrorists, who had seized one of the most secure buildings in the country (the Ambassador's home resembled a fortress surrounded by a high wall, with bullet proof glass and iron gates in front of its windows). The hostage crisis propelled the MRTA onto the world stage, when it became clear that the terrorists had outwitted more than 300 heavily armed police units stationed outside the residence. According to Enrique Obando, a Peruvian authority on civil-military relations "the security forces were sloppy and overconfident. This attack could have been prevented with the same measures that any airline takes when passengers go onto an airplane."[54]

The official Japanese position encouraged a negotiated settlement to the hostage situation. Japanese Prime Minister Ryutaro Hashimoto publicly urged Peru to avoid taking actions that endangered the hostages, since one-third of them were Japanese citizens.[55] Among the other high-value hostages were the Peruvian foreign minister, the Peruvian minister of agriculture, the president of the Peruvian supreme court, five congressmen, (ironically) the current and former anti-terror police chiefs, President Fujimori's brother, the Japanese Ambassador to Peru, and Bolivia's Ambassador to Peru.

Right from the beginning of the crisis, the Peruvian government employed disturbing tactics of psychological warfare to unsettle and worry the MRTA. For example, water and electricity were cut off, but the terrorists quickly learned that the Ambassador's compound had its own generators. Then the Peruvian anti-terror units attempted to disrupt sleeping patterns by setting up an enormous sound system with an amplifier to project military music into the compound. In addition, Peruvian helicopters buzzed the residence, seemingly indicating an imminent frontal assault. Occasionally hundreds of heavily armed men encircled the residence pointing their guns at the entrance in a menacing way, provoking a burst of fire from the MRTA.

It is entirely unclear what advantage these actions could have created for the anti-terror units. The MRTA terrorists were prepared for an eventual assault, and the provocative tactics displayed by the Peruvian armed forces caused significant distress for the large number of hostages who were robbed of what little sleep they might have gotten since the loud military music and buzzing helicopters kept them up day and night. This

Just days after the raid, the left-wing Peruvian newspaper *La República* published articles alleging that several MRTA members had tried to surrender but were extra-judicially executed. Grainy images showed bodies of mutilated, perhaps even dismembered terrorists. Based on eye-witness accounts of former hostages, including Japanese embassy employee Hidetaka Ogura, three terrorists were alive and tied up in the garden after the raid. Ogura stated that they had been extra-judicially executed and that at least one begged for his life.[61] According to documents from the Inter-American Court of Human Rights (Inter.-Am. C.H.R.), a human rights case was filed by family members of MRTA terrorists to investigate the circumstance under which the 14 MRTA members perished. The Inter.-Am. C.H.R. document states that

> When the military rescue operation was over, the bodies [of the MRTA members] were removed by military prosecutors; representatives from the Attorney General's Office were not permitted entry. The corpses were not taken to the Institute of Forensic Medicine for the autopsy required by law; in a highly irregular move, the bodies were taken instead to the morgue at the Police Hospital. It was there that the autopsies would be performed. The autopsy reports were kept secret until 2001. Next of kin of the deceased were not allowed to be present for the identification of the bodies and the autopsies. The bodies were buried in secrecy in various cemeteries throughout Lima.[62]

CONCLUSIONS

The country's handling of the hostage drama must be considered within the larger context of Peru's repressive and corrupt national security state. It is therefore essential to examine the government's misguided management of the media, its collusion with corrupt military and police, and its embrace of tactics of intimidation, abduction, torture, and a series of other horrific human rights offenses. In light of these parameters, the Peruvian government's handling of the MRTA hostage crisis in 1997 represents a worthy case study of counterterrorism measures in a Praetorian society with fledging democratic institutions.

The Peruvian counterterrorism directorate committed horrendous errors in the decade prior to the hostage crisis. First and foremost, the Peruvian government lost its public relations battle with the MRTA. Inexplicably, consecutive Peruvian governments lacked the insight to include television and radio messaging into their arsenal of counterterrorism measures. The MRTA nourished its membership by engaging in publicity stunts that embarrassed the government, and resulted in beneficial media coverage. While the García government failed to utilize media for its own purposes, Fujimori made targets out of journalists who expressed any criticism. Secondly, the anti-terrorism campaign was almost exclusively dominated by a military strategy, which allowed key figures within the armed forces to control all levels of decision-making. By marginalizing the civilian oversight, a closed and authoritarian inner circle determined the direction of the domestic security apparatus. This resulted in policies of intimidation and victimization of entire segments of the population, rather than encouraging cooperation between the armed forces and peasants or workers. Finally, most troops and police units lacked proper training and equipment to address the terrorist surge in the country during the 1980s. In addition, their leadership lacked the sophistication to conceive of a simple I.D. check at the service entry gates of the Ambassador's residence. In summary, the anti-terrorism measures applied by Peruvian officials before the 1997 raid can be characterized as myopic and crude, but as the crisis continued, more effective and productive strategies were planned and carried out.

The masterful rescue of the hostages, however, was profoundly tainted by the unlawful executions of members of the MRTA and the subsequent cover-up. This behavior is indicative of contempt for the most fundamental principles of democracy—particularly the rule of law and justice, including due process. The Peruvian police and military forces have a long history of grave misconduct, disregard for the law, and excessive brutality. In many ways, the execution of the MRTA members in the Ambassador's residence was not surprising, since a pattern of extra-judicial executions had already emerged. In 1986, when terrorists in prisons across the country staged a coordinated uprising, the government reacted with extreme levels of violence. After quelling the riots at Lurigancho prison and regaining control, at least 90 prisoners were executed by military police.[63] Evidence also exists that MRTA members were executed in a similar fashion at Los Molinos, where after their arrest the terrorists were briefly held, then shot to death. It is no surprise, then, that after the raid on the Ambassador's residence in 1997, many of the surrendering terrorists were doomed to the same fate—execution at the hands of the anti-terror commandos. According to Peruvian Deputy State Attorney for Human Rights, Ronald Gamarra, unofficial post mortems were carried out after the siege indicating (along with eyewitness reports) that a crime was committed.[64] Reportedly, several MRTA terrorists were killed by gunshots to the forehead after their capture.[65]

During the Fujimori government Peruvian armed forces desperately needed civilian oversight, professionally trained anti-terrorism units and police, and new leadership at the highest ranks. The findings of the Peruvian Truth and Reconciliation Commission represent the beginning of such a process. The challenge remains for the Peruvian government to pursue counterterrorism measures that do not compromise democratic principles and ideals. In an ironic twist, Peruvian voters endorsed the return of former President Alan García for another term starting in June

2006. His first presidency from 1985 to 1990 was marked by severe economic crises, social unrest, the maturing of both Peruvian terror groups, and a disturbing upsurge in the activities of death squads. After some 10 years of experience with a failed national security state under Fujimori, 52 percent of Peru's voters decided to embrace another *caudillo*. The other Peruvian voters are hoping, at least, that García has learned some important lessons from the past—namely that fighting terrorism with state-terrorism leads to the breakdown of the fabric of civil society.

NOTES

1. Gabriela Tarazona-Sevillano, who called the Shining Path "possibly the most violent, vindictive, and elusive terrorist insurgency in the Western Hemisphere," served as criminal affairs prosecutor of the Public Ministry in the judicial system of Peru from 1984 to 1986. The quote is taken from her book *Sendero Luminoso and the Threat of Narcoterrorism* published jointly by Praeger and The Center for Strategic and International Studies, Washington, DC, 1990, 133.

2. For information about Lori Berenson's situation and her family's campaign to free her from the Peruvian jail, see http://www.freelori.org/ (accessed in June, 2006).

3. The U.S. State Department continues to list the MRTA among active terror organizations in the Western hemisphere, but estimates that its membership is limited to 100 cadres. In 2003, Peruvian authorities arrested the last remaining MRTA leader from the original organization, Julio César Vásquez. See *Country Reports on Terrorism*, released by the Office of the Coordinator for Counterterrorism, April 28, 2006. The U.S. Department of State makes the Western Hemisphere Overview available at http://www.state.gov/documents/organization/65473.pdf (accessed in June, 2006).

4. Curbstone press published the English version of Alegría's *Fuga de Canto Grande* as *Tunnel to Canto Grande: The Story of the Most Daring Prison Escape in Latin American History* in 1996.

5. See for example Clifford Krauss, "Fujimori's Fall: From Nation's Lion to Broken Man," *The New York Times*, Dec. 3, 2000: 1.

6. For a Peruvian perspective about Haya de La Torre, see the APRA Web site at http://www.apra.org.pe/victorraul.asp (accessed in June, 2006).

7. Carol Graham, "Peru's Apra Party in Power: Impossible Revolution, Relinquished Reform," *Journal of Interamerican Studies and World Affairs* 32, No. 3. (Autumn 1990): 75. Graham currently serves as senior fellow for the Brookings Institution.

8. Guillermo Rochabrun Silva, "Crisis, Democracy, and the Left in Peru," *Latin American Perspectives* 15, Issue 58, No. 3 (Summer 1988): 88. Rochabrun Silva teaches at the Pontifica Universidad Católica del Perú.

9. Mariátegui's most well-known work is a collection called *Siete ensayos de interpretación de la realidad peruana* [*Seven Interpretive Essays on Peruvian Reality* was published in translation by the University of Texas in 1971]. Mariátegui coined the phrase "sendero luminoso al futuro [the shining path to the future]" in reference

to Marxism as the solution to economic and social problems in Peru, but the terror organization *Sendero Luminoso* later appropriated this term for its own purposes.

10. In 1965 Luis de la Puente Uceda founded the Movement of the Revolutionary Left (MIR), and was killed within the year. Héctor Béjar Rivera was captured months after initiating guerrilla warfare as leader of the National Liberation Army (ELN).

11. Graham: p. 81.

12. Rochabrun Silva: pp. 88–89.

13. Graham discusses Huntington's praetorian society in her article "Peru's Apra Party in Power: Impossible Revolution, Relinquished Reform," and Rochabrun Silva inspired the comments on decay in the levels of public trust in "Crisis, Democracy, and the Left in Peru."

14. Samuel Huntington, *Political Order in Changing Societies* (New Haven, CT: Yale University, 1968).

15. Huntington: p. 196.

16. For an interesting interview with MRTA leader Polay Campos including his references to Mariátegui and President García, see the epilogue in Alegria's *Tunnel to Canto Grande*: pp. 185–193.

17. Graham: p. 109

18. Ibid.: p. 110.

19. For an excellent analysis of the MRTA's revolutionary strategy, see Gordon H. McCormick, *Sharp Dressed Men: Peru's Túpac Amaru Revolutionary Movement* (Santa Monica, CA: Rand [National Defense Research Institute], 1993).

20. Ward Stavig, "Túpac Amaru, the Body Politic, and the Embodiment of Hope: Inca Heritage and Social Justice in the Andres," in *Death, Dismemberment, and Memory in Latin America*, ed. Lyman L. Johnson (Albuquerque, NM: University of New Mexico Press, 2004) 27–62.

21. Ibid.: p. 35.

22. Tarazona-Sevillano: p. 14.

23. McCormick: pp. 8–10.

24. Ibid.: pp. 15–16.

25. Tarazona-Sevillano: pp. 79–98.

26. Ibid.

27. Ibid.: p. 84.

28. The death squads were named after a 1932 revolutionary fighter by the name of Manuel "Búfalo" Barreto.

29. For information about the crimes committed by the Commando Rodrigo Franco, see the Truth and Reconciliation Commission's final report. The document is available in Spanish at http://www.cverdad.org.pe/ifinal/pdf/TOMO%20VII/Casos%20Ilustrativos-UIE/2.19.%20COMANDO%20RODRIGO%20FRANCO.pdf(accessed in June, 2006).

30. Graham: pp. 100–102.

31. Ibid.: p. 102.

32. The Truth and Reconciliation Commission's final conclusions are available (in English) at http://www.cverdad.org.pe/ingles/ifinal/conclusiones.php (accessed in June, 2006).

33. Dartnell: p. 79.

34. Ibid.: p. 77.

35. For the most interesting and detailed analysis of the importance of media for the MRTA, see Michael Y. Dartnell, *Insurgency Online, Web Activism and Global Conflict* (Toronto: University of Toronto Press, 2006). Both Dartnell's assessments and McCormick's outstanding work in "Sharp Dressed Men" must be acknowledged for shaping this section.

36. Ibid.: p. 21.

37. For the MRTA perspective (in Spanish), see the following site http://www.voz-rebelde.de/ (accessed in June, 2006).

38. Dartnell: p. 79.

39. See "Peru Rebel Leader Polay of Tupac Amaru Faces Civilian Trial," June 12, 2004, Bloomberg, http://www.bloomberg.com/apps/news?pid=10000086&sid=aCl2_yn41FTw&refer=latin_america(accessed in June, 2006).

40. M-19 refers to the Colombian *Movimiento Abril 19*, an organization similar to the MRTA in its use of publicity stunts and kidnappings. On February 27, 1980, M-19 raided an Embassy reception in Colombia, held 52 hostages including ambassadors for 61 days of negotiations. The guerrillas then flew to Cuba with ransom money and the promise of an international commission to monitor human rights. They returned after an amnesty arrangement.

41. McCormick: pp. 20–29.

42. Ibid.: p. 23.

43. For the final conclusions of the Truth and Reconciliation Committee's findings in English, see http://www.cverdad.org.pe/ingles/ifinal/conclusiones.php (accessed in June, 2006).

44. McCormick: p. 32.

45. For names and comments about other kidnapping victims, see Alegría: pp. 100, 124.

46. McCormick: p. 41.

47. Alegría: p. 125.

48. Eight members of local communities disappeared after they were arrested by the military following the shootout with the MRTA. For further information, see the attached case addressed by the Inter-American Court of Human Rights at http://www1.umn.edu/humanrts/cases/9-93-PERU.htm (accessed in June, 2006). Also, for details about extrajudicial executions carried out by the military, see TRC final report, Vol. 5, section 2.7 entitled Molinos.

49. Alegría: pp.103–105. She offers a short MRTA perspective on the battle at Los Molinos.

50. Dartnell: p. 80.

51. Cynthia McClintock, *Revolutionary Movements in Latin America, El Salvador's FMLN and Peru's Shining Path* (Washington, DC: USIP, 1998,) 47–48.

52. The details are taken from the 1997 World Press Freedom Review on Peru (International Press Institute), which can be found at http://www.infoamerica.org/documentos_pdf/ipi_pe_00.pdf (accessed in June, 2006).

53. Ibid.

54. Steve Macko, "Day 3 of the Peru Hostage Crisis," ENN Special Report from December 19, 1996, http://www.emergency.com/peruhos2.htm (accessed in June, 2006).

55. Online PBS Newshour from February 7, see www.pbs.org/newshour/forum/february97/peru_2-7.html (accessed in June, 2006).

56. Online PBS Newshour from December 23, see www.pbs.org/newshour/bb/latin_america/december96/peru_12-23.html (accessed in June, 2006).

57. Ibid.

58. Online PBS Newshour from January 27, see www.pbs.org/newshour/bb/latin_america/jauary97/peru_1-27.html (accessed in June, 2006).

59. For the full text of the Canadian meeting, see http://www.mofa.go.jp/region/latin/peru/incident/0201.html (accessed in June, 2006).

60. For a BBC report on the day of the raid, see http://news.bbc.co.uk/onthisday/hi/dates/stories/april/22/newsid_4297000/4297347.stm (accessed in June, 2006).

61. "Peru State Attorney Seeks Fujimori Murder Charges," CNN online, March 9, 2001, http://www.latinamericanstudies.org/peru/fujimori-mrta.htm (accessed in June, 2006).

62. For further details, see the attached information of a case addressed by the Inter-American Court of Human Rights at http://www1.umn.edu/humanrts/cases/13-04.html (accessed in June, 2006).

63. Human Rights Watch, *Global Report on Prisons* (New York: Human Rights Watch, 1993).

64. "Fujimori Accused of Murders," BBC News online, March 11, 2001, http://news.bbc.co.uk/1/hi/world/americas/1212557.stm(accessed in June, 2006).

65. Ibid. Also, for access to declassified CIA documents on Peru go to The National Security Archive at George Washington University http://www.gwu.edu/~nsarchiv/NSAEBB/NSAEBB96/#docs(accessed in June, 2006).

Chapter 27

MORO INSURGENTS AND THE PEACE PROCESS IN THE PHILIPPINES

Robin L. Bowman

Since the coordinated attacks on American soil by al Qaeda operatives the morning of September 11, 2001 (aka 9/11), the United States has been waging the Global War on Terrorism (GWOT). President George W. Bush stated, "We will prosecute the war on terror with patience and focus and determination. With the help of a broad coalition, we will make certain that terrorists and their supporters are not safe in any cave or corner of the world."[1] Many states condemned the terror acts of 9/11 and partnered with the United States in the fight against terrorism. In Southeast Asia, the strongest response came from Philippine President Gloria Macapagal-Arroyo: "The Philippines stands together with the United States and the community of nations in a common effort to contain and to destroy terrorists and their global networks."[2] Hers was the first voice in Asia to support U.S. action in Afghanistan by offering access to Philippine airspace and former American military installations Clark Airbase and Subic Bay Naval Base, as well as deploying combat troops and humanitarian relief toward the war effort. For Manila, terrorism is an acute threat extending throughout the archipelago. For many years, the Philippines has been wrought with its fair share of domestic uprisings, guerilla warfare, and terror tactics from various insurgent groups, especially Muslim separatists in the south. Additionally, with a clear presence of international terrorist organizations al Qaeda and Jemaah Islamiyah (JI), Southeast Asia is considered the "second front" in the Global War on Terrorism.

This chapter addresses the "whys" (goals, motivations, and leadership) and "hows" (including organization and tactics) behind the violent

Muslim separatist movements in the Philippines, and their well-documented connections with foreign jihadists, as well as Manila's responses to its homegrown insurgencies and international terrorism. The experience of the Philippines offers an interesting case study of political violence. The archipelago is considered highly vulnerable to foreign terrorist penetration and prolific domestic attacks due to its abundant Christian and Western targets, its fluid borders, weak political institutions and responses, and general lack of governmental reach into the Muslim regions. Before examining the violent separatist movements themselves, it is important to understand the formation of Moro identity, and how and why this community turned to violence and militancy in order to assert their goals of a distinct and independent Muslim homeland.

CONSOLIDATING A DISTINCT MORO IDENTITY

"Moro," the Spanish word for Moor, is the collective name given to the Muslim population in the Philippines. The various Moro communities, are subdivided into separate tribes[3] based on territory, language, and customs, and are geographically concentrated in the southern islands of Mindanao and Sulu, an estimated 20 percent of the subregion's population. However, altogether there are roughly 4.5 million Muslims, only 5 percent of the entire population of over 89 million in the Philippines.[4] Christianity, particularly Catholicism, is practiced by 90 percent of the Filipinos.[5] What unifies these various Moros tribes is *dar al-Islam*, membership into the world of Islam. According to Vincent Houben, "Islam is more than a religion; it is a 'way of life' that encompasses all areas of human activity, private and public, ranging from the theological to the political."[6]

Though the majority of the population is Christian, Christianity was not the first monotheistic religion to reach the islands from foreign shores. Islam made its presence in southern Philippines as early as the fourteenth century;[7] Muslim traders, settlers, and missionaries brought their religion to the various tribes and villages. During initial adoption, Islam was blended into syncretic local traditions and customs, which included elements of animism, a polytheistic belief system based on spirits in nature and ancestor-worship. By the early 1500s, Islam took root in Mindanao and the Sulu islands, and continued to spread throughout the Philippines, reaching as far north as Luzon.

Western colonization halted the further transmission of Islam. Spanish traders and colonizers arrived in the Philippines in the mid-sixteenth century with high hopes of acquiring a large share of the lucrative South and Southeast Asian spice trade. However, their most successful endeavor was the conversion of the indigenous population, particularly the northern islands of Luzon and the Visayas, to Christianity. The southern regions, where Islam had taken strong root, never fully came under colonial control and conversion. Under Spanish administration, the Moros were politically, economically, and socially disenfranchised and alienated, in favor of their Christian counterparts. According to Pute Rahimah Makol-Abdul, colonial rule and policies sowed the seeds of socioeconomic and political degeneration of Muslim community, and unleashed divisive forces of Muslim-Christian alienation in the country.[8]

With the American victory over Spain in the 1898 war and the signing of the Treaty of Paris, the United States gained Spanish territories, including the Philippines. Moro communities, also included in the concessions, refused to acknowledge American annexation and tried to reassert their ancestral rights to Mindanao through armed resistance, but were quickly defeated by the powerful U.S. military.[9] Similar to Spanish control, direct rule over the Moro regions had disastrous effects on the indigenous population. First, despite much Muslim resistance, the colonial administration encouraged and supported Christian resettlement into the southern islands through various governmental policies, like the Public Land Acts that granted low-cost loans and land to individual settlers.[10] As a result, rapid migration of Christian Filipinos reduced the Muslim population to a numeric minority; the percentage of Moros residing in their "ancestral lands" fell from 98 percent to 40 percent of the population in less than 50 years.[11]

Western-style education was a second point of contention. The Moros believed that this was another direct assault on traditional religious learning, and another attempt at training them to be "good colonials" for easier subjugation and exploitation of natural resources.[12] Distrust in the education system led many Moros to refuse the American-style secular learning, which led to rampant illiteracy and a widened education gap between the Muslims and the Christians, who embraced the American education system.[13]

The Philippines gained its independence from the United States on July 4, 1946. While Filipinos celebrated their new-found freedom, the Muslims protested against the inclusion of the Moroland in any independence talks. The legacy of colonization left the Muslim population disenfranchised from the political system, exacerbating the educational, employment, and socioeconomic disparity between them and their Christian counterparts. However, the United States rejected their calls for independence. For the Moros, they felt they were effectively colonized once again—this time by Christian Filipinos.

The new government in Manila continued the policies and practices of displacement and subjugation. Transmigration continued, and more and more Christians settled in the south, both driving out and breeding out the Muslim populations. This influx and its encouragement from the state inflamed Moro hostilities. Muslims, now a minority, had to compete with immigrants over land, economic resources, and political power within their traditional ancestral territories. It was under these conditions that segments of the Moro population cried *no more*—the beginnings of an armed Muslim rebellion emerged in the 1970s.

The Moros resisted Manila's rule, and throughout the 1970s, widespread violence targeting ethnicity and religion subsumed much of Mindanao and the Sulu Archipelago. Amidst this conflict, Philippine President Ferdinand Marcos declared martial law in 1972, citing rampant violence as the main cause of his decision. Daniel Joseph Ringuet claimed that the oppressiveness of martial law and the Marcos regime made Muslims realize their own situation; the Moros demanded recognition from Manila as a distinctive ethno-religious group.[14] As a response to political and economic neglect from Christian leaders and perceived anti-Muslim policies from Manila, three major separatist organizations emerged: the Moro Nationalist Liberation Front (MNLF), the Moro Islamic Liberation Front (MILF), and the Abu Sayyaf Group (ASG). Analyst Peter Chalk contends that there were four main factors that underscored this separatist sentiment:

> First is resentment of Catholic transmigration from the north. This has not only dispossessed many Muslims of what are considered to be ancient and communal land rights; it has also reduced the Moro population to a minority in their own homeland. Second is an unwillingness to subscribe to Manila's secular civil, political, judicial, and penal constitutional system. Third is frustration borne of Mindanao's lack of economic and infrastructural development. Fourth is fear of having religious, cultural, and political traditions weakened (or possibly destroyed) by forced assimilation into a Catholic-dominated Philippine Republic.[15]

Moro homeland, traditions, and opportunities were again in jeopardy, and again it was time to take up arms; this time not for the preservation of Moro cultures and traditions within the state, but for a new goal: secession from the Philippine state.

MNFL: MILITANT NATIONALIST MOVEMENT

The Moro National Liberation Front (MNLF) was formed in 1972 primarily by Muslim students and educators seeking complete liberation of the Moroland from the Philippine state. Founder Nur Misuari believed in Moro self-determination and independence through armed revolt.[16] The organization quickly swelled to 30,000 members.[17] With foreign support, to include arms, supplies, and funding from Libya and Malaysia, MNLF led a jihad against the Marcos regime and engaged the Armed Forces of the Philippines (AFP) in many bloody battles. At the height of violence between 1973 and 1975, an estimated 50,000 military and civilians were killed.[18] Marcos and his successor, Corazon Aquino, attempted some reconciliation with the MNLF, from ceasefire agreements to negotiated limited autonomy. Each instance failed to bring about peace, and more fighting ensued from both sides.

President Fidel Ramos tried to restore MNLF confidence in the central government and offered a new settlement. The 1996 Agreement emphasized peace and development in southern Philippines. It called for the establishment of the Autonomous Region in Muslim Mindanao (ARMM), the Southern Philippines Council for Peace and Development (SPCPD), representation in some institutions of national government, creation of Special Regional Security Forces, inclusion of Islamic curriculum in education system, and authority of shariah court. Misuari was placed as governor of ARMM. This agreement ended not only the MNLF issue for Manila, but also two decades of hostilities.

However, problems still remained. The 1996 Agreement had little support from splinter Moro separatist groups, which continued their armed struggle against the central government. Additionally, many Moros criticized Manila for a lack of true commitment to, and resources for, the ARMM. The agreement, like previous attempts at peace, did not improve the living standards of Muslim Filipinos; poverty rates remained high, infrastructure development was slow, and investment levels were still low.[19] Lastly, Misuari and other SPCPD officials were accused of mismanagement and corruption, producing little faith in the ARMM structure among the masses.

THE MILF SPLINTERS

One major splinter group arose in the late 1970s, as the MNLF experienced an organizational shake-up. A political rift split top leadership in half; Misuari and second-in-command Hashim Salamat, aka Salamat Hashim, disagreed over "questions of leadership and the questions of Islam and ideology."[20] Salamat accused Misuari of corruption and abuse of power, and subsequently—along with several top officers—he broke away from the MNLF and established the Moro Islamic Liberation Front (MILF) in 1984.[21] Aside from these allegations of dictatorial leadership, ethnic favoritism, and leftist leanings, the two rival organizations fundamentally differed in the desired political end-state: the MNLF pushed for the creation of a separate Moro state from the Philippine government (ethnic nationalist identity) while the MILF sought to establish a separate Islamic Moro state (ethnic Muslim identity).[22] As Peter Chalk has observed, the MILF "is far more religiously oriented than its parent movement, emphasizing the promotion of Islamic ideals rather than the simple pursuit of Moro nationalist objectives," including governance by shariah law.[23] Salamat declared: "We want an Islamic political system and way of life that can be achieved through effective Da'wah, Tarbiyyah, and Jihad."[24] This new, more militant and faith-based Moro liberation organization's main objective is the creation of a separate and independent Islamic state in all Muslim-majority areas in the southern Philippines.[25]

The current strength of the MILF (as of this writing) ranges from 12,000 to 15,000. Within the Front are two "military" type organizations: the larger Bangsamoro Islamic Armed Forces (BIAF), in which military instructors have trained and fought with the mujahideen in the Soviet-Afghan War; and the clandestine Special Operations Group (SOG) that conducts the subversive, more terrorist-type attacks.[26] In 2001, the MILF restructured into a "Base Command" system to allow for more autonomy of command, flexibility, and mobility to better suit and accommodate the group's guerilla and urban warfare.[27] A change in top leadership occurred in July 2003, when Salamat died due to poor health; he reportedly had a heart condition, asthma, and a peptic ulcer.[28] Upon his passing, according to the International Crisis Group (ICG), the MILF became further divided along tribal, generational, and ideological grounds.[29] Al-Haj Murad Ebrahim, aka Murad, soon arose as the new MILF chairman. However, although the leadership and organizational structure has changed, the rhetorical goal has not changed since the Front's inception and later passing of its founder: the creation of an independent Islamic homeland in the southern Philippines.

The MILF is currently not considered a Foreign Terrorist Organization (FTO) by the U.S. government. In fact, MILF leaders publicly denounce terrorism. According to Chalk, "Generally speaking, the group has not emphasized indiscriminant violence against civilian and non-combatants targets," claiming that this "self-restraint" separates the MILF from other "terrorist" organizations, and maintains its own self-image as a revolutionary force.[30] However, terror tactics have been (and arguably still are) employed against their Christian, private-sector, infrastructure, and governmental (political officials, police, and military) targets (see Table 27.1 for a summation of MILF incidents). The most recent attacks of significance have been the Davao bombings in the spring of 2003. On March 4, 2003, a bomb in a backpack was remotely detonated inside the Davao City International Airport, killing 24 and injuring 100. Less than one month later, on April 2, 2003, another bomb—this time hidden near food stalls— exploded in a wharf near the airport, killing 16 and injuring over 50.[31]

Additionally, amidst leadership denials, the MILF has reportedly been linked to various FTOs—including al Qaeda, JI, ASG, and even the Philippine Communist Party's New People's Army (NPA)—for ideological, personal, and pragmatic reasons. Moro rebels have been studying, training, fighting, and forging personal ties with other Muslim insurgents in Middle East schools and South Asian training camps. For nearly 30 years,

Table 27.1   MILF Incidents, 1968–Present

Incidents	Injuries	Fatalities
30	311	105

Targets:		
Government	10%	
Private Citizens & Property	33%	
Airports & Airlines	10%	
Business	13%	
Journalists & Media	10%	
Educational Institutions	3%	
Other	6%	
Religious Figures/Institutions	10%	
Transportation	3%	

Notes:
Data for 1968–1997 covers only international incidents.
Data for 1998–Present covers both domestic and international incidents.
Source: MIPT Terrorism Knowledge Base, 2006.

the MILF has been benefiting from the patronage of foreign jihadists, including Osama bin Laden. According to Zachary Abuza, MILF leadership believes that the interaction with the mujahideen is vital to the education and indoctrination of the new generation of members in explosives and bomb-making, as well as guerilla and urban warfare.[32] The close pragmatic ties between MILF and JI have led to the establishment of a JI-run training camp and military academy for Moro recruits.[33] Furthermore, both organizations have cooperated on a number of attacks. Although the two Davao airport bombings were not claimed by any group or individual, investigators suggest that both incidents were joint MILF-JI efforts.[34] These relationships are also reciprocal, as foreign jihadists can benefit from MILF positioning in the southern Philippines. ICG reports that JI, as well as other small Indonesia-based groups, continue to send their young recruits to train in Mindanao.[35]

Though the MNLF and the central government reached an agreement in the mid-1990s, peace with the other Moro secessionist movements was not guaranteed after the creation of the ARMM. The MILF rejected the accord, arguing that regional autonomy was a mere placative conciliation prize to the group's ultimate goal of independence. Manila, for their part, recognized that the various Moro insurgent groups had to be included in negotiations in order for peace and stability to have any true merit.

The strongest show of commitment to peace and stability came from President Ramos, who sponsored cease-fire and confidence-building agreements, including socioeconomic development programs in the southern Philippines. Many were pleased by these ambitious plans. Yet, other Moro leaders spurned these projects, claiming that money and promises could not simply rectify the problem.[36] Moro grievances—such as internal displacement, discrimination and marginalization, socioeconomic inequalities, and exploitation of natural resources—could only be remedied through establishing a system of life and governance acceptable to the Muslim population.[37] Further attempts at peace and stability were suspended during the Estrada years, as the administration regarded these socioeconomic programs as "unnecessary" and "simply coddling the MILF."[38] President Estrada resumed military offensives against the Front.

But in 2001, an end to hostilities again looked possible when, according to Abuza, President Arroyo surprised the Moro separatists by announcing a unilateral ceasefire and calling for renewed negotiations.[39] That June, the MILF and Manila signed a peace agreement, but again peace was not guaranteed. The southern Philippines is still plagued with violence, as conflict between Moro insurgents and the police and military continued; the delicate ceasefire had been suspended as both sides pointed fingers. The MILF accused the AFP of derailing the peace process. The AFP accused Muslim rebels of ceasefire violations and terror tactics. Yet, pundits do admit that relations between Moro separatists and the government have substantially improved since the signing of the 2001 peace agreement, to include the December 22, 2004 MILF-Manila announcement for joint action to rid the southern Philippines of criminal and terrorist elements, particularly ASG and JI.[40]

Other rounds of peace negotiations followed, with the most recent beginning in April 2005, brokered by the Malaysian government and monitored by international representatives including from the United States, represented by United States Institute of Peace (USIP). Washington, by way of the USIP, is pledging $30 million in development aid for Muslim areas if and when a solid agreement is reached.[41] Yet one major issue looms over these proceedings: the main Moro concern over "ancestral domain" and access to its natural resources.[42] The MILF leadership seeks independence, coupled with economic rehabilitation programs. Other, less hardline Moros want governmental acknowledgments of Muslim grievances and land rights. The Arroyo administration claims to be committed to peace and stability in the southern Philippines, and is pursuing negotiated regional autonomy.[43] The central government has also demanded that the MILF sever all ties with terrorist organizations. Since Salamat had publicly denounced terrorism, Arroyo has "sought to insulate the MILF conflict from the war on terror, prevailing on the United States not to add the organization to its blacklist."[44] But these agreements are precarious, as both sides continue to engage in violent standoffs and public censure of each other.

THE ABU SAYYAF GROUP FORMS

Abu Sayyaf[45] may be the smallest (in terms of membership) of the three separatist organizations, but is considered the most radical and violent. With an estimated core of 200 to 500 of mostly Muslim young adults between the ages of 16 and 35, this designated FTO mixes political extremism, terrorism, and criminal activities, such as kidnappings for ransom, bombings, and extortion.[46] The ASG operates and trains primarily in the jungles, hills, and coastal areas of Zamboanga, Basilan, Sulu (where the main training camp is located), Tawi-Tawi, and pockets throughout Mindanao.[47]

Like other groups in Southeast Asia, the origins of Abu Sayyaf can be traced back to the Soviet-Afghan War. The U.S. State Department claims that many of the ASG top leadership fought, trained, and studied in Afghanistan and Pakistan with the mujahideen during the 1980s. Having been part of a successful effort to drive back the foreign invaders, these Moro rebels returned home to the southern Philippines as proponents of radical Islamic teachings, guerilla tactics, and Muslim self-determinism.[48] According to Daniel Ringuet, the ASG believes it is continuing the 300-year-long tradition of armed Muslim opposition against Christians.[49]

Abu Sayyaf formally split from the other Moro movements in the early 1990s. Its founder, Aburajak Janjalani (also spelled Abdurajik Abubakar Janjalani or Ustadz Abdurajak Janjalani), declared that the organization's goal was establishing an independent, theocratic, and exclusive (pure) Islamic state in the Southern Philippines.[50] In his research of political violence in Southeast Asia, Chalk highlights how this is a different goal than the MILF:

> Whereas the [MILF] merely aims for independence, the [ASG] additionally espouses violent religious intolerance, advocating the deliberate targeting of all southern Filipino Catholics including the beheading of women, children, and the elderly) to this effect. The ASG also sees its objectives in Mindanao as intimately tied to an integrated effort aimed at asserting the global dominance of Islam through armed struggle—an extreme religious fervor not generally shared (at least overtly) by the MILF.[51]

According to Filipino scholar Rommel C. Banlaoi, although Janjalani was a veteran of Afghan-Soviet war, he was "no mere Muslim fighter or mujahideen; he was a charismatic and a serious Muslim scholar."[52] Himself a son of an Islamic scholar, Janjalani studied theology in Islamic universities in Libya and Saudi Arabia, and was heavily influenced by strict Wahhabi tradition.[53] In 1987, he joined the mujahideen, first training in Peshawar, Pakistan, where he met and forged close ties with both Osama Bin Laden and Ramzi Yousef.[54] In fact, it was Janjalani who opened up the

Table 27.2   ASG Incidents, 1968–Present

Incidents	Injuries	Fatalities
55	515	197

Targets:

Tourists	3%
Government	3%
Military	3%
Private Citizens & Property	40%
Airports & Airlines	1%
NGO	1%
Business	18%
Journalists & Media	10%
Religious Figures/Institutions	7%
Police	1%
Transportation	7%

Notes:
Data for 1968–1997 covers only international incidents.
Data for 1998–Present covers both domestic and international incidents.
Source: MIPT Terrorism Knowledge Base, 2006.

southern Philippines to the al Qaeda network. After the war, Janjalani returned home to Basilan, and with a handful of followers, established Abu Sayyaf. He viewed the Quran "as the only worthy guide for human life since it is perfect creation of Allah who cannot err and who knows everything," and urged Moros to fight and die for their religion and way of life, thus earning "paradise as martyrs."[55]

Modeled after the Taliban, Janjalani's main goal for ASG was to create a highly organized and disciplined secessionist movement with the ultimate aim of establishing an Islamic state. Within the organization, the Islamic Executive Council was the main planning cell, while various special committees ran fundraising, Islamic education, propaganda, and "agitation" activities. The Mujahidden Al-Sharifullah served as the militant wing of ASG, comprised mostly of former members of MNLF and MILF.[56]

Early on, the group established itself as a small but highly lethal and effective organization, engaging the police and military not only in urban and maritime assaults, but also in assassinations, bombings, and kidnappings—particularly of Western (foreign) and Christian (religious) targets (see Table 27.2 for a summary of ASG incidents).[57] In the first 5 years of the group's inception, the ASG was responsible for 67 terrorist attacks, resulting in 58 deaths and 398 injuries.[58] Additionally, according to Philippine intelligence, the group sought to sabotage the 1996 peace negotiations between Manila and the MNFL.[59]

Abu Sayyaf received considerable funding from outside Muslim sources, including the governments of Malaysia and Libya, and particularly by bin Laden and other wealthy Saudi/Wahhabi financiers. But in the late 1990s, funding sources began to dry up.

One major blow to the organization came in December 1998, when Janjalani—the group's organizational and ideological authority—was killed in a gun battle with the police. Despite his efforts to forge a highly systematic organization, ASG was essentially left leaderless. His younger brother Khaddafy was appointed the head of the group, but did not have the impact or power of his brother. The ASG factionalized, leaving some to wonder whether the group's ideology and direction died with the elder Janjalani. Many turned toward more lucrative criminal activities, including piracy, extortion, and kidnapping for ransom. Because of this tactical turn, many Moros themselves contend that the ASG is currently just a band of rogue thugs and extreme bandits looking for a quick profit, lacking any real ideology.

However, according to Abuza, as of late, Abu Sayyaf "has re-emerged as one of the more important terrorist groups confronting the Government of the Republic of the Philippines, the United States, and our allies in Southeast Asia."[60] Hostage-taking and execution is slowly replacing mere kidnapping-for-ransom profiteering. Khaddafy Janjalani is reasserting himself as the true organizational and theological leader, "working very hard to get the ASG back to its roots" as the premier and legitimate Moro nationalist liberation movement.[61] Others claim that ASG has undergone a renewed sense of Islamic secessionist militancy.

Chalk claims that "in terms of revolutionary political violence, virtually all of the ASG's activities are terroristic in nature."[62] While the group's trademark tactics are piracy, robbery, extortion, and kidnapping, members typically and regularly engage in ambushing government forces, urban assaults, beheadings, brutal bombings, and assassinations.[63] The two most recent large-scale terror attacks are the *Superferry 14* bombing in 2004 and the Valentine's Day bombings in 2005.

On February 27, 2004, a bomb detonated aboard *Superferry 14*, a commuter ferry boat in Manila harbor, killing over 130 of its 900 passengers—the worst terror attack in Southeast Asia since the 2002 Bali bombings.[64] Abu Sayyaf claimed responsibility for this explosion. The group's spokesperson, Abu Soliman, declared that this was revenge for the ongoing violence in Mindanao, taunting: "Still doubtful about our capabilities? Good. Just wait and see. We will bring the war that you impose on us to your lands and seas, homes, and streets. We will multiply the pain and suffering that you have inflicted on our people."[65]

A year later, the ASG also claimed responsibility for the simultaneous bombings in three different cities throughout the archipelago: Manila, Davao City, and General Santos City. This "Valentine's Day gift to

Mrs. Arroyo," which resulted in 12 deaths and over 150 injuries, was declared by Abu Sayyaf to be retaliation for the government's "atrocities committed against Muslims."[66] According to several reports, the ASG has become more tactically innovative and more sophisticated in their development and use of explosive devices and technology.[67]

Unlike the MILF, Manila views the ASG as a true terrorist organization. The Philippine police and military can boast a number of successes against Abu Sayyaf, engaging the group in over 100 armed conflicts and standoffs, resulting in the capture or killing of over 175 members and top leaders, including the high-profile deaths of Father Roman Al-Ghozi and founder Janjalani.[68] Yet, despite these successes, both the government and military recognize that a military solution alone cannot defeat Abu Sayyaf; a holistic package encompassing civil and military cooperation is much needed. Arroyo advocates this "right-hand and left-hand approach . . . [where the] right hand is the full force of the law and the left hand is the hand of reconciliation and the hand of giving support to our poorest brothers so that they won't be encouraged to join the rebels," to include socioeconomic, political, and security efforts to address local grievances.[69]

Recent events are promising. Khaddafy Janjalani was killed in a raid by the Philippine military in September 2006 in Jolo (Southern Philippines). His apparent successor as ASG leader, senior commander Abu Sulaiman (who claimed responsibility for the superferry bombing as well as the high-profile kidnapping of American and Filipino tourists in Palawan in 2001) was also killed by troops in January 2007. But despite military successes against the group, Abu Sayyaf continues to be a lethal terrorist threat "because its membership includes well equipped, highly trained fighters with significant experience in both day and night...combat operations."[70] Experts warn that ASG should not be merely discounted as a band of thugs, but is in fact reasserting itself under new leadership as an ideologically and politically driven violent separatist organization, capable of high-impact terrorist activities and lucrative foreign patronage.

PHILIPPINE RESPONSES TO THE WAR ON TERRORISM WRIT LARGE

Aside from specific responses to domestic insurgent and terrorist groups, the Philippines is a partner nation in the United States-led Global War on Terrorism. President Arroyo was one of the first world leaders to condemn the 9/11 actions and to join the international coalition against terrorism. She offered Philippine airspace and seaports, intelligence sharing, law enforcement cooperation, and logistical support.

New policies and legislation were proposed and enacted as a result of 9/11. Almost immediately, Arroyo announced her "14 pillars of policy and action against terrorism." According to Francisco L. Tolin, retired AFP officer and vice-president for Research and Special Studies at the

National Defense College of the Philippines, this national framework was aimed at strengthening internal anti-terrorism and counterterrorism efforts through delineation of responsibilities, modernization of the military and police force, anticipation and preparation for future attacks, enlisting the cooperation of other sectors in the society such as the media, and addressing the varied underpinnings of terrorism.[71]

With presidential approval, Congress passed the Anti-Money Laundering Act on September 29, 2001, which froze financial assets of (alleged) international terrorists and targeted the flow of illegal monies from criminal activities.[72] This act was the country's first-ever law to criminalize money laundering. In addition, Arroyo ordered the Securities and Exchange Commission and the Department of the Interior and Local Government to identify and neutralize "dubious personalities and organizations" that may be operating as fronts for terrorist and criminal activities.[73]

Turning to the economy, the president clearly believes in the causal linkage between war on terrorism and the war on poverty: "I see that the world needs to fight poverty as the highest of all priorities because it breeds division and conflict and terrorism ... There is no denying that poverty provides the breeding grounds for the recruitment of terrorists." Her administration has put economic recovery at the top of the priority list. She argues that the developing world needs access to the West's markets, currently obstructed by agricultural subsidies.[74] She has sought to increase more open trade relations with the United States.[75] She also encourages much-needed foreign investment into the Philippines; by actively combating terrorism, the risk to investors will decrease and allow new possibilities of funds flow into the country.[76]

The Arroyo administration implemented the "strategy of holistic approach," or SHA, as a comprehensive plan to eradicate both the domestic and foreign terrorist threats on many different levels. Banlaoi's research examines the four major components of the SHA. The first, "political/legal/diplomatic component" focuses on strengthening democratic institutions and public involvement in the political process to propagate democracy to confront the communist and Islamic fundamentalist ideology. Secondly, the "socioeconomic/psychosocial component" encompasses development and poverty-alleviation programs to strengthen a shared national identity. The "peace and order/security component" seeks to provide a secure environment for the population and development programs, as well as deny insurgents "access to their most important resource—popular support." Lastly, the "information component" refers to "the overall effort to advocate peace, promote public confidence in government and support government efforts to overcome insurgency through tri-media and interpersonal approaches."[77]

The administration also created the Inter-Agency Task Force Against International Terrorism, also known as the Anti-Terrorism Task Force (ATTF). The ATTF coordinates with other coalition partners on strategies, policies, plans, and intelligence operations to prevent, identify, and suppress terrorism in the Philippines.[78] Manila attests that the task force has been hard at work at counterterrorism efforts, including the surveillance of foreign JI members in the Philippines.[79] Moreover, the president contended that a "Madrid-level" attack was prevented with the arrest of four al Qaeda-linked extremists and the seizure of an 80-pound explosives cache intended for shopping mall and train bombings throughout Manila.

Along with a comprehensive response by the government, the Philippine armed forces were quick to support the war on terrorism. As the organization primarily responsible for conducting counterterrorism and counterinsurgency operations, the military had two main security goals in mind with the onset of the GWOT. First, the AFP wanted to restore close military-to-military ties with the United States that had been weakened by the 1991 base closures. Second, it needed to enhance counterterrorism capabilities. The Philippines has recommitted itself to the 1952 Mutual Defense Treaty with the United States, declaring full support of American/Coalition operations in Afghanistan and Iraq, offering intelligence, airspace, military bases, and ground forces, in exchange for military hardware and supplies under the Mutual Logistics Support Agreement.[80]

Another counterterrorism response by the military as well as law enforcement includes the creation of both the Joint Task Force within the AFP and the AFP-PNP Joint Task Forces in Mindanao. The AFP Joint Task Force, composed of special units from the different branches of service, promotes the application of the joint concept of operations and command and control. The AFP-PNP Joint Task Force was created to enhance joint capabilities through working together toward preventing, suppressing, and neutralizing terrorist acts and lawless violence in Mindanao.[81]

According to Patricia Paez, a spokeswoman at the Philippine Embassy in Washington, President Arroyo was looking for "an expansion in U.S. military assistance in terms of equipment, training and advisers. The U.S. forces will not play any combat role, but they will help us in routing out the terrorists ourselves."[82] "Balikatan 02-1" was the largest joint and combined military exercise between Philippine and American forces. According to Tolin, the four main objectives of Balikatan 02-1 were: to improve the counterterrorism interoperability of Philippine and America forces; to enhance the combat capability of AFP infantry battalions based in Mindanao; to ensure quality in intelligence processing; and to upgrade Philippine-United States capability to wage effective civil, military, and psychological operations.[83]

Criticisms of the Philippines' Responses

Although seemingly a robust response package to 9/11, the Philippine government and military have been under heavy criticism as to their actions—as well as lack of—in the war on terrorism. Some experts argue that the situation in the Philippines has not changed in the new security environment; Manila is still battling the same insurgent and terrorist groups as it had decades before. Moreover, ICG reports that the Philippines is considered Southeast Asia's "weakest link" in ongoing counterterrorism efforts, with relatively low arrest rates despite the presence of many top JI operatives.[84] Thus "internationalizing" or "globalizing" this terrorist issue has not changed the internal threats and responses from the Philippine government and military.

Furthermore, other critics claim that nothing substantial has been accomplished in the form of true counterterrorism policy reform: this administration lacks the political will to provide anything more than a superficial show of support to the United States and the GWOT coalition partners. Others contend that the Anti-Money Laundering Act had little effectiveness for curbing the use of Filipino financial institutions by supposed terrorist organization.[85] Additionally, Manila passed another antiterrorism bill in February 2007 called the Human Security Act. The crackdown on terrorism is really the president projecting a tough image amidst declining domestic support.[86] Many charge that the government's efforts to deal with insurgents have led to serious accusations of human rights violations and unwarranted militarization.[87] Still others point out that much-needed counterterrorism reforms that address the prosecution of convicted terrorists and the consequences of graft and corruption within the system have not yet been passed.

Political opponents of the Arroyo administration claim that GWOT responses are in effect guises to promote other interests. Some leftist groups claim that the government "is colluding with the U.S. government and using the anti-terrorist hysteria to underhandedly justify the heightened U.S. military presence in the Philippines," warning that current responses could leave the country open to future retaliation.[88] The Moro community has also criticized the administration's response. Although Arroyo has previously stated that the government's antiterrorism drive "will continue to be carried out without any ethnic or religious bias, and with only the enforcement of impartial justice in mind," some Muslim critics claim that the counterterrorism campaign has a suspiciously anti-Islam bias, and that this is an opportunity for Manila to continue its "crusade."[89] In sum, critics from all sides claim that the Philippine government has done very little to affect counterterrorism policy within the country.

IN SEARCH OF PEACE AND SECURITY IN THE PHILIPPINES

Much terrorism and counterterrorism attention, particularly by the United States, is focused on actions and groups in the Middle East and South Asia. These regions are host to rampant anti-America/anti-Western sentiments, religious extremism, and high-profile FTOs such as Hamas, Hizbollah, and al Qaeda. However, one cannot overlook what has been transpiring in Southeast Asia over the past few decades. Numerous terror acts and a growing foreign jihadist presence prior to 9/11 were regarded as by-products of local political grievances and minority uprisings. Unlike the Middle East, this region was not considered a major center of transnational terrorism. However, Southeast Asian nations, particularly the Philippines, have been a breeding ground for international terrorist cells and radical jihadists. Since 9/11, perceptions of the terrorist threat in this region have been radically reshaped, culminating with the Bali bombing in 2002 and further documented evidence of international terrorist interactions. Rohan Gunaratna asserts that since the winter of 2001, several thousand jihadists have been driven out of Afghanistan into other lawless locations and comfort zones worldwide, including the southern Philippines.[90] If the Middle East is the front line of the war on terror, then Southeast Asia is considered the "second front."

Of all the countries in this second front, the Philippines proves to be the most interesting case to study. Its multilayered domestic problems have spilled into the international arena, impacting not only its immediate region (especially Indonesia and Malaysia), but across the oceans to South and Southwest Asia (particularly Pakistan, Afghanistan, and Saudi Arabia), as well as the United States. Its homegrown Muslim separatists groups—the MNLF, MILF, and ASG—have attracted considerable foreign attention, funding, training, and presence.

The MILF and ASG have forged ideological, personal, and pragmatic relationships with Middle East jihadists and foreign extremists. Many Southeast Asian Muslims trained in al Qaeda-run camps in Pakistan and Afghanistan in the 1980s. Moro radicals returned home with both renewed vigor for their liberation cause and newly gained expertise, including sophisticated techniques in bomb-making, guerrilla warfare, and terror.[91] At these camps, they established a sense of brotherhood and camaraderie with other jihadists, who in turn came to the archipelago to hide, train, organize, and plan. Al Qaeda is reported to have funneled money, weapons, and training to Moro separatists, and has used the Philippines as a major planning bed for many high-profile international acts of terror, including the unearthed "Bojinka plots."[92]

What makes the Philippines attractive to terrorism and insurgency? Let's highlight a few key summations from the experts. According to Banlaoi, the region is vulnerable to terrorist penetration because of its porous borders, weak law enforcement capabilities, and governmental institutions, as well as its close ties with the United States and other Western states.[93] Abuza explains that there are three main reasons why foreign terrorist groups such as al Qaeda have been attracted to the Philippines as a major hub of operations: "the Afghan connection to Middle East extremists, the growth of Islamic grievances within states since the 1970s for socioeconomic and political reasons, and, most important, that Southeast

Asian states are 'countries of convenience' for international terrorists."[94] In a 2004 report by ICG the archipelago is described as playing a vital role in the evolving terrorist threat in Southeast Asia for three main reasons:

> First ... it has become, since the mid-1990s, a primary training ground for JI and a number of like-minded groups that remain determined to acquire a military capacity, either to further their goal of establishing an Islamic state in Indonesia or to defend the faith against its enemies more generally. Secondly, the lack of state capacity to effectively police borders and movements of people, money and contraband, particularly in the south, continues to make it a country of convenience for "lone wolf" operators and cells of various jihadist organizations. Thirdly—and most fundamentally—operatives of jihadist groups, including in the past al Qaida, rely on the enabling environment of long-term separatist insurgencies in the southern Philippines.... The most significant threat of all for the Philippines and the wider region is the possibility of international terrorism and domestic insurgency becoming ever more closely interwoven and mutually reinforcing.[95]

Moreover, the Philippines is a critical ally in the War on Terror for the United States. Historically, the Philippines has been pro-America. The government, as well as the majority of the people, maintains close political, economic, and even cultural ties that both countries actively seek to maintain. Additionally, national and international security interests of both countries converge, as the archipelago is a classic manifestation of one of the United States's major goals of regional stability, as outlined in the most current *National Security Strategy*. Decades of hostilities and conflict between various secessionist and communist groups with the Philippine government have plagued the island nation. Manila seeks and accepts political, military, and development assistance, as the state is aware of its current limitations.

Lastly, both Manila and the Moro separatists can take monumental steps forward, building upon the foundations left by past attempts at peace, from the Tripoli Agreement to the establishment of the ARMM. Both sides must be committed to lasting peace, security, stability, and prosperity in the Philippines, and must realize the sacrifices and compromises necessary to forge lasting agreements. According to USIP, the U.S. observer at the Manila-MILF peace talks in Malaysia, in order to reach a consensus, both parties must explore all options that can meet their conflicting interests. Furthermore, the peace pact must: (1) "reconcile their divergent positions" on the controversial issue of autonomy versus independence, (2) "be able to offer a detailed roadmap that directly addresses the grievances of Muslims in the Philippines," and (3) "provide strong mechanisms for implementation."[96]

In order to pursue our goals of peace and security in this post-9/11 environment, it is still critical to study the "whys" (motivations and goals), the "hows" (tactics and strategies), and the differences and convergences of transnational terrorism and domestic insurgencies. The Philippine example offers more than a case study on domestic ethno-religious grievances, separatist movements, and links to foreign terrorism. It is a rich and multi-faceted case highlighting the intersection amongst these differing yet connected issues. Moreover, positive change has affected (and will continue to affect) the lives of Filipinos, both Muslim and Christian. Peace is possible, with political and economic commitment from Manila and cession of hostilities from violent Moro groups. The Philippines can prove to be a successful case of peace, security, and prosperity in the War on Terrorism.

ACKNOWLEDGMENTS

The views expressed in this paper are those of the author and do not reflect the official policy or position of the United States Air Force, Department of Defense, or the U.S. Government.

NOTES

1. Office of the Coordinator for Counterterrorism, *Patterns of Global Terrorism 2002*, April 30, 2003, Section A: Introduction, http://www.state.gov/s/ct/rls/pgtrpt/2002/.

2. Office of the President, "PGMA's Message Reiterating the Philippine Government Support on the US Action Against Terrorism," October 8, 2001, http://www.opnet.ops.gov.ph/ops-speeches2001.htm.

3. The main tribal groups are the Magindanaos of the Cotabato region, the Maranaos of the Lanao provinces, the Tausugs in Jolo, and the Samals of Sulu.

4. CIA World Factbook 2006, http://www.cia.gov/cia/publications/factbook/geos/rp.html.

5. Ibid.

6. Vincent J. Houben, "Southeast Asia and Islam," *The Annals of the American Academy*, No. 588 (July 2003): 149.

7. Some, including Syed Serajul Islam, have even claimed that Islam arrived in the Philippines as early as the eighth century.

8. Pute Rahimah Makol-Abdul, "Colonialism and Change: The Case of Muslims in the Philippines," *Journal of Muslim Minority Affairs* 17, no. 2 (October 1997): 323.

9. Daniel Joseph Ringuet, "The Continuation of Civil Unrest and Poverty in Mindanao," *Contemporary Southeast Asia* 24, no. 1 (April 2002): 35.

10. Syed Serajul Islam, "The Islamic Independence Movements in Patani of Thailand and Mindanao of the Philippines," *Asian Survey* 38, No. 5 (May 1998): 445.

11. United States Institution of Peace, *Special Report 131—The Mindanao Peace Talks: Another Opportunity to Resolve the Moro Conflict in the Philippines*, February 2005, http://www.usip.org/pubs/specialreports/sr131.html.

12. Pute Rahimah Makol-Abdul, "Colonialism and Change: The Case of Muslims in the Philippines," *Journal of Muslim Minority Affairs* 17, no. 2 (October 1997): 317.

13. Syed Serajul Islam, "The Islamic Independence Movements in Patani of Thailand and Mindanao of the Philippines," *Asian Survey* 38, No. 5 (May 1998): 445; and Pute Rahimah Makol-Abdul, "Colonialism and Change: The Case of Muslims in the Philippines," *Journal of Muslim Minority Affairs* 17, no. 2 (October 1997): 315.

14. Daniel Joseph Ringuet, "The Continuation of Civil Unrest and Poverty in Mindanao," *Contemporary Southeast Asia* 24, no. 1 (April 2002): 40.

15. Peter Chalk, "Separatism and Southeast Asia: The Islamic Factor in Southern Thailand, Mindanao, and Aceh," *Studies in Conflict and Terrorism* 24 (2001): 247.

16. Daniel Joseph Ringuet, "The Continuation of Civil Unrest and Poverty in Mindanao," *Contemporary Southeast Asia* 24, no. 1 (April 2002): 40.

17. Graham H. Turbiville, Jr., "Bearer of the Sword," *Military Review* (March–April 2002): 42.

18. Syed Serajul Islam, "The Islamic Independence Movements in Patani of Thailand and Mindanao of the Philippines," *Asian Survey* 38, No. 5 (May 1998): 448.

19. Jacques Bertrand, "Peace and Conflict in the Southern Philippines: Why the 1996 Peace Agreement is Fragile," *Pacific Affairs* 73, no. 1 (Spring 2000): 37–42.

20. Zachary Abuza, *Militant Islam in Southeast Asia: Crucible of Terror* (Boulder: Lynne Rienner, 2003) 39.

21. Daniel Joseph Ringuet, "The Continuation of Civil Unrest and Poverty in Mindanao," *Contemporary Southeast Asia* 24, no. 1 (April 2002): 41.

22. Thomas M. McKenna, *Muslim Rulers and Rebels: Everyday Politics and Armed Separatism in the Southern Philippines* (Berkeley: University of California Press, 1998) 208; and Zachary Abuza, *Militant Islam in Southeast Asia: Crucible of Terror* (Boulder: Lynne Rienner, 2003) 39.

23. Peter Chalk, "Separatism and Southeast Asia: The Islamic Factor in Southern Thailand, Mindanao, and Aceh," *Studies in Conflict and Terrorism* 24 (2001): 247–248.

24. Syed Serajul Islam, "The Islamic Independence Movements in Patani of Thailand and Mindanao of the Philippines," *Asian Survey* 38, No. 5 (May 1998): 450.

25. *Southern Philippines Backgrounder: Terrorism and the Peace Process ICG Asia Report N°80,* 13 July 2004, p. 4, http://www.crisisgroup.org/home/index.cfm?id=2863&l=1; and Peter Chalk, "Separatism and Southeast Asia: The Islamic Factor in Southern Thailand, Mindanao, and Aceh," *Studies in Conflict and Terrorism* 24 (2001): 247.

26. Peter Chalk, "Separatism and Southeast Asia: The Islamic Factor in Southern Thailand, Mindanao, and Aceh," *Studies in Conflict and Terrorism* 24 (2001): 248.

27. *Southern Philippines Backgrounder: Terrorism and the Peace Process ICG Asia Report N°80,* 13 July 2004, p. 10, http://www.crisisgroup.org/home/index.cfm?id=2863&l=1.

28. *Southern Philippines Backgrounder: Terrorism and the Peace Process ICG Asia Report N°80,* 13 July 2004, p. 9, http://www.crisisgroup.org/home/index.cfm?id=2863&l=1.

29. *Southern Philippines Backgrounder: Terrorism and the Peace Process ICG Asia Report N°80*, 13 July 2004, p. 2. http://www.crisisgroup.org/home/index.cfm?id=2863&l=1.

30. Peter Chalk, "Separatism and Southeast Asia: The Islamic Factor in Southern Thailand, Mindanao, and Aceh," *Studies in Conflict and Terrorism* 24 (2001): 248.

31. http://www.tkb.org/Incident.jsp?incID=15685.

32. Zachary Abuza, *Militant Islam in Southeast Asia: Crucible of Terror* (Boulder: Lynne Rienner, 2003): 91.

33. *Southern Philippines Backgrounder: Terrorism and the Peace Process ICG Asia Report N°80*, 13 July 2004, p. 13, http://www.crisisgroup.org/home/index.cfm?id=2863&l=1.

34. MIPT Terrorism Knowledge Base, Incident Profile: MILF Attacked Transportation Target (Apr. 2, 2003, Philippines) http://www.tkb.org/Incident.jsp?incID=15685.

35. *Southern Philippines Backgrounder: Terrorism and the Peace Process ICG Asia Report N°80*, 13 July 2004, p. 13, http://www.crisisgroup.org/home/index.cfm?id=2863&l=1.

36. Zachary Abuza, *Militant Islam in Southeast Asia: Crucible of Terror* (Boulder: Lynne Rienner, 2003) 45.

37. United States Institution of Peace, *Special Report 131–The Mindanao Peace Talks: Another Opportunity to Resolve the Moro Conflict in the Philippines*, February 2005, p. 5, http://www.usip.org/pubs/specialreports/sr131.html.

38. Zachary Abuza, *Militant Islam in Southeast Asia: Crucible of Terror* (Boulder: Lynne Rienner, 2003) 46; and United States Institution of Peace, *Special Report 131– The Mindanao Peace Talks: Another Opportunity to Resolve the Moro Conflict in the Philippines*, February 2005, p. 5, http://www.usip.org/pubs/specialreports/sr131.html.

39. Zachary Abuza, *Militant Islam in Southeast Asia: Crucible of Terror* (Boulder: Lynne Rienner, 2003) 46.

40. MIPT Terrorism Knowledge Base, Group Profile: Moro Islamic Liberation Front, http://www.tkb.org/Group.jsp?groupID=3631.

41. "Al-Qaeda and the Separatists," *The Economist* 370, no. 8364 (February 28, 2004): 41–42.

42. MIPT Terrorism Knowledge Base, Group Profile: Moro Islamic Liberation Front, http://www.tkb.org/Group.jsp?groupID=3631.

43. Zachary Abuza, *Militant Islam in Southeast Asia: Crucible of Terror* (Boulder: Lynne Rienner, 2003) 208.

44. *Southern Philippines Backgrounder: Terrorism and the Peace Process ICG Asia Report N°80*, 13 July 2004, p. 7, http://www.crisisgroup.org/home/index.cfm?id=2863&l=1.

45. While most of the translations for Abu Sayyaf claim that the literal Arabic-to-English translation is "bearer of the sword," Rommel C. Banlaoi contends that this is a mistranslation; Abu Sayyaf actually means "Father of the Swordsman" in reference to (and in honor of) the Afghan resistance leader Abdul Rasul Sayyaf. Rommel C. Banlaoi, "Maritime Terrorism in Southeast Asia: The Abu Sayyaf Threat," *Naval War College Review* 58, no. 4 (Autumn 2005): 66.

46. Office of the Coordinator for Counterterrorism, *Country Reports on Terrorism*, April 28, 2006, p. 185, http://www.state.gov/s/ct/rls/crt/2005/; and Peter Chalk, "Separatism and Southeast Asia: The Islamic Factor in Southern Thailand, Mindanao, and Aceh," *Studies in Conflict and Terrorism* 24 (2001): 249.

47. Graham H. Turbiville, Jr., "Bearer of the Sword," *Military Review* (March–April 2002): 38; Peter Chalk, "Separatism and Southeast Asia: The Islamic Factor in Southern Thailand, Mindanao, and Aceh," *Studies in Conflict and Terrorism* 24 (2001): 249; Office of the Coordinator for Counterterrorism, "Chapter 8: Foreign Terrorist Organizations," *Country Reports on Terrorism*, April 28, 2006, p. 185, http://www.state.gov/s/ct/rls/crt/2005/.

48. Office of the Coordinator for Counterterrorism, *Country Reports on Terrorism*, April 28, 2006, p. 185, http://www.state.gov/s/ct/rls/crt/2005/; and Graham H. Turbiville, Jr., "Bearer of the Sword," *Military Review* (March–April 2002): 38, 43.

49. Daniel Joseph Ringuet, "The Continuation of Civil Unrest and Poverty in Mindanao," *Contemporary Southeast Asia* 24, no. 1 (April 2002): 41.

50. John Gee, *The Washington Report on Middle East Affairs* 19, no. 7 (September 2000): p. 60; and Rommel C. Banlaoi, "Maritime Terrorism in Southeast Asia: The Abu Sayyaf Threat," *Naval War College Review* 58, no. 4 (Autumn 2005): 66–67.

51. Peter Chalk, "Separatism and Southeast Asia: The Islamic Factor in Southern Thailand, Mindanao, and Aceh," *Studies in Conflict and Terrorism* 24 (2001): 248.

52. Rommel C. Banlaoi, "Maritime Terrorism in Southeast Asia: The Abu Sayyaf Threat," *Naval War College Review* 58, no. 4 (Autumn 2005): 66.

53. Graham H. Turbiville, Jr., "Bearer of the Sword," *Military Review* (March–April 2002): 42; and Zachary Abuza, *Militant Islam in Southeast Asia: Crucible of Terror* (Boulder: Lynne Rienner, 2003) 100.

54. Graham H. Turbiville, Jr., "Bearer of the Sword," *Military Review* (March–April 2002): 42–43; Rommel C. Banlaoi, "Maritime Terrorism in Southeast Asia: The Abu Sayyaf Threat," *Naval War College Review* 58, no. 4 (Autumn 2005): 66; and Abuza: p. 100.

55. Rommel C. Banlaoi, "Maritime Terrorism in Southeast Asia: The Abu Sayyaf Threat," *Naval War College Review* 58, no 4 (Autumn 2005): 66.

56. Rommel C. Banlaoi, "Maritime Terrorism in Southeast Asia: The Abu Sayyaf Threat," *Naval War College Review* 58, no 4 (Autumn 2005): 68.

57. For a detailed account of some of these activities, please see Maria Ressa, *Seeds of Terror* (New York: Free Press, 2003) 104–123.

58. Zachary Abuza, *Militant Islam in Southeast Asia: Crucible of Terror* (Boulder: Lynne Rienner, 2003) 101.

59. Zachary Abuza, "Balik Terrorism: The Return of the Abu Sayyaf," *Strategic Studies Institute*, U.S. Army War College (September 2005): 3.

60. Ibid.: p. vii.

61. Ibid.: p. 13.

62. Peter Chalk, "Separatism and Southeast Asia: The Islamic Factor in Southern Thailand, Mindanao, and Aceh," *Studies in Conflict and Terrorism* 24 (2001): 249.

63. Graham H. Turbiville, Jr. "Bearer of the Sword." *Military Review*. March–April 2002, p. 43.

64. "Vote-Winning," *The Economist* 371, no. 8369 (April 3, 2004); and Office of the Coordinator for Counterterrorism, "Chapter 8: Foreign Terrorist Organizations," *Country Reports on Terrorism* April 28, 2006, p. 185, http://www.state.gov/s/ct/rls/crt/2005/.

65. Rommel C. Banlaoi, "Maritime Terrorism in Southeast Asia: The Abu Sayyaf Threat," *Naval War College Review* 58, no. 4 (Autumn 2005): 71–72.

66. "New Abu Sayyaf," *The Economist* 374, no. 8414 (February 19, 2005); and Office of the Coordinator for Counterterrorism, "Chapter 8: Foreign Terrorist Organizations," *Country Reports on Terrorism*, April 28, 2006, p. 185, http://www.state.gov/s/ct/rls/crt/2005/.

67. Office of the Coordinator for Counterterrorism, "Chapter 8: Foreign Terrorist Organizations," *Country Reports on Terrorism*, April 28, 2006, p. 185, http://www.state.gov/s/ct/rls/crt/2005/; and Rommel C. Banlaoi, "Maritime Terrorism in Southeast Asia: The Abu Sayyaf Threat," *Naval War College Review* 58, no. 4 (Autumn 2005): 71–72.

68. Rommel C. Banlaoi, "Maritime Terrorism in Southeast Asia: The Abu Sayyaf Threat," *Naval War College Review* 58, no. 4 (Autumn 2005): 73.

69. Ibid.: pp. 74–75.

70. Ibid.: p. 73.

71. Francisco L. Tolin, "The Response of the Philippine Government and the Role of the AFP in Addressing Terrorism," National Defense College of the Philippines online featured paper, http://www.ndcp.edu.ph/tokyopaper.htm.

72. Rommel C. Banlaoi, *The War on Terrorism in Southeast Asia* (Quezon City: Strategic and Integrative Studies Center, 2003) 48.

73. The Philippines in America's War," *Philippine Star Online*, www.philstar.com/philstar/newwar6.htm.

74. Arnaud de Borchgrave, "Arroyo to Warn Bush of Poverty-Terror Link," *The Washington Times Online*, October 16, 2003, http://www.washingtontimes.com/functions/print.php?StoryID=20031016-120033-8644r.

75. Deb Riechmann, "Philippine Leader Seeks More US Aid," *Monterey Herald Online*, May 18, 2003, www.bayarea.com/mld/montereyherald/5892303.htm.

76. Francisco L. Tolin, "The Response of the Philippine Government and the Role of the AFP in Addressing Terrorism," National Defense College of the Philippines online featured paper, http://www.ndcp.edu.ph/tokyopaper.htm.

77. Rommel C. Banlaoi, "Maritime Terrorism in Southeast Asia: The Abu Sayyaf Threat," *Naval War College Review* 58, no. 4 (Autumn 2005): 74–75.

78. Marichu Villanueva and Christina Mendez, "Anti-Terror Task Force Keeps Watch on Foreigners in RP," *Philippine Headline News Online*, April 8, 2004, http://www.newsflash.org/2004/02/hl/hl100199.htm; and Rommel C. Banlaoi, "Maritime Terrorism in Southeast Asia: The Abu Sayyaf Threat," *Naval War College Review* 58, no. 4 (Autumn 2005): 75.

79. Marichu Villanueva and Christina Mendez, "Anti-Terror Task Force Keeps Watch on Foreigners in RP," *Philippine Headline News Online*, April 8, 2004, http://www.newsflash.org/2004/02/hl/hl100199.htm.

80. Rommel C. Banlaoi. "The Role of Philippine-American Relations in the Global Campaign Against Terrorism: Implications for Regional Security," *Contemporary Southeast Asia* 24, no. 2 (August 2002): 302; and Zachary Abuza, *Militant Islam in Southeast Asia: Crucible of Terror* (Boulder: Lynne Rienner, 2003) 203.

81. Francisco L. Tolin, "The Response of the Philippine Government and the Role of the AFP in Addressing Terrorism," National Defense College of the Philippines online featured paper, http://www.ndcp.edu.ph/tokyopaper.htm.

82. Deb Riechmann, "Philippine Leader Seeks More US Aid," *Monterey Herald Online*, May 18, 2003, www.bayarea.com/mld/montereyherald/5892303.htm.

83. Francisco L. Tolin, "The Response of the Philippine Government and the Role of the AFP in Addressing Terrorism," National Defense College of the Philippines online featured paper, http://www.ndcp.edu.ph/tokyopaper.htm.

84. *Southern Philippines Backgrounder: Terrorism and the Peace Process ICG Asia Report N°80,* 13 July 2004, p. 1, http://www.crisisgroup.org/home/index.cfm?id=2863&l=1.

85. Zachary Abuza, *Militant Islam in Southeast Asia: Crucible of Terror* (Boulder: Lynne Rienner, 2003) 211.

86. Marichu Villanueva and Christina Mendez, "Anti-Terror Task Force Keeps Watch on Foreigners in RP," *Philippine Headline News Online*, April 8, 2004, http://www.newsflash.org/2004/02/hl/hl100199.htm.

87. Graham H. Turbiville, Jr., "Bearer of the Sword," *Military Review* (March–April 2002): 46.

88. Zachary Abuza, *Militant Islam in Southeast Asia: Crucible of Terror* (Boulder: Lynne Rienner, 2003) 203.

89. Marichu Villanueva and Christina Mendez, "Anti-Terror Task Force Keeps Watch on Foreigners in RP," *Philippine Headline News Online*, April 8, 2004, http://www.newsflash.org/2004/02/hl/hl100199.htm.

90. Rohan Gunaratna, "The Prospects of Global Terrorism," *Society* (September/October 2005): 32.

91. *Southern Philippines Backgrounder: Terrorism and the Peace Process ICG Asia Report N°80,* 13 July 2004, p. 25, http://www.crisisgroup.org/home/index.cfm?id=2863&l=1.

92. Brian Nichiporuk, "Regional Demographics and the War on Terrorism," *RUSI Journal* 148, no. 1 (February 2003): 26. For a full account of this plot, see Rohan Gunaratna, "Al Qaeda's Lose and Learn Doctrine: The Trajectory from Oplan Bojinka to 9/11," in *Teaching Terror: Strategic and Tactical Learning in the Terrorist World,* ed. James J. F. Forest (Lanham, MD: Rowman & Littlefield, 2006) 171–188.

93. Rommel C. Banlaoi, *The War on Terrorism in Southeast Asia* (Quezon City: Strategic and Integrative Studies Center, 2003) 17.

94. Zachary Abuza, *Militant Islam in Southeast Asia: Crucible of Terror* (Boulder: Lynne Rienner, 2003) 9–10, 18.

95. Southern Philippines Backgrounder: Terrorism and the Peace Process ICG Asia Report N°80, 13 July 2004, p. 2, http://www.crisisgroup.org/home/index.cfm?id=2863&l=1.

96. United States Institution of Peace, *Special Report 131–The Mindanao Peace Talks: Another Opportunity to Resolve the Moro Conflict in the Philippines* (February 2005): 1–2, 8–11, http://www.usip.org/pubs/specialreports/sr131.html.

CHAPTER 28

TERRORISM AND UZBEKISTAN: THE THREAT AND THE RESPONSE

Joshua Sinai

Uzbekistan is a highly authoritarian regime that has faced a terrorist insurgency by radical Islamists since the early 1990s. Uzbekistan is the former Soviet Union's largest Muslim nation, with a population of 27.3 million people.[1] Until its human rights abuses led to a fallout with the United States in 2005,[2] Uzbekistan was an ally in the United States-led coalition against the global Salafi Jihadists, represented by Osama bin Laden's al Qaeda network of terrorist groupings. The Islamic insurgency in Uzbekistan is part of a wider conflict being waged by other radical Islamists in Central Asia who were inspired by the early success of the Taliban in Afghanistan.[3] In the case of Uzbekistan, the policies and methods utilized by the government in responding to the Islamic insurgency (as well as to any semblance of democratic opposition) pose myriad dilemmas for the Karimov regime and its allies, such as Russia, that seek to assist in restoring stability and prosperity to this geo-strategically important and yet troubled region.

The primary dilemma facing Uzbekistan is how an effective counterterrorism (CT) policy against militant Islamic terrorist groups can be pursued by a relatively secular yet highly authoritarian state with a large Muslim population that maintains its power by means of the secret police and restricting political participation rather than through popular support. This is the main weakness of the Uzbekistan government's CT policy against the Islamic Movement of Uzbekistan (IMU) terrorist group, which throughout the 1990s until late 2001 maintained links to Afghanistan's Taliban rulers. With other opposition groups excluded from the political process, the IMU has come to represent the primary opposition to the Uzbekistan government's harsh rule.

The IMU connection to the Taliban was significant. While the Taliban's leaders lacked the military capability to invade and overtake Uzbekistan, they hoped that by sponsoring terrorist groups, such as the IMU, their influence would spread throughout the neighboring Central Asian countries. This desire came to a crashing end following the Taliban's overthrow by the United States-led coalition in late 2001, although affiliated Islamic groups in the region have continued to mount their own insurgencies.

THE ISLAMIC INSURGENTS

The IMU is considered the most dangerous of the several Muslim terrorist groups currently operating in Central Asia. The IMU emerged in the 1990s to capitalize on the region's impoverished and politically disaffected populace to mobilize support and recruits for its insurgency. The IMU has sought to destabilize and overthrow the Uzbek government in order to establish a Taliban-type regime that would lay the foundation for a future Islamic caliphate in Central Asia. Accordingly, in September 1999 the IMU declared a jihad against the Uzbekistan government.[4] The IMU's propaganda has also been directed against Uzbekistan's Western allies and Israel.

In Uzbekistan, the IMU has operated out of the Fergana Valley, and has also established bases in Tajikistan and Kyrgyzstan. The IMU was estimated to have between 1,000 and 2,000 members, with the lower estimate likely after 2001, when the group was hunt by the U.S.-led war against the Taliban.[5] In the late 1990s, its forces underwent training in Afghanistan and Pakistan (and reportedly also in Chechnya), and it has also operated out of Iran, where it has broadcast statements over the Tehran government's radio station.

The IMU has obtained funding from Islamic groups and individuals in Pakistan, Afghanistan, Turkey, Saudi Arabia, and other states. It is reported to have received $25 million from its foreign sponsors in 1999, and its activities have been subsidized by profits from narcotrafficking.[6] The IMU has also engaged in kidnapping foreigners to extort money for its activities. For example, in late October 1999, the IMU gained a reported $3–5 million in ransom for the release of four Japanese geologists who were abducted (along with eight Kyrgystan hostages, including military personnel) in the mountains of southern Kyrgystan on August 22 that year.

The IMU has carried out numerous terrorist operations. In 1998, the group was responsible for two bombings in Osh, Kyrgyzstan's second-largest city, killing several persons and wounding others. On February 16, 1999, the IMU carried out five coordinated car bomb attacks against Uzbek government facilities, killing 16 persons and wounding more than 100 others. In November 1999, the IMU initiated a shoot-out near the capital city of Tashkent, killing 10 government officials, with 15 insurgents killed.

During the period of March 28–April 1, 2004, a series of bombings and armed attacks took place in Uzbekistan that killed 47 persons.[7] The group that claimed responsibility for the attacks, the previously unknown Islamic Jihad Group of Uzbekistan (IJG), was alleged to have been an alias of the IMU. These attacks were followed by attacks against the U.S. and Israeli embassies and the Uzbek Prosecutor-General's Office in Tashkent on July 30, 2004, for which the IMU and IJG claimed responsibility. In September 2000, in response to the IMU's terrorist activities, the U.S. State Department designated it as a Foreign Terrorist Organization.

The IMU's top leader is Takhir Yoldashev, an Islamic extremist. Until the Taliban's overthrow, he maintained an office in Kandahar, Afghanistan (which was also the headquarters of the Taliban's spiritual leader, Mullah Omar). Under Yoldashev's leadership, the IMU carried out a series of multiple bombings in Tashkent in February 1999.[8] Yoldashev's deputy was Djumaboy Hadjiev (a.k.a. "Juma Namangany"), who headed the IMU's paramilitary group. In 1992–1997 Namangany's militia—together with the United Tajik Opposition—was also involved in an insurgency against Tajikistan's government, and later assisted the Taliban in its military campaign to achieve power in Afghanistan. He was killed in Afghanistan in November 2001 while fighting alongside Taliban and al Qaeda forces. Yoldashev, however, survived the fighting, and is believed to be hiding in Pakistan.

A third IMU leader is Muhammad Salih (original name, Salai Madaminov), a former presidential candidate in Uzbekistan's 1991 elections and leader of the banned "Erk" (Freedom) party, who joined the IMU in mid-1997. Salih was born in 1949 in the Kharezm province of western Uzbekistan. During the 1970s and 1980s he became widely known as a poet and a philosopher. Following the arrests of many of his "Erk" party colleagues by the Uzbekistan government in April 1993, Salih moved to Turkey, where he and his associates provided ideological and subversive training to a group of Uzbekistanis. In 1994, he was expelled from Turkey. According to some reports, in June 1994 Salih met with Chechen militants in Grozny, and shortly thereafter Uzbek nationals began to participate in the insurgency in Chechnya, which also served as a training ground to improve their combat skills. After living in Germany, Salih returned to Turkey, although illegally. It is reported that at an October 1998 meeting in Turkey, Yoldashev offered Salih the post of president of the "Islamic Democratic State of Uzbekistan" in return for his help in securing financial assistance to the IMU for the procurement of weapons and military equipment from a Turkish-based "Muslim Mukhadjir Assistance Fund." Salih accepted the proposal, and promised to ensure full financial support. Under this agreement, Salih would become the political leader and Yoldashev the military leader of the new Islamic state. After residing in Turkey during much of the 1990s, in February (or March) 1999, Salih took up residence in Norway, where he sought asylum. He later moved to Germany (where he resided, as of 2006).

Interestingly, in his public pronouncements in 2005–2006, Salih attempted to distance himself from the IMU, portraying himself as the leader of the newly formed United Uzbek Democratic Coalition. In fact, Salih even visited the United States in July 2005, urging the United States and the European Union to support democracy activists in Uzbekistan. This followed the Uzbekistan government's harsh crackdown against demonstrators in the city of Andijan in May 2005—an event that gave additional credence to any group, even one tainted with an association with the IMU that claimed to represent the country's democratic opposition.

A second Islamic insurgent group that poses a threat to the Uzbek government is the Hizb ut-Tahrir (HT, the Islamic Liberation Party), a clandestine organization that seeks to establish an Islamic state in Uzbekistan. It is also active in neighboring Central Asian states, particularly Kyrgyzstan. In February 1999, President Karimov accused it of infiltrating Uzbekistan to establish an Islamic caliphate. The group has gained a following in Uzbekistan, particularly among the country's young population. The group's alleged leader, Hafizulloh Nasirov, was arrested by Uzbekistan authorities in December 1999.[9] The IMU's Yoldashev is reportedly the HT's chief ideological inspiration. In 1999, the group was blamed for a series of bomb attacks in the capital, Tashkent, which led to the detainment of hundreds of HT supporters.

THE ROOTS OF INSURGENCY

The terrorist insurgency in Uzbekistan is the product of several factors, most notably its highly authoritarian political system, rule by a closed oligarchy, economic dislocation, poverty, and harsh crackdowns on all internal dissidents, with the only plausible alternative to President Karimov represented by the Islamist movement.

Uzbekistan's political system is highly authoritarian. President Karimov has no designated successor. In fact, the post of vice president had been abolished to prevent the emergence of any potential rival. In 1998–1999, Karimov carried out an extensive purge within his administration to maintain his full control. It is also illegal for any political party that aims to "change the existing order" to be permitted to register. As a result, all opposition parties are banned and no fair or free elections can be held. Opponents of Karimov have complained that they are barred from taking part in elections and that only progovernment parties are permitted to compete. Thus, in the January 2000 election, President Karimov returned to office with almost 92 percent of the vote.[10] In that election, Abdulkhafiz

Jalolov, the sole candidate allowed to oppose Karimov, was the nominee of the People's Democratic Party (PDP), which Karimov had previously headed. In fact, Jalolov admitted that he had voted for the president. In response to such a closed electoral system, the Organization of Security and Cooperation in Europe (OSCE) refused to send a monitoring team to the election, accusing the government of failing to give voters a real choice.

These conditions have radicalized segments of Uzbekistan's Muslim population, who have looked to Afghanistan's previous Taliban rulers or bin Laden's al Qaeda and its global Salafi Jihadi networks as examples of populist Islamic power. The IMU's emergence is also due to the collapse of law and order in Tajikistan during the Tajik civil war in 1992–1997, which provided Uzbekistan's Islamist resistance movement with a safe haven and a base of operations.

A final condition for the insurgency is the country's poverty. Uzbekistan is the poorest of its resource-rich neighbors among the southern former Soviet republics (Azerbaijan, Kazakhstan, and Turkmenistan). The country's resource base is relatively modest and there is little foreign investment. As a result, there is no likelihood in Uzbekistan of the kind of rapid economic growth that its oil- and gas-rich neighbors are experiencing.

UZBEKISTAN'S COUNTERTERRORISM POLICY

The cornerstone of President Karimov's counterterrorism policy has been to maintain stability and security, not to promote increased democratization in the form of wide political participation. This has led to the outlawing of numerous Islamic groups accused of trying to destabilize the country by spreading Islamic radicalism from Afghanistan. As a result, many of President Karimov's opponents now live in exile. A second component of Uzbekistan's CT campaign is to bombard the Uzbek rebels at their Tajikistan bases. A third component is to assist the Kyrgyzstan government in forcing the IMU guerrillas out of their country by providing assistance in the form of air strikes, border troops, and military materiel. A fourth component is participation in military exercises to combat terrorism jointly with the other Central Asian states (except Turkmenistan), such as the "Southern Shield" exercise held in late 1999 and March 2000. Uzbekistan also conducts joint military exercises with Russian troops. A fifth component is to recruit moderate Islamic voices to join the Uzbekistan government to help counteract the extremists' ideology.

The Uzbekistan government has also sought U.S. counterterrorism assistance in its campaign against the IMU. While the United States provided Uzbekistan with financial assistance for border control and other security measures, Washington stated that a country's counterterrorism campaign should not be based on human rights violations. Until November 2005, U.S. troops were deployed at Qarshi-Khonobod ("K2") airbase in southern Uzbekistan, not far from the Afghan border, but following their expulsion, U.S. assistance for counterterrorism ceased.

The Uzbekistan government believes that its counterterrorism strategy will enable it to avoid the fate of its smaller southern neighbor Tajikistan, which has been engulfed in a civil war since independence. So far, however, such a strategy has not succeeded in rooting out Uzbekistan's extremist Islamic insurgency, because its military campaign has been ineffective and solutions still need to be provided to tackle the country's internal problems, particularly the lack of full political participation in the form of free, fair, and competitive elections.

It is important that an effective response to the radical Islamic insurgency in Uzbekistan is found and implemented, because this insurgency is part of a wider series of insurgencies facing the Central Asian states that pose a major threat to their stability and prospects for increased democratization and economic well-being. However, until Uzbekistan adopts a more democratic course, there will be few internal or external allies to help it defeat the IMU's insurgency.

NOTES

1. "Uzbekistan" in *The World Factbook* (Washington, DC: Central Intelligence Agency, 2006).

2. See John C.K. Daly, Kurt H. Meppen, Vladimir Socor, and S. Frederick Starr eds., *Anatomy of a Crisis: U.S.-Uzbekistan Relations, 2001–2005* (Washington, DC: Central Asia-Caucasus & Silk Road Studies Program, Johns Hopkins University-SAIS, February 2006).

3. For an analysis of the rise of radical Islam in Central Asia, see Ahmed Rashid, *Jihad: The Rise of Militant Islam in Central Asia* (New York: Penguin, 2002).

4. Poonam Mann, "Islamic Movement of Uzbekistan: Will it Strike?", *Strategic Analysis: A Monthly Journal of the IDSA*, April–June 2002, Vol. XXVI, No, 2, p. 8.

5. Audrey Kurth Cronin, et al, "Foreign Terrorist Organization," *CRS Report for Congress*, February 6, 2004, p. 38.

6. Mann, "Islamic Movement of Uzbekistan: Will it Strike Back?", p. 3.

7. Human Rights Watch, "Uzbekistan," *World Report 2005*.

8. "Islamic Movement of Uzbekistan (IMU)," *Patterns of Global Terrorism 2001*, (Washington: United States Department of State, May 21, 2002).

9. Louise Hidalgo, "Uzbekistan arrests leading Islamist," *BBC News*, December 2, 1999.

10. CIA, "Uzbekistan," *The World Factbook*, March 15, 2007.

CHAPTER 29

INDIA'S RESPONSE TO TERRORISM IN KASHMIR

Behram A. Sahukar

Pakistan-sponsored terrorism remains one of the gravest threats to India's security and stability. Full-blown separatist Islamist violence against India erupted in Jammu and Kashmir (shortened to 'Kashmir' throughout this chapter) in 1989 at the end of the Afghan jihad and has taken a tragic toll of human life on both sides. It is estimated that over 63,000 persons have been killed in India as a result of terrorist-related violence, and that over 850,000 persons have been displaced from their homes. Of this, about 18,000 civilian deaths have occurred in Kashmir alone.[1] This chapter will primarily address the issue of cross-border terrorism in Kashmir, and the Indian response to Pakistan's proxy war and jihad in Kashmir.

BACKGROUND

The origins of the Kashmir issue go back to 1947, when the British planned to grant India its independence on August 15, 1947. To meet the demands of the Muslim League, the British decided to create Pakistan out of the Muslim majority area of British India to serve as a homeland for the Muslims of the Indian subcontinent. The rulers of the 565 Princely states were to accede at the time of independence to either India or Pakistan. In most cases, the dictates of contiguous borders or geography made the decision a simple one.

However, the case of Jammu and Kashmir posed a peculiar problem: a Hindu raja, Hari Singh ruled over the Muslim majority state, and its borders were contiguous to both India and Pakistan.[2] Hari Singh asked Lord Mountbatten for additional time to reach a final decision and did not accede to either India or Pakistan. To force the issue, Pakistan attacked

Kashmir on October 22, 1947, and Hari Singh turned to India for military assistance. On October 26, 1947, the beleaguered Maharaja signed the Instrument of Accession, legally joining the Indian Union. The following day, India sent troops to counter the aggression and stemmed the Pakistani advance.

India then took the case to the United Nations (UN), which brokered a conditional ceasefire in January 1949 that established (roughly) the present-day Line of Control. Pakistan was subsequently instructed to withdraw all its troops from Kashmir and this was to be followed by a plebiscite. However, Pakistan continues to occupy approximately one third of Kashmir to this day, and considers the Kashmir issue to be the "unfinished agenda of Partition." It still feels wronged by the legal decision of the Hindu ruler to accede to India when it was under Pakistani attack.

In September 1965, Pakistan launched another unsuccessful military attack (Operation Gibraltar) seeking to wrest Kashmir from India. In December 1971, civil war in East Pakistan escalated to an all-out war with India. Pakistan suffered a humiliating defeat in the West, and lost all of East Pakistan. Over 93,000 men of the Pakistan Army were taken prisoner.[3] Bangladesh emerged as a new independent nation from the ashes of East Pakistan.

The 1971 war had an important impact on the Kashmir issue. The Simla Agreement, which was signed in July 1972, stated that all issues between India and Pakistan—including Kashmir—would be resolved bilaterally in a peaceful manner. The 1949 UN ceasefire line in Kashmir was formalized as the "Line of Control" (LOC). No change in the status quo was permissible unless this was done peacefully and by the mutual consent of both India and Pakistan (see Figure 29.1).

The humiliation of the 1971 war also scarred the psyche of the Pakistani Army, which vowed to avenge its defeat by India at an opportune time. Despite its failed attempts in the past, Pakistan remained obsessed with the idea of taking all of Kashmir from India by force.

The Afghan Jihad

When General Zia ul Haq came to power in 1975, he intensified the policy of Islamization of Pakistani society and the Pakistani Army. The Soviet invasion of Afghanistan in 1979 made Pakistan a frontline state in the United States-funded jihad against the Soviet Union. The infusion of CIA-funded arms, equipment, and other forms of support into Pakistan legitimized the use of Islam to fight an Islamic holy war. The end of the Afghan jihad in 1989 left Pakistan flooded with surplus arms and equipment, as well as a cadre of fighters with experience in a prolonged low-intensity conflict. Mujahideen who had completed their successful mission against

Figure 29.1   Map of Jammu and Kashmir
Source: Embassy of India, Washington, DC.

the Soviets were diverted to Kashmir to continue their fight for Islam in Kashmir against "infidel" Hindu India.

Operation Topac

In 1988, Pakistan prepared a strategy "to bleed India by a thousand cuts" (code named Op Topac). Having lost three conventional wars against India, it planned to fight an asymmetrical war by waging a low-intensity proxy war in Kashmir and then extend it to the rest of India.[4] According to this plan, the Inter Services Intelligence (ISI) would fund and train the jihadi insurgents and coordinate the Islamist agenda against India. The Pakistan-sponsored Islamist campaign of terror that began in 1989 has ravaged Kashmir and spilled over to the rest of India. Hundreds of terrorist cells have been established in Nepal, Bangladesh, Myanmar, and Bhutan, encircling India in a web of terror backed by Islamic extremism.

Kargil Conflict

Emboldened further after it acquired the nuclear bomb in May 1998, Pakistan sent its Army and mujahideen fighters in May 1999 to occupy the icy heights of eastern Kashmir at Kargil on the Indian side of the LOC. Pakistan sought to internationalize the Kashmir issue and to test India's response to an armed Pakistan intrusion under the backdrop of nuclear weapons. India launched a costly limited military response to dislodge the intruders, but refrained from expanding the conflict to other sectors. U.S. diplomatic pressure and the Indian military successes forced Pakistan to withdraw its troops. Following this, a military coup led by the Army Chief General Pervez Musharraf in October 1999 ousted the elected government of Nawar Sharif. The army was back in power in Pakistan, and soon after, terrorism in Kashmir surged. Since many Indian units had been diverted to the Kargil sector, terrorist attacks in various parts of the region met with initial success. Suicide attacks in particular increased against security forces, and additional Indian troops were sent into Kashmir in order to counter the growing frequency and intensity of terror attacks.[5]

TERRORISM AND COUNTERTERRORISM IN KASHMIR

Countering terrorism in Kashmir has posed a serious challenge to India. India's 150 million Muslims form approximately 12 percent of its billion-plus population. The Indian Muslim population is second in size only to Indonesia, and outnumbers the Muslim population of Pakistan. The vast majority of Indian Muslims are moderate in their views and do not take part in terrorist-related activities. The Muslims and other minority communities of India have integrated well in all areas of Indian society and government.[6] India is very mindful of the fact that its counterterrorism policies in Kashmir must not radicalize its Indian Muslims.

Admittedly, the complex situation in Kashmir has been exacerbated by Indian political bungling and manipulation. The genesis of present-day terrorism in Kashmir can be traced to alleged electoral manipulation in the 1986 state elections, which led to disgruntlement and a loss of faith in the Central government. Pakistan was quick to seize the opportunity and began to arm and train Kashmiri youth in Pakistani camps to fight against Indian misrule. The LOC afforded many gaps in the physical border and concealed routes through which militants could cross into and out of Pakistan (often with assistance from the Pakistan Army). The terrain in Kashmir is mainly mountainous and forested, providing ideal conditions for infiltration and quick exfiltration. Observation is limited and movement of conventional forces is slow and arduous.

Some of the objectives of the terrorists in this contested region are:

- Destabilize India by inciting large-scale communal violence between Hindus, Muslims, and other minorities;
- Subvert the loyalty of Indian Muslims and incite them to conduct antinational activities by coercion, fear, and religious indoctrination;
- Restore the glory of former Muslim rule over all of India and annex Kashmir to Pakistan by waging a jihad; and
- Terrorize all non-Muslims in Kashmir and force them out of Kashmir.

Terrorist Targets

Initially, the targets of these terror attacks were the security forces and military installations. However, the focus has more recently shifted to soft targets, including a mix of the following:

- Attacks on civilians in buses, trains, marketplaces, and families of soldiers deployed on the borders;
- Attacks on places of Hindu worship and pilgrims on their way to holy mountain shrines in Kashmir;
- Forcing security forces to attack mosques and religious places in which terrorists were hiding, such as the Charar-e-Sharif, and the Hazrat Bal Mosques, in response to the Akshardham and Raghunath Hindu Temple attacks.
- Killings and abduction of tourists and foreigners;
- Attacks on symbols of Indian democracy, such as the State Legislature building, the Indian Parliament, and the Red Fort;
- Disruption of free and fair elections, attacks on security forces, assassination of politicians, political candidates, and killing of voters; and
- Attacks on India's economic progress such as the Mumbai bombings of 1993 (that killed over 257), the 2002 bombings (that killed over 52), and the July 2006 train bombings that killed over 200 and injured over 800.

Methods and Trends

Among these terrorist attacks in (or related to) Kashmir, the following trends are prevalent:

- Use of roadside improvised explosive devices especially against military convoys and civilian transport.
- Kidnapping and killing of government officials and innocent civilians traveling by bus or in their own transport.
- Indiscriminate grenade attacks in busy marketplaces, bus stations, railway stations, and during gatherings to celebrate holy Hindu festivals.

- Use of car bombs to cause mayhem and panic at odd hours and in busy city centers.
- Suicide attacks by fidayeen who gain entry into government buildings and places of worship, and carry out indiscriminate firing until security forces eliminate the fidayeen.
- Large-scale infiltration across the LOC to establish bases and weapons caches within the wooded and mountainous areas, so that terrorist operations can continue into the winter when snow makes infiltration difficult.
- Efforts to expand operations into the rest of India with the help of sleeper terrorist cells, and establish bases in Bangladesh and Nepal.
- Use of women for surveillance, as couriers, and for active operations.
- Use of madrasas as schools of jihad and hate; opening up of new madrasas in Bangladesh, India-Nepal border areas, and along the Rajasthan border with India.
- Equipping insurgents and terrorists with modern communication, weapons, and explosives to inflict maximum damage, including surface-to-air missiles and chemical weapons capability.
- Increased use of military uniforms, fake documents, and military vehicles to gain entry into sensitive areas to launch suicide and car bomb attacks.

THE INDIAN RESPONSE

The "no war, no peace" low-intensity conflict situation prevailing in the sensitive region of Kashmir has posed a serious challenge to India, particularly in determining proper rules of engagement and in supporting the democratic process.

Rules of Engagement

In dealing with terrorism, the fight has been led mainly by the Army, supported on the ground by a mix of paramilitary forces and law enforcement agencies. India follows a very strict policy with regard to the rules of engagement. These are based on "the use of minimum force" and acting in "good faith." The Indian army has almost never used its heavy weapons, tanks, artillery fire, or air support when combating terrorism. Also, India's counterterrorism operations have been conducted within the recognized boundaries of India. India has never attacked another country or used preemptive force to counter terrorism. India's responses have been reactive and restrained rather than proactive or overly belligerent.

India has learned that while military force may kill terrorists, it cannot defeat terrorism unless the real or perceived grievances in Kashmir are also addressed. India is in a difficult position, as terrorism and jihad against it is being sustained from across its borders by a hostile nuclear-armed Pakistan. India's strategy in fighting terrorism in Kashmir has been derived from the successes and failures of its vast experience in counterterrorism and insurgency operations in the Northeast, Punjab, Sri Lanka, and Kashmir.[7]

India's response to terrorism in Kashmir is multidimensional, to include the military response to tackle violence, border management to prevent infiltration, political dialogue and negotiations with all parties that have given up violence, economic measures to improve the living conditions and job prospects of the local population, diplomatic initiatives toward peace to include confidence-building measures with Pakistan, and international counterterrorism cooperation with friendly countries.

Democratic Process and Elections

India has ensured that despite the turmoil and instability in Kashmir, the democratic process is kept alive. Elections have been held regularly, and these are both free and fair. Though over 800 people were killed by terrorists in the 2002 elections to the Kashmir State Assembly, over 28 percent in the Valley and 70 percent in Ladakh voted. In the April 2006 by-elections to the State Legislature, over 70 percent voted. In the February 2005 elections to 63 urban civic bodies, there was an average of 48 percent voter turnout. Surprisingly, in many of the terrorism-affected areas of Srinagar, over 80 percent of the registered voters cast their vote.[8] The transparency of the electoral process has done much to restore the faith of the people in good governance and fairness, and undermined the false propaganda by Pakistan that the wishes of the people in Kashmir have been muzzled.

Military and Civic Aspects

The Army's Northern Command has the prime responsibility of tackling terrorism and insurgency in Kashmir. After the Kargil war of 1999, an additional Corps Headquarters (HQ) was set up to control operations in eastern Kashmir and Ladakh sectors. India has approximately 300,000 troops in Kashmir. It is willing to reduce this number if Pakistan shuts down the 58 existing terrorist training camps in Pakistan Occupied Kashmir, and stops Islamic extremists from using Pakistan as a launch pad for terrorist activities against India.

The whole area has been divided into an interlocking and mutually supporting "counterinsurgency grid." The size of each grid varies according to the terrain. Normally each grid is looked after by a battalion or a brigade-sized formation that is responsible for operations within the grid. These areas of responsibilities have been subdivided laterally into tiers extending rearwards in depth, so that any terrorists that manage to evade the first tier or second tier are subsequently trapped in the rear areas, and apprehended or killed.

Operations of the Army, police, and the paramilitary forces are coordinated by a Unified Headquarters. The paramilitary forces include the Border Security Force (BSF), Central Reserve Police Force (CRPF), Central Industrial Security Force (CISF), Indo-Tibetan Border Police (ITBP), and elements of the National Security Guard (NSG—a specially equipped counterterrorism unit manned by the police and the Army).

In addition, the Rashtriya Rifles (RR) is a specially organized force to deal specifically with counterinsurgency. The RR will free the Army from counterinsurgency duties in the long term. The RR battalions are deployed under Five Sector Headquarters covering all the vital terrorist-prone areas of Kashmir.

Pre-Induction Training

Theater and Corps Battle Schools have been set up in Kashmir for mental and physical pre-induction training to units as a whole. They impart a four-week syllabus in which the units are "fine tuned" to the peculiarities of waging a successful counterterrorism and counterinsurgency campaign in Kashmir. In addition, a new Army Doctrine has been published in 2006 that includes a special chapter on counterinsurgency operations.[9] A special training manual on counterinsurgency operations is being updated and will be published shortly.

Specialized Training

The Counter Insurgency and Jungle Warfare (CIJW) school in Mizoram in India's Northeast province gives special emphasis to the importance of winning popular support and respecting human rights in counterinsurgency operations. In many cases, the Army units have to "un-learn" the lessons of conventional warfare, and change not only their way of functioning in war but also their mental attitude to fighting in an insurgency-prone area that is rural and semiurban.[10] Joint training between the U.S. and Indian Special Forces has been conducted recently at the CIJW school and also in the Ladakh sector of eastern Kashmir. These exercises revealed valuable lessons in counterinsurgency operations for both sides.

Employment of Surrendered Militants

A policy for the voluntary surrender and rehabilitation of misguided Indian Kashmiri militants was introduced in August 1995. The main objective of this policy is to offer monetary rewards and incentives to Kashmiri militants who were lured by Pakistan and now want to give up terrorism. The Indian government has recently increased the monthly incentive given to these surrendered militants to $40, which is a welcome induce-ment because jobs are hard to find. The government also invests approx-imately $3,000 in a fixed deposit account for a period of 3 years in each surrendered militant's name. At the end of this period, the money with in-terest is handed over to him for his use if he maintains good behavior and proves continued loyalty to India. Additional incentives are also offered for turning in weapons, and for providing actionable real-time intelligence such as current infiltration routes, location of training camps, weapon and explosives caches, and providing the names of terrorist leaders and the exact location of their cells. Vocational training for gainful employment is also offered.

So far, the policy has proved to be fairly successful, and about 3,700 militants have willingly surrendered. They have been organized into a Special Operations Group called the *Ikhwans,* and have been employed in the forefront of successful offensive operations that have killed or captured militant leaders and unearthed caches of arms, explosives, and ammunition.

COUNTERINFILTRATION AND BORDER MANAGEMENT

It is estimated that at any given time there are about 3,000 militants op-erating inside Kashmir, and about 300 trained militants are waiting to in-filtrate into India from Pakistan. The prevailing conditions along the LOC are ideal for small armed groups to move with impunity from bases in Pakistan into Kashmir. To plug the major infiltration routes, India has re-cently built a fence along the entire 470 miles of the LOC, and deployed surveillance radars, ground sensors, and early warning detectors. Un-manned aerial vehicles and drones are also used to monitor any hostile movement near the LOC.

To secure the rear areas, retired Army soldiers from the local villages have been organized into Village Defense Committees. They have been organized into a lightly armed force to prevent terrorists from gaining a foothold in the vulnerable villages of the hinterland. Terrorists are there-fore forced out of the semiurban areas into the inhospitable open terrain, where they can be hunted down by the security forces.

Following the brazen attack by Pakistan-based militants on India's par-liament on December 13, 2001, India mobilized its armed forces to pun-ish Pakistan by launching an all-out punitive war to destroy its terror-ist infrastructure. However, India was prevented from attacking Pakistan by the United States and intense international pressure, as it was feared that India's action might escalate into a nuclear exchange with Pakistan. After assurances from Pakistani President Pervez Musharraf in January and May 2002 that it would take necessary steps to rein in the terrorists, India held off its advance and troops returned to peacetime locations in October 2002.[11]

Modernization and Training of the Security Forces

India has initiated an extensive modernization plan for its Armed Forces and units engaged in counterterrorism operations. These include the development of additional Special Forces units and introduction of modern communications, night fighting equipment, and lightweight body armor. Large-scale imports of defense equipment have been ordered from the United States, Israel, Russia, and other friendly countries. Concurrently, a concerted effort has been made to modernize and reequip the Jammu and Kashmir police and the Rashtriya Rifles with the latest weapons and equipment, in order to ensure interoperability with the Army and to keep up with the modern arms and equipment used by the terrorists. Improved pay scales and increased benefits for the families of those killed in action, coupled with intensive counterinsurgency training have raised the morale of the police.

Intelligence Reorganization

Intelligence agencies have been reorganized and allotted additional funding to make them more reliable in providing actionable real-time intelligence. A new Defense Intelligence Agency has been established, as recommended by the Kargil Review Committee, to coordinate military intelligence inputs.[12] Successful relentless offensive operations based on accurate, actionable intelligence, have raised the morale of the security forces and decimated the leadership of the terrorist organizations operating within Kashmir. Enhanced surveillance of the LOC has reduced the infiltration across the LOC. Though sporadic incidents of grenade throwing and car bombings continue, the overall incidents of violence have reduced from 3,479 incidents in 2003 to 2,586 in 2004, a reduction of 26 percent, while the comparative figures between 2004 and 2005 show a reduction of 34 percent. The daily rate of killings including—security forces, civilians, and terrorists—fell from 10 in 2003, to 7 in 2004, to 3 in 2005. The estimated terrorist strength has been reduced from about 3,400 to 1,800. During the last few months, over 75 top leaders of various militant groups have been killed by the security forces.[13]

Special Legislation to Empower the Security Forces and Protection of Human Rights

Several areas of Kashmir have been designated as "disturbed areas," and the security forces have been given special powers of search and arrest. They have limited immunity from prosecution under the Armed Forces Special Powers Act (1990). However, judicial review and activism has ensured that any excesses are promptly investigated, and the guilty parties promptly punished.

The security forces and the Army in particular are very conscious of the human rights of the civilians and the rights of captured terrorists. The central and state governments have been very mindful of the conduct of its soldiers in counterterrorism operations. Any misuse or abuse of power has been dealt with severely. The Governor of Kashmir, Lieutenant General S. K. Sinha (a former Army general), stated recently that in the past 16 years, 134 personnel of the Army had been convicted on charges of human rights abuses in Kashmir. They were given punishments ranging from life imprisonment to dismissal from the Service and civil imprisonment. General N. C. Vig, a former Army Chief, reports that from 1990–2000, there were 1,340 cases of alleged human rights abuses by the Army, but only 33 were substantiated by any evidence. On investigation by the Army, 71 personnel were punished for various human rights violations.[14]

A Human Rights Cell has been operating for years at the Discipline and Vigilance Directorate at Army Headquarters. In addition, the Army has laid down its version of the "Ten Commandments" to be carried by every soldier serving in terrorism-prone areas. They include "no rape, no molestation or torture, no meddling in civil administration, respect for human rights, develop interaction with the media, restriction in the use of excessive force, upholding the code of conduct and honored traditions of the military, avoiding indiscriminate firing or harassment of civilians, impartiality during cordon and search operations, no acceptance of presents or gifts for performance of duty or otherwise, acting within the bounds of the law, avoiding the 'body count' approach in counterinsurgency operations and maintaining relentless offensive pressure against terrorists."

At the national level, the National Human Rights Commission has been established for many years. It has limited judicial powers and acts as a watchdog to safeguard the human rights of all concerned.[15] A similar organization designated as the State Human Rights Commission has been established in each state. The Unlawful Activities (Prevention) Act 2004 recently replaced the more draconian Prevention of Terrorism Act of 2002. It introduces a fairer justice system with avenues for appeal and speedy justice that are not prone to misuse or political manipulation. This has boosted the confidence of the public in the rule of law and the fairness of the judicial system.

Improving Media and Public Relations

A concerted effort has been made to improve the Army's relations with the media, so that a balanced picture of military operations is projected. The Army has its own publication *Sainik Samachar*, which is a monthly newsletter covering all aspects of the military and its interaction with the local population throughout India. It is published in several Indian languages.

To counter terrorist propaganda that usually aims to malign the conduct of the security forces, and to enable better media-military interaction to repudiate false rumors, a Public Information Directorate has been established at Army HQ. Qualified public relations officers have been posted in the forward Corps HQ as spokesmen for the Army. Media and diplomatic personnel are now encouraged to visit forward locations to see for themselves the situation in Kashmir. They are also shown captured arms, ammunition, and explosives. Proof of Pakistani involvement in terrorism is also produced in the form of captured documents and photographs. The Army has also involved the media in projecting a positive and friendly image of the security forces. Some programs highlight the sacrifices the forces make everyday in fighting terrorism and to ensure the safety and security of Kashmir and its inhabitants. The Army is also involved in using the Internet to neutralize jihadi Web sites and has its own Web site that is used to counter Islamist ideology. An Information Warfare Directorate has been established, which explores all facets of cyber security and the use of cyberspace.

Op Sadbhavna: Winning the Hearts and Minds

The Army has been actively involved in a large scale "winning the hearts and minds" campaign, called Op Sadbhavna, to improve the living conditions and educational standards of the locals by establishing schools and computer learning centers, vocational training centers, organizing health camps and medical treatment centers in far flung areas, constructing and repairing bridges and houses damaged by enemy action or by the weather, assisting in farming by providing pumps for irrigation and provision of drinking water, adopting children made orphans by terrorist violence, providing veterinary cover for farm livestock, arranging for the village seniors and children to visit various cities in India and in Kashmir to get a broader perspective of India, and offering assistance in the provision of radios, television sets, and computers.

Films and entertainment programs showing the rich cultural and religious diversity and unity of India have been a great draw and have helped in healing communal disharmony and allaying suspicion. The Army and the Air Force have always helped the locals during natural calamities such as heavy snowfalls, floods, drought, and earthquakes. Op Sadbhavna and disaster management by the Armed Forces have been a great success in changing the attitude of the people toward the security forces for the better, and in weaning the people away from supporting the terrorists.

Economic Development

The central government has infused millions of dollars to give a boost to the flagging economy of Kashmir that has been ravaged by terrorism. In particular, the central government has loaned Kashmir 100 percent of the state's budget since 1990. In November 2004, the Central government announced a reconstruction plan for Kashmir involving an outlay of approximately $5.3 billion to expand the economic infrastructure and provide basic services, imparting a thrust to employment and income generation, and providing relief and rehabilitation to the displaced families of the state. Infrastructure sectors include power generation, construction of roads, education, health, civic amenities, tourism, agriculture and food processing, and generation of employment. In addition, $1.3 billion has been earmarked to extend the existing railway network from Jammu to Srinagar in the Kashmir Valley. This will give a boost to the economy of the region and is expected to be completed by 2007. However, despite Kashmir's natural resources and potential for economic development, terrorism and instability have kept Indian business houses and foreign companies away from investing in Kashmir's economic improvement. Tourism inflow, which at one time was the mainstay of Kashmir's economy, improved slightly during the last 2 years, but terrorism and the continuing instability in the state have kept most investors away.

International Cooperation and Diplomatic Pressure

India strongly supports the United Nations Security Council resolution 1373 and has signed all 12 UN Conventions on Terrorism. It is also a signatory to the 1987 South Asia Association of Regional Cooperation Convention on Suppression of Terrorism. India participates in Joint Working Groups on Terrorism with over 15 countries, including the United States, United Kingdom, Israel, Germany, France, Canada, Russia, the European Union, and China. These focus on bilateral cooperation in criminal matters such as drug trafficking, as well as the exchange of information about terrorist groups and joint antiterrorism training, among other activities.

Diplomatic pressure has worked to some extent in convincing Pakistan's leadership to crack down on the terrorist infrastructure within the country. However, the military government in Pakistan—which receives military and economic support from the United States for its support in the war against global terrorism—also has a vested interest in supporting the insurgency and terrorism against India, and in keeping the Kashmir issue unresolved. The Pakistani terror groups have been known to maintain links with al Qaeda and other international jihad organizations, and will sooner or later pose a threat to the United States as well.[16] India has achieved only limited diplomatic success with Pakistan. The United

States has confirmed that terrorist groups on its list of "Foreign Terrorist Organizations" such as Lashkar-e-Taiba, Jaish-e-Muhammad, and Harkat ul-Mujahidin have bases in Pakistan. In addition, other terrorist groups such as Al Badr Mujhahidin, Harkat ul-Jihad-e-Islami, and the Jamat ul-Mujahidin also operate from within Pakistan.[17] However, India has failed to have Pakistan designated as a state sponsor of terrorism by the United States.

Peace Initiatives and Confidence-Building Measures with Pakistan

Several peace initiatives and confidence-building measures have being initiated by India to bring down the level of mistrust between India and Pakistan. Since November 2003, there has been a ceasefire along the LOC between the two armies, which is still holding. However, Pakistan has not yet dismantled the infrastructure of terror as it had promised to do repeatedly in January and May 2002, June 2003, and January 2004.

Both Pakistan and India have now taken a pragmatic approach to the Kashmir issue. The LOC has been transformed into a "soft border," and people-to-people contact across it has been encouraged. The Srinagar-Muzaffarabad bus service was inaugurated in April 2005, and has become a regular feature reuniting many families on either side of the LOC. Additional routes linking other towns have been planned. During the October 2005 earthquake that caused extensive damage in Pakistan Occupied Kashmir, India offered to help and opened up five crossing points along the LOC to facilitate easier movement of the affected people.

There have also been talks on Nuclear Confidence Building Measures. President Musharraf had proposed a seven-point plan for Kashmir—which includes joint control of some areas of Kashmir and demilitarization of the region—that India has considered to be unrealistic until Pakistan stops supporting terrorist groups operating against India.

Pakistani Mindset

India has also ruled out any change in the international borders of Kashmir and has suggested that the beginning of a resolution of the Kashmir issue could be made by converting the LOC into an international border. This is unacceptable to Pakistan, as President Musharraf has said that the LOC is "part of the problem and therefore cannot be the solution." President Musharraf has often stated that Kashmir runs in the "blood of every Pakistani," and that "waging a jihad is not terrorism." On several occasions he has referred to Pakistani militants and terrorists as "freedom fighters." Such remarks do little to control terrorism and the Islamist ideology of exporting terror. Pakistani complicity has also been linked to several bomb blasts that caused many deaths to innocent Indian civilians in 2005 and 2006 in Varanasi, Mumbai, Malegaon, and Ayodhya.

Dialogue with Separatist Groups

The Indian government has initiated talks with several political parties in Kashmir with the support of the state government, and allowed them to visit Pakistan for talks with Pakistani officials. India has nominated Mr. N. N. Vohra, a well-known and respected senior figure, to be its interlocutor on Kashmir. India has also offered to talk with separatist groups if they give up violence. Two roundtable meetings have been held with various groups in the past two years, though no real breakthrough has been achieved so far. Pakistan has also been more flexible in its approach, and is willing to discuss other matters in addition to Kashmir (which was previously considered the "core issue" between India and Pakistan). Under U.S. pressure, it has acted against Muslim extremists within Pakistan, but still allows terrorist training camps to function. Terrorist attacks against India from Pakistan have not stopped. Despite the peace initiatives and improved relations, a mutually acceptable resolution of the Kashmir conflict does not seem any closer than before.

CONCLUSION AND RECOMMENDATIONS

Terrorism in Kashmir has brought death and destruction to a large segment of the Kashmiri population, and adversely affected regional stability and the security of the whole of India. Since 1989, separatist violence in Kashmir has been backed by a radical Islamist ideology that aims to annex Kashmir to Pakistan and extend Islamic rule over India. Pakistan considers the issue of Kashmir as the "unfinished agenda of partition," and remains in occupation of one-third of the Indian state. It has tried to take the rest of the state by force several times in the past and failed. In 1998, both India and Pakistan acquired nuclear weapons, and the conventional military superiority India had over Pakistan has in some ways been nullified. India's resolute military response to the unsuccessful Kargil war that Pakistan initiated in May 1999 underscored the fact that India was determined to thwart any attempt to change the status quo in Kashmir. The military coup in October 1999 that put Pervez Musharraf in power saw a sudden upsurge in terrorism against India. Finally in December 2001—only months after 9/11—India's Parliament was attacked by Pakistan-backed terrorists, and India mobilized for war to punish Pakistan. Pakistan's repeated assurances that it would dismantle the terrorist infrastructure on its soil, coupled with U.S. pressure on both India and Pakistan, prevented an outbreak of a war that could have had a disastrous outcome. Both sides realized that continued hostility and acrimony was counterproductive to the peace and stability of the region. This realization led to the beginning of a comprehensive dialogue and peace process in April 2003, and the confidence-building measures that India initiated. Unfortunately, the jihadi factor and the anti-India military in Pakistan has been a hindrance to any lasting peaceful solution to Kashmir.[18]

Unless Pakistan gives up its fixation with Kashmir and returns to a democracy, the military and the ISI will continue to fuel a proxy war against India.

India has the will and the means to counter Pakistan's proxy war in Kashmir. However, the need of the hour is for a realistic negotiated settlement and a firm policy against the terrorist infrastructure in Pakistan. India must continue with good governance and the people-friendly approach in Kashmir. The practical approach could include the following:

- Pakistan must stop aiding and abetting Islamist groups on its territory and shut down all terrorist training camps on its soil.
- Both sides must accept the division of Kashmir along the LOC and convert it to an international border between India and Pakistan.[19]
- Trifurcation of Kashmir into three new states—namely Jammu, Kashmir, and Ladakh, to satisfy the disparate regions of Kashmir—each with its own government and legislature within the Union could be considered.[20]
- Continue with the peace process and the comprehensive dialogue with Pakistan and keep up the pressure against the terrorists.
- Continue with the people-friendly approach and democratic process in Kashmir.

India's multidimensional policy for fighting terrorism in Kashmir seems to be working. However, for the terrorist attacks to end and to find a just and lasting solution to the Kashmir conflict, India needs a genuine partner in a Pakistan that will first act against the terrorist infrastructure on its soil.

NOTES

1. Figures compiled from the Government of India and other sources from the media. Details of major terrorist attacks in Kashmir and in India can be viewed at http://www.satp.org. India has been fighting terrorism in the North East since 1956, in Punjab from 1981–1995, and in Kashmir soon after independence. Naxalites, a right-wing group, have resorted to domestic terrorism since the 1960s.

2. In 1846, The British made Maharaja Gulab Singh who was a minor Hindu chieftain, ruler of Jammu and Kashmir under the Treaty of Amritsar for his help in defeating the Sikh king Ranjit Singh. Gulab Singh consolidated his kingdom by annexing the Buddhist and Shiite regions of Ladakh to the east, and also advanced to the north to Gilgit. Jammu and Kashmir comprises three major regions: Jammu

in the south-west, which is predominantly Hindu, Kashmir, which is overwhelmingly Muslim and includes the fiercely contested Valley of Kashmir, and Ladakh, which is mainly Buddhist. Overall, 80 percent of the state is Muslim.

3. For a brief account of India's wars with Pakistan, see Sumit Ganguly, *Conflict Unending: India-Pakistan Tensions Since 1947* (New Delhi: Oxford University Press, 2002).

4. The operation was code-named Op Topac. See details in Rajeev Sharma, *Pak Proxy War: A Story of ISI, Bin Laden and Kargil* (New Delhi: South Asia Books, 2002).

5. See Ashley Tellis, C. Christine Fair, and Jamison Jo Medby, *Limited Conflict Under a Nuclear Umbrella: India and Pakistan Lessons from the Kargil Crisis,* (MR 1450-USCA) (Santa Monica, CA: RAND, 2001); and Ganguly, Note 3 for an account of the Kargil War.

6. Presently (July 2006) India's head of State is a Muslim, both the prime minister and the chief of the Army are Sikhs. During the 1971 war, the president and prime minister were Hindus, the chief of the Army was a Parsi Zoroastrian, the Eastern Army commander who led operations against Pakistan was a Sikh, and his chief of staff was Jewish.

7. For some of the lessons learned see, Yonah Alexander (ed.), *Combating Terrorism: Strategies of Ten Countries* (New Delhi: Manas Publications, 2003).

8. Figures compiled from Annual Reports of the Government of India, Ministry of Home Affairs 1999–2006.

9. The unclassified portion can be viewed at www. http://indianarmy.nic.in/indianarmydoctrine.htm.

10. Also see C. Christine Fair, *Urban Battle Fields of South Asia: Lessons Learnt from Sri Lanka, India, and Pakistan* (RAND Arroyo Center, 2004).

11. For a good account of India's dilemmas and inaction during this period, see Lt Gen V. K. Sood and Pravin Sawhney, *Operation Parakram War Unfinished* (New Delhi: Sage Publications, 2003).

12. See The Kargil Review Committee Report released December 15, 1999 and republished in book form, K. Subrahmanyam, *From Surprise to Reckoning* (New Delhi: Sage Publications, 2000); and the Government of India, Group of Ministers, *Reforming the National Security System: Recommendations of the Group of Ministers* (New Delhi: Government of India, February 2001). Available http://mod.nic.in/newadditions/rcontents.htm.

13. Lieutenant General (r) S. K. Sinha, Governor of Jammu and Kashmir during an address to the United Service Institution (USI) of India, New Delhi, reproduced as "Jammu and Kashmir: Past, Present and Future," *The Journal of the USI of India*, no. 560 (April –June 2005): 182–199.

14. See U.S. State Department Web site http://www.state.gov/g/drl/frl/hrrpt/2005/61707.htm; Lt Gen S. K. Sinha, Note 13 ante; and http://mod.nic.in/samchar/jan15-03/html/ch/htm. Also see Prabhu Ghate, "Kashmir, The Dirty War," *Economic and Political Weekly*, January 26, 2002: 313–322.

15. See http://nhrc.nic.in.

16. See Congressional Research Service, The Library of Congress, "Terrorism in South Asia," March 8, 2004: 11.

17. Ibid. Also see U.S. Department of State, "Pattern 5 of Global Terrorism," Year 2003 onwards.

18. See the Wilson John, "The Jihad Factor in India-Pakistan Peace Process," http://www.observerindia.com/publication/IssueBrief/Pak.pdf; Jonah Blank, "Kashmir: Fundamentalism Takes Root," *Foreign Affairs,* November–December 1999: 37–53; Yoginder Sikand, "Changing Course of Kashmiri Struggle: From National Liberation to Islamist Jihad?" *Economic and Political Weekly,* January 20, 2001: 218–227.

19. This has been mooted many times in the past by India, and it reported that the same was suggested at the Simla Agreement in 1972. Also see Jasjit Singh, "The Line of Control as Border," *World Focus*, October–December 2002.

20. See Om Hari, "Kashmir Impasse: Trifurcation is the only Way Out," *World Focus*, October–December 2002.

CHAPTER 30

COMBATING TERRORISM IN NEPAL

Thomas A. Marks

Preoccupation in the West with violent political Islam has allowed the emerging global left-wing challenge to established governments to become lost in the shuffle. Yet from Latin America to South Asia, left-wing extremism—once thought vanquished—has reared its ugly head again. No country has suffered more in this regard than the Himalayan kingdom of Nepal. In less than a decade, since the formal declaration on February 13, 1996, of "people's war" by the Communist Party of Nepal (Maoist), or CPN(M), more than 13,000 Nepalis have lost their lives, many to insurgent torture and murder.[1]

Difficult enough to grapple with on its own terms, the conflict in Nepal is further complicated by its location at a "crease" in the Global War on Terrorism (GWOT). The struggle fits neatly into none of our familiar categories, thus playing to insurgent strengths and government weakness. In the GWOT, much that we lump into the strategic category of terrorism is actually tactical use of terror by insurgency—as in Nepal. Far from being a matter of academic hair-splitting, the distinction is critical to constructing proper response.

As many scholars have observed, terrorism is propaganda by the deed, a form of political communication through violence. In contrast, insurgency is the mobilization of a counterstate with which to attack the state.[2] Insurgency always incorporates terror as a weapons system; but terrorism eschews the painstaking work of mobilizing a mass base. Counterinsurgency must incorporate counterterrorism as a campaign element. However, focusing upon this single facet to the exclusion of others guarantees a response that is neither correct nor sustainable. In fact, counterinsurgency as a term has meaning only if one considers its target, insurgency.

An armed *political* movement attempts to seize control of the state or to separate from it. Therefore, the response—counterinsurgency—must also be an armed *political* movement.

To mobilize such a response in today's global environment, though, is not nearly as straightforward a proposition as implied above. Bin Laden, to cite but the most obvious case, has an ample base of popular support worldwide. So, too, do left-wing groups. Any state response is bound to be controversial, and an array of actors are more than willing to enlist in support of the very philosophy, communism, which gave us the greatest crimes of the twentieth century.

PARAMETERS OF THE OLD REGIME

In mid-2006, negotiations between the Maoists and the restored forces of parliamentary democracy in Nepal, the Seven-Party Alliance (SPA), had reached preliminary agreement on a power-sharing arrangement. Nepal's monarchy, which had unsuccessfully sought to use more than a year of direct royal rule to deal with ever greater pressures, had been vanquished and relegated to the sidelines, together with the intact, undefeated (but sidelined nonetheless) Royal Nepal Army, or RNA (along with, to a lesser extent, the Civil Police, or CP, and paramilitary Armed Police Force, or APF). In a profound case of "déjà vu all over again," at least within the South Asian regional context, an unlikely alliance of democracy and terrorism was hatched in New Delhi and facilitated by India. The claim was that the Maoists had "developed a new maturity" and conceded that they were unable to complete their "capture of state power through the barrel of the gun." Hence, they had agreed to practice peaceful politics. The future of Nepali democracy is dependent upon the correctness of that judgment.

Known as a premier tourist destination, the site of the mighty Himalayas (the tallest being Mt. Everest), Nepal would hardly seem a candidate for what had become, halfway through the first decade of the twenty-first century, a state locked in a costly stalemate.[3] Indeed, if anything, its population was recognized not as rebels but for its loyal service as Gurkhas, perhaps the single most legendary infantry in the world. The combination, though—dominant peaks and service as infantry in foreign armies—actually goes to the heart of the matter. It is no accident that over the past nearly two centuries, a small, land-locked mountain kingdom has sent hundreds of thousands of its young men into combat for others. Indeed, Nepalese have flocked abroad not due to martial bent, rather for the oldest reason known to recruiters: need.

Far from being a Shangri-la, Nepal is home to 24 million people competing for livelihood in a country about the size of Florida (which has half as large a population). More than two-thirds of Nepal's population lives in the central belt of hills, where population densities are very high. Living conditions are among the worst in the world, according to the United Nations, because an effective lack of any industrial base means 90 percent of the population is rural, with 80 percent of the total population working directly on the land. Skewed resource distribution is further exacerbated by the top castes in the Hindu structure (*Brahmins* and *Chhetris*) controlling most positions of power and authority. Particularly unempowered are the lowest caste, the *dalits*, and the one-third of the population that is "ethnic," or tribal. Traditional out-migration has involved service as soldiers in either the British or Indian armies,[4] but this is no longer a preferred option. In any case, most job-seekers are unable to obtain external employment and so find themselves mired in poverty. Statistics show that at least 20 percent of the population lives in extreme, abject circumstances.

It would be expected that politics would play a significant role in mediating contending demands, for the country is nominally a parliamentary democracy. Yet this has not been the case. A democracy only since 1990, Nepal has suffered from the (by now, all-too-familiar) problems of the genre "emerging democracy": corruption, inefficiency, and lack of focus. Compounded by a lack of state integration, the political system has been able to foster except for a lack of legitimacy.

Thus, even as Nepal has all the organization and bureaucracy of a modern nation-state, in reality it remains a backwater. Heightened expectations that democracy could make a difference in the lives of the populace have not been met. Though there were improvements during the 1990s, particularly in the areas of health and education, these were minor bright spots in an overall dark picture of self-absorption by the major political parties. The Nepali Congress (NC) ruled for all but less than a single year of the democratic era, with the legal leftist coalition, the United Marxist-Leninists (UML), the major opposition. The monarch, who might have been expected to serve a mediating and leadership role similar to that played so effectively by King Bhumipol in Thailand, was killed in June 2001 in the so-called "Royal Massacre" (described later in this chapter) and was replaced by his brother, who, to many, lacked legitimacy.

COMMUNIST OPPOSITION TO THE OLD-REGIME

Into this dynamic, the left interjected itself early as an active player, even heading the government for slightly less than a year. Yet, as happened in Peru with the restoration of democracy in 1980, expectations and unleashed passions led to the proliferation of ever-more radical options.[5] The result, in the early 1990s, was the Communist Party of Nepal (Maoist), or CPN(M). Committed to "Gang of Four" Maoism, as had emerged during the Great Proletarian Cultural Revolution—which convulsed China with its attempt to "internalize" the dialectic—it demanded a solution to Nepal's problems by the establishment of a Maoist "people's republic." It declared "people's war" on February 13, 1996.

In implementing this approach, the CPN(M) examined the numerous "people's war" struggles which had been carried out in the post-World War II era. The two insurgencies that exercised the most influence early on were *Sendero Luminoso* (Shining Path) in Peru[6] and the so-called "Naxalites," or Indian Maoists. What both of these key influences share is that they are distinguished by their use of terror as an integral component of mass mobilization. The practical result was that the CPN(M) initially looked for inspiration to two of the more radical insurgent movements to have appeared in the heyday of post-World War II insurgency.

There is some irony in this, since the CPN(M)'s leadership, like that of both *Sendero* and the Naxalites (not to mention the Khmer Rouge, another Maoist group which adopted extreme violence), is drawn overwhelmingly from the very "class enemies" attacked by the party's doctrine. The two key figures in the Politburo, Pushba Kamal Dahal (a.k.a. "Prachanda," or "Fierce One") and Baburam Bhattarai, for instance, are both *Brahmins* with educational backgrounds. Followers, as might be expected, are drawn from altogether different strata, the marginalized of society, those who become the so-called "grievance guerrillas." That the CPN(M) has had little difficulty tapping such individuals stems from the abundance of socioeconomic-political contradictions compounded by issues of gender. Women have been prominent in the recruiting profile.

Organizationally, there was nothing unexpected in the CPN(M)'s approach. In areas they seized, the Maoists laid their own radical alternative upon the existing regime structure. By the close of the first 5 years of conflict, the government's presence in the six districts of Mid-Western hills was limited to only the district capitals, with the Maoists effectively providing the ruling structure. The heartland of the early Maoist position was the area straddling either side of the border between the districts of Rolpa and Rukkum in the Mid-Western Region. There, Kham Magars responded to CPN(M) guidance and became guerrillas generally supported by the population.[7] Further expansion proved more difficult and the level of popular involvement was commensurately lower, the role of terror higher. Available figures on CPN(M) strength did not inspire confidence, but government estimates provided in early 2003 seemed reasonable: 5,500 combatants; 8,000 militia; 4,500 cadre; 33,000 hard-core followers; and 200,000 sympathizers.

The Maoists were thus able to dominate the districts in the Mid-Western Region and use them as base areas. In the absence of external input—as provided, for instance, by drugs in the cases of FARC in Colombia and *Sendero Luminoso* in Peru—CPN(M) was forced to rely upon the more traditional but limited insurgent methodology of criminal activity for generating funds (in aggregate, perhaps several million US dollars per year), especially bank-robbing, kidnapping-for-ransom, and extortion. These activities, though they could at times produce windfalls, were not able to meet the demands of rapid expansion.

Neither could external links make up shortfalls, since the allied movements of the "Coordination Committee of Maoist Parties and Organizations of South Asia" (CCOMPOSA)—created in July 2001 after a meeting of nine South Asian Maoist parties in West Bengal—were actually in an inferior position logistically to their Nepalese compatriots. These stark realities left the movement with a character, in many areas, as much *jacquerie* peasant revolt as disciplined insurgency.

DYNAMICS OF "PEOPLE'S WAR"

Progress of the insurgency was steady but more a product of government lack of capacity than insurgent power. Their methodology was predictable and mirrored that of other insurgent movements following the people's war approach. While "winning the hearts and minds" was important in the base areas, terror was indispensable for expansion into contested populations. This was supplemented by guerrilla action and ultimately, with the launching of the November 2001 general offensive, the mobile warfare (or main force) phase.

The lynchpin of the Maoist effort was its drive to neutralize the state. District and Village Development Committee (VDC) offices (75 and 3,913, respectively), for example, were systematically razed, their records and equipment destroyed. Post offices were eliminated. All other elements of the state likewise found themselves attacked. Roads were cut; bridges, dams and hydropower facilities, aqueducts, telephone towers and electric lines, airport control towers were systematically destroyed. Such action was the essence of the approach of *Sendero Luminoso*. Not surprisingly, the CPN(M) blueprint for anticipated societal transformation was contained in the thoughts and dictums of the leader, "Prachanda Path," a deliberate echoing of *Sendero*'s "Gonzalo Path" ("President Gonzalo" was party leader Abimael Guzman Reynoso).

Though the campaign was rural-based, urban action was not eschewed. Just as *Sendero* eventually extended its campaign into urban spaces, so did the CPN(M). Of course, urban spaces were limited in Nepal, so the main targets were the three most important cities and their surrounding productive lands: Kathmandu, the capital; Pokhara, to the west, on the doorstep of the Mid-Western Region; and Nepalgunj, on the Indian border. In these cities, united front activity of the CPN(M)'s United Revolutionary People's Council (URPC) was most important, supplemented by a terror campaign of bombings and assassinations initiated in Kathmandu in August 2002.

Even as terror forced society in upon itself, the principal target of guerrilla action was the 46,500-man national police force—the first line of armed defense, since Nepal possessed no local forces of any kind. An essentially unarmed "watcher" force, two-thirds of whom carried nothing heavier than a patrol stick, the Civil Police were quite unprepared for the demands of counterinsurgency. Emergency response units, typically armed with the 1941 version of the 303 Lee Enfield (a bolt-action rifle), were likewise found lacking.

Patrols sent to the scenes of incidents were ambushed, while numerous small police stations were overrun, attacked in the dead of night in assaults initiated with homemade explosives, then overwhelmed by human wave assaults. Efforts to stand up a more properly armed and equipped police field force, Armed Police Force (APF, with approximately 25,000 men), made slow progress under the pressure of operational demands. By January 2003, the Civil Police and Armed Police Force together had suffered some 1,300 dead. (In contrast, a total of 850 civilians were listed as having been killed.)

Predictably, the only possible police response was to abandon outlying stations and consolidate in defensible mass. In the hills—where terrain, lack of communication, and difficulty of movement favored the guerrillas—this process of withdrawal was inexorable across the entire breadth of the country. By early 2003, half of all police stations nationwide had been abandoned. Such was the lack of national integration that once the police presence was eliminated, the insurgents became the state. All that remained to serve as a reminder of far-off Kathmandu were the minor functionaries (e.g., teachers, postmen, and VDC personnel) who could not flee lest they should lose their meager salaries.

The critical insurgent component at the local level, of course, was the CPN(M) cadre. These were of remarkably uneven quality and presence. It would be expected that the level of ideological knowledge would be low among movement "followers," but this generally has proved the case for the cadre, as well. Participation in the movement resulted from a variety of local and personal factors, and cadre generally did their best to reproduce the procedures and symbology of the movement. But outside the core areas, they held sway only through terror, through their ability to call upon guerrilla formations to act as enforcers.

This reality revealed a peculiarity observed by virtually all observers: the dependence of the Maoist main force campaign upon tribal manpower, especially Magars. That guerrilla formations at this time were dominated numerically by Magars stemmed from the ethnic composition of the core areas in which the Maoists had long worked, such as the Rukkum-Rolpa border corridor. That entire tribal communities would become involved in the insurgency was predictable once government miscues allowed the CPN(M) to tap the self-defense dynamic.

If this dynamic fingered the CPN(M), in a sense, as a tribal revolt, a different process was at work in more mixed areas. Here, cadre were the movement, and they, as indicated, were a product of local realities and thus of mixed ethnic and class composition. Though they did participate directly in terror actions, especially in villages targeted for movement expansion, within their own areas of responsibility, they were more likely to call upon outsiders, often the guerrillas.

These guerrillas, who initially were formed in small units, eventually (certainly by early 2003) were overwhelmingly assigned to main force units, battalion facsimiles of 400–600 men each. Later, copying government forms of organizing forces, brigades and even divisions were added. Their weaponry was similar to that possessed by the Nepalese government, with older types dominating. These were primarily captured pieces and those bought on the black market using looted funds. For training, ex-servicemen were both coerced and hired.

Even if terror was not the most salient issue in the minds of villagers, contact between them and the guerrillas was a recurring factor in life, since the combatants were dependent upon the villagers for the necessities of life. All movement, for instance, occurred through the preparation of caches of necessities, ranging from food and water to firewood, and such activity occurred through orders issued to villagers by the cadre at the behest of the guerrilla chain-of-command. Similarly, mandatory attendance by villagers at political rallies was enforced by the combatants, with the cadre issuing the orders and fingering those who resisted or malingered. The end product was a high level of popular fear but an inability to do anything save reach accommodation—unless flight was adopted as a course of action. As the conflict wore on—and kidnapping of the young became ever more prominent in Maoist recruiting—a growing number of villagers appeared to be opt for this choice.

SYSTEMIC RESPONSE TO THE MAOIST CHALLENGE

Only with the November 2001 general offensive by the Maoists did Nepal take the necessary step of reinforcing the overwhelmed police force by committing the 54,000 troops of the Royal Nepalese Army (RNA) and passing antiterrorism legislation. Spread throughout areas of the country that could be reached by road, quartered in battalion (but more often company) cantonments, the RNA was a largely ceremonial force better known for its contribution to United Nations peacekeeping missions than for martial prowess. The result was a number of serious reverses, as the RNA went through the painful transformation required for dealing with guerrilla warfare.[8]

Faced with the Maoist campaign, the Nepalese state reeled.[9] Though the number of dead was not as severe as that of many other insurgencies, they were concentrated in the relatively short period following November 2001 and produced a powerful shock. Democracy effectively collapsed and the kingdom was ruled by prime ministers appointed by the monarch. Even as the RNA expanded to some 75 battalions (and approximately 80,000 men), the government's response was hampered by political shortcomings. Not only did governments change regularly, self-interest was the order of the day among the marginalized political forces, illustrated by rampant corruption and policy drift. Consequently, even substantial foreign development assistance was not incorporated in a systematic manner.

One advantage for the state was that numerous individuals, both civilians and security force, had served abroad with the United Nations in peacekeeping situations. Thus they were well-versed in the "hearts and minds" approach to internal pacification as opposed to pure repression. Approximately a year before the Maoist general offensive, the RNA was deployed in limited fashion in support of the government's Integrated Security and Development Programme (ISDP), a "hearts and minds"-driven area domination effort. With the November 2001 offensive, the ISDP was suspended and the RNA deployed to engage in area domination.

A critical weakness in the government's approach was intelligence, the essential element of any counterinsurgency effort. Nepal's various sources for information-gathering and processing—the police, Armed Police Force, RNA, and National Investigation Department (NID)—were quite unprepared for the demands of internal war and generally deficient in both information gathering and intelligence production/dissemination. Exacerbating the situation, these bodies functioned as separate entities with little coordination or data sharing. Only at the very highest levels of the bureaucracy was raw input brought together for analysis, but this, too, was provided for in an ad hoc and undermanned fashion.

Still, dramatic strides were made in standing up the command and control architecture necessary for counterinsurgency. At the cutting edge, especially in the districts, coordinating committees—comprising the local police, RNA, civil, and intelligence representatives—met to determine policy and implementation. A unified command, with the RNA having authority over all elements of the armed response, eventually came into existence, giving fiber to the ad hoc but functioning coordination cells that had been formed at RNA headquarters. APF platoons were deployed as if they were "light" RNA units, and the police were given primacy in the defense of most urban areas.

Where difficulties occurred was in overcoming the substantial baggage of past political conflicts: in particular, none of the security forces worked well together, and the government bureaucracy saw the conflict as something quite outside its mandate. A highly centralized decision-making machinery meant that even the best of motives could often not overcome bureaucratic inertia or implement decisions when they were forthcoming. Foreign support hence became crucial in efforts to address these flaws. Britain, as might be expected from its long and deep involvement in Nepal, played an important role in providing training of all sorts. India, concerned lest it should see another security headache develop on a crucial border (Nepal is considered a buffer between New Delhi and Beijing), responded initially with training and material support, eventually moving vigorously to suppress substantial Maoist activity within India's own borders. Ironically, China, having moved in its foreign policy beyond supporting "Maoist insurgents," also provided equipment.

The United States, which long had been a major development actor through its USAID, moved vigorously in all areas from supplying arms and equipment to training. An emergency appropriation brought the combined military aid (Foreign Military Financing) for Fiscal Years 2002 and 2003 (FY02/FY03) to US $17 million. Assessment teams from the United States, Britain, and India were supplemented by personnel for actual training, to include US special operations personnel. Eventually, the United States equipped and partially trained a highly effective Ranger battalion.

Where no amount of foreign input could compensate, though, was in overcoming the shortfalls of a traditional system, which organizationally manifested themselves in extreme deference to authority and a consequent lack of initiative. Combined with the intelligence shortcomings cited above, this resulted in a failure to come to grips with the struggle operationally and tactically—even as a general strategic grasp of overall parameters could be judged reasonably accurate. While it was understood with considerable clarity how socioeconomic-political shortcomings had produced the insurgency, a proper response seemed largely elusive. Above all else, there was no mobilization of the people into a structure of self-defense. Thus insurgent terror had maximum effect because it allowed the mobilization of the Maoist counter-state to proceed virtually unchecked. Consequently, a comparatively weak insurgent movement, which drew its combatant strength from minimally armed tribal revolt and could expand beyond core regions mainly through terror, was allowed to go unchecked for want of application of any systematic counterforce.[10]

No event was more critical than the "Royal Massacre" of June 2001.[11] The Crown Prince, angry at his parents' position toward his significant other, gunned down his entire family, then turned a weapon upon himself. Birendra, the deceased monarch, was followed by his less-popular brother, Gyanendra. The latter's missteps saw democracy increasingly marginalized, with direct royal rule instituted in February 2005 (in effect, martial law—controversial, but arguably legal). In a process that could only call forth echoes of Ferdinand Marcos, the royal decision was initially welcomed but became ever more controversial as it was judged corrupt, ineffective, and overbearing. The Maoists made opposition to the monarch a salient theme of their propaganda.

By November 2005, a 12-point letter of understanding emerged between the Maoists and the principal legal parliamentary opposition, the Seven-Party Alliance (SPA). The latter claimed they had cut a deal with the Maoists, whereby the insurgents had agreed to give up armed struggle in favor of participation in a republican scheme of parliamentary democracy. Astonishing on its face, the deal was hatched in New Delhi and facilitated by India, which saw a desperate need to "manage" events spiraling beyond its control, even as its own Maoist problem produced an increasing number of casualties (in the first quarter of 2006, more than the running sore that was Jammu and Kashmir).[12]

Only knowledge of SPA's long battle with the monarchy, combined with India's inability to give up playing the Great Game at the expense of its democratic neighbors, could make such a situation comprehensible to an outsider. There followed classic united front action by the Maoists, with massive SPA demonstrations in major urban centers, especially the capital, even as the Maoists attacked in other areas and infiltrated operatives into the demonstrations in an effort to provoke violence. International NGOs and even some foreign official elements actively sided with the demonstrators, as did key segments of the Nepali press, thus bringing into play the same type of *netwar* seen earlier in Chiapas during the Zapatista uprising.[13] In the end, isolated and cut off from its foreign sources of supply, the regime capitulated and restored the dismissed parliament. The negotiations mentioned earlier in this text were occurring as the volume went to press.

EXPLAINING PRACHANDA

In people's war terms, what has occurred in Nepal is textbook. In waging insurgency, all Maoist movements have before them a "play book" of five major campaigns:

- *Mass line*—functioning as a political party.
- *United front*—getting others to share tactical and operational actions even while perhaps disagreeing strategically (which normally means ideologically).
- *Violence*—fielded in different forms, from terror to guerrilla to main force warfare, but always used to facilitate political action.
- *Political warfare*—using nonviolent means (such as talks) to facilitate violence.
- *International action*—using international substate and state actors to apply pressure in such manner as to advance the internal struggle.

Any Maoist movement weights these elements, moving back and forth among them. The Nepali Maoists certainly do. In claiming they have examined their mistakes, what the Maoists mean is that they recognize militarism has brought them to an impasse. The essence of an earlier debate within the CPN(M) leadership—between number one, Prachanda, and number two, Bhattarai—was over just this issue: whether military action (violence) must lead, or if the path can be forged by any of the other (four) campaign elements above. Obviously, by late 2005, the correlation of forces strategically told a good Maoist to shift gears, to use *violence* not in the lead but to support the mass line, the united front, political warfare, and international action as the leading elements. Each of these four elements are described below.

Mass Line

The Maoists had consolidated a political base in the west. It had been achieved by armed political action. Terror, always important, could give way to *menace*. The base areas were consolidated relatively quickly and at acceptable cost. Yet the Maoists found it increasingly tough going to do anything decisive strategically decisive from those base areas.

United Front

The events of February 2005, when the king took over direct rule, provided the chance for a strategically decisive shift by delivering the political parties into Maoist hands. That the political parties were making a "mistake" was quite irrelevant to the fact that the mistake was made. A combination of "ceaseless waves" of protest inside with armed action outside, all held together by dramatically enhanced use of terror against the state and security forces (especially through Improvised Explosive Devices, IEDs, and unconventional actions) was seen as an unbeatable combination.

The most significant element in Prachanda's various statements was his advancing the next step in the united front process: his proposal that the political parties jointly form an army with the Maoists, sharing all positions and authority. He further proposed that democratic elements within the RNA join with the Maoists and the parties. He raised the question as to who controlled whom, monarch or RNA. The bottom line was the same: the Maoists recognized that the RNA was the lynchpin. If it could be neutralized, the game was over.

Political Warfare

Here again, circumstances delivered up to the Maoists a blue-chip item, "peace." The longing for peace was so great that Maoist propaganda built around the "peace now" theme undermined the *will* of all concerned to continue the struggle. It mattered not one bit that "peace" meant nothing tangible, neither did it matter that the Maoists had created the situation they were exploiting, or that the political parties of SPA were the very ones who had enabled Maoist progress by inept, corrupt administration. The longing for "peace" could be used at all levels of war (strategic, operational, and tactical) to neutralize the *ability* of the government to continue.

International

What the Maoists saw was a global situation where the trends were in their favor. Even those opposed to their dated, left-wing Fascist views were unwilling to grapple with the situation due to their preoccupation with *Islamofascism* (which the Nepalese Maoists claimed to support). As the CPN(M) saw it, everything was flowing its way. At least in part, the party declared its several earlier ceasefires as gambits to see if it could neutralize government armed action. This did not happen, but strategically the government in each case took a black eye as the entity that "wouldn't give peace a chance." That the Maoists used the ceasefires in each case to prepare for operations was known, most particularly by international non-governmental organizations and certain foreign embassies. India, as the prime offender, decided that playing its usual version of "the Great Game" was preferable to supporting the Kathmandu government. New Delhi was not totally committed negatively, but it made a calculation that it could contain the Nepali situation by fostering a "West Bengal solution" (i.e., legal Maoists participating in democratic governance).

POST-COLD WAR INSURGENCY

It is useful to place this Maoist effort within the global context, since "everything has changed" is a common refrain in US strategic literature of the GWOT. Insurgency, to fall back upon a useful definition advanced by Larry Cable, is "the armed expression of organic disaffiliation."[14] Insurgencies have traditionally taken place within nation-states. Yet a series of shifts in the post-Cold War world has dramatically affected most, if not all, insurgencies in subtle ways relevant to our discussion.

First, the end of generalized state support has left insurgent movements struggling financially and logistically to ensure that supply meets demand in the actual making of internal war. Movements that continue to enjoy external largess are a minority. Self-sustaining insurgencies have become potent only to the extent they have been able to tap sources (of support) *external to the target population.* Those movements that have not found such sources normally have remained weak (e.g., the CPP Maoists in the Philippines, or the various Maoist movements in India). There are always exceptions, where unique circumstances alter the playing field. This is what we see in Nepal. There, India's actions against the present Nepali state have been an important factor in making both the political opposition and the Maoists more powerful than objective circumstances would predict.

Second, this reality accounts for the present very mixed character of so many movements. In the past, external assistance provided ideologically and operationally viable movements with the critical margin that allowed focus upon ideological ends. Now, insurgencies must devote extraordinary amounts of time to criminal activity. This has created the "gang-like" behavior so typical of many movements, such as the Nepalese Maoists. The challenge for insurgents: how to squeeze blood from the turnip? What the state terms extortion and kidnapping, a group such as the Nepali Maoists calls "revolutionary taxation." A small shopkeeper in the hills, for instance, will be taxed NR 50 per month (less than US $1), a salaried teacher NR 200 (less than US $3). But kidnapping these same individuals and getting their families to come up with their life's savings will produce a ransom of NR 30,000 (about US $400). Demands from urban businesses or infrastructure development projects (funded from abroad) are much higher. Robbing banks produces still more. Crime does pay.

Third, at issue remains the question of *balance*. Engaging in criminal behavior has never been atypical of insurgencies; the behavior merely has been kept subordinate to larger ends. A movement which effectively turns its back upon its target population, which becomes mainly or wholly a criminal enterprise, is no longer an insurgency. The CPN(M) has not reached this point, but in certain areas it has come dangerously close.

Fourth, just as the relationship between various insurgent movements and their mass base has shifted, so the "negotiated" quality of many movements has changed. The implicit bargain reached—between the ideological designs of leadership and the "solve my grievances" demands of followers—has been altered. The result is an absence of the "checks and balances" provided by Mao's imperative of "the fish to swim in the sea." The scales have been tipped dramatically in favor of the leaders. Their insurgencies consequently are able to function far more as alternative, violent political organizations *in being* rather than as armed protest movements. We see this prominently in the present character of the CPN(M). The combatants and the mass base know little about Maoism (one could argue that this includes district level cadre). Yet it is Maoism that animates the strategy and plans of the upper leadership. They simply deny that such an ideology has produced tragedy throughout history. They claim that communism in Nepal will work out differently, that all Nepal's problems will be solved in the new order. Such assurances have thus far proved sufficient to keep mobilized the "grievance guerrillas" who are the party's critical element.

Fifth, extreme voluntarism, therefore, has become not the exception but the norm in insurgencies worldwide. To the extent that particular socioeconomic-political circumstances allow *foco*-like behavior to mobilize a following, there is the appearance of insurgent strength. Where such conditions are absent, terror has been used with increasing frequency to propel movements along. It is terror that has been essential to the Maoist mass mobilization effort in Nepal, with kidnapping of the young the key element at present.[15] One point must be highlighted here: The issue in insurgency is never the use of terror—*terror is integral to insurgency.* For the insurgent, the primary issue is one of balancing its use within a larger political framework.

THE GOVERNMENT'S CURRENT SITUATION

Where does all this leave Nepal? The conflict is now at a turning point. From the insurgent standpoint, united fronts are always a preferable way of waging people's war, because they are less dangerous for the movement. No one in the Maoist movement wants to die (as opposed to *Salafist* fanatics seeking Paradise). As to how matters will play themselves out, the chaos that has accompanied the present negotiations bears witness to how effective united fronts can be—the system dies the death of the thousand cuts.

As always, the task at hand is to discern insurgent intentions, even as they agree to become part of the interim government.[16] The Maoists are portraying themselves as having had a change of heart. That is not true. They have simply chosen to lead with a different combination of punches, to use a boxing metaphor. They see violence and nonviolence as complementary, just as the Provisional Irish Republican Army (PIRA) did in its famous maxim that it would fight with a ballot in one hand, an *Armalite* (rifle) in the other. It may be recalled that when the PIRA moved to emphasize the ballot, the question was whether the shift was "real." The intelligence on this matter was very mixed. On the one hand, significant steps were taken that indicated a PIRA willingness to participate peacefully in politics. On the other hand, there were serious actions that demonstrated the armed option was not being foreclosed (such as working with FARC in Colombia).

In the end, the strength of the state and the willingness of the PIRA insurgents to reintegrate produced a tenuous peace. Neither of those factors is present in the Nepali case. To the contrary, in the Irish case, "reintegration" was the end-state. In Nepal, the Maoists see themselves as offering the terms of surrender. Though the Maoists claim they are willing to accept the outcome of a vote on the future shape of the system, they refuse to allow political action that would create a level playing field. Instead, as the *Sandinistas* did in Nicaragua, they disingenuously assert—having altered the playing field and gained armed control of the areas that will produce the vote—they will allow "peaceful measures" to hold sway.

Though the Maoists claim they will participate in the system if they lose a referendum on its future shape, there are two critical sticking points that make it unlikely such will happen. First, it does not appear that even the Maoist leadership could simply order the local elements of the movement to "go back inside the system." Second, all Maoist internal discourse is predicated upon a belief that the present united front line of operation will deliver victory at less cost than the alternative, "violence leads," course. It is most unlikely that a campaign setback (i.e., defeat in the united front effort) would lead to renunciation of the strategic approach (people's war), because the other campaign elements offer ways to continue the struggle. The movement, in other words, is currently on Maoist auto-pilot: its strategy has not changed, only emphasized a different campaign element (or "weapons system," if you like). Violence and nonviolence are still just two sides of the same coin.

What should be obvious is that Nepali counterinsurgency strategy also should have been an armed political movement, a blend of the violent and the nonviolent. This was recognized by many security force personnel but they were unable to prevail upon their superiors.[17] In the view of the former, the security forces needed to be the shield for *reform and counter-mobilization*. Counterterrorism would be an important element, but should have been only one campaign among many in a comprehensive approach that addressed the roots of conflict and created good governance.

ACKNOWLEDGMENTS

The views expressed in this chapter are those of the author and do not reflect the official policy or position of the National Defense University, the Department of Defense, or the US Government.

NOTES

1. For an earlier discussion, see Thomas A. Marks, *Insurgency in Nepal* (Carlisle, PA: Army War College, 2003).

2. "Terror," as a term, needs little elaboration, but the present use of "terrorism" as a virtual synonym for "nastiness" obscures the essentials that distinguish a terrorist group from an insurgent body: the inversion undergone by the former in categories of reference so that there remain no essential connections with the purported mass base. Terror, then, for the terrorist, becomes both tactic and strategy, both goal and means. It determines even operational art. For the insurgent, in contrast, terror is more instrumental, a tactic for furthering the construction of an alternate polity. See Michel Wieviorka, "Terrorism in the Context of Academic Research," in *Terrorism in Context*, ed. Martha Crenshaw (University Park, PA: The Pennsylvania State University Press, 1995) 597–606. For Wieviorka's seminal work,

see *The Making of Terrorism*, trans. David Gordon White (Chicago, IL: The University of Chicago Press, 1993).

3. For a general history, see John Whelpton, *A History of Nepal* (New York: Cambridge, 2005).

4. The United Kingdom establishment has been run down to just two infantry battalions and limited support units, with another battalion-equivalent (3 rifle companies) assigned to round-out under-strength British infantry battalions. Brunei, where one of the two UK battalions is based on a rotational basis, has two Gurkha battalions of its own, though they apparently have declined in strength after agitation concerning pay and allowances. Manpower for these two battalions comes from prior-service British Gurkhas who are recruited upon separation from UK service. Singapore Police has a Gurkha battalion that is recruited as part of the normal British scheme. India apparently has at least 42 battalions of Gurkha infantry (one-eighth of its infantry manpower) and some 10–12 battalions of other formations, such as Assam Rifles, which, though not nominally "Gurkha," are in fact manned by them. At an May 11, 2003, presentation in Kathmandu, Major (Ret) Deepak Gurung presented figures which placed 35,000 Nepalese in the Indian Army, with over 115,000 receiving pensions, and 3,500 men in the British establishment, with 26,000 receiving pensions. If the number of "other formations" is included, it would appear that the number of Nepali citizens serving in the Indian armed and paramilitary forces is possibly as high as 50,000. For origins of the Gurkha tradition, see A.P. Coleman, *A Special Corps: The Beginnings of Gorkha Service With the British* (Cambridge: Pentland, 1999). Particularly revealing in its discussion of Gurkha strategic influence is Raffi Gregorian, *The British Army, the Gurkhas and Cold War Strategy in the Far East, 1947–1954* (New York: Palgrave, 2002). Especially useful for its insights is Lionel Caplan, *Warrior Gentlemen: "Gurkhas" in the Western Imagination* (Oxford: Berghahn Books, 1995).

5. A noteworthy effort to explore the relationship between structure and agency in the Nepali conflict is Bishnu Raj Upreti, *The Price of Neglect: From Resource Conflict to Maoist Insurgency in the Himalayan Kingdom* (Kathmandu: Bhrikuti Academic Publications, 2004). A complementary effort is Bishnu Pathak, *Politics of People's War and Human Rights in Nepal* (Kathmandu: BIMIPA, 2005). For the Maoist analysis of the problem, written by the penultimate figure in the movement, see Baburam Bhattarai, *The Nature of Underdevelopment and Regional Structure of Nepal: A Marxist Analysis* (Delhi: Adroit, 2003).

6. See the chapter by David Scott Palmer in this volume.

7. See especially Anne de Sales, "The Kham Magar Country: Between Ethnic Claims and Maoism," in *Resistance and the State: Nepalese Experiences*, ed. David N. Gellner (New Delhi: Social Science Press, 2003) 326–357. It is useful to compare her findings to my own work in the Hmong areas of Northern Thailand that were mobilized by the Maoist insurgency there. See Thomas A. Marks, "The Meo Hill Tribe Problem in North Thailand," *Asian Survey* XIII, no. 10 (October 1973): 929–944; as well as appropriate sections in my *Making Revolution: The Communist Party of Thailand in Structural Perspective* (Bangkok: White Lotus, 1994). More recent work I have done inside Laos among Hmong messianic insurgents explores many of the same issues. Among a number of possibilities, see esp. Tom Marks, "Guerrillas in the Mist: Hmong Resistance Continues in Laos," *Combat and Survival* 8, no. 5 (August 1996): 4–11 (w/ photos by author).

8. Virtually no analytical work exists on RNA. Single best source is Prakesh Nepali and Phanindra Subba [pseudonyms], "Civil-Military Relations and the Maoist Insurgency in Nepal," *Small Wars and Insurgencies* 16, no. 1 (March 2005): 83–100. Not as complete but widely available is Ashok K. Mehta, *The Royal Nepal Army: Meeting the Maoist Challenge* (New Delhi: Rupa, 2005).

9. Useful for the period under discussion is Deepak Thapa, ed., *Understanding the Maoist Movement of Nepal* (Kathmandu: Chautari, 2003). See also the earlier work by Thapa, "The Maobadi of Nepal," in *State of Nepal*, eds. Kanak Mani Dixit and Shastri Ramachandaran (Kathmandu: Himal, 2002) 77–99; as well as the appropriate chapters Gellner, ed., *Resistance and the State: Nepalese Experiences.*

10. Best single volume discussion of the Maoist movement is the now dated but still indispensable Michael Hutt, ed., *Himalayan People's War: Nepal's Maoist Rebellion* (Bloomington, IN: Indiana University Press, 2004). A complementary effort is Arjun Karki and David Seddon, eds., *The People's War in Nepal: Left Perspectives* (Delhi: Adroit, 2003).

11. A number of works are available. Among the best, despite its drift at times into conspiracy theory, is Aditya Man Shrestha, *The Dreadful Night: Carnage at Nepalese Royal Palace* (Kathmandu: Ekta, 2001).

12. For assessment by an Indian specialist apparently consulted in this effort, see S.D. Muni, *Maoist Insurgency in Nepal: The Challenge and the Response* (New Delhi: Rupa, 2003).

13. A particularly useful recent contribution is Thomas Olesen, *International Zapatismo: The Construction of Solidarity in the Age of Globalization* (London: Zed, 2005).

14. This insightful definition was coined by Larry Cable; see his "Reinventing the Round Wheel: Insurgency, Counter-Insurgency, and Peacekeeping Post Cold War," *Small Wars and Insurgencies* 4, no. 2 (Autumn 1993): 228–262.

15.. It is significant that this kidnapping—the ultimate obscenity, seizing the young—has been all but ignored by international human rights organizations.

16. Bhattarai, in particular, has taken me to task (in Nepali) for misstating Maoist intentions. I think the point is rather that I have accurately rendered just what the Maoists say to themselves and to the public. We only differ in that they claim what they say represents the legitimate forces of history.

17. Police understanding of the conflict was surprisingly astute. For one work, by a fairly senior officer, see Chuda Bahadur Shrestha, *Nepal: Coping With Maoist Insurgency* (Kathmandu: Nepal Lithographing, 2004).

CHAPTER 31

JAPAN AND AUM SHINRIKYO

James M. Smith

The case of Aum Shinrikyo ("Supreme Truth," referred to generally here as Aum), a Japanese "new religion" and cult that also embraced and practiced chemical and biological terrorism, and of the restrained and delayed Japanese government response, provides significant lessons for those seeking to better understand and respond to terrorism—domestic, religion-based terrorism, and weapons of mass destruction (WMD) terrorism. While Aum has never risen to the level of any realistic threat to Japanese governmental order or national survival, it did cause a notable level of mass injury and disruption, and it did in fact employ—with little or limited effect in most cases—both biological and chemical weapons as its tactic of choice. The Aum case also demonstrates the utility to terrorism of "sanctuary under national law," and of the acquisition of chemical and biological materials and production equipment under the sanctuary of legitimate business operations. And this case raises issues of—and consequences from—governmental restraint and the persistent challenge of balancing civil liberties and national security. Finally, as described in this chapter, the case of Aum Shinrikyo also illustrates the utility of a culturally based analytical framework in examining terrorist groups and political violence, terrorist decisions and actions regarding WMD acquisition and use, and government response options, and constraints.

This chapter first examines Aum Shinrikyo within the specific context of post-World War II Japan. It does so from a strategic, culturally based analytical framework tailored to the WMD acquisition and use decisions and actions of violent nonstate actors. It then addresses the Japanese government's decisions and actions in response to Aum and its terrorist attacks from a similar cultural lens tailored to Japan. Finally, it suggests lessons learned from this case and its cultural analysis specifically for Japan and Aum, and for WMD terrorism in general. It begins by setting Aum and its resort to WMD terrorism firmly within the context of modern Japanese history and culture.

AUM SHINRIKYO

This chapter applies a tailored, strategic, culturally based framework in analyzing Aum Shinrikyo and its employment of WMD terrorism.[1] It begins with an examination of Aum as both a new religion and political/economic entity employing violence to further its distinct agenda. The strategic analysis of its internal cult and terrorist core provides insight into the identity and belief structure of the group, its rationale for resorting to political violence, and its perspective on the legitimacy and optimal utility of WMD terrorism. This analysis thus provides the foundation for examining the group's organizational, human, technical, and operational dynamics, and its ultimate employment of terror using WMD.

Aum Roots in Japanese History and Culture

Aum Shinrikyo as a religion, cult, and terrorist group, and the Japanese governmental responses to its activities and attacks, are all solidly rooted in distinct elements of Japanese tradition as affected by World War II, its climax, and aftermath. The Japanese responses to Western technological superiority—particularly military technologies—as they played into and across the War, and also the realities of Hiroshima and Nagasaki and of the vast changes in Japanese society following the War, combined to create the context within which Aum grew and operated.

Modern Japanese attempts to remain insolated from Western influence were dashed with the forced "opening" at the hands of armed Western fleets, but Japan did manage to maintain a level of insulation from Western domination. The major impact and legacy from the opening was not the supremacy of Western values, but was primarily a recognition of Western technological superiority and military might derived from technology. The Japanese reaction then was to adopt and adapt selected military technologies while maintaining the traditional Japanese system and values.

This technology was applied in the military campaigns of World War II with mixed success. One noteworthy outcome often undervalued or even overlooked in the West is the Japanese preeminence in Asia throughout the war, which is a source of quiet pride to the Japanese and a source of continuing animosity among those whom the Japanese invaded. Technology was the vehicle to regional superiority and is seen as the key to strength for many Japanese to this day. Only the United States' sustained industrial capacity and its atomic technology could overcome Japanese technology and strength. And even the atomic bomb that caused so much death and destruction in Japan is sometimes viewed with respect beneath outward fears.

The period following the war was pivotal in forming today's Japan, with its many strengths but also its weaknesses, from which societal dislocation and terrorism have found root. Japan literally rose from the atomic ashes of Hiroshima and Nagasaki, and also from the fire bomb ashes of the raids on Tokyo and elsewhere. More was destroyed than the physical cities. Much of the Japanese tradition was seen as having precipitated militarism, and the combined impact of both Japanese-initiated changes and those imposed by the Western occupation authorities was to create a very different Japan. The extent and depth of the changes in Japanese society—from urbanization and industrialization to shifting family patterns and demographics—are chronicled elsewhere;[2] however, the net effect as relevant to this discussion has been termed "psychohistorical dislocation,"[3] where "the disaster of defeat . . . discredited all traditional authorities and values."[4] The results included a loss of confidence in traditional authorities, a generational stratification, new and stovepiped hierarchies around school and job, and a fractured society.

Japan had traditionally been organized according to a "vertical principle" that ordered all behaviors and relationships and was based in the core family group.[5] With the destruction of so much of the social and economic infrastructure due to the war, the progression of vertical structures for the new, urban, industrial Japan soon became family only for youth, followed by educational institution for young adults, and employer after graduation. When isolated from family and village within the new urban environment, the company becomes the "whole social existence of a person, and has authority over all aspects of his life."[6] So the progression of gaining entry into the "right" university as a stepping stone to employment with the "right" company became absolutely central to the young person's entire future. Social status was dependent on "making" this series of "gates," and failure at any level would leave the individual lost and adrift with no anchoring identity or structure. The "vertical principle" dictated societal structure and dynamics.

In such a vertically ordered society, the individual takes his identity from an institutional unit (family/school/company). That institutional identity subjugates individualism and becomes the "whole social existence of a person, and has authority over all aspects of his life."[7] The individual, "completely enveloped" within the group, attaches to a single loyalty—substantive and emotional—and displays very little individualism or autonomy. Group membership is the sole source of status and prestige. So even if you are at the bottom of the group hierarchy, the status derived from group membership places you above all outsiders. The social order is anchored in the group; a collective "us" versus all external "thems."

Within the group there is a small functional, superior core with a tiered hierarchy for all others. Across the tiers of this rigid, internal stratification there is a single, shared group loyalty. A top-down consensus is forged, and all agree and act accordingly. The alternative is forced conformity or expulsion and loss of all identity. When the group consensus is challenged from the outside, the "us/them" relationship becomes aggravated, the already extreme group loyalty is enhanced, and outsiders cease to be considered even human. Individual identity, perspective, and loyalty are then all directed to (and flow from) the in-group, and all out-groups and individuals are ignored or treated with hostility, sometimes extreme. This "localism" pervades all fields of activity, and cross-group communication—let alone cooperation—is supremely difficult.

Again, this vertical society had been originally based on the family unit within the village but post-war Japan saw vast disruption and change. The emerging pattern was focused on the concurrent increase in urbanization, as the country rebuilt its physical and economic infrastructure, but with little popular confidence in the future or expectation that the discredited organs of government could steer a productive course. As the economy began to rebound, centered on urban enterprise and technological sectors, confidence and hope shifted from family and government to industry and to education, which became the pathway into the main technical economic sectors. These sectors—technical industry and educational institutions—became themselves fairly closed and rigid stovepipes, with difficult standards set for entry and advancement. So, Japanese society was divided on several planes: generational; urban/rural; education level and focus, even specific school attended; and industrial sector, specific industry and individual company—all were delineated externally and stratified internally due to "deep social and intellectual cleavages."[8]

Japanese economic success accelerated during the 1970s, but even then Japan was left in what has been described as a "spiritual void."[9] Japan's economic success had failed to bring it wide international respect or power in the world. Japan remained in the shadow of the United States, sometimes seen as an American "puppet," and subject to being drawn into United States conflicts—including nuclear conflicts. Doubts about the present course and its uncharted, uncertain future cut deep, and this was an overlay atop the disruption of urban life and corporate technical hierarchy. The compounding pressure-cooker environment of school entry exams to get into the right school, educational success to be able to be hired by the right company, and workplace success along with the strict internal etiquette, hierarchy, and demands on the "salaryman" all created extreme pressure with little outlet for the new urbanite. This void began to be filled by "new religions," often eclectic blends of traditional religions adapted to the new environment that became a mainstay of

Japanese life. These religions received a second boost from the economic downturn of the 1980s, when even the economic anchor failed to provide stability.

Unease about the future and about Japanese national identity, compounded by a lack of trust in or clear identification with national leaders, created a quest for moral and societal vision that these new religions sought to fill. According to Mark Juergensmeyer, they "spoke to the needs of people to find certainty and a framework for understanding the unseen forces in the world around them."[10] Aum Shinrikyo emerged in this second 1980s wave of new religions in Japan.

Aum Identity, Structure, and Belief System

Aum was at its core one of several Japanese "new religions," an inclusive blending of elements of traditional Eastern religions (in this case Buddhism, Taoism, Hindu) adapted to modern themes and societal dynamics (for Aum, mixing in some aspects of the Christian book of "Revelations" and American pop cultural new age elements). The resulting mix promised both enlightenment and empowerment and proved attractive to many disaffected Japanese youth, including many educated, technically competent young people. But Aum was not simply another of the many new religions in Japan. At the head of it all was a charismatic guru, within the religion was also a cult, and within the cult grew a political entity that resorted to violence and ultimately to terrorism and employing WMD.[11]

To examine Aum's identity and core beliefs relative to terrorism, one must understand its tiered structure. As a religion, Aum accepted an apocalyptic vision that society was so badly spiritually polluted and flawed that only near-total destruction could create the conditions necessary for salvation. Aum's founder and leader, Shoko Asahara, the blind guru, taught that salvation required destruction, that society's corruption was so advanced that the world would have to be destroyed to be saved, and that a coming Armageddon perpetrated by United States' employment of nuclear weapons would initiate that destruction. Aum filed for official recognition as a religious entity and was granted that official status under the "Religious Corporations Law" in August 1989. While Aum the religion claimed tens of thousands of adherents, its inner core membership consisted of approximately 1,400 "renunciants" who surrendered all of their possessions, outside contact, and identity—even their name—to move into one of approximately 30 communes in Japan. These closed societies offered both the salvation of current living removed from the flawed values of the outside world, and also promised that these inner core members would survive and arise from the destruction of the coming Armageddon to reestablish a new society in Aum's image. These communal adherents formed what is described here as Aum the cult (see Table 31.1).[12]

Table 31.1   **The Multiple Faces of Aum Shinrikyo**

New Religion	– Thousands to Tens of Thousands of Adherents – Official status under "Religious Corporations Law" from 1989
Cult	– Residential Compounds (1,400 "Renunciants" at 30 Compounds) – Business Enterprises (37 Companies/300 Scientists) – Political Party (25 Candidates Ran for Diet) – Shadow Government (24 Distinct Branches)
Terrorist Organization	– 115 Indicted/20–30 in Core Cell

Source: Author

Aum the cult exercised primary control and provided most of the workers for Aum the corporate empire. Aum's holdings included religious item sales and combined religious and secular publishing, but it also included more purely "business" pursuits from noodle shops and restaurants to computer assembly operations, from a fitness club and baby sitting service to chemicals and pharmaceuticals, and from dating services and travel and real estate agencies to a weapons factory. "Aum Incorporated" also reached overseas with a presence, for example, in Australia, Russia, Sri Lanka, Taiwan, and the United States. Since Aum recruited specifically from college dropouts and college graduates who subsequently dropped out of corporate life or failed to gain entry into the most prestigious companies—semisuccessful and technically educated "losers"— they were able to operate high-technology economic concerns. These corporate enterprises made significant profits, largely tax exempt under Religious Corporations Law status, which Aum could then use to fund its entire range of activities, including WMD terrorism. The chemical companies also gave cover and legitimacy to obtaining equipment and precursors used for weapons manufacturing,[13] as well as for the manufacturing and sale of illicit drugs that brought in even more profits. Besides technical cover, it is estimated that by 1995 Aum had amassed wealth from these activities in the amount of $1 billion (US).[14]

Aum also formed a short-lived political party that put forward 25 candidates for election to the Diet, the Japanese parliament, in 1990. All of these candidates, including guru Asahara, went down to swift defeat. Also on the political side, Aum eventually formed a "shadow government" made up of 24 ministries and agencies to be ready to step in and assume government functions at the time of the coming Armageddon. This structure has been variously reported as mirroring the contemporary Japanese government or as reflecting the fascist government of World War II. The seemingly conflicting descriptions may result from its incorporation of both the executive governmental functions and parts of the imperial structure surrounding the Emperor. In essence, there was an imperial structure for Asahara and his family, and there was an executive structure manned by those inner sanctum members of the highest three levels of the seven-tier religious hierarchy of Aum's renunciant followers. The central members of the core Aum decision and action structure, including the terrorist core members, are also seen on the list of "ministers."[15]

Aum's inner core's embrace of violence and ultimate resort to WMD terror is best understood by examining the turning point year of 1990. Asahara had earlier embraced an apocalyptic vision, with Japan destroyed in the coming nuclear fire, but (as opposed to 1945) now arising from the ashes spiritually reborn (with Aum as its spiritual savior). In early 1990, both with newly won official religion status and in the wake of its overwhelming and humiliating electoral defeat (and bearing the brunt of unflattering press caricatures), Asahara began to preach a religion of heightened violence linked to the coming end of the millennium. Influences on this shift also included the build-up to and conduct of the Gulf War, where Asahara identified with Saddam Hussein as a "victim" of United States' aggression. He also saw the futility of seeking to stand up to the U.S. military superiority, the conventional military supremacy that might make the predicted nuclear destruction avoidable (coupled with the end of the Cold War also lowering the likelihood of nuclear exchange). And he saw the respect—even fear—shown by the U.S. military of the possibility of Iraqi chemical or biological weapons employment. Asahara now shifted to put emphasis on hastening and ensuring Armageddon, and also shifted to obtaining and using his own WMD weapons. He undertook a retreat into the southern islands to announce and recast his vision, and simultaneously ordered the initial biological weapons test back on the main Japanese island. Aum the terrorist core was launched in the guru's vision. As Lifton observes, "Asahara's shifting predictions and lurid descriptions of the sequence of events by which the world would end became Aum's controlling narrative, the story that subsumed all else and into which every struggle had to fit."[16]

Against this backdrop, Aum had also—concurrently with gaining official religion status in late 1989—come under attack from families and their lawyers complaining of the cult's aggressive recruitment and virtual "kidnapping" of renunciants into its isolated compounds. It was also criticized for some of its property and land acquisition practices, and the net effect was to perceive these complaints as threatening its recognition under the Religious Corporations Law. Aum reacted by murdering the primary lawyer involved in the challenge (Tsutsumi Sakamoto) and his family. Aum had been (and continued to be) strident and violent in its internal "control and discipline" of its members (police reports subsequently held that Aum had killed 33 of its own members as well as several outside challengers), and now it also turned to attack all significant external challenges. A relatively nonchallenging police raid on one compound in 1990 over a land dispute compounded the other 1990 influences, and Aum turned its violence both at its challengers and in pursuit of its religious beliefs.

This reaction to external challenges combined with the embrace of "endism" (actively seeking Armageddon) to create a self-sustaining cycle: endism justified, even drove, extremism; extremism alienated some members; dealing with potential and actual dropouts brought on "persecution;" persecution and criticism fueled the Armageddon prophecy while underscoring and heightening endism. As Lifton reports, to Asahara a direct linkage was cemented between the "end of the self"—challenges to Aum and its religion status—and to the "end of the world" as central to the religious core; thus, "Weapons-centered destruction of the defiled world had to be achieved for the survival of that self."[17] Aum embarked upon an active biological and chemical weapons program (and unsuccessfully sought nuclear weapons) to ensure its survival to and through the "end of the world." Aum's resulting violent action, then, developed in three phases: retribution and enforcement against external critics and internal turncoats; WMD terrorism to force the predicted Armageddon; and WMD terrorism against external challenges that rose to threaten the continued health and existence of Aum the cult and its core leadership.

Aum Operations and WMD[18]

Aum carried out several "disciplinary" operations—including murder—against defectors or others that defied the central authority of Asahara or otherwise incurred his wrath. These acts of non-WMD control and retribution are believed to have begun with the murder of cult member Shuji Taguchi in February 1989, proceeded to the brutal killing of lawyer Sakamoto and his family in November 1989, and continued on to the pivotal February 1995 Tokyo kidnapping and murder of Kiyoshi Kariya, brother of an escaped cult member.[19]

To detail one example of an act of political violence in this category, Aum's first major violent action outside of the cult was the murder of the Sakamoto family in Yokohama in November 1989. Sakamoto was a lawyer who was calling on families of Aum renunciants to bring suit over the cult's "fraudulent message," aggressive recruitment, harsh treatment, and removal of all personal wealth and property from its inner members. Sakamoto was seen as a threat to the official religion status and even existence of Aum, and thus to its ability to fulfill its religious destiny. The threat must be removed, its leaders felt, and such opposition deterred from happening again. Asahara dispatched a team to meet Sakamoto at the commuter train station on his way home, kidnap him, and kill him. In their first illustration of their "keystone cops" ineptitude (as opposed to hardened terrorists), the Aum team failed to realize that they were standing on the platform on a national holiday, and Sakamoto was not working or commuting that day. They were forced to invade the Sakamoto home in the middle of the night and kill the entire family. Press and some local police following of this case would dog Aum across the next several years until their eventual fall.

Most notably, the group also carried out at least 14 WMD operations across the 6-year period 1990–1995.[20] The most significant of these WMD operations are summarized in Table 31.2 (Biological Agent Attacks) and Table 31.3 (Chemical Agent Attacks). Note that Aum began with an active bio-weapons program. However, its use of bio-weapons was limited by repeated failure to achieve successful effects with those weapons. As a result, the focus fell upon more tactical chemical weapons, and as the group succeeded in producing sarin, that chemical became the weapon of choice.[21]

Aum's use of biological weapons came primarily early in the cult's efforts to facilitate Armageddon, and these attacks were attempts to both validate the technology and perfect the employment of the agents. The initial test in April 1990, this of botulinus toxin sprayed from vehicles, was timed to coincide with Aum's core leadership retreat on Ishigaki Island, during which they sought to articulate the new and more strident religious doctrine of hastening Armageddon. Reports indicate that these vehicles traveled around the Japanese Diet (to which Aum had just failed in their attempt to be elected), U.S. military installations in the Tokyo vicinity, and even out to Narita airport. However, the cult failed in its attempt to disperse the bacillus in lethal form.

Similarly, Aum had not solved its dispersal problems 3 years later when it again sought to spray botulinus from vehicles in Tokyo, this time around the Imperial Palace in conjunction with the visits from many foreign dignitaries to attend the Crown Prince's royal wedding. Even a switch a few weeks later to anthrax dispensed from blowers on the roof of an Aum-owned building in Tokyo was no more successful. Aum then largely abandoned active attempts at bio-terrorism until its again-unsuccessful use, this time in the form of botulinus released in the Tokyo subway's Kasumigaseki Station, in March 1995, in an attempt to save the cult just days before its Tokyo subway sarin attack centered on the same station.

With the failures across 1993 in its use of bio-weapons to achieve fulfillment of its Armageddon narrative, and faced with a range of growing popular and press criticisms and legal challenges, Aum embarked on a chemical weapons program centered on sarin. Sarin became the central element of Aum's most notorious and dangerous WMD terrorism. Indeed, Lifton notes that "Aum's embrace of sarin had to do, at first, with the cult's success in producing it as a weapon. Once established, however, sarin became an organizing principle for Asahara's megalomania, for Aum's rhetoric of persecution, and ultimately for its Armageddon project."[22]

Table 31.2 Aum Shinrikyo and Major Biological Agent Attacks[27]

Date	Agent(s)	Location(s)	Victim(s)	Rationale	Results
April 1990	Botulinus Toxin	Tokyo Area	Japanese Diet; U.S. military installations at Yokohama and Yokosuka; Narita airport	Agent/System Test; Force Armageddon	Failed: Dispersal problems
June 9, 1993	Botulinus Toxin	Tokyo	Imperial Wedding	Force Armageddon	Failed: Dispersal problems
Late June 1993	Anthrax	Tokyo	Downtown Tokyo	Force Armageddon	Failed: Agent, dispersal problems
March 15, 1995	Botulinus Toxin	Tokyo	Kasumigaseki subway station	Retribution/Survival	Failed: Agent problems

Source: Author

Table 31.3 Aum Shinrikyo and Major Chemical Agent Attacks[28]

Date	Agent(s)	Location(s)	Victim(s)	Rationale	Results
Spring 1994	Sarin	Tokyo	Soka Gakkai Leader	Agent/System Test; Retribution	Failed: Dispersal problems
June 27, 1994	Sarin	Matsumoto Village	Three judges	Retribution/Survival	Failed: Seven dead, over 200 affected; wind blew away from judges
March 20, 1995	Sarin	Tokyo	Subway system	Preemption/Survival	Failed (?): 12 dead, over 5,500 affected
May 5, 1995	Hydrogen Cyanide	Tokyo	Subway system	Retribution/Survival	Failed: Dispersal problems

Source: Author

As Aum succeeded in producing sarin in weaponized form, its first attempt to disperse sarin in gas form (through heating) was targeted at an auditorium in which the leader of a rival new religion, Soka Gakkai, was speaking. Heating the liquid sarin to produce gas failed, and the truck carrying the Aum team caught fire, ending that test. Aum switched to heavy, refrigerator trucks, but still did not find total success in employment of sarin gas.

In June 1994 Aum sent its sarin trucks to Matsumoto Village, in the center of Honshu, to attack the courthouse where three district court judges were hearing a property challenge involving Aum land. The plan was to spray sarin gas into the courthouse and kill the principals in the case. The new, heavy trucks may have been better vehicles for producing sarin gas, but they were also very slow, and they arrived at Matsumoto after court had adjourned for the day. The target was switched to the neighborhood compound where the judges lived. This time the winds did not cooperate, and the judges' homes were spared attack. However, 7 were killed and over 200 made ill by the sarin.

Aum's signature sarin attack was on the central Tokyo subway system on March 20, 1995, and involved five nearly simultaneous sarin releases on four separate rail lines, all converging on the Kasumigaseki Station. By early 1995 the weight of evidence against Aum was becoming so great as to overcome cultural and structural barriers that affected the Japanese police and government response (as addressed in the following section of this chapter). Multiple police raids were planned on Aum compounds for March 19–21, and one was actually carried out on March 19. Aum was tipped off about these raids, and the cult first staged a failed botulinus attack, attempting to use briefcase dispersal on Kasumigaseki Station on March 15. Kasumigaseki Station serves the Tokyo district that houses the headquarters of the Japanese National Police Agency and Ministry of Justice, as well as several other government agencies. With the raids imminent and the botulinus attack having failed, Aum hastily dispatched five teams to dispense sarin by simply using sharpened umbrella tips to release liquid sarin contained in plastic bags. The plan was to have five trains from multiple directions converging on Kasumigaseki to bring mass death that would affect the investigation and prosecution of Aum. The primitive dispersal limited that mass effect, but still 12 died and over 5,500 people were made ill by the attack. Aum leadership was subsequently brought to justice following this attack, and the core terrorist membership removed from the religion. The religion remains today, but without the vision and resources to recreate the level of danger it once posed, and with more direct monitoring by authorities to ensure it limits its activities to more traditional religious practices.

Summary

To summarize, Aum Shinrikyo—one of Japan's second wave of new religions—operated under the Japanese vertical principle to provide a "total envelopment" of its members, becoming the single focal point of their identity. Its unique draw fell upon educated but less than totally successful youth, particularly many with technical knowledge and skills. As many of these youth were drawn into Aum's inner cult, which increasingly embraced a vision of Armageddon and societal rebirth, a few were enticed to turn their technical skills to produce biological and chemical weapons, and to assist in employing those agents and toxins both to protect Aum against official challenge and to hasten the coming Armageddon.

Aum first employed violence without the use of WMD both to control its members and to attack its active detractors. The religious narrative of violence became one with the cult itself, particularly among its core leadership, and violence produced a cycle of action, reaction, and escalated action. Aum then began to test and employ biological weapons to seek to hasten and ensure the Armageddon, but the cult was unable to successfully dispense the toxins. Aum had, after initial failure, slightly more success with sarin, which it employed in an effort to stave off challenges to its official religion status and survival.

Aum's recruitment of technically able young people and its acquisition and employment of WMD were enabled by legal protections for religions and corporate enterprises. Aum built a significant corporate structure, including chemical and pharmaceutical companies that provided access to the materials and precursors for biological and chemical terrorism, and that also provided up to $1 billion American dollars to back the effort. But even with this technical, financial, and resources base, Aum was unable to fully successfully produce and employ WMD. The problems of agent weaponization and dispersal are very real, and Aum did not quite reach the level of capability to employ its full lethal potential. Given these setbacks and the accumulation of evidence and incentive over almost 6 years, Japanese national and local authorities had sufficient opportunity and push to finally bring to bear a culturally determined and delayed response.

THE JAPANESE RESPONSE

Even though Aum succeeded in developing biological and chemical weapons, the cult never developed the operational expertise to allow it to carry out a fully successful operation, nor to provide complete cover and deniability for its acts. In fact, its operational activities should have been challenged and stopped much earlier, given the errors made at each action and the evidence provided from those errors. But Japanese culture and the changes in Japanese society following World War II also shaped the response to Aum by both local and national officials. And even after Japan was faced with largely external violence from the terrorist group of the 1970s, the Japanese Red Army, the nation remained unprepared to face terrorist challenges.

The primary impediments to a Japanese response to Aum stemmed from the same "vertical principle" within Japanese society and culture that helped to shape Aum and enable its path to violence. Each police force and justice jurisdiction was in fact its own stovepiped vertical structure, with limited initiative at lower levels internally and little communication or contact—let alone cooperation—between agencies, jurisdictions, or levels of government. As Nakane puts it, "localism characterizes all fields of activity," rendering any crossgroup cooperation very difficult.[23]

Further, and compounding this already difficult response context, the police legacy of prewar religious repression had two compounding effects. First, the police at every level were very slow and reluctant to challenge any religious entity. For Aum and other groups with official religion status, they enjoyed a "great deal of latitude and considerable government leniency regarding their freedom of action and range of public expression."[24] This also extended to latitude to employ violence with only a much delayed and muted response. A second effect on the police response was to limit their expertise to deal with complex and technical criminal or terrorist acts. After the war, and to prevent the creation of a strong national police capability that might once again become a vehicle for centralized national control, the Japanese and American architects of postwar Japan created a decentralized system, with no central national investigation authority. This resulted in fragmented efforts at investigation of multijurisdictional activities, interjurisdictional rivalries, and little to no information sharing. Even the national body that might have brought coordinated focus on Aum and its activities, the Security Bureau of Japanese intelligence, focused on leftists not terrorism. And because of the legacy of abuse, this bureau is reported to have great reluctance to wire tap or use undercover agents. Similar deliberate weakness extended to corporate oversight, where the Japanese Ministry of Health took a hands-off approach to registration of bio-technology firms and activities, allowing mail order of dangerous organisms if the order appeared on an "official" letterhead and contained a self-statement of a legitimate purpose for the order.[25] As Kaplan and Marshal note, "The nation, in effect, had a nineteenth-century police force trying to fight a twenty-first century crime."[26] So, while Aum almost tried to get caught at virtually every step of violence, the police response was fragmented and ineffectual for several years.

As early as the Sakamoto family murder in late 1989, an Aum badge or medallion was found at the scene. At that time only the top 100 or so members of the inner core had these badges, and this might have been a red flag pointing to the cult as responsible for the crime. However, the police argued internally that this evidence might be an attempt to "get" Aum approaching the election in which Aum was running 25 candidates for parliament. The decision to even request an interview to question Aum leadership about the badge was delayed for 16 days, during which Aum manufactured many hundred more badges.

This Sakamoto case illustrates one other aspect of the Japanese delay in acting against Aum. The press pointed to Aum as primary culprit immediately upon the disappearance of the Sakamoto family. However, much of the Japanese press tends toward sensationalized stories, and for years they had a love-hate relationship with Aum. Aum made the news in many ways, and it sought to use the press for publicity and recruitment. Meanwhile, the press covered Aum, often ridiculing or criticizing Asahara and some of the group's eccentricities. So, even when the press correctly identified Aum as the culprit and published evidence of its crimes and terrorist acts, the police exhibited great reluctance to investigate based solely or primarily on press reports. Even later, when local press in the villages bordering Aum's Kamikuishiki Compound near Mount Fuji (and the site of Aum's Satyam 7 biological and chemical weapons production facility) made claims of stunted crops and dead animals resulting from a sarin leak at the compound, the police were slow to react until prodded by further evidence and inputs. In response to these reports, Asahara reported multiple sarin attacks on the compound by United States and Japanese aircraft, but even such outrageous claims actually naming sarin as the source of the village effects failed to move the police to quick action.

In the end, it was a combination of evidence from two attacks, ironically one against a member of the press whose persistent investigation got under cult leadership's skin, that brought on police cooperation and a more effective, coordinated response. A former Yokohama press reporter and then freelance investigator with two critical books on Aum to her credit continued to press her attempts to prove Aum's responsibility for the Sakamoto family murders, and then almost 5 years after that crime was seeking to prove the link between Aum and the Matsumoto Village sarin attack. Aum gassed her home in the night with World War I-era phosgene gas, and this attack prompted the Yokohama police to finally pass on evidence of Aum's interest in sarin to the Japanese National Police Agency, which finally began a coordinated, multijurisdictional investigation. Ultimately this investigation linked the sarin used at Matsumoto Village to the sarin leaked from Satyam 7, thus linking Aum to the Matsumoto deaths.

Just after the New Year's day 1995 report of this sarin linkage on the front pages of *Yomiuri Shimbun*, the largest circulation Japanese newspaper, Aum was implicated in the kidnapping from Tokyo and murder of Kiyoshi Kariya, the brother and protector of a woman who had escaped from Aum. In this case, the rental van used in the kidnapping in Tokyo was identified and traced to Aum. Key here is that at last the Tokyo police, the nation's most capable force, was also brought to the center of the growing effort to investigate Aum. From here it was a short few weeks until the planned combined police raids precipitated Aum's Tokyo subway attack.

In sum, a decentralized and fragmented police structure within a society in which crossgroup communication and cooperation is rare and far from facilitated, provided Aum with cover—both religious and corporate—under which it carried out an escalating series of violent acts, ultimately incorporating WMD into those actions. The press was in front of the police in pointing fingers at Aum, but press sensationalism and a confrontational relationship with Aum delayed and muted the impact of their reporting. As Aum's acts and activities spanned several prefectures and thus jurisdictions, no one police force gathered sufficient evidence to overcome the legal and cultural barriers behind which Aum the religious cult and Aum Incorporated stood. It finally took courage and an accumulation of evidence to force a coordinated response to Aum. But overall, across 6 years of violence and really 2 years of repeated WMD employment, the Japanese government and police failed to act. Even after the Tokyo subway attacks, all of the deaths, arrests, and evidence accumulation, the Japanese government still stopped short of amending its broad grant of religious and corporate freedom in general, treating Aum as an aberration, but it also declined to ban Aum or withdraw its official religion status. With Asahara and the core cult/terrorist leadership in jail, Aum the religion still endures.

LESSONS LEARNED

While in many ways this case is a unique reflection of both traditional and contemporary Japanese culture and society, and the product of the unique blend that became the conjoined personality of Shoko Asahara and Aum Shinrikyo, we can still draw some general lessons to improve our ability to analyze and respond to national, religious-based, and WMD terrorism. These lessons are drawn from the potential and problems of WMD as terror weapons, the underlying political purpose of the use of violence by nominally "religious" organizations, the implications of special treatment of religious groups and seemingly legitimate businesses, and the overall utility of expanding more widely used tactical and operational analysis tools with the addition of cultural perspectives and culture-based analysis.

Both the Potential and Problems of WMD Terrorism

The Aum case at once underscores the very real potential for WMD weapons acquisition/development and use by a national, not externally sponsored entity, and of the significant technical barriers to the successful employment of such weapons by even highly technically competent and well-resourced groups. Aum membership was attractive to well-educated, technically competent young Japanese, and thus Aum had an internal recruitment base of literally hundreds of scientists and technicians from which to draw the handful they needed for their WMD terror program. Aum also developed a significant and overt business enterprise that provided legitimate cover that allowed—within admittedly lax Japanese government regulation—the acquisition of the needed equipment, precursors, and materials for the development of biological and chemical weapons. However, even with those advantages and with the availability of technically competent personnel to be included on its operational WMD employment teams, Aum was not fully successful in dispersing its toxins and agents during any of its WMD attacks.

Aum's success in developing the weapons stands as a red flag that others will try to gain and some will likely succeed in gaining chemical and biological terror capabilities. But Aum's failure to fully succeed in weaponization and dispersal also provides a note of reality that somewhat lowers the "terror" of WMD terrorism. It must also remind us that this only means that, at this moment, we have won a brief period in which to improve our WMD controls, detection mechanisms, and response capabilities. WMD terrorism is not easy, but in all probably it is inevitable.

Political Foundations of "Religious" Terrorism

The Aum case reminds us that the "new" terrorism—religious-based terrorism—is both new and old simultaneously. Yes, self-proclaimed limits on mass, indiscriminate violence may be removed by the new narratives, opening both the possibility and desirability of WMD employment by the "new" generation of terrorists. But this new terrorism retains an underlying foundation of political purpose, in Aum's case an explicit underlying political structure closely linked to its religious hierarchy and the ultimate political objectives behind its resort to violence. Terrorism is at base political violence in one of its many guises and incarnations; indirect violence applied for psychological effect toward political goals whether toward fulfilling an ideologically or a religiously defined destiny. And responding to religious-based terrorism must put emphasis on that political foundation and the terrorist actions, ultimately forcing questions about the balance of civil/religious liberty and security. These questions are not easy or comfortable for any society, and the answers are far from preordained regardless of the type or level of violence. However, those questions cannot be ignored without consequences.

Essential Sanctuary Can Be Anchored in Law and/or Business Status

The Aum case underscores that one of those consequences of deferring or avoiding addressing the religious-based terrorism questions is the creation of "sanctuary under the law" and/or "sanctuary of legitimate business." Sanctuary has long been established as a central goal of and aid to transborder and transnational groups. This sanctuary has come in the form of borders, "ungoverned" remote regions, and today even "ungoverned" urban sectors. Aum illustrates how emphasizing the "religion" dimension of a religious-based terrorist group can lead to significant legal protections that provide "sanctuary" for the organization's operations, as well as cause delays and even form barriers to government and police response. Similarly, economic freedom can be used by a terrorist group to establish the cover for dual-use enterprises (those using processes and materials that have both legitimate and nefarious purposes). When economic regulation is too lax, or especially when a trend toward loose regulation is heightened by a hands-off approach to religion-affiliated businesses, a form of economic sanctuary results. As chemical and biological weapons are both associated with the dual-use problem, this sanctuary is particularly relevant to WMD terrorism. Sanctuary is indeed a critical element to insurgents and terrorists, and it can come from internal sources.

Cultural Determinism of Both Terrorism and the Response

There are several strengths to a strategic, culturally focused perspective for terrorism analysis. Terrorism is a complex, multifaceted phenomenon and it is best addressed through multiple levels of analysis and the application of multiple lenses. The cultural, strategic lens expands the focus well beyond simply the weapons, the victims, and the acts. It allows full attention to the rationale and objectives behind the acts, and it links the ultimate targets to the tactical victims. Significantly, it also delves into the terrorist identity and belief structure, providing a hint of their "rationality" behind what often appears to us as totally non-rational decisions and actions. So while not ignoring the important *what, who, when,* and *where* questions and answers of operational analysis, it also provides the fundamental *why,* the essential second-order *who,* and the ever-critical *so what* of a strategic focus. Only understanding all of these dimensions of terrorism will allow a full set of tailored response actions and effects. It forms a valuable additional arrow in the quiver of those seeking to respond to and ultimately defeat terrorism, and no weapon can be ignored in that fight.

ACKNOWLEDGMENTS

The views expressed in this case study are those of the author and do not necessarily reflect the official policy or position of the Department of the Air Force, the Department of the Army, The Department of Defense, or the U.S. Government.

NOTES

1. The Defense Threat Reduction Agency's Advanced Systems and Concepts Office (DTRA/ASCO) has sponsored a project across 2005 and 2006 to advance the academic study of strategic culture and to demonstrate the utility of cultural analysis and intelligence to examine state and "rogue" state weapons of mass destruction acquisition and use decisions and actions. This case author's USAF Institute for National Security Studies has participated in the project workshops, and the author contributed a template extending the project focus to violent nonstate actors (VNSAs) and WMD terrorism. The discussion and framework development and application in this section is based on that work. See James M. Smith, "Strategic Culture, VNSAs, and WMD," paper presented at DTRA/Utah State University Comparative Strategic Cultures III Workshop, Park City, UT, May 3–5, 2006.

2. For just three such classic studies that were reviewed for this chapter see R. P. Dore, *City Life in Japan: A Study of a Tokyo Ward* (Berkeley, CA: University of California Press, 1967); Chie Nakane, *Japanese Society* (Berkeley, CA: University of California Press, 1970); and Edwin O. Reischauer, *Japan: The Story of a Nation*, revised ed. (New York: Knopf, 1974).

3. Robert Jay Lifton, *Destroying the World to Save It: Aum Shinrikyo, Apocalyptic Violence, and the New Global Terrorism* (New York: Metropolitan Books, 1999) 236.

4. Reischauer: p. 249.

5. This section is based on the analysis presented in Nakane.

6. Nakane: p. 3.

7. Nakane: p. 3.

8. Reischauer: p. 262.

9. Reischauer: p. 316.

10. Mark Juergensmeyer, *Terror in the Mind of God: The Global Rise of Religious Violence* (Berkeley, CA: University of California Press, 2000) 116. See Chapter 6, "Armageddon in a Tokyo Subway," for details about Aum the new religion.

11. This analysis is focusing on broad aspects of culture and their shaping influence on the organizational, operational, and behavioral dynamics of Aum's practice of WMD terrorism and concurrent cultural shaping effects on the Japanese response. For equally important detail, not included here, and psychological analysis of cult guru Shoko Asahara and of Aum the cult see Lifton, *Destroying the World to Save It*; for equally important detail on Aum the religion see Juergensmeyer, *Terror in the Mind of God*; and for additional detail on operational and response issues see D. W. Brackett, *Holy Terror: Armageddon in Tokyo* (New York:

Weatherhill, 1996); and David E. Kaplan and Andrew Marshall, *The Cult at the End of the World* (New York: Crown, 1996).

12. For more on the power of cults to control members' behavior, please see Mark Galanter and James J. F. Forest, "Cults, Charismatic Groups and Social Systems: Understanding the Transformation of Terrorist Recruits," in *The Making of a Terrorist, Vol. 2*, ed. James J. F. Forest (Westport, CT: Praeger, 2005) 51–70; and Arthur J. Deikman, "The Psychological Power of Charismatic Leaders in Cults and Terrorist Organizations," in *The Making of a Terrorist, Vol. 2*: pp. 71–83.

13. For a detailed description of the Satian 7 chemical weapons manufacturing compound, see John V. Parachini, "The Making of Aum Shinrikyo's Chemical Weapons Program," in *The Making of a Terrorist, Vol. 2*: pp. 277–295.

14. Lifton: p. 37.

15. See Brackett: pp. 103–104, for graphic depictions of the religious and shadow government hierarchies.

16. Lifton: p. 44.

17. Lifton: p. 201.

18. For more detail specifically on Aum's WMD terrorism, see James M. Smith, "Aum Shinrikyo," in *Weapons of Mass Destruction: An Encyclopedia of Worldwide Policy, Technology, and History,* eds. Eric Croddy and James Wirtz (Santa Barbara, CA: ABC CLIO, 2005).

19. Brackett: p. 19, cites the strangulation of Taguchi as the cult's first murder.

20. Accounts and numbers vary, but the number 14 incidents appears supportable. It is offered by Lifton: p. 6.

21. See John V. Parachini, "The Making of Aum Shinrikyo's Chemical Weapons Program."

22. Lifton: p. 179.

23. Nakane: p. 131.

24. Juergensmeyer: p. 116.

25. Kaplan and Marahall: p. 56.

26. Kaplan and Marshall: p. 149.

27. Derived from Brackett, *Holy Terror*; Kaplan and Marshall, *The Cult at the End of the World*; Lifton, *Destroying the World to Save It*; and U.S. Congress, Senate Government Affairs Permanent Subcommittee on Investigations (Minority Staff), *Global Proliferation of Weapons of Mass Destruction: A Case Study on the Aum Shinrikyo,* Washington, DC, October 31, 1995.

28. Derived from Brackett, *Holy Terror*; Kaplan and Marshall, *The Cult at the End of the World*; Lifton, *Destroying the World to Save It*; and Senate Government Affairs Permanent Subcommittee on Investigations (Minority Staff), *Global Proliferation of Weapons of Mass Destruction: A Case Study on the Aum Shinrikyo.*

CHAPTER 32

THE STRUGGLE WITH VIOLENT RIGHT-WING EXTREMIST GROUPS IN THE UNITED STATES

Eric Y. Shibuya

Though most attention today is focused on foreign terrorist organizations against the United States, it would be a grave mistake to discount the dedication of and danger posed by domestic violent movements. Though there have been incidents of violence perpetuated by left-wing movements (notably groups like the Weathermen in the 1960s, the nearly two decade-long threat of Theodore Kaczynski, the "Unabomber," and radical environmental groups like the Earth Liberation Front), it has been the right-wing movements that have been responsible for the rising lethality of incidents in the last quarter century. It is important to recall that, prior to the September 11, 2001 (9/11) attacks, the most lethal terrorist event on U.S. soil was the bombing of the Murrah Federal Building in Oklahoma City. This chapter charts the evolution of violent right-wing movements in the United States and attempts to curtail their activities. It will look at the post-9/11 effects on these movements and possible future developments. The final sections will discuss the potential for greater violence on their part in the future as well as shifts in their organizational structure and their consequences.

Rather than discussing right-wing "groups," it may be more valuable to conceptualize them as facets of a larger movement. Political scientist Paul De Armond's typology classifies four "movement networks" under the larger umbrella of violent right-wing movements: Wise Use, Anti-Abortion, Klan/neo-Nazi, and Patriot.[1] The first group focuses on the use of natural resources, usually timber and mining, and frequently come in conflict with environmental movements. The Wise Use movement is the least prone to violence and is also generally the least likely to express its concerns in religious terms. However, the latter three groups exhibit significant overlap, and are more prone to acts of violence in general and mass casualty violence in particular. All three will frequently express their aims and concerns in religious terminology, but the anti-abortion movement draws mainly from very conservative elements of mainstream Christianity. In very sharp contrast, the Klan/neo-Nazi and Patriot movements are more likely to espouse a form of religious radicalism known as Christian Identity. (There are some exceptions to this that reveal the slight difference between the Klan/neo-nazi and Patriot movements. Christian Identity, as will be discussed later in this chapter, espouses a racist, white-supremacist philosophy, while there are non-white members of Patriot organizations). The Christian Identity movement is a significant departure from the doctrines of mainstream Christianity, most notably in its outright racism. As journalist Joel Dyer notes, "Fundamentalists make no argument to justify racism biblically, but Identity-influenced groups ... attempt to do so."[2] This division is clear evidence, according to Identity adherents, that it is "mainstream" Christianity that has been corrupted away from the "truth."

THE DOCTRINE OF CHRISTIAN IDENTITY

Christian Identity thought has its roots in British-Israelism, a religious movement that developed during the nineteenth century. British-Israelism argued that the British were actually descendants of the lost tribes of Israel. However, British-Israelism differs from its offshoot in that it is nonviolent and not anti-Semitic. Rather, Jews are viewed as members of a different tribe. This differs significantly from the beliefs espoused by Christian Identity, which claim not only that white "Aryans" are the true chosen people, but that the Jews are in fact the product of a union between Eve and Satan. Finally, and perhaps most importantly, Christian Identity adherents believe that the world is on the brink of a great apocalyptic conflict between the Aryans and the Jews (and their followers).[3]

The Christian Identity ideology argues that the Book of Genesis describes two distinct creations. The first, described in the first chapter of Genesis, is said to detail the creation of the "subhuman" races (non-whites). It is in the second chapter of Genesis that the term "Adam" is first used. Identity believers argue that the term means to be fair skinned, to show color in the face.[4] In contrast, Jerome Walters points to the word-play inherent in the Hebrew words *adam* (man) and *adamah* (ground). The term does describe ruddiness, but points to Adam's connection to the red earth, not to the color of his skin.[5]

While the "pre-Adamite" peoples are considered inferior to the Aryan race in this ideology, they are not necessarily considered evil—unlike the Jews, who are literally considered to be the children of Satan. Between the Aryans and Jews, there can be no negotiation; no peaceful coexistence is possible between the two. Identity adherents believe that the rest of the world has been duped into believing that the Jews are the Chosen People of the Old Testament of the Bible. This has occurred, according to Identity thought, due to a powerful conspiracy of power and control over the media and over governments, led by the Jews. Identity adherents and other conspiracy theorists believe this conspiracy extends through history as is described in the infamous *Protocols of the Elders of Zion*. This text is one of the major readings of the Identity (and other anti-Semitic) movements and its power remains seemingly undiminished.

The Protocols of the Elders of Zion

The Protocols of the Elders of Zion (sometimes referred to as the *Protocols of the Learned Elders of Zion,* and hereafter referred to simply as the *Protocols*) purports to document the minutes of a secret meeting in 1840 of a Jewish cabal detailing their plans for global domination. This domination would not occur openly, but rather through the control of major areas of industry (notably the media) and via compliant government leaders. Despite the fact that the *Protocols* has been exposed as a forgery (the "authoritative" version of the *Protocols* was created in tsarist Russia and taken from a text of an 1864 French play, *The Dialogues in Hell Between Machiavelli and Montesquieu*[6]), its popularity remains undiminished, with published versions available in several different languages. (Beyond the early editions in English, Russian, and French, other languages include Polish, Spanish, and Arabic, and the list continues to grow). The weight of evidence against the authenticity of the *Protocols* has led, however, to a shift in thought and tactics on the part of Identity adherents and other anti-Semitic movements/conspiracy theorists. Rather than argue the authenticity of the document itself, they argue over the *veracity* of its claims (or at least, the perceived veracity of its claims). The *Protocols* themselves may not be an actual description of a secret meeting, this new argument goes, but the views and modes of thought it presents can nevertheless be taken as accurate reflections of reality.[7]

The longevity of the *Protocols* is certainly testimony to the fact that ideas have power, but this does not fully explain the ebb and flow of the intensity of action surrounding beliefs like Identity thought. Conspiracy theory may be a powerful seed, but other events are required to provide suitable soil for this mode of thought to flourish.

THE FARM CRISIS AND THE RISE OF ANTI-GOVERNMENT SENTIMENT IN THE UNITED STATES

It is no coincidence that the heartland of the United States has also been the hotbed of the antigovernment movement. During the 1970s, a major push on the part of the Department of Agriculture (as well as bankers) encouraged farmers to buy more and more farmland. This led to severe consequences when larger forces in the economy shifted, notably in 1979, when Federal Reserve Chairman Paul Volcker raised interest rates to curb inflation. That decision had the side-effect of causing the nationwide farm crisis. "Property values collapsed at the same time the interest rates on the farmer's loans climbed out of sight. The men and women who had listened to the experts and had done exactly as they were told lost everything."[8]

The loss of a farmer's land means more than the loss of a source of income. For many, the farm had been passed on through generations; its loss signified the end of a way of life and, most fundamentally, a loss of identity. Over time, the despair connected with such a situation has turned both inward (in the form of suicide) and, more importantly for this chapter, outward in the form of antigovernment sentiment, which in turn provided a fruitful ground for the spread of the Christian Identity ideology. Dyer notes that this ideology has transformed "the 'economic' war that can't be fought . . . into the 'holy' war that must be,"[9] and two major events followed the farm crisis that would coalesce the various groups and philosophies into just such a movement.

Shock Events: Ruby Ridge and the "Siege on Waco"

On August 21, 1992, U.S. marshals and agents of the Federal Bureau of Investigation (FBI) attempted to apprehend Randy Weaver at his home in Ruby Ridge, Idaho. Weaver was an antigovernment and Christian Identity adherent, and had missed a court date for a firearms dispute. During surveillance of the Weaver property, family's dog began to bark at the hidden U. S. Marshals, who subsequently shot the dog. This shooting was witnessed by Sammy Weaver, Randy's 14-year-old son, who fired his rifle in the direction of the Marshals and then began to run back to his home. The U.S. Marshals shot Sammy in the back, killing him. Randy Weaver and a friend placed Sammy's body in a shed and ran back to the home, while Vicky Weaver—holding her 10-month-old daughter—opened the door and was fatally shot by an FBI sniper. Randy Weaver and the surviving members of his family barricaded themselves inside the home, but surrendered 9 days later. The government's actions at Ruby Ridge fueled the flames of the antigovernment movement and the dead at Ruby Ridge would eventually become martyrs.[10]

As a response to this event, a gathering of antigovernment activists was convened in Estes Park, Colorado, on October 22, 1992. As Louis Beam—a Christian Identity adherent and a speaker at the "Rocky Mountain Rendezvous"—argued, "the two murders of the Weaver family have shown us all that our religious, our political, our ideological differences mean nothing to those who wish to make us all slaves. We are viewed by the government as the same—the enemies of the state."[11] Ruby Ridge was a major catalyst in drawing together the disparate movements who united in their recognition that the Federal government of the United States was their common enemy. The point would be reinforced after the events in Waco, Texas, the following year.

David Koresh was the leader of the Branch Davidians, a cult that believed Koresh to be a new prophet—the "Lamb" foretold in the Book of Revelation who would open the "seals" that would bring about the end of the world. (Mainstream Christianity believes the Lamb is Jesus Christ). The Branch Davidians established a compound in Waco that included a stockpile of weapons in preparation for this coming apocalypse. In April 1993, agents of the Bureau of Alcohol, Tobacco, and Firearms (ATF) attempted to enter the compound to serve a warrant and investigate claims of illegal firearms possession. A standoff ensued, and on April 19, 1993, ATF agents attempted to storm the compound. In the ensuing chaos, a fire resulted that led to the deaths of Koresh and 74 followers. Koresh was not an Identity believer; indeed, he led a cult of personality in the truest sense of the term. However, his belief in an impending battle between good and evil, his fear of oppressive control by the federal government, and his belief in the right to bear arms struck strong elements of common bond between him and other facets of the violent right-wing movement. The Waco Siege would become another ground of martyrs, another symbol of the danger of the federal government. Koresh may not have been one of them, but as the argument went, all antigovernment activists would be treated in the same fashion if something was not done. The antigovernment response to Waco would eventually become violent and devastating.

The Oklahoma City Bombing: The Apex of the Violent Right-Wing Movement

On April 19, 1995, the Murrah Federal Building in Oklahoma City was bombed, killing 168 men, women, and children. The date of the attack, the second anniversary of the Waco Siege, was not an accident, but the date has an even longer and deeper symbolic meaning. April 19 is "Patriot's Day," the day of the battles at Lexington and Concord that signaled the beginning of the American Revolution. Despite early arguments that the attack had been perpetrated by foreign agents, Timothy McVeigh (and coconspirator Terry Nichols) was soon apprehended. McVeigh, a Gulf War veteran, had seen the destruction at Waco and became enraged with what he saw as an overly oppressive federal government. McVeigh was inspired by *The Turner Diaries*, a novel that described a race war in the United States that begins after the federal government begins a program to remove all privately owned firearms. *The Turner Diaries* was written by William Pierce under the pseudonym "Andrew Macdonald." Pierce was a leader of the National Alliance, a White supremacist, Christian Identity organization. The *Diaries*, first published in 1978, is significant for two major reasons. First, the book's detailed description of how to build, deliver, and detonate a truck bomb was used by McVeigh to construct the device used in Oklahoma City. Second, in a somewhat prophetic manner, the book ends with the protagonist flying a small plane loaded with a nuclear device into the Pentagon.

McVeigh's action was certainly shocking, but more ominous for policymakers dealing with terrorism was the fact that McVeigh had seemingly acted with very little organizational support. McVeigh was viewed by many in the movement to be emblematic of the concept of "leaderless resistance," which would be the necessary model for future attacks against the federal government.

Leaderless Resistance

The aftermath of the Oklahoma City bombing should have been the downfall of the violent right-wing movement. Indeed, membership in many groups did decline drop after the bombing. The violence, it was felt, had gone too far. That said, the bombing also brought about a rededication among those who remained. As Dyer quotes Ron Cole, leader of what remains of the Branch Davidians, "[The bombing] created a weeding-out process . . . You knew you could count on the people who didn't run away after Oklahoma City. It made the militias stronger."[12] More importantly, McVeigh's action suggested that centrally organized groups may not be the most effective way to strike against the federal government. McVeigh put the concept of leaderless resistance into action, and others would follow in his footsteps.

Another example of leaderless resistance was Eric Rudolph, the man responsible for the bombing at the 1996 Olympics in Atlanta. Rudolph was also convicted of bombings at an abortion clinic and a gay nightclub. While there have been allegations that Rudolph was also an Identity adherent, he denied such in his court confession, arguing instead that his actions were driven by extremely conservative (but nonetheless closer to mainstream) Christian beliefs. In any case, Rudolph had been adopted as a "hero" by the Identity movement, and many Web sites called for acts of violence patterned after Rudolph's attacks.[13] Rudolph may not have belonged to any specific group, but it is clear that his actions have contributed to a much larger ideology and movement. This is exactly what was hoped for by the originator of the principle of leaderless resistance.

Leaderless resistance was first developed in the 1960s by Colonel Ulius Amoss as a proposed response to a communist takeover of the United States. The concept would be expanded by white supremacist Louis Beam in 1983 as a method to attack the federal government. In many ways, the idea came about as a reaction to the breakdown of many centralized white supremacist organizations. In particular, the use of civil actions that bankrupted many groups increased the desire of these groups to find different ways of organizing that would lessen their vulnerability to this tactic.[14] Furthermore, centralized groups such as the "Order" (patterned after the organization in *The Turner Diaries* and responsible for the June 1984 murder of Denver radio talk show host Alan Berg) were decimated when federal agents captured members who gave information on others in the organization. Beam argues that the ability for highly technical societies to conduct surveillance and penetrate highly centralized organizations is what makes that type of organizing principle useless when fighting the state. "Experience has revealed over and over again that anti-state, political organizations utilizing this method of command and control are easy prey for government infiltration, entrapment, and destruction of the personnel involved."[15] Therefore, rather than a hierarchical arrangement, the establishment of "phantom cells" tied together only by common philosophy would be the way of the future for the movement. Beam notes himself that this may not be the best way to organize a movement, but argues that in the confrontation with the federal government, it is the only hope for success.[16]

The main advantage of leaderless resistance is obvious. The lack of a coordinated leadership structure makes it virtually impossible to tie cells together and map the network of the organization. In many cases, members of various cells do not know of each other's existence at all. The major disadvantage is also readily apparent. There is no way to know for sure who is doing what. As Beam notes, "It becomes the responsibility of the individual to acquire the necessary skills and information as to what is to be done."[17] There is a general decline in the quality of the actors, as training and indoctrination can no longer be conducted in a single location. However, this disadvantage has been overcome somewhat by the rise of the internet, as training videos (some of very high quality) can be found on various Web sites. This improvement has made increasingly possible the worst-case scenario of a terrorist group effectively mounting an attack using a weapon of mass destruction.

EVOLUTION OF ACTION IN VIOLENT RIGHT-WING MOVEMENTS: THE USE OF WEAPONS OF MASS DESTRUCTION

The nexus between terrorist movements and their potential use of Weapons of Mass Destruction (WMD) is not a recent phenomenon. Indeed, because the motivations of right-wing movements in the United States are frequently expressed in religious terms, there are fewer psychological and political limitations toward mass casualty actions. Although none of the individuals or groups of concern thus far have been able to successfully execute a WMD attack, right-wing movements in the United States have made very credible attempts at conducting just such an attack. Unfortunately, as Roberts notes, "partially successful attacks get recorded for what the terrorists achieved rather than what he or she attempted."[18] This has the dangerous effect of downplaying the intensity of the threat posed by terrorist organizations of whatever stripe. Limitations on WMD use by violent right wing groups in the United States have been mostly limitations of resources and capability, not of intention.

The anthrax attacks that came soon after 9/11 led to the death of five people, but the intention was clearly to cause a high number of casualties. There is some dispute as to the quality of the anthrax, but this is not an event that should be quickly dismissed, and it remains unsolved as of mid-2006. An earlier significant event involved The Covenant, Sword, and Arm of the Lord, a Christian Identity group whose members were apprehended in 1985 with a large drum of potassium cyanide (along with a substantial arsenal of conventional weapons) in their possession. Their plan of attack included poisoning water supplies of major U.S. cities. Although technically, their plan would not have led to the casualties the group aspired to (the amount of cyanide was inadequate to actually poison a reservoir), it is possible that the group would have found a different and more effective method of dispersal if they had not been caught by the FBI.[19]

While the use of a WMD by a terrorist group has become the source of increasing concern for analysts generally, there has been a more insidious evolution of thought on the part of the violent right-wing movement in the United States. In particular, there has been a notable shift in rhetorical tone on the part of many groups in the movement that have allowed them to cloak their more controversial ideas in milder forms. This may be the most dangerous aspect of the movement today, as this shift may allow for greater access into the mainstream.

EVOLUTION OF THOUGHT IN THE VIOLENT RIGHT-WING MOVEMENT: SEPARATISM, NOT SUPREMACY

As noted earlier, there has been a subtle shift among Christian Identity adherents and other violent right-wing movements in their treatment of the *Protocols of the Elders of Zion,* from viewing it as a document about an actual meeting to promoting it as a document whose ideas are true. Similarly, there has been a shift in description and rhetoric from some groups calling themselves white *separatists* (or nationalists) rather than white *supremacists*. This shift has two consequences, one subtle and one more overtly dangerous. The consequence is that this simple shift has allowed the Christian Identity movement to recast its rhetoric within the United States as another expression of "equal opportunity." Examples of the subtle aspect of this movement include the National Association for the Advancement of White People (NAAWP), established by David Duke, a former candidate for the governorship of Louisiana, U.S. Senate, and Presidency of the United States. Groups such as the NAAWP argue that legislation such as Affirmative Action and the consideration of race for university admittance are examples of "reverse discrimination" and argue for their elimination on the grounds of equal opportunity. More overtly, this shift from supremacy to separatism has allowed for these groups to draw common cause with other racist organizations. White "Separatist" groups have issued statements in support of groups such as Louis Farrakhan's Nation of Islam, arguing that his "Black Nationalism" corresponds with their own views. This does not mean peaceful coexistence, except in perhaps the same fashion as it did during the Cold War, where two opposing entities had their own separate spheres of influence. Nowhere is this expression of common cause more evident than the response of many in the right-wing movement to the September 11 attacks.

September 11 and Domestic Extremist Movements in the United States

The 9/11 attacks returned, in much more lethal fashion, international terrorism to the United States. Al Qaeda was able to accomplish what Ramzi Yousef failed to do in 1993. Since then, concerns have focused on the potential for "sleeper agents" in the service of al Qaeda or other organizations to threaten other targets in the United States. However, this rising concern has not led to a resurgence of interest regarding more homegrown violent movements in the United States. And yet, while there were no connections between the hijackers and domestic extremist movements, the 9/11 attacks were praised by many among the latter. Indeed, the Aryan Nations proclaimed the hijackers to be "Islamic Freedom Fighters."[20] William Pierce, author of *The Turner Diaries* and leader of the National Alliance, proclaimed that the attacks were the price for the U.S. government's support for Israel. Pierce's argument was the most prevalent among the right-wing movement in the United States, which put the blame of the attacks on the Jewish lobby's excessive control over the U.S. government. On the Aryan Nations Web site, the Phineas Priesthood—an

Identity group—issued a text entitled "Jihad, in the Bible," ending the essay with "Let the Islamic world know, Jihad is not just their ideal; it is not alone in this Holiest of causes, we are here to join them in Holy Worldwide Jihad. Death to the Infidels! Death to the jEw!"[sic][21] The same Web site included an essay on "Aryan Islam." The essay praises the "Aryan youth who embrace the TRUE [sic] Islam of the Qu'ran and Sunnah. *They include those who join or support the honorable warriors of Islam, the Mujahideen.*"[22] This tactic of drawing common cause and building a bigger "umbrella" movement has not (thus far) led to actual evidence of cooperation, but the potential for that kind of alliance—even in the forms of tactical "marriages of convenience"—could have dire long-term implications for security practitioners in the years to come.

CONCLUSION: LONG-TERM IMPLICATIONS

Three major trends are the most significant when considering the threat of violent right-wing groups in the United States. The first is the potential for a WMD attack. The use of a WMD in a terrorist attack is clearly not beyond the scope of possibility for violent right-wing actors, in terms of motivation or in (growing) capability. Authorities would be remiss in dismissing the potential for this threat by focusing on past failures and the relative incompetence of these groups' actions so far. A consideration of the intentions and growing capability of this movement to procure WMD should be a major focus in analyzing the future threat of this movement.

The second trend is the increasing value of the Internet in putting the leaderless resistance form of operation into practice. The Internet has been a boon to the movement by allowing for the creation of virtual communities of interest that are more anonymous and physically disconnected, making investigation and surveillance much more difficult. The Internet has also been able to lessen one of the major flaws in the leaderless resistance concept—the ability of the lone actor to acquire adequate information, ideological support, and tactical training for conducting violent operations. Copies of texts like *The Protocols of the Elders of Zion* and *The Turner Diaries* (among others) are easily found on the Web. More importantly, "how-to" videos and instructions on constructing explosive devices are appearing faster than authorities can track and/or shut them down.

The third and perhaps most significant trend is the growing statements of common cause between the violent right-wing movement and other terrorist movements. It may be an exaggeration to consider groups like al Qaeda and the Aryan Nations to be part of a single "movement," but it is certainly true that both groups find common cause in their hatred for the U.S. government. While strategic alliances may be less likely, tactical relationships may increase as both groups find areas of mutual benefit to work together. Certainly, in the area of tactical training, especially on the Internet, knowledge is already being diffused between terrorist groups.[23]

ACKNOWLEDGMENTS

The views presented in this chapter are the author's alone, and do not reflect the official policy of the Marine Corps University or any other U.S. Governmental Agency.

NOTES

1. Paul de Armond, "Right-Wing Terrorism and Weapons of Mass Destruction: Motives, Strategies, and Movements," in *Hype or Reality: The "New Terrorism" and Mass Casualty Attacks,* ed. Brad Roberts (Alexandria, VA: Chemical and Biological Arms Control Institute, 2000) 55–56.

2. Joel Dyer, *Harvest of Rage: Why Oklahoma City is Only the Beginning* (Boulder, CO: Westview, 1998) 80.

3. Michael Barkun, *Religion and the Racist Right: The Origins of the Christian Identity Movement* (Chapel Hill, NC: University of North Carolina Press, 1997) x–xi. Also, see James Aho, "Christian Fundamentalism and Militia Movements in the U.S," in *The Making of a Terrorist, Vol. 1,* ed. James Forest (Westport, CT: Praeger, 2005).

4. Jerome Walters, *One Aryan Nation under God: How Religious Extremists Use the Bible to Justify Their Actions* (Naperville, IL: Sourcebooks, 2001) 14.

5. Walters: p. 121.

6. The definitive history of the *Protocols* is Norman Cohn, *Warrant for Genocide: The Myth of the Jewish World-Conspiracy and "The Protocols of the Elders of Zion"* (Chicago, IL: Scholars Press, 1981), though Barkun notes an error in attribution of the authorship of the prefaces to the publication of the *Protocols* in Henry Ford's paper, the *Dearborn Independent* (see Barkun: p. 246, n.14). A more accessible (but no less effective) piece is Wil Eisner, *The Plot: The Secret Story of the Protocols of the Elders of Zion* (New York: W.W. Norton, 2005).

7. On Web sites such as Amazon.com, several online reviews of the *Protocols,* as well as reviews of books detailing its inauthenticity, can be found to show that this line of argument is still quite prevalent and powerful.

8. Dyer: p. 15.

9. Dyer: p. 79.

10. A fairly sympathetic portrayal of the Weaver family in the aftermath of Ruby Ridge can be found in Jon Ronson, *Them: Adventures with Extremists* (New York: Simon and Schuster, 2002).

11. Dyer: p. 83.

12. Dyer: p. 108.

13. "Extremist Chatter Praises Eric Rudolph as 'Hero'," http://www.adl.org/PresRele/ASUS_12/4264_72.htm, June 3, 2003 (accessed June 6, 2006).

14. The use of civil suits against white supremacist organizations was pioneered by Morris Dees. See Morris Dees and Steve Fiffer, *A Season for Justice: The*

Life and Times of Civil Rights Lawyer Morris Dees (New York: Charles Scribner's Sons, 1991).

15. Louis Beam, "Leaderless Resistance," *The Seditionist* 12 (February 1992), http://www.louisbeam.com (accessed June 5, 2006).

16. Beam, "Leaderless Resistance."

17. Beam, "Leaderless Resistance."

18. Brad Roberts, "Conclusion: The Prospects for Mass Casualty Terrorism," in *Hype or Reality: The "New Terrorism" and Mass Casualty Attacks*, ed. Brad Roberts (Alexandria, VA: Chemical and Biological Arms Control Institute, 2000) 268.

19. Jessica Eve Stern, "The Covenant, the Sword, and the Arm of the Lord (1985)," in *Toxic Terror: Assessing Terrorist Use of Chemical and Biological Weapons*, ed. J. B. Tucker (Cambridge, MA: MIT Press, 2000) 154.

20. Brad Knickerbocker, "White Supremacy Groups Use Terrorist Attacks to Recruit New Members," *White Supremacy Groups*, ed. Claire Kreger (San Diego: Greenhaven Press, 2003) 10.

21. "Jihad, in the Bible," http://www.aryan-nations.org, no date (accessed February 21, 2006).

22. "What is Aryan Islam?" http://www.aryan-nations.org, no date (accessed February 21, 2006), emphasis added.

23. For more on the topic of knowledge diffusion, including via the Internet, please see James Forest, ed., *Teaching Terror: Strategic and Tactical Learning in the Terrorist World* (Lanham, MD: Rowman & Littlefield, 2006).

BIBLIOGRAPHY

Abbas, Mazhar. "Al-Qaeda Terror Mastermind Gives Pakistani Security the Slip." *Agence France-Presse*, November 14, 2002.

Abd-Allah, Umar. *The Islamic Struggle in Syria*. Berkeley, CA: Mizan Press, 1983.

Abuza, Zachary. "Balik Terrorism: The Return of the Abu Sayyaf." Strategic Studies Institute. U.S. Army War College, September 2005.

———. *Militant Islam in Southeast Asia: Crucible of Terror*. Boulder, CO: Lynne Rienner, 2003.

Achcar, Gilbert. *The Clash of Barbarisms: The Making of the New World Disorder*. London: Saqi Books, 2006.

Alegria, Claribel, and Darwin Flakoll. *Tunnel to Canto Grande: The Story of the Most Daring Prison Escape in the History of Latin America*. Willimantic, CT: Curbstone Press, 1996.

Alexander, Yonah (ed.). *Combating Terrorism: Strategies of Ten Countries*. Ann Arbor, MI: University of Michigan Press, 2002.

——— (ed.). *Combating Terrorism: Strategies of Ten Countries*. New Delhi, Manas Publications, Indian Edition, 2003.

Alexander, Yonah, and Dennis Pluchinsky. *Europe's Red Terrorists: The Fighting Communist Organizations*. London: Frank Cass, 1992.

Alonso, Rogelio. "El Nuevo Terrorismo: Factores de Cambio y Permanencia." In *Un análisis del mal y sus consecuencias*, edited by Amalio Blanco, Rafael del Águila, and José Manuel Sabucedo. Madrid: Editorial Trotta, 2005.

"Al-Qaeda and the Separatists." *The Economist* 370, no. 8364, February 28, 2004.

Anderson, Sean K., and Stephen Sloan. *Historical Dictionary of Terrorism*, Second Edition. Lanham, MD and London: Scarecrow Press, 2002.

———. *Terrorism: Assassins to Zealots*. Lanham, MD: Scarecrow Press, 2003.

Arend, Anthony Clark. "International Law and the Use of Military Force." *The Washington Quarterly* (Spring 2003): 89–103.

Arendt, Hannah. *The Origins of Totalitarianism*. New York: Harcourt, 1966.

Arquilla, John, and David Ronfelt. *Networks and Netwar: The Future of Terrorism, Crime and Militancy*. Santa Monica, CA: Rand Corporation, 2001.

Auda, Gehad. "An Uncertain Response: The Islamic Movement in Egypt." In *Islamic Fundamentalisms and the Gulf Crisis*, edited by James Piscatori. Chicago, IL: American Academy of Arts and Sciences with the Fundamentalism Project, 1991.

Aust, Stefan. *The Baader-Meinhof Group*, translated by Anthea Bell. UK: The Bodley Head, 1987.

Aydinli, Ersel, and Umit Ozdag. "Winning a Low Intensity Conflict: Drawing Lessons from the Turkish Case." *Review of International Affairs* 2 (2003): 101–121.

Azzam, Maha. "Egypt: The Islamists and the State under Mubarak." In *Islamic Fundamentalism*, edited by Abdel Salam Sidahmed and Anoushirvan Ehteshami. Boulder, CO: Westview Press, 1996.

Baiev, Khassan. *The Oath. Surgeon Under Fire.* New York: Walker and Co., 2004.

Baker, Raymond William. *Islam without Fear: Egypt and the New Islamists.* Cambridge, MA: Harvard University Press, 1993.

Bal, Ihsan, and Sedat Laciner. "The Ideological and Historical Roots of the Kurdist Movement in Turkey: Ethnicity, Demography and Politics." *Nationalism and Ethnic Politics* 10, no. 3 (Autumn 2003): 473–504.

Balbi, Carmen Rosa, and David Scott Palmer. "'Reinventing' Democracy in Peru." *Current History* 100, no. 643 (February 2001): 65–72.

Banlaoi, Rommel C. "Maritime Terrorism in Southeast Asia: The Abu Sayyaf Threat." *Naval War College Review* 58, no 4 (Autumn 2005): 63–80.

Barkey, Henri J., and Graham E. Fuller. *Turkey's Kurdish Question.* Lanham Maryland, MD: Roman Littlefield, 1998.

Barkun, Michael. *Religion and the Racist Right: The Origins of the Christian Identity Movement.* Chapel Hill, NC: University of North Carolina Press, 1997.

Barletta, Michael. "Chemical Weapons in the Sudan: Allegations and Evidence." *The Nonproliferation Review* 6, no. 1 (Fall 1998): 115–136.

Baumann, Bommi. *How it All Began.* Vancouver, Canada: Arsenal Pulp Press, 2000.

Beam, Louis. "Leaderless Resistance." *The Seditionist* 12 (February 1992). http://www.louisbeam.com.

Becker, Jillian. *Hitler's Children: The Story of the Baader-Meinhof Terrorist Gang.* Philadelphia, PA: Lippincott Williams & Wilkins, 1977.

Beitler, Ruth M., and Cindy R. Jebb. "Egypt as a Failing State: Implications for US National Security." INSS Occasional Paper #51, July 2003.

Benjamin, Daniel, and Steven Simon. *The Age of Sacred Terror.* New York: Random House, 2002.

Bergen, Peter L. *Holy War, Inc.: Inside the Secret World of Osama bin Laden.* New York: The Free Press, 2001.

———. *The Osama Bin Laden I Know: An Oral History of al Qaeda's Leader.* New York: Free Press, 2005.

Bertrand, Jacques. "Peace and Conflict in the Southern Philippines: Why the 1996 Peace Agreement is Fragile." *Pacific Affairs* 73, no. 1 (Spring 2000): 37–54.

Bhattarai, Baburam. *The Nature of Underdevelopment and Regional Structure of Nepal: A Marxist Analysis.* Delhi: Adroit, 2003.

Binder, Leonard. "The Religious Aesthetic of Sayyid Qutb: A Non-Scriptural Fundamentalism." In *Islamic Liberalism: A Critique of Development Ideologies*, edited by Binder. Chicago, IL: University of Chicago Press, 1988.

Black, Cofer J. "Testimony of J. Cofer Black—Director of CIA Counterterrorist Center (1999–2002)." *National Commission on Terrorist Attacks Upon the United States.* April 13, 2004.

Black, Crispin. *7/7: The London Bombs: What Went Wrong?* London: Gibson Square Books, 2005.

Blanchard, Cristopher. "Al Qaeda: Statements and Evolving Ideology." CRS Report in Congress. RS 21973, November 16, 2004.

Blank, Jonah. "Kashmir, Fundamentalism Takes Root." *Foreign Affairs* (November–December 1999): 37–53.

Blank, Stephen J., and Earl H. Tilford, Jr. "Russia's Invasion of Chechnya: A Preliminary Assessment." Carlisle, PA: Strategic Studies Institute, January 13, 1995.

———. *Russia's Invasion of Chechnya: A Preliminary Assessment.* Carlisle Barracks, PA: U.S. Army War College, 1995.

Bohn, Michael K. *The Achille Lauro Hijacking; Lessons in the Politics and Prejudice of Terrorism.* Washington, DC: Brassey's Inc., 2004.

Bonner, Raymond, and James Risen. "Nairobi Embassy Received Warning of Coming Attack." *The New York Times,* October 23, 1998.

Borja, Luis Arce, and Janet Talavera Sánchez. "La entrevista del siglo: El Presidente Gonzalo rompe el silencio." *El Diario,* July 24, 1988: 2–48.

Bougereau, Jean. *Memoirs of an International Terrorist. Conversations with Hans Joachim Klein.* Orkney, UK: Cienfuegos Press, 1981.

Bowen, Sally. *The Fujimori File: Peru and its President, 1990–2000.* Lima: Peru Monitor, 2000.

Boyne, Sean. "PKK May Go Back on Offensive, Claims Ocalan." *Jane's Intelligence Review* 11, no. 2 (February 1, 1999). http://www.janes.org

Brackett, D. W. *Holy Terror: Armageddon in Tokyo.* New York: Weatherhill, 1996.

Brandon, James. "Yemen Attempts to Rein in Outlaw Tribes." *Christian Science Monitor,* January 24, 2006.

Briand, J. P. "The Achille Lauro Rescue." *The Maine Observer* 65, no. 329 (1995): 117.

Brinton, Crane. *The Anatomy of Revolution.* Upper Saddle River, NJ: Prentice-Hall, 1965.

Bunker, Robert J. (ed.). *Networks, Terrorism and Global Insurgency,* Oxford: Routledge, 2005.

Burke, Jason. *Al-Qaeda: Casting a Shadow of Terror.* London: I. B. Taurus, 2003.

Buse, Uwe, Ullrich Fichtner, Mario Kaiser, Uwe Klussmann, Walter Mayr, and Christian Neef, "Putin's Ground Zero." *Der Spiegel,* December 27, 2004: 65–101.

Byman, Daniel, Peter Chalk, Bruce Hoffman, William Rosenau, and David Brannan. *Trends in Outside Support for Insurgent Movements.* Santa Monica, CA: RAND, 2001.

Cable, Larry. "Reinventing the Round Wheel: Insurgency, Counter-Insurgency, and Peacekeeping Post Cold War." *Small Wars and Insurgencies* 4, no. 2 (Autumn 1993): 228–262.

Caplan, Lionel. *Warrior Gentlemen: "Gurkhas" in the Western Imagination.* Oxford: Berghahn Books, 1995.

Carlson, Kurt. *One American Must Die: A Hostage's Personal Account of the Hijacking of Flight 847.* New York: Congdon and Weed, 1986.

Cassese, Antonio. *Terrorism, Politics, and Law: The Achille Lauro Affairs.* Princeton, NJ: Princeton University Press, 1989.

Catanzaro, Raimondo (ed.). *The Red Brigades and Left Wing Terrorism in Italy.* New York: St. Martin's Press, 1991.

Chalk, Peter. "Separatism and Southeast Asia: The Islamic Factor in Southern Thailand, Mindanao, and Aceh." *Studies in Conflict and Terrorism* 24 (2001): 241–269.

Chivers, C. J., "The School: The Inside Story of the 2004 Attack in Beslan." *Esquire* 145, no. 6 (June 2006). http://www.esquire.com/features/articles/2006/060512_mfe_beslan.html.

Clarke, Richard. *Against All Enemies: Inside America's War on Terror*. New York: Free Press, 2004.

Coleman, A. P. *A Special Corps: The Beginnings of Gorkha Service with the British*. Cambridge: Pentland, 1999.

Coll, Steve. *Ghost Wars: The Secret History of the CIA, Afghanistan, and Bin Laden, from the Soviet Invasion to September 10, 2001*. New York: The Penguin Press, 2004.

Combs, Cindy C. *Terrorism in the Twenty-First Century*, 2nd edition. Upper Saddle River, NJ: Prentice Hall, 2000.

———. *Terrorism in the Twenty-First Century*. Saddle River, NJ: Prentice Hall, 1997.

Comisión de Juristas Internacionales. *Informe sobre la administración de justicia en el Perú*, 30 de noviembre de 1993, typescript.

Comisión de la Verdad y Reconciliación Perú, *Informe Final: Tomo I: Primera parte: El proceso, los hechos, las víctimas*. Lima: Navarrete, 2003.

Commission of Enquiry set up by the Spanish Parliament to investigate the March 11 attacks. Cortes Generales. Diario de Sesiones del Congreso de los Diputados. Comisiones de Investigación, 2004.

Congressional Research Service. "The Beirut Hostages: Background to the Crisis." Washington, DC: Foreign Affairs and National Defense Division, CRS, The Library of Congress, June 21, 1985.

———. "TWA Hijacking, A Chronology of Events." Washington, DC: Foreign Affairs and National Defense Division, CRS, The Library of Congress, June 21, 1985.

———. "Terrorism in South Asia." Washington, DC: CRS, The Library of Congress, March 8, 2004.

Coronel, José. "Violencia política y respuestas campesinas en Huanta." In *Las rondas campesinas y la derrota de Sendero Luminoso*, edited by Carlos Iván Degregori, José Coronel, Ponciano Del Pino, and Orin Starn. Lima: Instituto de Estudios Peruanos, 1996.

Cotler, Julio. *Peru Problema*. Lima: Instituto de Estudios Peruanos, 1969.

Crabtree, John. "Neopopulismo y el fenómeno Fujimori." In *El Perú de Fujimori*, edited by John Crabtree and Jim Thomas. Lima: Universidad del Pacífico y el Instituto de Estudios Peruanos, 2000.

Cragin, Kim, and Bruce Hoffman. *Arms Trafficking and Colombia*. Santa Monica, CA: RAND National Defense Research Institute, 2003.

Cragin, Kim, and Scott Gerwehr. *Dissuading Terror: Strategic Influence and the Struggle Against Terrorism*. Santa Monica, CA: RAND Corporation, 2005.

Craig, Wesley W., Jr. "Peru: The Peasant Movement of La Convención." In *Latin American Peasant Movements*, edited by Henry A. Landsberger. Ithaca, NY: Cornell University Press, 1969.

Crelinsten, Ronald D., and Iffet Özkut. "Counterterrorism Policy in Fortress Europe: Implications for Human Rights." In *European Democracies against Terrorism. Governmental policies and intergovernmental cooperation*, edited by Fernando Reinares. Aldershot: Ashgate, 2000.

Daly, John C. K., et al. (eds.). *Anatomy of a Crisis: U.S.-Uzbekistan Relations, 2001–2005*. Washington, DC: Central Asia-Caucasus & Silk Road Studies Program, Johns Hopkins University-SAIS, February 2006.

Davis, Anthony. "Tamil Tiger International," *Jane's Intelligence Review* (October 1996): 469–473.

Dawoud, Khaled. "Concepts of Jihad." *Al-Ahram Weekly Online*, January 11–17, 2001. http://weekly.Ahram.org.eg.

"Days of terror: Turkey and the Kurds." *The Economist* 376, no. 8436, July 23, 2005.

de Armond, Paul. "Right-Wing Terrorism and Weapons of Mass Destruction: Motives, Strategies, and Movements." In *Hype or Reality: The "New Terrorism" and Mass Casualty Attacks*, edited by Brad Roberts. Alexandria, VA: Chemical and Biological Arms Control Institute, 2000.

de la Puente Uceda, Luis. "The Peruvian Revolution: Concepts and Perspectives." *Monthly Review* 17 (November 1965): 12–28.

De Sales, Anne. "The Kham Magar Country: Between Ethnic Claims and Maoism." In *Resistance and the State: Nepalese Experiences*, edited by David N. Gellner. New Delhi: Social Science Press, 2003, 326–357.

Degregori, Carlos Iván. "After the Fall of Abimael Guzmán: The Limits of Sendero Luminoso." In *The Peruvian Labyrinth: Polity, Society, Economy*, edited by Maxwell A. Cameron and Philip Mauceri. University Park, PA: Pennsylvania State University Press, 1997.

———. "Harvesting Storms: Peasant Rondas and the Defeat of Sendero Luminoso in Ayacucho." In *Shining and Other Paths: War and Society in Peru, 1980–1995*, edited by Steve J. Stern. Durham, NC: Duke University Press, 1998.

———. *Ayacucho 1969–1979: El surgimiento de Sendero Luminoso*. Lima: Instituto de Estudios Peruanos, 1990.

del Pino, Ponciano. "Family, Culture, and 'Revolution:' Everyday Life with Sendero Luminoso." In *Shining and Other Paths: War and Society in Peru, 1980–1995*, edited by Steve Stern. Durham, NC: Duke University Press, 1998.

———. "Tiempos de guerra y de dioses: Ronderos, evangélicos y senderistas en el valle del río Apurímac." In *Las Rondas campesinas y la Derrota de Sendero Luminoso*, edited by Carlos Iván Degregori, et al. Lima: Instituto de Estudios Peruanos, 1996, 117–188.

Dees, Morris, and Steve Fiffer. *A Season for Justice: The Life and Times of Civil Rights Lawyer Morris Dees*. New York: Charles Scribner's Sons, 1991.

Della Porta, Donatella. "Left-Wing Terrorism in Italy." In *Terrorism in Context*, edited by Martha Crenshaw. State College, PA: Penn State University Press, 1995.

Desai, Jatin. *India and the U.S. on Terrorism*. New Delhi: Commonwealth, 2002.

Dixit, J. N. "Reality Check: India Must Structure its Response to Pervez Musharraf's Postures." *The Hindustan Times*, January 8, 2003.

———. *India's Foreign Policy Challenges on Terrorism: Fashioning New Inter State Equations*. New Delhi: Gyan Publishers, 2002.

Donahoe, John J. "The Moscow Hostage Crisis: An Analysis of Chechen Terrorist Goals." *Strategic Insights* 2, no. 5 (May 2003). http://www.ccc.nps.navy.mil/si/may03/russia.pdf.

Dowden, Richard. "The War that Cannot Speak its Name." *The Economist* 339, no. 7969, June 8, 1996.

Drake, Richard. *The Aldo Moro Murder Case*. Cambridge, MA and London: Harvard University Press, 1995.

Dunlop. John B. "Beslan: Russia's 9/11?" The American Committee for Peace in Chechnya and The Jamestown Foundation, October 2005.

Dwyer, Jim, David Kocieniewski, Deidre Murphy, and Peg Tyre. *Two Seconds Under the World*. New York: Ballantine Books, 1994.

Dyer, Joel. *Harvest of Rage: Why Oklahoma City is Only the Beginning*. Boulder, CO: Westview, 1997.

Echandía, Camilo. *El Conflicto Armado y las Manifestaciones de la Violencia en las Regiones de Colombia*. Bogotá: Presidencia de la República-Oficina del Alto Comisionado para la Paz, 1999.

Edwards, John, Jack Kemp, and Stephen Sestanovich. *Russia's Wrong Direction: What the United States Can and Should Do*. New York: Council on Foreign Relations, 2006. http://www.cfr.org/publication/9997

Engene, Jan Oskar. *Terrorism in Western Europe: Explaining the Trends since 1950*. Cheltenham, UK: Edward Elgar, 2004.

Europol. *Terrorist Activity in the European Union: Situation and Trends Report* (TESAT) October 2002–15 October 2003.

Evangelista, Matthew. *The Chechen Wars: Will Russia Go the Way of the Soviet Union?* Washington, DC: Brookings, 2003.

Fair, C. Christine. *Urban Battlefields of South Asia: Lessons Learnt from Sri Lanka, India, and Pakistan*. Santa Monica, CA: RAND, 2004.

Fall, Bernard. *The Two Viet-Nams: A Political and Military Analysis*, 2nd edition, Revised. New York: Praeger, 1967.

Fanon, Frantz. *The Wretched of the Earth*. Harmondsworth, UK: Penguin, 1967.

Farral, William Regis. *The U.S. Government Response to Terrorism: In Search of an Effective Strategy*. Boulder, CO: Westview Press, 1982.

Federal Bureau of Investigation. "Executive Summary of FBI's Investigation into the Embassy Bombings." Federal Bureau of Investigation. November 19, 1998.

Federal Bureau of Investigation. "The War on Terrorism: Remembering the losses of KENBOM/TANBOM." Federal Bureau of Investigation. August 6, 2003.

Ferro, Juan Guillermo, and Graciela Uribe. *El Orden de la Guerra. Las FARC-EP: Entre la Organización y la Política*. Bogotá: Centro Editorial Javeriano, 2002.

Fetscher, Iring. "Terrorism and Reaction." *International Summaries–A Collection of Selected Translations in Law Enforcement and Criminal Justice*. Washington, DC: US Department of Justice, National Criminal Justice Reference Service, 1979.

Fischer, Thomas. "La Constante Guerra Civil en Colombia." In *Sociedades en Guerra Civil: Conflictos violentos de Europa y Latin America*, edited by Peter Waldman and Fernando Reinares. Barcelona: Paidos, 1999.

Forest, James J. F. "The Democratic Disadvantage in the Strategic Communications Battlespace." *Democracy and Security* 2, no. 1 (2006): 73–102.

Franchetti, Mark, and Matthew Campbell. "How a Repressed Village Misfit Became the Butcher of Beslan." *The Sunday Times*, September 12, 2004. http://www.timesonline.co.uk/article/0,2089-1257953_1,00.html.

"Freedom Calls: Turkey's Kurds." *The Economist* 371, no. 8379, June 12, 2004.

Friedman, Thomas. *From Beirut to Jerusalem*. New York: Farrar Straus Giroux, 1989.

Gall, Carlotta, and Thomas de Waal. *Chechnya: Calamity in the Caucasus.* New York: New York University Press, 1998.

Ganguly, Sumit. *Conflict Unending: India–Pakistan Tensions since 1947.* New Delhi, Oxford University Press, 2002.

Gellner, David N. (ed.). *Resistance and the State: Nepalese Experiences.* New Delhi: Social Science Press, 2003.

Gerges, Fawaz. *The Far Enemy: Why Jihad Went Global.* New York: Cambridge University Press, 2005.

Ghate, Prabhu. "Kashmir: The Dirty War." *Economic and Political Weekly* (January 26, 2002): 313–322.

Giles, Kepel. *Muslim Extremism in Egypt: The Prophet and the Pharaoh.* Berkeley, CA: University of California Press, 1984.

Gonzales, José E. "Guerrillas and Coca in the Upper Huallaga Valley." In *Shining Path of Peru*, 2nd edition, edited by David Scott Palmer. New York: St. Martin's, 1994.

Goodspeed, Michael. *When Reasons Fail.* London: Praeger, 2002.

Gorriti, Gustavo. "El día que cayó Sendero Luminoso." *Selecciones de Reader's Digest* (December 1996): 117–142.

———. "Shining Path's Stalin and Trotsky." In *Shining Path of Peru*, 2nd edition, edited by David Scott Palmer. New York: St. Martin's, 1994.

———. *Sendero: La historia de la guerra milenaria en el Perú.* Lima: Editorial Apoyo, 1990.

———. *The Shining Path: A History of the Millenarian War in Peru*, translated, with an introduction, by Robin Kirk. Chapel Hill, NC: University of North Carolina Press, 2000.

Graham, Carol. *Peru's APRA: Parties, Politics, and the Elusive Quest for Democracy.* Boulder, CO: Lynne Rienner, 1992.

Gregorian, Raffi. *The British Army, the Gurkhas and Cold War Strategy in the Far East, 1947–1954.* New York: Palgrave, 2002.

Guenena, Nemat. "The 'Jihad': An 'Islamic Alternative' in Egypt." *Cairo Papers in Social Science* 9, Monograph 2. Cairo: American University in Cairo Press, 1986.

Guevara, Che. "Guerrilla Warfare." In *Mao Tse-Tung and Che Guevara: Guerrilla Warfare*, edited by F. A. Praeger, Inc. London, UK: Cassell, 1962.

Gunaratna, Rohan. "Al Qaeda's Lose and Learn Doctrine: The Trajectory from Oplan Bojinka to 9/11." In *Teaching Terror: Strategic and Tactical Learning in the Terrorist World*, edited by James J. F. Forest. Lanham, MD: Rowman & Littlefield, 2006.

———. *Indian Intervention in Sri Lanka: The Role of India's Intelligence Agencies*, 2nd ed. Colombo: South Asian Network on Conflict Research (SANCOR), 1994.

———. *Inside Al Qaeda: Global Network of Terror.* New York: Berkley Books, 2002.

Gunter, Michael M. "The Continuing Kurdish Problem in Turkey after Ocalan's Capture." *Third World Quarterly* 21, no. 5 (2000): 849–869.

Hacaoglu, Selcan. "Kurdish Success in Iraq Raises Hope, Fear in Turkey," *Associated Press*, April 9, 2006.

Hajjar, Sami G. "Hizballah: Terrorism, National Liberation, or Menace?" Monograph for the Strategic Studies Institute. Carlisle: U.S. Army War College, 2002.

Hammond, Andrew. "Between the Ballot and the Bullet: Egypt's War on Terrorism." *World Press Review Online*, November 15, 2001. http://www.worldpress.org/mideast/1114web_egypt.htm.

Hamud, Randall B (ed.). *Osama Bin Laden: America's Enemy in His Own Words*. San Diego, CA: Nadeem, 2005.

Hamzeh, Ahmad Nizar. *In the Path of Hizbullah*. Syracuse, NY: Syracuse University Press, 2004.

Harris, Paul. "Bitter Lessons for the SLA." *Jane's Intelligence Review* (October 1996): 466–468.

Henzel, Christopher. "The Origins of al Qaeda's Ideology: Implication for US Strategy." *Parameters* 35, no. 1 (2005): 69–80.

Hill, Eleanor. *Staff Statement: Joint Inquiry Staff Statement*. September 18, 2002.

Hill, Fiona, Anatol Lieven, and Thomas de Waal. "A Spreading Danger: Time for a New Policy toward Chechnya." *Carnegie Endowment for International Peace*. Policy Brief no. 35, March 2005.

Hoffman, Bruce. *Inside Terrorism*. New York: Columbia University Press, 1998.

Honderich, Ted. *Humanity, Terrorism, Terrorist War: Palestine, 9/11, Iraq, 7/7*. London: Continuum, 2006.

"Hope Versus Fear: Turkey's Kurds." *The Economist* 368, no. 8335 (August 2, 2003).

Hosmer, Stephen T. and Sybylle O. Crane. "Counterinsurgency: A Symposium, April 16–20, 1962." Santa Monica, CA: RAND, 1963.

Houben, Vincent J. "Southeast Asia and Islam." *The Annals of the American Academy*, no. 588 (July 2003): 149–170.

Howe, Marvine. "As Generals Seek Military Solution, Kurdish Problem Poisons Turkish Life." *The Washington Report on Middle East Affairs* 15, no. 4 (October, 1996): 8, 107–108.

Howitt, Arnold M., and Robyn L. Pangi (eds). *Countering Terrorism: Dimensions and Preparedness*. Cambridge, MA: The MIT Press, 2003.

Huntington, Samuel P. *Political Order in Changing Societies*. New Haven, CT: Yale University Press, 1968.

Hutt, Michael (ed.). *Himalayan People's War: Nepal's Maoist Rebellion*. Bloomington, IN: Indiana University Press, 2004.

Ibrahim, Saad Eddin. "Egypt's Islamic Activism in the 1980s." *Third World Quarterly* 10 (April 1988): 632–657.

Iguíñiz, Javier. "La estrategia económica del gobierno de Fujimori: Una visión global." In *El Perú de Fujimori*, edited by John Crabtree and Jim Thomas. Lima: Universidad del Pacífico y el Instituto de Estudios Peruanos, 2000.

International Crisis Group. *Southern Philippines Backgrounder: Terrorism and the Peace Process*. ICG Asia Report No. 80, July 13, 2004. http://www.crisisgroup.org/home/index.cfm?id=2863&l=1.

International Institute for Strategic Studies. *The Military Balance 2002–2003*. London: IISS, 2005.

Irujo, José María. *El agujero. España invadida por la yihad*. Madrid: Aguilar, 2005.

Irving, Clive (ed.). *In Their Name*. New York: Random House, 1995.

Isbell, Billy Jean. "Shining Path and Peasant Responses in Rural Ayacucho." In *Shining Path of Peru*, 2nd edition, edited by David Scott Palmer. New York: St. Martin's, 1994.

Islam, Syed Serajul. "The Islamic Independence Movements in Patani of Thailand and Mindanao of the Philippines." *Asian Survey* 38, no. 5 (May 1998): 441–456.

Jamieson, Alison. *Identity and Morality in the Italian Red Brigades*. London: Frank Cass, 1990.

Jebb, Cindy R., Peter H. Liotta, Thomas Sherlock, and Ruth Margolies Beitler. *The Fight for Legitimacy: Democracy vs. Terrorism*. Westport, CT: Praeger, 2006.

Jenkins, Brian M. "Defense against Terrorism." *Political Science Quarterly* 101, no. 5 (1986): 773–786.

———. *International Terrorism: A New Mode of Conflict*. Los Angeles: Crescent Publications, 1974.

Jenkins, Gareth. "Good Neighbor, Bad Neighbor." *Al Ahram Weekly*, no. 794 (May 11–17, 2006).

Jenkins, Vlad. *The Achille Lauro Hijacking*. Boston: President and Fellows of Harvard College, 1988.

Jha, Nalini Kant. "Countering Anti-India Terror: Beyond and Surrender." *Journal of Peace Studies* 9, no. 4 (July/August 2002): 20–38.

Jiménez Bacca, Benedicto. *Inicio, desarrollo, y ocaso del terrorismo en el Perú (2 Volumes)*. Lima: SANKI, 2000.

Joshi, Manoj. "The Indo-Pak Military Balance and Limited War." *Harvard Asia Quarterly* 6, no. 4 (Autumn 2002): 35–43.

Juergensmeyer, Mark. "Holy Orders: Religious Opposition to Modern States." *Harvard International Review* 25 (Winter 2004): 34–38.

———. *Terror in the Mind of God: The Global Rise of Religious Violence*. Berkeley, CA: University of California, 2000.

Kaplan, David E. "On Terrorism's Trail." *U.S. News & World Report*, November 23, 1998.

Kaplan, David E., and Andrew Marshall. *The Cult at the End of the World*. New York: Crown, 1996.

Karki, Arjun, and David Seddon (eds.). *The People's War in Nepal: Left Perspectives*. Delhi: Adroit, 2003.

Karnad, Bharat. "A New Strategy for the LoC and Low Intensity Conflict in Kashmir." *Faultlines* 4 (February 2000): 116–137.

———. *Nuclear Weapons and Indian Security: The Realist Foundations of Strategy*. New Delhi: Macmillan India, 2002.

Kassem, Naim. *Hizbullah: The Story from Within*. http://www.naimkassem.org.

Katz, Mark N. "Breaking the Yemen-Al Qaeda Connection." *Current History* 102 (January 2003): 40–43.

Kaumik, Shubir. "Insurgency in North East India." *Aakrosh* 1, no. 1 (October 1998): 78–88.

Keeley, Brian L. "Of Conspiracy Theories." *The Journal of Philosophy* 96, no. 3. (March 1999): 109–126.

Killcullen, David. "Countering Global Insurgency." *Journal of Strategic Studies* (August 24, 2005): 597–617.

Klarén, Peter Flindell. *Peru: Society and Nationhood in the Andes*. New York: Oxford University Press, 2000.

Knickerbocker, Brad. "White Supremacy Groups Use Terrorist Attacks to Recruit New Members." In *White Supremacy Groups*, edited by Claire Kreger. San Diego, CA: Greenhaven Press, 2003.

Knights, Michael. "Internal Politics Complicate Counterterrorism in Yemen." *Jane's Intelligence Review* (February 1, 2006).

———. "The Moral Logic of Hizballah." In *Confronting Fear*, edited by Issac Cronin. New York: Thunder's Mouth Press, 2002.

Kramer, Mark. "The Perils of Insurgency." *International Security* 29, no. 3 (Winter 2004–2005): 5–62.

Kutschera, Chris. "Abdullah Ocalan: The End of a Myth." *Middle East*, no. 298 (February 2000): 12–14.

Kux, Dennis. "India's Fine Balance." *Foreign Affairs* 81, no. 3 (May/June 2002): 93–106.

Kuzma, Lynn M. "Trends: Terrorism in the United States." *The Public Opinion Quarterly* 64, no.1 (Spring 2000): 90–105.

Lago, Ignacio, and José Ramón Montero. "Los mecanismos del cambio electoral. Del 11-M al 14-M." *Claves de Razón Práctica* 149 (2005): 36–45.

Laquer, Walter. *The Age of Terrorism.* Boston, MA: Little Brown Publishing Company, 1987.

Larsson, J. P. "The Role of Religious Ideology in Terrorist Recruitment." In *The Making of a Terrorist (Volume 1: Recruitment)*, edited by James J. F. Forest. Westport, CT: Praeger Security International, 2005.

Leavitt, Geoffrey M. *Democracies against Terror: The Western Response to State-Sponsored Terrorism.* Washington Paper, published by the Center for Strategic and International Studies. New York: Praeger, 1988.

Lesser, Ian O., Bruce Hoffman, John Arquilla, David Ronfeldt, and Michele Zanini. *Countering the New Terrorism.* Santa Monica, CA: RAND, 1999.

Levy, Jack. "The Diversionary Theory of War: A Critique." In *Handbook of War Studies,* edited by Manus I. Midlarsky. Boston, MA: Unwin Hyman, 1989.

Lieven, Anatol. "Russia's Military Nadir: The Meaning of the Chechen Debacle." *The National Interest* (Summer 1996): 24–33.

Lifton, Robert Jay. *Destroying the World to Save It: Aum Shinrikyo, Apocalyptic Violence, and the New Global Terrorism.* New York: Metropolitan Books, 1999.

Mahler, Horst. *Kollectiv RAF: über den bewaffneten Kampf in Westeuropa.* West Berlin: Wagenbuch-Rotbuch, 1971.

Makol-Abdul, Pute Rahimah. "Colonialism and Change: The Case of Muslims in the Philippines." *Journal of Muslim Minority Affairs* 17, no. 2 (October 1997): 311–323.

Mansfield, Edward, and Jack Snyder. "Democratization and War." *Foreign Affairs* 74, no. 3 (May/June 1995): 79–97.

Maoz, Zeev. *Defending the Holy Land.* Ann Arbor, MI: University of Michigan Press, 2006.

Marcuse, Herbert. "Ethics and Revolution." In *Ethics and Society*, edited by Richard De George. New York: Doubleday, 1968.

———. "Re-examination of the Concept of Revolution." *New Left Review* 56 (1969): 27–34.

Marighella, Carlos. "Minimanual of the Urban Guerrilla." Reprinted as an appendix to R. Moss, "Urban Guerrilla Warfare." *Adelphi Paper* 79. London: IISS, 1971.

Marks, Thomas A. "At the Frontlines of the GWOT: State Response to Insurgency in Sri Lanka." *Journal of Counterterrorism & Homeland Security International* 10, no. 3 (2004): 34–46.

———. *Colombian Army Adaptation to FARC Insurgency.* Carlisle: Strategic Studies Institute, U.S. Army War College, 2002.

———. "Counterinsurgency and Operational Art." *Low Intensity Conflict & Law Enforcement* 13, no. 3 (Winter 2005): 168–211.

———. "Guerrillas in the Mist: Hmong Resistance Continues in Laos." *Combat and Survival* 8, no, 5 (August 1996): 4–11.

———. "India is the Key to Peace in Sri Lanka." *Asian Wall Street Journal* (September 19–20, 1986): 8.

———. *Insurgency in Nepal.* Carlisle: Army War College, 2003.

———. *Making Revolution: The Communist Party of Thailand in Structural Perspective.* Bangkok: White Lotus, 1994.

———. *Maoist Insurgency since Vietnam.* London: Frank Cass, 1996.

———. "The Meo Hill Tribe Problem in North Thailand." *Asian Survey* 13, no. 10 (October 1973): 929–944.

———. "Peace in Sri Lanka." *Daily News* [Colombo], 3 parts, 6-7-8 July 1987: "I. India Acts in its Own Interests," 6 July: 6; "II. Bengali Solution: India Trained Personnel for Invasion of Sri Lanka," 7 July: 8; "III. India's Political Solution Narrow and Impossible," 8 July: 6.

Martin, David C., and John Walcott. *Best Laid Plans: The Inside Story of America's War against Terrorism.* New York: Harper and Row Publishers, 1988.

Mater, Nadire. "Iraq: Turkey's Kurds Maintain Hope for Recognition." *Global Information Network*, March, 31, 2003.

Matthews, Owen. "Sliding Backward: An Ugly Nationalist Mood is Brewing in Ankara, Stalling Once Hailed Reforms." *Newsweek*, April 24, 2006.

Mauceri, Philip. "Military Politics and Counter-Insurgency in Peru." *Journal of Interamerican Studies and World Affairs* 33, no. 4 (Winter 1991): 83–129.

———. *State under Siege: Development and Policy Making in Peru.* Boulder, CO: Westview, 1996.

Mazzetti, Mark. "C.I.A. Closes Unit Focused on Capture of bin Laden." *The New York Times*, July 4, 2006.

McCarthy, Rory. "Al-Qaida Linchpin Eludes His Pursuers, Most Wanted is Elusive Quarry." *The Guardian*, September 23, 2002.

McClintock, Cynthia. "The Prospects for Democratic Consolidation in a 'Least Likely' Case: Peru." *Comparative Politics* 21, no. 2 (January 1989): 127–148.

———. *Revolutionary Movements in Latin America: El Salvador's FMLN and Peru's Shining Path.* Washington, DC: U.S. Institute of Peace Press, 1998.

———. "Theories of Revolution and the Case of Peru." In *Shining Path of Peru*, 2nd edition, edited by David Scott Palmer. New York: St. Martin's Press, 1994.

McClintock, Cynthia, and Fabian Vallas. *The United States and Peru: Cooperation at a Cost.* New York: Routledge, 2003.

McCormick, Gordon H. *Sharp Dressed Men: Peru's Tupac Amaru Revolutionary Movement.* Santa Monica, CA: RAND, 1993.

McDermott, Jeremy. "Financing Insurgents in Colombia." *Jane's Intelligence Review* 15, no. 2 (2003): 16–19.

McDowall, David. *A Modern History of the Kurds*. London: I. B. Tauris, 1996.

McKenna, Thomas M. *Muslim Rulers and Rebels: Everyday Politics and Armed Separatism in the Southern Philippines*. Berkeley, CA: University of California Press, 1998

McKiernan, Kevin. "Turkey's War on the Kurds." *Bulletin of the Atomic Scientists* 55, no. 2 (Mar/Apr, 1999): 26–37.

Meade, Robert C. *Red Brigades: The Story of Italian Terrorism*. New York: St. Martin's, 1990.

Mehta, Ashok K. *The Royal Nepal Army: Meeting the Maoist Challenge*. New Delhi: Rupa, 2005.

Merritt, Richard. "The Student Protest Movement in West Berlin." *Comparative Politics* (July 1969): 516–533.

Michel, Lou, and Dan Herbeck. *American Terrorist: Timothy McVeigh and The Oklahoma City Bombing*. New York: Regan Books, 2001.

Miller, John, Michael Stone, and Chris Mitchell. *The Cell: Inside the 9/11 Plot, and Why the FBI and CIA Failed to Stop It*. New York: Hyperion, 2002.

Mitchell, Richard P. *The Society of the Muslim Brothers*, revised edition. New York: Oxford University Press, 1993.

Mohan, C. Raja. "Vajpayee and Pre-emptive War." *The Hindu*, September 12, 2002.

Mullen. Robert K. "Mass Destruction and Terrorism," *Journal of International Affairs* 32 (1978): 63–89.

Muni, S. D. *Maoist Insurgency in Nepal: The Challenge and the Response*. New Delhi: Rupa, 2003.

Murphy, Caryle. *Passion for Islam: Shaping the Modern Middle East, The Egyptian Experience*. New York: Scribner, 2002.

Muslim Youth in Europe: Addressing Alienation and Extremism. Report on Wilton Park Conference, WPSO5/3, February 7–10, 2005.

Mylroie, Laurie. *Study of Revenge: The First World Trade Center Attack and Saddam Hussein's War Against America*. Lanham, MD: AEI, 2001.

National Commission on Terrorist Attacks upon the United States. *The 9/11 Commission Report*. New York: W. W. Norton & Co., 2004.

Nepali, Prakesh, and Phanindra Subba [pseudonyms]. "Civil-Military Relations and the Maoist Insurgency in Nepal." *Small Wars and Insurgencies* 16, no. 1 (March 2005): 83–100.

Netanyahu, Benjamin (ed.). *Terrorism: How the West Can Win*. New York: The Jonathan Institute, 1986.

"New Abu Sayyaf." *The Economist* 374, no. 8414, February 19, 2005.

Nichiporuk, Brian. "Regional Demographics and the War on Terrorism." *RUSI Journal* 148, no. 1 (February 2003): 22–29.

Nigosian, S. A. *World Religions: A Historical Approach*. Boston, MA: Bedford/St. Martin's Press, 2000.

Noel Moral, Roberto C. Gen. *Ayacucho: Testimonio de un soldado*. Lima: Publinor, 1989.

Norton, Augustus Richard. "Hizballah: From Radicalism to Pragmatism?" *Middle East Policy Council Journal* 5, no. 4 (January 1998): 147–158.

Norton, Richard Augustus. *AMAL and the Shi'a, Struggle for the Soul of Lebanon*. Austin, TX: University of Texas Press, 1987.

Nye, Joseph. *The Paradox of American Power: Why the World's Superpower Can't Go it Alone.* New York: Oxford University Press, 2002.

Obando, Enrique. "Fujimori y las Fuerzas Armadas." In *El Perú de Fujimori,* edited by John Crabtree and Jim Thomas. Lima: Universidad del Pacífico y el Instituto de Estudios Peruanos, 2000.

Olesen, Thomas. *International Zapatismo: The Construction of Solidarity in the Age of Globalization.* London: Zed, 2005.

Oliverio, Annamarie. "Chapter 4. (Re)Constructing the Event: The Achille Lauro Plot." In *The State of Terror.* Albany, NY: State University of New York Press, 1998.

Oppenheimer, Martin. "The Criminalization of Political Dissent in the Federal Republic of Germany." *Contemporary Crises* 2 (1978): 97–103.

Orbach, Benjamin. "Usama Bin Ladin and Al-Qa'ida: Origins and Doctrines." *Middle East Review of International Affairs* 5, no. 4 (2001): 54–68.

Ortiz, Román D. "El Estado Colombiano Frente a las FARC: Buscando respuestas a una nueva amenaza insurgente." In *Terrorismo y Seguridad,* edited by Reinaldo Botero. Bogotá: Planeta-Semana, 2003.

———. "The Human Factor in Insurgency: Recruitment and Training in the Revolutionary Armed Forces of Colombia (FARC)." In *The Making of a Terrorist: Recruitment, Training and Root Causes (Vol. 2),* edited by James J. F. Forest. Westport, CT: Praeger Security International, 2005.

———. "Renew to Last: Innovation and Strategy of the Revolutionary Armed Forces of Colombia (FARC)." In *Teaching Terror: Strategic and Tactical Learning in the Terrorist World,* edited by James J. F. Forest. Lanham, MD: Rowman & Littlefield, 2006.

Ostrovsky, Simon. "PKK Guerrillas Sacrifice Love, Marriage and a Family for their Cause." *Agence France Presse,* May 10, 2006.

Ozcan, Nihat Ali, and M. Hakan Yavuz. "The Kurdish Question and Turkey's Justice and Development." *Middle East Policy* 13, no. 1 (Spring, 2006): 102–119.

Palmer, David Scott. "Citizen Responses to Conflict and Political Crisis in Peru: Informal Politics in Ayacucho." In *What Justice? Whose Justice? Fighting for Fairness in Latin America,* edited by Susan Eva Eckstein and Timothy P. Wickham-Crowley. Berkeley, CA: University of California Press, 2003.

———. "FONCODES y su impacto en la pacificación en el Perú: Observaciones generales y el caso de Ayacucho." In Fondo Nacional de Compensación y Desarrollo Nacional (FONCODES), *Concertando para el desarrollo: Lecciones aprendidas del FONCODES en sus estratégias de intervención.* Lima: Gráfica Medelius, 2001.

———. "National Security." In *Peru: A Country Study,* edited by Rex A. Hudson. Area Handbook Series, 4th edition. Washington, DC: Federal Research Division of the Library of Congress, 1993.

———. *Peru: The Authoritarian Tradition.* New York: Praeger, 1980.

———. "Peru's Persistent Problems." *Current History* 89, no. 543 (January 1990): 5-8, 31–34.

———. "Rebellion in Rural Peru: The Origins and Evolution of Sendero Luminoso." *Comparative Politics* 18, no. 2 (January 1986): 127–146.

———. "The Revolutionary Terrorism of Peru's Shining Path." In *Terrorism in Context*, edited by Martha Crenshaw. University Park, PA: Pennsylvania State University Press, 1995.

———. "Soluciones ciudadanas y crisis política: El caso de Ayacucho." In *El juego politico: Fujimori, la oposición y las reglas*, edited by Fernando Tuesta Soldevilla. Lima: Fundación Fredrich Ebert, 1999.

———. *Revolution from Above: Military Government and Popular Participation in Peru, 1968-1972*. Ithaca: Cornell University Latin American Studies Program, 1973.

Pathak, Bishnu. *Politics of People's War and Human Rights in Nepal*. Kathmandu: BIMIPA, 2005.

Perl, Raphael, and Ronald O'Rourke. "Terrorist Attack on the USS *Cole*: Background and Issues for Congress." CRS Report for Congress # RS20721.http://www.fas.org/sgp/crs/index.html.

Perl, Raphael. "Terrorism: U.S. Response to Bombings in Kenya and Tanzania: A New Policy Direction?" CRS Report for Congress, September 1, 1998.

Peterson, Scott. "Is Yemen a Conduit for Global Terrorism?" *Christian Science Monitor*, March 31, 2000.

Pillar, Paul R. *Terrorism and U.S. Foreign Policy*. Washington, DC: Brookings Institution Press, 2001.

Pizarro, Eduardo. *Insurgencia sin Revolución. La Guerrilla en Colombia en una Perspectiva Comparada*. Bogotá: Tercer Mundo Editores-IEPRI, 1996.

———. *Las FARC 1949–1966. De la Autodefensa de Masas a la Combinación de Todas las Formas de Lucha*. Bogotá: Tercer Mundo Editores-IEPRI, 1992.

———. *Una democracia asediada. Balance y Perspectivas del Conflicto Armado en Colombia*. Bogotá: Norma, 2004.

Pluchinsky, Dennis A. "Western Europe's Red Terrorists: The Fighting Communist Organizations." In *Europe's Red Terrorists: The Fighting Communist Organizations*, edited by Yonah Alexander and Dennis Pluchinsky. London: Frank Cass, 1992.

Posner, Richard A. *Preventing Surprise Attacks: Intelligence Reform in the Wake of 9/11*. New York: Rowman & Littlefield, 2005.

Priest, Dana, and Susan Schmidt. "Hunt Grows in Yemen for Al Qaeda: Persian Gulf Nation's Links to Terror Fuel U.S. Resolve." *Washington Post*, September 15, 2002.

Qutb, Sayyid. *al-Ma'alim fi tariq*. Beirut: Dar al-Shuruq, 1980.

Rabasa, Angel, and Peter Chalk. *Colombian Labyrinth. The Synergy of Drugs and Insurgency and its Implications for Regional Stability*. Santa Monica, CA: Rand, 2001.

Radu, Michael. "The Rise and Fall of the PKK." *Orbis* 45, no. 1 (Winter 2001) 47–63.

RAF statement, *Der Spiegel*, January 2, 1975.

Rai, Milan. *7/7: The London Bombings, Islam, and the Iraq War*. Ann Arbor, MI: University of Michigan Press, 2006.

Rajagopalan, Rajesh. "Restoring Normalcy: The Evolution of the Indian Army's Counterinsurgency Doctrine." *Small Wars and Insurgencies* (Spring 2000): 44–68.

Rangel, Alfredo. "Las FARC-EP: Una Mirada Actual." In *Reconocer la guerra para construir la paz*, edited by Malcom Deas and María Victoria Llorente. Bogota: Cerec-Uniandes-Norma, 1999.

————. "Parasites and Predators: Guerrillas and the Insurrection Economy of Colombia." *Journal of International Affairs* 53, no. 2 (2000): 577–601.

Rapoport, David, and Leonard Weinberg. "Elections and Violence." *Terrorism and Political Violence* 12 (2000): 15–50.

Rashid, Ahmed. *Jihad: The Rise of Militant Islam in Central Asia.* New York: Penguin, 2002.

————. *Taliban: Militant Islam, Oil, & Fundamentalism in Central Asia.* New Haven, CT: Yale University Press, 2000.

Reeve, Simon. *The New Jackals: Ramzi Yousef, Osama bin Laden and the Future of Terrorism.* Boston, CA: Northeastern University, 1999.

Reinares, Fernando. "Al Qaeda, neosalafistas magrebíes y 11-M: sobre el nuevo terrorismo islamista en España." In *El nuevo terrorismo islamista. Del 11-S al 11-M*, edited by Fernando Reinares and Antonio Elorza. Madrid: Temas de Hoy, 2004.

Ressa, Maria. *Seeds of Terror.* New York: Free Press, 2003.

Ringuet, Daniel Joseph. "The Continuation of Civil Unrest and Poverty in Mindanao." *Contemporary Southeast Asia* 24, no. 1 (April 2002): 33–49.

Risen, James. "To Bomb Sudan Plant, or Not; A Year Later, Debates Rankle." *The New York Times*, October 27, 1999.

————. "U.S. Directs International Drive on Bin Laden Networks." *The New York Times*, September 25, 1998.

Robbins, James S. "Sovereignty-Building: The Case of Chechnya." *The Fletcher Forum of World Affairs* (Summer/Fall 1997): 17–36.

Roberts, Brad. "Conclusion: The Prospects for Mass Casualty Terrorism." In *Hype or Reality: The "New Terrorism" and Mass Casualty Attacks*, edited by Brad Roberts. Alexandria, VA: Chemical and Biological Arms Control Institute, 2000.

Saad-Ghorayeb, Amal. *Hizbu'llah, Politics and Religion.* Sterling, UK: Pluto Press, 2002.

Sageman, Marc. *Understanding Terrorist Networks.* Philadelphia, PA: University of Pennsylvania Press, 2004.

Santamaría, Julián. "El azar y el contexto." *Claves de Razón Práctica* 146 (2004): 28–40.

Saribrahimoglu, Lale. "Turkey Attacks PKK: 130 killed." *Jane's Defense Weekly*, April 17, 1996.

————. "Turkish Troops Kill 45 in Latest Deep Strike against PKK." *Jane's Defense Weekly*, July 3, 1996.

Sartre, Jean Paul. "Preface." In *The Wretched of the Earth*, by Frantz Fanon. Harmondsworth, UK: Penguin, 1967.

Sayyid Ahmed, Rif'at (ed.). *The Militant Prophet. 2 Vols.* London: Riad El-Rayyes, 1991.

Schalk, Peter. "Resistance and Martyrdom in the Process of State Formation of Tamil Eelam." In *Martyrdom and Political Resistance: Essays From Asia and Europe*, edited by Joyce Pettigrew, accessed at http://www.tamilnation.org/ideology/schalkthiyagam.htm. Amsterdam: Centre for Asian Studies/Vu University Press, 1997.

————. "The Revival of Martyr Cults Among Havar, *Temenos* 33 (1997): 151–190, accessed at http://tamilnation.org/ideology/schalk01.htm.

Schanzer, Jonathan. "Yemen's Al Qaeda Amnesty: Revolving Door or Evolving Strategy?" PolicyWatch #808. Washington Institute for Near East Policy, November 26, 2003. http://www.washingtoninstitute.org.

———. "Yemen's War on Terror," *Orbis* (Summer 2004): 517–531.

Schmid, Alex P. "Terrorism and Democracy." In *Western Responses to Terrorism*, edited by Alex P. Schmid and Ronald D. Crelinsten. Londres: Frank Cass, 1993.

———. "Terrorism and the Media: The Ethics of Publicity." *Terrorism and Political Violence* 1 (1989): 539–565.

———. "Towards Joint Political Strategies for De-legitimising the use of Terrorism." In *Countering Terrorism through International Cooperation.* Proceedings of the International Conference on "Countering Terrorism through Enhanced international Cooperation," Courmayeur, Mont Blanc, Italy, September 22–24, 2000.

Schmid, Alex P., and A. J. Jongman. *Political Terrorism: A Research Guide to Concepts, Theories, Data Bases and Literature.* Amsterdam: Royal Netherlands Academy of Arts and Sciences Social Science Research Center (SWIDOC) and New York: Transaction Books, 1981.

Schmitz, Charles. "Investigating the *Cole* Bombing." *Middle East Report Online*, September 6, 2001. http://www.merip.org/mero/mero090601.html.

Schultz, Richard. "Showstoppers: Nine Reasons Why We Never Sent Our Special Operations Forces After al Qaeda Before 9/11." *The Weekly Standard*, January 26, 2004: 25–33.

Schwedler, Jillian. "Yemen's Aborted Opening," *Journal of Democracy* 13, no. 4 (October 2002): 48–55.

Schweitzer, Yoram. "The Capture of Khalid Sheikh Mohammad." Herziliya, Israel: Jaffee Center for Strategic Studies, March 5, 2003.

Scott, Roddy. "Ankara's PKK Hunt Leaves Regional Conflict Cycle Intact." *Jane's Intelligence Review*, August 1, 1997.

———. "PKK is Down But Not Out as Leaders Talk of Three Front War." *Jane's Intellignece Review* 11, no. 5 (May 1, 1999): 24–27.

———. "PKK Policy Switch." *Jane's Defense Weekly* 32, no. 24 (December 15, 1999).

Seale, Patrick. *Asad: The Struggle for the Mideast.* Berkeley, CA: University of California Press. 1988.

Sharma, Rajeev. *Proxy War: A Story of ISI, Bin Laden and Kargil.* New Delhi: South Asia Books, 2002.

Shell, Kurt. "Extraparliamentary Opposition in Postwar Germany." *Comparative Politics* (July 1970): 563–680.

Shelton, Henry. "Professional Education: The Key to Transformation." *Parameters* (Autumn 2001): 4–16.

Shrestha, Aditya Man. *The Dreadful Night: Carnage at Nepalese Royal Palace.* Kathmandu: Ekta, 2001.

Shrestha, Chuda Bahadur. *Nepal: Coping With Maoist Insurgency.* Kathmandu: Nepal Lithographing, 2004.

Shukrallah, Hani. "Political Crisis/Conflict in Post-1967 Egypt." In *Egypt under Mubarak*, edited by Charles Tripp and Roger Owen. London: Routledge, 1989.

Shultz, Richard, Jr., and Ruth Margolies Beitler. "Tactical Deception and Strategic Surprise in Al Qai'ida's Operations." *Middle East Review of International Affairs* 8, no. 2 (June 2004). http://meria.idc.ac.il/journal/2004/issue2/jv8n2a6.html.

Shvarev, Aleksander. "'Man With a Gun' From Engenoy." *Moscow Vremya Novostey*, September 16, 2004.

Sidoti, Francesco. "Terrorism Supporters in the West: The Italian case." In *Tolerating Terrorism in the West: An International Survey*, edited by Noemi Gal-Or. London and New York: Routledge, 1991.

Sikand, Yoginder. "Changing Course of Kashmiri Struggle: From National Liberation to Islamist Jihad?" *Economic and Political Weekly* (January 20, 2001): 218–227.

———. *The Implications of the Achille Lauro Hijacking for the Maritime Community.* (RAND Papers Series). Santa Monica, CA: RAND, 1986.

Simon, Jeffrey D. *The Terrorist Trap: America's Experience with Terrorism.* Bloomington, IN: Indiana University Press, 1994.

Sinha, S. K. "Jammu and Kashmir: Past, Present, and Future." *The Journal of the USI of India*, no. 560 (April–June 2005): 182–199.

Sloan, Stephen. *The Anatomy of Nonterritorial Terrorism: An Analytical Essay.* Gaithersburg, MD: International Association of Chiefs of Police, 1979.

Slocombe, Walter B. "Force Pre-emption and Legitimacy." *Survival* 45, no. 1 (Spring 2003): 117–130.

Smith, Dennis Mack. *Modern Italy: A Political History.* Ann Arbor, MI: University of Michigan Press, 1997.

Smith, James M. "Aum Shinrikyo." In *Weapons of Mass Destruction: An Encyclopedia of Worldwide Policy, Technology, and History*, edited by Eric Croddy and James Wirtz. Santa Barbara, CA: ABC CLIO, 2005.

Sood, V. K., and P. Sawhney. *Operation Parakram: The War Unfinished.* New Delhi: Sage, 2003.

Spencer, David. "A Lesson for Colombia." *Jane's Intelligence Review* 9, no. 10 (1997): 474–477.

Starn, Orin (ed.). *Hablan Los Ronderos: La búsqueda por la paz en los Andes.* Documento de Trabajo No. 45. Lima: Instituto de Estudios Peruanos, 1993.

———. "Sendero, Soldados y Ronderos en el Mantaro." *Quehacer* 74 (November–December 1991): 60–68.

———. "Villagers at Arms: War and Counterrevolution in the Central-South Andes." In *Shining and Other Paths: War and Society in Peru, 1980–1995*, edited by Steve J. Stern. Durham, NC: Duke University Press, 1998.

Starr, S. Frederick. "A Solution for Chechnya." *Washington Post*, September 17, 2004.

Stavig, Ward. "Tupac Amaru, The Body Politic, and The Embodiment of Hope: Inca Heritage and Social Justice in the Andes." In *Death, Dismemberment, and Memory*, edited by Lyman L. Johnson. Albuquerque, NM: University of New Mexico Press, 2004.

Stern, Jessica. *Terror in the Name of God.* Cambridge, MA: Harvard University Press, 2003.

———. "The Covenant, the Sword, and the Arm of the Lord (1985)." In *Toxic Terror: Assessing Terrorist Use of Chemical and Biological Weapons*, edited by J. B. Tucker. Cambridge, MA: MIT Press, 2000.

Storn, Orin, Carlos I. Degregori, and Robin Kirk (eds.). *The Peru Reader: History, Culture, Politics.* Durham, NC: Duke University Press, 1995.

Stortoni-Wortmann, Luciana. "The Political Response to Terrorism in Italy from 1969 to 1983." In *European Democracies against Terrorism: Governmental Policies and Intergovernmental Cooperation*, edited by Fernando Reinares. Burlington, VT: Ashgate, 2000.

Strasser, Steve (ed.). *The 9/11 Investigations: Staff Report of the 9/11 Commission*. New York: Public Affairs Reports, 2004.

Strong, Simon. *Sendero Luminoso: El Movimiento Subversivo más Letal del Mundo*. Lima: Peru Reporting, 1992.

Subramanyam, K. *From Surprise to Reckoning: The Kargil Review Committee Report*. New Delhi: Sage Publications, 2000.

Sullivan, Denis, and Sana Abed-Kotob, *Islam in Contemporary Egypt: Civil Society vs. the State*. Boulder, CO: Lynne Rienner, 1999.

Swamy, M. R. Narayan. *Tigers of Lanka: From Boys to Guerrillas*, 3rd ed. New Delhi: Konark, 2002.

Taber, Robert. *The War of the Flea*. London: Paladin, 1970.

Talhami, Ghada Hashem. "Syria: Islam, Arab Nationalism and the Military." *Middle East Policy* 8, no. 4 (December 2001): 110–127.

Tapia, Carlos. *Las Fuerzas Armadas y Sendero Luminoso: Dos estratégias y un final*. Lima: Instituto de Estudios Peruanos, 1997.

Tarazona Sevillano, Gabriela. *Sendero Luminoso and the Threat of Narcoterrorism*. Center for Strategic and International Studies, Washington Papers 144. New York: Praeger, 1990.

Tarrow, Sidney. *Democracy and Disorder: Protest and Politics in Italy 1965–1975*. Oxford: Clarendon Press, 1989.

Taylor, Lewis. "La estratégia contrainsurgente: El PCP-SL y la guerra civil en el Perú, 1980–1996." *Debate Agrario* 26 (July 1997): 81–110.

Tellis, Ashleyl C. Christine Fair and Jamison Jo Medby. *Limited Conflict Under the Nuclear Umbrella: Indian and Pakistani Lessons from the Kargil Crisis*. Santa Monica, CA: RAND, 2001.

Tenet, George. "Written Statement for the Record of the Director of Central Intelligence." *National Commission on Terrorist Attacks upon the United States*, March 24, 2004.

———. "The Maobadi of Nepal." In *State of Nepal*, edited by Kanak Mani Dixit and Shastri Ramachandaran. Kathmandu: Himal, 2002.

Thapa, Deepak (ed.). *Understanding the Maoist Movement of Nepal*. Kathmandu: Chautari, 2003.

Thomas, Timothy L. "Grozny 2000: Urban Combat Lessons Learned." *Military Review* (July–August 2000): 50–58.

———. "The Battle of Grozny: Deadly Classroom for Urban Combat." *Parameters* (Summer 1999): 87–102.

Thomas, Ward. "Norms and Security: The Case of International Assassination." International Security 25, no. 1 (Summer 2000): 105–133.

Tulloch, John. *One Day in July: Experiencing 7/7*. London: Little, Brown Book Group, 2006

Turbiville, Graham H., Jr. "Bearer of the Sword." *Military Review* (March–April 2002): 38–48.

"Turkey: Springtime Means Wartime (Turkey vs. the Kurdish Workers (PKK)), *The Economist*, 339, no. 7965, May 11, 1996.

"Turkey's Kurds Fight on Alone." *The Nation* 258, no. 1 (January 3, 1994): 8–10.

Turner, Stansfield. *Terrorism and Democracy*. Boston, MA: Houghton Mifflin Company, 1991.

U.S. Congress. Senate Government Affairs Permanent Subcommittee on Investigations (Minority Staff). *Global Proliferation of Weapons of Mass Destruction: A Case Study on the Aum Shinrikyo*. Washington, DC, October 31, 1995.

U.S. Department of State. *Report of the Accountability Review Boards: Bombings of the US Embassies in Nairobi, Kenya and Dar es Salaam, Tanzania on August 7, 1998*. U.S. Department of State. January 8, 1999.

United States Institution of Peace. *The Mindanao Peace Talks: Another Opportunity to Resolve the Moro Conflict in the Philippines*. USIP Special Report 131, February 2005. http://www.usip.org/pubs/specialreports/sr131.html.

United States of America v Ramzi Ahmed Yousef, Eyad Ismoil, Abdul Hakim Murad, Wali Khan Amin Shah. S 1239 Cr.180 (KTD) (S.D. New York, 1996).

United States of America v Ramzi Ahmed Yousef, Eyad Ismoil. S 1239 Cr.180 (KTD) (S.D. New York, 1997).

United States of America v. Usama Bin Laden et al. S 98 Cr. 539 (S.D. New York, 1998).

Upreti, Bishnu Raj. *The Price of Neglect: From Resource Conflict to Maoist Insurgency in the Himalayan Kingdom*. Kathmandu: Bhrikuti Academic Publications, 2004.

Uzzell, Lawrence. "Reporter Puts Forward Another Version of Events." *Chechnya Weekly* 5, no. 35 (September 15, 2004): 5–8.

Valenzuela, Javier. *España en el punto de mira. La amenaza del integrismo islámico*. Madrid:Temas de Hoy, 2002.

van Creveld, Martin. *The Transformation of War*. New York: The Free Press, 1991.

Van Dam, Nikolaos. *The Struggle for Power in Syria*. London: I.B. Tauris.

Varon, Jeremy. *Bringing the War Home: The Weather Underground, the Red Army Faction, and Revolutionary Violence in the Sixties and Seventies*. Berkeley, California, CA: The University of California Press, 2004.

Vick, Karl. "Assault on a U.S. Embassy: A Plot Both Wide and Deep." *The Washington Post*, November 23, 1998.

Vistica, Gregory L., and Daniel Klaidman. "Tracking Terror." *Newsweek*, October 19, 1998.

Walters, Jerome. *One Aryan Nation under God: How Religious Extremists Use the Bible to Justify Their Actions*. Naperville, IL: Sourcebooks, 2001.

Weaver, Mary Anne. "Pharoahs-in Waiting. Who Will Succeed Egypt's Hosni Mubarak as the Ruler of the World's Most Populous and Important Arab Country?" *The Atlantic* (October 2003): 79–92.

Weinberg, Leonard, and William Lee Eubank. *The Rise and Fall of Italian Terrorism*. Boulder, CO: Westview Press, 1987.

Weiner, Tim, and James Risen. "Decision to Strike Factory in Sudan Based on Surmise Inferred From Evidence." *The New York Times*, September 21, 1998.

Weiser, Benjamin. "U.S. Says Bin Laden Aide Tried to Get Nuclear Material." *The New York Times*, September 26, 1998.

Whelpton, John. *A History of Nepal*. New York: Cambridge, 2005.

————. *The Making of Terrorism*, translated by David Gordon White. Chicago, IL: The University of Chicago Press, 1993.

Wieviorka, Michel. "Terrorism in the Context of Academic Research." In *Terrorism in Context*, edited by Martha Crenshaw. University Park, PA: The Pennsylvania State University Press, 1995.

Wilkinson, Paul. *Terrorism Versus Democracy.* London: Frank Cass Publishers, 2000.

————. *Terrorism Versus Democracy: The Liberal State Response.* London: Frank Cass, 2001.

Wills, David C. "Hijacking of the *Achille Lauro.*" In *The First War on Terrorism: Counter-Terrorism Policy During the Reagan Administration.* Lanham, MD: Rowman & Littlefield, 2003.

Yekaterina, Blinova, and Anton Trofimov. "Beslan Hostage Takers May Have Included Arrested Terrorist, Basayev Link Likely." *Nezavisimaya Gazeta*, September 8, 2004.

Zimmermann, Tim. "Coercive Diplomacy and Libya." In *The Limits of Coercive Diplomacy*, 2nd edition, edited by Alexander L. George and William E. Simons. Boulder, CO: Westview Press, 1994.

Zuhur, Sherifa. "A New Phase for Jihad in Egypt?" In *Unmasking Terror: A Global Review of Terrorist Activities*, edited by Christopher Heffelfinger. Washington, DC: Jamestown Foundation, 2006.

Web Sites

Al Manar Television
   http://www.almanar.com
Al Jazeera Television
   http://english.aljazeera.net
Aryan Nations
   http://www.aryan-nations.org
Center for Defense Information
   http://www.cdi.org
Chechnya Weekly
   http://www.jamestown.org
CIA World Factbook
   http://www.cia.gov/cia/publications/factbook
Colombian Ministry of Defense
   http://www.mindefensa.gov.co
Combating Terrorism Center at West Point
   http://ctc.usma.edu
Convention against Torture and Other Cruel, Inhuman or Degrading Treatment or Punishment
   http://www.ohchr.org/english/law/cat.htm
International Crisis Group
   http://www.crisisgroup.org
London Assembly
   http://www.london.gov.uk/assembly

London Resilience Forum
   http://www.londonprepared.gov.uk
Louis Beam's Seditionist Website
   http://www.louisbeam.com
Metropolitan Police Service
   http://www.met.police.uk
MI5 The Security Service
   http://www.mi5.gov.uk
Middle East Media Research Institute
   http://www.memri.org
Ministry of Defence of India
   http://mod.nic.in
MIPT Terrorism Knowledge Base
   http://www.tkb.org
National Defence College of the Philippines
   http://www.ndcp.edu.ph
Open Source Center (U.S. Government)
   http://www.opensource.gov
RAND Corporation
   http://www.rand.org
Teaching Terror
   http://www.teachingterror.net
Terrorism Monitor
   http://www.jamestown.org
UK Government Foreign Office
   http://www.fco.gov.uk
UK Government, Home Office
   http://www.homeoffice.gov.uk
UK Government Security Service
   http://www.mi5.gov.uk
UK Resilience
   http://www.ukresilience.info/terrorism.htm
US Department of Defense
   http://www.defenselink.mil
US Department of State
   http://www.state.gov
US Institute of Peace
   http://www.usip.org

INDEX

Prisoner/prison conditions
RAF sympathy, 287–89
West German response, 276–77, 282–85
Project Heartland, Murrah bombing response, 250
Pronichev, Vladimir, Beslan school crisis, 187
"Propaganda by deed," 15
Protection, CONTEST strategy, 231, 236–37
Protocols of the Elder of Zion, Christian Identity movement, 571, 576–78
Provisional Irish Republican Army (PIRA), 545
Proxy war, Kashmir, 516, 529
Psychological warfare, Israel, 419–20
Psychology departments, terrorism studies, 21, 25
Pubblica Sicurezza (PS), Italian antiterrorist police, 356
Public health education, sarin attack, 22
Public morale, Israel, 417
Puerto Rican separatist groups, domestic terrorism, 22
Pulikovsky, Lt. Gen. Konstantin, Chechen crisis, 97–98
"Pure liberals," Columbia, 314
Pursuit, CONTEST strategy, 231, 234–36
Putin, Vladimir
acting president, 338
Beslan school crisis, 179–81, 187
Chechen crisis, 100
Chechenization strategy, 342–46
current Chechen policy, 346–47
Dagestan crisis, 337
Second Chechen War, 339–41

Qadus, Ahmed Abdul, capture of, 170
al-Qantari, Samir, *Achille Lauro* demand, 58
Quso, Fahd, *USS Cole* bombers, 153–54 al
Qutb, Sayyid, 433, 445–46

Rabin, Yitahak
on Tunis PLO attack, 52–53
on TWA 847 detainee release, 46
Racism, Peruvian politics, 295
Radicals Edict, response to RAF, 285–86
"Radio Imperial," 472
Raduyev, Salman, Chechen rebellion, 90
Rafaat, Samir, 454
al-Rahal, Muhammad Salim, 448
al-Rahman, Mullah Omar (Umar Abd), 73, 75, 170, 451
and bin Laden, 111–12, 117–18
al-Rahman, Mohammad Abd, capture of, 170
Ramonova, Ala, Beslan school crisis, 189
Ramos, Fidel, 489, 491
Ramzanov, Vakha, Grozny seizure, 95
Rand Corporation, terrorism studies, 14
Rand study. *See* "Counterinsurgency: A Symposium"
Rantitisi, Abdel Azia, 418
Rapse, Jan-Carl, death of, 275–76, 283, 287
Rashtriya Rifles (RR), Kashmir, 521
Rawalpindi (Pakistan), KSM capture, 162
Reagan, Ronald
Achille Lauro crisis, 60–61
terrorism policy, 46–47
TWA 847 crisis, 41–43
Red Aid, RAF support group, 284
Red Army Faction (RAF)
attempted NATO destabilization, 81
background of, 277
East German police links, 276
ideology of, 277–81
Lufthansa hijacking, 276
meeting with Red Brigade, 360–61
prisoner treatment, 282–83
Schleyer kidnapping, 275–76
sympathy toward, 282, 287–89
Red Brigade (*Brigate Rosse*, BR)
early activities, 354–56

ABOUT THE EDITOR
AND CONTRIBUTORS

JAMES J. F. FOREST is Director of Terrorism Studies and Associate Professor of Political Science at the U.S. Military Academy at West Point, where he teaches undergraduate courses on terrorism, counterterrorism, and information warfare, and directs research initiatives for the Combating Terrorism Center. His recent publications include *Teaching Terror: Strategic and Tactical Learning in the Terrorist World* (2006); *Homeland Security: Protecting America's Targets* (2006); and *The Making of a Terrorist: Recruitment, Training and Root Causes* (2005). His research has also appeared in the *Cambridge Review of International Affairs*, the *Journal of Political Science Education*, and *Democracy and Security*. Dr. Forest received his graduate degrees from Stanford University and Boston College, and undergraduate degrees from Georgetown University and De Anza College.

GARY A. ACKERMAN is Director of the Center for Terrorism and Intelligence Studies and Research Director of the National Consortium for the Study of Terrorism and the Response to Terrorism. He received his M.A. from Yale University and his bachelor's and honors degrees from the University of the Witwatersrand in Johannesburg, South Africa. Ackerman has published extensively in a variety of academic and popular media, and has also been invited to present briefings and talks before a variety of government and academic audiences.

ROGELIO ALONSO is a Lecturer in Politics and Terrorism at Universidad Rey Juan Carlos of Madrid and coordinator of the Unit for Documentation and Analysis on Terrorism at this university. He is the author of three books on terrorism, and a fourth—*The IRA and Armed Struggle*—will be published by Routledge in 2007. He has also written numerous chapters in collective books as well as articles in academic journals such as *Terrorism and Political Violence* as well as *Studies in Conflict and Terrorism*. His latest publications include several chapters on international terrorism, anti-terrorist responses in liberal democracies as well as the radicalization processes of Salafist Jihadist. He serves as book review editor for the journal *Democracy and Security*.

SEAN K. ANDERSON is Professor of Political Science at Idaho State University. From 1980 to 1982, Dr. Anderson worked as chief editor in the International Department of the Pars News Agency in Tehran, Iran. He has published several studies concerning state sponsorship of terrorism in the Middle East, including articles in *Conflict Quarterly* and *Studies in Conflict and Terrorism*. Together with Stephen Sloan, he has published the *Historical Dictionary of Terrorism* (Scarecrow Press, 2002, 2nd ed.). Dr. Anderson also works with state and local emergency planning and disaster relief agencies.

DANIEL BARACSKAY is Assistant Professor of Political Science and Public Administration at Valdosta State University. He holds five academic degrees, including an M.B.A. from Cleveland State University, and a Ph.D. in Political Science from the University of Cincinnati. He has also taught at Cleveland State University, the University of Akron, and University of Cincinnati. Dr. Baracskay has contributed to several books and academic journals and published a book entitled *The Rise and Destruction of the Warner & Swasey Company* in 2003 with co-author Peter Rebar. His research interests are diverse, covering American politics, public administration, international relations, and comparative politics.

RUTH MARGOLIES BEITLER is Associate Professor of International Relations and Comparative Politics in the Department of Social Sciences. She serves as course director for Middle East Politics and Cultural Anthropology. She is author of *The Path to Mass Rebellion: An Analysis of Two Intifadas* (2004), and co-author of *The Fight for Legitimacy: Democracy vs. Terrorism* (2006). She has written numerous articles and chapters on the Middle East, and has appeared on the CBS Morning Show and MSNBC as a commentator on Middle East affairs. A graduate of Cornell University with a B.A. in Near Eastern Studies, Dr. Beitler holds a M.A. in Law and Diplomacy from the Fletcher School of Law and Diplomacy, Tufts University, where she also received her Ph.D. in International Relations.

ROBIN L. BOWMAN is a Captain in the United States Air Force, and currently serves as an Assistant Professor of Political Science at the United States Air Force Academy. She holds a Bachelors degree in Political Science from the University of California, Berkeley, a Masters degree in National Security Affairs from the Naval Postgraduate School, and is working toward her Ph.D. in Political Science at the University of California, Irvine. Her areas of interest include South/Southeast/East Asian politics, security, ethnic conflict, religious extremism, and terrorism.

ERICA CHENOWETH is a doctoral candidate at the University of Colorado at Boulder and a fellow at Harvard University. Her primary research emphases are terrorism and counterterrorism in democracies. She has presented her research nationwide, having published articles and book reviews in venues such as the *Review of Policy Research, Terror and Conflict Monitor, the International Criminal Justice Review,* and *e-Extreme.* Her work has also appeared in several edited volumes, including *The Making of a Terrorist: Recruitment, Training, and Root Causes* (2005) and *Homeland Security: Protecting America's Targets* (2006).

ADAM DOLNIK is Director of Research Development and Senior Research Fellow at the Centre for Transnational Crime Prevention (CTCP), University of Wollongong, Australia. He has also worked as a researcher at the Institute of Defense and Strategic Studies in Singapore, the WMD Terrorism Research Program at the Monterey Institute of International Studies, and at the United Nations Terrorism Prevention Branch in Vienna. His research has been published in a number of books and journals, including *Terrorism and Political Violence, Studies in Conflict and Terrorism, International Negotiation: Journal of Theory and Practice, Perspectives: Central European Review of International Affairs,* and *Yaderny Kontrol.*

VERA ECCARIUS-KELLY is an Assistant Professor of Political Science at Siena College in Albany, NY, and specializes in comparative Latin American and Middle East politics. In 2002, she received her Ph.D. from The Fletcher School of Law and Diplomacy at Tufts University in Boston. Dr. Eccarius-Kelly has spent extended periods of time researching revolutionary movements in Central America and among her recent publications are "Guatemalan Women's Cooperatives and State Neglect," *Peace Review: A Journal of Social Science* 18, no. 1 (2006): 37–43, "Political Movements and Leverage Points: Kurdish Activism in the European Diaspora," *The Journal of Muslim Minority Affairs* 22 (2002): 91–118, and "Radical Consequences of Benign Neglect: The Rise of the PKK in Germany," *The Fletcher Forum of World Affairs* 24 (2000): 161–174.

BRIAN FISHMAN is a Senior Associate at the Combating Terrorism Center at West Point and an Instructor in the Department of Social Sciences. His research interests include Abu Mus'ab al-Zarqawi and the insurgency in Iraq, and American grand strategy. Previously, Fishman worked as a Legislative Assistant on Capitol Hill. He has a Master's degree from Columbia University and a B.A. from the University of California Los Angeles.

JOSHUA L. GLEIS is a Research Fellow at the Belfer Center for Science and International Studies at Harvard University and a Ph.D. candidate at the Fletcher School of Law and Diplomacy at Tufts University. As an analyst at the Jebsen Center for Counter Terrorism Studies at the Fletcher

School, his areas of focus are counterterrorism, counterinsurgencies, and the Middle East.

LYDIA KHALIL is a Counterterrorism Analyst for the New York Police Department and is also affiliated with Jamestown Foundation where she is a regular contributor to *Terrorism Focus* and *Terrorism Monitor*. She previously worked in Iraq as a policy advisor for the Coalition Provisional Authority in Baghdad. Prior to that Lydia was appointed to the White House Office of Homeland Security. Lydia has worked at home and abroad for the U.S. government, international organizations, private companies, and think tanks on a variety of Middle East and terrorism issues. Born in Cairo and raised in the United States, Lydia received her B.A. from Boston College in International Relations and her M.A. from Georgetown University in International Security.

TOM MALEY is a lecturer in the Security Studies Institute of Cranfield University, part of the Defence College of Management and Technology at the Defence Academy of the United Kingdom. Prior to joining Cranfield University, he was a career officer in the Educational and Training Services Branch of the British Army, where he specialized in officers' education, most notably teaching war studies and international relations at the Royal Military Academy, Sandhurst, and, latterly, security studies at the George C. Marshall European Center for Security Studies in Garmisch-Partenkirchen, Germany. His primary areas of interest lie in nontraditional security threats and challenges. He specializes in the teaching of terrorism and political violence at the postgraduate level.

THOMAS A. MARKS is a Professor of Insurgency, Terrorism, and Counterterrorism at the School for National Security Executive Education (SNSEE) of National Defense University (NDU) in Washington, DC, and the author of *Maoist Insurgency Since Vietnam* (London, 1996), considered the current standard on the subject of "people's war." A former U.S. government officer who is a member of the editorial board of *Small Wars and Insurgencies* (London), he previously served as the Oppenheimer Chair of Warfighting Strategy at the Marine Corps University (Quantico), where he taught "Insurgency and Operational Art."

ROMÁN D. ORTIZ is the Coordinator of the *Grupo de Estudios de Seguridad y Defensa* (Group for the Study of Security and Defense) within the Political Science Department, School of Social Sciences at the Universidad de los Andes (Bogotá), where he focuses on the analysis of political violence and terrorism phenomena in Latin America. He has previously taught and researched these topics at Spanish academic institutions such as the General Gutiérrez Mellado Institute and the Ortega y Gasset

Institute. His most recent publications include "Renew to Last: Innovation and Strategy of the Revolutionary Armed Forces of Colombia (FARC)" in James Forest (ed.) *Teaching Terror: Strategic and Tactical Learning in the Terrorist World*, 2006.

DAVID SCOTT PALMER is a Professor of International Relations and Political Science at Boston University. His research and writing has focused on political development dynamics and challenges in Latin America generally and the Andean republics in particular, with particular concern for guerrilla movements, drug production and trafficking, organized local citizen networks of informal politics, and U.S. policy. His most recent published work includes "Revolution in the Name of Mao: Revolution and Response in Peru," in *Democracy and Counterterrorism: Lessons from the Past* (2006), and *U.S. Relations with Latin America during the Clinton Years: Opportunities Lost or Opportunities Squandered?* (2006).

JAMES S. ROBBINS is a Professor of International Relations at the National Defense University in Washington, DC, and Senior Fellow in National Security Affairs at the American Foreign Policy Council. Dr. Robbins is a former Special Assistant in the Office of the Secretary of Defense, and frequent commentator on national security issues for *National Review, The Wall Street Journal,* and other publications. He holds a Ph.D. from the Fletcher School of Law and Diplomacy. His research interests include terrorism and national security strategy, political theory, and military history. He is author of *Last in Their Class: Custer, Pickett and the Goats of West Point* (2006).

BEHRAM A. SAHUKAR retired in November 2003 at the rank of Colonel after 34 years in the Parachute Regiment of the Indian Army. He is a combat veteran of the 1971 India–Pakistan war and operations in Jammu and Kashmir. He is a former Research Fellow (Terrorism and Security Studies) at the Institute for Defense Studies and Analyses, New Delhi, and the United Service Institution of India, New Delhi. He is a member of the International Institute for Strategic Studies, London, and is currently working on a project on suicide terrorism. He holds an M.Sc. degree in Defense and Strategic Studies and an M.Phil. degree in Middle Eastern Security Studies. He is based in Amman, Jordan.

THOMAS SHERLOCK is Associate Professor of Political Science at the U.S. Military Academy at West Point, where he teaches courses on international relations, comparative politics, democracy and democratization, and the politics of the former Soviet Union. He has published widely in scholarly journals (in both English and Russian) as well as several books, including *The Fight for Legitimacy: Democracy vs. Terrorism* (Praeger, 2006).

ERIC Y. SHIBUYA is Associate Professor at the U.S. Marine Corps Command and Staff College. His interests include political violence and the politics of Oceania. His most recent publication is "Pacific Engaged, or Washed Away? Implications of Australia's New Activism in Oceania," *Global Change, Peace and Security* (June 2006).

JOSHUA SINAI is Program Manager for counterterrorism studies and education at The Analysis Corporation, in McLean, VA. His areas of specialization focus on developing curriculum, methodologies, and tools to conduct research on terrorism and counterterrorism, as well as regional studies. In addition to publishing articles in academic publications he writes a regular Terrorism Books column for *The Washington Times* book review section. He obtained his Ph.D. in Political Science/Comparative Politics from Columbia University.

STEPHEN SLOAN is a University Professor and Fellow in the Office of Global Perspectives at the University of Central Florida. His latest book is *Terrorism: The Present Threat in Context* (2005). Dr. Sloan has engaged in the study of terrorism since the 1970s. He pioneered simulation techniques to assist authorities in responding to incidents of terrorism. He frequently consults internationally with military, police and security forces responsible for combating terrorism. Dr. Sloan is also involved in formulating policies in the public and corporate sectors for those involved in dealing with the continuity and change that characterizes modern terrorism.

JAMES M. SMITH is Director of the USAF Institute for National Security Studies (INSS) and Professor of Military Strategic Studies at the U.S. Air Force Academy. His recent publications on terrorism include *The Terrorism Threat and U.S. Government Response: Operational and Organizational Factors* (2001); "Aum Shinrikyo," in *Weapons of Mass Destruction: An Encyclopedia of Worldwide Policy, Technology, and History* (2005); "A Strategic Response to Terrorism," in *After 9/11: Terrorism and Crime in a Globalised World* (2005); and (with Brent J. Talbot) "Terrorism and Deterrence by Denial," in *Homeland Security: The Strategic Quest* (2006).

PETER N. SPAGNOLO teaches counterterrorism/antiterrorism and SWAT tactics at The Government Training Institute in Boise, Idaho. He holds a Master of Arts in Diplomacy from Norwich University and served over 20 years in the U.S. Army. For his last 11 years of service, he was a member of the 5th Special Forces Group where he worked closely with militaries and governments of states throughout the Middle East and Africa.

NICOLÁS URRUTIA is a Research Assistant with the *Grupo de Estudios de Seguridad y Defensa* (Group for the Study of Security and Defense) within the Political Science Department, School of Social Sciences at the University of Los Andes (Bogotá). He has worked as a defense policy and procurement analyst for the Colombian government and as an independent researcher. Nicolás' primary areas of interest are organizational change, command and control, defense budgeting, and counterinsurgency. He is a M.A. candidate in Political Science at the University of Los Andes and holds a B.A. in international relations from Stanford University.

SUNDARA VADLAMUDI is a Research Associate in the Monterey Terrorism Research and Education Program (MonTREP), where he provides day-to-day maintenance and qualitative review of the WMD Terrorism Database. Mr. Vadlamudi's research interests include terrorist groups in South Asia, the linkages between South Asian terrorists and both transnational and regional terrorist networks, technology assimilation by terrorist organizations, the ideologies and motivations of terrorist groups, and proliferation of nuclear weapons and missile systems in South Asia. Mr. Vadlamudi received his M.A. in International Policy Studies from the Monterey Institute of International Studies and his B.E. (Computer Science) from Thiagarajar College of Engineering, India.

ROBERT N. WESLEY is a terrorism expert focusing on emerging trends in Islamist militancy and weapons of mass destruction. He has extensive experience analyzing the motivations and activities of terrorist groups. He has worked closely with governments, international organizations, and the private sector on combating these threats.

JOANNE WRIGHT is currently Pro-Vice-Chancellor at the University of Sussex in the United Kingdom. She has published several books and articles on terrorism and other issues of state and non-state security. She is particularly interested in how terrorists manipulate messages to target particular audiences.

RICHARD M. WRONA, JR. is an Infantry officer and Strategist of the United States Army presently serving as an assistant professor in the Department of Social Sciences, United States Military Academy. A graduate of the United States Naval Academy (1994) and the Nitze School of Advanced International Studies (2004), Major Wrona is a term member of the

Council on Foreign Relations. His research interests include Hizbollah, insurgency and counterinsurgency, and American civil-military relations.

SHERIFA ZUHUR is Professor of Islamic and Regional Studies at the Strategic Studies Institute, U.S. Army War College, Carlisle Barracks, Pennsylvania. She has written extensively on Islamist movements, and many other subjects concerning Egypt, including the military, politics, women's rights, and the arts. She has held faculty positions at MIT, the University of California, Berkeley, and the American University in Cairo. She has published 12 books and monographs and more than 40 articles and book chapters.